Practical Quantitative Finance with ASP.NET Core and Angular

Building Ultra-Modern, Responsive Single-Page Web Applications for Quantitative Finance Using ASP.NET Core and Angular

Practical Quantitative Finance with ASP.NET Core and Angular

Building Ultra-Modern, Responsive Single-Page
Web Applications for Quantitative Finance
Using ASP.NET Core and Angular

Jack Xu, PhD

UniCAD Publishing

Practical Quantitative Finance with ASP.NET Core and Angular

Published by UniCAD Publishing.
New York, USA
ISBN-13: 978-0-9793725-6-8
ISBN-10: 0-9793725-6-9

Publisher's Cataloging-in-Publication Data

Xu, Jack
Practical Quantitative Finance with ASP.NET Core and Angular – Building Ultra-Modern, Responsive Single-Page Web Applications for Quantitative Finance Using ASP.NET Core and Angular/ Jack Xu
– 1st ed.
p.cm.
ISBN 978-0-9793725-6-8

1. .NET Programming. 2. Finance. 3. Quant. 4. ASP.NET Core. 5. Angular. 6. Quant Developer. 7. Quant Analyst. 8. Stock Trading. 9. Option Trading. 10. SQL Database. 11. Pricing Engines.
I. Title. II. Title. III Title: Practical Quantitative Finance with ASP.NET Core and Angular

Contents

Introduction

Overview

Welcome to *Practical Quantitative Finance with ASP.NET Core and Angular*. This book will provide all the tools you need to develop ultra-modern financial web applications using ASP.NET Core and Angular. I hope that this book will be useful for quant developers, quant analysts, individual traders, .NET programmers, web developers, and students of all skill levels.

In recent years, quantitative finance has been an attractive field due to the intellectual challenge and high remuneration. Many scientists, engineers, and students wish to change their careers to become a quant developer or analyst in investment banks or hedge fund firms. Most of them have solid background in mathematics, statistical analysis, physics modeling, and programming, but lack knowledge and experience in quantitative finance. A question that they constantly ask is "what do I need to prepare myself to become a quant developer/analyst?" This book will provide answer to this question and prepare you with solid technical skills in quantitative analysis and development.

On the other hand, more and more individuals want to become independent ("retail") quantitative traders who are looking to start their own quantitative or algorithmic trading business. The most common issue they are facing is what kind of background do they need in order to be success in quantitative trading? Most of those individuals received their advanced degrees in physics, math, engineering, or computer science. This kind of training in hard sciences will give them an edge in quantitative analysis and pricing complex derivative instruments. However, the capability to convert trading ideas into trading strategies and the programming skill in implementing the automatic trading system are equally important. This book will prepare you with all the necessary analysis and programming techniques to become a well-equipped individual quant trader.

So what kinds of applications, desktop or web, are more suitable in quantitative finance? Financial applications development began with desktop applications, which can be used in specific machines in which the applications have been installed. Generally, writing code for desktop application is relatively easier, and you have much greater control over how your application works. Another benefit is that desktop applications are always offline because they are executable programs that need not to be accessed over the internet. In my previously published book, *Practical C# and WPF for Financial Markets*, I presented the detailed explanation on how to build desktop applications in finance using C#, WPF, MVVM, and .NET framework.

In contrast to desktop applications, a web-based application is a software that can be accessed through the internet. The software and database are resided in a central server rather than being in the local desktop system. Web based applications are the better way to take advantage of today's technology to enhance the productivity and efficiency. Web or distributed applications are mostly used on client-server networks where the user's computer accesses information from the server or cloud computing server. There are some obvious advantages of web applications over desktop applications. Web applications need to be installed only once, which can avoid the burden in deploying in each client machine and make software updates and maintenance much easier. They are platform independent, adaptable in mobile application, and can be accessed from anywhere in the world.

Here, I would like to point out the difference between the website and web application, even though they are not entirely exclusive and the difference is simply a matter of perspective. Websites are primarily informational and defined by their content. In this sense, https://www.cnn.com and http://www.espn .com are websites, not web applications. Web applications are primarily interactive, and allow users to perform actions. Google Gmail and Google Maps are examples of web applications. That is, a website consists of static content repository that is dealt out to all visitors, while a web application depends on interaction and requires user input and data processing.

If you are thinking about creating your own web applications, you have probably heard that there are two main design patterns: multi-page application (MPA) and single-page application (SPA). MPA works in a more traditional way. It has slower speed because it needs to fetch pages from the server for each request. The main advantage of MPA is its simple search engine optimization (SEO) scheme. The architecture of MPA allows you to optimize every page for search engines. Developer can easily add the meta tags for any page. Another advantage is that developing a multi-page application is much easier than SPA because MPA requires a smaller stack of technologies. MPA is more suitable for developing websites.

SPA is a web application that fits on a single web page with dynamic actions without the need to refresh the page. It is fast, as most resources like HTHL, CSS, and Scripts are only loaded once throughout the lifespan of application. SPA allows you to simulate the work of a desktop application. The architecture of SPA is arranged in such a way that when you go to a new page, only a portion of the content is updated. Thus, there is no need to reload the same elements from the server.

SPA is highly decoupled between client-side and server, and the codes for both ends can be kept separately. SPA interacts with the server only through the web service (or web API) built by server-side developers to fetch and display data. On the other hand, MPA has a tight coupling of front-end and back-end. It is usually one big project, which will house all the codes together. The codes in MPA for both ends are often inter-dependent. SPA also simplifies mobile development as we can reuse the same backend for web application and native mobile application, while MPA usually requires separate code base for mobile application.

SPA is a good fit for web application development. However, building single-page applications is a complicated task. It can be challenge to integrate server-side and client-side code well or even just to choose a productive project setup in the first place. This means that SPA usually requires more development effort to build than MPA.

I write this book with the intention of providing a complete and comprehensive explanation of ultra-modern web application development in quantitative finance using the latest technology stacks: ASP.NET Core 2.2 and SPA framework Angular 7. This book pays special attention to creating various business applications and reusable .NET/TypeScript libraries that can be used directly in real-world finance applications. Much of this book contains the original work based on my own programming experience when I was developing business applications for quantitative analysis in financial field.

Practical Quantitative Finance with ASP.NET Core and Angular provides everything you need to create your own advanced single-page web applications in quantitative finance and reusable packages using ASP.NET Core and Angular. Individually, each of these two frameworks is powerful and feature-rich, but using them together combines the dynamic flexibility of Angular with the solid infrastructure of ASP.NET Core. This book shows you how to use ASP.NET Core together with Angular to build a variety of financial applications that range from simple database, market data API, data visualization, quantitative analysis to pricing equity options and complex fixed income instruments, machine learning, and trading strategy development. I will try my best to introduce you to ultra-modern web application development in quantitative finance in a simple way – simple enough to be easily followed by a quant or .NET/web developer who has basic prior experience in developing business applications using .NET technology or JavaScript framework.

What this Book Includes

This book and its sample code listings, which are available for download at my website at https://drxudotnet.com, provide you with:

- A complete, in-depth instruction to ultra-modern web application development in quantitative finance with ASP.NET Core and Angular. After reading this book and running the example programs, you will be able to create various sophisticated business applications in quantitative finance using the .NET technology and JavaScript framework.

- Ready-to-run example programs that allow you to explore the quantitative finance programming techniques and understand how the algorithms work. You can modify the code examples or add new features to them to form the basis of your own projects. Some of the example code listings provided in this book are already sophisticated programming packages in quantitative finance that you can use directly in your own real-world business applications.

- Many classes and components in the sample code listings that you will find useful in your quant development. These classes and components include charting libraries, various quantitative analysis models, pricing engines for options and fixed income instruments, machine learning for trading strategy development and back-testing, and the other useful utility classes. You can extract these classes and components and plug them into your own business applications.

Is This Book for You?

You do not have to be an experienced quant developer/analyst or .NET/web developer to use this book. I designed this book to be useful to people of all levels of .NET/web programming experience and financial background. In fact, I believe that if you have some prior experience with quantitative analysis/development and programming language C++, Java, R, Python, VBA, C#, or JavaScript, you will be able to sit down in front of your computer, start up Microsoft Visual Studio Community 2017, follow the examples provided in this book, and quickly become proficient with quantitative application development. For those of you who are already experienced quant analyst/developer or .NET programmers, I believe this book has much to offer as well. A great deal of the information in this book about .NET/web programming in quantitative finance is not available in other tutorial and reference books. In addition, you can use most of the example programs in this book directly in your own real-world application development. This book will provide you with a level of detail, explanation, instruction, and sample program code that will enable you to do just about anything related to quantitative finance application development using ASP.NET Core and Angular.

Perhaps you are a scientist, an engineer, a mathematician, or a student, rather than a professional quant developer/analyst, .NET programmer, or web developer; nevertheless, this book is still a good bet for you. In fact, my own background is in theoretical physics, a field involving extensive physical modeling, numerical calculations, and graphical representations of calculated data. I devoted my effort to this field for many years, starting from undergraduate up to PhD. My first computer experience was with FORTRAN. Later on, I had programming experience with Basic, C, C++, R, Python, JavaScript, and Matlab. I always tried to find an ideal development tool that would allow me not only to generate data easily (computation capability) but also to represent data graphically (graphics and chart power). The .NET Core and Microsoft Visual Studio development environment made it possible to develop such integrated applications. Ever since Microsoft .NET 1.0 came out, I have been in love with the C# language, and able to use this tool successfully to create powerful business applications for quantitative analysis.

Quant analysts/developers, individual quant traders, and .NET/web developers can use the majority of the example programs in this book routinely. Throughout the book, I emphasize the usefulness of web application development to real-world quantitative finance problems. If you follow the instructions presented in this book closely, you will easily be able to develop various practical business applications in quantitative finance, from linear analysis, machine learning to pricing engines, and trading strategy development. At the same time, I will not spend too much time discussing the programming style, execution speed, and code optimization, because a plethora of books out there already deals with these topics. Most of the example programs you will find in this book omit error handlings, which makes the code easier to understand by focusing only on the key concepts and practical applications.

What Do You Need to Use This Book?

You will need no special equipment to make the best use of this book and understand the algorithms. This book will take full advantage of open source frameworks and libraries. To run and modify the sample programs, you will need a computer capable of running either Windows 7, 8, or 10. The server-side software installed on your computer should include Visual Studio 2017 (Community version is fine), the .NET Core 2.2 SDK or higher, and SQL Server Express 2016 or higher. For the front end, you need to install Node.js version 8.x or 10.x, Angular 7, and Angular 7 CLI.

If you have .NET Core 2.1 SDK or older version, SQL Server Express 2014 or older versions, and Angular 6 or older version, you can also run most of the sample code with few modifications. Please remember, however, that this book is intended for .NET Core 2.2, SQL Server Express 2016, and Angular 7 and that all of the example programs were created and tested on this platform, so it is best to run the sample code on the same platform.

How the Book Is Organized

This book is organized into eleven chapters, each of which covers a different topic about quantitative finance applications using .NET Core and Angular. The following summaries of each chapter should give you an overview of the book's content:

Chapter 1, *Overview of ASP.NET Core and Angular*

This chapter provides an overview of ASP.NET Core and Angular, which explains how to set up the tools, packages, and development environment required for building a single-page application using ASP.NET Core and Angular with the Visual Studio IDE.

Chapter 2, *Angular Basics*

This chapter provides a quick review of various features available in the Angular framework, including one- and two-way data binding, components, templates, routing, dependency injection, directives, and Inputs/Output decorators.

Chapter 3, *Database and Web Services*

This chapter introduces the SQL Server and Entity Framework Core, which are built-in features and shipped as part of the core product of Visual Studio 2017. It shows you how to create simple database and how to interact with the data in Angular applications via ASP.NET API web service.

Chapter 4, *Market Data*

This chapter explains how to interact with market data providers' API and retrieve the free market data from online data source. These market data includes the end of the day (EOD) stock data, intraday data, real-time stock price quotes, and interest rate data.

Chapter 5, *Data Visualization*

Data visualization plays a critical role in quantitative finance and trading. Quant analysts and traders need to monitor the real-time changes in market and trading signals visually on their screen. In this chapter, I will show you how to use a client chart library called ECharts to create various charts and display the market data in an Angular singe-page application.

Chapter 6, *Linear Analysis*

This chapter presents the most fundamental analysis approach in quantitative finance based on linear analysis. I will discuss how to develop different business applications using the linear regression, principal component analysis (PCA), and correlation.

Chapter 7, *Technical Indicators*

This chapter discusses various technical indicators, which are often used in quantitative analysis. A technical indicator is just a mathematical calculation based on historic market data, which is used to predict market direction. I will show you how to convert various indicators provided in TA-Lib library into web services and how to apply them to your Angular applications.

Chapter 8, *Machine Learning*

This chapter discusses the advanced quantitative analysis techniques: machine learning. Machine-learning technique has become one of the most promising fields in quantitative finance. It is widely used in quantitative finance for predicting the future stock prices. This chapter will concentrate on the supervised learning and covers several commonly used machine-learning algorithms in finance, including the K-nearest neighbors, support vector machines, and neural networks.

Chapter 9, *Options Pricing*

This chapter covers the Black-Scholes formula used for options pricing. It shows how to use an open source library called QuantLib to calculate the price and Greeks of the European and American options. It also discusses how to use this library to price the other options, including barrier options, Bermudan options, and other exotic options.

Chapter 10, *Pricing Fixed-Income Instruments*

This chapter demonstrates how to price the fixed-income instruments, including interest rates, bonds, and credit default swaps. It also discusses various related topics, such as cash flows, term structures, yield curves, discount factors, and zero-coupon bonds. I will provide the detailed procedures on how to use the open-source QuantLib library to price these complex financial instruments.

Chapter 11, Trading Strategies and Backtesting

This chapter presents several trading strategies using the simple quantitative analysis techniques, including crossovers and z-score based on commonly used technical indicators. I will also present a long-short based backtesting framework, which allows you to examine the historical performance of your strategies in stock trading.

Using Code Examples

You may use the code in this book in your own applications and documentation. You do not need to contact the author for permission unless you are reproducing a significant portion of the code. For example, writing a program that uses several chunks of code from this book does not require permission. Selling or distributing the example code listings does require permission. Incorporating a significant amount of example code from this book into your applications and documentation also requires permission. Integrating the example code from this book into commercial products is not allowed without written permission of the author.

Customer Support

I am always interested in hearing from readers, and enjoy learning of your thoughts on this book. You can send me comments by e-mail to jxu@DrXuDotNet.com. I also provide updates, bug fixes, and ongoing support via my website:

https://DrXuDotNet.com

You can also obtain the complete source code for all of examples in this book from the foregoing website. At the same time, I created a code demonstration website at https://quant.gincker.com that shows a live demo for all examples included in this book.

Chapter 1
Introduction to ASP.NET Core and Angular

In this chapter, I will explain how to set up the tools and packages required for ASP.NET Core and Angular development. Both ASP.NET Core and Angular frameworks are cross-platform and independent of operating systems. However, in this book, we choose Windows 10 and Visual Studio 2017 as our development environment. If you use the other platforms like Linux or macOS, you can use Visual Studio Code as your IDE to build and run the example projects.

The following sections describe the setup required for building a single-page application based on ASP.NET Core and Angular. All the tools used here are available as open sources (free of charge), although some are offered in commercial versions with additional features (but these are not needed for the examples in this book).

Install Visual Studio and .NET Core

Since we want to use the Windows operating system, we can use either Visual Studio, which is a traditional IDE for .NET projects, or Visual Studio Core, which is a light-weight alternative. Here, we choose to use Visual Studio 2017 because it offers a full-featured development environment.

First, download visual studio installer from https://visualstudio.microsoft.com/downloads/. There are different editions available, but the free Community edition is sufficient for the examples in this book. Run the installer and ensure that the .NET Core cross-platform development workload is selected. Click the Install button to begin the process of downloading and installing the visual studio features.

Next, we need to install the .NET Core. The .NET Core software development kit (SDK) includes the runtime and development tools required to start the development project and perform database operations. Download the installer from https://www.microsoft.com/net/download/thank-you/dotnet-sdk-2.2.100-preview3-windows-x64-installer. This URL is for 64-bit .NET Core SDK, which is the version that I use throughout this book and which you should install to ensure that you get the expected results from the examples.

Run the installer. Once the install process is complete, open a new command prompt window and run the following command to check that .NET Core is working:

```
dotnet -version
```

The output from this command will display the latest version of the .NET Core runtime that is installed. At the time of writing, the latest version of .NET Core SDK is 2.2.101. The examples included in this book should run on this version or later.

Install Node.js

Node.js is a runtime for server-side JavaScript applications and has become a popular platform for development tools. In this book, Node.js is used by the Angular build tools to compile and prepare the code that ASP.NET Core will send to the browser.

To install Node.js, download the installer from https://nodejs.org/en/. You can select version 8.x (recommended for most users) or 11.x (the latest features). Run the installer and ensure that the *npm* package manager and "Add to PATH" options are selected. The *npm* package manager is used to download and install Node packages. Adding Node.js to the PATH ensures that you can use the Node.js runtime at the command prompt just typing node. Once you have completed the installation, you can open a new command prompt window and run the following command:

```
node -v
```

You should see the version number displayed: v8.9.3 (you may see a different version number depending on which version installed on your machine).

You do not need to install Angular manually. You will use the Angular SPA project template with ASP.NET Core project. When you run the project, Visual Studio 2017 will install Angular CLI and corresponding packages for you automatically.

Create the SPA Project

The Angular SPA project template provides a convenient starting point for ASP.NET Core applications using Angular and the Angular CLI to implement a rich, client-side user interface (UI). The template is equivalent to creating an ASP.NET Core project to act as an API backend and an Angular CLI project to act as a front end. The template offers the convenience of hosting both project types in a single application project. Consequently, the project can be built and published as a single unit.

Create a New Application

Open Visual Studio 2017, create a new ASP.NET Core Web Application project, and name it Quant. Click OK button to bring up the Quant project window, as shown in Fig.1-1. Now complete the dialog on this window: in the version selector drop-down box select ASP.NET Core 2.2. Choose the Angular template and tap the OK button.

The project template creates an ASP.NET Core application and an Angular application. The ASP.NET Core app is intended to be used for data access, authorization, and other server-side concerns. The Angular app, residing in the ClientApp subdirectory, is intended to be used for all UI concerns.

You have a working application now by simply entering a project name and selecting a few options. This is a basic starter project, but it is a good place to start.

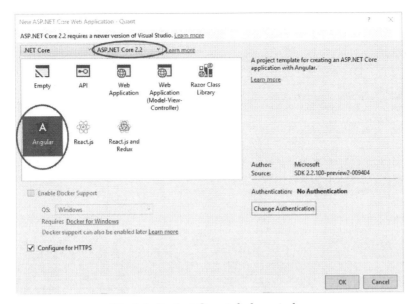

Fig.1-1. Project Quant dialog window.

Tap F5 to run the application. Note that the build process restores *npm* dependencies on the first run, which may take several minutes. Subsequent builds will be much faster.

If everything goes smoothly, Visual Studio will start IIS Express and run your app. The default template gives you working *Home*, *Counter*, and *Fetch Data* links, shown in Fig.1-2.

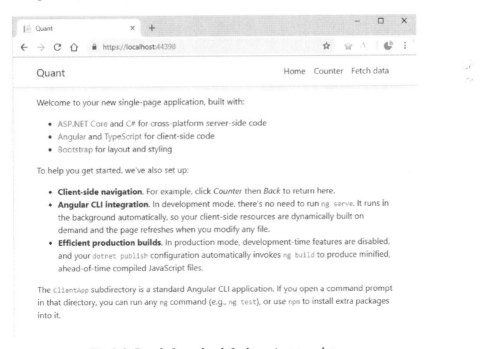

Fig.1-2. Result from the default project template.

Update Angular

In the preceding section, we have successfully created a single-page web application with the ASP.NET Core and the Angular template. The problem with that template is that it scaffolds an Angular 6 project, while Angular release new version 7 in October of 2018. In this section, I show you how to update the project to the latest Angular, which is version 7 as of this writing.

First, from the solution explorer, open the *package.json* file from the *ClientApp* folder. You can see from this file that the template uses Angular 6, as shown in the following:

```
// package.json file:
{
  "name": "Quant",
  "version": "0.0.0",
  "scripts": {
    "ng": "ng",
    "start": "ng serve",
    "build": "ng build",
    "build:ssr": "ng run Quant:server:dev",
    "test": "ng test",
    "lint": "ng lint",
    "e2e": "ng e2e"
  },
  "private": true,
  "dependencies": {
    "@angular/animations": "^6.0.0",
    "@angular/common": "^6.0.0",
    "@angular/compiler": "^6.0.0",
    "@angular/core": "^6.0.0",
    "@angular/forms": "^6.0.0",
    "@angular/http": "^6.0.0",
    "@angular/platform-browser": "^6.0.0",
    "@angular/platform-browser-dynamic": "^6.0.0",
    "@angular/router": "^6.0.0",
"@nguniversal/module-map-ngfactory-loader": "6.0.0",

// ... other code omitted for brevity ...

  },
  "devDependencies": {
    "@angular-devkit/build-angular": "~0.6.0",
    "@angular/cli": "~6.0.0",
    "@angular/compiler-cli": "^6.0.0",
    "@angular/language-service": "^6.0.0",
"@angular/platform-server": "6.0.0",

// ... other code omitted for brevity ...

  }
}
```

In order to update to Angular 7 from 6, open a new command prompt window, navigate to the *ClientApp* directory (where the *package.json* file is present), and run the following command:

```
ng update @angular/cli @angular/core
```

This update process may take up to few seconds. After completing the update, reopen the *package.json* file to ensure that all the packages related to Angular are now updated to version, as shown in the following code:

```
// package.json file:
{
  "name": "Quant",
  "version": "0.0.0",
  "scripts": {
    "ng": "ng",
    "start": "ng serve",
    "build": "ng build",
    "build:ssr": "ng run Quant:server:dev",
    "test": "ng test",
    "lint": "ng lint",
    "e2e": "ng e2e"
  },
  "private": true,
  "dependencies": {
    "@angular/animations": "^7.2.0",
    "@angular/common": "^7.2.0",
    "@angular/compiler": "^7.2.0",
    "@angular/core": "^7.2.0",
    "@angular/forms": "^7.2.0",
    "@angular/http": "^7.2.0",
    "@angular/platform-browser": "^7.2.0",
    "@angular/platform-browser-dynamic": "^7.2.0",
    "@angular/router": "^7.2.0",

    // ... other code omitted for brevity ...

  },
  "devDependencies": {
    "@angular/cli": "^7.2.1",
    "@angular/compiler-cli": "^7.2.0",
    "@angular/language-service": "^7.2.0",
    "@angular/platform-server": "^7.2.0",

    // ... other code omitted for brevity ...

  }
}
```

At the time of writing, the latest version of Angular is 7.2.0. After the update, build and run the application to see if it is running properly. If you face any issue, visit https://update.angular.io for detailed information and guidance on updating your Angular application.

Project Structure

Combining ASP.NET Core and Angular in a single project produces a complex file structures. When working with a combined project, it is important to remember that you are developing two distinct applications whose files happen to be collocated. The folder structure of our *Quant* project is shown in Fig.1-3.

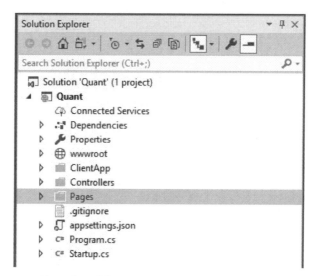

Fig.1-3. Folder structure of the Quant project.

The following listing describes the files and folders in the above screenshot:

- *ClientApp* folder contains the Angular application and its configuration files.
- *Controllers* folder contains the ASP.NET Core controller classes.
- *Pages* folder contains the Razor page files (will not be used in this project).
- *wwwroot* folder contains the static content files that ASP.NET Core app requires.
- The *Program.cs* file has the *Main* method to start the application.
- The *Startup.cs* file sets up the services and middlewares for the ASP.NET Core app.

Fig.1-4 shows structure of the *ClientApp* folder:

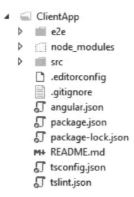

Fig.1-4. File structure of the ClientApp folder.

If you were familiar with the files generated by Angular CLI, most of the files in the *ClientApp* folder would look familiar to you. The following listing explains the files and folders shown in Fig.1-4:

- *e2e*: This folder is used to add end-to-end tests. These tests have to be written using protractor. This folder contains some sample tests for the application added by the Angular CLI. We will not use this folder in this book.

- *node_modules*: This folder contains the *npm* packages that are required for the application and for the Angular development tools. All of the JavaScript packages installed using the *npm* package manager or through *package.json* will go to this folder.

- *src*: This folder contains the source files, resources, configuration files, and the *index.html* file.

- *.editorconfig*: This file contains settings that configure text editors.

- *.gitignore*: This file contains a list of files and folders that are excluded from version control when using Git.

- *angular.json*: This file contains the configuration for the Angular development tools.

- *package.json*: This file contains details of the *npm* packages required by the applications and the development tools and defines the commands that run the development tools.

- *Package-lock.json*: This file contains version information for all the packages that are installed in the *node_modules* folder.

- *README.md*: This readme file contains the list of commands for the development tools.

- *tsconfig.json*: This file contains the configuration settings for the TypeScript compiler.

- *tslint.json*: This file contains the settings for the TypeScript linter.

You would not always need all of these files in every project, and you can remove the ones you do not require. In our Quant project, we do not want to create Angular test files (i.e., **.spec.ts*) when generating components or services. This can be achieved by adding the following highlighted code to the *angular.json* file:

```
{
    "$schema": "./node_modules/@angular/cli/lib/config/schema.json",
    // ... other code omitted for brevity ...

    "defaultProject": "Quant",
    "schematics": {
      "@schematics/angular": {
        "class": {
          "spec": false
        },
        "component": {
          "spec": false
        },
        "directive": {
          "spec": false
        },
        "module": {
          "spec": false
        },
        "service": {
          "spec": false
        }
      }
    }
}
```

Here, we simply set the *spec* property to *false* for components, modules, services, etc.

Now, let us consider the src folder, as shown in Fig.1-5.

Fig.1-5. File structure of the src folder.

The *src* folder contains the Angular app's files, including the source code and static assets, such as images. This folder is the focus of most development activity for the Angular app. The following listing explains the files and folders shown in Fig.1-5:

- *app*: This folder contains an Angular app's source code and content. It is where you will add the custom code and content for the Angular app, and its structure becomes more complex as you add features.

- *assets*: This folder is used for the static resources required by the Angular app, such as images.

- *environments*: This folder contains configuration files that define settings for different environments. By default, the only configuration setting is the production flag, which is set to true when the application is built for deployment.

- *browserlist*: This file is used to support the CSS processing packages that are used by the development tools.

- *index.html*: This HTML file is sent to the browser during development.

- *karma.conf.js*: This file contains the configuration for the Karma testing tool.

- *main.ts*: This file contains the TypeScript statements that start the Angular app when they are executed.

- *polyfills.ts*: This file is used to include polyfills in the project to provide support for features that are not available natively in some browsers, especially Internet Explorer.
- *styles.css*: This file is used to define CSS styles that are applied throughout the application.
- *tests.ts*: This is the configuration file for the Karma test package.
- *tsconfig.app.json*: This is the configuration file for the TypeScript compiler that is used during development.
- *tsconfig.server.json*: This is the configuration file for the TypeScript compiler that is used during server-side rendering.
- *tsconfig.spec.json*: This is the configuration file for the TypeScript compiler that is used during testing.
- *tslint.json*: This file contains the settings for the TypeScript linter.

Configure ASP.NET Core App and Angular

The template ASP.NET Core and Angular SPA project is configured to start its own instance of the Angular CLI server in the background when the ASP.NET Core app starts in development model. This is convenient because you do not have to run a separate server manually.

There is a drawback to the default setup for the template project. Each time you modify your C# code and your ASP.NET Core app needs to restart, the Angular CLI server restarts too. Over 10 seconds are required to start back up. If you are making frequent C# code changes and do not want to wait for Angular CLI to restart, you can run the Angular CLI server externally, independently of the ASP.NET Core process.

First, modify your ASP.NET Core app to use the external Angular CLI instance instead of launching one of its own. Open the *Startup.cs* file and replace the **spa.UseAngularCliServer** invocation with the following:

```
// Startup.cs file:

// ... other code omitted for brevity ...

app.UseSpa(spa =>
{
    spa.Options.SourcePath = "ClientApp";

    if (env.IsDevelopment())
    {
        //spa.UseAngularCliServer(npmScript: "start");
        spa.UseProxyToSpaDevelopmentServer("http://localhost:4200");
    }
});
```

Next, open a command prompt window, navigate to the *ClientApp* directory, and run the following command:

npm start

Note that here we use **npm start** to launch the Angular CLI development server, not **ng serve**, so that the configuration in the *package.json* file is respected.

Now, start your ASP.NET Core app, it would not launch an Angular CLI server. The instance you started manually is used instead. This enables it to start and restart faster. It is no longer waiting for Angular CLI to rebuild your client app each time. We will use this approach for building SPA project throughout this book.

We also need to add the following code snippet to *PropertyGroup* of the *Quant.csproj* file:

```
<TypeScriptExperimentalDecorators>true</TypeScriptExperimentalDecorators>
```

Then save the file and reload the project. This will avoid the TypeScript warning in the development mode like the following:

```
[ts] Experimental support for decorators is a feature that is subject to change in
a future release. Set the 'experimentalDecoratos' option to remove this warning.
```

Set up Angular Material

Twitter's Bootstrap is the most popular HTML, CSS, and JavaScript framework for developing websites and web applications. Angular is a JavaScript framework used for creating dynamic web applications. Both Bootstrap and Angular are great tools for front-end web development.

Bootstrap

There are some issues when using Bootstrap and Angular together in the same project. These issues arise because Bootstrap JS uses the jQuery library. Bootstrap has a dependency on jQuery. It uses jQuery library for components like tooltips, modals, popovers, etc. When using Angular in your projects, you should not add jQuery library with Angular. Otherwise, Bootstrap JS will create a conflict with Angular. The reason for this conflict is that the way jQuery and Angular manipulates the view is completely different. The jQuery library manipulates the data in the view by grabbing and injecting DOM based on events. The data manipulation in Angular takes place by data binding. This means that a variable is bound to the component. The state of the component is changed based on the true or false value of the variable.

Microsoft's solution is to use Bootstrap CSS only in the ASP.NET Core Angular template. You can clearly see this from the package.json and angular.json file in the ClientApp directory of our Quant project. The following content of the package.json file shows that the template project pre-installed Bootstrap 4:

```
// package.json file:
"dependencies": {

    // ... other packages omitted for brevity ...

    "bootstrap": "4.1.3",
},
```

And from *angular.json*, you see that only Bootstrap CSS was used:

```
//  angular.json file:
{
  "$schema": "./node_modules/@angular/cli/lib/config/schema.json",
  "version": 1,
  "newProjectRoot": "projects",
```

```
"projects": {
  "Quant": {
    "root": "",
    "sourceRoot": "src",
    "projectType": "application",
    "prefix": "app",
    "schematics": {},
    "architect": {
      "build": {
        "builder": "@angular-devkit/build-angular:browser",
        "options": {
          "progress": true,
          "extractCss": true,
          "outputPath": "dist",
          "index": "src/index.html",
          "main": "src/main.ts",
          "polyfills": "src/polyfills.ts",
          "tsConfig": "src/tsconfig.app.json",
          "assets": [
            "src/assets"
          ],
          "styles": [
            "node_modules/bootstrap/dist/css/bootstrap.min.css",
            "src/styles.css"
          ],
          "scripts": []
        },

        // ... the other code omitted for brevity ...
}
```

With the Bootstrap CSS only, you can create Bootstrap components that do not use JavaScript, however, you will have to build your components that require JavaScript on your own from scratch.

The other option is to use the libraries like *ng-bootstrap*, which is the Angular version of the Angular UI Bootstrap library. This library uses TypeScript and targets the Bootstrap 4 CSS framework.

Bootstrap or Angular Material?

Currently, Twitter's Bootstrap is the most popular HTML, CSS, and JavaScript framework for developing responsive projects on the web. Angular Material is an alternative to Bootstrap as a responsive design framework. Material Design is a specification for a unified system of visual, motion, and interaction that adapts across different devices. It delivers a lean, lightweight set of Angular-native UI elements that implement the material design system for use in Angular SPAs.

Bootstrap and Angular Material have many common components, including Card, Panel, Forms, Inputs, Dialog, Menu, List, etc. However, there are some components found on Bootstrap but not found in Angular Material, and verse visa.

Both Bootstrap and Angular Material have many amazing components. While in the case of Bootstrap there is more than just component, it has utilities and a lot of helper classes and responsive grid design all rolled up in one package. On the other hand, Angular Material does have some helper classes and better interaction with Material Icons. On its own, it does not provide responsive web design but can be used together with Angular Flex Layout to achieve that.

So which framework should we choose? One may say "Bootstrap" while the others may say "Material Design" – there is no correct answer. In this book, I will use Angular Material because it moves a step forward adding fresh styles and animations to its components. The web applications will become more interactive, which is one of the greatest features making user experience more pleasing than ever before.

In order to use the pure Angular Material, we need to remove the Bootstrap package from the *package.json* file in the *ClientApp* folder. We also need to remove or comment out the following code from the *angular.json* in the *ClientApp* folder:

```
"node_modules/bootstrap/dist/css/bootstrap.min.css",
```

Install Angular Material

There are two ways to install the JavaScript packages: using the *npm* package manager or adding packages directly to the *package.json* file. Here, we will use the latter method. Add the following commands to the *dependencies* section of the *package.json* file:

```
"@angular/material": "^7.0.1",
"@angular/cdk": "^7.0.1",
"@angular/flex-layout": "7.0.0-beta.19",
```

The *@angular/cdk* package is a common development kit, which contains a set of tools that implement common interaction patterns. It represents an abstraction of the core functionalities found in the Angular Material library, without any styling specific to Material Design. The Angular Flex Layout package provides a responsive layout API using Flexbox CSS + mediaQuery. It enables you to easily specify different layouts, sizing, visibilities for different viewport sizes and display devices.

Now if you save the file, Visual Studio will install the above packages and add corresponding files to the *ClientApp/node_modules* directory automatically for you.

After installing Angular Material, you will need to configure a theme that defines what colors will be used in your Angular Material components. There are four prebuilt themes, including *deeppurple-amber*, *indigo-pink*, *pink-bluegrey*, and *purple-green*. The theme file are stored in the *ClientApp/node_modules /@angular/material/prebuilt-themes* folder. In this book, we will choose the *indigo-pink* theme. Open the *styles.css* file in the ClientApp/src folder and add the following code to it:

```
// styles.css file:
@import"~@angular/material/prebuilt-themes/indigo-pink.css";

html, body {
  height: 100%;
}

body {
  margin: 0;
  font-family: Roboto, "Helvetica Neue", sans-serif;
}
```

Some Material components like *Slide Toggle, Slider*, and *Tooltip* depend on a library called *HammerJS* to capture touch gestures. So, we need to install *HammerJS* and load it into our Quant application. Add the following code to the *dependencies* section of the *package.json* file in the *ClientApp* folder:

```
// package.json file:
"dependencies": {
```

```
// ... other packages omitted for brevity ...

  "hammerjs": "2.0.8"
},
```

After installing it, add the following code to the *main.ts* file:

```
// main.ts file:

// ... other imports omitted for brevity ...

import 'hammerjs';

export function getBaseUrl() {
  return document.getElementsByTagName('base')[0].href;
}

// ... other code omitted for brevity ...
```

If you want to use icons in your project, you can use the Material Icons library. To access this library, update the *index.html* file in the *ClientApp/src* folder as followings:

```
// index.html file:
<!doctype html>
<html lang="en">
<head>

  <!-- ... other tags omitted for brevity ... -->

  <link href="https://fonts.googleapis.com/icon?family=Material+Icons"
        rel="stylesheet">
</head>
<body>
  <app-root>Loading...</app-root>
</body>
</html>
```

After setting up the Angular project structure and corresponding dependencies, you need to import the corresponding Material modules to be used in your project.

Import Material Modules

Add a new folder named *material* in the *ClientApp/src/app* folder. Add a module file named *material.module.ts* to this new folder. The following is the code listing for this module:

```
// material.module.ts file:
import { NgModule } from '@angular/core';
import {
  MatAutocompleteModule,
  MatButtonModule,
  MatButtonToggleModule,

  // ... other modules omitted for brevity ...

} from '@angular/material'
```

```
@NgModule({
  imports: [
    MatAutocompleteModule,
    MatButtonModule,
    MatButtonToggleModule,

  // ... other modules omitted for brevity ...

  ],
  exports: [
    MatAutocompleteModule,
    MatButtonModule,
    MatButtonToggleModule,

  // ... other modules omitted for brevity ...

  ]
})
export class MaterialModule { }
```

The purpose of creating the *material.module* is to centralize what we import from Angular Material in a single file. In this module, we import all of the Material modules, so that all of the Material components will be available to our *Quant* project.

Before using Angular Material components, we need to import and configure the *material.module* in our root module, *app.module.ts*, in the *ClientApp/src/app* folder as follows:

```
// app.module.ts file:

// ... other imports omitted for brevity ...

import { FlexLayoutModule } from '@angular/flex-layout';
import { MaterialModule } from './material/material.module';
@NgModule({
  declarations: [
AppComponent,

// ... other components omitted for brevity ...

  ],
  imports: [

// ... other modules omitted for brevity ...

    FlexLayoutModule,
    MaterialModule,
  ],
  providers: [],
  bootstrap: [AppComponent]
})
export class AppModule { }
```

In this file, we register both the Material module and Flex Layout module.

Set up Navigation

In this section, we make changes to the layout and navigation of our *Quant* project using Angular Material.

Change Layout

First, we need to remove the Bootstrap elements from the root template. Open the *app.component.html* file from the *ClientApp/src/app* folder and replace the class attribute for the *div* element by an inline style, as shown in the following listing:

```
// app.component.html file:
<body>
  <app-nav-menu></app-nav-menu>
  <div style="margin:10px">
    <router-outlet></router-outlet>
  </div>
</body>
```

Next, we change the file structure in order to manage the Angular component files easily. Add a new folder named *chapter01* to the *ClientApp/src/app* folder, and move the *counter* and *fetch-data* folders and corresponding files to the *chapter01* folder, as shown in Fig.1-6.

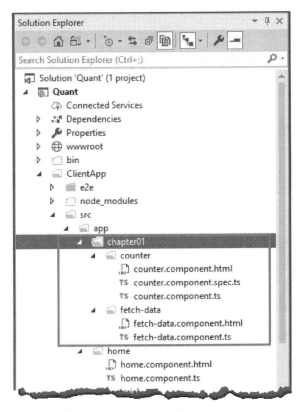

Fig.1-6. Change the file structure.

Open the root module file, *app.module.ts*, from the *ClientApp* directory and make changes to *CounterComponent* and *FetchDataComponent* to reflect the changes to the new file structure:

```
import { CounterComponent } from './chapter01/counter/counter.component'
import { FetchDataComponent } from './chapter01/fetch-data/fetch-data.component';

// ... other code omitted for brevity ...

{ path: 'chapter01/counter', component: CounterComponent },
{ path: 'chapter01/fetch-data', component: FetchDataComponent }
```

Update Home Page

Now, open the *home.component.html* file in the *Client/src/app/home* folder and replace its content with the following code list:

```
// home.component.html file:
<h1>Welcome to Quant Book Project</h1>
<h2>This project provides example code for the book of <i>Practical ASP.NET Core and
    Angular for Quantitative Finance</i></h2>
<h4>This page is a gateway. You can access various examples by clicking
    corresponding links.</h4>

<ul style="margin-top:50px;list-style:none">
  <li><p><a [routerLink]='["/"]'>Quant Book Home</a></p></li>
  <li>
    <p>Chapter 1</p>
    <ul>
      <li><a [routerLink]='["/chapter01/counter"]'>Counter</a></li>
      <li style="margin-top:5px"><a [routerLink]='["/chapter01/fetch-data"]'>
          Fetch Data</a></li>
    </ul>
  </li>
  <li><p>Chapter 2</p></li>
  <li><p>Chapter 3</p></li>
</ul>
```

This page will be a gateway, from which you can access the examples by clicking corresponding links. With the progress of the book, we will add more links to this page later.

Update Navigation Menu

In addition to the home page, we will provide another convenient way to access the examples in this book using the dropdown menu. Now, open the *nav-menu.component.css* file from the *ClientApp/ src/app/nav-menu* directory and add the following code to this file:

```
// nav-menu.component.css file:
.fill-remaining-space {
  flex: 1 1 auto;
}
```

The *flex* property in the above CSS file is a sub-property of the *Flexbox* layout module. The code sizes the item based on its width, but makes it fully flexible so that the width property absorbs any extra space along the horizontal direction.

Open the *nav-menu.component.html* file from the *ClientApp/src/app/nav-menu* directory and replace its content with the following code listing:

```html
// nav-menu.component.html file:
<mat-toolbar color="primary">
  <button mat-button (click)="sidenav.toggle()" fxShow fxHide.gt-sm>
    <mat-icon>menu</mat-icon>
  </button>

  <button mat-button routerLink="/">
    <mat-icon>book</mat-icon>
    <span style="font-size:20px">Quant Book</span>
  </button>

  <span class="fill-remaining-space"></span>
  <div fxLayout="row" fxHide fxShow.gt-sm>
    <button mat-button [matMenuTriggerFor]="menu1">Ch1<mat-
icon>arrow_drop_down</mat-icon></button>
    <mat-menu #menu1="matMenu">
      <button mat-menu-item routerLink="/chapter01/counter">Counter</button>
      <button mat-menu-item routerLink="/chapter01/fetch-data">Fetch Data</button>
    </mat-menu>
    <button mat-button [matMenuTriggerFor]="menu2">Ch2<mat-
icon>arrow_drop_down</mat-icon></button>
    <mat-menu #menu2="matMenu">
      <a mat-menu-item href="https://gincker.com">Gincker</a>
      <a mat-menu-item href="https://gincker.com/AI">Gincker AI</a>
      <a mat-menu-item href="https://gincker.com/Graphics">Gincker Graphics</a>
    </mat-menu>
    <button mat-button [matMenuTriggerFor]="menu3">Ch3<mat-
icon>arrow_drop_down</mat-icon></button>
    <mat-menu #menu3="matMenu">
      <a mat-menu-item href="https://gincker.com">Gincker</a>
      <a mat-menu-item href="https://gincker.com/AI">Gincker AI</a>
      <a mat-menu-item href="https://gincker.com/Graphics">Gincker Graphics</a>
    </mat-menu>
  </div>
</mat-toolbar>

<mat-sidenav-container>
  <mat-sidenav #sidenav mode="push" opened="false" fixedInViewport="true">
    <mat-tree [dataSource]="dataSource" [treeControl]="treeControl">
      <mat-tree-node *matTreeNodeDef="let node" matTreeNodeToggle
                     matTreeNodePadding>
        <span *ngIf="node.type.indexOf('http') < 0">
          <a (click)="sidenav.toggle()" mat-button routerLink="{{node.type}}">
            {{node.filename}}
          </a>
        </span>
        <span *ngIf="node.type.indexOf('http') > -1">
          <a (click)="sidenav.toggle()" mat-button href="{{node.type}}">
            {{node.filename}}
          </a>
        </span>
      </mat-tree-node>
```

```
<mat-tree-node *matTreeNodeDef="let node;when: hasChild" matTreeNodePadding>
  <button mat-button matTreeNodeToggle
          [attr.aria-label]="'toggle ' + node.filename">
    <mat-icon class="mat-icon-rtl-mirror">
      {{treeControl.isExpanded(node) ? 'expand_more' : 'chevron_right'}}
    </mat-icon>
      {{node.filename}} {{node.type}}
  </button>
</mat-tree-node>
    </mat-tree>
  </mat-sidenav>
  <mat-sidenav-content fxFlexFill>
    <div style="margin:10px">
      <router-outlet></router-outlet>
    </div>
  </mat-sidenav-content>
</mat-sidenav-container>
```

Angular Material supports the ability for a *mat-menu-item* to open a sub-menu. To do so, we define a root menu and submenus whose names starts with the **#** character, and then use [**matMenuTriggerFor**] on the mat-menu-item that should trigger the submenu.

We also use the Angular Flex-Layout to build a responsive navigation menu. The following code

```
<div fxLayout="row" fxHide fxShow.gt-sm>

        // ... other code omitted for brevity ...

</div>
```

indicates that the above element will be hidden by default and only shown on viewport sizes greater than mobile.

On the other hand, the following code snippet

```
<button mat-button (click)="sidenav.toggle()" fxShow fxHide.gt-sm>
  <mat-icon>menu</mat-icon>
</button>
```

is used to triggers the sidenav component. Here, **fxShow fxHide.gt-sm** means that the above element will be shown by default and only hidden on viewport size > *sm* mediaQuery ranges. Here, we also add a *mat-icon* named *menu* to the element. You can find all of the Material Icons and corresponding icon names from the web site https://material.io/tools/icons/?style=baseline.

The sidenav.toggle() triggers the open or close state for the *sidenav* component. The *sidenav* is an Angular Material element deigned to add collapsible side content for navigation alongside some primary content. To set up a *sidenav* we use three components: *mat-sidenav-container*, which acts as a structural container for our content and *sidenav*, *mat-sidenav*, which represents the added side content, and *mat-sidenav-content*, which represents the main content.

Inside the *sidenav* element, we implement a *mat-tree*, which provides a Material Design styled tree view that can be used to display hierarchy data or URL links. The mat-tree requires a *dataSource*, which we create in the *nav-menu.component.ts* file, whose code listing is provided as follows:

```
// nav-menu.component.ts file:
import { Component, Injectable } from '@angular/core';
import { FlatTreeControl } from '@angular/cdk/tree';
```

```
import { MatTreeFlatDataSource, MatTreeFlattener } from '@angular/material/tree';
import { BehaviorSubject, Observable, of as observableOf } from 'rxjs';

@Injectable()
export class FileData {
  dataChange = new BehaviorSubject<FileNode[]>([]);

  get data(): FileNode[] { return this.dataChange.value; }

  constructor() {
    this.initialize();
  }

  initialize() {
    const dataObject = JSON.parse(TREE_DATA);
    const data = this.buildFileTree(dataObject, 0);
    this.dataChange.next(data);
  }

  buildFileTree(obj: { [key: string]: any }, level: number): FileNode[] {
    return Object.keys(obj).reduce<FileNode[]>((accumulator, key) => {
      const value = obj[key];
      const node = new FileNode();
      node.filename = key;

      if (value != null) {
        if (typeof value === 'object') {
          node.children = this.buildFileTree(value, level + 1);
        } else {
          node.type = value;
        }
      }

      return accumulator.concat(node);
    }, []);
  }
}

@Component({
  selector: 'app-nav-menu',
  templateUrl: './nav-menu.component.html',
  styleUrls: ['./nav-menu.component.css'],
  providers: [FileData]
})
export class NavMenuComponent {
  treeControl: FlatTreeControl<FileFlatNode>;
  treeFlattener: MatTreeFlattener<FileNode, FileFlatNode>;
  dataSource: MatTreeFlatDataSource<FileNode, FileFlatNode>;

  constructor(database: FileData) {
    this.treeFlattener = new MatTreeFlattener(this.transformer, this._getLevel,
      this._isExpandable, this._getChildren);
    this.treeControl = new FlatTreeControl<FileFlatNode>(this._getLevel,
this._isExpandable);
```

```
    this.dataSource = new MatTreeFlatDataSource(this.treeControl,
this.treeFlattener);

    database.dataChange.subscribe(data => this.dataSource.data = data);
  }

  transformer = (node: FileNode, level: number) => {
    return new FileFlatNode(!!node.children, node.filename, level, node.type);
  }

  private _getLevel = (node: FileFlatNode) => node.level;

  private _isExpandable = (node: FileFlatNode) => node.expandable;

  private _getChildren = (node: FileNode): Observable<FileNode[]> =>
observableOf(node.children);

  hasChild = (_: number, _nodeData: FileFlatNode) => _nodeData.expandable;
}

export class FileNode {
  children: FileNode[];
  filename: string;
  type: any;
}

export class FileFlatNode {
  constructor(
    public expandable: boolean,
    public filename: string,
    public level: number,
    public type: any) { }
}

const TREE_DATA = JSON.stringify({
  'Chapter 1': {
    'Counter': '/chapter01/counter',
    'Fetch Data': '/chapter01/fetch-data'
  },
  'Chapter 2': {
    'Gincker': 'https://gincker.com',
    'Gincker AI': 'https://gincker.com/AI',
    'Gincker Graphics': 'https://gincker.com/Graphics'
  },
  'Chapter 3': {
    'Gincker': 'https://gincker.com',
    'Gincker AI': 'https://gincker.com/AI',
    'Gincker Graphics': 'https://gincker.com/Graphics'
  },
});
```

Here, we implement several TypeScript classes, which will be explained in the following chapters. The *FileNode* class provides the file node data with nested structure, and each node has a filename, and a type or a list of children. The *FileFlatNode* class provides file node with expandable and level information. The *FileData* class builds a tree structured JSON object from string. Each node in JSON object represents a file (or link) or a directory. For a file, it has filename and type. While for a directory, it has filename and children (a list of files or directories). The input will be a JSON object string, and the output is a list of *FileNode* with nested structure. The *TREE_DATA* string represents the file structure of the tree data in string and can be parsed into a JSON object. We will update this data string when we add more examples to the project later.

Here, we implement three dropdown menus, *Ch1, Ch2, and Ch3* using the *mat-menu* from Angular Material. These menus are simply placeholders, to which we will add more corresponding links later. From these dropdown menus, you can navigate to different pages. For example, tap the *Ch1* dropdown menu and select *Counter*, which brings up the *Counter* page, as shown in Fig.1-7.

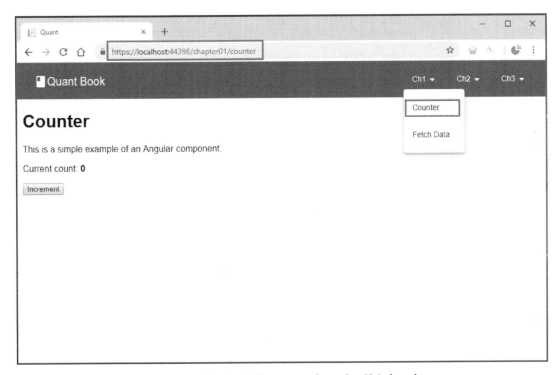

Fig.1-7. Navigate to the Fetch Data page from the Ch1 dropdown menu.

The dropdown menu in the mat-toolbar will be disappear and the menu icon will show up when reducing your browser's size. Click the menu icon to bring up the sidenav component, as shown in Fig.1-8.

Now click the Fetch Data link will lead to two results: navigating to the Fetch Data page and closing the *sidenav* component automatically, as shown in Fig.1-9.

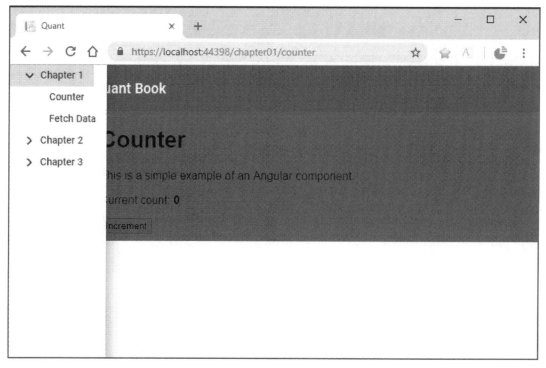

Fig.1-8. Sidenav component on the left.

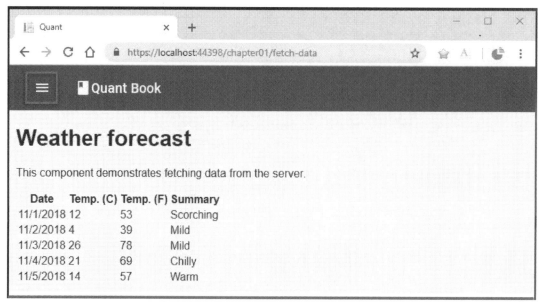

Fig.1-9. Responsive navigation from sidenav for small viewport.

Use Angular Material Table

You may notice from Fig.1-9 that the data shown in the table has no styling since we have removed the Bootstrap CSS framework from our project. Here, we will use Angular Material table component to display the data.

Open the *fetch-data.component.ts* file in the *ClientApp/src/chapter01/fetch-data* folder and add a *displayedColumns* property, as shown in the following listing:

```
// fetch-data.componnet.ts file:
import { Component, Inject } from '@angular/core';
import { HttpClient } from '@angular/common/http';

@Component({
  selector: 'app-fetch-data',
  templateUrl: './fetch-data.component.html'
})
export class FetchDataComponent {
  public forecasts: WeatherForecast[];

  public displayedColumns =
        ['dateFormatted', 'temperatureC', 'temperatureF', 'summary'];

    // ... other code omitted for brevity ...
}
......
```

Open the *fetch-data.component.html* from the same folder and replace its content with the following code listing:

```
// fetch-data.component.html file:
<h1>Weather forecast</h1>

<p>This component demonstrates fetching data from the server.</p>

<p *ngIf="!forecasts"><em>Loading...</em></p>

<mat-table [dataSource]="forecasts">
  <ng-container matColumnDef="dateFormatted">
    <mat-header-cell *matHeaderCellDef>Date</mat-header-cell>
    <mat-cell *matCellDef="let forecast">{{forecast.dateFormatted}}</mat-cell>
  </ng-container>
  <ng-container matColumnDef="temperatureC">
    <mat-header-cell *matHeaderCellDef>Temp. (C)</mat-header-cell>
    <mat-cell *matCellDef="let forecast">{{forecast.temperatureC}}</mat-cell>
  </ng-container>
  <ng-container matColumnDef="temperatureF">
    <mat-header-cell *matHeaderCellDef>Temp. (F)</mat-header-cell>
    <mat-cell *matCellDef="let forecast">{{forecast.temperatureF}}</mat-cell>
  </ng-container>
  <ng-container matColumnDef="summary">
    <mat-header-cell *matHeaderCellDef>Summary</mat-header-cell>
    <mat-cell *matCellDef="let forecast">{{forecast.summary}}</mat-cell>
  </ng-container>
  <mat-header-row *matHeaderRowDef="displayedColumns"></mat-header-row>
  <mat-row *matRowDef="let row; columns: displayedColumns;"></mat-row>
```

```
</mat-table>
```

Here we use *mat-table* that provides a Material design styled data-table, which can be used to display rows of data. First, we need to add **<table mat-table>** component to the template and passing in data. The simplest way to provide data to the table is by passing a data array to the table's *dataSource* input. The table will take the array and render a row for each object in the data array.

Next, we need to define the column templates. Each column definition should be given a unique name and contain the content for its header and row cells. Here is a simple column definition with the name '*summary*'. The header cell contains the text *Name* and each row cell will render the *name* property of each row's data:

```
<ng-container matColumnDef="summary">
    <mat-header-cell *matHeaderCellDef>Summary</mat-header-cell>
    <mat-cell *matCellDef="let forecast">{{forecast.summary}}</mat-cell>
</ng-container>
```

Finally, once we have defined columns, we need to tell the table which columns will be rendered in the header and data rows. Previously, we created a variable named *displayedColumns* in the *fetch-data.component.ts* file that contains the list of the columns we want to render. Now, we can add *mat-header-row* and *mat-row* to the content of our *mat-table* and provide the column variable as inputs:

```
<mat-header-row *matHeaderRowDef="displayedColumns"></mat-header-row>
<mat-row *matRowDef="let row; columns: displayedColumns;"></mat-row>
```

Note that this list of columns provided to the rows can be in any order, not necessary the order in which you wrote the column definitions. Also, you do not necessarily have to include every column that was defined in your template. This means that by changing your column list provided to the rows, you can easily re-order and include/exclude columns dynamically.

Saving the files and navigating to the fetch-data page produce the result shown in Fig.1-10. 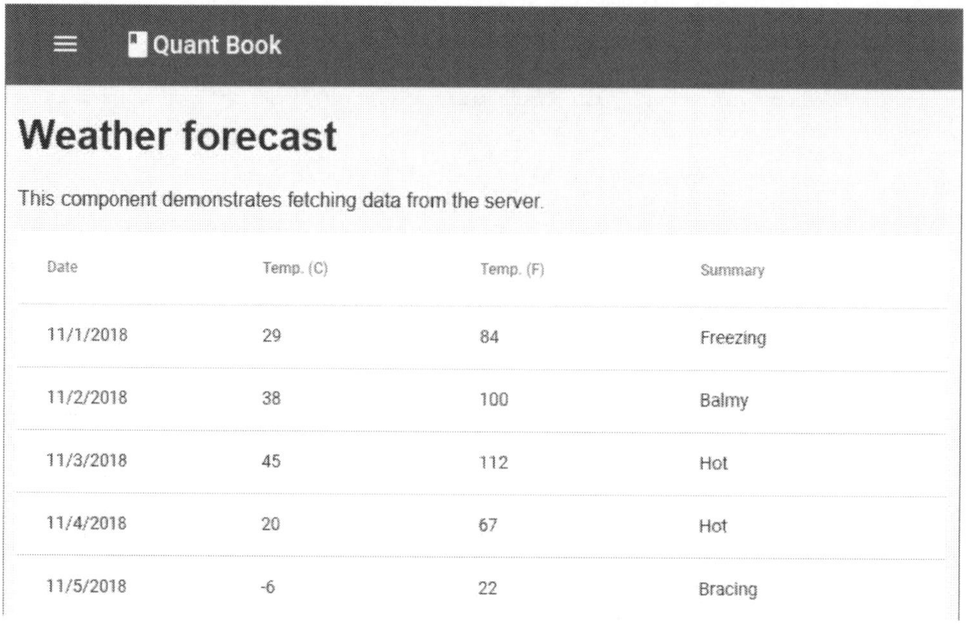

Fig.1-10. Data displayed in a mat-table.

If you do not like the looks of the default *mat-table*, you can changes its styles using CSS. Add the following code listing to the global styling file, *styles.css*, in the *ClientApp/src* folder:

```
// styles.css
@import"~@angular/material/prebuilt-themes/indigo-pink.css";

html, body {
  height: 100%;
}

body {
  margin: 0;
  font-family: "Roboto monospace", "Helvetica Neue", sans-serif;
}

.mat-row{
  min-height:30px;
  max-height:40px;
}
.mat-header-row {
  min-height: 40px;
  max-height: 50px;
  background-color: #7986CB;
}
.mat-header-cell{
  font-weight:400;
  font-size:medium;
  color:white;
}
```

Here, we set the min-height and max-height properties for the rows of the *mat-table*. We also change the background color and font for the table header. Saving the file and navigating to the *Fetch Data* page produce the result shown in Fig.1-11.

| | Quant Book |

Weather forecast

This component demonstrates fetching data from the server.

Date	Temp. (C)	Temp. (F)	Summary
11/6/2018	-9	16	Warm
11/7/2018	-13	9	Sweltering
11/8/2018	15	58	Warm
11/9/2018	41	105	Hot
11/10/2018	50	121	Bracing

Fig.1-11. Data displayed in a mat-table with new styles.

Chapter 2
Angular Basics

In this chapter, I provide a quick review for Angular framework. Angular is a web application framework developed and maintained by Google and the open-source community. The framework has many features, including one- and two-way data binding, templating, routing, components, dependency injection, etc. Unfortunately, like all framework of its breed, Angular has a steep learning curve due to many concepts you have to grasp in order to be fluent in it.

Here is a list of the most important Angular features:

- *Module*: a container that group together blocks of functionalities that belong together, like components, directives, services, etc.
- *Component*: a directive that defines its own HTML content and, optionally, CSS styles.
- *Template*: an HTML file that defines how the view for a component is rendered.
- *Data binding*: the process that connects a component to its template and allows data and events to flow between them.
- *Directive*: a custom attribute that enhances HTML syntax and is used to attach behaviors to specific elements on the page.
- *Service*: a reusable functionality that is independent from the views.
- *Dependency Injection (DI)*: a way to supply dependencies to classes.
- *Metadata*: instructs Angular on how to process a class, whether it is a component, a module, a directive, which services have to be injected, etc.

These terms might sound abstract at the moment, but they will become clear, as all of these features are used to build various SPA examples in the following chapters.

TypeScript

JavaScript (JS) and TypeScript (TS) are two widely known languages in the web development world. JS allows web pages to be interactive. It is created for client-side programming, which means it runs in the user's web browser without requiring resources from the server. It is used to perform dynamic tasks such as quizzes or polls and can be used with other technologies, including XML, REST APIs, etc.

TS is an object-oriented programming language developed and maintained by Microsoft. It is a superset of JS and contains all of JS elements. TS uses all the code found in JavaScript with other additional features such as modules, classes, interfaces, and types. It was created to make JS development easier. Because TS is a programming language, a compiler is required to convert it into plain JavaScript so it can run on web pages.

The benefits of TS arise from its additional features. Here are a few notable advantages over JS:

- Class and module support.
- Optional static type checking.
- Access to ES7 and ES7 features before they become supported by major browsers.
- Clear library API definition.
- Build-in support for JavaScript packaging.
- Ability to compile down to a version of JavaScript that runs on all browsers.
- Great tooling support with IntelliSense.

In fact, the modern Angular was built entirely in TypeScript, and as a result, using TypeScript with Angular provides a seamless experience. The Angular documentation not only supports TypeScript as a first-class citizen, but also uses it as its primary language. The TS's strong type system is very similar to the one you are already familiar with in C#. However, TypeScript is not C#, and working on a project that combines Angular and ASP.NET Core means writing code in two different languages, with two different sets of rules and features. There is a good deal of commonality between TS and C#, as you might expect from two languages created by Microsoft, but there are some import differences, too.

Static Types

TypeScript compiler will check the type. For example:

```
var name: string;
name = 2; // (TS) Type '2' is not assignable to type 'string'.

function foo(value: number) { }
foo(''); // (TS) Argument of type '""' is not assignable to parameter of
         // type 'string'.

interface Bar {
  setName: (name: string) => void;
  getName: () => string;
}

var bar: Bar = {
  getName: function () {
    return 'myName';
  }
} // (TS) Type '{ getName:()=> string;}' is not assignable to type 'Bar'.
  // Property 'setName' is missing in type '{getName()=>string;}'.
```

The IntelliSense in Visual Studio also gives your above code errors. This means that if you use the wrong data type in the TypeScript code, you will get compiling errors. Without TypeScript, these errors could only be found by testing against the back-end.

Class

The keywords like class, interface, extends, and module are available in TypeScript. You can define a *Person* class like this:

```
class Person {
  // properties
  firstName: string;
  lastName: string;

  // construtor
  constructor(frstName: string, lstName: string) {
    // fill the properties
    this.firstName = frstName;
    this.lastName = lstName;
  }
  // method
  getFullName() : string {
    return `${firstName} ${lastName}`;
  }
}
```

TypeScript compiler will convert the above class into the following plain JavaScript code:

```
var Person = /** @class */ (function () {
  // construtor
  function Person(frstName, lstName) {
    // fill the properties
    this.firstName = frstName;
    this.lastName = lstName;
  }
  // method
  Person.prototype.getFullName = function () {
    return firstName + " " + lastName;
  };
  return Person;
}());
```

From the above code for a simple *Person* class, you can clearly see that the TypeScript code is much concise, easier to read, and simpler to maintain than JavaScript. When Angular 2 was introduced, the use of TypeScript was optional, and it was possible to build Angular apps using plain JavaScript. The result was awkward and required some contorted code to recreate the effect of key TypeScript features. Therefore, to build applications in the Angular framework, you should master and use TypeScript.

TS also supports class inheritance by using the *extends* keyword. Here, we inherit a *Student* class from the *Person* class defined above:

```
class Student extends Person {
  // properties
  studentId: string;
  class: string;
  // construtor
  constructor(frstName: string, lstName: string,
    stdntId: string, clss: string) {
    // call the base class constructor
    super(rstName, lstName);
```

```
      // fill the other properties
      this.studentID = stdntId;
      this.class = clss;
    }
    // method
    toString() : string {
      return `${studentID} - ${firstName} ${lastName} => ${class}`;
    }
}
```

Here the *Student* class inherits its base *Person* class by writing **class Student extends Person**. In the derived class, **super (...)** can be used to call the constructor of the base class.

In this case, the TS compiler will convert the *Student* class into the following JavaScript code:

```
var __extends = (this && this.__extends) || (function () {
  var extendStatics = function (d, b) {
    extendStatics = Object.setPrototypeOf ||
        ({ __proto__: [] } instanceof Array && function (d, b) { d.__proto__ = b; })
        ||
        function (d, b) { for (var p in b) if (b.hasOwnProperty(p)) d[p] = b[p]; };
    return extendStatics(d, b);
  }
  return function (d, b) {
    extendStatics(d, b);
    function __() { this.constructor = d; }
d.prototype = b === null ? Object.create(b) :
(__.prototype = b.prototype, new __());
  };
})();
var Student = /** @class */ (function (_super) {
  __extends(Student, _super);
  // construtor
  function Student(frstName, lstName, stdntId, clss) {
    var _this =
      // call the base class constructor
      _super.call(this, rstName, lstName) || this;
    // fill the other properties
    _this.studentID = stdntId;
    _this.class = clss;
    return _this;
  }
  // method
  Student.prototype.toString = function () {
return studentID + " - " + firstName + " " + lastName + " => " + /** @class */
(function () {
      function class_1() {
      }
      return class_1;
    }());
  };
  return Student;
}(Person));
```

You can see that the JS code is very complex and hard to read.

Module

JavaScript files depend on each other, and, in large code bases, tracking their dependencies to decide which files to add to each HTML page, and in which order, is not a trivial task. The situation will soon become more complex if we try to optimize the downloading time of JavaScript files for HTML pages. In fact, the way to optimize the downloading time, other than the obvious minimization of JavaScript files, is to bundle together several files in a way to reduce the number of download operations, or to try downloading some files in parallel, while respecting all precedence constraints coming from the dependencies graph. In fact, if a file A depends on files B, then B must be downloaded and executed before A is executed.

Defining a single bundle per HTML page does not optimize cache usage, since common files are copied in several bundles instead of being cached once in the browser. An optimal strategy should factor out files used by several pages in separate bundles so that, when passing from one page to another, they may be found in the cache instead of being downloaded several times as part of different bundles.

Bundling, cache optimization, and parallel downloading may be taken care of by automatic tools, but this would require dependency relations be explicitly represented. This led the creation of the concept of a JavaScript module as a chunk of JavaScript code that explicitly represents its dependencies, and that can be asynchronously downloaded.

TypeScript modules, based on ECMAScript 6 type modules, combine asynchronous module-loaders with JavaScript module-bundlers. They can bundle several modules together to reduce download time and optimize cache usage. Modules are necessary in client-rich web applications where the entire presentation layer, such as Angular SPAs, is moved to the client side, since in this case both JavaScript files' optimization and dependencies tracking become extremely complex tasks.

A TypeScript file does not require any syntax to be interpreted as a module, but a TS file is considered a module just because another file tries to load it as a module. Like for classes, symbols are visible to the importing modules only if declarations are preceded by the *export* keyword. Unlike with classes, a module's code does not need to be enclosed in any syntax container – the boundary of a module is defined by the file it is in. For example:

```
// school.ts file:

export class Person {
    ...
}

export class Student extends Person {
    ...
}

class Teacher extends Person {
    ...
}
```

Thus, in the preceding module, just *Person* and *Student* are visible to importing modules, while *Teacher* is invisible. The name of the module is the name of the file containing it, that is, *school*.

The simplest way to import symbols from another module is something like the following:

```
// schoolImporter.ts file:

import * as school from "./school";
```

The preceding code import all symbols that are exported by *school.ts*. All symbols imported from *./school* are available through the identifies specified after the *as* keyword, that in the preceding example is *school* with expressions such as school.<imported module symbols>. For instance:

```
let aStudent: school.Student =
    new school.Student("John", "Smith", "ID123", "Class2018");
```

Only all *./school* exported symbols are visible, and they are visible with the names they are exported.

It is also possible to import just some symbols with a statement such as the following:

```
import { Student } from "./school";
```

With the preceding import statement, imported symbol is available as it is without being prefixed by any name:

```
let aStudent: Student = new Student("John", "Smith", "ID123", "Class2018");
```

It is also possible to provide alias while importing symbols by adding as clauses after symbols, as shown in the following example:

```
import { Student as Human } from "./school";
let aStudent: Human = new Human("John", "Smith", "ID123", "Class2018");
```

ES2017 (ES8) Feature Support

JavaScript implements ECMAScript and builds on top of it. ES is simply short for ECMAScript. Initial standards of ECMAScript were named numerically, increasing by 1, such as ES1 (1997), ES2 (1998), ES 3 (1999), ES4 (abandoned due to political reason), and ES5 (2009). The new editions, starting from 2015, will be named ES followed by the year of release, such as ES2015 (or ES6), ES2016 (or ES7), and ES2017 (or ES8).

If you open the *tsconfig.json* file in the *ClientApp* folder, you can check which ES version is used in building your application and which ES version is used to target your browser. Here is the content of the *tsconfig.json* file:

```
{
  "compileOnSave": false,
  "compilerOptions": {
    "baseUrl": "./",
    "outDir": "./dist/out-tsc",
    "sourceMap": true,
    "declaration": false,
    "moduleResolution": "node",
    "emitDecoratorMetadata": true,
    "experimentalDecorators": true,
    "target": "es5",
    "typeRoots": [
      "node_modules/@types"
    ],
    "lib": [
      "es2017",
      "dom"
    ]
  }
}
```

You can see that we have the latest version of ES2017 (or ES 8) in the **Lib** array, while we target ES5 in the *CompilerOptions* section. This means that we can use all the new features of ES 2017 during the course of application development, while the TypeScript compiler will convert it into JavaScript based on ES5 standard to support older browsers.

Some of new features in ES2017 are very handy. For example, the for-loop code:

```
// for … of loops
var ar = ['a', 'b', 'c'];
for (let item of ar) {
  console.log(item);
}
This will be compiled to the following:
// for … of loops
var ar = ['a', 'b', 'c'];
for (var i = 0, i < ar.length; i++) {
  var item = ar[i];
  console.log(item);
}
```

Refer to TypeScript ES2017 compatibility table (http://kangax.github.io/compat-table/es2016plus/) for more ES8 features you can use in your Angular project.

Structure of Angular App

With the skeleton of the default examples created via ASP.NET Core Angular template, as discussed in the Chapter 1, we can explore the basic components and structure of an Angular application (inside the *ClientApp/src* folder).

Angular App Entry Point

The entry point for Angular app in our *Quant* project or any other Angular application is the *main.ts* file in the *ClientApp/src* folder. Here is the code listing for this file:

```
// main.ts file:
import { enableProdMode } from '@angular/core';
import { platformBrowserDynamic } from '@angular/platform-browser-dynamic';
import { AppModule } from './app/app.module';
import { environment } from './environments/environment';
import 'hammerjs';

export function getBaseUrl() {
  return document.getElementsByTagName('base')[0].href;
}

const providers = [
  { provide: 'BASE_URL', useFactory: getBaseUrl, deps: [] }
];

if (environment.production) {
  enableProdMode();
}
```

```
platformBrowserDynamic(providers).bootstrapModule(AppModule)
  .catch(err => console.log(err));
```

This file is responsible for compiling the application with the just-in-time (JIT) compiler and bootstrapping the application's root module (*AppModule*) to run in the browser. You can see from the preceding code listing that it imports several modules to provide the very basic and initial setup to Angular:

- *enableProdMode*: disable Angular's development mode, which turns off assertions and other checks within the framework.

- *platformBrowserDynamic*: To bootstrap your app for browsers.

- *AppModule*: The root module that informs Angular about various files and codes.

- *environment*: Environment variables in Angular.

Root Module

The next file is the *app.module.ts* file in the *ClientApp/src/app* folder. This file defines the root module, which tells Angular how to assemble the application. By default, it declares only a few components for the default examples. Soon there will be more components to declare as our project grows. Here is the current code listing of this root module:

```
import { BrowserModule } from '@angular/platform-browser';
import { NgModule } from '@angular/core';
import { FormsModule, ReactiveFormsModule} from '@angular/forms';
import { HttpClientModule } from '@angular/common/http';
import { CommonModule } from '@angular/common';
import { RouterModule } from '@angular/router';
import { BrowserAnimationsModule } from '@angular/platform-browser/animations';
import { FlexLayoutModule } from '@angular/flex-layout';
import { MaterialModule } from './material/material.module';

import { AppComponent } from './app.component';
import { NavMenuComponent } from './nav-menu/nav-menu.component';
import { HomeComponent } from './home/home.component';
import { CounterComponent } from './chapter01/counter/counter.component'
import { FetchDataComponent } from './chapter01/fetch-data/fetch-data.component';
import { TestMaterialComponent }
        from './chapter01/test-material/test-material.component';

@NgModule({
  declarations: [
    AppComponent,
    NavMenuComponent,
    HomeComponent,
    CounterComponent,
    FetchDataComponent,
  ],
  imports: [
    BrowserModule.withServerTransition({ appId: 'ng-cli-universal' }),
    HttpClientModule,
    CommonModule,
    FormsModule,
```

```
    ReactiveFormsModule,
    BrowserAnimationsModule,
    FlexLayoutModule,
    MaterialModule,
    RouterModule.forRoot([
        { path: 'chapter01/counter', component: CounterComponent },
        { path: 'chapter01/fetch-data', component: FetchDataComponent },
        { path: '', component: HomeComponent, pathMatch: 'full' }
    ])
  ],
  providers: [],
  bootstrap: [AppComponent]
})
export class AppModule { }
```

The file starts by importing all the JavaScript classes that are referenced inside this class. There are three Angular modules, *BrowserModule, FormsModule, and HttpModule*, which are going to be used by almost any Angular app, and one decorator, *NgModule*, which is used to define the application root module. All the other modules are specifically required by our *Quant* project.

Then there is an actual module definition, the class *AppModule*, decorated by the *@NgModule* decorator, which contains four arrays:

- *declarations*: contains all the components belong to this module.

- *imports*: contains all the Angular modules used inside this module. This includes both structural modules and as the application evolves custom feature modules.

- *providers*: It is an empty array because at the moment the application is not using any service, but once we start creating services, they will need to be defined inside this array.

- *bootstrap*: contains the components that have to be created during the app's bootstrapping process. In our project, this is the *AppComponent*.

The *RouterModule* inside the *imports* array defines the routing paths for the application, which will be discussed in the "Routing and Navigation" section later.

Root Component

The following code listing is for the root component, *AppComponent*, defined in the file *app.component.ts* in the *ClientApp/src/app* folder:

```
// app.component.ts file:
import { Component } from '@angular/core';

@Component({
  selector: 'app-root',
  templateUrl: './app.component.html',
  styleUrls: ['./app.component.css']
})
export class AppComponent {
  title = 'app';
}
```

Defining the root component is just like defining the root module. It is done with decorator *@Component* and specifying the selector that is used in the HTML file to include the component, the URL of the view (or template) for the component (via the *templateUrl* property), and the styles specific for this view (with the *styleUrls* property).

Since a component, unlike a module, has behaviors, the class must do something, in this case just setting the value of the property title. In our project the view (or template) of the component is very simple, as shown in the following code:

```
// app.component.html file:
<body>
  <app-nav-menu></app-nav-menu>
  <!-- <router-outlet></router-outlet> -->
</body>
```

Since we have moved the *router-outlet* component to the *sidenav* section of the *nav-menu* component's template as discussed in Chapter 1, the *app* view now only contains the *nav-menu* directives. The *router-outlet* is a directive from the router library that is used like a component. It acts as a placeholder that makes the spot in the template where the router should display the component for that outlet.

Routing and Navigation

The *RouterModule* inside the *imports* array of the root module is an optional Angular routing service that presents a particular convenient view for a given URL. It is not part of the Angular core. It is in its own library *@angular/router*. By default, the ASP.NET Core and Angular SPA template automatically import it and use it to set up the URL paths to the default examples.

A routed Angular app has one singleton instance of the *Router* service. When the browser's URL changes, that router looks for a corresponding route from which it can determine the component to display. A router has no routes until you configure it. Angular configures the router via the *RouterModule.forRoot* method and adds the result to the *AppModule*'s imports array. Our current project has three route definitions:

```
RouterModule.forRoot([
  { path: 'chapter01/counter', component: CounterComponent },
  { path: 'chapter01/fetch-data', component: FetchDataComponent },
  { path: '', component: HomeComponent, pathMatch: 'full' }
])
```

Here each *Route* maps a URL path to a component. There are no leading slashes in the path. The router parses and builds the final URL for you, allowing you to use both relative and absolute paths when navigating between application views. The empty path corresponding the *HomeComponent* represents the default path for the application, the place to go when the path in the URL is empty. The default route goes to the home page of our application.

The order of the routes in the configuration matters and this is by design. The router uses a first-match wins strategy when matching routes, so more specific routes should be placed above less specific routes. In the configuration above, routes with a static path are listed first, followed by an empty path route, which matches the default route.

Now we have routes configured and a place to render them, but how do we navigate? The URL could arrive directly from the browser address bar. However, most of the time you navigate as a result of some user action such as the click of an anchor tag. This can be seen clearly by opening the *home.component.html* file in the *ClientApp/src/app/home* folder:

```
// home.component.html file:
```

```
// ... other code omitted for brevity ...

<ul style="margin-top:50px;list-style:none">
  <li><p><a [routerLink]='["/"]'>Quant Book Home</a></p></li>
  <li>
    <p>Chapter 1</p>
    <ul>
      <li><a [routerLink]='["/chapter01/counter"]'>Counter</a></li>
      <li style="margin-top:5px">
          <a [routerLink]='["/chapter01/fetch-data"]'>Fetch Data</a>
      </li>
    </ul>
  </li>
  <li><p>Chapter 2</p></li>
  <li><p>Chapter 3</p></li>
</ul>
```

The *routerLink* directive on the anchor tags gives the router control over those elements. In our project, the above navigation paths are fixed, so you can assign a string directly to the *routerLink* as follows:

```
<a routerLink="/chapter01/counter">Counter</a>
```

The above code is simply a "one-time" binding. Had the navigation path been more dynamic, you could have bound to a template expression that returned an array of route link parameters. In this case, you should use [*routerLink*] instead of *routerLink* to resolves that array into a complete URL.

Main HTML Page

The real entry point of the Angular app, which actually starts its bootstrapping process, is the main *index.html* file in the *ClientApp/src* folder. Here is the code for this file:

```
// index.html file:
<!doctype html>
<html lang="en">
<head>
  <meta charset="utf-8">
  <title>Quant</title>
  <base href="/">

  <meta name="viewport" content="width=device-width, initial-scale=1">
  <link rel="icon" type="image/x-icon" href="favicon.ico">
  <link href="https://fonts.googleapis.com/icon?family=Material+Icons"
        rel="stylesheet">
  <link href="https://fonts.googleapis.com/css?family=Roboto:300,400,500"
        rel="stylesheet">
</head>
<body>
  <app-root>Loading...</app-root>
</body>
</html>
```

As you can see, the **<app-root>** tag is the same as specified in the selector property of the root component (refer to *app.component.ts* file). Here is where the bootstrapping process will inject the view rendered by the root component.

Data Binding

Data binding is a core concept in Angular. It allows you to communication between a component and the view (or template), making it very easy to build interactive applications without worrying about pushing and pulling data. There are four types of data binding and they differ in the way the data is flowing.

- *Interpolation*: sends data from the component to the browser, rendering it as the content of a HTML tag.

- *One-way binding*: sends data from the component to the browser, but it assigns the value to an attribute or property of an HTML element.

- *Event binding*: sends data from the browser to the component.

- *Two-way binding*: keeps in sync a property of the component with what is rendered in an *input* element in the browser.

Interpolation Binding

An Angular application starts with a component and the basis of data binding involves displaying data in a template rendered using a component. If all you need to do is render a property value of the model of a component inside the browser as the content of an HTML element, the simplest way of binding is called interpolation. This is done by putting the expression you want to render inside double curly braces {{...}}. The content can be just the name of a component's property or a TypeScript expression.

Let us create a new component named interpolation using the Angular CLI tool. This tool is a command-line interface (CLI) tool, which can be used to initialize, develop, scaffold, and maintain Angular app. It is easy to invoke the tool on the command line through the *ng* executable.

Open a command prompt window, navigate to the *ClientApp* folder of our *Quant* project, and run the following command:

```
ng generate component charter02/interpolation --module=app.module
```

or use the equivalent short version:

```
ng g c charter02/interpolation --module=app.module
```

With the Angular CLI tool, we can use **ng generate** (or **ng g**) command to create blueprint for all kind of resources needed during the course of our Angular app development. Here, we use the **ng generate component** (or **ng g c**) to create a new Angular component called *interpolation* in the *ClientApp/src/app/chapter02* folder with the files that a typical component needs, as shown in Fig.2-1.

You can see from Fig.2-1 that there are three files with the extensions of *css*, *html*, and *ts*, representing the component styles, template, and class, respectively.

In the preceding command, we also add an option: *--module=app.module*. This option indicates that the new component should be declared into *app.module*. The *--module* option is required in our *Quant* project because there are two modules in the app root folder: *app.module.ts* and *app.server.module.ts*. If omitting this option, you will get an error like below:

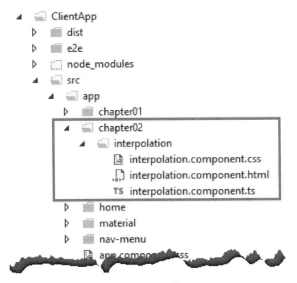

Fig.2-1. Files for the interpolation component.

More than one module matches. Use skip-import option to skip importing the component into the closest module.

With the preceding command, the new component is also added in the root module's declaration automatically, which can be seen from the following code snippet in the *app.module.ts* file:

```
// app.module.ts file:
// ... other imports omitted for brevity ...

import { InterpolationComponent } from
      './chapter02/interpolation/interpolation.component';

@NgModule({
  declarations: [
    // ... other declarations omitted for brevity ...

    InterpolationComponent
  ],
  imports: [
    BrowserModule.withServerTransition({ appId: 'ng-cli-universal' }),

    // ... other modules omitted for brevity ...

    RouterModule.forRoot([
      { path: 'chapter01/counter', component: CounterComponent },
      { path: 'chapter01/fetch-data', component: FetchDataComponent },
      { path: '', component: HomeComponent, pathMatch: 'full' }
    ])
  ],
  providers: [],
  bootstrap: [AppComponent]
})
export class AppModule { }
```

We need to manually add a path for this new component to the *RouterModule* of this file:

```
{ path: 'chapter02/interpolation', component: InterpolationComponent },
```

Then add the corresponding URL link to the *home* and *nav-menu* components.

Now, we need to add some properties to the component. Open the *interpolation.component.ts* file and replace its content with the following code:

```
// inoterpolation.component.ts file:
import { Component, OnInit } from '@angular/core';

@Component({
  selector: 'app-interpolation',
  templateUrl: './interpolation.component.html',
  styleUrls: ['./interpolation.component.css']
})
export class InterpolationComponent implements OnInit {
  public ticker: string = 'IBM';
  public date: Date = new Date('7/14/2015');
  public open: number = 169.43;
  public high: number = 169.54;
  public low: number = 168.24;
  public close: number = 168.61;

  constructor() {}

  ngOnInit() {
  }

  getAvgPrice() : number {
      return (this.open + this.high + this.low + this.close) / 4;
  }
}
```

You might wonder why the *interpolation* component class has a *constructor* and an *ngOnInit* method when you look at the code. The constructor method is a feature of a class itself in TypeScript, rather than an Angular feature. It might be out of Angular's control when the *constructor* is invoked, which means that it is not a suitable hook to let you know when Angular has finished initializing the component. By adding the *ngOnInit* method, Angular can fire a method once it has finished setting the component up.

In an Angular app, constructor can be used to initialize the fields and dependency injection. The *ngOnInit* method signals that Angular has finished initializing and setting up component. It is called after the constructor is executed. In *constructor,* Angular initializes and resolves all class members, so in *ngOnInit* you can initialize work and logic of the component. The *ngOnInit* lifecycle hook is a guarantee that your bindings are readily available.

The preceding class defines several properties used to specify the stock prices for IBM and a *getAvgPrice* method used to calculate the average stock price.

Then open the temple file, *interpolation.component.html*, in the *ClientApp/src/app/chapter02* folder and update its content with the following code:

```
// interpolation.component.html file:

<h2>
  Interpolation works!
```

```
</h2>

<p>Stock Ticker: {{ticker}}</p>
<p>Date: {{date | date: 'MM/dd/yyyy'}}</p>
<p>
   Stock Prices: open price = {{open}}, high price = {{high}}, low price = {{low}},
   close price = {{close}}
</p>
<p>Average Stock Price: {{getAvgPrice()}}</p>
<p>Total Price: {{200 + getAvgPrice()}}</p>
```

Here we use Angular pipe to display the date property, as shown in the bold code. Angular pipe is responsible for formatting data values so they can be represented to the user. Pipe is applied to a data value using the vertical bar, following by the name of the pipe and its configuration settings.

Note that the expression in the double curly braces can invoke methods of the host component such as `{{getAvgPrice()}}`. The following is also a valid expression for interpolation binding:

```
<p>Total price: {{200 + getAvgPrice()}}</p>
```

Angular evaluates all expressions in double curly braces, converts the expression results to strings, and links them with neighboring literal strings. Finally, it assigns this complete interpolated result to an element or directive property.

Saving the project and navigating to the */chapter02/interpolation* page produce the results shown in Fig.2-2.

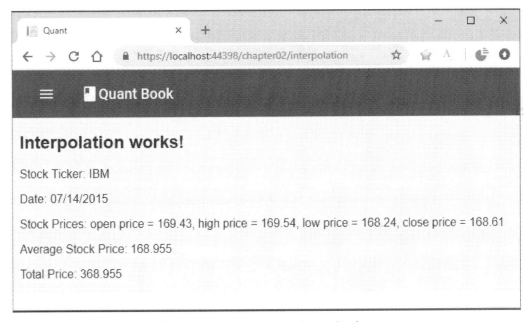

Fig.2-2. Results for interpolation binding.

Interpolation binding has some limitations. It works only for string type properties. We cannot assign an expression result to a variable using interpolation nor access global variables like *window.location.href*.

One-Way Binding

One-way binding, also called property binding, flows a value in one direction, from a component's data property into a target element property in the view. You cannot use property binding to pull values out of the target element, nor bind to a property of the target element to read it – you can only set it. Similarly, you cannot use property binding to call a method on the target element.

One-way binding can be achieved in Angular by wrapping the attribute name with square brackets [...] and assigning the value using the property name as if it was a static value. An element property between enclosing square brackets identifies the target property. Alternatively, you can also use the *bind-prefix*, known as the canonical form, for the property binding.

Let us consider an example for property binding. Open a command prompt window, navigate to the *ClientApp* directory, and run the following command:

ng g c charter02/one-way-binding --module=app.module

This creates a new component named *one-way-binding* in the *ClientApp/src/app/chapter02* folder. Open the *one-way-binding.component.css* file and add the following styles to it:

```
// one-way-binding.component.css file:
.example-form {
  min-width: 100px;
  max-width: 300px;
  width: 100%;
}

.example-full-width {
  width: 100%;
}
```

Open the class file for this component and replace its content with the following code:

```
// one-way-binding.component.ts file:
mport { Component, OnInit } from '@angular/core';

@Component({
  selector: 'app-one-way-binding',
  templateUrl: './one-way-binding.component.html',
  styleUrls: ['./one-way-binding.component.css']
})
export class OneWayBindingComponent implements OnInit {
  public ticker: string = 'IBM';
  public date: Date = new Date('7/14/2015');
  public open: number = 169.43;
  public high: number = 169.54;
  public low: number = 168.24;
  public close: number = 168.61;

  constructor() { }
  ngOnInit() {
  }
  getAvgPrice(): number {
    return (this.open + this.high + this.low + this.close) / 4;
  }
```

```
  getColor(price: number): string {
    return price < 169 ? 'red' : 'green';
  }
}
```

This component class is similar to that used in the preceding example, except that we add an additional method named *getColor* with an input parameter of price. If the price < 169, it returns a "red" string, otherwise it return a "green" color string.

Now, open the template file for this component and replace its content with the following code:

```
// one-way-binding.component.html file:
<h2>
  One-way-binding works!
</h2>


<form class="example-form" [style.color]="getColor(getAvgPrice())">
  <mat-form-field class="example-full-width">
    <input matInput placeholder="Stock Ticker" [value]="ticker">
  </mat-form-field>
  <mat-form-field class="example-full-width">
    <input matInput placeholder="Date" [value]="date | date:'MM/dd/yyyy'">
  </mat-form-field>
  <mat-form-field class="example-full-width">
<input matInput placeholder="Open Price" [value]="open"
      [style.color]="getColor(open)">
  </mat-form-field>
  <mat-form-field class="example-full-width">
<input matInput placeholder="High Price" [value]="high"
      [style.color]="getColor(high)">
  </mat-form-field>
  <mat-form-field class="example-full-width">
<input matInput placeholder="Low Price" bind-value="low"
      [style.color]="getColor(low)">
  </mat-form-field>
  <mat-form-field class="example-full-width">
<input matInput placeholder="Close Price" bind-value="close"
      [style.color]="getColor(close)">
  </mat-form-field>

  <mat-form-field class="example-full-width">
<input matInput placeholder="Average Price" bind-value="getAvgPrice()"
      bind-style.color="getColor(getAvgPrice())">
  </mat-form-field>
</form>
```

Here we use both the square brackets and bind-prefix for the property binding. We use the property binding to set not only the value of the *input* elements, but also their text color via [style.color]. We also use the *mat-form-field* and *matInput* from Angular Material to provide an ultra-modern feel to our application.

Finally, we need to add a path for this new component to the *RouterModule* of the root module (i.e., the *app.module.ts* file):

```
{ path: 'chapter02/one-way-binding', component: OneWayBindingComponent },
```

Then add the corresponding URL link to the *home* and *nav-menu* components.

Saving the project and navigating to the */chapter02/one-way-binding* page produce the results shown in Fig.2-3.

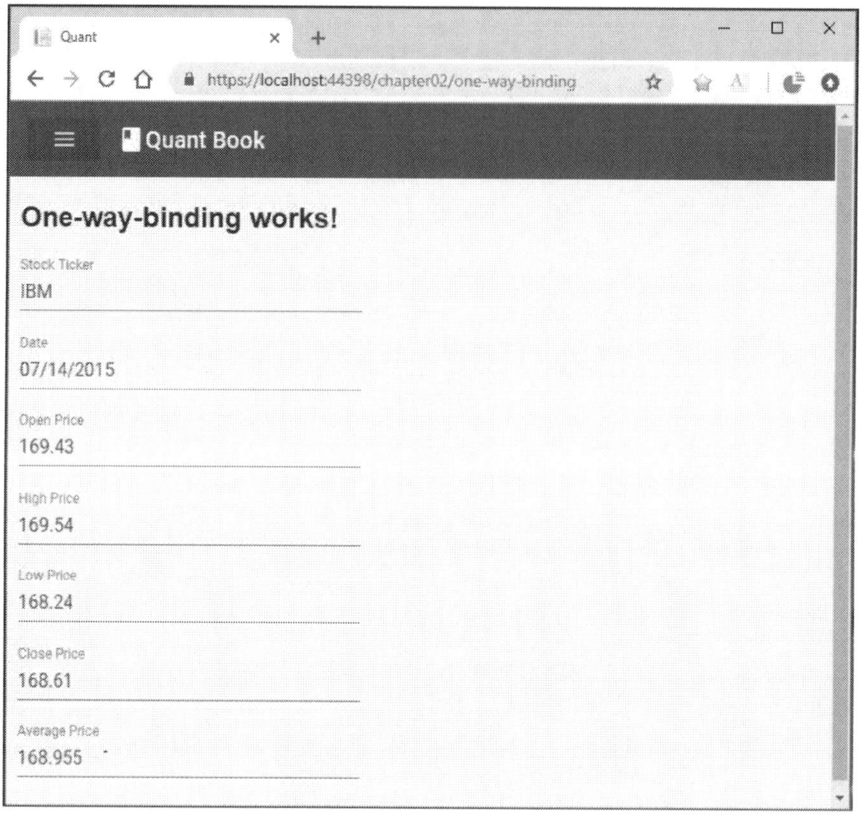

Fig.2-3. Results for one-way binding.

Event Binding

We can use the event binding to send data from the template to the component. This time we wrap the name of any valid HTML event with parentheses (…) and assign it to a method of the component.

Let us consider an example. Run the following command in a command prompt window:

```
ng g c charter02/event-binding --module=app.module
```

This creates a new component named *event-binding* in the *ClientApp/src/app/chapter02* folder. The style file for this component will be the same as preceding example. We need to make changes to the component class. Open the *event-binding.component.ts* file and replace its content with the following code:

```
// event-binding.component.ts file:
import { Component, OnInit } from '@angular/core';

@Component({
  selector: 'app-event-binding',
```

```
    templateUrl: './event-binding.component.html',
    styleUrls: ['./event-binding.component.css']
})
export class EventBindingComponent implements OnInit {
  public ticker: string = 'IBM';
  public date: Date = new Date('7/14/2015');
  public open: number = 169.43;
  public high: number = 169.54;
  public low: number = 168.24;
  public close: number = 168.61;
  public bgColor: string = 'white';

  constructor() { }

  ngOnInit() {
  }

  getAvgPrice(): number {
    return (this.open + this.high + this.low + this.close) / 4;
  }

  getColor(price: number): string {
    return price < 169 ? 'red' : 'green';
  }

  setBackgroundColor() {
    if (this.bgColor == 'white') this.bgColor = 'grey';
    else this.bgColor = 'white';
  }
}
```

This file is similar to that used in the preceding example, except we add a *bgColor* property and a method named *setBackgroundColor*.

Open the template file for this component and replace its content with the following code:

```
// event-binding.component.html file:
<h2>
  Event-binding works!
</h2>

<form class="example-form" [style.background-color]="bgColor">
  <mat-form-field class="example-full-width">
    <input matInput placeholder="Stock Ticker" [value]="ticker">
  </mat-form-field>
  <mat-form-field class="example-full-width">
    <input matInput placeholder="Date" [value]="date | date:'MM/dd/yyyy'">
  </mat-form-field>
  <mat-form-field class="example-full-width">
    <input matInput placeholder="Open Price" [value]="open"
      [style.color]="getColor(open)">
  </mat-form-field>
  <mat-form-field class="example-full-width">
    <input matInput placeholder="High Price" [value]="high"
      [style.color]="getColor(high)">
  </mat-form-field>
```

```html
<mat-form-field class="example-full-width">
  <input matInput placeholder="Low Price" bind-value="low"
    [style.color]="getColor(low)">
</mat-form-field>
<mat-form-field class="example-full-width">
  <input matInput placeholder="Close Price" bind-value="close"
    [style.color]="getColor(close)">
</mat-form-field>

<mat-form-field class="example-full-width">
  <input matInput placeholder="Average Price" bind-value="getAvgPrice()"
    bind-style.color="getColor(getAvgPrice())">
</mat-form-field>
</form>
```

```html
<button mat-raised-button (click)="setBackgroundColor()">
    Change Background Color
</button>
```

Here, we set the form's background color using the *bgColor* property defined in the component class. We also add a button that listens for its click event, calling the component's *setBackgroundColor* method whenever a click occurs. The name between parentheses – for example, **(click)** – identifies the target event. You can also use the *on-prefix* alternative to replace the parentheses. The following code snippet will work the same way as the **(click)**:

```html
<button mat-raised-button on-click="setBackgroundColor()">
  Change Background Color
</button>
```

Finally, we need to add a path for this new component to the *RouterModule* of the root module (i.e., the *app.module.ts* file):

```
{ path: 'chapter02/event-binding', component: EventBindingComponent },
```

Then add the corresponding URL link to the *home* and *nav-menu* components.

Saving the project and navigating to the */chapter02/event-binding* page produce the results shown in Fig.2-4. Now if you click the *Change Background Color* button, the form's background color will change.

Two-Way Binding

The most powerful of all bindings is the two-way binding, which keeps in sync templates and components' models. It allows you to both display a data property and update that property when the user makes changes. On the element side, that takes a combination of setting a specific element property and listening for an element change event. This is done using a new syntax [(…)], which combines the brackets of property binding, […], with the parentheses of event binding, (…).

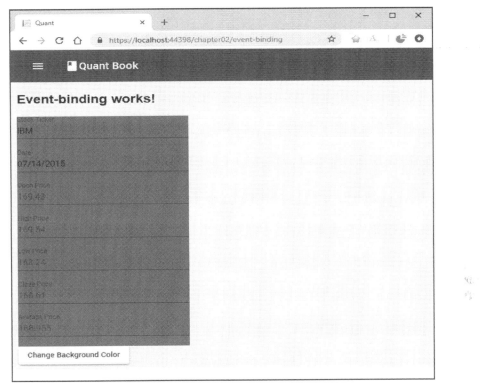

Fig.2-4. Results for event binding.

The [(ngModel)] directive can be used to simplify two-way bindings so that you do not have to apply both an event and a property binding to the same element. Here, I will use an example to illustrate how to use this directive for two-way bindings. First, we need to run the following command in a command prompt window from the *ClientApp* folder:

```
ng g c charter02/two-way-binding --module=app.module
```

This creates a new component named *two-way-binding* in the *ClientApp/src/app/chapter02* folder. Add the following code listing to the style file for the component:

```
// two-way.component.css file:
.example-form {
  min-width: 100px;
  max-width: 300px;
  width: 100%;
}

.example-full-width {
  width: 100%;
}

.mat-grid-list{
  min-width:300px;
  max-width:500px;
}
```

Open the *two-way-binding.component.ts* file and replace its content with the following code:

```
// two-way.component.ts file:
import { Component, OnInit } from '@angular/core';

@Component({
  selector: 'app-two-way-binding',
  templateUrl: './two-way-binding.component.html',
  styleUrls: ['./two-way-binding.component.css']
})
export class TwoWayBindingComponent implements OnInit {
  public ticker: string = 'IBM';
  public date: Date = new Date('7/14/2015');
  public open: number = 169.43;
  public high: number = 169.54;
  public low: number = 168.24;
  public close: number = 168.61;

  constructor() { }

  ngOnInit() {
  }

  getColor(price: number): string {
    return price < 169 ? 'red' : 'green';
  }
}
```

Next, replace the content of the component's template file with the following code:

```
// two-way-binding.component.html file:
<h2>
  Two-way-binding works!
</h2>

<mat-grid-list cols="2" rowHeight="400px">
  <mat-grid-tile>
    <form class="example-form">
      <mat-form-field class="example-full-width">
        <input matInput placeholder="Stock Ticker" [value]="ticker">
      </mat-form-field>
      <mat-form-field class="example-full-width">
        <input matInput type="date" placeholder="Date"
          [value]="date | date:'MM/dd/yyyy'">
      </mat-form-field>
      <mat-form-field class="example-full-width">
        <input matInput placeholder="Open Price" [(ngModel)]="open" name="open"
            [style.color]="getColor(open)">
      </mat-form-field>
      <mat-form-field class="example-full-width">
        <input matInput placeholder="High Price" [(ngModel)]="high" name="high"
            [style.color]="getColor(high)">
      </mat-form-field>
      <mat-form-field class="example-full-width">
        <input matInput placeholder="Low Price" [(ngModel)]="low" name="low"
            [style.color]="getColor(low)">
```

```
      </mat-form-field>
      <mat-form-field class="example-full-width">
        <input matInput placeholder="Close Price" [(ngModel)]="close" name="close"
             [style.color]="getColor(close)">
      </mat-form-field>
    </form>
  </mat-grid-tile>
  <mat-grid-tile>
    <div>
      <p>Open: {{open}}</p>
      <p>High: {{high}}</p>
      <p>Low: {{low}}</p>
      <p>Close: {{close}}</p>
      <p>Average: {{((+open) + (+high) + (+low) + (+close))/4 |
                number: '1.1-5'}}</p>
    </div>
  </mat-grid-tile>
</mat-grid-list>
```

Here, we apply [(*ngModel*)] two-way binding directive to the input elements for stock price *open*, *high*, *low*, and *close*. In fact, [(*ngModel*)] represents two bindings: event binding and property binding. For example, we can achieve the same result with these two separate bindings:

```
<input matInput placeholder="Open Price" [value]="open"
       (input)="open=$event.target.value" [style.color]="getColor(open)">
```

The [(*ngModel*)] directive hides these onerous details behind its own *ngModel* input and *ngModelChange* output properties.

In the above code listing, we also add interpolation bindings for stock prices and the average price. Note that we add extra + signs in font of *open, high, low*, and *close* when calculating the average price. This is necessary because HTML inputs are text by definition. The added + sign will convert it to number prior to being used.

Finally, we need to add a path for this new component to the *RouterModule* of the root module (i.e., the *app.module.ts* file):

```
{ path: 'chapter02/two-way-binding', component: TwoWayBindingComponent },
```

Then add the corresponding URL link to the *home* and *nav-menu* components.

Saving the project and navigating to the */chapter02/two-way-binding* page produce the results shown in Fig.2-5. Now if you change the values of *open*, *high*, *low*, and *close* from corresponding input fields, the fields and average price on the right will change correspondingly.

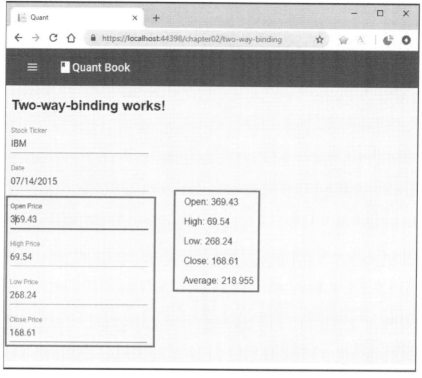

Fig.2-5. Results for two-way binding.

The two-way binding notation [( )] is also referred to as "banana in a box" because that is what the brackets and parentheses look like.

Directives

In Angular, there are three types of directives: components, structural directives, and attribute directives. Components are the most common of the three directives. A component is simply a directive with template. Structural directives change the structure of the view and modify the layout of the page by adding or removing DOM elements. Attribute directives are used as attributes of elements, and change the appearance of an existing elements.

Structural Directives

Structural directives are responsible for shape or reshape the DOM's structure, typically by adding, removing, or manipulating elements. Structural directive are easy to recognize – an asterisk (*) precedes the directive attribute name. It does not require brackets or parentheses like attribute directive. Three of the common, built-in structural directives are *ngIf, *ngFor, and *ngSwitch.

Here, I will use an example to demonstrate how to use Angular built-in directives. Run the following command in the Command prompt window from the *ClientApp* directory:

```
ng g c charter02/directive-test --module=app.module
```

This creates a new component named *directive-test* in the *ClientApp/src/app/chapter02* folder. Add the following code to the component class:

```
// directive-test.component.ts file:
import { Component, OnInit } from '@angular/core';

@Component({
  selector: 'app-directive-test',
  templateUrl: './directive-test.component.html',
  styleUrls: ['./directive-test.component.css']
})
export class DirectiveTestComponent implements OnInit {
  public stocks: Stock[];

  constructor() {
  }

  ngOnInit() {
    this.stocks = [
      new Stock(1, "AAPL", 207.48, true),
      new Stock(2, "AMZN", 1665.53, false),
      new Stock(3, "GOOG", 1057.79, true),
      new Stock(4, "IBM", 115.67, false),
      new Stock(5, "MSFT", 106.16, true),
    ];
  }

  getStock(key: number): Stock {
    return this.stocks.find(s => s.id == key);
  }

  getStockCount(): number {
    return this.stocks.length;
  }

  getStockColor(key: number) {
    switch (key) {
      case 1: return 'red';
      case 2: return 'green';
      case 3: return 'blue';
      case 4: return 'maroon';
      case 5: return 'black';
    }
  }
}

export class Stock {
  constructor(public id: number, public ticker: string, public price: number,
      public holdStock: boolean) {
  }
}
```

Here we define a *Stock* class and use it to create a *stocks* list. We also add several methods used to manipulate the *Stock* object.

First, we use *ngFor* to populate a table by generating a row for each *Stock* object. Add the following code to the template file:

```
// directive-test.component.html:
<h2>
  Directive-test works!
</h2>

<h3>Using *ngFor: </h3>
<table *ngIf="stocks">
  <thead>
    <tr>
      <th align="left">Ticker</th>
      <th align="left">Price</th>
      <th align="left">Hold Stock</th>
    </tr>
  </thead>
  <tbody>
    <tr *ngFor="let stock of stocks">
      <td>{{ stock.ticker }}</td>
      <td>{{ stock.price }}</td>
      <td>{{ stock.holdStock }}</td>
    </tr>
  </tbody>
</table>
```

The expression used with the *ngFor* directive includes two distinct parts, joined together with the *of* keyword. The right-hand part of the expression provides the data source that will be enumerated.

```
...
<tr *ngFor="let stock of stocks">
...
```

This example specifies the component's *stocks* list as the data source. The left-hand side of the *ngFor* expression defines a *template variable*, denoted by the *let* keyword, which is how data is passed between elements within an Angular template.

The *ngFor* directive assigns the variable to each object in the data source so that it is available for use by the nested elements. The local template variable in our example is *stock*, and it is used to access the *Stock* object's properties for the *td* elements.

Now, we need to add a path for this new component to the *RouterModule* of the root module (i.e., the *app.module.ts* file):

```
{ path: 'chapter02/directive-test', component: DirectiveTestComponent },
```

Then add the corresponding URL link to the *home* and *nav-menu* components.

Saving the files and navigating to the */chapter02/directive-test* page generate results shown in Fig.2-6.

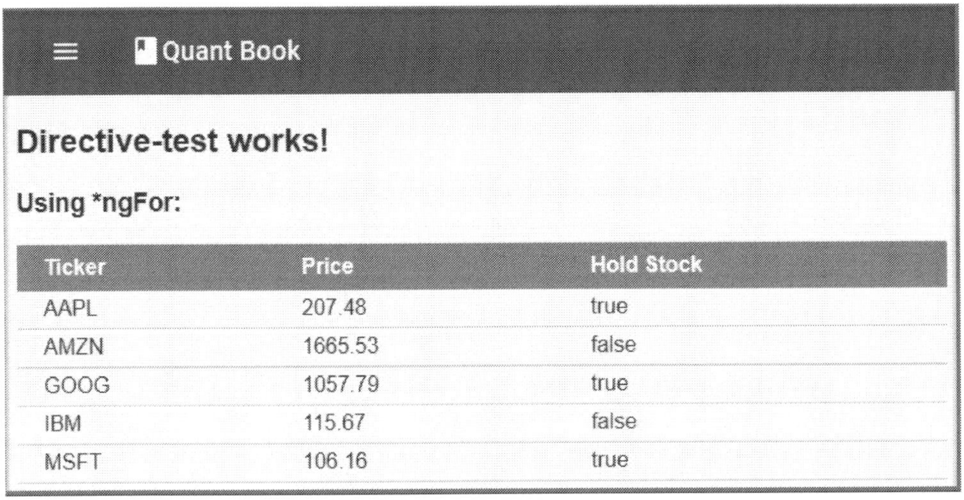

Ticker	Price	Hold Stock
AAPL	207.48	true
AMZN	1665.53	false
GOOG	1057.79	true
IBM	115.67	false
MSFT	106.16	true

Fig.2-6. Using the *ngFor directive to create table rows.

Next, we consider the **ngIf* directive, which is the simplest structural directive and the easiest to understand. It takes a Boolean expression and makes an entire chunk of the DOM appear or disappear.

Add the following code snippet to the directive-test.component.html:

```
// directive-test.component.html file:

// ... other code omitted for brevity ...

<h3>Uisng *ngIf:</h3>
<p *ngIf="getStockCount() > 3">
  There are more than 3 stocks in the list.
</p>
<p *ngIf="getStock(1).ticker=='FB'">
  The first stock is Facebook.
</p>
<p *ngIf="getStock(1).ticker!='FB'">
  The first stock is not Facebook.
</p>
```

The **ngIf* directive has been applied to three *p* elements, with expressions that check the number of *Stock* objects in the stock list and whether the ticker of the stock with `id = 1` is the Facebook stock or not. The first expression evaluates as true, which means that *p* element and its content will be included in the HTML document; the second expression evaluates as false (since no FB stock in the list), which means that the second *p* element will be excluded; the third expression evaluates as true, which means that the third *p* element will be included. Fig.2-7 shows the result.

Fig.2-7. Using the *ngIf directive.

Note that *ngIf directive adds or removes elements from the HTML document, rather than just showing or hiding them. Use the property or style bindings if you want to leave elements in place and control their visibility, either by setting the hidden element property to *true* or by setting the display style property to *none*.

The *ngSwitch* directive is actually a set of cooperating directives: *ngSwitch*, *ngSwitchCase*, and *ngSwitchDefault*. It selects one of several elements based on the expression result, similar to a JavaScript switch statement. Add the following code snippet to the *directive-test.component.html* file:

```
// directive-test.component.html file:

// ... other code omitted for brevity ...

<h3>Using ngSwitch</h3>
<p>There are {{getStockCount()}} stocks in the list.</p>
<p [ngSwitch]="getStockCount()">
  <span *ngSwitchCase="1">There is one stocks</span>
  <span *ngSwitchCase="3">There are three stocks</span>
  <span *ngSwitchDefault>This is the default</span>
</p>
```

The above code shows the *ngSwitch* directive being used to choose an element based on the number of *Stock* objects in the list. The element that the *ngSwitch* directive is applied to is always included in the HTML document, and the directive name is not prefixed with an asterisk. It must be specified within square brackets.

The *ngSwitchCase* directive is used to specify a particular expression result. If the *ngSwitch* expression evaluates to the specified result, then that element and its contents will be included in the HTML document. If the expression does not evaluate to the specified result, the element and its contents will be excluded from the HTML document.

The *ngSwitchDefault* directive is applied to a fallback element, which is included in the HTML document if the expression result does not match any of the results specified by the *ngSwitchCase* directives.

The above code produces the result shown in Fig.2-8.

Fig.2-8. Using the ngSwitch directive.

You can see that neither of the results for the first two *ngSwitchCase* directives matches the result from the length of the stock list, so the *ngSwitchDefault* element is included in the HTML document, as shown in Fig.2-8.

Attribute Directives

Here we consider two built-in attribute directives: *ngStyle* and *ngClass*. The *ngStyle* directive lets you set a given HTML element's style properties. One way to set styles is by using the *ngStyle* directive and assigning it an object literal:

```
<p [ngStyle]="{'color':'green'}">Set green color.</p>
```

This sets the color of the *p* element to green. The *ngStyle* directive becomes much more useful when the value is dynamic. The values in the object literal that we assign to *ngStyle* can be expressions, which are evaluated and the result of that expression is used as the value of the CSS property, like this:

```
<p [ngStyle]="{'color':getStock(1).ticker =='GOOG'?'green':'red'}">
   {{getStock(1).ticker}}
</p>
```

The above code snippet uses the ternary operator to set the color to green if the ticker of the stock with `id = 1` is GOOG; otherwise, the color is set to red.

Adding the above code snippet to the *directive-test.component.html* file produces the result shown in Fig.2-9.

Using ngStyle

Set green color.

AAPL

Fig.2-9. Using the ngStyle directive.

Note that the expression does not have to be inline; we can call a function on the component instead. To demonstrate this, we have implemented a *getStockColor* method in the component class (refer to the preceding code listing for *directive-test.component.ts*), where we set the color of the text according to the value that is returned from the *getStockColor* method. This method returns different colors depending on the stock `id` passed in.

Now, add the following code snippet to the *directive-test.component.html* file:

```
// directive-test.component.html file:

// ...other code omitted for brevity ...

<ul *ngFor="let stock of stocks">
  <li [ngStyle]="{'color':getStockColor(stock.id)}">
    id = {{stock.id}}, ticker = {{stock.ticker}}, price = {{stock.price}}
  </li>
</ul>
```

In this code snippet, we first use the **ngFor* directive to loop through all the *Stock* objects within the stock list, while the color of the displayed text is set by the [*ngStyle*] directive and determined by the **getStockColor(stock.id)** method, which gives different color for different *Stock* object.

The above code produces result shown in Fig.2-10.

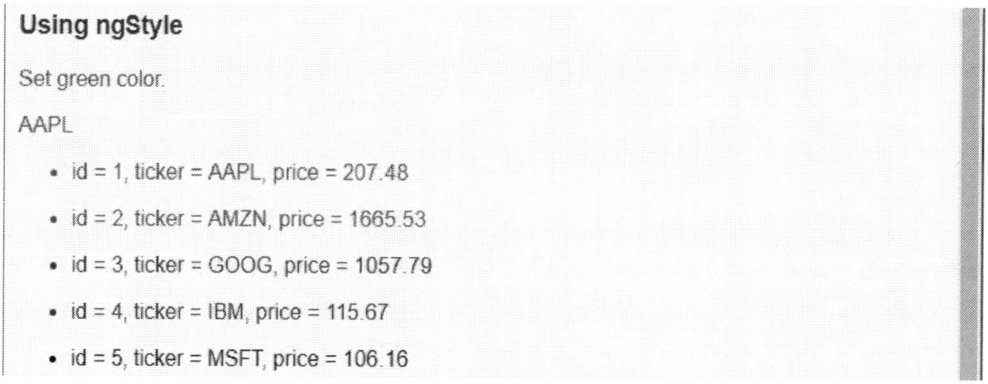

Using ngStyle

Set green color.

AAPL

- id = 1, ticker = AAPL, price = 207.48
- id = 2, ticker = AMZN, price = 1665.53
- id = 3, ticker = GOOG, price = 1057.79
- id = 4, ticker = IBM, price = 115.67
- id = 5, ticker = MSFT, price = 106.16

Fig.2-10. Result using the ngStyle and method defined in the component.

Next, we consider the *ngClass* directive, which allows you to set the CSS class dynamically for HTML elements. This directive is similar to what the *ngStyle* does in Angular.

Here, we recreate the stock color example using *ngClass* instead of *ngStyle*.

Add the following code to the component's style file, *directive-test.component.css*:

```
// directive-test.component.css file:
.class-red{
  color: red;
}
.class-green {
  color: green;
}
.class-blue {
  color: blue;
}
.class-maroon {
  color: maroon;
}
.class-black {
  color: black;
}
```

Here, we define five classes that represent five different colors. Now, add the following code snippet to the template file, *directive-test.component.html*:

```
// directive-test.component.html file:
<h3>Using ngClass</h3>
<ul *ngFor="let stock of stocks">
  <li [ngClass]="{
      'class-red':stock.id == 1,
      'class-green':stock.id == 2,
      'class-vlue':stock.id == 3,
      'class-maroon':stock.id == 4,
      'class-black':stock.id == 5
      }">
    id = {{stock.id}}, ticker = {{stock.ticker}}, price = {{stock.price}}
  </li>
</ul>
```

Here, the *ngClass* binding applied to the `li` elements sets the text color using a different class for different stock identified by its `id`. Saving the files produces result shown in Fig.2-11.

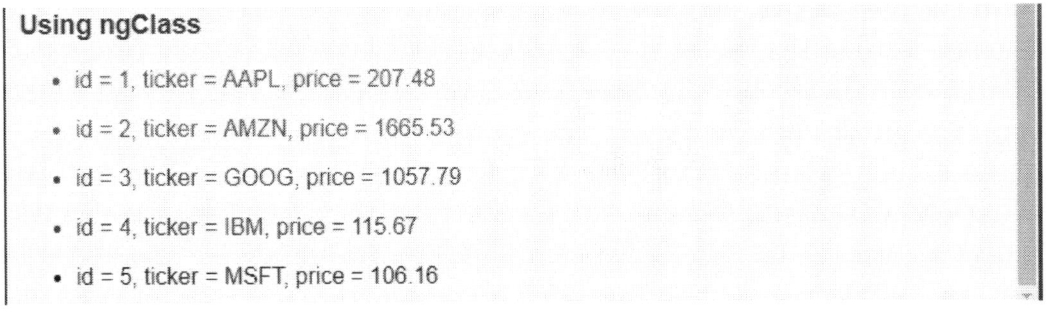

Using ngClass

- id = 1, ticker = AAPL, price = 207.48

- id = 2, ticker = AMZN, price = 1665.53

- id = 3, ticker = GOOG, price = 1057.79

- id = 4, ticker = IBM, price = 115.67

- id = 5, ticker = MSFT, price = 106.16

Fig.2-11. Using the ngClass directive.

Custom Directives

In addition to the built-in directives, Angular allows you to create your own custom directives. Here, I show you how to create a simple attribute directive (you can also create structural directives by following the similar procedure presented here).

A custom directive requires building a controller (or *ts* file) class annotated with *@Directive*, which specifies the selector that identifies the attribute. The *ts* class file implements the desired directive behavior.

Here, we build a simple *highlight* attribute directive to set an element's background color when the user hovers over that element. Now, run the following command in a command prompt window from the *ClientApp* directory:

`ng generate directive chapter02/highlight --module=app.module`

This creates a file named *highlight.directive.ts* in the *ClientApp/src/app/chapter02* folder, as shown in the follows:

```
// hightlight.directive.ts file:
import { Directive } from '@angular/core';

@Directive({
  selector: '[appHighlight]'
})
export class HighlightDirective {
  constructor() { }
}
```

The @Directive decorator's selector property specifies the directives's CSS attribute selector, [*appHighlight*]. Angular locates each element in the template that has an attribute named *appHighlight* and applies the logic of this directive to that element.

Now update the *highlight.directive.ts* file to look as follows:

```
// highlight.directive.ts file:
import { Directive, ElementRef, HostListener } from '@angular/core';

@Directive({
```

```
    selector: '[appHighlight]'
})
export class HighlightDirective {
  constructor(private el: ElementRef) {
  }

  @HostListener('mouseenter') onMouseEnter() {
    this.highlight('rgba(255,255,0,150)');
  }

  @HostListener('mouseleave') onMouseLeave() {
    this.highlight(null);
  }
  private highlight(color: string) {
    this.el.nativeElement.style.backgroundColor = color;
  }
}
```

The import statement specifies two additional symbols from the Angular core library: *ElementRef* and *HostListener*. You use the *ElementRef* in the directive's constructor to inject a reference to the host DOM element, the element to which you applied *appHighlight*. *ElementRef* grants direct access to the host DOM element through its *nativeElement* property.

HostListener binds a CSS event to a host listener and supplies configuration metadata. Angular invokes the supplied handler method when the host element emits the specified event and updates the bound element with the result. We add two event handlers that respond when the mouse enters or leaves, each adorned by the *HostListener* decorator. The *HostListener* decorator lets you subscribe to events of the DOM element that hosts an attribute directive.

The private helper method, *highlight*, is extracted from the constructor that declares the injected *el*: *ElementRef*.

To test our custom directive, add the following code snippet to the *directive-test.component.html* file in the *ClientApp/src/app/chapter02/directive-test* folder:

```
<h3>Custom Directive</h3>
<p appHighlight>Highlight me!</p>
```

Save the project and navigate to the *chaper02/directive-test* page to confirm that the background color appears when the mouse hovers over the *p* element and disappears as it moves out, as shown in Fig.2-12.

Fig.2-12. Custom directive test.

Input and Output Properties

In this section, we consider how to communicate and interact between components using the *@Input* and *@Output* decorators.

Multiple Components

So far, we only have worked with individual components of our Angular application, but this is not how things are typically done in more complex applications. Complex apps usually contain more nested components that can also contain other components. This splitting of the app into multiple components results in the need to manage communication and interaction between them.

Up to now, most components we created in our *Quant* project are isolated components, meaning that each of them does everything. For instance, in our stock list example (see the *directive-test* example), the component renders title, shows the list, and displays the details of each item. To make it more modular, a better approach is to separate this component into three components:

- A parent component named *input-output* just renders the application title and then included a child component named *stock-list*.

- A child component named *stock-list* creates the stock list and shows a list of the *Stock* object.

- Another child component named *stock-detail* display the details of a *Stock* object.

Now, run the following *ng* commands in a prompt window from the *ClientApp* folder to create these three components:

```
ng g c chapter02/input-output --module=app.module
ng g c chapter02/input-output/stock-list --module=app.module
ng g c chapter02/input-output/stock-detail --module=app.module
```

Here, we create the parent component in the *chapter02* directory and two children components in the *chapter02/input-output* subdirectory.

We also need to add a path for this new component to the *RouterModule* of the root module (i.e., the *app.module.ts* file):

```
{ path: 'chapter02/input-output, component: InputOutputComponent },
```

Then add the corresponding URL link to the *home* and *nav-menu* components.

Open the *stock-list.component.ts* file in the *ClientApp/src/app/chapter02/input-output/stock-list* folder and change its content with the following code:

```
// stock-list.component.ts file:
import { Component, OnInit} from '@angular/core';

@Component({
  selector: 'app-stock-list',
  templateUrl: './stock-list.component.html',
  styleUrls: ['./stock-list.component.css']
})
export class StockListComponent implements OnInit {
  public stocks: Stock[];

  constructor() { }

  ngOnInit() {
    this.stocks = [
      new Stock(1, "AAPL", 207.48, true),
      new Stock(2, "AMZN", 1665.53, false),
      new Stock(3, "GOOG", 1057.79, true),
      new Stock(4, "IBM", 115.67, false),
```

```
      new Stock(5, "MSFT", 106.16, true),
    ];
  }
}

export class Stock {
  constructor(public id: number, public ticker: string, public price: number,
      public holdStock: boolean) {
  }
}
```

This code simply defines a stock list named *stocks* using the *Stock* class object. The selector for this component is *app-stock-list*, which is the "tag" that will be used by its parent component to reference the *StockListComponent*.

The corresponding template for this component is very simple, as shown in in the following code:

```
// stock-list.component.html file:
<ol>
  <li *ngFor="let item of stocks">
      <p>{{stock.ticker}}, {{stock.price}}</p>
  </li>
</ol>
```

This code simply display the stock list.

At this moment, we do not need to make any change to the parent component class, but need only to update its template, as shown in the follows:

```
// input-output.component.html file:
<h2>
  Input-output works!
</h2>

<app-stock-list>Loading stock list...</app-stock-list>
```

The code simply references the stock-list component with its selector's name. At this point, the application simply displays the stock list, but each component serves its own task, achieving a better separation of concerns. But, we can bring it a level further and have the markup and logic display the details of a stock in their own component. Thus, we need to move the individual stock information code from the stock-list to the stock-detail component. For the stock-detail component, we change its template using the following code:

```
// stock-detail.component.html file:
<p>{{stock.ticker}}, {{stock.price}}</p>
```

Now, instead of rendering the ticker and price of the stock in the list directly, the *stock-list* component just needs to reference the *stock-detail* component using its selector, *app-stock-detail*, as seen here:

```
// stock-list.component.html file:
<ol>
  <li *ngFor="let item of stocks">
    <app-stock-detail></app-stock-detail>
  </li>
</ol>
```

There, however, is a problem here. How do you pass to the child component which stock to display?

Input Property

In order to solve the problem of passing stock to the child component (the *stock-detail* component in our example), the component must declare an input property. This is done in Angular using the @Input decorator inside the component that exposes the property.

Now, update the *stock-detail.component.ts* file with the following code:

```
// stock-detail.component.ts file:
import { Component, OnInit, Input } from '@angular/core';
import { Stock } from '../stock-list/stock-list.component'

@Component({
  selector: 'app-stock-detail',
  templateUrl: './stock-detail.component.html',
  styleUrls: ['./stock-detail.component.css']
})
export class StockDetailComponent implements OnInit {

  @Input() stock: Stock;

  constructor() { }

  ngOnInit() {
  }
}
```

Here, we first add *Input* to the list of symbols imported from @angular/core and the *Stock* class object from the *stock-list.component.ts* file. Next, we add a stock property to the directive class like this:

```
@Input() stock: Stock;
```

Notice the *@Input* decorator, which adds metadata to the class that makes the directive's stock property available for binding. It is called an *Input* property because data flows from the binding expression into the directive. Without that input metadata, Angular rejects the binding.

We also need to update the stock-list component's template as follows:

```
// stock-list.component.html file:
<ol>
  <li *ngFor="let item of stocks">
    <app-stock-detail [stock]= "item"></app-stock-detail>
  </li>
</ol>
```

The code creates a directive object for each *li* element, evaluates the expressions specified in the [*stock*] attribute and uses the result to set the values of the stock.

Saving the files and navigating to the */chapter02/input-output* page produce the result shown in Fig.2-13.

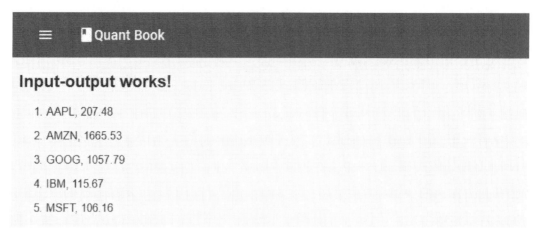

Fig.2-13. Showing stock list using @Input decorator.

Output Property

The Output property is the Angular feature that allows directives to add custom events to their host elements, through which details of important changes can be sent to the rest of the application. The output property is defined using the *@Output* decorator, which is defined in the *@angular/core* module.

Let us use a *@Output* directive in our example to show how to inform the parent component that user clicked on a stock, so that it can display a more detailed view on the stock.

For this to happen, the *stock-list* component must bind to the click event on the stock, and it must raise the custom event inside the handler for the click. The following listing highlights the new lines of code added to this component class:

```
// stock-list.component.ts file:
import { Component, OnInit, Output, EventEmitter } from '@angular/core';

@Component({
  selector: 'app-stock-list',
  templateUrl: './stock-list.component.html',
  styleUrls: ['./stock-list.component.css']
})
export class StockListComponent implements OnInit {
  public stocks: Stock[];

  @Output() selected = new EventEmitter<Stock>();

  constructor() { }

  ngOnInit() {
    this.stocks = [
      new Stock(1, "AAPL", 207.48, true),
      new Stock(2, "AMZN", 1665.53, false),
      new Stock(3, "GOOG", 1057.79, true),
      new Stock(4, "IBM", 115.67, false),
      new Stock(5, "MSFT", 106.16, true),
    ];
```

```
    }

  select(selectedStock: Stock) {
    this.selected.emit(selectedStock);
  }
}

export class Stock {
  constructor(public id: number, public ticker: string, public price: number,
    public holdStock: boolean) {
  }
}
```

The *EventEmitter* class provides the event mechanism for Angular directives. The code creates an *EventEmitter* object and assigns it to a variable called *selected*, like this:

```
@Output() selected = new EventEmitter<Stock>();
```

The *Stock* type parameter indicates that listeners to the event will receive a *Stock* class object when the event is triggered.

In our example, the custom event in the code listing is triggered when the mouse button is clicked on the host element.

We also need to make the corresponding changes to its template:

```
//stock-list.component.html file:
<ol>
  <li *ngFor="let item of stocks">
    <app-stock-detail [stock]="item" (click)="select(item)"></app-stock-detail>
  </li>
</ol>
```

Here, we bind the click event to the *select* method defined in the *stock-list* component class. This method relates to an *EventEmitter* object named *selected* defined inside the *@Output* decorator.

Now the parent component, the *input-output* component, listens to the *selected* event and handles it as any other event. The following code shows changes to the *input-output* component class:

```
// input-output.component.ts file:
import { Component, OnInit } from '@angular/core';
import { Stock } from './stock-list/stock-list.component';

@Component({
  selector: 'app-input-output',
  templateUrl: './input-output.component.html',
  styleUrls: ['./input-output.component.css']
})
export class InputOutputComponent implements OnInit {
  selectedStock: Stock;

  constructor() {
    this.selectedStock = null;
  }

  ngOnInit() {
  }
```

```
showStockDetails(stck: Stock) {
    this.selectedStock = stck;
  }
}
```

We also need to make corresponding changes to its template as shown in the following code:

```
// input-output.component.html file:
<h2>
  Input-output works!
</h2>
<app-stock-list (selected)="showStockDetails($event)">
  Loading stock list...
</app-stock-list>

<p *ngIf="selectedStock" style="color:red">
  You selected stock: {{selectedStock.ticker}}, {{selectedStock.price}}
  <span *ngIf="selectedStock.holdStock">, you hold this stock.</span>
  <span *ngIf="!selectedStock.holdStock">, you do not hold this stock.</span>
</p>
```

The parameter of the event, which contains the stock being selected, is referenced by the **$event** variable. The detailed information of the selected stock is then displayed at the bottom of the screen when clicking a stock, as shown in Fig.2-14.

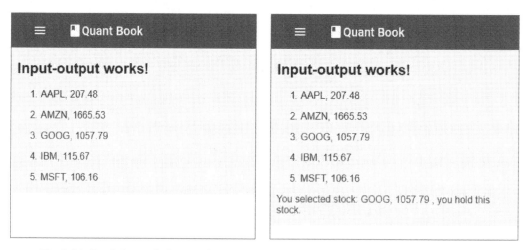

Fig.2-14. Stock list with Output decorator: without (left) and with (right) selected stock.

Chapter 3
Database and Web Services

For the past several years, I have worked with a financial firm as a quant analyst/developer on Wall Street. The most important thing I deal with every day is the market data. Most finance applications in different fields also need to interact with data stored in databases. Therefore, in my opinion, every quant developer/analyst should be familiar with the database and should know how to access the database data.

In this chapter, we start adding functionality to our *Quant* project created in the preceding chapters. We will set up a SQL Server (Expression Edition) database to store the application data, and define the model classes that Entity Framework Core will use to represent the data.

On the Angular part of our project, we will define corresponding TypeScript classes that will represent the data, and a repository that will make the data available throughout the application. We will also build an HTML web service that the Angular app can use to request data from ASP.NET Core API.

Data Model

Here, we will use the so-called code first approach to create database. In this method, we first create entity classes with properties defined in it. Entity Framework Core will create the database and tables based on the entity classes defined. So database is generated from the code. The database will be created automatically when you run the application for the first time.

Connection String

To provide Entity Framework Core with details of how to connect to the database, open the *appsettings.json* file and add the following statements, making sure to enter the connection string on a single line:

```
// appsettings.json file:
{
  "Logging": {
    "LogLevel": {
      "Default": "Warning"
    }
  },
  "AllowedHosts": "*",
```

```
"Data": {
  "Quant": {
    "ConnectionString": "Server=(localdb)\\mssqllocaldb;Database=QuantDb;
        Trusted_Connection=True;MultipleActiveResultSets=true"
  }
}
}
```

The connection string specifies a SQL Server LocalDB database with a database name of *QuantDb*. LocalDB is a lightweight version of the SQL Server Express Database Engine and is intended for application development, not production use. LocalDB starts on demand and runs in user mode, so there is no complex configurations. By default, LocalDB creates *.mdf* files in the *C:/users/<user>* directory.

Here, we set the **Trusted_Connection** option to **True**, indicating that Windows credentials are used, which is equivalent to **Integrated Security=SSPI** or **Integrated Security=true**. If you do not like the integrated security or trusted connection, you need to specify the user ID and password explicitly in your connection string. In this case, the SQL Server authentication mode is used.

Define Model Data Types

The purpose of creating a data model for the ASP.NET Core part of the application will be familiar to most .NET developers – a series C# model classes is used to create a database schema, which is used to prepare database to store the app's data.

The main difference from conventional ASP.NET Core development is that we do not need to create a repository interface and implementation class in the ASP.NET Core part of the project. Instead, we will create the repository in the Angular app, which is where the data is consumed.

Now, it is time to define a context and entity classes that make up our finance database model. Create a *Quant/Models* folder and add three new C# classes, *Symbol*, *Price*, and *IndexData* to this new folder.

```
using System.Collections.Generic;
namespace Quant.Models
{
    public class Symbol
    {
        public int SymbolId { get; set; }
        public string Ticker { get; set; }
        public string Region { get; set; }
        public string Sector { get; set; }

        public virtual ICollection<Price> Prices { get; set; }
    }
}

using System;
namespace Quant.Models
{
    public class Price
    {
        public int PriceId { get; set; }
        public int SymbolId { get; set; }
        public DateTime Date { get; set; }
        public decimal Open { get; set; }
```

```
        public decimal High { get; set; }
        public decimal Low { get; set; }
        public decimal Close { get; set; }
        public decimal CloseAdj { get; set; }
        public decimal Volume { get; set; }
    }
}

using System;
namespace Quant.Models
{
    public class IndexData
    {
        public int Id { get; set; }
        public DateTime Date { get; set; }
        public decimal IGSpread { get; set; }
        public decimal HYSpread { get; set; }
        public decimal SPX { get; set; }
        public decimal VIX { get; set; }
    }
}
```

We will use the classes, *Symbol* and *Price*, to store stock tickers and the stock data. The *IndexData* class will be used to store the market data from a CSV file for some indices, including SPX 500, VIX (volatility index), HY (high-yield CDX index), and IG (investment-grade CDX index). The properties with ID, such as *Id*, *SymbolId*, and *PriceId* will be the primary keys. By default, the Entity Framework Core interprets a property that is named *Id* or *classnameId* as the primary key. The *Prices* property in the *Symbol* class is a navigation property, which holds *Price* entities that are related to the *Symbol* entity.

Navigation properties are typically defined as *virtual* so that they can take advantage of certain Entity Framework Core functionalities such as *lazy loading*. If a navigation property can hold multiple entities, its type must be a list or collection, in which entries can be added, deleted, and updated, such as *ICollection*.

Define Data Context

The next step is to create the database context class that provides access to the data through Entity Framework Core. Add a C# class named *QuantDataContext* to the *Models* folder with the following code:

```
using Microsoft.EntityFrameworkCore;

namespace Quant.Models
{
    public class QuantDataContext : DbContext
    {
        public QuantDataContext(DbContextOptions<QuantDataContext> options)
            : base(options) { }

        public DbSet<Symbol> Symbols { get; set; }
        public DbSet<Price> Prices { get; set; }
        public DbSet<IndexData> IndexDatas { get; set; }

        protected override void OnModelCreating(ModelBuilder modelBuilder)
```

```
        {
            modelBuilder.Entity<Symbol>().ToTable("Symbol");
            modelBuilder.Entity<Price>().ToTable("Price");
            modelBuilder.Entity<IndexData>().ToTable("IndexData");
        }
    }
}
```

The context class follows the standard pattern for Entity Framework Core and defines a constructor that accepts a **DbContextOptions<T>** object and that is configured during the ASP.NET Core startup sequence. When database is created, Entity Framework Core generates tables that have names the same as the *DbSet* property names. Property names for collection are typically plural, but developers disagree about whether table names should be pluralized or not. Here, we override the default behavior by specifying singular table names in the *QuantDataContext* class. We create this class by deriving from the *DbContext* class. We also specify which entities are included in the data model. The code creates a *DbSet* property for each entity set. In Entity Framework Core terminology, an entity set typically corresponds to a database table, while an entity corresponds to a row in the table.

To register the context class with Entity Framework Core, add the following highlighted code snippet to the *Startup.cs* class:

```
using Microsoft.AspNetCore.Builder;
using Microsoft.AspNetCore.Hosting;
using Microsoft.AspNetCore.HttpsPolicy;
using Microsoft.AspNetCore.Mvc;
using Microsoft.AspNetCore.SpaServices.AngularCli;
using Microsoft.Extensions.Configuration;
using Microsoft.Extensions.DependencyInjection;
using Quant.Models;
using Microsoft.EntityFrameworkCore;

namespace Quant
{
    public class Startup
    {
        public Startup(IConfiguration configuration)
        {
            Configuration = configuration;
        }

        public IConfiguration Configuration { get; }

        public void ConfigureServices(IServiceCollection services)
        {
            services.AddDbContext<QuantDataContext>(options =>
                options.UseSqlServer(Configuration["Data:Quant:ConnectionString"]));

            services.AddMvc().SetCompatibilityVersion(
                CompatibilityVersion.Version_2_2);

            // In production, the Angular files will be served from this directory
            services.AddSpaStaticFiles(configuration =>
            {
                configuration.RootPath = "ClientApp/dist";
            });
```

```
    }

    // ... other code omitted for brevity ...

    }
}
```

Initialize Database

Entity Framework Core will create an empty database if the seed data is not provided. Here, we will implement a method that is called after database is created in order to populate it with the seed data. Add a new C# class named *DbInitializer* to the *Models* folder and replace its content with the following code, which causes a database to be created when needed and loads the seed data into the new database:

```
using System;
using System.Linq;
using System.Text.RegularExpressions;

namespace Quant.Models
{
    public static class DbInitializer
    {
        public static void Initialize(QuantDataContext context)
        {
            context.Database.EnsureCreated();
            if (context.IndexDatas.Any() && context.Symbols.Any())
            {
                return;
            }

            string path = AppContext.BaseDirectory;
            string[] ss = Regex.Split(path, "bin");
            string filePath = ss[0] + @"Models\";

            var data = ModelHelper.CsvToIndexData(filePath + "indices.csv");
            foreach (IndexData d in data)
                context.IndexDatas.Add(d);
            context.SaveChanges();

            if (context.Symbols.Any())
            {
                return;
            }

            var symbols = ModelHelper.CsvToSymbolList(filePath +
                    "StockTickers.csv");
            foreach (Symbol s in symbols)
                context.Symbols.Add(s);
            context.SaveChanges();

            var prices = ModelHelper.CsvToIbmPrices("IBM", context,
                    filePath + "IBM.csv");
            foreach (Price p in prices)
                context.Prices.Add(p);
```

```
            context.SaveChanges();
        }
    }
}
```

The code checks whether there are any symbols and index data in the database. If not, it assumes that the database is new and needs to be seeded with the seed data.

Here, we use the *EnsureCreated* method to create the database automatically. When we develop a new application, our data model may change, and each time the model changes, it gets out of sync with the database. We use this method for Entity Framework Core to create the database if it does not exist. Then each time we change the data model – add, remove, or change entity classes or change the *DbContext* class – we can delete the database and Entity Framework Core will create a new one that matches the model, and seeds it with the seed data.

The approach of keeping the database in sync with the data model works well until you deploy the application to production. When the application is running in production, it is usually storing data that you want to keep, and you do not want to lose everything each time you make a change such as adding a new column. In this case, you need to use the Entity Framework Core migrations feature to solve this problem by enabling Entity Framework Core to update the database schema instead of creating a new database. For the stock price database in this example, our data model is fixed. Therefore, the *EnsureCreated* method should work just fine.

In *Startup.cs*, modify the *Configure* method to call this *seed* method on application startup. First, add the context to the method signature so that ASP.NET dependency injection can provide it to our *DbInitializer* class, and then call the *DbInitializer.Initialize* method at the end of the *Configure* method as shown in the following highlighted code snippet:

```
public void Configure(IApplicationBuilder app, IHostingEnvironment env,
    QuantDataContext context)
{

    // ... Other code omitted for brevity ...

    DbInitializer.Initialize(context);
}
```

Add Stock Tickers to Database

You can see that inside the *Initialize* method in the *DbInitializer* class, we want to use the CSV files to add the seed data to the database. Here, I will show you how to do it.

I have already created a CSV file named *StockTicker.csv* that contains the stock tickers to be inserted into the *Symbol* table. This file is located in the *Models/Data* folder. The following list shows the format for this CSV file:

```
Ticker,Region,Sector
A,US,information Technology
AA,US,Materials
ABK,US,Financials
ACE,US,Financials
ACGL,US,Financials
ACN,US,Information Technology
ADI,US,Information Technology
```

```
ADP,US,Information Technology
AFG,US,Financials
AFL,US,Financials
```

```
// ... more tickers omitted for brevity ...
```

The first line in the file is the header, and the comma is used to separate data fields. In the *ModelHelper.cs* class located in the *Models* folder, I implemented a *CsvToSymbolList* method, which can be used to convert a CSV file into a *Symbol* list. Here is the code snippet for this method:

```
public static List<Symbol> CsvToSymbolList(string csvFile)
{
    FileStream fs = new FileStream(csvFile, FileMode.Open, FileAccess.Read,
        FileShare.ReadWrite);
    StreamReader sr = new StreamReader(fs);
    List<String> lst = new List<string>();
    while (!sr.EndOfStream)
        lst.Add(sr.ReadLine());
    string[] fields = lst[0].Split(new char[] { ',' });
    var res = new List<Symbol>();
    for (int i = 1; i < lst.Count; i++)
    {
        fields = lst[i].Split(',');
        res.Add(new Symbol
        {
            Ticker = fields[0],
            Region = fields[1],
            Sector = fields[2]
        });
    }
    return res;
}
```

We will use this method to add the stock tickers to database.

Add Stock Prices to Database

Inside the *Initialize* method in the *DbInitializer* class, we want to use a CSV file to add the seed data to the *Price* table. I have already created a CSV file named *IBM.csv* that contains one years of stock price data for IBM. This file is located in the *Models/Data* folder. The following list shows the format for this CSV file:

```
Date,Open,High,Low,Close,AdjClose,Volume
2017-11-07,151.369995,151.509995,150.500000,151.350006,145.193344,3701100
2017-11-08,151.600006,151.789993,150.279999,151.570007,145.404404,4634400
2017-11-09,149.929993,151.800003,149.860001,150.300003,145.627243,4776500
2017-11-10,150.649994,150.889999,149.139999,149.160004,144.522675,4307300
2017-11-13,148.880005,149.000000,147.919998,148.399994,143.786301,5107500
2017-11-14,147.949997,148.970001,147.490005,148.889999,144.261078,3758000
2017-11-15,148.000000,148.710007,146.210007,147.100006,142.526733,4773300
2017-11-16,147.729996,149.649994,147.500000,149.119995,144.483917,5446500
... ...
```

The first line in the file is the header, and the comma is used to separate data fields. In the *ModelHelper.cs* class in the *Models* folder, I implemented a *CsvToImbPrices* method, which can be used to convert a CSV file into a *Price* list. Here is the code snippet for this method:

```
public static List<Price> CsvToIbmPrices(string ticker, QuantDataContext context,
    string csvFile)
{
    var symbolId = TickerToId(ticker, context);
    FileStream fs = new FileStream(csvFile, FileMode.Open, FileAccess.Read,
        FileShare.ReadWrite);
    StreamReader sr = new StreamReader(fs);
    List<String> lst = new List<string>();

    while (!sr.EndOfStream) lst.Add(sr.ReadLine());
    string[] fields = lst[0].Split(new char[] { ',' });
    var res = new List<Price>();
    for (int i = 1; i < lst.Count; i++)
    {
        fields = lst[i].Split(',');
        res.Add(new Price
        {
            SymbolId = symbolId,
            Date = DateTime.Parse(fields[0]),
            Open = double.Parse(fields[1]),
            High = double.Parse(fields[2]),
            Low = double.Parse(fields[3]),
            Close = double.Parse(fields[4]),
            CloseAdj = double.Parse(fields[5]),
            Volume = double.Parse(fields[6])
        });
    }
    return res;
}
```

We will use this method to add IBM stock prices to database.

Add Index Data to Database

Inside the *Initialize* method in the *DbInitializer* class, we also want to use a CSV file to add the seed data to the *IndexData* table. I have already created a CSV file named *indices.csv* that contains over 10 years of market data for different indices starting from 9/21/2004 to 5/15/2015. This file is located in the *Models* folder. The following shows the format for this CSV file:

```
Date,IGSpread,HYSpread,SPX,VIX
9/21/2004,53.93,363,1129.3,13.66
9/22/2004,55.18,367.5,1113.56,14.74
9/23/2004,54.69,371.2,1108.36,14.8
9/24/2004,55.11,374.5,1110.11,14.28
9/27/2004,54.59,370.5,1103.52,14.62
... ...
5/12/2014,62.54275824,337.9057833,1896.65,12.23
5/13/2014,62.48443231,337.2766355,1897.45,12.13
5/14/2014,63.24887055,338.1121574,1888.53,12.17
5/15/2014,65.21262904,346.5008667,1870.85,13.17
```

The first line in the file is the header, and the comma is used to separate data fields. In the *ModelHelper.cs* class located in the *Models* folder, I implemented a *CsvToIndexData* method, which can be used to convert a CSV file into an *IndexData* list. Here is the code snippet for this method:

```
public static List<IndexData> CsvToIndexData(string csvFile)
{
    FileStream fs = new FileStream(csvFile, FileMode.Open,
    FileAccess.Read, FileShare.ReadWrite);
    StreamReader sr = new StreamReader(fs);
    List<String> lst = new List<string>();
    while (!sr.EndOfStream)
        lst.Add(sr.ReadLine());

    string[] fields = lst[0].Split(new char[] { ',' });
    var res = new List<IndexData>();
    for (int i = 1; i < lst.Count; i++)
    {
        fields = lst[i].Split(',');
        res.Add(new IndexData
        {
            Date = DateTime.Parse(fields[0]),
            IGSpread = double.Parse(fields[1]),
            HYSpread = double.Parse(fields[2]),
            SPX = double.Parse(fields[3]),
            VIX = double.Parse(fields[4])
        });
    }
    return res;
}
```

We will use this method to add the index data to database.

The first time you run the application the database will be created and seeded with the seed data. Here, we will use the database migration feature provided by ASP.NET Core to create database. Tap the *Tools* dropdown menu and select *NuGet Package Manager/Package Manager Console* to open the manager console window. From this console, run the following command:

Add-Migration Initial

The result of running this command is that a Migrations folder is added to the project, containing C# class files that include statements that generate the database schema when the migration is applied to the database. The files created for a migration start with a timestamp. If you examine the code in the <timestamp>_Initial.cs file in the *Migrations* folder, you will see how Entity Framework Core stores the application's data. The database will contains three tables, *Symbol*, *Price*, and *IndexData*, corresponding to each of the three data model types.

Whenever you change your data model, you can delete the database, update your seed method, and start afresh with a new database the same way; or you can use the migration to update your database.

Check Database

Now, run the project by pressing F5 within the Visual Studio or run the command **dotnet run** from the command prompt window. If everything goes smoothly, the database named *QuantDb* should have been created in the *LocalDB* server. Inside the Visual Studio, go to the *View* menu and select SQL Server

Object Explorer. You should see the *QuantDb* database in there, which contains three tables: *Symbol*, *Price*, and *IndexData*, as shown in Fig.3-1, corresponding to the three data model Types.

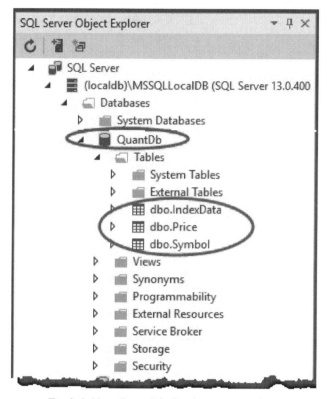

Fig.3-1. New QuantDb database in LocalDB.

You can examine if *Symbol* and *IndexData* tables contain the seed data. Right clicking on the *dbo.Symbol* table and choosing *View Data*, you should see the results on your screen, as shown in Fig.3-2. There should be more than 180 tickers in the *Symbol* table. If you could not add those tickers to this table, you need to redo it by closely following the instruction provided in this example. You will need the tickers in the *Symbol* table in the following chapters of this book.

The *Price* table should contain one-year stock prices for IBM. Right clicking on the *dbo.Price* table and choosing *View Data*, you should see the results on your screen, as shown in Fig.3-3.

You can also check the *IndexData* table to see if it contains the test data. Right clicking on the *dbo.IndexData* table and choosing *View Data*, you should see the results on your screen, as shown in Fig.3-4. There should be about 1000 records of the test data in this table.

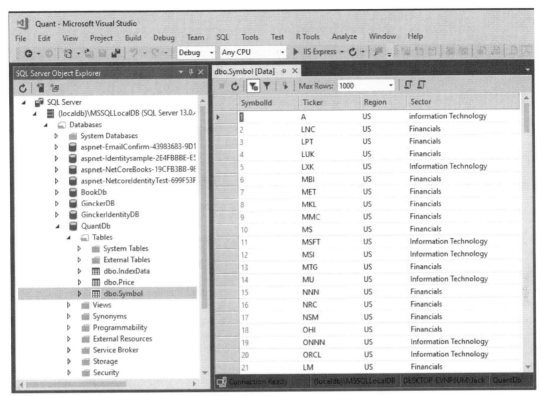

Fig.3-2. Stock tickers in the Symbol table.

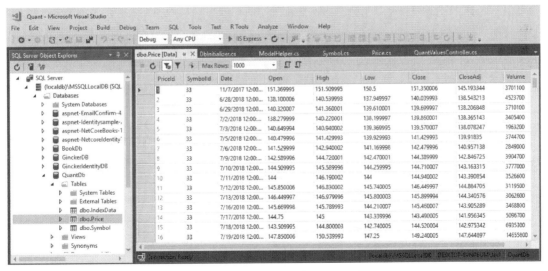

Fig.3-3. Stock prices in the Price table.

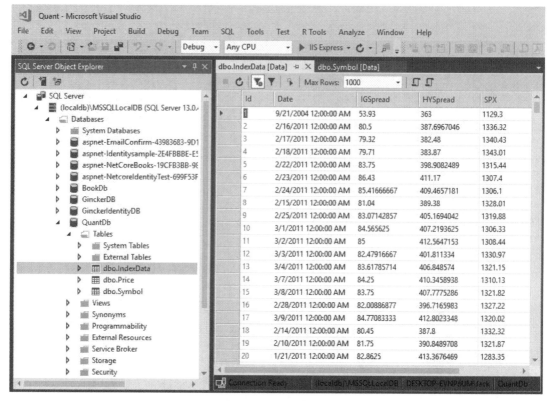

Fig.3-4. Seed data in the IndexData table.

ASP.NET Core Web Service

ASP.NET Core Web API controller provides access to application's data. It is a framework that makes it easy to build HTTP service that can reach a broad range of clients, including browsers, mobile devices, and traditional desktop applications. Web API can be used as Representational State Transfer (REST) API. It is an idea platform for building RESTful applications on the ASP.NET Core Framework.

The key promise of REST API is that a web service defines an API through a combination of the URLs and HTTP methods such as GET and POST, which are also known as the HTTP verbs. The verb specifies the type of operation, while the URL specifies the data object that the operation applies to.

Create Web Service

ASP.NET Core makes it easy to add web services to an application using standard MVC controller features. Add a C# class file named *StockValuesController.cs* to the *Controllers* folder and replace its content with the following code:

```
// StockValuesController.cs file:

using Microsoft.AspNetCore.Mvc;
using Quant.Models;
```

```csharp
using System;
using System.Collections.Generic;
using System.Globalization;
using System.Linq;

namespace Quant.Controllers
{
    [Route("api/Stocks")]
    public class StockValuesController : Controller
    {
        private readonly QuantDataContext context;
        public StockValuesController(QuantDataContext ctx)
        {
            context = ctx;
        }

        [HttpGet]
        public IEnumerable<Symbol> GetSymbols()
        {
            return context.Symbols;
        }

        [HttpGet("{id}")]
        public Symbol GetSymbol(int id)
        {
            return context.Symbols.Find(id);
        }


        [HttpGet("{id}/{start}/{end}")]
        public Symbol GetSymbolAndPrice(int id, string start, string end)
        {
            var startDate = DateTime.ParseExact(start, "yyyy-MM-dd",
                CultureInfo.InvariantCulture);
            var endDate = DateTime.ParseExact(end, "yyyy-MM-dd",
                CultureInfo.InvariantCulture);
            var stock = context.Symbols.Find(id);
            stock.Prices = context.Prices.Where(p => p.SymbolId == id &&
                p.Date>=startDate && p.Date<=endDate).OrderBy(d=>d.Date).ToList();
            return stock;
        }

        [HttpPost]
        public IActionResult CreateStock([FromBody] Symbol stock)
        {
            if (ModelState.IsValid)
            {
                var stk = GetSymbolwithTicker(stock.Ticker);
                if (stk == null)
                {
                    context.Add(stock);
                    context.SaveChanges();
                    return Ok(stock.SymbolId);
                }
                else return Ok(stk.SymbolId);
```

```csharp
        }
        else
        {
            return BadRequest(ModelState);
        }
    }

    [HttpPut("{id}")]
    public IActionResult UpdateSymbol(int id, [FromBody] Symbol stock)
    {
        if (ModelState.IsValid)
        {
            stock.SymbolId = id;
            context.Update(stock);
            context.SaveChanges();
            return Ok();
        }
        else
        {
            return BadRequest(ModelState);
        }
    }

    [HttpDelete("{id}")]
    public void DeleteStock(int id)
    {
        var prices = context.Prices.Where(p => p.SymbolId == id);
        if (prices != null) context.Prices.RemoveRange(prices);
        context.Symbols.Remove(new Symbol { SymbolId = id });
        context.SaveChanges();
    }

    // the following four methods override the default routing schema:

    [Route("~/api/stockwithticker/{ticker}")]
    [HttpGet]
    public Symbol GetSymbolwithTicker(string ticker)
    {
        return context.Symbols.Where(t => t.Ticker == ticker).FirstOrDefault();
    }

    [Route("~/api/stockwithticker/{ticker}/{start}/{end}")]
    [HttpGet]
    public Symbol GetSymbolAndPricewithTicker(string ticker, string start,
        string end)
    {
        var startDate = DateTime.ParseExact(start, "yyyy-MM-dd",
            CultureInfo.InvariantCulture);
        var endDate = DateTime.ParseExact(end, "yyyy-MM-dd",
            CultureInfo.InvariantCulture);
        var id = ModelHelper.TickerToId(ticker, context);
        var stock = context.Symbols.Find(id);
        stock.Prices = context.Prices.Where(p => p.SymbolId == id &&
            p.Date >= startDate && p.Date <= endDate).OrderBy(d =>
            d.Date).ToList();
```

```
        return stock;
    }

    [Route("~/api/IndexData")]
    [HttpGet]
    public IEnumerable<IndexData> GetIndexData()
    {
        return context.IndexDatas.OrderBy(d => d.Date);
    }

    [Route("~/api/IndexData/{start}/{end}")]
    [HttpGet]
    public IEnumerable<IndexData> GetIndexData(string start, string end)
    {
        var startDate = DateTime.ParseExact(start, "yyyy-MM-dd",
            CultureInfo.InvariantCulture);
        var endDate = DateTime.ParseExact(end, "yyyy-MM-dd",
            CultureInfo.InvariantCulture);
        return context.IndexDatas.Where(d => d.Date >= startDate &&
            d.Date <= endDate).OrderBy(d => d.Date);
    }
  }
}
```

This is a regular ASP.NET Core MVC controller, derived from the *Controller* class in the *Microsoft. AspNetCore.Mvc* namespace. The name of this new controller class is *StockValuesController*, which follows the convention of including the word *Values* in the name to indicate that the controller will return data to its clients rather than HTML.

Another convention for web service controllers is to create a separate part of the routing schema dedicated to handling requests for data. The most common way to do this is to create URLs for web services that start with */api*, followed by the plural form of the name of the data type that the web service handles. For web service handling *Stock* (or *Symbol*) object, this means that HTTP requests should be sent to the */api/stocks* URL, which we have configured using the Route attribute, like this:

```
[Route("api/Stocks")]
```

In this new controller, we implement a standard CRUD (create, read, update, and delete) operations for the stock objects. In the following sections, I will explain the various action methods for these CRUD operations.

GET Method

In a RESTful web service, the HTTP GET method typically does double duty – it is used to denote queries for one object and queries for multiple objects, with the request URL being used to specify the purpose of the query.

The *GET* action method is decorated with the *HttpGet* method, which will allow ASP.NET Core to use this action to handle HTTP GET request:

```
[HttpGet]
public IEnumerable<Symbol> GetSymbols(){
... ...
```

This method retrieves all stock objects in the database, which can be reached by a URL in the form */api/stocks*.

To test the new action, restart the application and use a browser to request *https://localhost:5001/api /stocks*. This URL requests will produce a result with data shown in Fig.3-5.

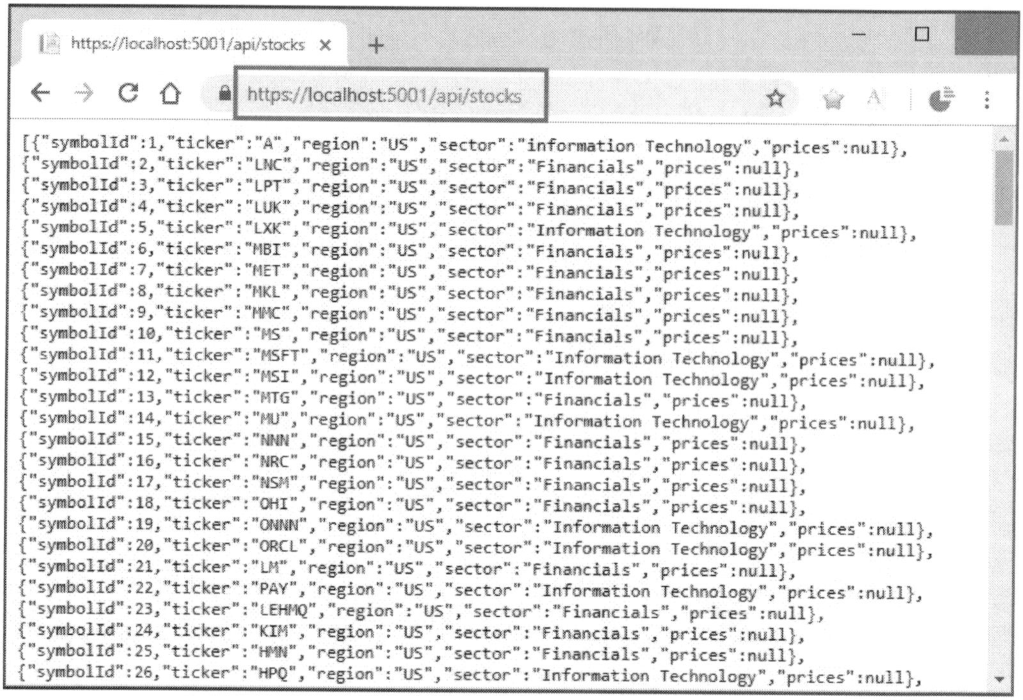

Fig.3-5. Retrieve stock list using web service.

While the action method, *GetSymbol*, returns object based on its primary key, which is the value assigned to its *SymbolId* property:

```
[HttpGet("{id}")]
public Symbol GetSymbol(int id){
... ...
```

The attribute's argument extends the URL schema defined by the Route attribute so that the *GetSymbol* method can be reached by a URL in the form */api/stocks/{id}*.

To test this method, request the URL, *https://localhost:5001/api/stocks/33*, in your browser. The stock with *SymbolId* = 33 will be returned to your browser, which will display the data it receives:

```
{
   "symbolId":33,"ticker":"IBM","region":"US","sector":"Information Technology",
   "prices":null
}
```

The stock object is serialized into JSON, which is the standard data format for web services. Note that the navigation property for *Price* object has been included in the JSON data but set to null. This is because Entity Framework Core does not load related data unless specifically asked to. The next *GET* method, *GetSymbolAndPrice*, shows how to get the related *Price* data:

```
[HttpGet("{id}/{start}/{end}")]
public Symbol GetSymbolAndPrice(int id, string start, string end){
... ...
    stock.Prices = context.Prices.Where(p => p.SymbolId == id && p.Date>=startDate
        && p.Date<=endDate).OrderBy(d=>d.Date).ToList();
    return stock
}
```

Inside this action method, we specifically request the related price data. This method add two more attribute arguments, *start* and *end*, which extends the URL schema defined by the Route attribute so that the *GetSymbolAndPrice* can be reached by a URL in the form */api/stocks/{id}/{start}/{end}*. The *start* and *end* arguments are used to specify the start date and end date when retrieving the related stock price data.

To test this new web service, request the URL, https, *https://localhost:5001/api/stocks/33/2018-01-01/2018-01-10*, in your browser, which will return the data shown in Fig.3-6.

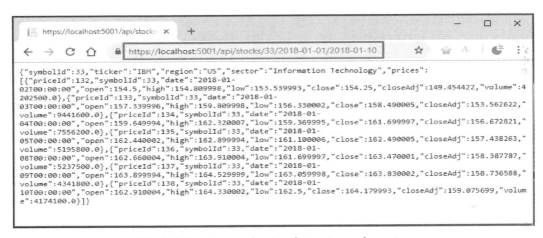

Fig.3-6. Retrieve stock price data using web service.

We also use the GET method to retrieve data from the *IndexData* table in the databased:

```
[Route("~/api/IndexData")]
[HttpGet]
public IEnumerable<IndexData> GetIndexData(){
... ...
```

This method redefine the Route explicitly for the *IndexData* object, so that the *GetIndexData* method can be reached by a URL in the form */api/indexdata*. To test this method, request the URL *https://localhost:5001/api/indexdata* in your browser, which will return the result shown in Fig.3-7.

The other *GetIndexData* method with input parameters *start* and *end* allows you to retrieve index data in a specified time interval:

```
[Route("~/api/IndexData/{start}/{end}")]
[HttpGet]
public IEnumerable<IndexData> GetIndexData(string start, string end)
{
... ...
```

This method can be reached by a URL in the form */api/indexdata/{start}/{end}*.

Fig.3-7. Retrieve all index data using web service.

Two more *GET* methods, *GetSymbolwithTicker* and *GetSymbolAndPricewithTicker*, were also added to the web API, which allow you to retrieve stock and price data using the stock ticker instead of ID.

POST Method

We use the HTTP POST method to store new data objects in the database. It allows clients to supply new data in a request so that a *Stock* object is received and stored in the database. In the *StockValuesController* class, we add a *CreateStock* method:

```
[HttpPost]
public IActionResult CreateStock([FromBody] Symbol stock)
{
... ...
```

This method has a *Symbol* input parameter, which will be populated by the model binder with the data sent by the client. This parameter is decorated with the *FromBody* attribute, which tells the model binder to get data values from the request body (and without which the JSON data sent by the client will be ignored).

The *CreateStock* method return an *IActionResult* object, which provides flexibility for returning an error if the data sent by the client does not pass the validation checks. The database context's *Add* method tells Entity Framework Core that the *Symbol* object should be stored in the database and the operation is performed when the *SaveChanges* method is called.

When the data is stored, the database generates a value for the *SymbolId* property, and it will automatically update the *Symbol* object with that value.

PUT Method

The HTTP PUT method is used to update (or edit) an existing data object and requires an approach similar to the one required by the POST method discussed in the preceding section. To support for updating *Stock* data, we add an action method named *UpdateSymbol* to the *StockValuesController* class:

```
[HttpPut("{id}")]
public IActionResult UpdateSymbol(int id, [FromBody] Symbol stock)
{
... ...
```

The ASP.NET Core model binder will create the *Symbol* object from the request data, whose *SymbolId* property is set from the *id* parameter so that Entity Framework Core knows which existing object is to be updated. The database is updated by calling the *SaveChanges* method.

DELETE Method

The last HTTP method that the web service should support is *DELETE*, which is used to remove data from the database.

Database would not allow data to be deleted if doing so creates an inconsistency. For our *Quant* project, an inconsistency would be to delete a *Stock* object but leave its related *Price* objects in the database, resulting in table rows that have a foreign key relationship to nonexistent data. To avoid inconsistencies we need to remove the related *Price* data when deleting a *Stock* object.

To add support for deleting *Stock* data, we add an action method named *DeleteStock* method to the *StockValuesController* class:

```
[HttpDelete("{id}")]
public void DeleteStock(int id)
{
... ...
```

This method first check if the stock has the *Price* data. If yes, it removes the *Price* objects first and then creates a new *Stock* object that has the ID value provided by the client and passes it to the database context's *Remove* method. This gives Entity Framework Core enough information to perform the delete operation when the *SaveChanges* method is called.

Angular Data Model

Creating a data model in the Angular part of the project makes it easier to work with the data received from ASP.NET Core web service. It can also take full advantage of Visual Studio's Intellisence.

Model Classes

Create a new directory named *models* in the *ClientApp/src/app* folder and add it a TypeScript class file called *symbol.model.ts*. Here is the code for this model:

```
// symbol.model.ts file:
import { Price } from './price.model';

export class Symbol {
  constructor(
    public symbolId?: number,
    public ticker?: string,
    public region?: string,
    public sector?: string,
    public prices?: Price[]
```

```
  ) { }
}
```

This class contains only a constructor, which is typical for a TypeScript data model class. Each parameter in the constructor receives a value that can be used to configure a new instance of the class. The question mark that follows a parameter name indicates that the parameter is optional:

```
...
public symbolId?: number,
...
```

Optional parameter are useful for model classes because you will not always have values for all the fields available when you create a new object. Making all the constructor parameters optional gives you extra flexibility, allowing you to create new objects with all, some, or even no data values.

The reason that the *symbol.model.ts* class contains only a constructor is that TypeScript has a useful feature for avoiding a common coding pattern that especially prevalent in model classes. When you include an access modifier on a constructor parameter, such as *public* or *private*, TypeScript creates a property with the same name and access level as the parameter and assigns it the value received by the constructor.

For example, the following constructor only class has the following code:

```
export class ConstructorOnly {
  constructor(
    public parameter1?: number,
    private parameter2?:string,
  ) { }
}
```

This class is equivalent to the following code:

```
export class ConstructorWithProperties {
  public parameter1: number;
  private parameter2: string;

  constructor(parameter1?: number, parameter2?: string) {
    this.parameter1 = parameter1;
    this.parameter2 = parameter2;
  }
}
```

It is easy to make mistake when defining properties and copying values to them manually, either forgetting to assign a value to a property or assigning the wrong value. The TypeScript feature that automates this process produces identical results but in a more concise and less error-prone way.

Next, add a file called *price.model.ts* in the *ClientApp/src/app/models* folder and add it the following code:

```
// price.model.ts file:
export class Price {
  constructor(
    public priceId?: number,
    public symbolId?: number,
    public date?: Date,
    public open?: number,
    public high?: number,
    public low?: number,
```

```
      public close?: number,
      public closeAdj?: number,
      public volume?: number
   ) { }
}
```

Finally, add a file called *indexData.model.ts* in the *ClientApp/src/app/models* folder and add it the following code:

```
// indexData.model.ts file:
export class IndexData {
   constructor(
      public id?: number,
      public date?: Date,
      public igSpread?: number,
      public hySpread?: number,
      public spx?: number,
      public vix?: number
   ) { }
}
```

Repository Service

The repository pattern isolates the code that manages the data from the rest of the application and makes it easy to provide access to data to any part of the application that requires it. To create a repository service in Angular, run the following command in a command prompt window:

ng g s models/repository

This will generates a skeleton *RepositoryService* class in the *ClientApp/src/app/models/repository. service.ts* file. The *RepositoryService* class looks like the following:

```
// repository. service.ts file
import { Injectable } from '@angular/core';

@Injectable({
   providedIn: 'root'
})
export class RepositotyService {

   constructor() {}
}
```

Notice that the service imports the Angular *Injectable* symbol and annotates the class with *@Injectable()* decorator. This marks the class as one that participates in the dependency injection system. However, you must make the *RepositoryService* available to the dependency injection system before Angular can inject it into Angular components. You can do this manually by registering a provider in the *app.module.ts* file. However, by default, the Angular CLI automatically registers a provider with the *root injector* for your service by including provider metadata in the *@Injectable* decorator, as shown in the above highlighted code snippet. When you provide the service at the *root* level, Angular creates a single, shared instance of your service and injects into any class that asks for it.

Now, open the *repository.service.ts* class file in the *ClientApp/src/app/models* folder and replace its content with the following code:

```typescript
// repository.service.ts file:
import { Injectable, Inject} from '@angular/core';
import { HttpClient } from '@angular/common/http';
import { Symbol } from './symbol.model';
import { Price } from './price.model';
import { IndexData } from './indexData.model';

@Injectable({
  providedIn: 'root'
})
export class Repository {
  stock: Symbol = new Symbol();
  stocks: Symbol[] = [];
  stock1: Symbol = new Symbol();
  prices: Price[] = [];
  indexData: IndexData[] = [];
  private url;

  constructor(private http: HttpClient, @Inject('BASE_URL') baseUrl: string) {
    this.url = baseUrl;
    this.getStocks();
    this.getIndexDataPeriod("2005-01-01", "2005-03-01");
    this.getStock(1);
  }

  getStock(id: number) {
    this.http.get<Symbol>(this.url + 'api/stocks/' + id).subscribe(
        result => { this.stock = result });
  }

  getStockWithTicker(ticker: string) {
    this.http.get<Symbol>(this.url + 'api/stockwithticker/' +
        ticker).subscribe(result => { this.stock1 = result });
  }

  getStockAndPriceWithTicker(ticker: string, start: string, end: string) {
    let url1 = this.url + 'api/stockwithticker/' + ticker + '/' + start + '/' + end;
    this.http.get<Symbol>(url1).subscribe(result => { this.stock1 = result });
  }

  getStocks() {
    this.http.get<Symbol[]>(this.url + 'api/stocks').subscribe(result => {
        this.stocks = result});
  }

  getStockAndPrice(id: number, start: string, end: string) {
    let url1 = this.url + 'api/stocks/' + id + '/' + start + '/' + end;
    this.http.get<Symbol>(url1).subscribe(result => { this.stock = result });
  }

  getIndexData() {
    this.http.get<IndexData[]>(this.url + 'api/indexdata').subscribe(result => {
        this.indexData = result });
  }
```

```
getIndexDataPeriod(start: string, end: string) {
  let url1 = this.url + 'api/indexdata' + '/' + start + '/' + end;
  this.http.get<IndexData[]>(url1).subscribe(result => {
      this.indexData = result });
}

createStock(stck: Symbol) {
  let data = {
    ticker: stck.ticker,
    region: stck.region,
    sector: stck.sector
  };
  this.http.post<number>(this.url + 'api/stocks', data).subscribe(result => {
    stck.symbolId = result;
    this.stocks.push(stck);
  });
  return stck;
}

updateStock(stck: Symbol) {
  let data = {
    ticker: stck.ticker,
    region: stck.region,
    sector: stck.sector
  };
  this.http.put(this.url + 'api/stocks/' + stck.symbolId, data).subscribe(
    result => this.getStocks());
}

deleteStock(id: number) {
  this.http.delete<any>(this.url + 'api/stocks/' + id).subscribe(
    result => this.getStocks(),
    error => console.log('error = ' + JSON.stringify(error, null, 4)));
}
}
```

Here, we use Angular's built-in service called *HttpClient* to request the configuration object from ASP.NET Core web API. Both the *HttpClient* service and application's BASE_URL are injected into the constructor of the *repository.service.ts* class. BASE_URL provides the application's root address which we will call back to reach the web API.

We then create various methods to perform necessary CRUD operations. The *HttpClient* object received through the constructor is used to make HTTP GET, POST, PUT, and DELETE requests. For example, to make an HTTP GET request, we use the following method:

```
getStock(id: number) {
  this.http.get<Symbol>(this.url + 'api/stocks/' + id).subscribe(
    result => { this.stock = result });
}
```

The *getStock* method accept a URL as its argument. The result of the *http.get* method is an Observable<Response> object. Observables are part of a library called Reactive Extensions (rxjs), which is used by Angular to connect different parts of the application. For the most part, you do not work directly with observables in an Angular app because they are used behind the scenes.

The *subscribe* method is used to invoke a function when the work represented by the *Observable* has completed. The function receives the *Observable* result, which is a response result object that is assigned to the *stock* property.

The overall effect is that when a new instance of the *RepositoryService* class is created, the constructor calls various methods, which send HTTP requests to the web service and use the results received in response to set corresponding properties, which can be accessed by the rest of applications.

Access Web Service Data

The basic infrastructure for the Angular data model is complete. There is a repository service that has been configured for use with the Angular dependency injection. The repository obtains its data from the TypeScript model classes that correspond to the ASP.NET Core web service.

In this section, I demonstrate how to use this repository to perform various CRUD operations.

Display Stock Data

Here, we want to use the repository service to access the stock data and display it to the user. In an Angular app, the key building block is the component, which provides the logic and data required to display HTML content. In loose term, an Angular component class is equivalent to an ASP.NET Core MVC controller, while an Angular component's template is equivalent to a Razor view. The key difference is that the MVC controllers and views are used to generate a response to an HTTP request, after which they have finished their job. But, an Angular component and its template have an ongoing responsibility to manage the HTML displayed to the user and respond to user interaction and changes to the data model.

Run the following command in a command prompt window from the *ClientApp* folder:

```
ng g c charter03/all-stocks --module=app.module
```

This creates a new component named *all-stocks* in the *ClientApp/src/app/chapter03* folder. We will use this component to display all stock tickers. Open the *all-stocks.component.ts* file and replace its content with the following code:

```
// all-stocks.component.ts file:
import { Component, OnInit } from '@angular/core';
import { RepositoryService } from '../../models/repository.service';
import { Symbol } from '../../models/symbol.model';

@Component({
  selector: 'app-all-stocks',
  templateUrl: './all-stocks.component.html',
  styleUrls: ['./all-stocks.component.css']
})
export class AllStocksComponent implements OnInit {
  public displayedCols = ['id', 'ticker', 'region', 'sector'];

  constructor(private repository: RepositoryService) { }

  ngOnInit() {
  }
```

```
  get stocks(): Symbol[] {
    return this.repository.stocks;
  }
}
```

The constructor has a *RepositoryService* parameter called *repository*, which is how dependencies are declared in an Angular app. The parameter tells Angular that the component class needs a *RepositoryService* object and provides it when a new *AllStocksComponent* object is created. The private keyword has been applied to the repository parameter, meaning that a property with the same name will be defined and assigned the value of the constructor parameter and that can be accesses only within the *AllStocksComponent* class.

The other addition in this class is a read-only property called *stocks* that returns the value of the *RepositoryService* object's *stocks* property.

To display the data to the user, edit the *all-stocks.component.html* file and replace the contents with the following code:

```
// all-stocks.component.html file:
<h2>
  All-stocks works!
</h2>

<mat-table [dataSource]="stocks">
  <ng-container matColumnDef="id">
    <mat-header-cell *matHeaderCellDef>Symbol ID</mat-header-cell>
    <mat-cell *matCellDef="let stock">{{stock?.symbolId}}</mat-cell>
  </ng-container>
  <ng-container matColumnDef="ticker">
    <mat-header-cell *matHeaderCellDef>Ticker</mat-header-cell>
    <mat-cell *matCellDef="let stock">{{stock?.ticker}}</mat-cell>
  </ng-container>
  <ng-container matColumnDef="region">
    <mat-header-cell *matHeaderCellDef>Region</mat-header-cell>
    <mat-cell *matCellDef="let stock">{{stock?.region}}</mat-cell>
  </ng-container>
  <ng-container matColumnDef="sector">
    <mat-header-cell *matHeaderCellDef>Sector</mat-header-cell>
    <mat-cell *matCellDef="let stock">{{stock?.sector}}</mat-cell>
  </ng-container>
  <mat-header-row *matHeaderRowDef="displayedCols"></mat-header-row>
  <mat-row *matRowDef="let row; columns: displayedCols;"></mat-row>
</mat-table>
```

Here, we use the Angular one-way data binding to display the stock data defined by the `Symbol[]` object returned by the component's *stocks* property. The question mark is the TypeScript safe navigation operator, and it has the same purpose as the C# equivalent, preventing the properties from being read when the *stocks* property has not been initialized.

Finally, we need to add a path for this new component to the *RouterModule* of the root module (i.e., the *app.module.ts* file):

```
{ path: 'chapter03/all-stocks, component: AllStocksComponent },
```

Then add the corresponding URL link to the *home* and *nav-menu* components.

Saving the project and navigating to the */chapter03/all-stocks* page produce the results shown in Fig.3-8.

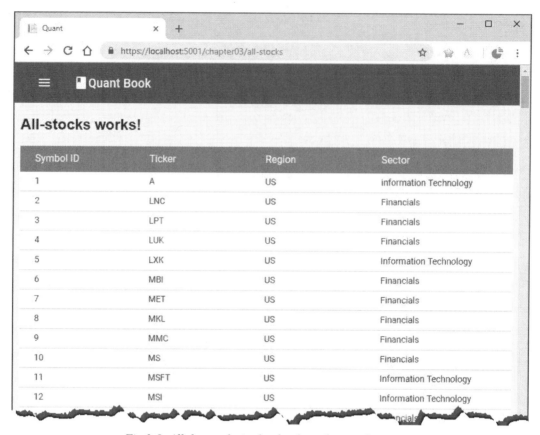

Fig.3-8. All the stocks in the database from web service.

Display Stock Price Data

In this section, we illustrate how to display the detailed information for a single stock, including its price data if it is available in database. We will use two approaches to access the stock details; i.e., using either stock ID or stock ticker.

Run the following command in a command prompt window from the *ClientApp* folder:

```
ng g c charter03/stock-price --module=app.module
```

This creates a new component named *stock-price* in the *ClientApp/src/app/chapter03* folder. We will use this component to display details for a specified stock. Open the *stock-price.component.ts* file and replace its content with the following code:

```
// stock-price.component.ts file:
import { Component, OnInit } from '@angular/core';
import { RepositoryService } from '../../models/repository.service';
import { Symbol } from '../../models/symbol.model';
```

```
@Component({
  selector: 'app-stock-price',
  templateUrl: './stock-price.component.html',
  styleUrls: ['./stock-price.component.css']
})
export class StockPriceComponent implements OnInit {
  public stockId: number = 1;
  public ticker = 'A';
  public startDate: string = '2018-07-01';
  public endDate: string = '2018-08-01';
  public startDate1: string = '2018-07-01';
  public endDate1: string = '2018-08-01';

  constructor(private repository: Repositoryservice) { }

  ngOnInit() {
    this.getStockAndPrice(this.stockId, this.startDate, this.endDate);
    this.getStockAndPriceWithTicker(this.ticker, this.startDate1, this.endDate1);
  }

  get stock(): Symbol {
    return this.repository.stock;
  }

  get stock1(): Symbol {
    return this.repository.stock1;
  }

  getStockAndPrice(id: number, start: string, end: string) {
    this.repository.getStockAndPrice(id, start, end);
  }

  getStockAndPriceWithTicker(ticker: string, start: string, end: string) {
    this.repository.getStockAndPriceWithTicker(ticker, start, end);
  }
}
```

Here, we add two read-only properties *stock* and *stock1*, which are updated using the *getStockAndPrice* and *getStockAndPriceWithTicker* methods respectively. For the *getStockAndPrice* method, we use stock *Id*, *startDate*, and *endData* as its input arguments, while for the *getStockAndPriceWithTicker* method, we use *ticker*, *startDate1*, and *endDate1* as its input arguments. Using two sets of start and end dates allows you to specify the time periods independently for these two methods.

To avoid the repeated coding, we will create a child component to display the detailed information for a specified stock.

Run the following command in a command prompt window from the *ClientApp* folder:

ng g c charter03/stock-price/stock-price-child --module=app.module

This creates a new component named *stock-price-child* in the *ClientApp/src/app/chapter03/stock-price* folder. We will use this component to display details for a specified stock. Open the *stock-price-child.component.ts* file and replace its content with the following code:

```
// stock-price-child.ts file:
import { Component, OnInit, Input } from '@angular/core';
```

```
import { Symbol } from '../../../models/symbol.model';

@Component({
  selector: 'app-stock-price-child',
  templateUrl: './stock-price-child.component.html',
  styleUrls: ['./stock-price-child.component.css']
})
export class StockPriceChildComponent implements OnInit {

  @Input() stock: Symbol;

  public displayedCols =
    ['date', 'open', 'high', 'low', 'close', 'closeAdj', 'volume'];

  constructor() { }

  ngOnInit() {
  }
}
```

The child component needs to know which *stock* object it is responsible for, and for this we have used an Angular *Input* property, which has been discussed in the preceding chapter. The *Input* property allows this child component to receive *stock* data from its parent component's template in which it is applied.

Open its template file named *stock-price-child.component.html* in the *ClientApp.src/app/chapter03/stock-price* folder and replace its content with the following code:

```
// stoc-price-child.html file:
<h3>Stock Details:</h3>
<p><b>ID:</b> {{stock.symbolId}}, <b>Ticker:</b> {{stock.ticker}},
  <b>Region:</b> {{stock.region}}, <b>Sector:</b> {{stock.sector}}</p>

<div *ngIf="stock.prices">
  <div *ngIf="stock.prices.length>0">
    <h4>Prices:</h4>
    <mat-table [dataSource]="stock.prices">
      <ng-container matColumnDef="date">
        <mat-header-cell *matHeaderCellDef>Date</mat-header-cell>
        <mat-cell *matCellDef="let item">{{item.date |
          date: 'MM/dd/yyyy'}}</mat-cell>
      </ng-container>
      <ng-container matColumnDef="open">
        <mat-header-cell *matHeaderCellDef>Open</mat-header-cell>
        <mat-cell *matCellDef="let item">{{item.open}}</mat-cell>
      </ng-container>
      <ng-container matColumnDef="high">
        <mat-header-cell *matHeaderCellDef>High</mat-header-cell>
        <mat-cell *matCellDef="let item">{{item.high}}</mat-cell>
      </ng-container>
      <ng-container matColumnDef="low">
        <mat-header-cell *matHeaderCellDef>Low</mat-header-cell>
        <mat-cell *matCellDef="let item">{{item.low}}</mat-cell>
      </ng-container>
      <ng-container matColumnDef="close">
        <mat-header-cell *matHeaderCellDef>Close</mat-header-cell>
        <mat-cell *matCellDef="let item">{{item.close}}</mat-cell>
```

```
          </ng-container>
          <ng-container matColumnDef="closeAdj">
            <mat-header-cell *matHeaderCellDef>Close Adj</mat-header-cell>
            <mat-cell *matCellDef="let item">{{item.closeAdj}}</mat-cell>
          </ng-container>
          <ng-container matColumnDef="volume">
            <mat-header-cell *matHeaderCellDef>Volume</mat-header-cell>
            <mat-cell *matCellDef="let item">{{item.volume}}</mat-cell>
          </ng-container>
          <mat-header-row *matHeaderRowDef="displayedCols"></mat-header-row>
          <mat-row *matRowDef="let row; columns: displayedCols;"></mat-row>
        </mat-table>
      </div>
</div>
```

Here, we simply use a *mat-table* to display the detailed information for a specified stock object. Note that we use *ngFor* directive to show the *stock.prices* collection object.

Now, we can use this child component directive in the *stock-price* component's template like the follows:

```
// stock-price.component.html file:
<h2>
  Stock-price works!
</h2>

<mat-tab-group>
  <mat-tab label="Using Stock ID">
    <br /><br />
    <mat-form-field>
      <input matInput placeholder="stock Id" [(ngModel)]="stockId" name="stockId">
    </mat-form-field>
    <mat-form-field>
      <input matInput placeholder="Start Date" [(ngModel)]="startDate"
             name="startDate">
    </mat-form-field>
    <mat-form-field>
      <input matInput placeholder="End Date" [(ngModel)]="endDate" name="endDate">
    </mat-form-field>
    <button mat-raised-button (click)="getStockAndPrice(stockId,startDate,
            endDate)"> Get Stock Details</button>
    <app-stock-price-child [stock]="stock"></app-stock-price-child>
  </mat-tab>

  <mat-tab label="Using Stock Ticker">
    <br /><br />
    <mat-form-field>
      <input matInput placeholder="ticker" [(ngModel)]="ticker" name="ticker">
    </mat-form-field>
    <mat-form-field>
      <input matInput placeholder="Start Date" [(ngModel)]="startDate1"
             name="startDate1">
    </mat-form-field>
    <mat-form-field>
      <input matInput placeholder="End Date" [(ngModel)]="endDate1" name="endDate1">
    </mat-form-field>
    <button mat-raised-button (click)="getStockAndPriceWithTicker(ticker,
```

```
                  startDate1, endDate1)">Get Stock Details</button>
    <app-stock-price-child [stock]="stock1"></app-stock-price-child>
  </mat-tab>
</mat-tab-group>
```

Here, we use Angular Material tabs (*mat-tab*) to organize content into separate views where only one view can be visible at a time. Each tab's label is shown in the tab header and the active tab's label is designed with the animated ink bar. In our case, the tab contains two labels: *Using Stock ID* and *Using Stock Ticker*, representing the stock details queried using the stock *Id* or *ticker* respectively.

The *stock-price* component includes a child component named *app-stock-price-child* inside each tab, binding its *stock* or *stock1* property to the child's *stock* property depending on which tab is selected.

Finally, we need to add a path for the parent component to the *RouterModule* of the root module (i.e., the *app.module.ts* file):

```
{ path: 'chapter03/stock-price, component: StockPriceComponent },
```

Then add the corresponding URL link to the *home* and *nav-menu* components.

Saving the project and navigating to the */chapter03/stock-price* page will give the default result for stock with *Id* = 1. In this case, the page will display the stock details without the price data because this stock has no price data in the database. Now, change the stock *Id* to 33, which is for the IBM stock, make changes to *Start Date* and *End Date* fields, and click the *Get Stock Details* button, which creates the result shown in Fig.3-9.

If you tap the *Using Stock Ticker* tab and set ticker to IBM, you will get the similar result shown in Fig.3-9, except that in this case, we use the stock ticker to retrieve data from the web service.

Display Index Data

In this section, we want to display the index data to the user. Run the following command in a command prompt window from the *ClientApp* folder:

```
ng g c charter03/index-data --module=app.module
```

This creates a new component named *index-data* in the *ClientApp/src/app/chapter03* folder. We will use this component to display the default index data. Open the *index-data.component.ts* file and replace its content with the following code listing:

```
// index-data.component.ts file:
import { Component, OnInit } from '@angular/core';
import { RepositoryService } from '../../models/repository.service';
import { IndexData } from '../../models/indexData.model';

@Component({
  selector: 'app-index-data',
  templateUrl: './index-data.component.html',
  styleUrls: ['./index-data.component.css']
})
export class IndexDataComponent implements OnInit {

  public displayedCols = ['date', 'ig', 'hy', 'spx', 'vix'];

  constructor(private repository: RepositoryService) { }
```

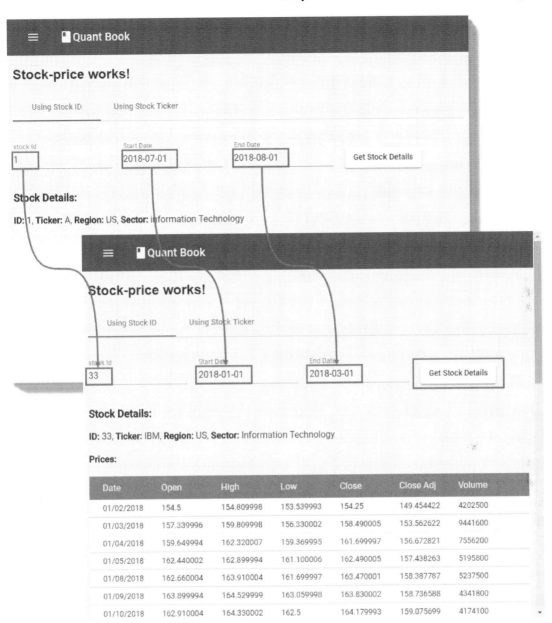

Fig.3-9. Stock price from web service.

```
ngOnInit() {
}

get indexData(): IndexData[] {
  return this.repository.indexData;
}
}
```

The read-only property *indexData* returns the default index data defined in the constructor of the *repository.service.ts* class:

Open this component's template file *index-data.component.html* and replace its content with the following code:

```
// index-data.component.html file:
<h2>
  Index-data works!
</h2>

<mat-table [dataSource]="indexData">
  <ng-container matColumnDef="date">
    <mat-header-cell *matHeaderCellDef>Date</mat-header-cell>
    <mat-cell *matCellDef="let item">{{item.date | date: 'MM/dd/yyyy'}}</mat-cell>
  </ng-container>
  <ng-container matColumnDef="ig">
    <mat-header-cell *matHeaderCellDef>IG Spread</mat-header-cell>
    <mat-cell *matCellDef="let item">{{item.igSpread}}</mat-cell>
  </ng-container>
  <ng-container matColumnDef="hy">
    <mat-header-cell *matHeaderCellDef>HY Spread</mat-header-cell>
    <mat-cell *matCellDef="let item">{{item.hySpread}}</mat-cell>
  </ng-container>
  <ng-container matColumnDef="spx">
    <mat-header-cell *matHeaderCellDef>SPX</mat-header-cell>
    <mat-cell *matCellDef="let item">{{item.spx}}</mat-cell>
  </ng-container>
  <ng-container matColumnDef="vix">
    <mat-header-cell *matHeaderCellDef>VIX</mat-header-cell>
    <mat-cell *matCellDef="let item">{{item.vix}}</mat-cell>
  </ng-container>
  <mat-header-row *matHeaderRowDef="displayedCols"></mat-header-row>
  <mat-row *matRowDef="let row; columns: displayedCols;"></mat-row>
</mat-table>
```

Here, we use the Angular one-way data binding to display the index data defined by the `IndexData[]` object returned by the component's *indexData* property.

Finally, we need to add a path for this new component to the *RouterModule* of the root module (i.e., the *app.module.ts* file):

```
{ path: 'chapter03/index-data, component: IndexDataComponent },
```

Then add the corresponding URL link to the *home* and *nav-menu* components.

Saving the project and navigating to the */chapter03/index-data* page produce the results shown in Fig.3-10.

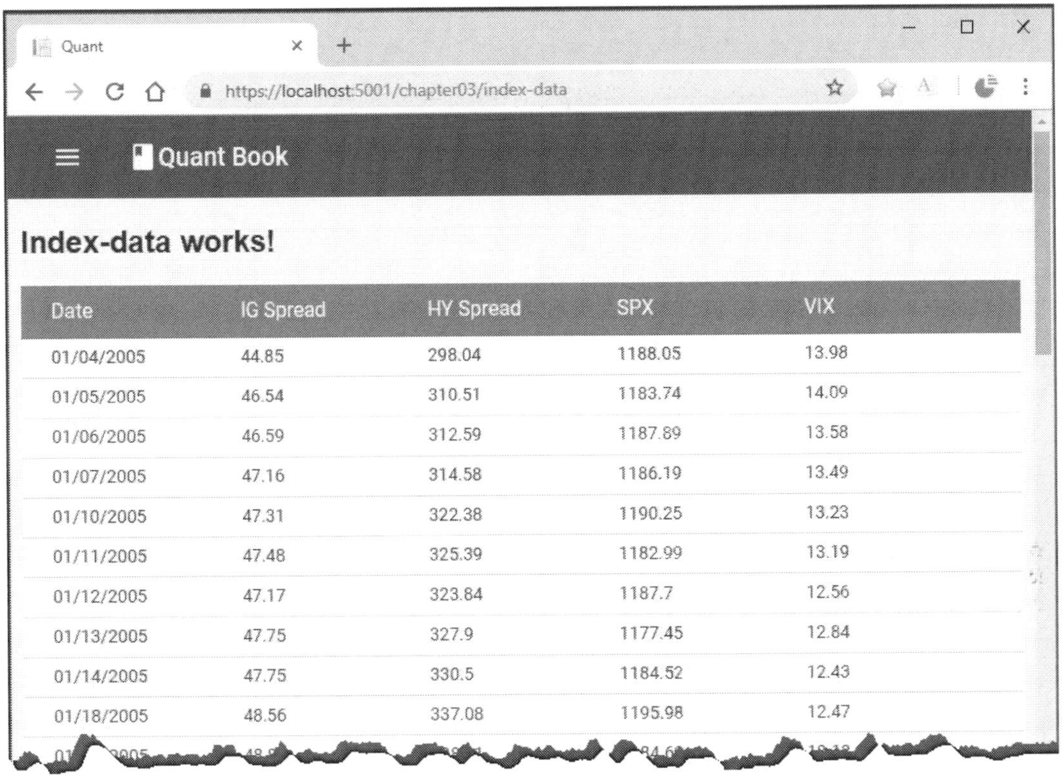

Fig.3-10. Index data from web service.

Perform CRUD Operations

In the *repository.service.ts* class, we implemented various CRUD operations for *Stock* (or *Symbol*) objects. In this section, I will use examples to illustrate how to perform these CRUD operations.

Here, we will use Angular material tabs to organize the CRUD operations into three separate views with labels, *Create Stock*, *Update Stock*, and *Delete Stock*.

Run the following command in a command prompt window from the *ClientApp* folder:

```
ng g c charter03/stock-crud --module=app.module
```

This creates a new component named *stock-crud* in the *ClientApp/src/app/chapter03* folder. Here, we can simply use the default component class, while only need to replace its template with the following code:

```
// stock-crud.component.html file:
<h2>
  Stock CRUD Operations
</h2>

<mat-tab-group>
  <mat-tab label="Create Stock">
    <app-stock-create></app-stock-create>
```

```
  </mat-tab>

  <mat-tab label="Update Stock">
    <app-stock-update></app-stock-update>
  </mat-tab>

  <mat-tab label="Delete Stock">
    <app-stock-delete></app-stock-delete>
  </mat-tab>
</mat-tab-group>
```

This template is very simple – it contains three new component directives: *app-stock-create*, *app-stock-update*, and *app-stock-delete*, which will be implemented in the following subsections.

Next, we need to add a path for this new component to the *RouterModule* of the root module (i.e., the *app.module.ts* file):

```
{ path: 'chapter03/stock-crud, component: StockCrudComponent },
```

Then add the corresponding URL link to the *home* and *nav-menu* components.

Perform Create Operation

In this section, we create the *app-stock-create* component that can be called when the user wants to create a new stock.

Run the following command in a command prompt window from the *ClientApp* folder:

ng g c charter03/stock-crud/stock-create --module=app.module

This creates a new component named *stock-create* in the *ClientApp/src/app/chapter03/stock-crud* folder. Open the *stock-create.component.ts* file and replace its content with the following code:

```
// stock-create.component.ts file:
import { Component, OnInit } from '@angular/core';
import { RepositoryService } from '../../../models/repository.service';
import { Symbol } from '../../../models/symbol.model';

@Component({
  selector: 'app-stock-create',
  templateUrl: './stock-create.component.html',
  styleUrls: ['./stock-create.component.css']
})
export class StockCreateComponent implements OnInit {
  public ticker: string;
  public region: string;
  public sector: string;
  public stock: Symbol;

  constructor(private repository: RepositoryService) { }

  ngOnInit() {
  }

  createStock() {
    let symbol = new Symbol(0, this.ticker, this.region, this.sector);
```

```
    this.stock = this.repository.createStock(symbol);
    this.ticker = null;
    this.region = null;
    this.sector = null;
  }
}
```

The *createStock* method creates a new *Symbol* object that is defined using the properties, *ticker, region,* and *sector*. This method also asks the repository to send it to the web service.

Next, open the template file, *stock-create.component.html*, and replace its content with the following code:

```
// stock-create.component.html file:
<h3 style="margin-top:50px">
  Create a New Stock Object
</h3>
<form>
  <mat-form-field>
    <input matInput placeholder="Ticker" [(ngModel)]="ticker" #tk="ngModel"
name="ticker">
  </mat-form-field>
  <mat-form-field>
    <input matInput placeholder="Region" [(ngModel)]="region" name="region">
  </mat-form-field>
  <mat-form-field>
    <input matInput placeholder="Sector" [(ngModel)]="sector" name="sector">
  </mat-form-field>
</form>

<span *ngIf="stock" style="color:red">
  The stock: ID = {{stock.symbolId}}, Ticker = {{stock.ticker}},
  Region = {{stock.region}}, Sector = {{stock.sector}}
  has been saved to database.
</span>

<br /><br />
<button mat-raised-button (click)="createStock()">Create Stock</button>
```

This template contains three inputs: *ticker, region,* and *sector,* which defines a new stock object, and can be specified by the user. The click event of the *Create Stock* button is triggered when the user clicks it, at which point Angular invokes the component's *CreateStock* method. The result is that clicking the button will create a new stock object and add it to database.

Now, save the project and navigate to the */chapter03/stock-crud* page to bring up the stock creation window. Enter a fake stock as shown in Fig.3-11 and then click the *Create Stock* button. A confirmation message will appear to tell you that the new stock is saved to database. The *stockId* (= 189 in our example) for this new stock object is assigned automatically by the database (see Fig.3-11).

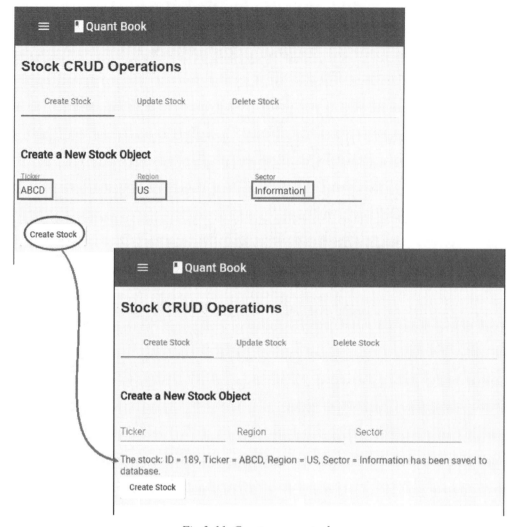

Fig.3-11. Create a new stock.

Perform Update Operation

In this section, we create the *app-stock-update* component that can be called when the user wants to update existing stocks in the database.

Run the following command in a command prompt window from the *ClientApp* folder:

```
ng g c charter03/stock-crud/stock-update --module=app.module
```

This creates a new component named *stock-update* in the *ClientApp/src/app/chapter03/stock-crud* folder. Open the *stock-update.component.ts* file and replace its content with the following code:

```
// stock-update.component.html file:
import { Component, OnInit } from '@angular/core';
import { RepositoryService } from '../../../models/repository.service';
```

```
import { Symbol } from '../../../models/symbol.model';

@Component({
  selector: 'app-stock-update',
  templateUrl: './stock-update.component.html',
  styleUrls: ['./stock-update.component.css']
})
export class StockUpdateComponent implements OnInit {
  public stockId: number;
  public stck: Symbol;

  constructor(private repository: RepositoryService) {
    this.stck = null;
    this.stockId = 1;
  }

  ngOnInit() {
  }

  get stock() {
    return this.repository.stock;
  }

  getStock() {
    this.stck = null;
    this.repository.getStock(this.stockId);
  }

  updateStock() {
    this.stck = new Symbol(this.stock.symbolId, this.stock.ticker,
      this.stock.region, this.stock.sector);
    this.repository.updateStock(this.stck);
  }
}
```

The read-only *stock* property and the *getStock* method let you check the stock status (whether it is in the database or not) before updating the stock. While the *updateStock* method creates an updating object and uses the repository to send it to the web service.

Add the following code listing to the component's template so that the new component methods can be invoked:

```
// stock-update.component.html file:
<h3 style="margin-top:50px">
  Update a Stock Object
</h3>

<h4>Enter a stock Id to be updated:</h4>
<mat-form-field>
  <input matInput placeholder="Stock Id" [(ngModel)]="stockId" name="stockId">
</mat-form-field>
<button mat-raised-button (click)="getStock()">Get Stock</button>

<br /><br />
<div *ngIf="stock">
  <h4>Update this Stock:</h4>
```

```
<mat-form-field>
  <input matInput placeholder="Ticker" [(ngModel)]="stock.ticker" name="ticker">
</mat-form-field>
<mat-form-field>
  <input matInput placeholder="Region" [(ngModel)]="stock.region" name="region">
</mat-form-field>
<mat-form-field>
  <input matInput placeholder="Sector" [(ngModel)]="stock.sector" name="sector">
</mat-form-field>

<p *ngIf="stck" style="color:red">
  The stock with ID = {{stck.symbolId}} has been updated.
</p>

<br />
<button mat-raised-button (click)="updateStock()">Update Stock</button>
</div>

<p *ngIf="!stock" style="color:red">
  The stock with Id = {{stockId}} is not in database.
</p>
```

This template allows you to enter a *stockId* to check the stock status by clicking the *Get Stock* button. If the stock is in the database, its attributes will be used to fill out the corresponding input fields in the *Update this stock* section. Otherwise, it will display a warning message telling you that the stock you specified is not in database.

You can make any changes to the stock's attributes, including ticker, region, and sector. After completing the changes, click the *Update Stock* button to save your changes to the database.

Now, save the project, navigate to the */chapter03/stock-crud* page, click the *Update Stock* tab to bring up the stock creation window. Enter 189 (which is the fake stock we just created) in the *stock Id* field and click the *Get Stock* button. In the *Update this stock* part, make some changes to the stock attributes, and finally click the *Update Stock* button to save your changes, as shown in Fig.3-12.

Perform Delete Operation with Confirmation

In this section, we create the *app-stock-delete* component that can be called when the user wants to delete an existing stock object from the database. Here, we want to have a confirmation mechanism to avoid accidental deletions, which can be done using Angular Material Dialog (*MatDialog*).

Run the following command in a command prompt window from the *ClientApp* folder:

```
ng g c charter03/stock-crud/stock-delete --module=app.module
```

This creates a new component named *stock-delete* in the *ClientApp/src/app/chapter03/stock-crud* folder. Open the *stock-delete.component.ts* file and replace its content with the following code:

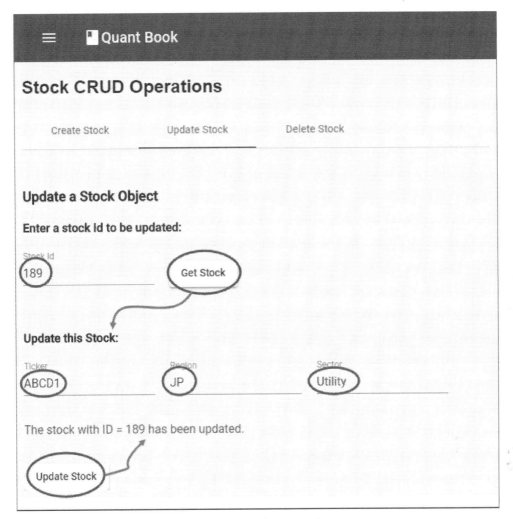

Fig.3-12. Update a stock.

```
// stock-delete.component.ts file:
import { Component, OnInit } from '@angular/core';
import { MatDialog, MatDialogConfig } from "@angular/material";
import { RepositoryService } from '../../../models/repository.service';
import { Symbol } from '../../../models/symbol.model';
import { StockDeleteDialogComponent } from './stock-delete-dialog/
        stock-delete-dialog.component';

@Component({
  selector: 'app-stock-delete',
  templateUrl: './stock-delete.component.html',
  styleUrls: ['./stock-delete.component.css']
})
export class StockDeleteComponent implements OnInit {
  public stockId: number;
  public isDeleted: boolean;
```

```
constructor(private repository: RepositoryService, private dialog: MatDialog) {
  this.stockId = 1;
  this.isDeleted = false;
}

ngOnInit() {
}

get stock() {
  return this.repository.stock;
}

getStock() {
  this.isDeleted = false;
  this.repository.getStock(this.stockId);
}

deleteStock() {
  this.repository.deleteStock(this.stockId);
  this.isDeleted = true;
}

openDialog() {
  const dialogConfig = new MatDialogConfig();
  dialogConfig.disableClose = true;
  dialogConfig.autoFocus = true;

  dialogConfig.data = {
    stock: this.stock
  }

  const dialogRef = this.dialog.open(StockDeleteDialogComponent, dialogConfig);
  dialogRef.afterClosed().subscribe(result => {
    if (result) {
      this.deleteStock();
    }
  });
}
}
```

In order to create Material Dialog instance, we inject the *MatDialog* service in the constructor. Inside the *openDialog* method, we create a *MatDialogConfig* instance used to configure the dialog with a set of parameters. In particular, we can pass data to the dialog component using the *data* property of the dialog configuration object, as shown in the following code snippet:

```
dialogConfig.data = {
  stock: this.stock
}
```

Here, we pass *stock* property to the dialog. We also need a way to pass the data back from the dialog to the component that created the dialog. We receive the dialog data by using the dialog reference to subscribe to the *afterClosed* observable, which emits a value containing the output data passed to *dialogRef.close* method.

Open the component's template and replace its content with the following code:

```
// stock-delete.component.html file:
<h3 style="margin-top:50px">
  Delete a Stock Object
</h3>

<h4>Enter a stock Id to be deleted:</h4>
<mat-form-field>
  <input matInput placeholder="Stock Id" [(ngModel)]="stockId" name="stockId">
</mat-form-field>
<button mat-raised-button (click)="getStock()">Get Stock</button>

<br /><br />
<div *ngIf="stock">
  <mat-form-field>
    <input matInput placeholder="Ticker" [(ngModel)]="stock.ticker" name="ticker">
  </mat-form-field>
  <mat-form-field>
    <input matInput placeholder="Region" [(ngModel)]="stock.region" name="region">
  </mat-form-field>
  <mat-form-field>
    <input matInput placeholder="Sector" [(ngModel)]="stock.sector" name="sector">
  </mat-form-field>
  <p *ngIf="isDeleted" style="color:red">
    The stock: ID = {{stockId}} has been deleted from database.
  </p>
  <br /><br />
  <button mat-raised-button (click)="openDialog()">Delete This Stock</button>
</div>

<p *ngIf="!stock" style="color:red">The stock with Id = {{stockId}} is not in
database.</p>
```

This template allows you to enter a *stockId* to check the stock status by clicking the *Get Stock* button. If the stock is in the database, its attributes will be used to fill out the corresponding input. Otherwise, it will display a warning message telling you that the stock you specified is not in database.

Clicking the *Delete This Stock* button will bring up the dialog modal window that let you confirm the stock deletion. Next, we will implement this dialog.

Run the following command in a command prompt window from the *ClientApp* folder:

```
ng g c charter03/stock-crud/stock-delete/stock-delete-dialog
       --module=app.module
```

This will create a new *stock-delete-dialog* component in the *ClientApp/src/app/chapter03/stock-delete* folder. In order for this component to be usable as a dialog body, we need to declare it as an *entryComponent* in the root module file, *app.module.ts*:

```
// app.module.ts file:
... ...

@NgModule({
  declarations: [
    AppComponent,

    //... other components omitted for breviry ...
```

```
  ],
  imports: [
    BrowserModule.withServerTransition({ appId: 'ng-cli-universal' }),
    HttpClientModule,
    CommonModule,

  // ... other imports omitted for breviry ...

  ],
  providers: [Repository],
  bootstrap: [AppComponent],
  entryComponents: [StockDeleteDialogComponent]
})
export class AppModule { }
```

If forgetting to resister it in the *entryComponents* decorator, you will get the following error while opening the dialog:

```
Error: No component factory found for StockDeleteDialogComponent. Did you add it to
@NgModule.entryComponents?
```

With this in place, we are ready to start building our dialog. Open the dialog component class and replace its content with the following code:

```
// stock-delete-dialog.ts file:
import { Component, OnInit, Inject } from '@angular/core';
import { MAT_DIALOG_DATA, MatDialogRef } from "@angular/material";
import { Symbol } from '../../../../models/symbol.model';

@Component({
  selector: 'app-stock-delete-dialog',
  templateUrl: './stock-delete-dialog.component.html',
  styleUrls: ['./stock-delete-dialog.component.css']
})
export class StockDeleteDialogComponent implements OnInit {
  stock: Symbol;
  isdelete: boolean = false;

  constructor(private dialogRef: MatDialogRef<StockDeleteDialogComponent>,
    @Inject(MAT_DIALOG_DATA) data) {
    this.stock = data.stock;
  }

  ngOnInit() {
  }

  close() {
    this.isdelete = false;
    this.dialogRef.close(this.isdelete);
  }

  deleteStock() {
    this.isdelete = true;
    this.dialogRef.close(this.isdelete);
  }
}
```

Here, we get a reference to the *data* object defined in the *stock-delete* component (i.e., the parent component) using the MAT_DIALOG_DATA injectable, that is, the *data* object initially passed as part of the dialog configuration object can now be directly injected into the constructor.

We also inject a reference to the dialog instance named *dialogRef*, which will be used to close the dialog and pass output data (the *isdelete* property in our example) back to the parent component.

The template of the dialog component is very simple:

```
// stock-delete-dialog.html file:
<h2 mat-dialog-title>Delete Stock</h2>

<mat-dialog-content>
  <p>StockId: {{stock.symbolId}}, Ticker: {{stock.ticker}}</p>
  <p style="color:red">Do you really want to delete this stock?</p>
</mat-dialog-content>

<mat-dialog-actions>
  <button class="mat-raised-button" (click)="close()">Cancel</button>
  <button class="mat-raised-button mat-primary"
(click)="deleteStock()">Delate</button>
</mat-dialog-actions>
```

Here, we build the template using the *mat-dialog* directives that have the typical Angular Material Design look and feel. There are three main directives in this template: *mat-dialog-title* identifies the title of the dialog; *mat-dialog-content* contains the body of the dialog (in this case, it displays the stock *Id* and *ticker*); and *mat-dialog-actions* consists of the action buttons at the bottom of the dialog.

Now, save the project, navigate to the */chapter03/stock-crud* page, click the *delete Stock* tab to bring up the stock deletion window. Enter 189 (which is the fake stock we just created) in the *stock Id* field and click the *Get Stock* button to display the stock's attribute on the screen, as shown in Fig.3-13. Click the *Delete This Stock* button to bring up the delete confirmation dialog. At this moment, you can double check whether you really want to delete this stock. If not, click the *Cancel* button to go back to the parent component window. While if yes, click the *Delete* button to delete this stock object, which will bring back to the parent component window with a message telling you that the stock has been deleted from database, as shown in Fig.3-13.

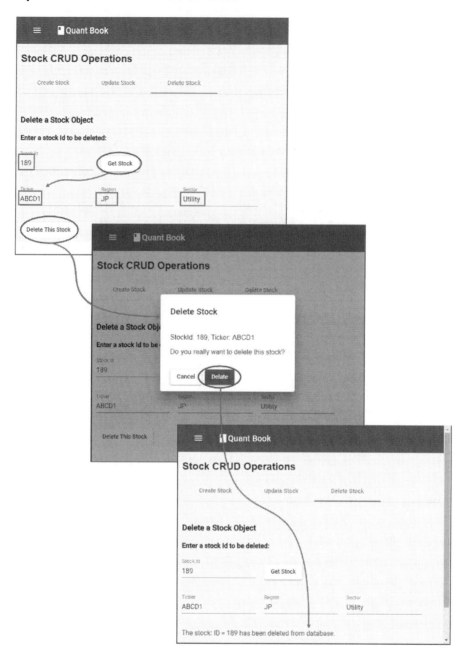

Fig.3-13. Delete stock with confirmation dialog.

Chapter 4
Market Data

Market data in finance is the most important part of any successful trading business. Regardless you are a quant analyst, quant developer, trader, or independent investor, you always have to deal with market data. Market data is price, volume, and trade-related data for a financial instrument reported by a trading venue such as a stock exchange. Market data allows you to know the latest price and see historical trends for instruments such as equities, fixed-income products, derivatives, and currencies. There are a number of market data vendors, which specialize in collecting, cleaning, collating and distributing market data. This has become the most common way that you get access to market data.

Delivery of price data from exchanges to users is highly time-sensitive, and specialized technologies designed to handle collection and throughput of massive data streams are used to distribute the information to traders and investors. The speed that market data is distributed can become critical when trading systems are based on analyzing the data before others are able to, such as in high frequency trading.

In this chapter, I will implement various interfaces that allow you to access some popular free online data sources, including Yahoo Finance, IEX API, Alpha Vantage, and Quandl. We will utilize the market data from these free data source heavily in this book. These data sources usually provide the end-of-day (EOD) market data for stocks, currencies, and fixed-income instruments. You may also access the 15-minute delayed or real-time stock quotes as well as the historical intraday bar data.

Market Data from Yahoo

Yahoo Finance had a popular API that allows you to download daily stock data and 15-minute delayed stock quotes from its library. However, starting May 16, 2017, Yahoo Finance has discontinued its service of stock data download without notice or warning. Fortunately, the EOD stock data are still available on Yahoo Finance pages. To access these data, you will now require "crumb" and cookie "B" for authentication.

In this section, I will show you how to use a NuGet package called *YahooFinanceApi* to access the historical stock data from Yahoo and how to store the data into database.

Warning: *YahooFinanceApi* is a non-official API that cannot be assumed stable, and might break any time. So use it at your own risk.

Stock Data from Yahoo

The NuGet package, *YahooFinanceApi*, can be found from the URL at https://www.nuget.org/packages/ YahooFinanceApi. You can install it from the Package Manager Console inside Visual Studio using the following command:

```
PM> Install-Package YahooFinanceApi -Version 2.1.1
```

Add a new class called *StockData.cs* to the *Quant/Models* folder. Here is the code listing for this class:

```
using System;

namespace Quant.Models
{
    public class StockData
    {
        public string Ticker { get; set; }
        public DateTime Date { get; set; }
        public double Open { get; set; }
        public double High { get; set; }
        public double Low { get; set; }
        public double Close { get; set; }
        public double CloseAdj { get; set; }
        public double Volume { get; set; }
    }
}
```

Now, add a new web service controller named *MarketDataValuesController.cs* to the *Controllers* folder and replace its content with the following code:

```
using System;
using System.Collections.Generic;
using System.Linq;
using System.Threading.Tasks;
using Microsoft.AspNetCore.Mvc;
using Microsoft.Extensions.Options;
using Quant.Models;
using YahooFinanceApi;

namespace Quant.Controllers
{
    [Produces("application/json")]
    public class MarketDataValuesController : Controller
    {
        #region Yahoo
        [Route("~/api/YahooStock/{ticker}/{start}/{end}/{period}")]
        [HttpGet]
        public async Task<List<StockData>> GetYahooStock(string ticker,
            string start, string end, string period)
        {
            var p = Period.Daily;
            if (period.ToLower() == "weekly") p = Period.Weekly;
            else if (period.ToLower() == "monthly") p = Period.Monthly;
            var startDate = DateTime.Parse(start);
            var endDate = DateTime.Parse(end);
            var hist = await Yahoo.GetHistoricalAsync(ticker, startDate, endDate, p);
```

```csharp
            List<StockData> prices = new List<StockData>();
            foreach (var r in hist)
            {
                prices.Add(new StockData
                {
                    Ticker = ticker,
                    Date = r.DateTime,
                    Open = (double)r.Open,
                    High = (double)r.High,
                    Low = (double)r.Low,
                    Close = (double)r.Close,
                    CloseAdj = (double)r.AdjustedClose,
                    Volume = r.Volume
                });
            }
            return prices;
        }
        #endregion
    }
}
```

Here, we set the router specifically using

[Route("~/api/YahooStock/{ticker}/{start}/{end}/{period}")]

This means that an HTTP request should be sent to the **/api/yahoostock/{ticker}/{start}/{end}/{period}**. The *period* property can be *daily*, *weekly* or *monthly*.

To test the new web service, run the *Quant* project, open a web browser, and request the following URL:

https://localhost:5001/api/yahoostock/ibm/2018-01-01/2018-02-01/daily

This will produce the results shown in Fig.4-1.

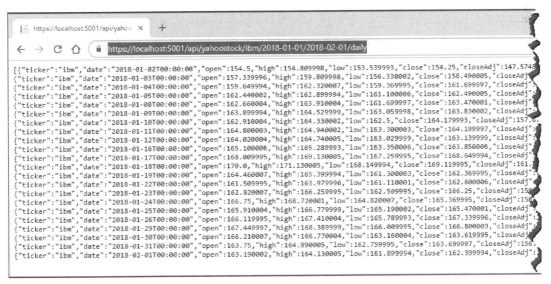

Fig.4-1. Test web service using YahooFinanceApi.

Here, the stock data is serialized into JSON, which is the standard data format used for the web services.

Create Repository Service in Angular

The process of sending a request from the Angular application to access the Yahoo market data following the same basic repository patterns presented in the preceding chapter. The first step is to define a model for the market data. Add a TypeScript class called *market-data.model.ts* to the *ClientApp/src/app/models* folder. Here is the code listing for this class:

```
//market-data.ts file:
export class MarketData {
  constructor(
    public ticker:string,
    public date?: Date,
    public open?: number,
    public high?: number,
    public low?: number,
    public close?: number,
    public closeAdj?: number,
    public volume?: number
  ) { }
}
```

This class corresponds to the C# *StockData.cs* class defined in the preceding section. Next, we need to add a repository service called *market-data.service.ts* to the *ClientApp/src/app/models* folder by running the following command in a command prompt window:

ng g s models/market-data

Open the *market-data.service.ts* file and replace its content with the following code:

```
// market-data.service.ts file:
import { Inject } from '@angular/core';
import { HttpClient } from '@angular/common/http';
import { MarketData } from './market-data.model';

@Injectable({
  providedIn: 'root'
})
export class MarketDataService {
  yahooStock: MarketData[] = [];
  private url;

  constructor(private http: HttpClient, @Inject('BASE_URL') baseUrl: string) {
    this.url = baseUrl;
  }

  getYahooStock(ticker: string, start: string, end: string, period: string) {
    let url1 = this.url + 'api/yahoostock/' + ticker + '/' + start + '/' + end +
      '/' + period;
    this.http.get<MarketData[]>(url1).subscribe(result => { this.yahooStock =
      result});
  }
}
```

This service is very similar to the *repository.service.ts* class implemented in Chapter 3. The *getYahooStock* method sends an HTTP request to a specified URL, which gets the stock data from Yahoo Finance.

Download Market Data from Yahoo

Now, I will use an example to show you how to use the *market-data-service* repository implemented in the preceding section to download the market data from Yahoo Finance.

Run the following command in the command prompt window from the *ClientApp* folder:

```
ng g c chapter04/yahoo-stock --module=app.module
```

This will generate a new component named *yahoo-stock* in the *ClientApp/src/app/chapter04* folder. Open the component class file and replace its content with the following code:

```
// yahoo-stock.componnet.ts file:
import { Component, OnInit } from '@angular/core';
import { MarketDataService } from '../../models/market-data.service';
import { MarketData } from '../../models/market-data.model';

@Component({
  selector: 'app-yahoo-stock',
  templateUrl: './yahoo-stock.component.html',
  styleUrls: ['./yahoo-stock.component.css']
})
export class YahooStockComponent implements OnInit {
  ticker = 'A';
  startDate: string = '2018-8-01';
  endDate: string = '2018-11-01';
  period = 'daily';
  displayedCols = ['date', 'open', 'high', 'low', 'close', 'closeAdj', 'volume'];

  constructor(private repository: MarketDataService) { }

  ngOnInit() {
    this.getStock(this.ticker, this.startDate, this.endDate, this.period);
  }

  get stock(): MarketData[] {
    return this.repository.yahooStock;
  }

  getStock(ticker: string, start: string, end: string, period: string) {
    this.repository.getYahooStock(ticker, start, end, period);
  }
}
```

The constructor has a *MarketDataService* parameter called *repository*, which is how dependencies are declared in an Angular app. The parameter tells Angular that the component class needs a *MarketDataService* object and provides it when a new *YahooStockComponent* object is created. The *private* keyword has been applied to the repository parameter, meaning that a property with the same name will be defined and assigned the value of the constructor parameter and that can be accesses only within the *YahooStockComponent* class.

The other addition in this class is a read-only property called *stock* that returns the value of the *MarketDataService* object's *yahooStock* property. The *getStock* method calls the *getYahooStock* method defined in the *MarketDataService* class, which will update the *stock* property according to the user's input.

We need also to update the component's template with the following code:

```html
// yahoo-stock.component.html file:
<h2>
  Yahoo-stock works!
</h2>

<mat-form-field>
  <input matInput placeholder="ticker" [(ngModel)]="ticker" name="ticker">
</mat-form-field>
<mat-form-field>
  <input matInput placeholder="Start Date" [(ngModel)]="startDate" name="startDate">
</mat-form-field>
<mat-form-field>
  <input matInput placeholder="End Date" [(ngModel)]="endDate" name="endDate">
</mat-form-field>
<mat-form-field>
  <mat-select placeholder="Select a period" [(value)]="period">
    <mat-option value="daily">daily</mat-option>
    <mat-option value="weekly">weekly</mat-option>
    <mat-option value="monthly">monthly</mat-option>
  </mat-select>
</mat-form-field>
<button mat-raised-button (click)="getStock(ticker,startDate, endDate,period)">Get
Stock Data</button>

<div *ngIf="stock">
  <div *ngIf="stock.length>0">
    <br />
    <h4>Stock Price</h4>
    <mat-table [dataSource]="stock">
      <ng-container matColumnDef="date">
        <mat-header-cell *matHeaderCellDef>Date</mat-header-cell>
        <mat-cell *matCellDef="let item">{{item.date |
          date: 'MM/dd/yyyy'}}</mat-cell>
      </ng-container>
      <ng-container matColumnDef="open">
        <mat-header-cell *matHeaderCellDef>Open</mat-header-cell>
        <mat-cell *matCellDef="let item">{{item.open}}</mat-cell>
      </ng-container>
      <ng-container matColumnDef="high">
        <mat-header-cell *matHeaderCellDef>High</mat-header-cell>
        <mat-cell *matCellDef="let item">{{item.high}}</mat-cell>
      </ng-container>
      <ng-container matColumnDef="low">
        <mat-header-cell *matHeaderCellDef>Low</mat-header-cell>
        <mat-cell *matCellDef="let item">{{item.low}}</mat-cell>
      </ng-container>
      <ng-container matColumnDef="close">
        <mat-header-cell *matHeaderCellDef>Close</mat-header-cell>
```

```
      <mat-cell *matCellDef="let item">{{item.close}}</mat-cell>
    </ng-container>
    <ng-container matColumnDef="closeAdj">
      <mat-header-cell *matHeaderCellDef>Close Adj</mat-header-cell>
      <mat-cell *matCellDef="let item">{{item.closeAdj}}</mat-cell>
    </ng-container>
    <ng-container matColumnDef="volume">
      <mat-header-cell *matHeaderCellDef>Volume</mat-header-cell>
      <mat-cell *matCellDef="let item">{{item.volume}}</mat-cell>
    </ng-container>
    <mat-header-row *matHeaderRowDef="displayedCols"></mat-header-row>
    <mat-row *matRowDef="let row; columns: displayedCols;"></mat-row>
  </mat-table>
  </div>
</div>
```

You should be familiar with most part of this template, except that we set the *period* property using a *mat-select* directive with a two-way binding. This *select* directive has three options: *daily*, *weekly*, and *monthly*, corresponding to Yahoo stock data with different periods.

Finally, we need to add a path for this new component to the *RouterModule* of the root module (i.e., the *app.module.ts* file):

```
{ path: 'chapter04/yahoo-stock, component: YahooStockComponent },
```

Then add the corresponding URL link to the *home* and *nav-menu* components.

Saving the project and navigating to the */chapter04/yahoo-stock* page produce the results shown in Fig.4-2. Here, we download the weekly stock data for MSFT from 5/1/2018 to 11/1/2018.

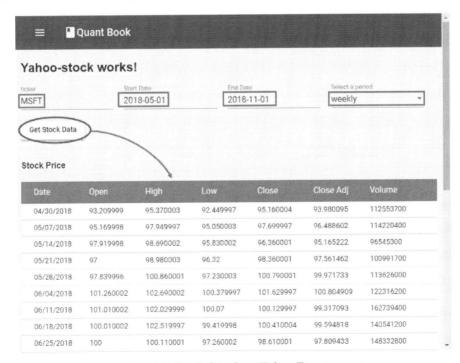

Fig.4-2. Stock data from Yahoo Finance.

You can download over 20-year market data for any stock ticker using the method discussed here.

Save Market Data to Database

In the preceding sections, you learned how to download historical stock data from Yahoo Finance. For trading strategy development and backtesting, you usually need to store the market data into database. In this section, we will add the historical EOD (end of day) stock data to database.

In Chapter 3, we have created a database called *QuantDb* and shown how to add new stock tickers to the *Symbol* table. The *Price* table in the database is basically empty except for IBM that has one-year seed data. Here, we will create an interface, which can be used to insert the stock price data into the *Price* table via downloading the market data from Yahoo Finance.

First, add a method called *AddStockPrice* to the *StockValuesController.cs* in the *Controllers* folder with the following code listing:

```
[Route("~/api/addStockPrice")]
[HttpPost]
public IActionResult AddStockPrice([FromBody] List<StockData> stocks)
{
    if (stocks.Count < 1) return BadRequest("No price data.");
    var symbol = GetSymbolwithTicker(stocks[0].Ticker);
    if (symbol == null) return BadRequest("The ticker = " + stocks[0].Ticker +
        "is not in database.");

    if (ModelState.IsValid)
    {
        var prices = new List<Price>();
        foreach (var stock in stocks)
        {
            if (!context.Prices.Any(p => p.Date == stock.Date &&
                p.SymbolId == symbol.SymbolId))
            {
                prices.Add(new Price
                {
                    SymbolId =symbol.SymbolId,
                    Date = stock.Date,
                    Open = stock.Open,
                    High = stock.High,
                    Low = stock.Low,
                    Close = stock.Close,
                    CloseAdj = stock.CloseAdj,
                    Volume = stock.Volume
                });
            }
        }
        context.Prices.AddRange(prices);
        context.SaveChanges();
        return Ok(prices);
    }
    else  return BadRequest(ModelState);
}
```

This method has a *StockData* list input argument, which will be downloaded from Yahoo Finance API. This argument is decorated with the *FromBody* attribute, which tells the model binder to get data values from the request body (and without which the JSON data sent by the client will be ignored).

The *AddStockPrice* method first check whether the list contains any data and then examine if the ticker is in the database. If the ticker is not in database yet, you need to add it to the *Symbol* table (see Chapter 3) before adding stock price data to the database. We then try to convert the *StockData* object into *Price* object, and at the same time, we check if the *Price* object is already in the database to avoid the duplicated records in the database.

Next, we need to add a TypeScript post method named *addStockPrice* method to the *repository.service.ts* file in the *ClientApp /src/app/models folder*. Here is the code for this method:

```
addStockPrice(stockData: MarketData[]) {
  this.errorMsg = null;
  this.http.post<any>(this.url + 'api/addstockprice', stockData)
    .subscribe(result => console.log(result),
    error => {this.errorMsg = error.error});
}
```

The method accept a *MarketData* array and send it using a POST request. Here, we also define an *errorMsg* property that allows you to pass the error message to the template element.

Now, we can create a new component to save the market data to database using this method. Run the following command in the command prompt window from the *ClientApp* folder:

ng g c chapter04/yahoo-stock-save --module=app.module

This command creates a new component named *yahoo-stock-save* in the *ClientApp/src/app/chapter04* folder. Open this new component class file and replace its content with the following code listing:

```
// yahoo-stock-save.component.ts file:
import { Component, OnInit } from '@angular/core';
import { RepositoryService } from '../../models/repository.service';
import { MarketDataService } from '../../models/market-data.service';
import { MarketData } from '../../models/market-data.model';

@Component({
  selector: 'app-yahoo-stock-save',
  templateUrl: './yahoo-stock-save.component.html',
  styleUrls: ['./yahoo-stock-save.component.css']
})
export class YahooStockSaveComponent implements OnInit {
  ticker = 'A';
  startDate: string = '2017-11-01';
  endDate: string = '2018-11-01';
  period = 'daily';
  displayedCols = ['date', 'open', 'high', 'low', 'close', 'closeAdj', 'volume'];
  isSaved = false;

  constructor(private marketRepo: MarketDataService,
    private repo: RepositoryService) { }

  ngOnInit() {
    this.getStock(this.ticker, this.startDate, this.endDate, this.period);
  }
```

```
get stock(): MarketData[] {
  return this.marketRepo.yahooStock;
}

getStock(ticker: string, start: string, end: string, period: string) {
  this.isSaved = false;
  this.marketRepo.getYahooStock(ticker, start, end, period);
}

saveStock() {
  this.repo.addStockPrice(this.stock);
  this.isSaved = true;
}
}
```

Note that we inject both the *MaketDataService* and *RepositoryService* dependencies into the constructor, where the former, combining with the *stock* property and the *getStock* method, is responsible for downloading the market data from Yahoo Finance, while the latter, combining with the *saveStock* method, is responsible for saving the market data to database.

Open its template file and replace its content with the following code listing:

```
// yahoo-stock-save.cmponent.html file:
<h2>
  Yahoo-stock-save works!
</h2>
<mat-form-field>
  <input matInput placeholder="ticker" [(ngModel)]="ticker" name="ticker">
</mat-form-field>

<!-- ... other fields omitted for brevity ... -->

<button mat-raised-button (click)="getStock(ticker,startDate, endDate,period)">
  Get Stock Data
</button>
<button mat-raised-button (click)="saveStock()" style="margin-left:10px">
  Save to Database
</button>

<p *ngIf="isSaved" style="color:red">
  <span *ngIf="errorMsg==null">The stock data has been saved to database.</span>
  <span *ngIf="errorMsg!=null">{{errorMsg}}. Please click
    <a [routerLink]='["/chapter03/stock-crud"]'>this link</a> to add {{ticker}}
      to database.
  </span>
</p>

<div *ngIf="stock">
  <div *ngIf="stock.length>0">
    <br />
    <h4>Stock Price</h4>
    <mat-table [dataSource]="stock">
      <ng-container matColumnDef="date">
        <mat-header-cell *matHeaderCellDef>Date</mat-header-cell>
        <mat-cell *matCellDef="let item">{{item.date |
          date: 'MM/dd/yyyy'}}</mat-cell>
```

```
    </ng-container>

    <!-- ... other code omitted for brevity ... -->

  </mat-table>
 </div>
</div>
```

This template is basically the same as that used in the preceding example, except that we add a *Save to Database* button that binds its *click* event to the *saveStock* method defined in the component class. We also add several *ngIf* directives to display messages whether the data is saved to database or not. Here we omit irrelevant code for brevity.

Finally, we need to add a path for this new component to the *RouterModule* of the root module (i.e., the *app.module.ts* file):

```
{ path: 'chapter04/yahoo-stock-save, component: YahooStockSaveComponent },
```

Then add the corresponding URL link to the *home* and *nav-menu* components.

Save the project and navigate to the */chapter04/yahoo-stock-save* page to bring up the *save stock data* page, from which you can specified a stock ticker and periods to download the stock data and then save the data to database.

Let us take AAPL as an example. We first download 5-year stock EOD data for AAPL and then click the *Save to Database* button. However, we get an error message – "The ticker = AAPL is not in database. ..." which means that AAPL is not in database yet, as shown in Fig.4-3.

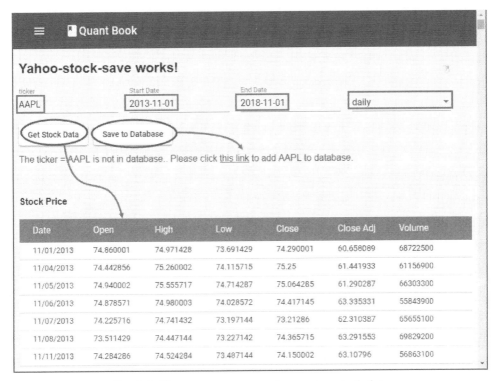

Fig.4-3. Show error message when saving stock data.

Simply follow the link to add the AAPL ticker to database. The procedure of adding ticker to database has been described in the preceding chapter, and we will not discuss it here.

After adding AAPL ticker to database, we can go back to the save stock data page again. Download the stock data and click the *Save to Database* button. This time, you get a message saying, "The stock data has been saved to database", as shown in Fig.4-4.

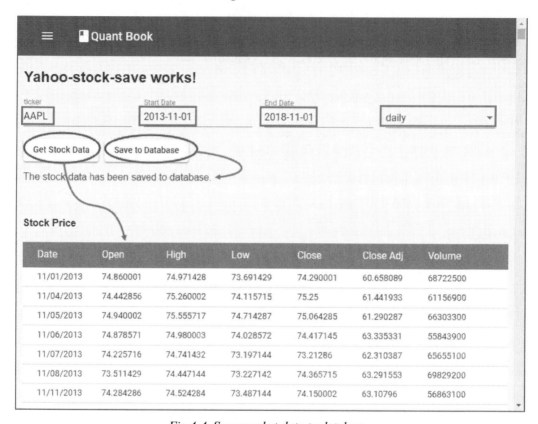

Fig.4-4. Save market data to database.

Following the above procedure, we have added stock EOD data for some commonly traded stocks, including A, AMAT, IBM, INTL, MSFT, GS, SPY, etc.

Market Data from IEX

In the preceding section, I showed you how to get market data from Yahoo and save the data into database. In fact, you can also get market data from other free sources. In this section, we consider the IEX (Investors Exchange) API that allows you to integrate tools for monitoring and transacting stocks in financial markets. You can use the API's endpoint at https://iextrading.com to integrate an analytical portal for prices, market data, and stats. The API currently supports only the HTTP GET methods and conveys requests and responses in JSONP (JSON with Padding) format. JSONP is a way to get data from another domain that bypasses CORS (cross origin resource sharing) rules.

For convenience, we will use IEXTradingApi, which is a .NET Core API wrapper that allows you to retrieve market data from IEX Trading endpoint.

Historical Market Data

In this section, I will show how to get historical stock EOD data from IEX. First, we need to install the NuGet package, *IEXTradingApi*, which can be found from the URL at https://www.nuget.org/packages/IEXTradingApi. You can install it from the Package Manager Console inside Visual Studio using the following command:

PM> Install-Package IEXTradingApi -Version 1.0.26

The web service for IEX API is similar to Yahoo Finance API. To retrieve historical market data from IEX, add a new method named *GetIexStock* to the *MarketDataValuesController* in the *Controllers* folder. Here is the code listing for this method:

```
using System;
using System.Collections.Generic;
using System.Linq;
using System.Threading.Tasks;
using IEXTrading;
using IEXTradingDotNetCore.STOCK_CHART;
using Microsoft.AspNetCore.Mvc;
using Microsoft.Extensions.Options;
using Quant.Models;
using YahooFinanceApi;

namespace Quant.Controllers
{
    public class MarketDataValuesController : Controller
    {

        // ... other action methods omitted for brevity ...

        [Route("~/api/IexStock/{ticker}/{range}")]
        [HttpGet]
        public List<StockData> GetIexStock(string ticker,
            Const_STOCK_CHART.STOCK_CHART_input_options_fields range
            = Const_STOCK_CHART.STOCK_CHART_input_options_fields.OneMonth)
        {
            var connection = IEXTradingConnection.Instance;
            var operation = connection.GetQueryObject_STOCK_CHART();
            var response = operation.Query(ticker, range);
            var data = response.Data;

            var models = new List<StockData>();

            foreach (var d in data.TimeSeries)
            {
                models.Add(new StockData
                {
                    Ticker = ticker,
                    Date = DateTime.Parse(d.Date),
                    Open = double.Parse(d.Open),
```

```
                    High = double.Parse(d.High),
                    Low = double.Parse(d.Low),
                    Close = double.Parse(d.Close),
                    Volume = double.Parse(d.Volume)

                });
        }
        return models.OrderBy(d => d.Date).ToList();
    }
  }
}
```

This method has a route attribute like this

[Route("~/api/IexStock/{ticker}/{range}")]

For a web service handing market data from IEX, this means that HTTP requests should be sent to the above URL. This method also contains two parameters, *ticker* and *range*. The *range* parameter is an input field enumeration called **Const_STOCK_CHART.STOCK_CHART_input_options_fields** defined by the IEX API as follows:

```
public static class Const_STOCK_CHART
{
    public enum STOCK_CHART_input_options_fields
    {
        FiveYears = 0,
        TwoYears = 1,
        OneYear = 2,
        YearToDate = 3,
        SixMonths = 4,
        ThreeMonths = 5,
        OneMonth = 6,
    }
}
```

This *range* enum will return the historical EOD stock data. For example, **TwoYears = 1** will return the most recent two-year EOD stock data.

When retrieving market data using this web service, you can use either the enum string name or value. To test the service, run the *Quant* project, open a web browser, and request the following URL:

https://localhost:5001/api/iexstock/ibm/onemonth

This will give the same one-month data as that using the following URL request:

https://localhost:5001/api/iexstock/ibm/6

Fig.4-5 shows the results retrieved using these two different URLs.

Real-Time Stock Quotes

IEX API also allows you to access the real-time quotes for most of the US stocks. First, we need to create a generic interface for the stock quotes. Open the *StockData.cs* class file in the *Quant/Models* folder. Add a class called *IexStockQuote* to this file with the following code:

Fig.4-5. Stock data from IEX web service.

```csharp
using System;
namespace Quant.Models
{
    public class StockData
    {
        public string Ticker { get; set; }
        public DateTime Date { get; set; }
        public double Open { get; set; }
        public double High { get; set; }
        public double Low { get; set; }
        public double Close { get; set; }
        public double CloseAdj { get; set; }
        public double Volume { get; set; }
    }

    public class IexStockQuote
    {
        public string Ticker { get; set; }
        public decimal Open { get; set; }
        public DateTime OpenTime { get; set; }
```

```
            public decimal Close { get; set; }
            public DateTime CloseTime { get; set; }
            public decimal LatestPrice { get; set; }
            public DateTime LatestTime { get; set; }
            public DateTime LatestUpdateTime { get; set; }
            public double LatestVolume { get; set; }
            public decimal DelayedPrice { get; set; }
            public DateTime DelayedPriceTime { get; set; }
            public decimal PreviousClose { get; set; }
            public decimal IexRealTimePrice { get; set; }
            public double IexRealTimeSize { get; set; }
            public DateTime IexLastUpdated { get; set; }
            public decimal IexBidPrice { get; set; }
            public decimal IexBidSize { get; set; }
            public decimal IexAskPrice { get; set; }
            public decimal IexAskSize { get; set; }
            public double Change { get; set; }
            public double ChangePercent { get; set; }
            public double MarketCap { get; set; }
            public double PeRatio { get; set; }
            public decimal Week52High { get; set; }
            public decimal Week52Low { get; set; }
            public double YtdChange { get; set; }
        }
    }
```

The properties defined in this class provide a variety of attributes for the stock quote. In addition to the standard quote information, this class also consists of specific attributes from IEX. For example, **IexRealTimePrice** refers to last sale price of the stock on IEX market; **IexLasteUpdated** refers to the last update time or **-1** or **0**. If the value is **-1** or **0**, this means that IEX has not quoted the stock in the trading day.

To add support for retrieving real-time quotes from IEX, add a new method named *GetIexQuote* to the *MarketDataValuesController* in the *Controllers* folder. Here is the code listing for this method:

```
[Route("~/api/IexQuote/{ticker}")]
[HttpGet]
public IexStockQuote GetIexQuote(string ticker)
{
    var connection = IEXTradingConnection.Instance;
    var operation = connection.GetQueryObject_STOCK_QUOTE();
    var response = operation.Query(ticker);
    var data = response.Data;

    return new IexStockQuote
    {
        Ticker = ticker,
        Open = decimal.Parse(data.Open),
        OpenTime = FromUnixTime(data.OpenTime),
        Close = decimal.Parse(data.Close),
        CloseTime = FromUnixTime(data.CloseTime),
        LatestPrice = decimal.Parse(data.LatestPrice),
        LatestTime = DateTime.Parse(data.LatestTime),
        LatestUpdateTime = FromUnixTime(data.LatestUpdate),
        LatestVolume = double.Parse(data.LatestVolume),
        DelayedPrice = decimal.Parse(data.DelayedPrice),
```

```
            DelayedPriceTime = FromUnixTime(data.DelayedPriceTime),
            PreviousClose = decimal.Parse(data.PreviousClose),
            IexRealTimePrice = decimal.Parse(data.IEXRealtimePrice),
            IexRealTimeSize = double.Parse(data.IEXRealtimeSize),
            IexLastUpdated = FromUnixTime(data.IEXLastUpdated),
            IexBidPrice = decimal.Parse(data.IEXBidPrice),
            IexBidSize = decimal.Parse(data.IEXBidSize),
            IexAskPrice = decimal.Parse(data.IEXAskPrice),
            IexAskSize = decimal.Parse(data.IEXAskSize),
            Change = double.Parse(data.Change),
            ChangePercent = double.Parse(data.ChangePercent),
            MarketCap = double.Parse(data.MarketCap),
            PeRatio = double.Parse(data.PeRatio),
            Week52High = decimal.Parse(data.Week52High),
            Week52Low = decimal.Parse(data.Week52Low),
            YtdChange = double.Parse(data.YtdChange)
        };
}

private DateTime FromUnixTime(string utime)
{
    return DateTimeOffset.FromUnixTimeMilliseconds(long.Parse(utime))
                         .DateTime.ToLocalTime();
}
```

For real-time stock quotes, the timestamp is usually represented in term of the UNIX timestamp, i.e., milliseconds since January 1, 1970 UTC. Here, we add a private method named *FromUnixTime*, which converts the UNIX timestamp into the normal date time.

To test the service, run the *Quant* project, open a web browser, and request the following URL:

https://localhost:5001/api/iexquote/ibm

This will produce the results shown in Fig.4-6.

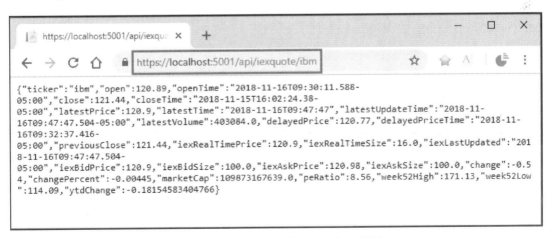

Fig.4-6. Real-time stock quote from IEX.

Stock Data in Angular

To add support for retrieving historical stock data from IEX in the Angular application, we need to add a method named *getIexStock* shown in the following code listing to the *market-data.service.ts* class in the *ClientApp/src/app/models* folder so that it can send GET requests to the web service:

```
// market-data.service.ts file:
import { Inject } from '@angular/core';
import { HttpClient } from '@angular/common/http';
import { MarketData } from './market-data.model';

export class MarketDataRepository {
  yahooStock: MarketData[] = [];
  iexStock: MarketData[] = [];

  private url;

  constructor(private http: HttpClient, @Inject('BASE_URL') baseUrl: string) {
    this.url = baseUrl;
  }

  getYahooStock(ticker: string, start: string, end: string, period: string) {
    let url1 = this.url + 'api/yahoostock/' + ticker + '/' + start + '/' + end
      + '/' + period;
    this.http.get<MarketData[]>(url1).subscribe(result => { this.yahooStock =
      result });
  }

  getIexStock(ticker: string, range: string) {
    this.http.get<MarketData[]>(this.url + 'api/iexstock/' + ticker + '/' +
      range).subscribe(result => { this.iexStock = result });
  }
}
```

The *getIexStock* method accepts ticker and range parameters, and sends an HTTP request to a specified URL, which retrieves the stock data from IEX.

Now, I will use an example to show you how to use this repository service to download the market data from IEX.

Run the following command in the command prompt window from the *ClientApp* folder:

```
ng g c chapter04/iex-stock --module=app.module
```

This will generate a new component named *iex-stock* in the *ClientApp/src/app/chapter04* folder. Open the component class file and replace its content with the following code:

```
// iex-stock.component.ts file:
import { Component, OnInit } from '@angular/core';
import { MarketDataService } from '../../models/market-data.service';
import { MarketData } from '../../models/market-data.model';

@Component({
  selector: 'app-iex-stock',
  templateUrl: './iex-stock.component.html',
  styleUrls: ['./iex-stock.component.css']
})
```

```
export class IexStockComponent implements OnInit {
  ticker = 'A';
  range = 'oneMonth';
  displayedCols = ['date', 'open', 'high', 'low', 'close', 'volume'];

  constructor(private repository: MarketDataService) { }

  ngOnInit() {
    this.getStock(this.ticker, this.range);
  }

  get stock(): MarketData[] {
    return this.repository.iexStock;
  }

  getStock(ticker: string, range: string) {
    this.repository.getIexStock(ticker, range);
  }
}
```

The constructor has a *MarketDataService* parameter called *repository*, which is how dependencies are declared in an Angular app. The other addition in this class is a read-only property called *stock* that returns the value of the *MarketDataService* object's *iexStock* property. The *getStock* method calls the *getIexStock* method defined in the *MarketDataService* class, which will update the *stock* property according to the user's input.

We also need to update the component's template with the following code:

```
// iex-stock.component.html file:
<h2>
  Iex-stock works!
</h2>
<mat-form-field>
  <input matInput placeholder="ticker" [(ngModel)]="ticker" name="ticker">
</mat-form-field>
<mat-form-field>
  <mat-select [(value)]="range">
    <mat-option value="0">Five Years</mat-option>
    <mat-option value="1">Two Years</mat-option>
    <mat-option value="2">One Year</mat-option>
    <mat-option value="3">Year to Date</mat-option>
    <mat-option value="4">Six Months</mat-option>
    <mat-option value="5">Three Months</mat-option>
    <mat-option value="oneMonth">One Month</mat-option>
  </mat-select>
</mat-form-field>
<button mat-raised-button (click)="getStock(ticker,range)">Get Stock Data</button>

<div *ngIf="stock">
  <div *ngIf="stock.length>0">
    <br />
    <h4>Stock Price</h4>
    <mat-table [dataSource]="stock">
      <ng-container matColumnDef="date">
        <mat-header-cell *matHeaderCellDef>Date</mat-header-cell>
        <mat-cell *matCellDef="let item">{{item.date |
```

```
            date: 'MM/dd/yyyy'}}</mat-cell>
    </ng-container>
    <ng-container matColumnDef="open">
      <mat-header-cell *matHeaderCellDef>Open</mat-header-cell>
      <mat-cell *matCellDef="let item">{{item.open}}</mat-cell>
    </ng-container>
    <ng-container matColumnDef="high">
      <mat-header-cell *matHeaderCellDef>High</mat-header-cell>
      <mat-cell *matCellDef="let item">{{item.high}}</mat-cell>
    </ng-container>
    <ng-container matColumnDef="low">
      <mat-header-cell *matHeaderCellDef>Low</mat-header-cell>
      <mat-cell *matCellDef="let item">{{item.low}}</mat-cell>
    </ng-container>
    <ng-container matColumnDef="close">
      <mat-header-cell *matHeaderCellDef>Close</mat-header-cell>
      <mat-cell *matCellDef="let item">{{item.close}}</mat-cell>
    </ng-container>
    <ng-container matColumnDef="volume">
      <mat-header-cell *matHeaderCellDef>Volume</mat-header-cell>
      <mat-cell *matCellDef="let item">{{item.volume}}</mat-cell>
    </ng-container>
    <mat-header-row *matHeaderRowDef="displayedCols"></mat-header-row>
    <mat-row *matRowDef="let row; columns: displayedCols;"></mat-row>
  </mat-table>
  </div>
</div>
```

Here, we set the *range* property using a *mat-select* directive with a two-way binding. This *select* directive has seven options that correspond to the C# range enumeration for the IEX stock object.

Finally, we need to add a path for this new component to the *RouterModule* of the root module (i.e., the *app.module.ts* file):

```
{ path: 'chapter04/iex-stock, component: IexStockComponent },
```

Then add the corresponding URL link to the *home* and *nav-menu* components.

Saving the project and navigating to the */chapter04/iex-stock* page produce the results shown in Fig.4-7.

Here, we download the latest three-month EOD stock data for MSFT. You can download market data for any ticker using the method discussed here.

Real-Time Stock Quote in Angular

In this section, we consider the real-time stock quotes in the Angular application. Before adding a method to the *market-data.service.ts* file for retrieving real-time stock quotes from IEX, we need to define a TypeScript stock quote model. Open the *market-data.model.ts* file and add a new class named *MarketQuote* as shown in the following code listing:

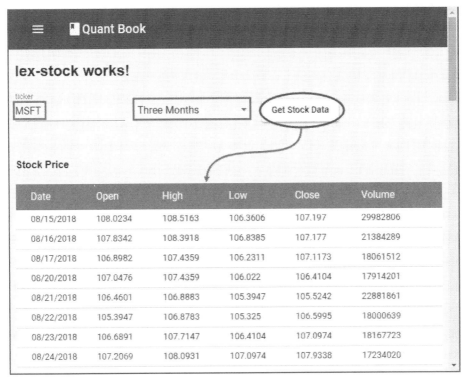

Fig.4-7. Stock data from IEX web service.

```
// market-data.model.ts file:
export class MarketData {
  constructor(
    public ticker:string,
    public date?: Date,
    public open?: number,
    public high?: number,
    public low?: number,
    public close?: number,
    public closeAdj?: number,
    public volume?: number
  ) { }
}

export class MarketQuote {
  constructor(
    public ticker: string,
    public open?: number,
    public openTime?: Date,
    public close?: number,
    public closeTime?: Date,
    public latestPrice?: number,
    public latestTime?: Date,
    public latestUpdateTime?: Date,
    public latestVolume?: number,
```

```
    public delayedPrice?: number,
    public delayedPriceTime?: Date,
    public previousClose?: number,
    public iexRealTimePrice?: number,
    public iexRealTimeSize?: number,
    public iexLastUpdated?: Date,
    public iexBidPrice?: number,
    public iexBidSize?: number,
    public iexAskPrice?: number,
    public iexAskSize?: number,
    public change?: number,
    public changePercent?: number,
    public marketCap?: number,
    public PeRatio?: number,
    public week52High?: number,
    public week52Low?: number,
    public ytdChange?: number,
  ) { }
}
```

This model corresponds to the C# *IexStockQuote* class defined previously.

The process of sending a request from the Angular app to get the real-time stock quotes follows the same basic patterns as for the historical stock data from IEX. The first step is to define a new method named *getIexQuote* method in the *market-data.service.ts* class to send the request and process the response, as shown in the following code:

```
// market-data.service.ts file:
import { Inject } from '@angular/core';
import { HttpClient } from '@angular/common/http';
import { MarketData, MarketQuote } from './market-data.model';

export class MarketDataRepository {
  yahooStock: MarketData[] = [];
  iexStock: MarketData[] = [];
  iexQuote: MarketQuote;

  private url;

  constructor(private http: HttpClient, @Inject('BASE_URL') baseUrl: string) {
    this.url = baseUrl;
  }

  // ... other methods omitted for brevity ...

  getIexQuote(ticker: string) {
    this.http.get<MarketQuote>(this.url + 'api/iexquote/' + ticker)
      .subscribe(result => { this.iexQuote = result });
  }
}
```

The *getIexQuote* method sends an HTTP request to the **/api/iexquote/{ticker}** URL, which gets the real-time quote if available.

Now, I will use an example to show you how to use this repository service to download the stock quote from IEX. Run the following command in the command prompt window from the *ClientApp* folder:

```
ng g c chapter04/iex-quote --module=app.module
```

This will generate a new component named *iex-quote* in the *ClientApp/src/app/chapter04* folder. Open the component class file and replace its content with the following code:

```
// iex-quote.component.ts file:
import { Component, OnInit } from '@angular/core';
import { MarketDataService } from '../../models/market-data.service';
import { MarketQuote } from '../../models/market-data.model';

@Component({
  selector: 'app-iex-quote',
  templateUrl: './iex-quote.component.html',
  styleUrls: ['./iex-quote.component.css']
})
export class IexQuoteComponent implements OnInit {
  ticker = 'A';

  constructor(private repository: MarketDataService) { }

  ngOnInit() {
    this.getQuote(this.ticker);
  }

  get quote(): MarketQuote {
    return this.repository.iexQuote;
  }

  getQuote(ticker: string) {
    this.repository.getIexQuote(ticker);
  }
}
```

The constructor has a *MarketDataService* parameter called *repository*, which is how dependencies are declared in an Angular app. The other addition in this class is a read-only property called *quote* that returns the value of the *MarketDataService* object's *iexQuote* property. The *getQuote* method calls the *getIexQuote* method defined in the *MarketDataService* class, which will update the *quote* property according to the user's input.

We also need to update the component's template with the following code:

```
//iex-quote.component.html file:
<h2>
  Iex-quote works!
</h2>
<mat-form-field>
  <input matInput placeholder="ticker" [(ngModel)]="ticker" name="ticker">
</mat-form-field>
<button mat-raised-button (click)="getQuote(ticker)">Get Stock Quote</button>

<div *ngIf="quote">
  <h4>Stock Quote</h4>
  <ul>
    <li>Ticker: {{quote.ticker}}</li>
    <li>Open: {{quote.open}}</li>
    <li>Open Time: {{quote.openTime}}</li>
```

```
    <li>Close: {{quote.close}}</li>
    <li>Close Time: {{quote.closeTime}}</li>
    <li>Latest Price: {{quote.latestPrice}}</li>
    <li>Latest Time: {{quote.latestTime}}</li>
    <li>Latest Update Time: {{quote.latestUpdateTime}}</li>
    <li>Latest Volume: {{quote.latestVolume}}</li>
    <li>Delayed Price: {{quote.delayedPrice}}</li>
    <li>Delayed Price Time: {{quote.delayedPriceTime}}</li>
    <li>Previous Close: {{quote.previousClose}}</li>
    <li>IEX Real-Time Price: {{quote.iexRealTimePrice}}</li>
    <li>IEX Real-Time Size: {{quote.iexRealTimeSize}}</li>
    <li>IEX Last Updated: {{quote.iexLastUpdated}}</li>
    <li>IEX Bid Price: {{quote.iexBidPrice}}</li>
    <li>IEX Bid Size: {{quote.iexBidSize}}</li>
    <li>IEX Ask Price: {{quote.iexAskPrice}}</li>
    <li>IEX Ask Size: {{quote.iexAskSize}}</li>
    <li>Change: {{quote.change}}</li>
    <li>Change Percent: {{quote.changePercent}}</li>
    <li>Market Cap: {{quote.marketCap}}</li>
    <li>PE Ratio: {{quote.peRatio}}</li>
    <li>52 Week High: {{quote.week52High}}</li>
    <li>52 Week Low: {{quote.week52Low}}</li>
    <li> Year-To-Date Change: {{quote.ytdChange}}</li>
  </ul>
</div>
```

Here, the button element is configured using the Angular event binding feature and its click event is triggered when the user clicks the button, at which point Angular evaluates the expression and invokes the component's *getQuote* method.

Finally, we need to add a path for this new component to the *RouterModule* of the root module (i.e., the *app.module.ts* file):

```
{ path: 'chapter04/iex-quote, component: IexQuoteComponent },
```

Then add the corresponding URL link to the *home* and *nav-menu* components.

Saving the project and navigating to the */chapter04/iex-quote* page produce the results shown in Fig.4-8.

Here, we download the real-time stock quotes for IBM. You can download stock quotes for any ticker using the method discussed here.

Market Data from Alpha Vantage

Alpha Vantage provides APIs for historical and real-time data on stocks, forex, and digital/crypto currencies. Alpha Vantage is free, but to use it you must sign up for an API key. You can follow this link to sign up: https://www.alphavantage.co/support/#api-key.

Please note that the free API from Alpha Vantage has the following limitations – the standard API call frequency is 5 calls per minute and 500 calls per day.

Fig.4-8. Real-time stock quote from IEX web service.

Create API Key Service

After receiving the API key from Alpha Vantage, you can make it as a service. You can then add this service to the dependency injection container, register it with the pipeline, and consume it in your application.

Open the *appsettings.json* file and add the highlighted code as shown in the follows:

```
{
  "Logging": {
    "LogLevel": {
      "Default": "Warning"
    }
  },
  "AllowedHosts": "*",
  "Data": {
    "Quant": {
```

```
  "ConnectionString":
    "Server=(localdb)\\mssqllocaldb;Database=QuantDb;Trusted_Connection
    =True;MultipleActiveResultSets=true"
},
"AlphaVantage": {
  "ApiKey": "your-av-api-key"
}
  }
}
```

Please remember to replace the parameter of *"your-av-api-key"* with your own Alpha Vantage API key.

ASP.NET Core has no default way to get settings from the *appsettings.json*. The recommended approach is to create a configuration class with a structure that matches a section in your configuration file. Add a C# class named *ApiKeySettings.cs* to the *Quant/Models* folder with the following code listing:

```
namespace Quant.Models
{
    public class ApiKeySettings
    {
        public class AlphaVantage
        {
            public string ApiKey { get; set; }
        }
    }
}
```

The *AlphaVatage* class contains only one property, *ApiKey*.

To register the API key as a service, add the following highlighted code snippet to the *Startup.cs* file:

```
// ... using statements omitted for brevity ...

namespace Quant
{
    public class Startup
    {
        public Startup(IConfiguration configuration)
        {
            Configuration = configuration;
        }

        public IConfiguration Configuration { get; }

        public void ConfigureServices(IServiceCollection services)
        {

            // ... other code omitted for brevity ...

            services.Configure<ApiKeySettings.AlphaVantage>(
                Configuration.GetSection("Data:AlphaVantage"));
        }

        // ... other methods omitted for brevity ...

    }
}
```

The *ConfigureServices* method adds the API key service to the service container, which makes it available in your application via dependency injection.

EOD Stock Data

In this section, I will show you how to retrieve the historical stock EOD data from Alpha Vantage. Add a new C# class named *AlphaVantageHelper* to the *Quant/Models* folder. Here is the code listing for this class:

```
using System;
using System.Net;

namespace Quant.Models
{
    public static class AlphaVantageHelper
    {
        public static string GetStockEod(string ticker, string start,
            string end,string period, string apiKey)
        {
            var startDate = DateTime.Parse(start);
            var endDate = DateTime.Parse(end);
            var size = "compact";
            if (startDate < DateTime.Today.AddDays(-120)) size = "full";
                var tseries = "TIME_SERIES_DAILY_ADJUSTED";
            if (period == "weekly") tseries = "TIME_SERIES_WEEKLY_ADJUSTED";
            else if (period == "monthly") tseries = "TIME_SERIES_MONTHLY_ADJUSTED";
            string url = "https://www.alphavantage.co/query?function=
                [tseries]&symbol=[ticker]&outputsize=[size]
                &apikey=[apiKey]&datatype=csv";
            url = url.Replace("[tseries]", tseries);
            url = url.Replace("[ticker]", ticker);
            url = url.Replace("[size]", size);
            url = url.Replace("[apiKey]", apiKey);

            string history = string.Empty;
            using (WebClient wc = new WebClient())
            {
                try
                {
                    history = wc.DownloadString(url);
                }
                catch { }
            }
            return history;
        }
    }
}
```

The *GetStockEod* method takes *ticker*, date range, *period* (= daily, weekly, or monthly), and *apiKey* as input parameters. The key step to access the Alpha Vantage market data is to construct the URL address with a suitable template.

To add web service support for retrieving market data from Alpha Vantage, add the following code statements to the *MarketDataValuesController* class in the *Controllers* folder:

```csharp
// ... using statements omitted for brevity ...

namespace Quant.Controllers
{
    public class MarketDataValuesController : Controller
    {
        private readonly ApiKeySettings.AlphaVantage avKey;
        public MarketDataValuesController(
            IOptions<ApiKeySettings.AlphaVantage> alpha)
        {
            avKey = alpha.Value;
        }

        // ... other methods omitted for brevity ...

        [Route("~/api/AvEod/{ticker}/{start}/{end}/{period}")]
        [HttpGet]
        public List<StockData> GetAvStockEod(string ticker,string start, string end,
            string period)
        {
            var startDate = DateTime.Parse(start);
            var endDate = DateTime.Parse(end);
            var history = AlphaVantageHelper.GetStockEod(ticker, start, end, period,
                avKey.ApiKey);
            history = history.Replace("\r", "");
            string[] rows = history.Split('\n');

            var models = new List<StockData>();
            for (var i = 1; i < rows.Length; i++)
            {
                var r = rows[i].Split(",");
                try
                {
                    var date = DateTime.Parse(r[0]);
                    if (date >= startDate && date <= endDate)
                    {
                        models.Add(new StockData
                        {
                            Ticker = ticker,
                            Date = date,
                            Open = double.Parse(r[1]),
                            High = double.Parse(r[2]),
                            Low = double.Parse(r[3]),
                            Close = double.Parse(r[4]),
                            CloseAdj = double.Parse(r[5]),
                            Volume = double.Parse(r[6])
                        });
                    }
                }
                catch { }
            }
            return models.OrderBy(d => d.Date).ToList();
        }
    }
}
```

Here, to access the value of *AlphaVantage* API key, we inject an instance of an *IOptions* call into the constructor. The *IOptions* service exposes a *Value* property that contains your configured API key settings.

For the *GetAvStockEod* method, we define the router specifically using

[Route("~/api/AvEod/{ticker}/{start}/{end}/{period}")]

This means that an HTTP request should be sent to the **/api/aveod/{ticker}/{start}/{end}/{period}**. The *period* property can be *daily*, *weekly* or *monthly*.

To test the new web service, run the *Quant* project, open a web browser, and request the following URL:

https://localhost:5001/api/aveod/ibm/2018-10-01/2018-11-19/daily

This will produce the results shown in Fig.4-9.

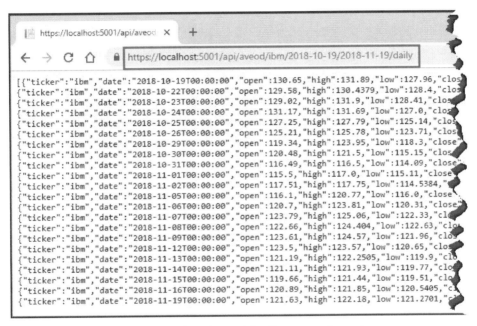

Fig.4-9. Stock data from Alpha Vantage web service.

Intraday Stock Data

Alpha Vantage also provides historical intraday stock bar data. Add a method called *GetStockBar* to the *AlphaVantageHelper* class with the following code snippet:

```
public static string GetStockBar(string ticker, int interval, int outputsize,
    string apiKey)
{
    var size = "compact";
    if (outputsize > 100) size = "full";
    var tseries = "TIME_SERIES_INTRADAY";
    string url = "https://www.alphavantage.co/query?function=[tseries]
        &symbol=[ticker]&outputsize=[size]&apikey=[apiKey]&datatype=csv
```

```
        &interval=[interval]min";
url = url.Replace("[tseries]", tseries);
url = url.Replace("[ticker]", ticker);
url = url.Replace("[size]", size);
url = url.Replace("[apiKey]", apiKey);
url = url.Replace("[interval]", interval.ToString());

string history = string.Empty;
using (WebClient wc = new WebClient())
{
    try
    {
        history = wc.DownloadString(url);
    }
    catch { }
}
return history;
}
```

This method takes the *ticker*, *interval*, *outputsize*, and *apiKey* as input arguments. The key step to access the Alpha Vantage stock bar data is to construct the URL address with a suitable template. The *interval* parameter can be specified by 1min, 5min, 15min, 30min, and 60-min, corresponding to one-minute, 5-minute, ,..., and 60-minute bar data.

To add web service support for retrieving historical intraday data from Alpha Vantage, add a new method named *getAvStockBar* to the *MarketDataValuesController* class in the *Controllers* folder. Here is the code for this method:

```
[Route("~/api/AvBar/{ticker}/{interval}/{outputsize}")]
[HttpGet]
public List<StockData> GetAvStockBar(string ticker, int interval, int outputsize)
{
    var history = AlphaVantageHelper.GetStockBar(ticker, interval, outputsize,
        avKey.ApiKey);
    history = history.Replace("\r", "");
    string[] rows = history.Split('\n');
    var models = new List<StockData>();

    for (var i = 1; i < rows.Length; i++)
    {
        var r = rows[i].Split(",");
        try
        {
            var date = DateTime.Parse(r[0]);
            models.Add(new StockData
            {
                Ticker = ticker,
                Date = date,
                Open = double.Parse(r[1]),
                High = double.Parse(r[2]),
                Low = double.Parse(r[3]),
                Close = double.Parse(r[4]),
                Volume = double.Parse(r[5])
            });
        }
        catch { }
```

```
    }
    return models.OrderBy(d => d.Date).ToList();
}
```

The *outputsize* parameter in the above method specifies the size of the data returned – the method returns the latest 100 data points if **outputsize** **<=100** while it returns the full-length intraday data if **outputsize > 100**.

For the *GetAvStockBar* method, we define the router specifically using

[Route("~/api/AvBar/{ticker}/{interval}/{outputsize}")]

This means that an HTTP request should be sent to the **/api/avbar/{ticker}/{interval}/** **{outputsize}**. To test the new web service, run the *Quant* project, open a web browser, and request the following URL:

https://localhost:5001/api/avbar/ibm/1/1

This will produce the results shown in Fig.4-10.

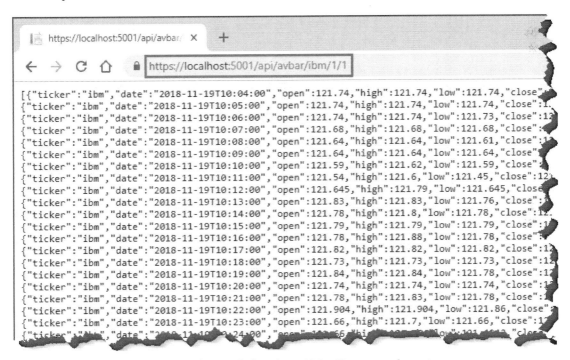

Fig.4-10. Intraday stock data from Alpha Vantage web service.

Real-Time Stock Quotes

Alpha Vantage also allows you to access the real-time stock quotes. First, we need to create a generic interface for the stock quotes. Open the *StockData.cs* file in the *Quant/Models* folder. Add a class called *AvStockQuote* to this file with the following code listing:

```
public class AvStockQuote
{
```

```
    public string Ticker { get; set; }
    public DateTime TimeStamp { get; set; }
    public decimal Open { get; set; }
    public decimal High { get; set; }
    public decimal Low { get; set; }
    public decimal Price { get; set; }
    public decimal Volume { get; set; }
    public decimal PrevClose { get; set; }
    public decimal Change { get; set; }
    public decimal ChangePercent { get; set; }
}
```

Add a new method called *GetStockQuote* to the *AlphaVantageHelper* class. Here is the code listing for this method:

```
public static string GetStockQuote(string ticker, string apiKey)
{
    var function = "GLOBAL_QUOTE";
    string url = "https://www.alphavantage.co/query?function=[function]&
        symbol=[ticker]&apikey=[apiKey]&datatype=csv";
    url = url.Replace("[function]", function);
    url = url.Replace("[ticker]", ticker);
    url = url.Replace("[apiKey]", apiKey);
    string history = string.Empty;
    using (WebClient wc = new WebClient())
    {
        try
        {
            history = wc.DownloadString(url);
        }
        catch { }
    }
    return history;
}
```

This method takes *ticker* and *apiKey* as input parameters. The key to access the Alpha Vantage real-time stock quotes is to construct the URL address with a suitable template.

To add web service support for retrieving real-time quotes from Alpha Vantage, add a new method named *GetAvStockQuote* to the *MarketDataValuesController* class in the *Controllers* folder. Here is the code listing for this method:

```
[Route("~/api/AvQuote/{ticker}")]
[HttpGet]
public AvStockQuote GetAvStockQuote(string ticker)
{
    var quote = AlphaVantageHelper.GetStockQuote(ticker, avKey.ApiKey);
    quote = quote.Replace("\r", "");
    string[] rows = quote.Split('\n');
    AvStockQuote model = null; ;
    if (rows.Length > 1)
    {
        var r = rows[1].Split(",");
        model = new AvStockQuote
        {
            Ticker = ticker,
```

```
            TimeStamp = DateTime.Now,
            Open = decimal.Parse(r[1]),
            High = decimal.Parse(r[2]),
            Low = decimal.Parse(r[3]),
            Price = decimal.Parse(r[4]),
            Volume = decimal.Parse(r[5]),
            PrevClose = decimal.Parse(r[7]),
            Change = decimal.Parse(r[8]),
            ChangePercent = decimal.Parse(r[9].TrimEnd(new char[] { '%', ' ' }))
                          / 100M
        };
    }
    return model;
}
```

For this method, we define the router specifically using

[Route("~/api/AvQuote/{ticker}")]

This means that an HTTP request should be sent to the **/api/avquote/{ticker}**. To test the new web service, run the *Quant* project, open a web browser, and request the following URL:

https://localhost:5001/api/avquote/ibm

This will produce the results shown in Fig.4-11.

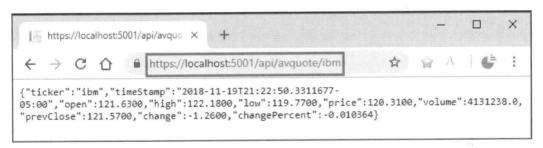

Fig.4-11. Real-time stock quote from Alpha Vantage web service.

EOD FX Data

In this section, we consider how to access historical Foreign Exchange (FX) data. First, we need to create a generic interface for the FX EOD data. Open the *StockData.cs* file in the *Quant/Models* folder. Add a class called *AvFxData* to this file with the following code:

```
public class AvFxData
{
    public string Ticker { get; set; }
    public DateTime Date { get; set; }
    public decimal Open { get; set; }
    public decimal High { get; set; }
    public decimal Low { get; set; }
    public decimal Close { get; set; }
}
```

Add a new method called *GetFxEod* to the *AlphaVantageHelper* class. Here is the code listing for this method:

```
public static string GetFxEod(string ticker, string start, string end,
    string period, string apiKey)
{
    string history = string.Empty;
    if(ticker.Length != 6) return history;
    var fromTicker = ticker.Substring(0, 3);
    var toTicker = ticker.Substring(3, 3);
    var startDate = DateTime.Parse(start);
    var endDate = DateTime.Parse(end);
    var size = "compact";
    if (startDate < DateTime.Today.AddDays(-120)) size = "full";
    var function = "FX_DAILY";
    if (period == "weekly") function = "FX_WEEKLY";
    else if (period == "monthly") function = "FX_MONTHLY";
    string url = "https://www.alphavantage.co/query?function=
        [function]&from_symbol=[fromTicker]&to_symbol=[toTicker]&
        outputsize=[size]&apikey=[apiKey]&datatype=csv";
    url = url.Replace("[function]", function);
    url = url.Replace("[fromTicker]", fromTicker);
    url = url.Replace("[toTicker]", toTicker);
    url = url.Replace("[size]", size);
    url = url.Replace("[apiKey]", apiKey);

    using (WebClient wc = new WebClient())
    {
        try
        {
            history = wc.DownloadString(url);
        }
        catch { }
    }
    return history;
}
```

Note that the *ticker* parameter for FX represents currency pairs, such as USDEUR, USDJPY, EURCAD, etc., and it must contains six characters.

To add web service support for retrieving FX data from Alpha Vantage, add a new method named *GetAvFxEod* to the *MarketDataValuesController* class in the *Controllers* folder. Here is the code listing for this method:

```
[Route("~/api/AvFxEod/{ticker}/{start}/{end}/{period}")]
[HttpGet]
public List<AvFxData> GetAvFxEod(string ticker, string start, string end,
    string period)
{
    var startDate = DateTime.Parse(start);
    var endDate = DateTime.Parse(end);
    var history = AlphaVantageHelper.GetFxEod(ticker, start, end, period,
        avKey.ApiKey);
    history = history.Replace("\r", "");
    string[] rows = history.Split('\n');

    var models = new List<AvFxData>();
    for (var i = 1; i < rows.Length; i++)
    {
```

```
        var r = rows[i].Split(",");
        try
        {
            var date = DateTime.Parse(r[0]);
            if (date >= startDate && date <= endDate)
            {
                models.Add(new AvFxData
                {
                    Ticker = ticker,
                    Date = date,
                    Open = decimal.Parse(r[1]),
                    High = decimal.Parse(r[2]),
                    Low = decimal.Parse(r[3]),
                    Close = decimal.Parse(r[4])
                });
            }
        }
        catch { }
    }
    return models.OrderBy(d => d.Date).ToList();
}
```

For this method, we define the router specifically using

[Route("~/api/AvFxEod/{ticker}/{start}/{end}/{period}")]

This means that an HTTP request should be sent to the **/api/avfxeod/{ticker}/{start}/{end} /{period}**. To test the new web service, run the *Quant* project, open a web browser, and request the following URL:

https://localhost:5001/api/avfxeod/usdjpy/2018-07-01/2018-08-10/daily

This will produce the results shown in Fig.4-12.

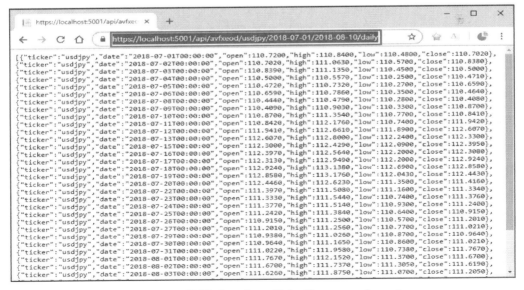

Fig.4-12. FX EOD data from Alpha Vantage web service.

Intraday FX Data

Alpha Vantage also provides historical intraday bar data for FX. Add a new method called *GetFxBar* to the *AlphaVantageHelper* class with the following code snippet:

```
public static string GetFxBar(string ticker, int interval, int outputsize,
    string apiKey)
{
    string history = string.Empty;
    if(ticker.Length != 6) return history;
    var fromTicker = ticker.Substring(0, 3);
    var toTicker = ticker.Substring(3, 3);
    var function = "FX_INTRADAY";
    var size = "compact";
    if (outputsize > 100) size = "full";

    string url = "https://www.alphavantage.co/query?function=
        [function]&from_symbol=[fromTicker]&to_symbol=[toTicker]&interval=
        [interval]min&outputsize=[size]&apikey=[apiKey]&datatype=csv";
    url = url.Replace("[function]", function);
    url = url.Replace("[fromTicker]", fromTicker);
    url = url.Replace("[toTicker]", toTicker);
    url = url.Replace("[size]", size);
    url = url.Replace("[interval]", interval.ToString());
    url = url.Replace("[apiKey]", apiKey);

    using (WebClient wc = new WebClient())
    {
        try
        {
            history = wc.DownloadString(url);
        }
        catch { }
    }
    return history;
}
```

This method takes the *ticker*, *interval*, *outputsize*, and *apiKey* as input arguments. The *interval* parameter can be specified by 1min, 5min, 15min, 30min, and 60-min, corresponding to one-minute, 5-minute, …, and 60-minute bar data, respectively.

To add web service support for retrieving historical intraday FX data from Alpha Vantage, add a new method named *GetAvFxBar* to the *MarketDataValuesController* class in the *Controllers* folder. Here is the code listing for this method:

```
[Route("~/api/AvFxBar/{ticker}/{interval}/{outputsize}")]
[HttpGet]
public List<AvFxData> GetAvFxBar(string ticker, int interval, int outputsize)
{
    var history = AlphaVantageHelper.GetFxBar(ticker, interval, outputsize,
        avKey.ApiKey);
    history = history.Replace("\r", "");
    string[] rows = history.Split('\n');

    var models = new List<AvFxData>();
    for (var i = 1; i < rows.Length; i++)
```

```
{
    var r = rows[i].Split(",");
    try
    {
        var date = DateTime.Parse(r[0]);
        models.Add(new AvFxData
        {
            Ticker = ticker,
            Date = date,
            Open = decimal.Parse(r[1]),
            High = decimal.Parse(r[2]),
            Low = decimal.Parse(r[3]),
            Close = decimal.Parse(r[4])
        });
    }
    catch { }
}
return models.OrderBy(d => d.Date).ToList();
}
```

The *outputsize* parameter in the above method specifies the size of the data returned – the method returns the latest 100 data points if **outputsize <=100** while it returns the full-length intraday data if **outputsize > 100**.

For the *GetAvFxBar* method, we define the router specifically using

[Route("~/api/AvFxBar/{ticker}/{interval}/{outputsize}")]

This means that an HTTP request should be sent to the **/api/avfxbar/{ticker}/{interval}/ {outputsize}**. To test the new web service, run the *Quant* project, open a web browser, and request the following URL:

https://localhost:5001/api/avfxbar/eurusd/1/1

This will produce the results shown in Fig.4-13.

Fig.4-13. FX minute-bar data from Alpha Vantage web service.

Sector Performance Data

Alpha Vantage also provides real-time and historical sector performance data calculated from S&P 500 incumbents. First, we need to create a generic interface for this data. Open the *StockData.cs* file in the *Quant/Models* folder. Add a class called *AvSectorPerf* to this file with the following code listing:

```
public class AvSectorPerf
{
    public string Rank { get; set; }
    public string CommunicationServices { get; set; }
    public string ConsumerDiscretionary { get; set; }
    public string ConsumerStaples { get; set; }
    public string Energy { get; set; }
    public string Financials { get; set; }
    public string HealthCare { get; set; }
    public string Industrials { get; set; }
    public string InformationTechnology { get; set; }
    public string Matericals { get; set; }
    public string Utilities { get; set; }
}
```

Add a new method called *GetSectorPerf* to the *AlphaVantageHelper* class. Here is the code listing for this method:

```
public static string GetSectorPerf(string apiKey) {
    string url = "https://www.alphavantage.co/query?function=
        SECTOR&apikey=[apiKey]";
    url = url.Replace("[apiKey]", apiKey);
    string result = string.Empty;

    using (WebClient wc = new WebClient())
    {
        try
        {
            result = wc.DownloadString(url);
        }
        catch { }
    }
    return result;
}
```

To add web service support for retrieving sector performance data from Alpha Vantage, add a new method named *GetAvSectorPerf* to the *MarketDataValuesController* class in the *Controllers* folder. Here is the code listing for this method:

```
[Route("~/api/AvSector/Perf")]
[HttpGet]
public List<AvSectorPerf> GetSectorPerformance()
{
    var result = AlphaVantageHelper.GetSectorPerf(avKey.ApiKey);
    List<AvSectorPerf> models = new List<AvSectorPerf>();
    var res = JsonConvert.DeserializeObject<dynamic>(result);
    string[] ranks = new string[]
    {
        "Rank A: Real-Time Performance",
        "Rank B: 1 Day Performance",
```

```
        "Rank C: 5 Day Performance",
        "Rank D: 1 Month Performance",
        "Rank E: 3 Month Performance",
        "Rank F: Year-to-Date (YTD) Performance",
        "Rank G: 1 Year Performance",
        "Rank H: 3 Year Performance",
        "Rank I: 5 Year Performance",
        "Rank J: 10 Year Performance"
    };

    foreach (var rank in ranks)
    {
        models.Add(new AvSectorPerf
        {
            Rank = rank,
            CommunicationServices = res[rank]["Communication Services"],
            ConsumerDiscretionary = res[rank]["Consumer Discretionary"],
            ConsumerStaples = res[rank]["Consumer Staples"],
            Energy = res[rank]["Energy"],
            Financials = res[rank]["Financials"],
            HealthCare = res[rank]["Health Care"],
            Industrials = res[rank]["Industrials"],
            InformationTechnology = res[rank]["Information Technology"],
            Matericals = res[rank]["Materials"],
            Utilities = res[rank]["Utilities"]
        });
    }
    return models;
}
```

This method first converts the JSON string into a JSON dynamic object using JSON deserialization and then converts this JSON dynamic object into C# *AvSectorPerf* objects for easy manipulation. We also define the router specifically for this method using

[Route("~/api/AvSector/Perf")]

This means that an HTTP request should be sent to the **/api/AvSector/Perf**. To test the new web service, run the *Quant* project, open a web browser, and request the following URL:

https://localhost:5001/api/AvSector/Perf

This will produce the results shown in Fig.4-14.

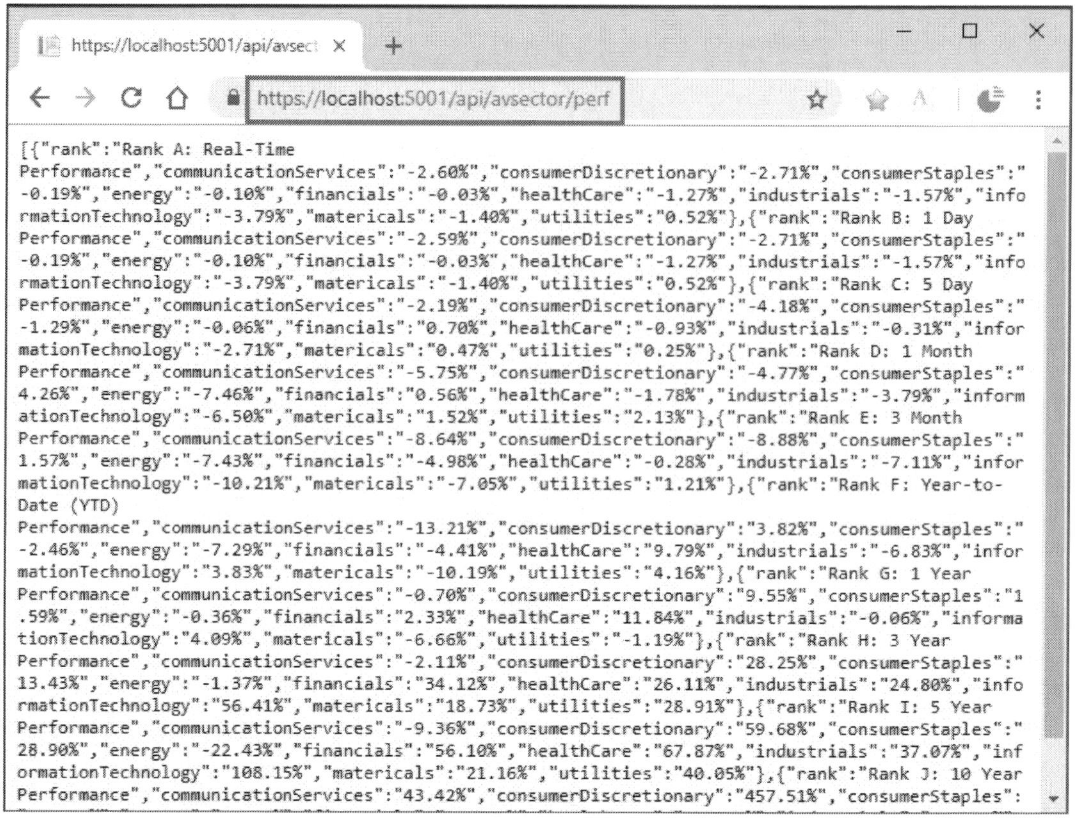

Fig.4-14. Sector performance data from Alpha Vantage web service.

Alpha Vantage Data in Angular

In this section, we will add various Alpha Vantage web services implemented in the preceding sections to the Angular application.

EOD Stock Data

To add support for retrieving historical stock data from Alpha Vantage in the Angular application, we need to add a method named *getAvStock* shown in the following code to the *market-data.service.ts* class in the *ClientApp/src/app/models* folder so that it can send GET requests to the web service:

```
// market-data.service.ts file:
import { Inject } from '@angular/core';
import { HttpClient } from '@angular/common/http';
import { MarketData } from './market-data.model';

export class MarketDataRepository {
  // ... other properties omitted for brevity ...

  avStock: MarketData[] = [];
```

```
  private url;

  constructor(private http: HttpClient, @Inject('BASE_URL') baseUrl: string) {
    this.url = baseUrl;
  }

  // ... other methods omitted for brevity ...

  getAvStock(ticker: string, start: string, end: string, period: string) {
    let url1 = this.url + 'api/aveod/' + ticker + '/' + start + '/' + end
      + '/' + period;
    this.http.get<MarketData[]>(url1).subscribe(result => { this.avStock =
      result });
  }
}
```

The *getAvStock* method accepts ticker, date range, and period parameters, and sends an HTTP request to a specified URL, which gets the stock data from Alpha Vantage.

Now, I will use an example to show you how to use this repository service to download the market data from Alpha Vantage.

Run the following command in the command prompt window from the *ClientApp* folder:

ng g c chapter04/av-stock --module=app.module

This will generate a new component named *av-stock* in the *ClientApp/src/app/chapter04* folder. Open the component class file and replace its content with the following code:

```
// av-stock.component.ts file:
import { Component, OnInit } from '@angular/core';
import { MarketDataService } from '../../models/market-data.service';
import { MarketData } from '../../models/market-data.model';

@Component({
  selector: 'app-av-stock',
  templateUrl: './av-stock.component.html',
  styleUrls: ['./av-stock.component.css']
})
export class AvStockComponent implements OnInit {
  ticker = 'MSFT';
  startDate: string = '2018-08-01';
  endDate: string = '2018-11-01';
  period = 'daily';
  displayedCols = ['date', 'open', 'high', 'low', 'close', 'closeAdj', 'volume'];

  constructor(private repository: MarketDataService) { }

  ngOnInit() {
    this.getStock(this.ticker, this.startDate, this.endDate, this.period);
  }

  get stock(): MarketData[] {
    return this.repository.avStock;
  }

  getStock(ticker: string, start: string, end: string, period: string) {
```

```
    this.repository.getAvStock(ticker, start, end, period);
  }
}
```

The constructor has a *MarketDataService* parameter called *repository*, which is how dependencies are declared in an Angular app. The other addition in this class is a read-only property called *stock* that returns the value of the *MarketDataService* object's *avStock* property. The *getStock* method calls the *getAvStock* method defined in the *MarketDataService* class, which will update the *stock* property according to the user's input.

We need also to update the component's template with the following code:

```html
// av-stock.component.html file:
<h2>
  AV-stock works!
</h2>
<mat-form-field>
  <input matInput placeholder="ticker" [(ngModel)]="ticker" name="ticker">
</mat-form-field>
<mat-form-field>
  <input matInput placeholder="Start Date" [(ngModel)]="startDate" name="startDate">
</mat-form-field>
<mat-form-field>
  <input matInput placeholder="End Date" [(ngModel)]="endDate" name="endDate">
</mat-form-field>
<mat-form-field>
  <mat-select [(value)]="period">
    <mat-option value="daily">daily</mat-option>
    <mat-option value="weekly">weekly</mat-option>
    <mat-option value="monthly">monthly</mat-option>
  </mat-select>
</mat-form-field>
<button mat-raised-button (click)="getStock(ticker,startDate, endDate,period)">Get
Stock Data</button>

<div *ngIf="stock">
  <div *ngIf="stock.length>0">
    <br />
    <h4>Stock Price</h4>
    <mat-table [dataSource]="stock">
      <ng-container matColumnDef="date">
        <mat-header-cell *matHeaderCellDef>Date</mat-header-cell>
        <mat-cell *matCellDef="let item">{{item.date |
            date: 'MM/dd/yyyy'}}</mat-cell>
      </ng-container>
      <ng-container matColumnDef="open">
        <mat-header-cell *matHeaderCellDef>Open</mat-header-cell>
        <mat-cell *matCellDef="let item">{{item.open}}</mat-cell>
      </ng-container>
      <ng-container matColumnDef="high">
        <mat-header-cell *matHeaderCellDef>High</mat-header-cell>
        <mat-cell *matCellDef="let item">{{item.high}}</mat-cell>
      </ng-container>
      <ng-container matColumnDef="low">
        <mat-header-cell *matHeaderCellDef>Low</mat-header-cell>
        <mat-cell *matCellDef="let item">{{item.low}}</mat-cell>
```

```
      </ng-container>
      <ng-container matColumnDef="close">
        <mat-header-cell *matHeaderCellDef>Close</mat-header-cell>
        <mat-cell *matCellDef="let item">{{item.close}}</mat-cell>
      </ng-container>
      <ng-container matColumnDef="closeAdj">
        <mat-header-cell *matHeaderCellDef>Close Adj</mat-header-cell>
        <mat-cell *matCellDef="let item">{{item.closeAdj}}</mat-cell>
      </ng-container>
      <ng-container matColumnDef="volume">
        <mat-header-cell *matHeaderCellDef>Volume</mat-header-cell>
        <mat-cell *matCellDef="let item">{{item.volume}}</mat-cell>
      </ng-container>
      <mat-header-row *matHeaderRowDef="displayedCols"></mat-header-row>
      <mat-row *matRowDef="let row; columns: displayedCols;"></mat-row>
    </mat-table>
  </div>
</div>
```

This template is very similar to that used in retrieving stock data from Yahoo Finance. Here, we also set the *period* property using a *mat-select* directive with a two-way binding. This *select* directive has three options: *daily*, *weekly*, and *monthly*, corresponding to the stock data with different periods.

Finally, we need to add a path for this new component to the *RouterModule* of the root module (i.e., the *app.module.ts* file):

```
{ path: 'chapter04/av-stock, component: AvStockComponent },
```

Then add the corresponding URL link to the *home* and *nav-menu* components.

Saving the project and navigating to the */chapter04/av-stock* page produce the results shown in Fig.4-15. Here, we download the weekly stock data for FB from 8/1/2018 to 11/1/2018.

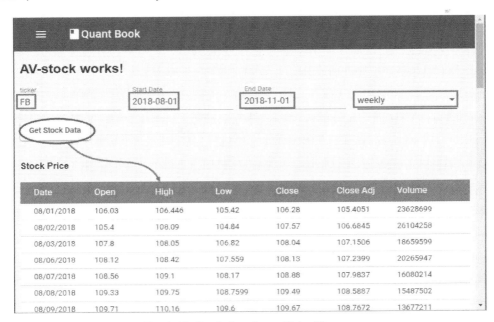

Fig.4-15. Stock data from Alpha Vantage.

You can retrieve stock EOD data for any ticker with a history back to January 1998 using the method discussed here.

Intraday Stock Data

To add support for retrieving intraday stock data from Alpha Vantage in the Angular application, we need to add a new method named *getAvStockBar* shown in the following code snippet to the *market-data.service.ts* class in the *ClientApp/src/app/models* folder so that it can send GET requests to the web service:

```
avStockBar: MarketData[] = [];
...


getAvStockBar(ticker: string, interval:string, outputsize: string) {
    let url1 = this.url + 'api/avbar/' + ticker + '/' + interval + '/' + outputsize;
    this.http.get<MarketData[]>(url1).subscribe(result => {
    this.avStockBar = result });
}
```

Here, we define a property named *avStockBar* in this repository class. The *getAvStockBar* method accepts *ticker*, *interval*, and *outputsize* parameters, and sends an HTTP request to a specified URL, which gets the intraday stock data from Alpha Vantage.

Now, I will use an example to show you how to use this repository service to download the intraday data from Alpha Vantage.

Run the following command in the command prompt window from the *ClientApp* folder:

ng g c chapter04/av-bar --module=app.module

This will generate a new component named *av-bar* in the *ClientApp/src/app/chapter04* folder. Open the component class file and replace its content with the following code:

```
//av-bar.component.ts file:
import { Component, OnInit } from '@angular/core';
import { MarketDataService } from '../../models/market-data.service';
import { MarketData } from '../../models/market-data.model';

@Component({
  selector: 'app-av-bar',
  templateUrl: './av-bar.component.html',
  styleUrls: ['./av-bar.component.css']
})
export class AvBarComponent implements OnInit {
  ticker: string = 'A';
  interval: string = "5";
  outputsize: string = "1"
  displayedCols = ['date', 'open', 'high', 'low', 'close', 'volume'];

  constructor(private repository: MarketDataservice) { }

  ngOnInit() {
    this.getBar(this.ticker, this.interval, this.outputsize);
  }
```

```
  get bar(): MarketData[] {
    return this.repository.avStockBar;
  }

  getBar(ticker: string, interval: string, outputsize: string) {
    this.repository.getAvStockBar(ticker, interval, outputsize);
  }
}
```

The constructor has a *MarketDataService* parameter called *repository*, which is how dependencies are declared in an Angular app. The other addition in this class is a read-only property called *bar* that returns the value of the *MarketDataService* object's *avStockBar* property. The *getBar* method calls the *getAvStockBar* method defined in the *MarketDataService* class, which will update the *bar* property according to the user's input.

We need also to update the component's template with the following code:

```
// av-bar.component.html file:
<h2>
  AV-bar works!
</h2>
<mat-form-field>
  <input matInput placeholder="ticker" [(ngModel)]="ticker" name="ticker">
</mat-form-field>
<mat-form-field>
  <mat-select [(value)]="interval">
    <mat-option value="1">1 Minute</mat-option>
    <mat-option value="5">5 minutes</mat-option>
    <mat-option value="15">15 Minutes</mat-option>
    <mat-option value="30">30 Minutes</mat-option>
    <mat-option value="60">60 Minutes</mat-option>
  </mat-select>
</mat-form-field>
<mat-form-field>
  <input matInput placeholder="outputsize" [(ngModel)]="outputsize"
    name="outputsize">
</mat-form-field>
<button mat-raised-button (click)="getBar(ticker,interval,outputsize)">
  Get Bar Data</button>

<div *ngIf="bar">
  <div *ngIf="bar.length>0">
    <h4>Stock Price</h4>
    <mat-table [dataSource]="bar">
      <ng-container matColumnDef="date">
        <mat-header-cell *matHeaderCellDef>Date</mat-header-cell>
        <mat-cell *matCellDef="let item">{{item.date |
          date: 'MM/dd/yyyy HH:mm'}}</mat-cell>
      </ng-container>
      <ng-container matColumnDef="open">
        <mat-header-cell *matHeaderCellDef>Open</mat-header-cell>
        <mat-cell *matCellDef="let item">{{item.open}}</mat-cell>
      </ng-container>
      <ng-container matColumnDef="high">
        <mat-header-cell *matHeaderCellDef>High</mat-header-cell>
        <mat-cell *matCellDef="let item">{{item.high}}</mat-cell>
```

```
      </ng-container>
      <ng-container matColumnDef="low">
        <mat-header-cell *matHeaderCellDef>Low</mat-header-cell>
        <mat-cell *matCellDef="let item">{{item.low}}</mat-cell>
      </ng-container>
      <ng-container matColumnDef="close">
        <mat-header-cell *matHeaderCellDef>Close</mat-header-cell>
        <mat-cell *matCellDef="let item">{{item.close}}</mat-cell>
      </ng-container>
      <ng-container matColumnDef="volume">
        <mat-header-cell *matHeaderCellDef>Volume</mat-header-cell>
        <mat-cell *matCellDef="let item">{{item.volume}}</mat-cell>
      </ng-container>
      <mat-header-row *matHeaderRowDef="displayedCols"></mat-header-row>
      <mat-row *matRowDef="let row; columns: displayedCols;"></mat-row>
    </mat-table>
  </div>
</div>
```

This template is very similar to that used in the previous example. Here, we set the *interval* property using a *mat-select* directive with a two-way binding. This *select* directive has five options that correspond to different types of bar data.

Finally, we need to add a path for this new component to the *RouterModule* of the root module (i.e., the *app.module.ts* file):

```
{ path: 'chapter04/av-bar, component: AvBarComponent },
```

Then add the corresponding URL link to the *home* and *nav-menu* components.

Saving the project and navigating to the */chapter04/av-bar* page produce the results shown in Fig.4-16.

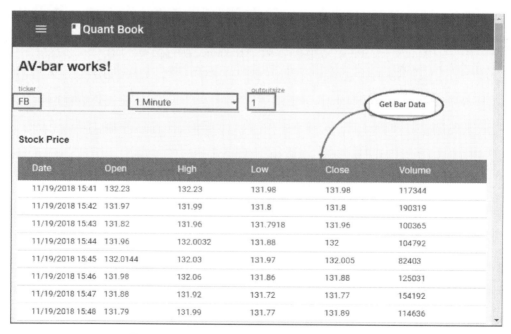

Fig.4-16. Intraday bar data from Alpha Vantage.

Real-Time Stock Quotes

In this section, we consider real-time stock quotes in the Angular application. Before adding a method to the *market-data.service* for retrieving real-time stock quotes from Alpha Vantage, we need to define a TypeScript stock quote model. Open the *market-data. model.ts* file and add a new class named *AvQuote* as shown in the following code listing:

```
export class AvQuote {
  constructor(
    public ticker: string,
    public timeStamp?: Date,
    public open?: number,
    public high?: number,
    public low?: number,
    public price?: number,
    public volume?: number,
    public prevClose?: number,
    public change?: number,
    public changePercent?: number
  ) { }
}
```

This model corresponds to the C# *AvStockQuote* class defined previously.

Next, we need to define a new method named *getAvQuote* in the *market-data.service.ts* class to send the request and process the response, as shown in the following code:

```
// market-data.service.ts file:
import { Inject } from '@angular/core';
import { HttpClient } from '@angular/common/http';
import { MarketData, MarketQuote, AvQuote} from './market-data.model';

export class MarketDataRepository {

  // ... other properties omitted for brevity ...
  avQuote: AvQuote = null;
  private url;

  constructor(private http: HttpClient, @Inject('BASE_URL') baseUrl: string) {
    this.url = baseUrl;
  }

  // ... other methods omitted for breviry ...

  getAvQuote(ticker: string) {
    this.http.get<AvQuote>(this.url + 'api/avquote/' + ticker)
      .subscribe(result => { this.avQuote = result });
  }
}
```

The *getAvQuote* method accepts *ticker* as input parameter, and sends an HTTP request to a specified URL, which gets the real-time quote data from Alpha Vantage.

Now, I will use an example to show you how to use this repository service to download the quote data from Alpha Vantage.

Run the following command in the command prompt window from the *ClientApp* folder:

```
ng g c chapter04/av-quote --module=app.module
```

This will generate a new component named *av-quote* in the *ClientApp/src/app/chapter04* folder. Open the component class file and replace its content with the following code:

```
// av-quote.ts file:
import { Component, OnInit } from '@angular/core';
import { MarketDataService } from '../../models/market-data.service';
import { AvQuote } from '../../models/market-data.model';

@Component({
  selector: 'app-av-quote',
  templateUrl: './av-quote.component.html',
  styleUrls: ['./av-quote.component.css']
})
export class AvQuoteComponent implements OnInit {
  ticker = 'A';
  constructor(private repository: MarketDataService) { }

  ngOnInit() {
    this.getQuote(this.ticker);
  }

  get quote(): AvQuote {
    return this.repository.avQuote;
  }

  getQuote(ticker: string) {
    this.repository.getAvQuote(ticker);
  }
}
```

The constructor has a *MarketDataService* parameter called *repository*, which is how dependencies are declared in an Angular app. The other addition in this class is a read-only property called *quote* that returns the value of the *MarketDataService* object's *avQuote* property. The *getQuote* method calls the *getAvQuote* method defined in the *MarketDataService* class, which will update the *quote* property according to the user's input.

We need also to update the component's template with the following code listing:

```
// av-quote.component.html file:
<h2>
  AV-quote works!
</h2>

<mat-form-field>
  <input matInput placeholder="ticker" [(ngModel)]="ticker" name="ticker">
</mat-form-field>
<button mat-raised-button (click)="getQuote(ticker)">Get Stock Quote</button>

<div *ngIf="quote">
  <h4>Stock Quote</h4>
  <ul>
    <li>Ticker: {{quote.ticker}}</li>
    <li>TimeStamp: {{quote.timeStamp}}</li>
```

```
      <li>Open: {{quote.open}}</li>
      <li>High: {{quote.high}}</li>
      <li>Low: {{quote.low}}</li>
      <li>Price: {{quote.price}}</li>
      <li>Volume: {{quote.volume}}</li>
      <li>Previous Price: {{quote.prevClose}}</li>
      <li>Change: {{quote.change}}</li>
      <li>Change Percent: {{quote.changePercent}}</li>
    </ul>
</div>
```

Here, the button element is configured using the Angular event binding feature, and its click event is triggered when the user clicks the button, at which point Angular evaluates the expression and invokes the component's *getQuote* method.

Finally, we need to add a path for this new component to the *RouterModule* of the root module (i.e., the *app.module.ts* file):

```
{ path: 'chapter04/av-quote, component: IexQuoteComponent },
```

Then add the corresponding URL link to the *home* and *nav-menu* components.

Saving the project and navigating to the */chapter04/av-quote* page produce the results shown in Fig.4-17.

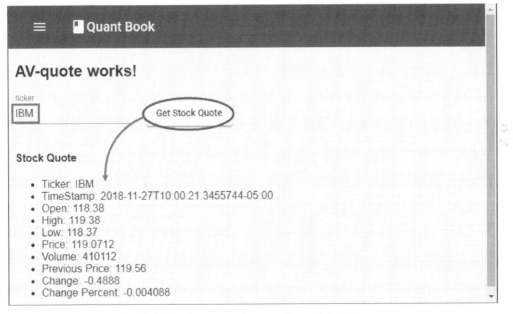

Fig.4-17.Real-time stock quote from Alpha Vantage.

EOD FX Data

In this section, I demonstrate how to add the web service for accessing historical FX data to the Angular application. Before adding a method to the *market-data.service* for retrieving FX data from Alpha

Vantage, we need to define a TypeScript FX data model. Open the *market-data. model.ts* file and add a new class named *AvFxData* as shown in the following code:

```
export class AvFxData {
  constructor(
    public ticker: string,
    public date?: Date,
    public open?: number,
    public high?: number,
    public low?: number,
    public close?: number,
  ) { }
}
```

This model corresponds to the C# *AvFxData* class defined previously.

Next, we need to define a new method named *getAvFx* method in the *market-data.service.ts* class to send the request and process the response, as shown in the following code:

```
// market-data.service.ts file:
import { Inject } from '@angular/core';
import { HttpClient } from '@angular/common/http';
import { MarketData, MarketQuote, AvQuote, AvFxData} from './market-data.model';

export class MarketDataRepository {

  // ... other properties omitted for brevity ...
  avFx: AvFxData[] = [];
  private url;

  constructor(private http: HttpClient, @Inject('BASE_URL') baseUrl: string) {
    this.url = baseUrl;
  }

  // ... other methods omitted for breviry ...

  getAvFx(ticker: string, start: string, end: string, period: string) {
    let url1 = this.url + 'api/avfxeod/' + ticker + '/' + start + '/' +
      end + '/' + period;
    this.http.get<AvFxData[]>(url1).subscribe(result => { this.avFx = result });
  }
}
```

The *getAvFx* method sends an HTTP request to a specified URL, which gets the FX EOD data from Alpha Vantage.

Now, I will use an example to show you how to use this repository service to download the FX data from Alpha Vantage.

Run the following command in the command prompt window from the *ClientApp* folder:

ng g c chapter04/av-fx --module=app.module

This will generate a new component named *av-fx* in the *ClientApp/src/app/chapter04* folder. Open the component class file and replace its content with the following code listing:

```
// av-fx.component.ts file:
import { Component, OnInit } from '@angular/core';
```

```
import { MarketDataService} from '../../models/market-data.service';
import { AvFxData } from '../../models/market-data.model';

@Component({
  selector: 'app-av-fx',
  templateUrl: './av-fx.component.html',
  styleUrls: ['./av-fx.component.css']
})
export class AvFxComponent implements OnInit {
  ticker = 'EURUSD';
  startDate: string = '2018-08-01';
  endDate: string = '2018-11-01';
  period = 'daily';
  displayedCols = ['date', 'open', 'high', 'low', 'close'];

  constructor(private repository: MarketDataService) { }

  ngOnInit() {
    this.getFx(this.ticker, this.startDate, this.endDate, this.period);
  }

  get fx(): AvFxData[] {
    return this.repository.avFx;
  }

  getFx(ticker: string, start: string, end: string, period: string) {
    this.repository.getAvFx(ticker, start, end, period);
  }
}
```

The constructor has a *MarketDataService* parameter called *repository*, which is how dependencies are declared in an Angular app. The other addition in this class is a read-only property called *fx* that returns the value of the *MarketDataService* object's *avFx* property. The *getFx* method calls the *getAvFx* method defined in the *MarketDataService* class, which will update the *fx* property according to the user's input.

We need also to update the component's template with the following code listing:

```
// av-fx.component.html file:
<h2>
  AV-fx works!
</h2>

<mat-form-field>
  <input matInput placeholder="ticker" [(ngModel)]="ticker" name="ticker">
</mat-form-field>
<mat-form-field>
  <input matInput placeholder="Start Date" [(ngModel)]="startDate" name="startDate">
</mat-form-field>
<mat-form-field>
  <input matInput placeholder="End Date" [(ngModel)]="endDate" name="endDate">
</mat-form-field>
<mat-form-field>
  <mat-select [(value)]="period">
    <mat-option value="daily">daily</mat-option>
    <mat-option value="weekly">weekly</mat-option>
    <mat-option value="monthly">monthly</mat-option>
```

```
    </mat-select>
  </mat-form-field>
  <button mat-raised-button (click)="getFx(ticker,startDate, endDate,period)">Get Fx
Data</button>

<div *ngIf="fx">
  <div *ngIf="fx.length>0">
    <br />
    <h4>Stock Price</h4>
    <mat-table [dataSource]="fx">
      <ng-container matColumnDef="date">
        <mat-header-cell *matHeaderCellDef>Date</mat-header-cell>
        <mat-cell *matCellDef="let item">{{item.date |
          date: 'MM/dd/yyyy'}}</mat-cell>
      </ng-container>
      <ng-container matColumnDef="open">
        <mat-header-cell *matHeaderCellDef>Open</mat-header-cell>
        <mat-cell *matCellDef="let item">{{item.open}}</mat-cell>
      </ng-container>
      <ng-container matColumnDef="high">
        <mat-header-cell *matHeaderCellDef>High</mat-header-cell>
        <mat-cell *matCellDef="let item">{{item.high}}</mat-cell>
      </ng-container>
      <ng-container matColumnDef="low">
        <mat-header-cell *matHeaderCellDef>Low</mat-header-cell>
        <mat-cell *matCellDef="let item">{{item.low}}</mat-cell>
      </ng-container>
      <ng-container matColumnDef="close">
        <mat-header-cell *matHeaderCellDef>Close</mat-header-cell>
        <mat-cell *matCellDef="let item">{{item.close}}</mat-cell>
      </ng-container>
      <mat-header-row *matHeaderRowDef="displayedCols"></mat-header-row>
      <mat-row *matRowDef="let row; columns: displayedCols;"></mat-row>
    </mat-table>
  </div>
</div>
```

Here, the button element is configured using the Angular event binding feature and its click event is triggered when the user clicks the button, at which point Angular evaluates the expression and invokes the component's *getFx* method.

Finally, we need to add a path for this new component to the *RouterModule* of the root module (i.e., the *app.module.ts* file):

```
{ path: 'chapter04/av-fx, component: IexQuoteComponent },
```

Then add the corresponding URL link to the *home* and *nav-menu* components.

Saving the project and navigating to the */chapter04/av-fx* page produce the results shown in Fig.4-18.

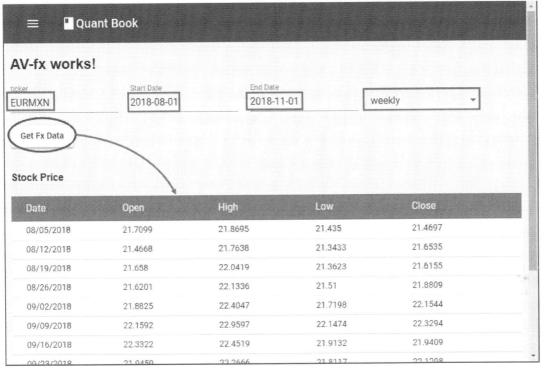

Fig.4-18. FX EOD data from Alpha Vantage.

Intraday FX Data

In this section, we consider how to add the web service for accessing intraday FX data to the Angular application. First, we need to define a new method named *getAvFxBar* method in the *market-data.service.ts* class to send the request and process the response, as shown in the following code snippet:

```
avFxBar: AvFxData[] = [];
getAvFxBar(ticker: string, interval: string, outputsize: string) {
  let url1 = this.url + 'api/avfxbar/' + ticker + '/' + interval + '/' +
    outputsize;
  this.http.get<AvFxData[]>(url1).subscribe(result => { this.avFxBar = result });
}
```

Here, we also define a property called *avFxBar*. The *getAvFxBar* method sends an HTTP request to a specified URL, which gets the FX intraday data from Alpha Vantage.

Now, I will use an example to show you how to use this repository service to download the FX intraday data from Alpha Vantage.

Run the following command in the command prompt window from the *ClientApp* folder:

```
ng g c chapter04/av-fx-bar --module=app.module
```

This will generate a new component named *av-fx-bar* in the *ClientApp/src/app/chapter04* folder. Open the component class file and replace its content with the following code listing:

```
// av-fx-bar.component.ts file:
```

```
import { Component, OnInit } from '@angular/core';
import { MarketDataService } from '../../models/market-data.service';
import { AvFxData } from '../../models/market-data.model';

@Component({
  selector: 'app-av-fx-bar',
  templateUrl: './av-fx-bar.component.html',
  styleUrls: ['./av-fx-bar.component.css']
})
export class AvFxBarComponent implements OnInit {
  ticker: string = 'EURUSD';
  interval: string = "5";
  outputsize: string = "1"
  displayedCols = ['date', 'open', 'high', 'low', 'close'];

  constructor(private repository: MarketDataService) { }

  ngOnInit() {
    this.getBar(this.ticker, this.interval, this.outputsize);
  }

  get bar(): AvFxData[] {
    return this.repository.avFxBar;
  }

  getBar(ticker: string, interval: string, outputsize: string) {
    this.repository.getAvFxBar(ticker, interval, outputsize);
  }
}
```

The constructor has a *MarketDataService* parameter called *repository*, which is how dependencies are declared in an Angular app. The other addition in this class is a read-only property called *bar* that returns the value of the *MarketDataService* object's *avFxBar* property. The *getBar* method calls the *getAvFxBar* method defined in the *MarketDataService* class, which will update the *bar* property according to the user's input.

We need also to update the component's template with the following code listing:

```
// av-fx-bar.component.html file:
<h2>
  AV-fx-bar works!
</h2>

<mat-form-field>
  <input matInput placeholder="ticker" [(ngModel)]="ticker" name="ticker">
</mat-form-field>
<mat-form-field>
  <mat-select [(value)]="interval">
    <mat-option value="1">1 Minute</mat-option>
    <mat-option value="5">5 minutes</mat-option>
    <mat-option value="15">15 Minutes</mat-option>
    <mat-option value="30">30 Minutes</mat-option>
    <mat-option value="60">60 Minutes</mat-option>
  </mat-select>
</mat-form-field>
<mat-form-field>
```

```
    <input matInput placeholder="outputsize" [(ngModel)]="outputsize"
      name="outputsize">
</mat-form-field>
<button mat-raised-button (click)="getBar(ticker,interval,outputsize)">
  Get Bar Data</button>

<div *ngIf="bar">
  <div *ngIf="bar.length>0">
    <h4>Stock Price</h4>
    <mat-table [dataSource]="bar">
      <ng-container matColumnDef="date">
        <mat-header-cell *matHeaderCellDef>Date</mat-header-cell>
        <mat-cell *matCellDef="let item">{{item.date |
          date: 'MM/dd/yyyy HH:mm'}}</mat-cell>
      </ng-container>
      <ng-container matColumnDef="open">
        <mat-header-cell *matHeaderCellDef>Open</mat-header-cell>
        <mat-cell *matCellDef="let item">{{item.open}}</mat-cell>
      </ng-container>
      <ng-container matColumnDef="high">
        <mat-header-cell *matHeaderCellDef>High</mat-header-cell>
        <mat-cell *matCellDef="let item">{{item.high}}</mat-cell>
      </ng-container>
      <ng-container matColumnDef="low">
        <mat-header-cell *matHeaderCellDef>Low</mat-header-cell>
        <mat-cell *matCellDef="let item">{{item.low}}</mat-cell>
      </ng-container>
      <ng-container matColumnDef="close">
        <mat-header-cell *matHeaderCellDef>Close</mat-header-cell>
        <mat-cell *matCellDef="let item">{{item.close}}</mat-cell>
      </ng-container>
      <mat-header-row *matHeaderRowDef="displayedCols"></mat-header-row>
      <mat-row *matRowDef="let row; columns: displayedCols;"></mat-row>
    </mat-table>
  </div>
</div>
```

This template is very similar to that used in the previous example. Here, we set the *interval* property using a *mat-select* directive with a two-way binding. This *select* directive has five options that correspond to different types of FX bar data.

Finally, we need to add a path for this new component to the *RouterModule* of the root module (i.e., the *app.module.ts* file):

```
{ path: 'chapter04/av-fx-bar, component: AvFxBaravComponent },
```

Then add the corresponding URL link to the *home* and *nav-menu* components.

Saving the project and navigating to the */chapter04/av-fx-bar* page produce the results shown in Fig.4-19.

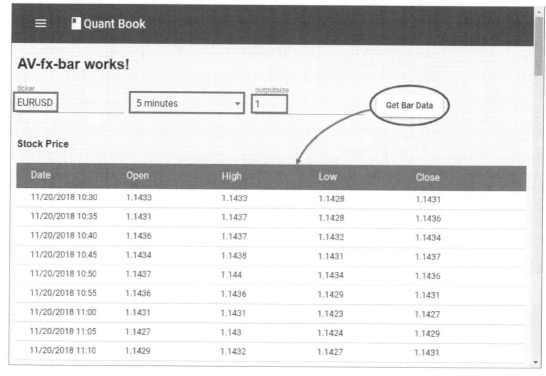

Fig.4-19. FX intraday data from Alpha Vantage.

Sector Performance Data

Here, we consider how to retrieve the sector performance data from Alpha Vantage in the Angular application. Before adding a method to the *market-data.service* for retrieving sector data from Alpha Vantage, we need to define a TypeScript data model for the performance data. Open the *market-data.model.ts* file and add a new class named *AvSectorPerf* as shown in the following code:

```
export class AvSectorPerf {
  constructor(
    public rank?: string,
    public communicationServices?: string,
    public consumerDiscretionary?: string,
    public consumerStaples?: string,
    public energy?: string,
    public financials?: string,
    public healthCare?: string,
    public industrials?: string,
    public informationTechnology?: string,
    public materials?: string,
    public utilities?: string,
  ) { }
}
```

This model corresponds to the C# *AvSectorPerf* class defined previously.

Next, we need to define a new method named *getAvSector* method in the *market-data.service.ts* class to send the request and process the response, as shown in the following code:

```
// market-data.service.ts file:
import { Inject } from '@angular/core';
import { HttpClient } from '@angular/common/http';
import { MarketData, MarketQuote, AvQuote, AvFxData, AvSectorPerf} from
  './market-data.model';

export class MarketDataRepository {

  // ... other properties omitted for brevity ...

  avSector: AvSectorPerf[] = [];
  private url;

  constructor(private http: HttpClient, @Inject('BASE_URL') baseUrl: string) {
    this.url = baseUrl;
  }

  // ... other methods omitted for breviry ...

  getAvSector() {
    this.http.get<AvSectorPerf[]>(this.url + 'api/avsector/perf')
      .subscribe(result => { this.avSector = result });
  }
}
```

The *getAvSector* method sends an HTTP request to a specified URL, which gets the sector performance data from Alpha Vantage.

Now, I will use an example to show you how to use this repository service to download the sector data from Alpha Vantage.

Run the following command in the command prompt window from the *ClientApp* folder:

ng g c chapter04/av-sector --module=app.module

This will generate a new component named *av-sector* in the *ClientApp/src/app/chapter04* folder. Open the component class file and replace its content with the following code:

```
// av-sector.component.ts file:
import { Component, OnInit } from '@angular/core';
import { MarketDataRepository } from '../../models/market-data.repository';
import { AvSectorPerf } from '../../models/market-data.model';

@Component({
  selector: 'app-av-sector',
  templateUrl: './av-sector.component.html',
  styleUrls: ['./av-sector.component.css']
})
export class AvSectorComponent implements OnInit {
  displayedCols = ['rank', 'service', 'desc', 'staple', 'energy', 'fin', 'health',
    'indu', 'it', 'material', 'util'];

  constructor(private repository: MarketDataRepository) { }
```

```
ngOnInit() {
  this.getSector();
}

get sector(): AvSectorPerf[] {
  return this.repository.avSector;
}

getSector() {
  this.repository.getAvSector();
}
}
```

The constructor has a *MarketDataService* parameter called *repository*, which is how dependencies are declared in an Angular app. The other addition in this class is a read-only property called *sector* that returns the value of the *MarketDataService* object's *avSector* property. The *getSector* method calls the *getAvSector* method defined in the *MarketDataService* class, which will update the *sector* property according to the user's input.

We need also to update the component's template with the following code listing:

```
// av-sector.component.html file:
<h2>
  AV-sector works!
</h2>
<button mat-raised-button (click)="getSector()">Get Sector Performance</button>

<div *ngIf="sector">
  <div *ngIf="sector.length>0">
    <h4>Sector Performance Data</h4>
    <mat-table [dataSource]="sector">
      <ng-container matColumnDef="rank">
        <mat-header-cell *matHeaderCellDef>Rank</mat-header-cell>
        <mat-cell *matCellDef="let item">{{item.rank}}</mat-cell>
      </ng-container>
      <ng-container matColumnDef="service">
        <mat-header-cell *matHeaderCellDef>Commu Services</mat-header-cell>
        <mat-cell *matCellDef="let item">{{item.communicationServices}}</mat-cell>
      </ng-container>
      <ng-container matColumnDef="desc">
        <mat-header-cell *matHeaderCellDef>Consumer Descretionary</mat-header-cell>
        <mat-cell *matCellDef="let item">{{item.consumerDiscretionary}}</mat-cell>
      </ng-container>
      <ng-container matColumnDef="staple">
        <mat-header-cell *matHeaderCellDef>Consumer Staples</mat-header-cell>
        <mat-cell *matCellDef="let item">{{item.consumerStaples}}</mat-cell>
      </ng-container>
      <ng-container matColumnDef="energy">
        <mat-header-cell *matHeaderCellDef>Energy</mat-header-cell>
        <mat-cell *matCellDef="let item">{{item.energy}}</mat-cell>
      </ng-container>
      <ng-container matColumnDef="fin">
        <mat-header-cell *matHeaderCellDef>Financials</mat-header-cell>
        <mat-cell *matCellDef="let item">{{item.financials}}</mat-cell>
      </ng-container>
      <ng-container matColumnDef="health">
```

```
      <mat-header-cell *matHeaderCellDef>Health Care</mat-header-cell>
      <mat-cell *matCellDef="let item">{{item.healthCare}}</mat-cell>
    </ng-container>
    <ng-container matColumnDef="indu">
      <mat-header-cell *matHeaderCellDef>Industrials</mat-header-cell>
      <mat-cell *matCellDef="let item">{{item.industrials}}</mat-cell>
    </ng-container>
    <ng-container matColumnDef="it">
      <mat-header-cell *matHeaderCellDef>Info Tech</mat-header-cell>
      <mat-cell *matCellDef="let item">{{item.informationTechnology}}</mat-cell>
    </ng-container>
    <ng-container matColumnDef="material">
      <mat-header-cell *matHeaderCellDef>Materials</mat-header-cell>
      <mat-cell *matCellDef="let item">{{item.materials}}</mat-cell>
    </ng-container>
    <ng-container matColumnDef="util">
      <mat-header-cell *matHeaderCellDef>Utilities</mat-header-cell>
      <mat-cell *matCellDef="let item">{{item.utilities}}</mat-cell>
    </ng-container>
    <mat-header-row *matHeaderRowDef="displayedCols"></mat-header-row>
    <mat-row *matRowDef="let row; columns: displayedCols;"></mat-row>
  </mat-table>
  </div>
</div>
```

Finally, we need to add a path for this new component to the *RouterModule* of the root module (i.e., the *app.module.ts* file):

```
{ path: 'chapter04/av-sector, component: AvSectorComponent },
```

Then add the corresponding URL link to the *home* and *nav-menu* components.

Saving the project and navigating to the */chapter04/av-sector* page produce the results shown in Fig.4-20.

Market Data from Quandl

Quandl is another open source website for financial data. The Quandl's database for stocks named WiKi EOD stock prices is probably the most reliable data source of this kind. It covers over 3000 stock names and includes dividends, splits, and adjustment in a single database. The stock EOD data from Yahoo Finance also includes a field called *Adjusted-Close*, but it does not have the adjusted fields for *Open*, *High*, *Low* and *Volume*. While the EOD stock price data from Quandl has all adjusted fields for *Open*, *High*, *Low*, *Close*, and *Volume*, which is very impressive and is very useful for back-testing your trading strategies.

However, as of April 11, 2013, Quandl no longer actively supported and updated the WiKi EOD and other free databases, even though Quandl will continue to host these free datasets. This means that you cannot develop trading strategies and make investment decision based on these databases. Nevertheless, these datasets are still useful resources for the purpose of research and backtesting.

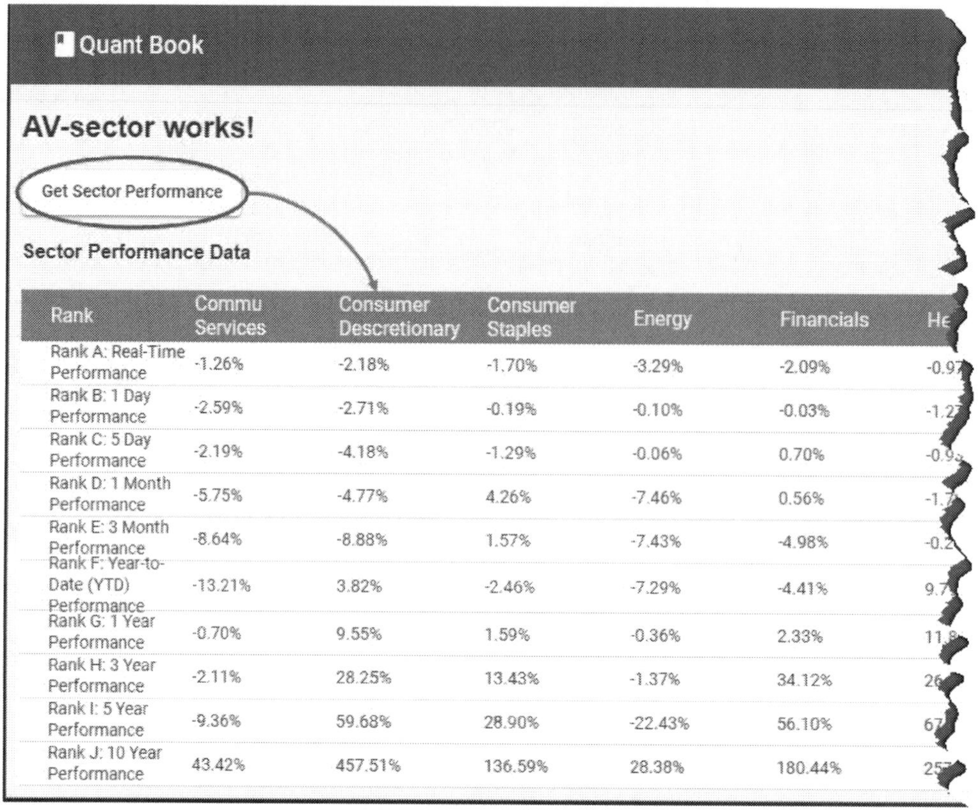

Rank	Commu Services	Consumer Descretionary	Consumer Staples	Energy	Financials	He
Rank A: Real-Time Performance	-1.26%	-2.18%	-1.70%	-3.29%	-2.09%	-0.97
Rank B: 1 Day Performance	-2.59%	-2.71%	-0.19%	-0.10%	-0.03%	-1.27
Rank C: 5 Day Performance	-2.19%	-4.18%	-1.29%	-0.06%	0.70%	-0.9
Rank D: 1 Month Performance	-5.75%	-4.77%	4.26%	-7.46%	0.56%	-1.7
Rank E: 3 Month Performance	-8.64%	-8.88%	1.57%	-7.43%	-4.98%	-0.2
Rank F: Year-to-Date (YTD) Performance	-13.21%	3.82%	-2.46%	-7.29%	-4.41%	9.7
Rank G: 1 Year Performance	-0.70%	9.55%	1.59%	-0.36%	2.33%	11.8
Rank H: 3 Year Performance	-2.11%	28.25%	13.43%	-1.37%	34.12%	26
Rank I: 5 Year Performance	-9.36%	59.68%	28.90%	-22.43%	56.10%	67
Rank J: 10 Year Performance	43.42%	457.51%	136.59%	28.38%	180.44%	25

Fig.4-20. Sector performance data from Alpha Vantage.

Create API Key Service

Like Alpha Vantage, Quandl API also requires an API key for using their RESTful API. You can follow the instruction of this link to sign up for your API key: https://docs.quandl.com/docs#section-authentication. After receiving the API key from Quandl, we can make it as a service, add this service to the dependency injection container, register it with the pipeline, and consume it in our application.

Open the *appsettings.json* file and add the highlighted code as shown in the follows:

```
{
  "Logging": {
    "LogLevel": {
      "Default": "Warning"
    }
  },
  "AllowedHosts": "*",
  "Data": {
    "Quant": {
      "ConnectionString":
        "Server=(localdb)\\mssqllocaldb;Database=QuantDb;Trusted_Connection
        =True;MultipleActiveResultSets=true"
    },
```

```
    "AlphaVantage": {
      "ApiKey": "your-av-api-key"
    },
    "Quandl": {
      "ApiKey": "your-quandl-api-key"
    }
  }
}
```

Please remember to replace the parameter of "*your-quandl-api-key*" with your own Quandl API key.

To access settings from the *appsettings.json*, we need to create a configuration class with a structure that matches a section in your configuration file. Add a C# class named *Quandl* to the *ApiKeySettings.cs* file in the *Quant/Models* folder with the following highlighted code snippet:

```
namespace Quant.Models
{
    public class ApiKeySettings
    {
        public class AlphaVantage
        {
            public string ApiKey { get; set; }
        }

        public class Quandl
        {
            public string ApiKey { get; set; }
        }
    }
}
```

The *Quandl* class contains only one property, *ApiKey*.

To register the API key as a service, add the following highlighted code snippet to the *Startup.cs* file:

```
// ... using statements omitted for brevity ...

namespace Quant
{
    public class Startup
    {
        public Startup(IConfiguration configuration)
        {
            Configuration = configuration;
        }

        public IConfiguration Configuration { get; }

        public void ConfigureServices(IServiceCollection services)
        {

            // ... other code omitted for brevity ...

            services.Configure<ApiKeySettings.AlphaVantage>(
                Configuration.GetSection("Data:AlphaVantage"));
            services.Configure<ApiKeySettings.Quandl>(
                Configuration.GetSection("Data:Quandl"));
```

```
    }

    // ... other methods omitted for brevity ...

  }
}
```

The *ConfigureServices* method adds the API key service to the service container, which makes it available in our application via dependency injection.

EOD Stock Data

In this section, I will show how to get historical stock EOD data from WIKI database. First, we need to install the NuGet package, *Quandl.NET*, which can be found from the URL at https://www.nuget.org/packages/Quandl.NET. You can install it from the Package Manager Console inside Visual Studio using the following command:

```
PM> Install-Package Quandl.NET -Version 1.2.1
```

The web service for Quandl API is similar to Yahoo Finance API. To add support for retrieving historical market data, we need to create a generic interface. Open the *StockData.cs* file in the *Quant/Models* folder. Add a class called *QuandlStockData* to this file with the following code:

```
public class QuandlStockData
{
    public string Ticker { get; set; }
    public DateTime Date { get; set; }
    public double Open { get; set; }
    public double High { get; set; }
    public double Low { get; set; }
    public double Close { get; set; }
    public double Volume { get; set; }
    public double OpenAdj { get; set; }
    public double HighAdj { get; set; }
    public double LowAdj { get; set; }
    public double CloseAdj { get; set; }
    public double VolumeAdj { get; set; }
    public double ExDividend { get; set; }
    public double SplitRatio { get; set; }
}
```

Next, add a new method named *GetQuandlStock* to the *MarketDataValuesController* in the *Controllers* folder. Here is the code listing for this method:

```
[Route("~/api/QuandlStock/{ticker}/{start}/{end}")]
[HttpGet]
public async Task<List<QuandlStockData>> GetQuandlStock(string ticker, string start,
    string end)
{
    var startDate = DateTime.Parse(start);
    var endDate = DateTime.Parse(end);
    var client = new QuandlClient(quandlKey.Value.ApiKey);
    var data = await client.Timeseries.GetDataAsync("WIKI", ticker,
        startDate: startDate, endDate: endDate);
```

```
var models = new List<QuandlStockData>();
foreach(var d in data.DatasetData.Data)
{
    models.Add(new QuandlStockData
    {
        Ticker = ticker,
        Date = DateTime.Parse(d[0].ToString()),
        Open = double.Parse(d[1].ToString()),
        High = double.Parse(d[2].ToString()),
        Low = double.Parse(d[3].ToString()),
        Close = double.Parse(d[4].ToString()),
        Volume = double.Parse(d[5].ToString()),
        ExDividend = double.Parse(d[6].ToString()),
        SplitRatio = double.Parse(d[7].ToString()),
        OpenAdj = double.Parse(d[8].ToString()),
        HighAdj = double.Parse(d[9].ToString()),
        LowAdj = double.Parse(d[10].ToString()),
        CloseAdj = double.Parse(d[11].ToString()),
        VolumeAdj = double.Parse(d[12].ToString())
    });
}
return models.OrderBy(d => d.Date).ToList();
}
```

Here, we define the router specifically using

[Route("~/api/QuandlStock/{ticker}/{start}/{end}")]

This means that an HTTP request should be sent to the **/api/quandlstock/{ticker}/{start}/{end}**. To test the new web service, run the *Quant* project, open a web browser, and request the following URL:

https://localhost:5001/api/quandlstock/ibm/2018-01-01/2018-03-01

This will produce the results shown in Fig.4-21.

Fig.4-21. Stock data from Quandl web service.

Stock Data in Angular

In this section, we consider how to add the web service for retrieving the historical stock data to the Angular application. Before adding a method to the *market-data.service* for retrieving stock data from Quandl, we need to define a TypeScript stock data model. Open the *market-data.model.ts* file and add a new class named *QuandlStockData* as shown in the following code:

```
export class QuandlStockData {
  constructor(
    public ticker: string,
    public date?: Date,
    public open?: number,
    public high?: number,
    public low?: number,
    public close?: number,
    public volume?: number,
    public exDividend?: number,
    public splitRatio?: number,
    public openAdj?: number,
    public highAdj?: number,
    public lowAdj?: number,
    public closeAdj?: number,
    public volumeAdj?: number,
  ) { }
}
```

This class corresponds to the C# *QuandlStockData* class defined in the preceding section.

To add support for retrieving historical stock data from Quandl to the Angular application, we need to add a method named *getQuandlStock* shown in the following code listing to the *market-data.service.ts* class in the *ClientApp/src/app/models* folder so that it can send GET requests to the web service:

```
// market-data.repository.ts file:
import { Inject } from '@angular/core';
import { HttpClient } from '@angular/common/http';
import { MarketData, MarketQuote, AvQuote, AvFxData, AvSectorPerf, QuandlStockData }
  from './market-data.model';
export class MarketDataRepository {
  // ... other properties omitted for brevity ...

  quandlStock: QuandlStockData[] = [];
  private url;

  constructor(private http: HttpClient, @Inject('BASE_URL') baseUrl: string) {
    this.url = baseUrl;
  }

  // ... other methods omitted for brevity ...

  getQuandlStock(ticker: string, start: string, end: string) {
    let url1 = this.url + 'api/quandlstock/' + ticker + '/' + start + '/' + end;
    this.http.get<QuandlStockData[]>(url1).subscribe(result => {
      this.quandlStock = result });
  }
}
```

The *getQuandlStock* method accepts ticker and date range parameters, and sends an HTTP request to a specified URL, which gets the stock data from Quandl.

Now, I will use an example to show you how to use this repository service to download the market data from Quandl.

Run the following command in the command prompt window from the *ClientApp* folder:

```
ng g c chapter04/quandl-stock --module=app.module
```

This will generate a new component named *quandl-stock* in the *ClientApp/src/app/chapter04* folder. Open the component class file and replace its content with the following code:

```
// quandl-stock.component.ts file:
import { Component, OnInit } from '@angular/core';
import { MarketDataService } from '../../models/market-data.service';
import { QuandlStockData } from '../../models/market-data.model';

@Component({
  selector: 'app-quandl-stock',
  templateUrl: './quandl-stock.component.html',
  styleUrls: ['./quandl-stock.component.css']
})
export class QuandlStockComponent implements OnInit {
  ticker = 'IBM';
  startDate: string = '2000-01-01';
  endDate: string = '2000-03-01';
  displayedCols = ['date', 'open', 'high', 'low', 'close', 'volume', 'openAdj',
  'highAdj', 'lowAdj', 'closeAdj', 'volumeAdj'];

  constructor(private repository: MarketDataService) { }

  ngOnInit() {
    this.getStock(this.ticker, this.startDate, this.endDate);
  }

  get stock(): QuandlStockData[] {
    return this.repository.quandlStock;
  }

  getStock(ticker: string, start: string, end: string) {
    this.repository.getQuandlStock(ticker, start, end);
  }
}
```

The constructor has a *MarketDataService* parameter called *repository*, which is how dependencies are declared in an Angular app. The other addition in this class is a read-only property called *stock* that returns the value of the *MarketDataService* object's *quandlStock* property. The *getStock* method calls the *getQuandlStock* method defined in the *MarketDataService* class, which will update the *stock* property according to the user's input.

We need also to update the component's template with the following code:

```
//quandl-stock.component.html file:
<h2>
  Quandl-stock works!
</h2>
```

```html
<mat-form-field>
  <input matInput placeholder="ticker" [(ngModel)]="ticker" name="ticker">
</mat-form-field>
<mat-form-field>
  <input matInput placeholder="Start Date" [(ngModel)]="startDate" name="startDate">
</mat-form-field>
<mat-form-field>
  <input matInput placeholder="End Date" [(ngModel)]="endDate" name="endDate">
</mat-form-field>

<button mat-raised-button (click)="getStock(ticker,startDate, endDate)">Get Stock
Data</button>

<div *ngIf="stock">
  <div *ngIf="stock.length>0">
    <h4>Stock Price</h4>
    <mat-table [dataSource]="stock">
      <ng-container matColumnDef="date">
        <mat-header-cell *matHeaderCellDef>Date</mat-header-cell>
        <mat-cell *matCellDef="let item">{{item.date |
          date: 'MM/dd/yyyy'}}</mat-cell>
      </ng-container>
      <ng-container matColumnDef="open">
        <mat-header-cell *matHeaderCellDef>Open</mat-header-cell>
        <mat-cell *matCellDef="let item">{{item.open}}</mat-cell>
      </ng-container>
      <ng-container matColumnDef="high">
        <mat-header-cell *matHeaderCellDef>High</mat-header-cell>
        <mat-cell *matCellDef="let item">{{item.high}}</mat-cell>
      </ng-container>
      <ng-container matColumnDef="low">
        <mat-header-cell *matHeaderCellDef>Low</mat-header-cell>
        <mat-cell *matCellDef="let item">{{item.low}}</mat-cell>
      </ng-container>
      <ng-container matColumnDef="close">
        <mat-header-cell *matHeaderCellDef>Close</mat-header-cell>
        <mat-cell *matCellDef="let item">{{item.close}}</mat-cell>
      </ng-container>
      <ng-container matColumnDef="volume">
        <mat-header-cell *matHeaderCellDef>Volume</mat-header-cell>
        <mat-cell *matCellDef="let item">{{item.volume}}</mat-cell>
      </ng-container>
      <ng-container matColumnDef="openAdj">
        <mat-header-cell *matHeaderCellDef>Open Adj</mat-header-cell>
        <mat-cell *matCellDef="let item">{{item.openAdj | number: '1.2-2'}}
        </mat-cell>
      </ng-container>
      <ng-container matColumnDef="highAdj">
        <mat-header-cell *matHeaderCellDef>High Adj</mat-header-cell>
        <mat-cell *matCellDef="let item">{{item.highAdj | number: '1.2-2'}}
        </mat-cell>
      </ng-container>
      <ng-container matColumnDef="lowAdj">
        <mat-header-cell *matHeaderCellDef>Low Adj</mat-header-cell>
        <mat-cell *matCellDef="let item">{{item.lowAdj | number: '1.2-2'}}
```

```
        </mat-cell>
      </ng-container>
      <ng-container matColumnDef="closeAdj">
        <mat-header-cell *matHeaderCellDef>Close Adj</mat-header-cell>
        <mat-cell *matCellDef="let item">{{item.closeAdj | number: '1.2-2'}}
        </mat-cell>
      </ng-container>
      <ng-container matColumnDef="volumeAdj">
        <mat-header-cell *matHeaderCellDef>Volume Adj</mat-header-cell>
        <mat-cell *matCellDef="let item">{{item.volumeAdj}}</mat-cell>
      </ng-container>

      <mat-header-row *matHeaderRowDef="displayedCols"></mat-header-row>
      <mat-row *matRowDef="let row; columns: displayedCols;"></mat-row>
    </mat-table>
  </div>
</div>
```

This template is very similar to that used in retrieving stock data from Yahoo Finance.

Finally, we need to add a path for this new component to the *RouterModule* of the root module (i.e., the *app.module.ts* file):

```
{ path: 'chapter04/quandl-stock, component: QuandlStockComponent },
```

Then add the corresponding URL link to the *home* and *nav-menu* components.

Saving the project and navigating to the */chapter04/quandl-stock* page produce the results shown in Fig.4-22. Here, we download the stock data for MSFT from 1/1/2000 to 3/1/2000.

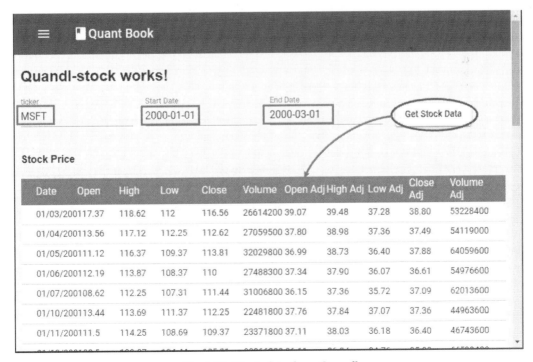

Fig.4-22. Stock data from Quandl.

You can see that the stock prices and volume are different from the adjusted stock prices and volume because the adjusted quantities take the stock split and dividend into account.

ISDA Rates from Markit

Interest rates play an important role in pricing fixed-income instruments such as bonds and CDS (credit default swap). In particular, ISDA (International Swaps and Derivatives Association) has set up a standard CDS model. In order to value the CDS contract consistently, you must use standardized inputs into the ISDA CDS model. Markit has published the standard interest rates daily for major global currencies in the XML format, including USD, JPY, EUR, etc.

Let us take USD interest rate as an example. The body of the XML includes the interest rates from the indicated sources for the following maturities, as shown in Fig. 4-23.

Maturity	USD Source	Day Count/Accual Convention
1MO	LIBOR	ACT/360
2MO	LIBOR	ACT/360
3MO	LIBOR	ACT/360
6MO	LIBOR	ACT/360
1Y	SWAP RATE	ACT/360
2Y	SWAP RATE	30/360 Semi-Annual
3Y	SWAP RATE	30/360 Semi-Annual
4Y	SWAP RATE	30/360 Semi-Annual
5Y	SWAP RATE	30/360 Semi-Annual
6Y	SWAP RATE	30/360 Semi-Annual
7Y	SWAP RATE	30/360 Semi-Annual
8Y	SWAP RATE	30/360 Semi-Annual
9Y	SWAP RATE	30/360 Semi-Annual
10Y	SWAP RATE	30/360 Semi-Annual
12Y	SWAP RATE	30/360 Semi-Annual
15Y	SWAP RATE	30/360 Semi-Annual
20Y	SWAP RATE	30/360 Semi-Annual
25Y	SWAP RATE	30/360 Semi-Annual
30Y	SWAP RATE	30/360 Semi-Annual

Fig.4-23. ISDA standard interest rate format for USD.

In fact, Markit provides the interest rates in a ZIP file. We need to first extract the ZIP file and then process the XML data. In the following section, I will show you how to implement the ISDA interest rate API.

ISDA Interest Rate API

First, we need to create a generic object that holds the interest rate data. Add an *IsdaHelper* class to the *Quant/Models* directory. Add a C# class named *IsdaRate* to the *IsdaHelper.cs* file. Here is the code for this class:

```
public class IsdaRate
{
    public string Currency { get; set; }
    public string EffectiveAsOf { get; set; }
```

```
public string BadDayConvention { get; set; }
public string Calendar { get; set; }
public DateTime SnapTime { get; set; }
public string SpotDate { get; set; }
public string Maturity { get; set; }
public string DayCountConvention { get; set; }
public string FixedDayCountConvention { get; set; }
public string FloatingPaymentFrequency { get; set; }
public string FixedPaymentFrequency { get; set; }
public string Tenor { get; set; }
public string Rate { get; set; }
}
```

The properties defined in this class correspond to the fields of the interest rate in the XML document. Once we have the generic object of how to hold the interest rate data, we need to get the data from Markit and process these data. The *IsdaHelper* class will perform this task:

```
using System;
using System.Collections.Generic;
using System.IO;
using System.IO.Compression;
using System.Net;
using System.Xml.Linq;

namespace Quant.Models
{
    public static class IsdaHelper
    {
        public static List<IsdaRate> GetIsdaRates(string currency,
            string date_yyyyMMdd)
        {
            string url = "https://www.markit.com/news/
                InterestRates_[ccy]_[date].zip";
            url = url.Replace("[ccy]", currency.ToUpper());
            url = url.Replace("[date]", date_yyyyMMdd);
            List<IsdaRate> rates = new List<IsdaRate>();
            using(WebClient wc = new WebClient())
            {
                try
                {
                    var data = wc.DownloadData(url);
                    var stream = new MemoryStream(data);
                    using(ZipArchive archive = new ZipArchive(stream))
                    {
                        foreach(ZipArchiveEntry entry in archive.Entries)
                        {
                            if(entry.FullName.EndsWith(".xml",
                                StringComparison.OrdinalIgnoreCase))
                            {
                                XDocument doc = XDocument.Load(entry.Open());
                                rates = ProcessIadaRates(doc, currency);
                            }
                        }
                    }
                }
                catch { }
```

```
        }
        return rates;
}

private static List<IsdaRate> ProcessIadaRates(XDocument doc,
    string currency)
{
    List<IsdaRate> rates = new List<IsdaRate>();
    XElement asof = doc.Root.Element("effectiveasof");
    XElement badday = doc.Root.Element("baddayconvention");

    //Process deposits:
    XElement deposits = doc.Root.Element("deposits");
    string dayConvention = deposits.Element("daycountconvention").Value;
    string calendar = deposits.Element("calendars")
        .Element("calendar").Value;
    string[] ss = deposits.Element("snaptime").Value.Split('T');
    string ts = ss[0] + " " + ss[1].Split('Z')[0];
    DateTime snapDate = Convert.ToDateTime(ts);
    string spotDate = deposits.Element("spotdate").Value;
    foreach (var e in deposits.Elements())
    {
        if (e.Name.ToString() == "curvepoint")
        {
            rates.Add(new IsdaRate
            {
                Currency = currency,
                EffectiveAsOf = asof.Value,
                BadDayConvention = badday.Value,
                Calendar = calendar,
                SnapTime = snapDate,
                SpotDate = spotDate,
                Maturity = e.Element("maturitydate").Value,
                DayCountConvention = dayConvention,
                Tenor = e.Element("tenor").Value,
                Rate = e.Element("parrate").Value
            });
        }
    }

    //Process swaps:
    XElement swaps = doc.Root.Element("swaps");
    dayConvention = swaps.Element("floatingdaycountconvention").Value;
    calendar = swaps.Element("calendars").Element("calendar").Value;
    string fixDayConvention =
        swaps.Element("fixeddaycountconvention").Value;
    ss = swaps.Element("snaptime").Value.Split('T');
    ts = ss[0] + " " + ss[1].Split('Z')[0];
    snapDate = Convert.ToDateTime(ts);
    spotDate = swaps.Element("spotdate").Value;
    string floatPay = swaps.Element("floatingpaymentfrequency").Value;
    string fixPay = swaps.Element("fixedpaymentfrequency").Value;
    foreach (var e in swaps.Elements())
    {
        if (e.Name.ToString() == "curvepoint")
```

```
                {
                    rates.Add(new IsdaRate
                    {
                        Currency = currency,
                        EffectiveAsOf = asof.Value,
                        BadDayConvention = badday.Value,
                        Calendar = calendar,
                        SnapTime = snapDate,
                        SpotDate = spotDate,
                        Maturity = e.Element("maturitydate").Value,
                        DayCountConvention = dayConvention,
                        FixedDayCountConvention = fixDayConvention,
                        FloatingPaymentFrequency = floatPay,
                        FixedPaymentFrequency = fixPay,
                        Tenor = e.Element("tenor").Value,
                        Rate = e.Element("parrate").Value
                    });
                }
            }
            return rates;
        }
    }
}
```

The *GetIsdaRates* method takes the currency and date as input parameters, and downloads the interest rate data. First, we download the ZIP file of interest rates from Markit and convert it into a memory stream; then use the .NET Core's *ZipArchive* utility to extract the ZIP file into the original XML document; finally process the XML file and convert it into an *IsdaRate* collection using a private method named *ProcessIsdaRates*.

To add web service support for ISDA interest rates, we need to add a GET method named *GetIsdaRate* to the *MarketDataValuesController.cs* file in the *Controllers* folder. Here is the code listing for this method:

```
[Route("~/api/IsdaRate/{currency}/{date}")]
[HttpGet]
public List<IsdaRate> GetIsdaRate(string currency, string date)
{
    return IsdaHelper.GetIsdaRates(currency, date);
}
```

Here, we define the router specifically using

[Route("~/api/IsdaRate/{currency}/{date}")]

This means that an HTTP request should be sent to the **/api/isdarate/{currency}/{date}**. To test the new web service, run the *Quant* project, open a web browser, and request the following URL:

https://localhost:5001/api/isdarate/usd/20181121

This will produce the results shown in Fig.4-24.

Fig.4-24. Interest rates from web service.

ISDA Interest Rates in Angular

In this section, we consider how to add the web service for retrieving ISDA interest rate data to the Angular application. Before adding a method to the *market-data.service* for retrieving interest rate data from Markit, we need to define a TypeScript stock data model. Open the *market-data.model.ts* file and add a new class named *IsdaRateData* as shown in the following code listing:

```
export class IsdaRateData {
  constructor(
    public currency?: string,
    public effectiveAsOf?: string,
    public calendar?: string,
    public snapTime?: Date,
    public spotDate?: string,
    public maturity?: string,
    public dayCountConvention?: string,
    public fixedDayCountConvention?: string,
    public floatingPaymentFrequency?: string,
    public fixedPaymentFrequency?: string,
    public tenor?: string,
    public rate?: string
  ) { }
}
```

This class corresponds to the C# *IsdaRate* class defined in the preceding section.

To add support for retrieving interest rate data from Markit to the Angular application, we need to add a method named *getIsdaRate* shown in the following code to the *market-data.service.ts* class in the *ClientApp/src/app/models* folder so that it can send GET requests to the web service:

```
// market-data.service.ts file:
import { Inject } from '@angular/core';
import { HttpClient } from '@angular/common/http';
```

```
import { MarketData, MarketQuote, AvQuote, AvFxData, AvSectorPerf, QuandlStockData,
   IsdaRateData } from './market-data.model';
export class MarketDataRepository {
  // ... other properties omitted for brevity ...

  isdaRate: IsdaRateData[] = [];
  private url;

  constructor(private http: HttpClient, @Inject('BASE_URL') baseUrl: string) {
    this.url = baseUrl;
  }

  // ... other methods omitted for brevity ...

  getIsdaRate(currency: string, date: string) {
    let url1 = this.url + 'api/isdarate/' + currency + '/' + date;
    this.http.get<IsdaRateData[]>(url1).subscribe(result =>
      { this.isdaRate = result });
  }
}
```

The *getIsdaRate* method accepts *currency* and *date* parameters, and sends an HTTP request to a specified URL, which gets the interest rate data from Markit.

Now, I will use an example to show you how to use this repository service to download the interest rate data from Markit.

Run the following command in the command prompt window from the *ClientApp* folder:

ng g c chapter04/isda --module=app.module

This will generate a new component named *isda* in the *ClientApp/src/app/chapter04* folder. Open the component class file and replace its content with the following code:

```
// isda.component.ts file:
import { Component, OnInit } from '@angular/core';
import { MarketDataService } from '../../models/market-data.service';
import { IsdaRateData } from '../../models/market-data.model';

@Component({
  selector: 'app-isda',
  templateUrl: './isda.component.html',
  styleUrls: ['./isda.component.css']
})
export class IsdaComponent implements OnInit {
  currency: string = 'USD';
  date: string = '20181120';
  displayedCols = ['cur', 'snap', 'mat', 'dayCount', 'fixedDay', 'tenor', 'rate'];

  constructor(private repository: MarketDataService) { }

  ngOnInit() {
    this.getRate(this.currency, this.date);
  }

  get rate(): IsdaRateData[] {
    return this.repository.isdaRate;
```

```
  }

  getRate(currency: string, date: string) {
    this.repository.getIsdaRate(currency, date);
  }
}
```

The constructor has a *MarketDataService* parameter called *repository*, which is how dependencies are declared in an Angular app. The other addition in this class is a read-only property called *rate* that returns the value of the *MarketDataService* object's *isdaRate* property. The *getRate* method calls the *getIsdaRate* method defined in the *MarketDataService* class, which will update the *rate* property according to the user's input.

We need also to update the component's template with the following code:

```html
// isda.component.html file:
<h2>
  Isda works!
</h2>

<mat-form-field>
  <input matInput placeholder="currency" [(ngModel)]="currency" name="currency">
</mat-form-field>
<mat-form-field>
  <input matInput placeholder="date" [(ngModel)]="date" name="date">
</mat-form-field>

<button mat-raised-button (click)="getRate(currency,date)">Get ISDA Rate</button>

<div *ngIf="rate">
  <div *ngIf="rate.length>0">
    <h4>ISDA Rate</h4>
    <mat-table [dataSource]="rate">
      <ng-container matColumnDef="cur">
        <mat-header-cell *matHeaderCellDef>Currency</mat-header-cell>
        <mat-cell *matCellDef="let item">{{item.currency}}</mat-cell>
      </ng-container>
      <ng-container matColumnDef="snap">
        <mat-header-cell *matHeaderCellDef>Snap Time</mat-header-cell>
        <mat-cell *matCellDef="let item">{{item.snapTime |
          date: 'MM/dd/yyyy'}}</mat-cell>
      </ng-container>
      <ng-container matColumnDef="mat">
        <mat-header-cell *matHeaderCellDef>Maturity</mat-header-cell>
        <mat-cell *matCellDef="let item">{{item.maturity}}</mat-cell>
      </ng-container>
      <ng-container matColumnDef="dayCount">
        <mat-header-cell *matHeaderCellDef>Day Count</mat-header-cell>
        <mat-cell *matCellDef="let item">{{item.dayCountConvention}}</mat-cell>
      </ng-container>
      <ng-container matColumnDef="fixedDay">
        <mat-header-cell *matHeaderCellDef>Fixed Day Count</mat-header-cell>
        <mat-cell *matCellDef="let item">{{item.fixedDayCountConvention}}</mat-cell>
      </ng-container>
      <ng-container matColumnDef="tenor">
        <mat-header-cell *matHeaderCellDef>Tenor</mat-header-cell>
```

```
      <mat-cell *matCellDef="let item">{{item.tenor}}</mat-cell>
    </ng-container>
    <ng-container matColumnDef="rate">
      <mat-header-cell *matHeaderCellDef>Rate</mat-header-cell>
      <mat-cell *matCellDef="let item">{{item.rate}}</mat-cell>
    </ng-container>
    <mat-header-row *matHeaderRowDef="displayedCols"></mat-header-row>
    <mat-row *matRowDef="let row; columns: displayedCols;"></mat-row>
  </mat-table>
</div>
</div>
```

This template is very similar to that used in retrieving stock data from Yahoo Finance.

Finally, we need to add a path for this new component to the *RouterModule* of the root module (i.e., the *app.module.ts* file):

```
{ path: 'chapter04/isda, component: IsdaComponent },
```

Then add the corresponding URL link to the *home* and *nav-menu* components.

Saving the project and navigating to the */chapter04/isda* page produce the results shown in Fig.4-25. Here, we download the interest rate data for EUR on 11/20/2018.

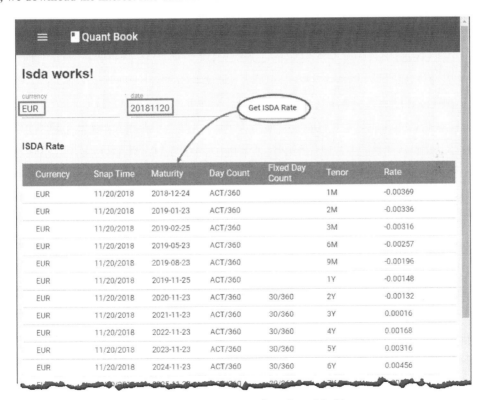

Fig.4-25. Interest rate data from Markit.

You can play around with this example by changing the currency (say USD, JPY, GBP, CAD, AUD, etc.) and date fields, and see how the interest rates change accordingly.

Chapter 5
Data Visualization

A picture is worth a thousand words. Charts and graphics play an important role in every business application. They make data easier to understand, interest to reports, and have wide applications in our daily life. With the use of advanced data visualization tools in finance, you can translate broad and deep sets of data into easily digested, actionable intelligence for your trading business.

In finance industry, you deal with data all over the place: in databases, in spreadsheets, in reports from various systems. However, if you can really see the data on charts rather than looking at endless rows and columns of numbers, you begin to comprehend what is going on much faster.

Previously, I have published several books on .NET chart programming, including *"Practical C# Charts and Graphics"*, *"Practical WPF Charts and Graphics"*, *"Practical .NET Chart Development and Applications"*, and *"Practical Cross-Platform Charts and Graphics with ASP.NET Core MVC"*. Those books show you how to use C#, WinForms, WPF, and ASP.NET Core to create your own charts and graphics, ranging from simple two-dimensional (2D) line plots to complicated three-dimensional (3D) surface graphs. In my work, I have extensively used these in-house chart tools based on the libraries included in my books.

Recently, we released a graphics playground named Gincker Graphics (https://gincker.com/graphics). With this playground, you can create a variety of charts and graphics, ranging from simple to sophisticated, just by typing in a mathematic formula, pasting a dataset, or uploading a data file; you do not need to write a single line of code or relay on any special software package. It converts different chart and graphics applications into templates and implements a common interface and standardized input/output format by encapsulating all the programming details internally. Gincker Graphics allows you to save your work into *gincker* – a unique URL link, which can be used to regenerate, manipulate, modify, and customize charts and graphics. Here are some charts and graphics created using this playground: https://gincker.com/Marketplace/FreeProductIndex and https://gincker.com/Marketplace/ProductIndex. This playground will be useful for prototyping your data visualization applications.

In this chapter, I will provide introduction to chart development for data visualization in ASP.NET Core Angular single-page applications. Instead of creating your own charting package from scratch, here we will go with a client-side JavaScript charting library named ECharts. There are many client-side JavaScript charting libraries, including HighCharts, Chartist, Chart.js, Google Charts API, etc. Any of these packages will work as long as it provides features you need in your applications.

ECharts, developed by Baidu, is an open-sourced, web-based, cross-platform framework that supports rapid construction of interactive data visualization. It has the most complete list of chart types, including

3D charts, globe visualization, and WebGL acceleration. It provides an awesome tool for manipulating data once it is charted because its unique drag-recalculate feature allows you to drag and drop sections of data from one chart to another and have the charts recalculate in real-time. ECharts supports visualization for big data – it can instantly plot up to 200,000 data points on a chart based on a unique rendering approach called ZRender, a lightweight canvas made specifically for ECharts. Furthermore, there is an Angular directive binding for ECharts, meaning that you can use ECharts in your Angular applications directly without any concerns.

In the following sections, I will show you how to use the ECharts library to create different types of charts, including line, area, bar, pie, polar, stock, and real-time charts.

Line Charts

The most basic and useful type of chart is a simple 2D line chart of numerical data. In this section, I illustrate how to create such a simple chart in an ASP.NET Core Angular application using ECharts.

Install ECharts package

Open the *package.json* file in the *ClientApp* folder and add the following highlighted statement to it:

```
// package.json file:
{
  "name": "Quant",
  "version": "0.0.0",
  "scripts": {
    "ng": "ng",
    "start": "ng serve",
    "build": "ng build",
    "build:ssr": "ng run Quant:server:dev",
    "test": "ng test",
    "lint": "ng lint",
    "e2e": "ng e2e"
  },
  "private": true,
  "dependencies": {

    // ... other dependencies omitted for brevity ...

    "echarts": "4.2.0-rc.2",
    "echarts-gl": "1.1.1",
    "ngx-echarts": "4.0.1",
    "@types/echarts": "4.1.3",
    "angular2-draggable": "2.1.8",
  },
  "devDependencies": {
    "@angular-devkit/build-angular": "^0.12.0",
    "@angular/cli": "^7.2.1",

    // ... other dependencies omitted for brevity ...

  },
  "optionalDependencies": {
```

```
    "node-sass": "^4.9.0",
    "protractor": "~5.3.0",
    "ts-node": "~5.0.1",
    "tslint": "~5.9.1"
  }
}
```

Note that here we add five packages: *echarts* is the standard ECharts package that includes commonly used chart types; *echarts-gl* is an extension pack of ECharts that provides 3D plots and WebGL acceleration; *ngx-echarts* is an Angular directive for ECharts; *@types/echarts* is TypeScript definitions for ECharts; and *angular2-draggable* provides draggable and resizable capabilities for ECharts.

Next, open the *app.module.ts* file in the *ClientApp/src/app* folder to register the ECharts module, as highlighted in the following code snippet:

```
//app.module.ts file:
import { BrowserModule } from '@angular/platform-browser';
import { NgModule } from '@angular/core';

// ... other imports omitted for brevity ...

import { NgxEchartsModule } from 'ngx-echarts';
import { AngularDraggableModule } from 'angular2-draggable';

@NgModule({
  declarations: [
    AppComponent,

    // ... other declarations omitted for brevity ...

  ],
  imports: [

    // ... other imports omitted for brevity ...

    NgxEchartsModule,
    AngularDraggableModule,
    RouterModule.forRoot([
      { path: 'chapter01/counter', component: CounterComponent },
      { path: 'chapter01/fetch-data', component: FetchDataComponent },

      // ... other paths omitted for brevity ...

      { path: '', component: HomeComponent, pathMatch: 'full' }
    ])
  ],
  providers: [
    Repository,
    MarketDataRepository
  ],
  bootstrap: [AppComponent],
  entryComponents: [StockDeleteDialogComponent]
})
export class AppModule { }
```

Open the *main.ts* in *ClientApp/src* folder to add a reference for the *echarts-gl* package:

```
// main.ts file:
import { enableProdMode } from '@angular/core';
import { platformBrowserDynamic } from '@angular/platform-browser-dynamic';

import { AppModule } from './app/app.module';
import { environment } from './environments/environment';

import 'hammerjs';
import 'echarts-gl';

export function getBaseUrl() {
  return document.getElementsByTagName('base')[0].href;
}

const providers = [
  { provide: 'BASE_URL', useFactory: getBaseUrl, deps: [] }
];

if (environment.production) {
  enableProdMode();
}

platformBrowserDynamic(providers).bootstrapModule(AppModule)
  .catch(err => console.log(err));
```

Now, we have set up the environment for ECharts, and we are ready to use this package to create various charts in our ASP.NET Core Angular applications.

Simple Line Charts

It is easy to use the ECharts package to create a simple 2D *X-Y* line chart. Run the following command in the command prompt window from the *ClientApp* folder:

ng g c chapter05/chart-line --module=app.module

This will generate a new component named *chart-line* in the *ClientApp/src/app/chapter05* folder. Run the following command to generate another component:

ng g c chapter05/chart-line/simple-line --module=app.module

This will generate a new component named *simple-line* in the *ClientApp/src/app /chapter05/chart-line* folder. Open the *simple-line* component class file and replace its content with the following code:

```
//simple-line.component.ts file:
import { Component, OnInit } from '@angular/core';

@Component({
  selector: 'app-simple-line',
  templateUrl: './simple-line.component.html',
  styleUrls: ['./simple-line.component.css']
})
export class SimpleLineComponent implements OnInit {
  options: any;

  constructor() { }
```

```
ngOnInit() {
  const data = [];

  for (let i = 0; i < 50; i++) {
    const x = i / 5.0;
    data.push([x, Math.sin(x)]);
  }

  this.options = {
    title: {
      text: 'Simple Line Chart',
      left: 'center'
    },
    tooltip: {
      trigger: 'axis',
      axisPointer: {
        type: 'cross'
      }
    },
    xAxis: {
      type: 'value',
      name: 'X Value',
      nameLocation: 'center',
      nameGap: '30',
      axisLine: { onZero: false }
    },
    yAxis: {
      type: 'value',
      name: 'Y Data',
      nameLocation: 'center',
      nameGap: '50'
    },
    series: [{
      name: 'line',
      type: 'line',
      data: data
    }],
  };
}
}
```

Note that ECharts uses an all-in-one JSON formatted *options* to declare the components, styles, data, and interactions, resulting in a logic-less and stateless mode. The main advantage of JSON format lies in that it is safe to store, transmit, and execute. For our simple line chart example, we first generate the data using a sine function and then declare the *options* where we set the *title*, *axes*, and *series*. The *series* field can contain one or more series of datasets and their chart types. Here, we set the *type* to '*line*', meaning that we want to create a line chart. The simple-line component exposes only one property: *options*, which will be bound to a DOM element in the template.

We need also to update the *simple-line* component's template with the following code:

```
//simple-line.component.html file:
<div echarts [options]="options" style="padding:30px"></div>
```

This template is so simple and only consists of a single line of code. It simply binds the *options* directive to the *options* property defined in the component class.

Now, open the *chart-line.component.html* file in the *ClientApp/src/app/chapter05/chart-line* folder and replace its content with the following code:

```
// chart-line.component.html file:
<h2>
  Chart-line works!
</h2>
<mat-tab-group>
  <mat-tab label="Simple Line">
    <app-simple-line></app-simple-line>
  </mat-tab>
</mat-tab-group>
```

Here, we simply add the directive for the *simple-line* component to a *mat-tab* control.

Finally, we need to add a path for this new component to the *RouterModule* of the root module (i.e., the *app.module.ts* file):

```
{ path: 'chapter05/chart-line, component: ChartLineComponent },
```

Then add the corresponding URL link to the *home* and *nav-menu* components.

Saving the project and navigating to the */chapter05/chart-line* page produce the results shown in Fig.5-1. You can interact with the chart by hovering over the line, which will display the data value.

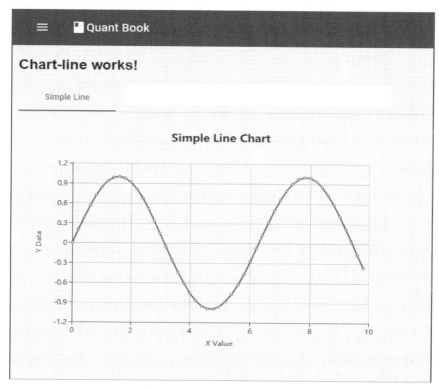

Fig.5-1. Simple 2D line chart.

Multiple-Line Charts

It is also easy to create a chart with multiple lines and legend. Run the following command in the command prompt window from the *ClientApp* folder:

```
ng g c chapter05/chart-line/multiple-lines --module=app.module
```

This will generate a new component named *multiple-lines* in the *ClientApp/src/app/chapter05/chart-line* folder. Open the component class file and replace its content with the following code:

```typescript
// multiple-lines.component.ts file:
import { Component, OnInit } from '@angular/core';

@Component({
  selector: 'app-multiple-lines',
  templateUrl: './multiple-lines.component.html',
  styleUrls: ['./multiple-lines.component.css']
})
export class MultipleLinesComponent implements OnInit {
  options: any;

  constructor() { }

  ngOnInit() {
    const data1 = [];
    const data2 = [];
    const data3 = [];

    for (let i = 0; i < 50; i++) {
      const x = i / 5.0;
      data1.push([x, Math.sin(x)]);
      data2.push([x, Math.cos(x)]);
      data3.push([x, Math.sin(x) * Math.sin(x)]);
    }

    this.options = {
      legend: {
        top: '8%',
        left: '10%',
      },
      title: {
        text: 'Multi-Line Chart',
        left: 'center'
      },
      tooltip: {
        trigger: 'axis',
        axisPointer: {
          type: 'cross'
        },
        backgroundColor: 'rgba(120, 120, 120, 0.9)',
        borderWidth: 1,
        borderColor: '#aaa',
        padding: 10,
        textStyle: {
          color: 'white'
        }
```

```
          },
          xAxis: {
            type: 'value',
            name: 'X Value',
            nameLocation: 'center',
            nameGap: '30',
            axisLine: { onZero: false }
          },
          yAxis: {
            type: 'value',
            name: 'Y Data',
            nameLocation: 'center',
            nameGap: '50'
          },
          series: [{
            name: 'sine',
            type: 'line',
            data: data1,
            symbol: 'circle',
            symbolSize: 8
          },
          {
            name: 'cosine',
            type: 'line',
            data: data2,
            symbol: 'diamond',
            symbolSize: 8
          },
          {
            name: 'sine^2',
            type: 'line',
            data: data3,
            symbol: 'triangle',
            symbolSize: 8
          }]
        };
      }
    }
```

This component class is very similar to that used in the preceding example, except that here we create three data arrays, representing three line curves. We also add a *legend* field, which shows symbol, color, and name of different series. ECharts allows you to click legend to toggle displaying series in the chart. The *legend* field would automatically collect from *series.name*. It also includes a *data* array field that allows you to manually specify an array item (usually a *name* representing a series).

The series contains an array of items, representing different line curves. For each series, we specify different *symbol* and *symbolSize*.

We need also to update the component's template with the following code listing:

```
// multiple-lines.component.html file:
<div echarts [options]="options" style="padding:30px"></div>
```

This template is also very simple and only consists of a single line of code. It simply binds the *options* directive to the *options* property defined in the component class.

Now, open the *chart-line.component.html* file in the *ClientApp/src/app/chapter05/chart-line* folder and add the highlighted code snippet to it:

```
// chart-line.component.html file:
<h2>
  Chart-line works!
</h2>

<mat-tab-group>
  <mat-tab label="Simple Line">
    <app-simple-line></app-simple-line>
  </mat-tab>
  <mat-tab label="multiple Lines">
    <app-multiple-lines></app-multiple-lines>
  </mat-tab>
</mat-tab-group>
```

Here, we simply add a directive for the *multiple-lines* component to a *mat-tab* control.

Saving the project, navigating to the */chapter05/chart-line* page, and tapping the *Multiple Lines* tab produce the results shown in Fig.5-2. You can interact with the chart by hovering over the lines, which will display the data values.

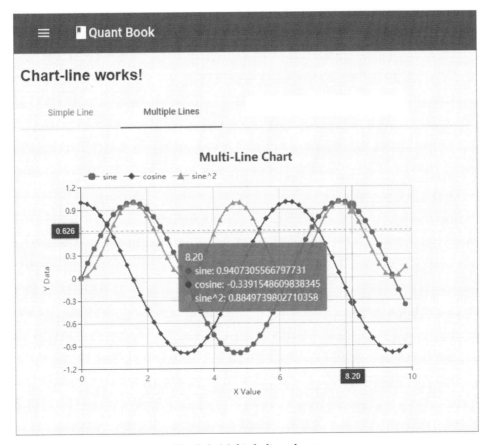

Fig.5-2. Multiple line charts.

Line Charts with Two *Y* Axes

In the previous sections, we created simple line charts using the *ECharts* library. This library has not restriction on the number of lines or curves you could add to a single chart. In this section, I will show you how to create line chart with an additional *Y*-axis.

In some instances, you may have multiple datasets you would like to display on the same chart. However, the *Y*-axis data values for each data set may not be within the same range. For example, consider the following two functions:

$$y1 = xcos(x)$$

$$y2 = 100 + 20x$$

If you want to display these two functions using the same scale in the *Y*-axis, you will get the results as shown in Figure 5-3.

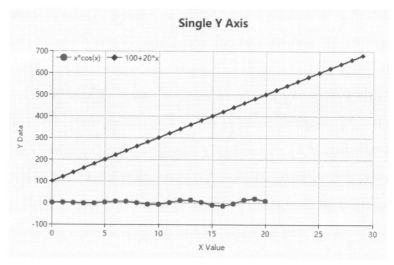

Fig.5-3. Line chart with two lines, whose data values fall in different ranges.

From the results displayed in Fig.5-3, you can see how difficult it is to view the values of the function *x*cos(*x*) because the *Y*-axis limits have been defined to display all of the data points on the same chart, while the values of these two functions have very different data ranges. We can solve this problem by adding another *Y*2-axis to the chart program.

Run the following command in the command prompt window from the *ClientApp* folder:

ng g c chapter05/chart-line/y2-axis --module=app.module

This will generate a new component named *y2-axis* in the *ClientApp/src/app/chapter05/chart-line* folder. Open the component class file and replace its content with the following code:

```
//y2-axis.component.ts file:
import { Component, OnInit } from '@angular/core';

@Component({
  selector: 'app-y2-axis',
  templateUrl: './y2-axis.component.html',
```

```
    styleUrls: ['./y2-axis.component.css']
})
export class Y2AxisComponent implements OnInit {
  option1: any;
  option2: any;

  constructor() { }

  ngOnInit() {
    const data1 = [];
    const data2 = [];

    for (let i = 0; i < 21; i++) {
      data1.push([i, i * Math.cos(i)]);
    }
    for (let i = 0; i < 30; i++) {
      data2.push([i, 100 + 20 * i]);
    }

    this.option1 = {

      // ... code for creating single y-axis chart omitted for brevity ...

    };

    this.option2 = {
      legend: {
        top: '15%',
        left: '10%',
        data: [
          { name: 'x*cos(x)' },
          { name: '100+20*x' }
        ]
      },
      title: {
        text: 'Two Y Axes',
        left: 'center'
      },
      tooltip: {
        trigger: 'axis',
        axisPointer: {
          type: 'cross'
        },
        backgroundColor: 'rgba(120, 120, 120, 0.9)',
        borderWidth: 1,
        borderColor: '#aaa',
        padding: 10,
        textStyle: {
          color: 'white'
        }
      },
      xAxis: {
        type: 'value',
        name: 'X Value',
        nameLocation: 'center',
```

```
            nameGap: '30',
            axisLine: { onZero: false }
        },
        yAxis: [{
            type: 'value',
            name: 'x*cos(x)',
            nameLocation: 'center',
            nameGap: '50'
        }, {
            type: 'value',
            name: '100+20*x',
            position: 'right',
            nameLocation: 'center',
            nameGap: '50'
        }],
        series: [{
            name: 'x*cos(x)',
            type: 'line',
            data: data1,
            symbol: 'circle',
            symbolSize: 8
        },
        {
            name: '100+20*x',
            type: 'line',
            data: data2,
            yAxisIndex: 1,
            symbol: 'diamond',
            symbolSize: 8
        }]
    };
  }
}
```

This component consists of two option properties: *option1* and *option2*. The *option1* property is used to create a single Y-axis chart (see Fig.5-3) for comparison, while *option2* is used to create a chart with two Y-axes. In *option2*, the *yAxis* field is an array of items with the first item representing the default left Y-axis while the second item representing the second Y-axis on the right (specified by *position*). Note that the second data series contains a *yAxisIndex* field that is set to 1, meaning the second Y-axis will be used for this series.

We need also to update the component's template with the following code:

```
// y2-axis.component.html file:
<div echarts [options]="option1" style="padding:30px"></div>
<div echarts [options]="option2" style="padding:30px;padding-top:0"></div>
```

This template contains two charts: the first one is a single Y-axis chart, while the second one is a line chart with two Y-axes.

Now, open the *chart-line.component.html* file in the *ClientApp/src/app/chapter05/chart-line* folder and add the highlighted code snippet to it:

```
// chart-line.component.html file:
<h2>
  Chart-line works!
```

```
</h2>
<mat-tab-group>
  <mat-tab label="Simple Line">
    <app-simple-line></app-simple-line>
  </mat-tab>
  <mat-tab label="Multiple Lines">
    <app-multiple-lines></app-multiple-lines>
  </mat-tab>
  <mat-tab label="Two Y Axes">
    <app-y2-axis></app-y2-axis>
  </mat-tab>
</mat-tab-group>
```

Here, we simply add a directive for the *y2-axis* component to a *mat-tab* control.

Saving the project, navigating to the */chapter05/chart-line* page, and then tapping the *Two Y Axes* tab produce the two line charts shown in Fig.5-3 and Fig.5-4 respectively.

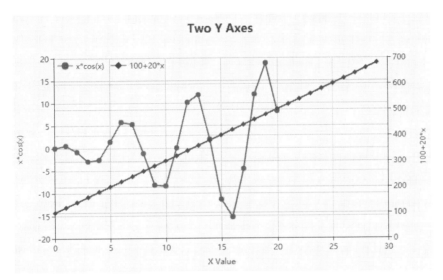

Fig.5-4. Line chart with two Y-axes.

You can see that both sets of data are clearly displayed in Figure 5-4, even though these two sets of data have dramatically different data ranges.

Resizable Charts

The charts created in the preceding sections are fixed inside your browser – you cannot resize them with your mouse. Here, I will show you how to create a resizable chart using both the ECharts and *angular2-draggable* packages.

Run the following command in the command prompt window from the *ClientApp* folder:

```
ng g c chapter05/chart-line/resize --module=app.module
```

This will generate a new component named *resize* in the *ClientApp/src/app/chapter05/chart-line* folder. Open the component class file and replace its content with the following code:

```
// resize.component.ts file:
import { Component, OnInit } from '@angular/core';

@Component({
  selector: 'app-resize',
  templateUrl: './resize.component.html',
  styleUrls: ['./resize.component.css']
})
export class ResizeComponent implements OnInit {
  options: any;
  autoResize: boolean = true;

  constructor() { }

  ngOnInit() {
    this.options = {
      grid: { left: 70 },
      xAxis: {
        type: 'category',
        data: ['Mon', 'Tue', 'Wed', 'Thu', 'Fri', 'Sat', 'Sun'],
        name: 'Date',
        nameLocation: 'center',
        nameGap: '30',
      },
      yAxis: {
        type: 'value',
        name: 'Temperature ( F )',
        nameLocation: 'center',
        nameGap: '40'
      },
      series: [{
        data: [42, 35, 27, 38, 49, 33, 25],
        type: 'line'
      }]
    };
  }
}
```

This component defines two properties, *options* and *autoResize*. The *options* property is used to create a simple line chart while the *autoResize* property is used to control whether the chart is resizable or not.

We need also to update the component's template with the following code listing:

```
// resize.component.html file:
<mat-card style="margin:30px">
  <mat-card-title>Resize Chart</mat-card-title>
  <button mat-raised-button (click)="autoResize=!autoResize" color="primary"
    style="margin-bottom:20px;margin-top:20px">
    {{autoResize ? 'Disable Resize' : 'Enable Resize' }}
  </button>
  <mat-card-content ngResizable class="resize-panel">
    <div echarts [options]="options" [autoResize]="autoResize" style="height:100%">
    </div>
```

```
  </mat-card-content>
</mat-card>
```

Note that ECharts exposes an *autoResize* directive that is bound to the *autoResize* property defined in the component class. The *ngResizable* directive, which is from the *angular2-draggable* package, is used to define a resizable element. The element's initial size is specified using a style class called *resize-panel* that is defined in the component's style file as shown in the following:

```
// resize.component.css file:
.resize-panel {
  width: 400px;
  height: 400px;
  background-color: #fff;
  border: solid 1px #869fac;
  padding: 0.5em;
}
```

Now, open the *chart-line.component.html* file in the *ClientApp/src/app/chapter05/chart-line* folder and add the highlighted snippet to it:

```
// chart-line.component.html file:
<h2>
  Chart-line works!
</h2>

<mat-tab-group>
  <mat-tab label="Simple Line">
    <app-simple-line></app-simple-line>
  </mat-tab>
  <mat-tab label="Multiple Lines">
    <app-multiple-lines></app-multiple-lines>
  </mat-tab>
  <mat-tab label="Two Y Axes">
    <app-y2-axis></app-y2-axis>
  </mat-tab>
  <mat-tab label="Auto Resize">
    <app-resize></app-resize>
  </mat-tab>
</mat-tab-group>
```

Here, we simply add a directive for the *resize* component to a *mat-tab* control.

Saving the project, navigating to the */chapter05/chart-line* page, and tapping the *Auto Resize* tab produce results shown in Fig.5-5.

You can trigger the *autoResize* property by clicking the button. When setting the *autoResize* property to *true*, you can resize the chart by resizing the panel, while the chart remains fixed when resizing the panel if the *autoResize* property is set to *false*.

Fig.5-5. Resizable chart (left) and fixed-size chart (right).

Specialized 2D Charts

ECharts also allows you to create various specialized 2D charts. In this section, I will show you how to create some commonly used specialized charts, including area, bar, pie and polar charts.

Area Charts

An area chart displays Y data values as one or more curves and fills the area beneath each curve. Run the following command in the command prompt window from the *ClientApp* folder:

```
ng g c chapter05/chart-specialized --module=app.module
```

This will generate a new component named *chart-specialized* in the *ClientApp/src/app/chapter05* folder. Run the following command to generate another component named *area-chart*:

```
ng g c chapter05/chart-specialized/area-chart --module=app.module
```

This will generate a new component named *area-chart* in the *ClientApp/src/app/chapter05/chart-specialized* folder. Open the *area-chart* component class file and replace its content with the following code:

```
// area-chart.component.ts file:
import { Component, OnInit } from '@angular/core';

@Component({
  selector: 'app-area-chart',
  templateUrl: './area-chart.component.html',
  styleUrls: ['./area-chart.component.css']
})
export class AreaChartComponent implements OnInit {
  simple: any;
  multiple: any;
  stack: any;

  private xdata = [];
  private data1 = [];
  private data2 = [];
  private data3 = [];

  constructor() { }

  ngOnInit() {
    this.getData();
    this.simple = this.getSimple();
    this.multiple = this.getMultiple();
    this.stack = this.getStack();
  }

  getData() {
    for (let i = 0; i <= 7; i++) {
      this.xdata.push(i);
      this.data1.push(1.2 + Math.sin(i));
      this.data2.push(1.2 + Math.cos(i));
      this.data3.push(1.2 + Math.sin(i) * Math.cos(i));
    }
  }

  private getSimple() {
    return {
      title: {
        text: 'Simple Area',
      },
      tooltip: {
        trigger: 'axis',
        axisPointer: {
          type: 'cross'
        }
      },
      xAxis: {
        data: this.xdata,
        type: 'category',
        boundaryGap: false
```

```
      },
      yAxis: {
        type: 'value'
      },
      series: [{
        data: this.data1,
        type: 'line',
        areaStyle: {},
        symbol: 'none'
      }]
    };
}

private getMultiple() {
  return {
    title: {
      text: 'Multiple Area',
    },
    legend: {
      top: '8%',
      left: '15%'
    },
    tooltip: {
      trigger: 'axis',
      axisPointer: {
        type: 'cross'
      }
    },
    xAxis: {
      data: this.xdata,
      type: 'category',
      boundaryGap: false
    },
    yAxis: {
      type: 'value'
    },
    series: [{
      data: this.data1,
      name: 'data1',
      type: 'line',
      areaStyle: {},
      symbol: 'none'
    }, {
      data: this.data2,
      name: 'data2',
      type: 'line',
      areaStyle: {},
      symbol: 'none'
    }, {
      data: this.data3,
      name: 'data3',
      type: 'line',
      areaStyle: {},
      symbol: 'none'
    }]
```

```
      };
  }

  private getStack() {
    return {
      title: {
        text: 'Stack Area',
      },
      legend: {
        top: '8%',
        left: '15%'
      },
      tooltip: {
        trigger: 'axis',
        axisPointer: {
          type: 'cross'
        }
      },
      xAxis: {
        data: this.xdata,
        type: 'category',
        boundaryGap: false
      },
      yAxis: {
        type: 'value'
      },
      series: [{
        data: this.data1,
        name: 'data1',
        type: 'line',
        areaStyle: {},
        stack: 'total',
        symbol: 'none'
      }, {
        data: this.data2,
        name: 'data2',
        type: 'line',
        areaStyle: {},
        stack: 'total',
        symbol: 'none'
      }, {
        data: this.data3,
        name: 'data3',
        type: 'line',
        areaStyle: {},
        stack: 'total',
        symbol: 'none'
      }]
    };
  }
}
```

This component defines three properties, simple, multiple, and stack, which are used for creating a simple area chart with a single data series, an area chart with multiple data series, and a stacked area chart. It also generates four datasets, *data1*, *data2*, *data3*, and *xdata*. The *xdata* is used for defining the categorized *x*-axis.

Let us first consider the simple area chart associated with the *simple* property that is created using a private method called *getSimple*. In ECharts, an area chart is specified by two fields:

```
type: 'line',
areaStyle: {},
```

That is, an area chart is basically a *line* chart type with an empty *areaStyle* field, indicating that the default parameter will be used. In fact, the *areaStyle* field consists of several properties that can be used to customize the area chart, including fill color, opacity, origin, shadow etc.

We also need to replace the component's template with the following code:

```
// area-chart.component.html file:
<h3>
  Area Charts
</h3>
<div class="cardList">
  <mat-card class="cardBorder">
    <div echarts [options]="simple" style="height:100%"></div>
  </mat-card>
  <mat-card class="card-border">
    <div echarts [options]="multiple" style="height:100%"></div>
  </mat-card>
  <mat-card class="card-border">
    <div echarts [options]="stack" style="height:100%"></div>
  </mat-card>
</div>
```

This template define three area charts using different options directives. It also uses the style classes, *cardList* and *card-border*, to set styles for the chart panels. Here is the code for the style file:

```
// area-chart.component.css file:
.cardList {
  display: flex;
  flex-direction: row;
  flex-wrap: wrap;
  justify-content: flex-start;
}

.card-border {
  margin: 10px;
  width: 400px;
  height: 400px;
}
```

Here, we use a row-based card list with flex-wrap

Now, open the *chart-specialized.component.html* file in the *ClientApp/src/app/chapter05/chart-specialized* folder and add the following code to it:

```
// chart-specialized.component.html file:
<h2>
  Chart-specialized works!
</h2>
```

```
<mat-tab-group>
  <mat-tab label="Area Charts">
    <app-area-chart></app-area-chart>
  </mat-tab>
</mat-tab-group>
```

Here, we simply add a directive for the *area-chart* component to a *mat-tab* control.

Finally, we need to add a path for this new component to the *RouterModule* of the root module (i.e., the *app.module.ts* file):

`{ path: 'chapter05/chart-specialized, component: ChartSpecializedComponent },`

Then add the corresponding URL link to the *home* and *nav-menu* components.

Saving the project and navigating to the */chapter05/chart-specialized* page produce the simple area chart shown in Fig.5-6.

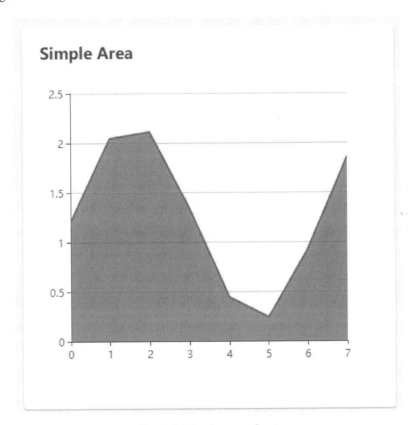

Fig.5-6. Simple area chart.

Like a line chart with multiple curves, an area chart can also contains multiple data series. The *multiple* property defined by the *getMultiple* method in the *area-chart* component class contains three data series, *data1*, *data2*, and *data3*. This produces the result shown in Fig.5-7.

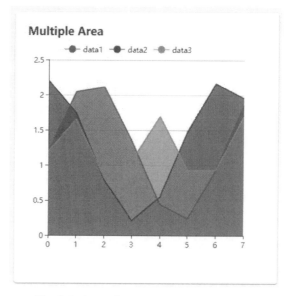

Fig.5-7. Area chart with three data series.

You can see from Fig.5-7 that the areas from different data series overlap together. In practice, an area chart with multiple data series is usually used to represent cumulated total, which is called the stacked area chart. In the *area-chart* component class, we use the *stack* property defined by the *getStack* method to create such a stacked area chart. In this case, we use the *stack* field for each data series to specify an area chart:

```
stack: 'total',
```

This produces a stacked area chart shown in Fig.5-8.

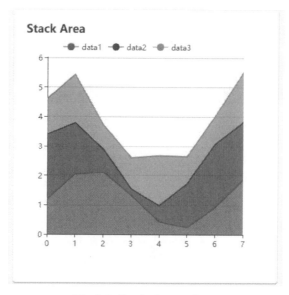

Fig.5-8. Stacked area chart.

Bar Charts

A bar chart is useful for comparing classes or group of data. In a bar chart, a class or group can contain a single category of data, or it can be broken down further into multiple categories for a greater depth of analysis. It is often used in exploratory data analysis to illustrate the major features of the distribution of the data in a convenient form. A bar chart displays the data using a number of rectangles of the same width, each of which represents a particular category. The length (and hence area) of each rectangle is proportional to the number of cases in the category it represents, for example, age group or religious affiliation.

We can easily create various bar charts in ECharts. Run the following command in the command prompt window from the *ClientApp* folder:

```
ng g c chapter05/chart-specialized/bar-chart --module=app.module
```

This will generate a new component named *bar-chart* in the *ClientApp/src/app/chapter05/chart-specialized* folder. Open the *bar-chart* component class file and replace its content with the following code:

```
// bar-chart.component.ts file:
import { Component, OnInit } from '@angular/core';

@Component({
  selector: 'app-bar-chart',
  templateUrl: './bar-chart.component.html',
  styleUrls: ['./bar-chart.component.css']
})
export class BarChartComponent implements OnInit {
  vertical: any;
  horizontal: any;
  group: any;
  stack: any;

  constructor() { }

  ngOnInit() {
    this.vertical = this.getVertical();
    this.horizontal = this.getHorizontal();
    this.group = this.getGroup();
    this.stack = this.getStack();
  }

  getVertical() {
    return {
      title: {
        text: 'Vertical Bar Chart',
        left: 'center'
      },
      tooltip: {},
      xAxis: {
        type: 'category',
        data: ['Mon', 'Tue', 'Wed', 'Thu', 'Fri', 'Sat', 'Sun']
      },
      yAxis: {
        type: 'value'
```

```
      },
      series: [{
        data: [120, 200, 150, 80, 70, 110, 130],
        type: 'bar'
      }]
    };
  }

  getHorizontal() {
    return {
      title: {
        text: 'Horizontal Bar Chart',
        left: 'center'
      },
      tooltip: {},
      xAxis: {
        type: 'value'
      },
      yAxis: {
        type: 'category',
        data: ['Mon', 'Tue', 'Wed', 'Thu', 'Fri', 'Sat', 'Sun']
      },
      series: [{
        data: [120, 200, 150, 80, 70, 110, 130],
        type: 'bar'
      }]
    };
  }

  getGroup() {
    return {
      title: {
        text: 'Group Bar Chart',
        left: 'center'
      },
      legend: {
        top: '15%',
        left: '15%',
        data: ['Houston', 'Los Angeles', 'New York', 'Chicago', 'Philadephia']
      },
      tooltip: {},
      xAxis: [
        {
          type: 'category',
          data: ['1990', '2000', '2005', '2010', '2015']
        }
      ],
      yAxis: [
        {
          type: 'value',
          name: 'Population (in millions)',
          nameLocation: 'center',
          nameGap: '25'
        }
      ],
```

```
    series: [
      {
        name: 'Houston',
        type: 'bar',
        data: [1.70, 1.98, 2.08, 2.10, 2.30],
      }, {
        name: 'Los Angeles',
        type: 'bar',
        data: [3.49, 3.70, 3.79, 3.79, 3.97]
      }, {
        name: 'New York',
        type: 'bar',
        data: [7.32, 8.02, 8.21, 8.18, 8.55]
      }, {
        name: 'Chicago',
        type: 'bar',
        data: [2.78, 2.90, 2.82, 2.70, 2.72]
      }, {
        name: 'Philadephia',
        type: 'bar',
        data: [1.59, 1.51, 1.52, 1.53, 1.57]
      }
    ]
  }
}

getStack() {
  return {
    title: {
      text: 'Stack',
    },
    legend: {
      left: '20%',
      data: ['Houston', 'Los Angeles', 'New York', 'Chicago', 'Philadephia']
    },
    tooltip: {},
    xAxis: [
      {
        type: 'category',
        data: ['1990', '2000', '2005', '2010', '2015']
      }],
    yAxis: [
      {
        type: 'value',
        name: 'Population (in millions)',
        nameLocation: 'center',
        nameGap: '25'
      }],
    series: [
      {
        name: 'Houston',
        type: 'bar',
        stack: 'Total',
        data: [1.70, 1.98, 2.08, 2.10, 2.30]
      }, {
```

```
            name: 'Los Angeles',
            type: 'bar',
            stack: 'Total',
            data: [3.49, 3.70, 3.79, 3.79, 3.97]
         }, {
            name: 'New York',
            type: 'bar',
            stack: 'Total',
            data: [7.32, 8.02, 8.21, 8.18, 8.55]
         }, {
            name: 'Chicago',
            type: 'bar',
            stack: 'Total',
            data: [2.78, 2.90, 2.82, 2.70, 2.72]
            }
         }, {
            name: 'Philadephia',
            type: 'bar',
            stack: 'Total',
            data: [1.59, 1.51, 1.52, 1.53, 1.57]
         }]
      }
   }
}
```

This component has four properties, *vertical*, *horizontal*, *group*, and *stack* defined by the methods *getVertical*, *getHorizontal*, *getGroup*, and *getStack* respectively. We will use these properties to create different types of bar charts.

Next, we need to update the component's template:

```
// bar-chart.component.ts file:
<h3>
  Bar Charts
</h3>

<div class="cardList">
  <mat-card class="card-border">
    <div echarts [options]="vertical" style="height:100%"></div>
  </mat-card>
  <mat-card class="card-border">
    <div echarts [options]="horizontal" style="height:100%"></div>
  </mat-card>
  <mat-card class="card-border">
    <div echarts [options]="group" style="height:100%"></div>
  </mat-card>
  <mat-card class="card-border">
    <div echarts [options]="stack" style="height:100%"></div>
  </mat-card>
</div>
```

Here, we also use style classes, *cardList* and *card-border*, to set styles for the chart panels. These style classes are defined in the *bar-chart.component.css* file:

```
// bar-chart.component.css file:
.cardList {
  display: flex;
```

```
  flex-direction: row;
  flex-wrap: wrap;
  justify-content: flex-start;
}

.card-border {
  margin: 10px;
  width: 400px;
  height: 400px;
}
```

Next, we need to add the *app-bar-chart* directive to the *chart-specialized* component's template:

```
// chart-specialized.component.html file:
<h2>
  Chart-specialized works!
</h2>

<mat-tab-group>
  <mat-tab label="Area Charts">
    <app-area-chart></app-area-chart>
  </mat-tab>
  <mat-tab label="Bar Charts">
    <app-bar-chart></app-bar-chart>
  </mat-tab>
</mat-tab-group>
```

Let us first consider the vertical bar chart. Inside the *getVertical* method, we set the *type* for *xAxis* to *category* and series to *bar*. Saving the project, navigating to */chapter05/chart-specialized*, and tapping the *Bar Charts* tab produce a vertical bar chart shown in Fig.5-9.

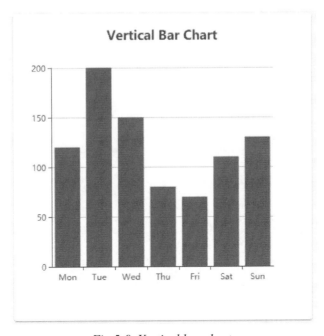

Fig.5-9. Vertical bar chart.

We can create a horizontal bar chart using the *horizontal* property defined in the *bar-chart* component class. Inside the *getHorizontal* method, we simply switch the X- and Y-axis, that is, we set the Y-axis to *category*. This generates a horizontal bar chart shown in Fig.5-10.

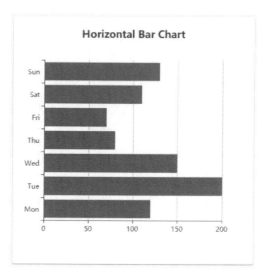

Fig.5-10. Horizontal bar chart.

We can then create a group bar chart using the *group* property. In this case, multiple sets of data have the same X-categories, and Y-values are distributed along the X-axis, with each Y at a different X drawn at a different location. All of the Y values at the same X are clustered around the same location on the X-axis. Inside the *getGroup* method, we simply set the *type* to *bar* for each data series. The *group* property produces the group bar chart shown in Fig.5-11.

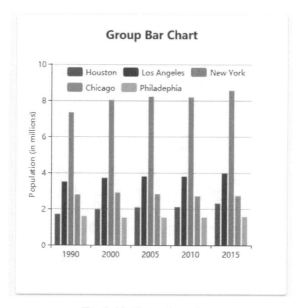

Fig.5-11. Group bar chart.

Bar charts can also show how different Y values at the same X point contribute to the sum of all of the Y values at the point. These types of bar charts are referred to as stacked bar charts.

Stacked bar charts display one bar per X category. The bars are divided into several fragments according to the number of Y values. The height of each bar equals the sum of all of the Y values at a given X category. Each fragment is equal to the value of its respective Y value.

We can create a stacked bar chart using the *stack* property defined in the *bar-chart* component class. Note that inside the *getStack* method, we specify both fields, *type* and *stack* for each data series:

```
type: 'bar',
stack: 'Total',
```

This produces the result shown in Fig.5-12.

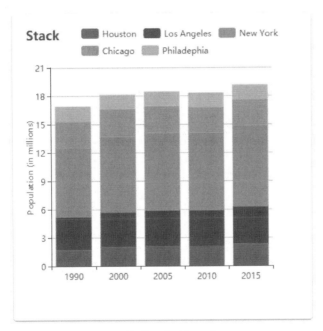

Fig.5-12. Stacked bar chart.

Pie Charts

We use pie charts mainly for showing proportion of different categories. Each arc length represents the proportion of data quantity.

We can easily create various pie charts in ECharts. Run the following command in the command prompt window from the *ClientApp* folder:

```
ng g c chapter05/chart-specialized/pie-chart --module=app.module
```

This will generate a new component named *pie-chart* in the *ClientApp/src/app/chapter05/chart-specialized* folder. Open the *pie-chart* component class file and replace its content with the following code:

```
// pie-chart.component.ts file:
```

```
import { Component, OnInit } from '@angular/core';

@Component({
  selector: 'app-pie-chart',
  templateUrl: './pie-chart.component.html',
  styleUrls: ['./pie-chart.component.css']
})
export class PieChartComponent implements OnInit {
  pie1: any;
  pie2: any;
  pie3: any;
  pie4: any;

  private data: any;
  constructor() { }

  ngOnInit() {
    this.getData();
    this.pie1 = this.getPie('Simple Pie', false, 0, '55%');
    this.pie2 = this.getPie('Doughnut', false, '30%', '55%');
    this.pie3 = this.getPie('Rose Area Pie', 'area', '10%', '55%');
    this.pie4 = this.getPie('Rose Radius Pie', 'radius', '10%', '55%');
  }

  getData() {
    this.data = [
      { value: 30, name: 'Soc. Sec. Tax' },
      { value: 8, name: 'Misc.' },
      { value: 15, name: 'Borrowing' },
      { value: 35, name: 'Income Tax' },
      { value: 12, name: 'Corp. Tax' }
    ];
  }

  getPie(title: string, rose: any, r1: any, r2: any) {
    return {
      title: {
        text: title,
      },
      tooltip: {},
      legend: {
        x: 'center',
        y: 'bottom'
      },
      series: [{
        data: this.data,
        type: 'pie',
        roseType: rose,
        radius: [r1, r2]
      }]
    };
  }
}
```

This component contains four properties, *pie1*, *pie2*, *pie3*, and *pie4*, which are defined using the *getPie* method with different sets of parameters. Inside the *getPie* method, we set the *type* to *pie* for the series. This data series also consists of the other two parameters, *roseType* and *radius*.

The *roseType* field can take three possible values:

- *false*: representing a standard pie chart.

- *radius*: representing a Nightingale rose chart using central angle to show the percentage of data and radius to show the data size.

- *area*, represent a Nightingale rose chart with all the sectors sharing the same central angle and data size being shown only through radii.

The *radius* field for the *series* represents the radius of a pie chart. It can take the following values:

- *Number*: specifying the outside radius directly.

- *String*: For example, '50%', means that the outside radius is 50% of the chart panel size.

- *Array.<number|string>*: The first item specifies the inside radius and second one specifies the outside radius.

Next, we need to update the component's template:

```
// pie-chart.component.html file:
<h3>
  Pie Charts
</h3>

<div class="cardList">
  <mat-card class="card-border">
    <div echarts [options]="pie1"></div>
  </mat-card>
  <mat-card class="card-border">
    <div echarts [options]="pie2"></div>
  </mat-card>
  <mat-card class="card-border">
    <div echarts [options]="pie3"></div>
  </mat-card>
  <mat-card class="card-border">
    <div echarts [options]="pie4"></div>
  </mat-card>
</div>
```

Here, we also use style classes, *cardList* and *card-border*, to set styles for the chart panels. These style classes are defined in the *pie-chart.component.css* file:

```
//pie-chart.component.css file:
.cardList {
  display: flex;
  flex-direction: row;
  flex-wrap: wrap;
  justify-content: flex-start;
}

.card-border {
  margin: 10px;
  width: 400px;
```

```
  height: 400px;
}
```

Next, we need to add the *app-pie-chart* directive to the *chart-specialized* component's template:

```
// chart-specialized.component.html file:
<h2>
  Chart-specialized works!
</h2>

<mat-tab-group>
  <mat-tab label="Area Charts">
    <app-area-chart></app-area-chart>
  </mat-tab>
  <mat-tab label="Bar Charts">
    <app-bar-chart></app-bar-chart>
  </mat-tab>
  <mat-tab label="Pie Charts">
    <app-pie-chart></app-pie-chart>
  </mat-tab>
</mat-tab-group>
```

Let us first consider a simple pie chart specified by the *pie1* property in the *pie-chart* component class:

```
this.pie1 = this.getPie('Simple Pie', false, 0, '55%');
```

Here, we set the *roseType* to false, which produces a simple pie chart shown in Fig.5-13.

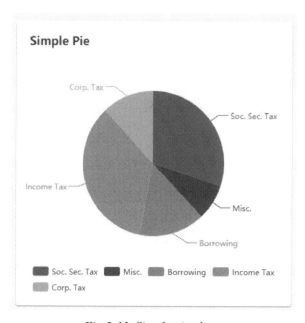

Fig.5-13. Simple pie chart.

Next, we consider a doughnut chart, which is essentially a pie chart with an area of the center cut out. A doughnut charts is specified by *pie2* property in the *pie-chart* component class:

```
this.pie2 = this.getPie('Doughnut', false, '30%', '55%');
```

Here, we also set the *roseType* to false, but specify two radius: '30%' and '50%'. This generates a doughnut chart shown in Fig.5-14:

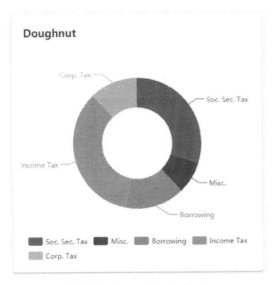

Fig.5-14. Doughnut chart.

We now consider a Nightingale rose chart. This type of chart also known as a Coxcomb chart or polar area diagram. A Nightingale area rose chart is similar to a pie chart, except that sectors are equal angles and differ in how far each sector extends from the center of the circle. This chart is specified by the *pie3* property in the *pie-chart* component class:

```
this.pie3 = this.getPie('Rose Area Pie', 'area', '10%', '55%');
```

This produces result shown in Fig.5-15.

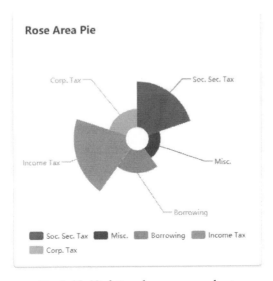

Fig.5-15. Nightingale area rose chart.

Finally, we discuss a Nightingale radius rose chart that uses the arc length to show the percentage of data and radius to show data size. This chart is specified by the *pie4* property in the *pie-chart* component class:

```
this.pie3 = this.getPie('Rose Radius Pie', 'radius', '10%', '55%');
```

This produces result shown in Fig.5-16.

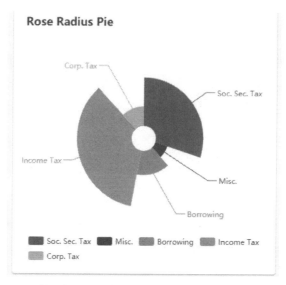

Fig.5-16. Nightingale radius rose chart.

Polar Charts

A polar chart is a common variation of circular plots. It is useful when relationships between data points can be displayed most easily in terms of angle and radius. The series is represented by a closed curve connecting points in the polar coordinate system. Each data point is determined by the distance from the center (the radial coordinate) and the angle from the fixed direction (the angular direction).

We can easily create a polar chart in ECharts. Run the following command in the command prompt window from the *ClientApp* folder:

ng g c chapter05/chart-specialized/polar-chart --module=app.module

This will generate a new component named *polar-chart* in the *ClientApp/src/app/chapter05/chart-specialized* folder. Open the *polar-chart* component class file and replace its content with the following code:

```
// polar-chart.component.ts file:
import { Component, OnInit } from '@angular/core';

@Component({
  selector: 'app-polar-chart',
  templateUrl: './polar-chart.component.html',
  styleUrls: ['./polar-chart.component.css']
})
export class PolarChartComponent implements OnInit {
```

```
polar1: any;
polar2: any;

private data1 = [];
private data2 = [];
private data3 = [];

constructor() { }
ngOnInit() {
  this.getData();
  this.polar1 = this.getPolar1();
  this.polar2 = this.getPolar2();
}

getData() {
  for (let i = 0; i <= 360; i++) {
    let theta = i / 180 * Math.PI;
    let r1 = Math.sin(2 * theta) * Math.cos(2 * theta);
    let r2 = Math.log(1 + Math.cos(2 * theta));
    let r3 = Math.log(1 + Math.sin(2 * theta));
    this.data1.push([r1, i]);
    this.data2.push([r2, i]);
    this.data3.push([r3, i]);
  }
}

getPolar1() {
  return {
    title: {
      text: 'Single Line'
    },
    tooltip: {
      trigger: 'axis',
      axisPointer: {
        type: 'cross'
      }
    },
    polar: {
      center: ['50%', '50%']
    },
    angleAxis: {
      type: 'value',
      startAngle: 0
    },
    radiusAxis: {
      min: 0
    },
    series: [{
      data: this.data1,
      type: 'line',
      coordinateSystem: 'polar',
      showSymbol: false
    }]
  };
}
```

```
getPolar2() {
    return {
        title: {
            text: 'Multiple Lines'
        },
        legend: {
            x: 'center',
            y: 'bottom'
        },
        tooltip: {
            trigger: 'axis',
            axisPointer: {
                type: 'cross'
            }
        },
        polar: {
            center: ['50%', '50%']
        },
        angleAxis: {
            type: 'value',
            startAngle: 0
        },
        radiusAxis: {
            min: -5,
            max: 1
        },
        series: [{
            data: this.data2,
            name: 'cosine',
            type: 'line',
            coordinateSystem: 'polar',
            showSymbol: false
        }, {
            data: this.data3,
            name: 'sine',
            type: 'line',
            coordinateSystem: 'polar',
            showSymbol: false
        }]
    };
  }
}
```

This class has two properties, *polar1* and *polar2*, defined using the methods *getPolar1* and *getPolar2* respectively. The polar chart created using *polar1* shows a single polar line while the chart created using *polar2* displays two polar curves. Inside these methods, we define the polar charts by specifying the *polar* coordinate with an *angleAxis* and a *radiusAxis*; and for each data series, we set the *coordinateSystem* field to *polar*.

Next, we need to update the component's template:

```
// polar-chart.component.html file:
<h3>
  Polar Charts
</h3>
```

```
<div class="cardList">
  <mat-card class="card-border">
    <div echarts [options]="polar1"></div>
  </mat-card>
  <mat-card class="card-border">
    <div echarts [options]="polar2"></div>
  </mat-card>
</div>
```

Here, we also use style classes, *cardList* and *card-border*, to set styles for the chart panels. These style classes are defined in the *polar-chart.component.css* file:

```
// polar-chart.component.css file:
.cardList {
  display: flex;
  flex-direction: row;
  flex-wrap: wrap;
  justify-content: flex-start;
}

.card-border {
  margin: 10px;
  width: 400px;
  height: 400px;
}
```

Next, we need to add the *app-polar-chart* directive to the *chart-specialized* component's template:

```
// chart-specialized.component.html file:
<h2>
  Chart-specialized works!
</h2>

<mat-tab-group>
  <mat-tab label="Area Charts">
    <app-area-chart></app-area-chart>
  </mat-tab>
  <mat-tab label="Bar Charts">
    <app-bar-chart></app-bar-chart>
  </mat-tab>
  <mat-tab label="Pie Charts">
    <app-pie-chart></app-pie-chart>
  </mat-tab>
  <mat-tab label="Polar Charts">
    <app-polar-chart></app-polar-chart>
  </mat-tab>
</mat-tab-group>
```

Saving the project, navigating to the */chapter05/chart-specialized* page, and tapping the *Polar Charts* tab produce the results shown in Fig.5-17.

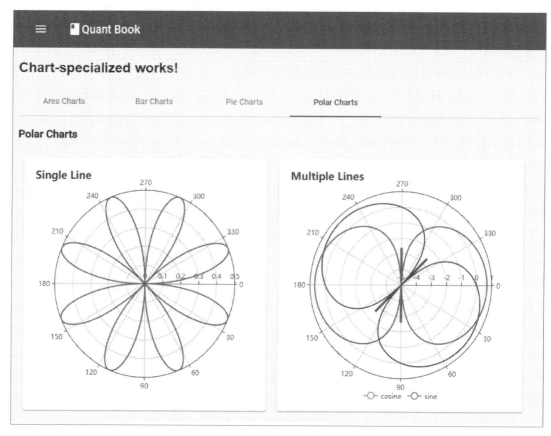

Fig.5-17. Polar charts.

Stock Charts

Stock charts play an important role in stock market research and analysis. Technical analysis, different from fundamental analysis, usually ignores the actual nature of the company, market, currency, or commodity. It is based solely on the stock charts, namely, the price and volume information. Stock charts usually show high, low, open, close, and volume data of a security. These charts allow you to plot the change of a stock price over time, analyze the history of stock price changes, and predict the future price movement of a stock based on prior price history.

In this section, I will show you how to create a candlestick and a candlestick + volume stock charts using ECharts. In addition, we will add a data-zoom component to these stock charts, used for zooming in a specific range that enables you to investigate data in detail or get an overview of the data. I will also demonstrate how to create real-time stock charts.

Candlestick Charts

A candlestick chart is like a combination of a line chart and a bar chart: each bar represents all four important pieces of price information for that bar – open, high, low, and close. Being densely packed with information, candlestick charts tend to represent trading patterns over short periods of time, often a few days or a few trading sessions. These charts are most often used in technical analysis of equity and currency price patterns.

First, we need to implement a helper class that converts the stock data from Yahoo Finance, database, or other source into a proper format for the stock charts. Add a TypeScript class named *stockChartHelper.ts* in the *ClientApp/src/app/models* folder with the following code:

```
import { MarketData } from './market-data.model';

export class StockChartHelper {

  processStockData(stockData: MarketData[]) {
    const categoryData = [];
    const values = [];
    const volume = [];
    for (let i = 0; i < stockData.length; i++) {
      categoryData.push(stockData[i].date.toString().substring(0, 10));
      values.push([stockData[i].open, stockData[i].close, stockData[i].low,
        stockData[i].high]);
      volume.push(stockData[i].volume);
    }
    return {
      categoryData: categoryData,
      values: values,
      volume: volume
    };
  }
}
```

The *processStockData* method takes the *MarketData* array as input and divides it into three parts: *categoryData* (date string array), *values* (prices array), and *volume* (volume array). These processed data arrays will be used to create stock charts.

Run the following command in the command prompt window from the *ClientApp* folder:

ng g c chapter05/chart-stock --module=app.module

This will generate a new component named *chart-stock* in the *ClientApp/src/app/chapter05* folder. Run the following command to generate another component named *candle-chart*:

ng g c chapter05/chart-stock/candle-chart --module=app.module

This will generate a new component named *candle-chart* in the *ClientApp/src/app/chapter05/chart-stock* folder. Open the *candle-chart* component class file and replace its content with the following code listing:

```
// candle-chart.component.ts file:
import { Component, OnInit, Input, OnChanges } from '@angular/core';
import { MarketData } from '../../../models/market-data.model';
import { StockChartHelper } from '../../../models/stockChartHelper'

@Component({
  selector: 'app-candle-chart',
  templateUrl: './candle-chart.component.html',
  styleUrls: ['./candle-chart.component.css']
})
```

```
export class CandleChartComponent implements OnInit, OnChanges {
  @Input() stockData: MarketData[];
  private stock: any;
  private helper: StockChartHelper = new StockChartHelper();
  options: any;

  constructor() { }

  ngOnInit() {
    this.stock = this.helper.processStockData(this.stockData);
    this.options = this.getOptions();
  }

  ngOnChanges() {
    this.stock = this.helper.processStockData(this.stockData);
    this.options = this.getOptions();
  }

  getOptions() {
    var downColor = '#ec0000';
    var downBorderColor = '#8A0000';
    var upColor = '#00da3c';
    var upBorderColor = '#008F28';

    return {
      title: {
        text: this.stockData[0].ticker + ': Stock Price',
        left: 'center'
      },
      tooltip: {
        trigger: 'axis',
        axisPointer: {
          type: 'cross'
        }
      },
      grid: {
        left: '10%',
        right: '10%',
        bottom: '15%'
      },
      xAxis: {
        type: 'category',
        data: this.stock.categoryData,
        scale: true,
        boundaryGap: false,
        axisLine: { onZero: false },
        splitLine: { show: false },
        splitNumber: 20,
        min: 'dataMin',
        max: 'dataMax'
      },
      yAxis: {
        scale: true,
        splitArea: {
          show: true
```

```
        }
      },
      dataZoom: [
        {
          type: 'inside',
          start: 70,
          end: 100
        },
        {
          show: true,
          type: 'slider',
          y: '90%',
          start: 70,
          end: 100
        }
      ],
      series: [
        {
          type: 'candlestick',
          data: this.stock.values,
          itemStyle: {
            color: upColor,
            color0: downColor,
            borderColor: upBorderColor,
            borderColor0: downBorderColor
          }
        }
      ]
    };
  }
}
```

This component has a *@Input()* property called *stockData*, which is a *MarketData* array. The private *stock* property is used to hold the processed stock data from the *processStockData* method defined in the *StockChartHelper* class.

Note that in addition to the *ngOnInit* method, this component also invokes a callback method named *ngOnChanges*. The *ngOnChanges* method will be invoked every time there is a change in one of the input properties of the component. In our case, this method ensure that the stock chart will be updated automatically whenever the input stock data changes,

The *getOptions* method sets up options for the candlestick chart. For the *xAxis*, we set the *type* and *data* fields to *category* and *stock.categoryData*, while for the *series*, we set the *type* and *data* to *candlestick* and *stock.values* respectively. There is also an *itemStyle* field for the *series*, which specifies the style of candlestick. Here, we set four items for the *itemStyle* field with different colors:

- *color*: fill color of bullish candlestick.
- *color0*: fill color off bearish candlestick.
- *borderColor*: border color of bullish candlestick.
- *borderColor0*: border color of bearish candlestick.

We also add a *dataZoom* component to the chart options. This component is used for zooming a specific range, which enables you to investigate data in detail or get an overview of the entire data range. We set the *type* to *slider* for this component, on which coordinate systems can be zoomed or roamed by mouse dragging or finger touch (in touch screen). We can set the default window for this component using the *start* and *end* fields: **start:70** and **end:100** means from 70% to 100% out of the **[xAxis.min, xAxis.max]**.

The template for this component is very simple, and only has a single line of code:

```
// candle-chart.component.html file:
<div echarts [options]="options" style="height:100%"></div>
```

Open the *chart-stock.component.ts* file in the *ClientApp/src/app/chapter05/chart-stock* folder and replace its content with the following code listing:

```
// chart-stock.component.ts file:
import { Component, OnInit } from '@angular/core';
import { MarketDataService } from '../../models/market-data.service';
import { MarketData } from '../../models/market-data.model';

@Component({
  selector: 'app-chart-stock',
  templateUrl: './chart-stock.component.html',
  styleUrls: ['./chart-stock.component.css']
})
export class ChartStockComponent implements OnInit {
  ticker = 'A';
  startDate: string = '2018-01-01';
  endDate: string = '2018-12-31';
  period = 'daily';

  constructor(private repository: MarketDataService) { }

  ngOnInit() {
    this.getStock(this.ticker, this.startDate, this.endDate, this.period);
  }

  get stock(): MarketData[] {
    return this.repository.yahooStock;
  }

  getStock(ticker: string, start: string, end: string, period: string) {
    this.repository.getYahooStock(ticker, start, end, period);
  }
}
```

This component should be familiar to you – it simply retrieves the stock data from web service through the market data service. The retrieved stock data will be the input for the candle-chart component.

Open the *chart-stock* component's template and replace its content with the following code:

```
// chart-stock.component.html file:
<h2>
  Stock Charts
</h2>

<mat-form-field>
  <input matInput placeholder="ticker" [(ngModel)]="ticker" name="ticker">
</mat-form-field>
<mat-form-field>
```

```
    <input matInput placeholder="Start Date" [(ngModel)]="startDate" name="startDate">
  </mat-form-field>
  <mat-form-field>
    <input matInput placeholder="End Date" [(ngModel)]="endDate" name="endDate">
  </mat-form-field>
  <mat-form-field>
    <mat-select [(value)]="period">
      <mat-option value="daily">daily</mat-option>
      <mat-option value="weekly">weekly</mat-option>
      <mat-option value="monthly">monthly</mat-option>
    </mat-select>
  </mat-form-field>
  <button mat-raised-button (click)="getStock(ticker, startDate, endDate, period)">
    Get Stock Chart</button>

<div *ngIf="stock">
  <div *ngIf="stock.length>0">
    <mat-tab-group>
      <mat-tab label="Candlestick Chart">
        <h3>Candlestick Chart</h3>
        <mat-card class="card-stock">
          <app-candle-chart [stockData]="stock"></app-candle-chart>
        </mat-card>
      </mat-tab>
    </mat-tab-group>
  </div>
</div>
```

The top part of the template specifies input parameters for retrieving stock data, which will be the input for the *app-candle-chart* directive. The container of this directive is a *mat-card* that is styled by a *card-stock* class defined in the component's style file:

```
//chart-stock.component.css file:
.card-stock {
  margin: 10px;
  width: 800px;
  height: 500px;
}
```

This simply specifies the size of the chart panel.

Finally, we need to add a path for this new component to the *RouterModule* of the root module (i.e., the *app.module.ts* file):

```
{ path: 'chapter05/chart-stock, component: ChartStockComponent },
```

Then add the corresponding URL link to the *home* and *nav-menu* components.

Saving the project and navigating to the */chapter05/chart-stock* page produce the result shown in Fig.5-18. Here, you can enter any valid stock ticker in US equity market and specify a date range to create corresponding candlestick stock chart. You can also zoom in to see the details or get an overview of the entire data range using the *dataZoom* component located at the bottom of the chart.

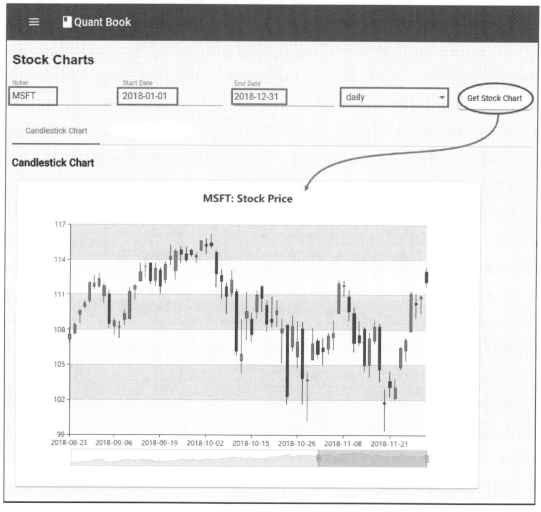

Fig.5-18. Candlestick stock chart.

Candlestick and Volume Charts

It is also easy to create a candlestick + volume stock chart in ECharts.

Run the following command in the command prompt window from the *ClientApp* folder:

```
ng g c chapter05/chart-stock/candle-volume --module=app.module
```

This will generate a new component named *candle-volume* in the *ClientApp/src/app/chapter05/chart-stock* folder. Open the *candle-volume* component class file and replace its content with the following code:

```
// candle-volume.component.ts file:
import { Component, OnInit, Input, OnChanges } from '@angular/core';
import { MarketData } from '../../../models/market-data.model';
import { StockChartHelper } from '../../../models/stockChartHelper';
```

```
@Component({
  selector: 'app-candle-volume',
  templateUrl: './candle-volume.component.html',
  styleUrls: ['./candle-volume.component.css']
})
export class CandleVolumeComponent implements OnInit, OnChanges {
  @Input() stockData: MarketData[];
  private stock: any;
  private helper: StockChartHelper = new StockChartHelper();
  options: any;

  constructor() { }

  ngOnInit() {
    this.stock = this.helper.processStockData(this.stockData);
    this.options = this.getOptions();
  }

  ngOnChanges() {
    this.stock = this.helper.processStockData(this.stockData);
    this.options = this.getOptions();
  }

  getOptions() {
    var downColor = '#ec0000';
    var downBorderColor = '#8A0000';
    var upColor = '#00da3c';
    var upBorderColor = '#008F28';

    return {
      title: {
        text: this.stockData[0].ticker + ': Stock Price',
        left: 'center'
      },
      tooltip: {
        trigger: 'axis',
        axisPointer: {
          type: 'cross'
        }
      },
      axisPointer: {
        link: { xAxisIndex: 'all' }
      },
      grid: [{
        left: 50,
        right: 20,
        top: '10%',
        height: '50%'
      }, {
        left: 50,
        right: 20,
        height: '20%',
        top: '65%'
      }],
```

```
xAxis: [{
  type: 'category',
  data: this.stock.categoryData,
  scale: true,
  boundaryGap: false,
  axisLine: { onZero: false },
  splitLine: { show: false },
  splitNumber: 20,
  min: 'dataMin',
  max: 'dataMax'
}, {
  type: 'category',
  gridIndex: 1,
  data: this.stock.categoryData,
  scale: true,
  boundaryGap: false,
  splitLine: { show: false },
  axisLabel: { show: false },
  axisTick: { show: false },
  axisLine: { lineStyle: { color: '#777' } },
  splitNumber: 20,
  min: 'dataMin',
  max: 'dataMax'
}
],
yAxis: [{
  scale: true,
  splitArea: {
    show: true
  }
}, {
  scale: true,
  gridIndex: 1,
  splitNumber: 2,
  axisLabel: { show: false },
  axisLine: { show: false },
  axisTick: { show: false },
  splitLine: { show: false }
}
],
dataZoom: [
  {
    show: true,
    type: 'slider',
    y: '90%',
    start: 70,
    end: 100,
    xAxisIndex: [0, 1],
  }
],
series: [
  {
    name: 'candlestock',
    type: 'candlestick',
    data: this.stock.values,
```

```
         itemStyle: {
           color: upColor,
           color0: downColor,
           borderColor: upBorderColor,
           borderColor0: downBorderColor
         }
      },
      {
        name: 'volume',
        type: 'bar',
        xAxisIndex: 1,
        yAxisIndex: 1,
        itemStyle: {
          normal: {
            color: '#7fbe9e'
          },
          emphasis: {
            color: '#140'
          }
        },
        data: this.stock.volume
      }
    ]
  };
}
}
```

This component is essentially similar to that used to create the candlestick chart, except that it adds a volume chart under the candlestick chart. Thus, we need to create two separate sets of *xAxis*, *yAxis*, and *series*, with the first set being for the candlestick chart and the second set for the volume chart.

The component's template is also very simple:

```
// candle-volume.component.html file:
<div echarts [options]="options" style="height:100%"></div>
```

Finally, we need to add the *app-candle-volume* directive to the *chart-stock* component's template:

```
// chart-stock.component.html file:
<h2>
  Stock Charts
</h2>

// ... other code omitted for previty ...

<div *ngIf="stock">
  <div *ngIf="stock.length>0">
    <mat-tab-group>
      <mat-tab label="Candlestick Chart">
        <h3>Candlestick Chart</h3>
        <mat-card class="card-stock">
          <app-candle-chart [stockData]="stock"></app-candle-chart>
        </mat-card>
      </mat-tab>
      <mat-tab label="Candlestick & Volume">
        <h3>Candlestick-Volume Chart</h3>
        <mat-card class="card-stock">
```

```
            <app-candle-volume [stockData]="stock"></app-candle-volume>
        </mat-card>
    </mat-tab>
  </mat-tab-group>
 </div>
</div>
```

Saving the project, navigating to the */chapter05/chart-stock* page, and tapping the *Candlestick & Volume* tab produce the result shown in Fig.5-19.

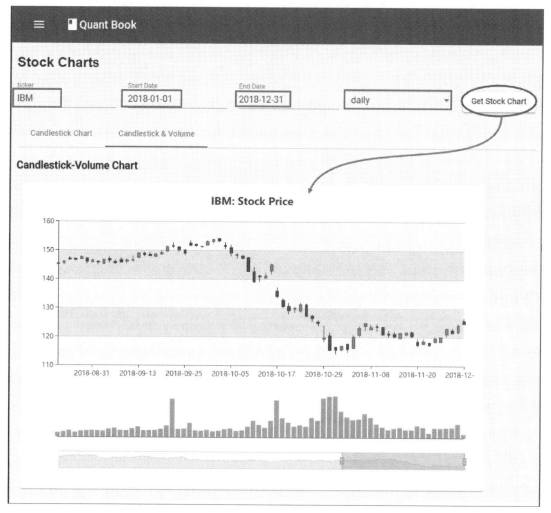

Fig.5-19. Candlestick & volume stock chart.

Real-Time Stock Charts

In this section, I will show you how to dynamically update the stock charts to display real-time data. Even though the example presented here uses the EOD stock data to demonstrate the concept of the real-time charts, it can be used as a guideline when creating your ASP.NET Core Angular single-page applications that monitor a stock's real-time tick or bar data.

Run the following command in a command prompt window from the *ClientApp* folder:

```
ng g c chapter05/realtime-stock --module=app.module
```

This will generate a new component named *realtime-stock* in the *ClientApp/src/app/chapter05* folder. Open the *realtime-stock* component class file and replace its content with the following code:

```typescript
// realtime-stock.component.ts file:
import { Component, OnInit, OnDestroy } from '@angular/core';
import { MarketDataService } from '../../models/market-data.service';
import { MarketData } from '../../models/market-data.model';
import { StockChartHelper } from '../../models/stockChartHelper';

@Component({
  selector: 'app-realtime-stock',
  templateUrl: './realtime-stock.component.html',
  styleUrls: ['./realtime-stock.component.css']
})
export class RealtimeStockComponent implements OnInit, OnDestroy {
  ticker = 'MSFT';
  startDate: string = '2015-01-01';
  endDate: string = '2018-12-31';
  interval: number = 1000;
  points: number = 50;
  private helper: StockChartHelper = new StockChartHelper();
  options: any;
  updateOptions: any;
  private data: any;
  private timer: any;
  constructor(private repository: MarketDataService) { }

  ngOnInit() {
  }

  ngOnDestroy() {
    clearInterval(this.timer);
    this.timer = null;
    this.data = null;
  }

  get stock(): MarketData[] {
    return this.repository.yahooStock;
  }

  getStock(ticker: string, start: string, end: string) {
    clearInterval(this.timer);
    this.timer = null;
    this.data = null;
    this.repository.getYahooStock(ticker, start, end, 'daily');
  }

  createChart() {
    let stock = this.helper.processStockData(this.stock);
```

```
    this.data = {
      categoryData: [stock.categoryData[0]],
      values: [stock.values[0]],
      volume: [stock.volume[0]]
    };
    this.options = this.getOptions();

    let i = 1;
    let subtitle;
    this.timer = setInterval(() => {
      this.data.categoryData.push(stock.categoryData[i]);
      this.data.values.push(stock.values[i]);
      this.data.volume.push(stock.volume[i]);
      if (this.data.values.length > this.points) {
        this.data.categoryData.shift();
        this.data.values.shift();
        this.data.volume.shift();
      }
      subtitle = '(' + (stock.values.length - i) + ' data points left)';
      if (i >= stock.values.length - 1) {
        subtitle = '(finished)';
        clearInterval(this.timer);
      }
      this.updateOptions = {
        title: {
          subtext: subtitle
        },
        xAxis: [
          { data: this.data.categoryData },
          { data: this.data.categoryData }
        ],
        series: [
          { data: this.data.values },
          { data: this.data.volume }
        ]
      };

      i++;
    }, this.interval);
}

stopChart() {
  clearInterval(this.timer);
  this.timer = null;
  this.data = null;
}

getOptions() {
  var downColor = '#ec0000';
  var downBorderColor = '#8A0000';
  var upColor = '#00da3c';
  var upBorderColor = '#008F28';

  return {
    title: {
```

```
    text: this.ticker + ': Stock Price',
    left: 'center',
    top: -5
},
tooltip: {
  trigger: 'axis',
  axisPointer: {
    type: 'cross'
  }
},
axisPointer: {
  link: { xAxisIndex: 'all' }
},
grid: [{
  left: 50,
  right: 20,
  top: '10%',
  height: '60%'
}, {
  left: 50,
  right: 20,
  height: '20%',
  top: '78%'
}],
xAxis: [{
  type: 'category',
  data: this.data.categoryData,
  scale: true,
  boundaryGap: false,
  axisLine: { onZero: false },
  splitLine: { show: false },
  splitNumber: 20,
  min: 'dataMin',
  max: 'dataMax'
}, {
  type: 'category',
  gridIndex: 1,
  data: this.data.categoryData,
  scale: true,
  boundaryGap: false,
  splitLine: { show: false },
  axisLabel: { show: false },
  axisTick: { show: false },
  axisLine: { lineStyle: { color: '#777' } },
  splitNumber: 20,
  min: 'dataMin',
  max: 'dataMax'
}
],
yAxis: [{
  scale: true,
  splitArea: {
    show: true
  }
}, {
```

```
            scale: true,
            gridIndex: 1,
            splitNumber: 2,
            axisLabel: { show: false },
            axisLine: { show: false },
            axisTick: { show: false },
            splitLine: { show: false }
        }
        ],
        series: [
          {
            name: 'candlestock',
            type: 'candlestick',
            data: this.data.values,
            itemStyle: {
              color: upColor,
              color0: downColor,
              borderColor: upBorderColor,
              borderColor0: downBorderColor
            }
          },
          {
            name: 'volume',
            type: 'bar',
            xAxisIndex: 1,
            yAxisIndex: 1,
            itemStyle: {
              normal: {
                color: '#7fbe9e'
              },
              emphasis: {
                color: '#140'
              }
            },
            data: this.data.volume
          }
        ]
    };
  }
}
```

This component first retrieves historical EOD stock data from the web service via the market data repository. It then defines two option properties for the stock chart, *options* and *updateOptions*. The former is defined using the *getOptions* method that sets up initial configurations for the stock chart, which is very similar to the options used to create the candlestick + volume chart in the preceding section. While the latter is defined inside the *setInterval* method, which needs to be updated over time. In the real-time stock chart, we only need to update the data for the *xAxis* and *series*. Here, we mimics the real-time data source by removing the oldest data point from the data series whenever a new data point is added to the data series after a specified time interval, so that we always keep 50 (you can change it as you like using the *points* property) data points in the data series.

In real-world problem, you should call the real-time stock quotes from the web service within the *setInterval* method. Here, we simply use the EOD historical stock data from Yahoo Finance to demonstrate the concept of the real-time stock charts.

Open the component's template and replace its content with the following code:

```
// realtime-stock.component.html file:
<h2>
  Real-Time Stock  Chart
</h2>
<mat-form-field>
  <input matInput placeholder="ticker" [(ngModel)]="ticker" name="ticker"
id="tickerId">
</mat-form-field>
<mat-form-field>
  <input matInput placeholder="startDate" [(ngModel)]="startDate" name="startDate">
</mat-form-field>
<mat-form-field>
  <input matInput placeholder="endDate" [(ngModel)]="endDate" name="endDate">
</mat-form-field>
<mat-form-field>
  <input matInput placeholder="interval" [(ngModel)]="interval" name="interval">
</mat-form-field>
<mat-form-field>
  <input matInput placeholder="points" [(ngModel)]="points" name="points">
</mat-form-field>
<br /><br />
<button mat-raised-button (click)="getStock(ticker,startDate,endDate)"
color="primary" style="margin-right:10px">Get Stock Data</button>

<button mat-raised-button (click)="createChart()" color="primary" style="margin-
right:10px">Start Stock Chart</button>

<button mat-raised-button (click)="stopChart()" color="primary" style="margin-
right:10px">Stop Chart</button>

<div *ngIf="stock" style="margin-top:20px">
  <div *ngIf="stock.length>0">
    <p>{{ticker}}: {{stock.length}}-day EOD stock data is available.</p>
    <mat-card class="card-stock">
      <div echarts [options]="options" [merge]="updateOptions" style="height:100%">
      </div>
    </mat-card>
  </div>
</div>
```

This template implements three buttons, *Get Stock Data*, *Start Stock Chart*, and *Stop Chart*, responsible for retrieving the stock data, starting real-time stock chart, and stopping the real-time stock chart, respectively. Here, we use the **[options]** and **[merge]** directives to bind the *options* and *updateOptions* properties defined in the component class.

The chart container is a *mat-card* that is styled using a *card-stock* class defined in the component's style file:

```
// realtime-stock.component.css file:
.card-stock {
  margin: 10px;
  width: 800px;
  height: 500px;
}
```

Finally, we need to add a path for this new component to the *RouterModule* of the root module (i.e., the *app.module.ts* file):

```
{ path: 'chapter05/realtime-stock, component: RealtimeStockComponent },
```

Then add the corresponding URL link to the *home* and *nav-menu* components.

Saving the project and navigating to the */chapter05/realtime-stock* page produce the result shown in Fig.5-20.

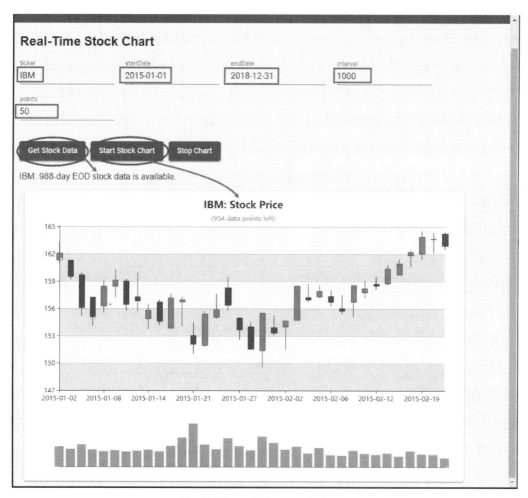

Fig.5-20. Real-time stock chart.

Here, you can enter any valid stock ticker in US equity market and specify a date range to create corresponding real-time stock chart. Note that the *interval* is in the unit of milliseconds, and 1000 means one second, that is, the chart is updated in every second.

Real-Time Stock Charts Using SignalR

In the preceding section, we created real-time stock charts using a JavaScript timer in client side. Here, I will show you another powerful method to create real-time charts using SignalR. ASP.NET Core SignalR is an open-source library that simplifies adding real-time functionality to your applications, which enables server-side code to push contents to clients instantly. It supports streaming return values of server methods. This is very useful for real-time stock charts where the stock quote data will come in continuously over time. When a return value is streamed to the client, each quote is sent to the client as soon as it becomes available, rather than waiting for all the stock data to become available.

The SignalR server library is included in the *Microsoft.AspNetCore.App* metapackage, while the JavaScript client library is not automatically included in the project. You can install the client SignalR library by adding the following statement to the *dependencies* section of the *package.json* file in the *ClientApp* folder:

```
"@aspnet/signalr": "1.1.0",
```

Here, I will show you how to dynamically update the stock charts to display real-time data. Even though the example presented here uses the EOD stock data to demonstrate the concept of the real-time charts, it can be used as a guideline when creating your ASP.NET Core Angular single-page applications that monitor a stock's real-time tick or quote data.

Add a helper method called *GetYahooStockData* to the *ModelHelper.cs* file in the *Quant/Models* folder with the following code:

```
public static List<StockData> GetYahooStockEodData(string ticker, string start,
string end)
{
    var startDate = DateTime.Parse(start);
    var endDate = DateTime.Parse(end);
    var hist = Task.Run(() => Yahoo.GetHistoricalAsync(ticker, startDate, endDate,
        Period.Daily)).Result;
    List<StockData> prices = new List<StockData>();
    foreach (var r in hist)
    {
        prices.Add(new StockData
        {
            Ticker = ticker,
            Date = r.DateTime,
            Open = (double)r.Open,
            High = (double)r.High,
            Low = (double)r.Low,
            Close = (double)r.Close,
            CloseAdj = (double)r.AdjustedClose,
            Volume = r.Volume
        });
    }
    return prices;
}
```

This method simply retrieves historical EOD stock data from Yahoo Finance.

Next, we need to create a SignalR hub class that serves as a high-level pipeline that handles client-server communication. In the *Quant* project folder, create a *Hubs* folder. In the *Hubs* folder, create a *Ch5Hub.cs* file with the following code:

```
using Microsoft.AspNetCore.SignalR;
using Quant.Models;
using System.Collections.Generic;
using System.Threading;
using System.Threading.Channels;
using System.Threading.Tasks;

namespace Quant.Hubs
{
    public class Ch5Hub : Hub
    {
        public ChannelReader<StockOutput> SendStock(string ticker, string start,
            string end, int updateInterval, CancellationToken token)
        {
            var channel = Channel.CreateUnbounded<StockOutput>();
            _ = GetStock(channel.Writer, ticker, start, end, updateInterval, token);
            return channel.Reader;
        }

        private async Task GetStock(ChannelWriter<StockOutput> writer,
            string ticker, string start, string end, int updateInterval,
            CancellationToken token)
        {
            List<StockData> stocks = ModelHelper.GetYahooStockEodData(ticker, start,
                end);
            var res = new StockOutput();
            res.Status = "starting";

            foreach (var stock in stocks)
            {
                token.ThrowIfCancellationRequested();
                res.Stock = stock;
                await writer.WriteAsync(res);
                await Task.Delay(updateInterval, token);
            }
            res.Status = "finished";
            writer.TryComplete();
        }
    }

    public class StockOutput
    {
        public string Status { get; set; }
        public StockData Stock { get; set; }
    }
}
```

Here, the *Ch5Hub* inherits from the SignalR *Hub* class. The *SendStock* method can be called by any connected clients. A hub method automatically supports a streaming hub method when it returns a **ChannelReader<T>** or a **Task<ChannelReader<T>>**. Inside the *GetStock* method, we first retrieve the stock data from Yahoo and then stream each day's stock data in every *updateInterval* (specified by user), which simulates the real-time stock quote. Note that in ASP.NET Core 2.2 or later, streaming *Hub* methods can accept a *CancellationToken* parameter that will be triggered when the client unsubscribes from the stream. Use this token to stop the server operation and release any resources if the client disconnects before the end of the stream.

Next, we need to configure SignalR. Add the following highlighted code to the *Startup.cs* file:

```
// ... other using statements omitted for brevity ...

using Quant.Hubs;

namespace Quant
{
    public class Startup
    {
        public Startup(IConfiguration configuration)
        {
            Configuration = configuration;
        }

        public IConfiguration Configuration { get; }

        public void ConfigureServices(IServiceCollection services)
        {
            // ... other service omitted for brevity ...

            services.AddSignalR();
        }

        public void Configure(IApplicationBuilder app, IHostingEnvironment env,
            QuantDataContext context)
        {
            // ... other code omitted for brevity ...

            app.UseSignalR(routes =>
            {
                routes.MapHub<Ch5Hub>("/ch5Hub");
            });

            // ... other spa-related code omitted for brevity ...
        }
    }
}
```

These changes add SignalR to the ASP.NET Core dependency injection system and the middleware pipeline.

Next, we need to create a SignalR service for the Angular client to subscribe the stream and the *SendStock* method. Run the following command in a command prompt window in the *ClientApp* folder:

```
ng g s models/signalr
```

This generates a new service class called *signalr.service.ts* in the *ClientApp/src/app/models* folder. Open this class and replace its content with the following code:

```
// signalr.service.ts file:
import { Injectable} from '@angular/core';
import { HubConnection,HubConnectionBuilder, IStreamResult } from '@aspnet/signalr';

@Injectable({
  providedIn: 'root'
})
```

```
export class Ch5HubService {
  private connection: HubConnection;

  constructor() {
    this.connection = new HubConnectionBuilder().withUrl('/ch5Hub').build();
    this.connection.start();
  }

  startStream(ticker: string, start: string, end: string, interval: number):
    IStreamResult<any> {
    if (this.connection.state == 0) this.connection.start();
    return this.connection.stream("SendStock", ticker, start, end, interval);
  }
}
```

Inside the constructor, we define and start the connection, which is responsible for creating connection with the SignalR hub, while the *startStream* method calls the *SendStock* method defined in the server to subscribe the stream data.

Now, we can use an example to test our SignalR service. Run the following command in a command prompt window from the *ClientApp* directory:

ng g c chapter05/realtime-server --module=app.module

This creates a new component named *realtime-server* in the *ClientApp/src/app/chapter05* folder. Open the component class file and replace its content with the following code:

```
// realtime-server.component.ts file:
import { Component, OnInit } from '@angular/core';
import { Ch5HubService } from '../../models/signalr.service';

@Component({
  selector: 'app-realtime-server',
  templateUrl: './realtime-server.component.html',
  styleUrls: ['./realtime-server.component.css']
})
export class RealtimeServerComponent implements OnInit {
  ticker: string = 'MSFT';
  startDate: string = '2010-01-01';
  endDate: string = '2018-12-31';
  interval: number = 1000;
  points: number = 50;
  options: any;
  updateOptions: any;
  private data: any;
  private subscription: any;

  constructor(private service: Ch5HubService) { }
    ngOnInit() {
  }

  getChart(ticker: string, start: string, end: string, interval: number) {
    const categoryData = [];
    const values = [];
    const volume = [];
    this.data = {
```

```
      categoryData: categoryData,
      values: values,
      volume: volume
    };

    this.options = this.getOptions();

    let i = 1;
    this.subscription = this.service.startStream(ticker, start, end,
      interval).subscribe({
      next: (item) => {
        if (item.status == 'starting') {
          this.data.categoryData.push(item.stock.date.toString().substring(0, 10));
          this.data.values.push([item.stock.open, item.stock.close, item.stock.low,
            item.stock.high]);
          this.data.volume.push(item.stock.volume);
          if (this.data.categoryData.length > this.points) {
            this.data.categoryData.shift();
            this.data.values.shift();
            this.data.volume.shift();
          }

          let subtitle = '(' + (item.totalDataPoints - i) + ' data points left)';
          if (item.status == 'finished') {
            subtitle = '(finished)';
            this.service.stopStream();
          }
          this.updateOptions = {
            title: {
              subtext: subtitle
            },
            xAxis: [
              { data: this.data.categoryData },
              { data: this.data.categoryData }
            ],
            series: [
              { data: this.data.values },
              { data: this.data.volume }
            ]
          };

          i++;
        }
      },
      complete: () => {
        console.log("finished.");
      },
      error: (err) => {
        console.log(err);
      }
    });
}

getOptions() {
```

```
    // ... this method is the same as that used in preceding section ...
    // ... the code omitted for brevity ...

  }

  stopChart() {
    this.subscription.dispose();
  }
}
```

In order to use the SignalR service, this component's constructor injects the *Ch5HubService* defined in the *signalr.service.ts* file. Inside the *getChart* method, we first define the *options* specified by the *getOptions* method, which is the same method we used in the preceding section. Next, we call the SignalR service's *startStream* method that returns an *IStreamResult*, which contains a subscribe method; and pass an *IStreamSubscriber* to *subscribe* and set the *next, error,* and *complete* callbacks to get notifications from the stream invocation.

In the *next* section of the *getChart* method, we can access the stream stock data via *item.stock*. In the real-time stock chart, we only need to update the data for the *xAxis* and *series*. Here, we define the data source for our real-time stock chart using each day's stream stock data and remove the oldest data point from the data source whenever a new stream data is added to the data source. We always keep 50 (you can change it as you like using the *points* property) data points in the data source.

To stop updating chart, we implement a *stopChart* method where we end the stream by calling the *dispose* method on the *ISubscription* that is returned from the *subscribe* method. Calling this *dispose* method will trigger the *CancellationToken* parameter and cause the *Hub* method to be cancelled.

Now, we need to update the component's template with the following code:

```
// realtime-server.component.html file:
<h2>
  realtime-server works!
</h2>

<mat-form-field>
  <input matInput placeholder="ticker" [(ngModel)]="ticker" name="ticker"
id="tickerId">
</mat-form-field>
<mat-form-field>
  <input matInput placeholder="startDate" [(ngModel)]="startDate" name="startDate">
</mat-form-field>
<mat-form-field>
  <input matInput placeholder="endDate" [(ngModel)]="endDate" name="endDate">
</mat-form-field>
<mat-form-field>
  <input matInput placeholder="interval" [(ngModel)]="interval" name="interval">
</mat-form-field>

<button mat-raised-button (click)="getChart(ticker,startDate,endDate,interval)"
color="primary" style="margin-right:10px">Start Stock Chart</button>

<button mat-raised-button (click)="stopChart()" color="primary" style="margin-
right:10px">Stop Stock Chart</button>
```

```
<div *ngIf="options" style="margin-top:20px">
  <mat-card class="card-stock">
    <div echarts [options]="options" [merge]="updateOptions"
      style="height:100%"></div>
  </mat-card>
</div>
```

This template implements two buttons, *Start Stock Chart* and *Stop Stock Chart*, responsible for starting the real-time stock chart and stopping the chart. Here, we use the **[options]** and **[merge]** directives to bind the *options* and *updateOptions* properties defined in the component class.

The chart container is a *mat-card* that is styled using a *card-stock* class defined in the component's style file, which is the same as that used in the previous example.

Finally, we need to add a path for this new component to the *RouterModule* of the root module (i.e., the *app.module.ts* file):

{ path: 'chapter05/realtime-server, component: RealtimeServerComponent },

Then add the corresponding URL link to the *home* and *nav-menu* components.

Saving the project and navigating to the */chapter05/realtime-server* page produce the result shown in Fig.5-21.

Fig.5-21. Real-time stock chart created using SignalR.

Chapter 6
Linear Analysis

Linear analysis is a widely used statistical tool in finance and trading. In this chapter, I will discuss two linear analysis techniques: linear regression and principal component analysis (PCA). In statistics, simple linear regression is a least squares estimator of a linear regression model with a single explanatory variable. In other words, simple linear regression fits a straight line through a set of n data points in such a way that minimizes the sum of squared residuals of the model. The PCA is a statistical procedure that uses an orthogonal transformation to convert a set of observations of possible correlated variables into a set of values of linearly uncorrelated variables called principal components. This transformation is defined in such a way that the first principal component has the largest possible eigenvalue.

In this chapter, I will first present the relevant mathematical background for simple linear regression and PCA. Next, I will show you how to carry out the multivariable line regression and multivariable PCA. We will use an open source package, Accord.NET, to perform these linear analyses.

Simple Linear Regression

Simple linear regression (SLR) refers to the fact that the resultant (or dependent) variable is related to a single predictor (or independent variable). The slope of the fitted line is equal to the correlation between these two variables corrected by the ratio of standard deviations of these variables.

We can construct a simple linear regression by fitting a line through a scatter plot of the prices for a pair of stocks. Suppose we have two stocks, x and y, which have n-day prices (x_0, y_0), $(x_1, y_1),\ldots,(x_n, y_n)$. The linear function that describes x and y is:

$$y_i = a + bx_i + \varepsilon_i$$

The goal is to find the equation of the straight line

$$y = a + bx$$

Which should provide a best fit for the data points. You can use the least-squares approach to achieve this goal. The least-squares technique minimizes the sum of squared residual of the linear regression model. You can get the parameters a (the intercept) and b (the slope) in the preceding equation from solving the following minimization problem:

$$\min_{a,b} \sum_{i=1}^{n} \epsilon_i^2 = \min_{a,b} \sum_{i=1}^{n} (y_i - a - bx_i)^2$$

Taking derivative to the above equation relative to a and b and setting them to zero generates the following equations:

$$\sum_{i=1}^{n} (y_i - a - bx_i) = 0$$

$$\sum_{i=1}^{n} x_i(y_i - a - bx_i) = 0$$

Solving these equation gives

$$b = \frac{\overline{xy} - \bar{x}\bar{y}}{\overline{x^2} - \bar{x}^2}, \qquad a = \bar{y} - b\bar{x}$$

Where $\bar{u}$ is the average value of the time series $u_0, u_1, \ldots u_n$.

Implementation

Here, we will use an open source package, Accord.NET, to perform simple linear regression. Search for Accord.NET in the NuGet package manager, and then choose to install the modules, *Accord.Math*, *Accord.Statistics*, and other modules you are interested.

Add a new class called *LinearAnalysisHelper* to the *Quant/models* folder and replace its content with the following code:

```
using Accord.Math;
using Accord.Statistics.Models.Regression.Linear;
using System.Collections.Generic;

namespace Quant.Models
{
    public static class LinearAnalysisHelper
    {
        public static SlrOutput GetSLR(string name1, string name2, double[] xdata,
            double[] ydata)
        {
            OrdinaryLeastSquares ols = new OrdinaryLeastSquares();
            SimpleLinearRegression regression = ols.Learn(xdata, ydata);
            var c = regression.Intercept;
            var s = regression.Slope;
            List<double[]> data = new List<double[]>();
            var predicted = xdata.Multiply(s).Add(c);
            for (var i = 0; i < xdata.Length; i++)
            {
                data.Add(new double[] { xdata[i], ydata[i], predicted[i]});
            }

            return new SlrOutput
            {
                Name1 = name1,
```

```
                Name2 = name2,
                Alpha = c,
                Beta = s,
                RSquared = regression.CoefficientOfDetermination(xdata, ydata),
                Data = data
            };
        }
    }

    public class SlrOutput
    {
        public string Name1 { get; set; }
        public string Name2 { get; set; }
        public double Alpha { get; set; }
        public double Beta { get; set; }
        public double RSquared { get; set; }
        public List<double[]> Data { get; set; }
    }
}
```

The *SlrOutput* class defines the output objects from the simple linear regression (SLR). Inside the *GetSlr* method, we use the ordinary least squares to learn the simple linear regression. We then extract the slope, intercept, and R-squared. We also calculate the predicted values for each of *x* data points.

In the following sections, we will discuss the meanings of Alpha, Beta, and R-squared.

R-Squared

R-squared, also called the coefficient of determination, is a statistical measure that indicates how well the data fits to a statistical model such as a linear regression. An R-Squared ~ 1 means that the regression line fits the data very well. In finance, R-Squared represents the percentage of a fund or stock's movements that can be explained by movements in a benchmark index. For equities, the benchmark is the S&P 500 index while the T-bill is usually used as the benchmark for fixed-income securities.

In a simple linear regression, R-squared equals the square of the Pearson correlation coefficient between the observed and modeled data values of the dependent variable. The Pearson correlation r can be calculated using the following equation:

$$r = \frac{\sum_{i=1}^{n}(x_i - \bar{x})(y_i - \bar{y})}{\sqrt{\sum_{i=1}^{n}(x_i - \bar{x})^2 \sum_{i=1}^{n}(y_i - \bar{y})^2}}$$

Where $\bar{u}$ is the average value of the time series $u_1, u_2,...u_n$.

In general, a data set has n values marked $y_1...y_n$, each associated with a predicted (modeled) value $f_1,... f_n$, then the variability of a data set can be measured using three sums of squares formula:

- The total sum of squares: $SS_{tot} = \sum_{i=1}^{n}(y_i - \bar{y})^2$

- The regression sum of squares: $SS_{reg} = \sum_{i=1}^{n}(f_i - \bar{y})^2$

- The sum of squares of residuals: $SS_{res} = \sum_{i=1}^{n}(y_i - f_i)^2$

The most general definition of R-squared (the coefficient of determination) is

$$R^2 = 1 - \frac{SS_{res}}{SS_{tot}}$$

What are Alpha and Beta?

In finance, *Alpha* and *Beta* are important tools when you try to figure out if your investments are performing well. *Alpha* is a measure of an investment's performance compared to a benchmark, such as the S&P 500 index. It is an estimate of the return based usually on the growth of earnings per share. On the other hand, *Beta* is based on the volatility, namely the movement of the fund or stock relative to its benchmark. If it goes up more when its benchmark goes up, then it has a higher beta. A beta of one means it moves just like its benchmark.

As discussed previously, the simple linear regression for the returns of a stock and a benchmark index is a mathematical process to produce a single straight line that best represents all the data points in a scatter chart. We can use two parameters, intercept and slope, to describe this regression line. Mathematically, we believe that the intercept is the *Alpha* and the slope is the *Beta*. Please note that both *Alpha* and *Beta* depend strongly on the date period you are choosing; they can have dramatically different values for different periods.

In the following section, we will look at how to calculate *Alpha* and *Beta* and how the linear regression looks like on the charts.

Web Service for Simple Linear Regression

In this section, I will show you how to perform simple linear regression for some securities and how to convert the results into web services.

Add an API controller named *LinearAnalysisValuesController* to the *Controllers* folder and replace its content with the following code listing:

```
using Accord.Math;
using Microsoft.AspNetCore.Mvc;
using Quant.Models;
using System;
using System.Linq;
using System.Threading.Tasks;
using YahooFinanceApi;

namespace Quant.Controllers
{
    public class LinearAnalysisValuesController : Controller
    {
        private readonly QuantDataContext context;
        public LinearAnalysisValuesController(QuantDataContext ctx)
        {
            context = ctx;
        }

        [Route("~/api/SlrIndex/{xName}/{yName}")]
        [HttpGet]
        public SlrOutput SlrIndex(string xName, string yName)
        {
            var data = context.IndexDatas.OrderBy(d => d.Date);
            double[] xdata = null;
            double[] ydata = null;
            xName = xName.ToLower();
            yName = yName.ToLower();
```

```
    if (xName == "ig") xdata = data.Select(x => x.IGSpread).ToArray();
    else if (xName == "hy") xdata = data.Select(x =>
        x.HYSpread).ToArray();
    else if (xName == "spx") xdata = data.Select(x => x.SPX).ToArray();
    else if (xName == "vix") xdata = data.Select(x => x.VIX).ToArray();
    if (yName == "ig") ydata = data.Select(x => x.IGSpread).ToArray();
    else if (yName == "hy") ydata = data.Select(x =>
        x.HYSpread).ToArray();
    else if (yName == "spx") ydata = data.Select(x => x.SPX).ToArray();
    else if (yName == "vix") ydata = data.Select(x => x.VIX).ToArray();
    return LinearAnalysisHelper.GetSlr(xName.ToUpper(), yName.ToUpper(),
        xdata, ydata);
}


[Route("~/api/SlrStock/{xTicker}/{yTicker}/{start}/{end}")]
[HttpGet]
public async Task<SlrOutput> SlrStock (string xTicker, string yTicker,
    string start, string end)
{
    xTicker = xTicker.ToUpper();
    yTicker = yTicker.ToUpper();
    var startDate = DateTime.Parse(start);
    var endDate = DateTime.Parse(end);
    var data1 = await Yahoo.GetHistoricalAsync(xTicker, startDate, endDate,
        Period.Daily);
    var data2 = await Yahoo.GetHistoricalAsync(yTicker, startDate, endDate,
        Period.Daily);
    var xdata = data1.Select(x => (double)x.AdjustedClose).ToArray();
    var ydata = data2.Select(x => (double)x.AdjustedClose).ToArray();
    return LinearAnalysisHelper.GetSlr(xTicker, yTicker, xdata, ydata);
}


[Route("~/api/SlrStockReturn/{xTicker}/{yTicker}/{start}/{end}")]
[HttpGet]
public async Task<SlrOutput> SlrStockReturn(string xTicker, string yTicker,
    string start, string end)
{
    xTicker = xTicker.ToUpper();
    yTicker = yTicker.ToUpper();
    var startDate = DateTime.Parse(start);
    var endDate = DateTime.Parse(end);
    var data1 = await Yahoo.GetHistoricalAsync(xTicker, startDate, endDate,
        Period.Daily);
    var data2 = await Yahoo.GetHistoricalAsync(yTicker, startDate, endDate,
        Period.Daily);
    var xdata1 = data1.Select(x => (double)x.AdjustedClose).ToArray();
    var ydata1 = data2.Select(x => (double)x.AdjustedClose).ToArray();
    int len = xdata1.Length;
    double[] xdata = new double[len - 1];
    double[] ydata = new double[len - 1];
    for(var i = 1; i < len; i++)
    {
        xdata[i - 1] = 100.0 * (xdata1[i] - xdata1[i - 1]) / xdata1[i - 1];
        ydata[i - 1] = 100.0 * (ydata1[i] - ydata1[i - 1]) / ydata1[i - 1];
    }
```

```
                return LinearAnalysisHelper.GetSlr(xTicker, yTicker, xdata, ydata);
        }
    }
}
```

Here, we implement three methods, *SlrIndex*, *SlrStock* and *SlrStockReturn*. The *SlrIndex* method is used to perform regression for any index pair using the index data stored in the database (see Chapter 3). The input arguments, *xName* and *yName*, can be any of four indices, IG, HY, SPX, and VIX. After assigning the *xdata* and *ydata* arrays, we call the *GetSlr* method in the *LinearAnalysisHelper* class to perform the regression computation.

Here, we also explicitly define the route for this API service. We can test this API service by running the project and entering the following URL in your browser:

https://localhost:5001/api/slrindex/vix/hyspread

This generates the result shown in Fig.6-1.

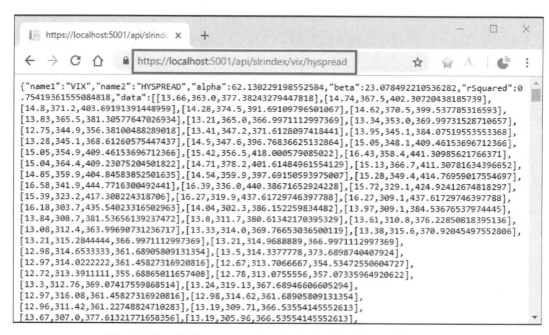

Fig.6-1. Simple linear regression for index data from web service.

The *SlrStock* method can be used to perform simple linear regression for any stock pair traded in the US equity market. It allows you to specify a pair of stock tickers and a data range. The data source is the historical EOD adjusted close price data from Yahoo Finance.

We can test this API service by running this project and entering the following URL in your browser:

https://localhost:5001/api/slrstock/ibm/msft/2017-01-01/2018-12-31

This produces the result shown in Fig.6-2.

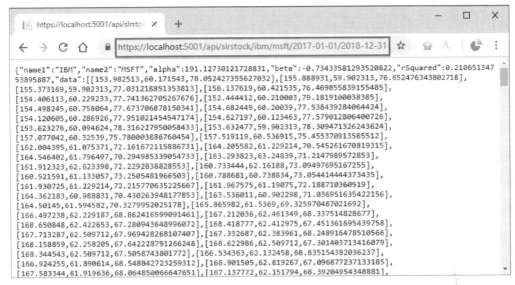

Fig.6-2. Simple linear regression for stock data from web service.

The *SlrStockReturn* method can be used to perform simple linear regression for price daily returns of any stock pair traded in the US equity market. It allows you to specify a pair of stock tickers and a data range. We can test this API service by running this project and entering the following URL in your browser:

`https://localhost:5001/api/slrstockReturn/ibm/msft/2017-01-01/2018-12-31`

This produces the result shown in Fig.6-3.

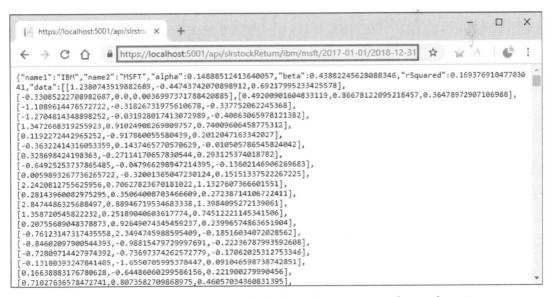

Fig.6-3. Simple linear regression for daily stock price returns from web service.

Simple Linear Regression in Angular

The process of sending a request from the Angular application to get the simple linear regression result following the same basic repository patterns presented in the preceding chapter. The first step is to define a model for the regression. Add a TypeScript class called *ch6.model.ts* to the *ClientApp/src/app/models* folder. The prefix *ch6* added to the model class is to avoid the name conflict. Here is the code listing for this class:

```
// ch6.model.ts file:
export class SlrOutput {
  constructor(
    public name1?: string,
    public name2?: string,
    public alpha?: number,
    public beta?: number,
    public rSquared?: number,
    public data?: any[]
  ) { }
}
```

This class corresponds to the C# *SlrOutput.cs* class defined in the preceding section. Next, we need to add a repository service called *ch6.service.ts* to the *ClientApp/src/app/models* folder by running the following command in a command prompt window from the *ClientApp* folder:

ng g s models/ch6

Open the *ch6.service.ts* class file and replace its content with the following code:

```
// ch6.service.ts file:
import { Injectable, Inject } from '@angular/core';
import { HttpClient } from '@angular/common/http';
import { SlrOutput } from './ch6.model'

@Injectable({
  providedIn: 'root'
})
export class Ch6Service {
  slrIndex: SlrOutput;
  slrStock: SlrOutput;
  slrStockReturn: SlrOutput;

  private url;
  constructor(private http: HttpClient, @Inject('BASE_URL') baseUrl: string) {
    this.url = baseUrl;
  }

  getSlrIndex(xname: string, yname: string) {
    let url1 = this.url + 'api/srlindex/' + xname + '/' + yname;
    this.http.get<SlrOutput>(url1).subscribe(result => { this.slrIndex = result });
  }

  getSlrStock(xticker: string, yticker: string, start: string, end: string) {
    let url1 = this.url + 'api/srlstock/' + xticker + '/' + yticker + '/'
      + start + '/' + end;
    this.http.get<SlrOutput>(url1).subscribe(result => { this.slrStock = result })
  }
```

```
getSlrStockReturn(xticker: string, yticker: string, start: string, end: string) {
    let url1 = this.url + 'api/slrstockreturn/' + xticker + '/' + yticker + '/' +
      start + '/' + end;
    this.http.get<SlrOutput>(url1).subscribe(result => {
      this.slrStockReturn = result })
  }
}
```

This service is very similar to the *repository.service.ts* class implemented in Chapter 3. The *getSlrIndex*, *getSlrStock*, and *getSlrStockReturn* methods send HTTP requests to specified URLs, which get the regression results for index data, stock data, and stock price returns respectively from the ASP.NET Core API service.

SLR Results for Index Data

Here, I will use an example to show you how to perform linear regression for index data and how to display the regression results.

First, we create a scatter chart with the regression line for simple linear regression. This chart component can be used to display various SLR results. Run the following command in a command prompt window:

ng g c chapter06/ch6-slr-chart --module=app.module

This will generate a new component named *ch6-slr-chart* in the *ClientApp/src/app/chapter06* folder. Open the component class file and replace its content with the following code:

```
// ch6-slr-chart.component.ts file:
import { Component, OnInit, Input, OnChanges } from '@angular/core';
import { SlrOutput } from '../../models/ch6.model';

@Component({
  selector: 'app-ch6-slr-chart',
  templateUrl: './ch6-slr-chart.component.html',
  styleUrls: ['./ch6-slr-chart.component.css']
})
export class Ch6SlrChartComponent implements OnInit, OnChanges {
  @Input() title: string;
  @Input() slrOutput: SlrOutput;
  options: any;

  constructor() { }

  ngOnInit() {

  }
  ngOnChanges() {
    this.options = this.getOptions();
  }

  getOptions() {
    return {
      title: {
        text: this.slrOutput.name2 + ' ~ ' + this.slrOutput.name1,
        subtext: 'α = ' + this.slrOutput.alpha.toFixed(4) + ', β = ' +
```

```
              this.slrOutput.beta.toFixed(4)
              + ', R2 = ' + this.slrOutput.rSquared.toFixed(4),
            left: 'center'
          },
          tooltip: {
            trigger: 'axis',
            axisPointer: {
              type: 'cross'
            }
          },
          dataset: {
            source: this.slrOutput.data
          },
          xAxis: {
            name: this.slrOutput.name1,
            scale: true,
            axisLine: {onZero: false}
          },
          yAxis: {
            name: this.slrOutput.name2,
            scale: true,
            axisLine: {onZero: false}
          },
          series: [
            {
              type: 'line',
              encode: {
                x: 0,
                y: 2
              },
              showSymbol: false,
              zlevel: 10
            },
            {
              type: 'scatter',
              encode: {
                x: 0,
                y: 1
              },
              symbolSize: 6,
              zlevel: 0
            }
          ]
        }
      }
    }
  }
}
```

This component takes *title* and *slrOutput* as input parameters that should be specified in its parent component. We also specify an *options* property, defined using the *getOptions* method. Inside this method, we set a global *dataset* field and set the *slrOutput.data* as its data source. This data source contains three columns: *xdata*, *ydata*, and *predicted*.

The chart we would like to create contains two series: a scatter chart and a line chart with the linear regression line. We use the *encode* field to indicate which columns should be used for each series. Here, we use the first column (column 0 or *xdata*) and second column (column 1 or *ydata*) for the scatter series, while use the first column and third column (column 2 or *predicted* from SLR) for the line series.

The template for this component is very simple:

```
// ch6-slr-chart.component.html file:
<div echarts [options]="options" style="height:100%"></div>
```

Now, we can use this component to display the SLR results for index and stock data.

Run the following command in a command prompt window:

ng g c chapter06/ch6-slr-index --module=app.module

This will generate a new component named *ch6-slr-index* in the *ClientApp/src/app/chapter06* folder. Open the component class file and replace its content with the following code listing:

```
// ch6-slr-index.component.ts file:
import { Component, OnInit } from '@angular/core';
import { SlrOutput } from '../../models/ch6.model';
import { Ch6Service } from '../../models/ch6.service'

@Component({
  selector: 'app-ch6-slr-index',
  templateUrl: './ch6-slr-index.component.html',
  styleUrls: ['./ch6-slr-index.component.css']
})
export class Ch6SlrIndexComponent implements OnInit {
  title: string = 'Simple Linear Regression';
  xname: string = 'SPX';
  yname: string = 'HY';

  constructor(private repository: Ch6Service) { }

  ngOnInit() {
    this.getSlrOutput(this.xname, this.yname);
  }

  get slrOutput(): SlrOutput {
    return this.repository.slrIndex;
  }

  getSlrOutput(xname: string, yname: string) {
    this.repository.getSlrIndex(xname, yname);
  }
}
```

This component simply retrieves the SLR results for the index data specified by the *xname* and *yname* properties with the default values of SPX and HY. We also define a *title* property to be used as input for the *ch6-slr-chart* component.

The following code is for this component's template:

```
// ch6-slr-index.component.html file:
<h2>
  ch6-slr-index works!
</h2>
```

```
<mat-form-field>
  <input matInput placeholder="xname" [(ngModel)]="xname" name="nxname">
</mat-form-field>
<mat-form-field>
  <input matInput placeholder="yname" [(ngModel)]="yname" name="yname">
</mat-form-field>
<button mat-raised-button color="primary" (click)="getSlrOutput(xname,yname)">Get
SLR Index Chart</button>

<div *ngIf="slrOutput">
  <div *ngIf="slrOutput.data.length>0">
    <mat-card class="card-chart">
      <app-ch6-slr-chart [title]="title" [slrOutput]="slrOutput">
      </app-ch6-slr-chart>
    </mat-card>
  </div>
</div>
```

This template allows you to specify a pair of index data for the regression. We also add the *app-ch6-slr-chart* directive and specify its *title* and *slrOutput* directives using corresponding properties. The *mat-card* container consists of a class named *card-chart* defined in the component's style file:

```
// ch6-slr-index.component.css file:
.card-chart {
  margin: 10px;
  width: 800px;
  height: 600px;
}
```

This simply defines the size of the chart.

Finally, we need to add a path for this new component to the *RouterModule* of the root module (i.e., the *app.module.ts* file):

```
{ path: 'chapter06/ch6-slr-index, component: Ch6SlrIndexComponent },
```

Then add the corresponding URL link to the *home* and *nav-menu* components.

Saving the project and navigating to the */chapter06/ch6-slr-index* page produce the default SLR results shown in Fig.6-4.

Now, changing the *xname* to VIX, keeping HY in the *yname* field, and clicking the *Get SLR Index Chart* button produce the results shown in Fig.6-5.

Note that the regression of SPX and VIX relative to HY has an R-squared = 0.4465 and 0.7542 respectively, indicating that VIX has a higher correlation to HY than SPX does during a 10-year period.

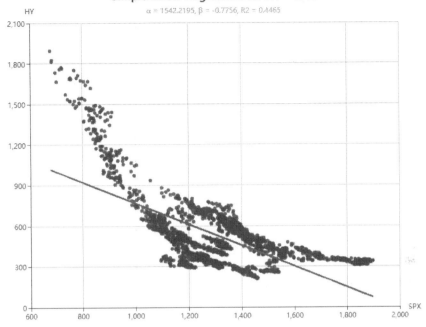

Fig.6-4. Simple linear regression result for HY and SPX.

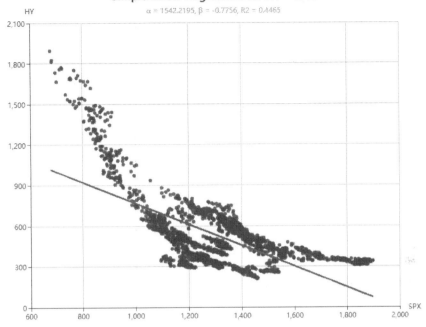

Fig.6-5. Simple linear regression results for HY and VIX.

SLR Results for Stocks

Similarly, we can create a component to display the regression results for a pair of stocks. Run the following command in a command prompt window:

```
ng g c chapter06/ch6-slr-stock --module=app.module
```

This will generate a new component named *ch6-slr-stock* in the *ClientApp/src/app/chapter06* folder. Open the component class file and replace its content with the following code:

```typescript
// ch6-slr-stock.component.ts file:
import { Component, OnInit } from '@angular/core';
import { SlrOutput } from '../../models/ch6.model';
import { Ch6Service } from '../../models/ch6.service'

@Component({
  selector: 'app-ch6-slr-stock',
  templateUrl: './ch6-slr-stock.component.html',
  styleUrls: ['./ch6-slr-stock.component.css']
})
export class Ch6SlrStockComponent implements OnInit {
  title: string = 'SLR Price';
  titleReturn: string = 'SLR Return';
  ticker1: string = '^GSPC';
  ticker2: string = 'C';
  start: string = '2013-01-01';
  end: string = '2018-01-01';

  constructor(private repository: Ch6Service) { }

  ngOnInit() {
    this.getSlrOutput(this.ticker1, this.ticker2, this.start, this.end);
  }

  get slrOutput(): SlrOutput {
    return this.repository.slrStock;
  }

  get slrOutputReturn(): SlrOutput {
    return this.repository.slrStockReturn;
  }

  getSlrOutput(ticker1: string, ticker2: string, start: string, end: string) {
    this.repository.getSlrStock(ticker1, ticker2, start, end);
    this.repository.getSlrStockReturn(ticker1, ticker2, start, end);
  }
}
```

This component simply retrieves the SLR results for the stock price data and price returns specified by the *ticker1, ticker2, start,* and *end* properties with the default stock tickers C (Citi) and ^GSPC (S&P 500 index). We also define *title* and *titleReturn* properties to be used as input for the *ch6-slr-chart* component.

The following code listing is for this component's template:

```
// ch6-slr-stock.component.html file:
```

```html
<h2>
  ch6-slr-stock works!
</h2>

<mat-form-field>
  <input matInput placeholder="ticker1" [(ngModel)]="ticker1" name="ticker1">
</mat-form-field>
<mat-form-field>
  <input matInput placeholder="ticker2" [(ngModel)]="ticker2" name="ticker2">
</mat-form-field>
<mat-form-field>
  <input matInput placeholder="start" [(ngModel)]="start" name="start">
</mat-form-field>
<mat-form-field>
  <input matInput placeholder="end" [(ngModel)]="end" name="end">
</mat-form-field>
<button mat-raised-button color="primary"
(click)="getSlrOutput(ticker1,ticker2,start,end)">Get SLR Stock Chart</button>

<div *ngIf="slrOutput">
  <div *ngIf="slrOutput.data.length>0">
    <div class="cardList">
      <mat-card class="card-border">
        <app-ch6-slr-chart [title]="title" [slrOutput]="slrOutput">
        </app-ch6-slr-chart>
      </mat-card>
      <mat-card class="card-border">
        <app-ch6-slr-chart [title]="titleReturn"
          [slrOutput]="slrOutputReturn"></app-ch6-slr-chart>
      </mat-card>
    </div>
  </div>
</div>
```

This template allows you to specify a pair of stocks and date range for the regression. We add two *app-ch6-slr-chart* directives and specify its *title* and *slrOutput* directives using corresponding properties, which are used to display regression results for stock prices and price returns. The *mat-card* container consists of style classes named *cardList* and *card-border* defined in the component's style file:

```css
// ch6-slr-stock.component.css file:
.cardList {
  display: flex;
  flex-direction: row;
  flex-wrap: wrap;
  justify-content: flex-start;
}

.card-border {
  margin: 10px;
  width: 600px;
  height: 500px;
}
```

Finally, we need to add a path for this new component to the *RouterModule* of the root module (i.e., the *app.module.ts* file):

```
{ path: 'chapter06/ch6-slr-stock, component: Ch6SlrStockComponent },
```

Then add the corresponding URL link to the *home* and *nav-menu* components.

Saving the project and navigating to the */chapter06/ch6-slr-stock* page produce the default SLR results shown in Fig.6-6.

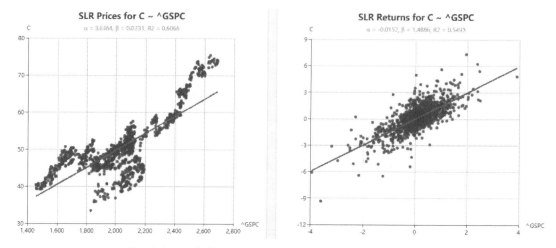

Fig.6-6. Simple linear regression results for C and ^GSPC.

Note that the price regression for C (Citi) and SPX (or ^GSPC) has an R-squared =0.6066, which is slightly higher than their daily return regression (0.5493). From their return regression, we can extract two important parameter, *Alpha* = -0.0152 and *Beta* = 1.4886, for the last 5-year period (from 2013-01-01 to 2018-01-01). You can see that the stock C underperforms the SPX index (*Alpha* < 0), and is almost 50% more volatile than the SPX index because Beta = 1.4886.

If we enter JPM in the ticker2 field, we will get the regression results shown in Fig.6-7.

In this case, the *Alpha* = 0.023 for the returns, meaning that the JPM outperforms the benchmark SPX index (*Alpha* > 0)

Investors can use both *Alpha* and *Beta* for the returns to examine a fund manager's or individual stock's performance. Most investors would prefer a high *Alpha* and a low *Beta*. However, other investors might like the higher *Beta*, trying to cash in on the stock or fund's volatility in price and shares sold.

We can check the ^DJI (Dow Jones Industrial Average index) regression relative to SPX. Figure 6-8 shows the regression results for ^DJI and SPX. You can see that both the price (left) and return (right) regressions have high R-squared (0.9589 and 0.9319), and Dow Jones index is slightly outperforms SPX (*Alpha* = 0.0038 > 0 for the return).

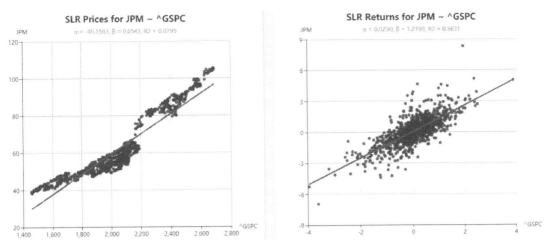

Fig.6-7. Simple linear regression results for JPM and ^GSPC.

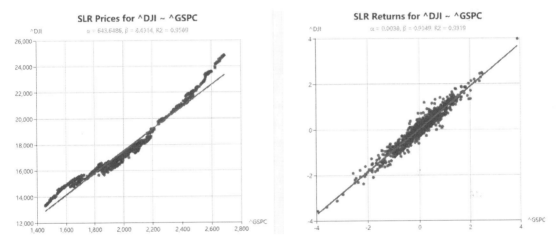

Figure 6-8. Simple linear regression results for ^DJI and ^GSPC.

Simple 2D PCA

PCA is a mathematical procedure that intends to replace a number of correlated variables with a new set of variables that are linearly uncorrelated. It is a way of identifying patterns in data, and expressing the data in such a way as to highlight their similarities and differences. Since patterns is hard to find in data of high dimension, PCA is a powerful tool for analyzing data. The other main advantage of PCA is that once you have found these patterns, you can compress the data by reducing the number of dimensions, without much loss of information.

In 2D case, PCA is very simple to analyze. Suppose we have a collection of data points (x_0, y_0), (x_1, y_1),...(x_n, y_n). In order for the PCA to work properly, we first need to subtract the mean from each data series. Therefore, all the x values have $\bar{x}$ (the mean of the x values of all the data points) subtracted, and all the y values have $\bar{y}$ subtracted. The new data points correspond to a translation: $(x, y) \rightarrow (x - \bar{x}, y -$

$\bar{y}$). In the new data space with the mean subtracted, the covariance matrix can be simply expressed in the form:

$$\sigma = \begin{pmatrix} \overline{x^2} & \overline{xy} \\ \overline{xy} & \overline{y^2} \end{pmatrix}, \quad \text{where: } \overline{x^2} = \frac{1}{n-1}\sum_{i=1}^{n} x_i x_i, \quad \overline{xy} = \frac{1}{n-1}\sum_{i=1}^{n} x_i y_i$$

The PCA components are just the eigenvectors of the covariance matrix. For a 2D covariance matrix, we can easily find the analytic solution for the eigenvalues and eigenvectors. The eigenvalues can be obtained by finding the roots of

$$\det \begin{pmatrix} a - \lambda & b \\ b & c - \lambda \end{pmatrix} = 0, \quad \text{with } a = \overline{x^2}, \quad b = \overline{xy}, \quad c = \overline{y^2}$$

This equation has two roots, and they are:

$$\lambda_{\pm} = \frac{(a+c) \pm d}{2}, \quad d = \sqrt{(a-c)^2 + 4b^2}$$

Corresponding to each eigenvalues, λ_i, there will be an eigenvector e_i that can be obtained by solving a set of linear equations. For 2D case, we need to solve

$$\begin{pmatrix} a - \lambda & b \\ b & c - \lambda \end{pmatrix} \begin{pmatrix} x \\ y \end{pmatrix} = \begin{pmatrix} 0 \\ 0 \end{pmatrix}$$

The normalized eigenvectors can be written in the form:

$$\frac{1}{\sqrt{2d[d \pm (c-a)]}} \begin{pmatrix} \pm 2b \\ d \pm (c-a) \end{pmatrix}$$

Any none-zero multiple of these vectors is, of course, also an eigenvector. It is important to note that these eigenvectors are unit eigenvectors, i.e. their lengths are 1. This is very important for PCA. Usually, the eigenvector with the highest eigenvalue is the principal component of the data set. In 2D PCA case, we usually pick the eigenvector with the higher eigenvalue and neglect the eigenvector with the lower eigenvalue.

Implementation

Here, we will also use Accord.NET to perform 2D PCA. Add a public method named *GetPca2D* and a private method named *GetRSquared* to the *LinearAnalysisHelper* class in the *Quant/models* folder. Here is the code for these two methods:

```
using Accord.Math;
using Accord.Statistics;
using Accord.Statistics.Analysis;
using Accord.Statistics.Models.Regression.Linear;
using System.Collections.Generic;

namespace Quant.Models
{
    public static class LinearAnalysisHelper
    {
        // ... other code omitted for brevity ...

        public static SlrOutput GetPca2D(string name1, string name2,
            double[] xdata, double[] ydata)
```

```
    {
        var xavg = xdata.Mean();
        var yavg = ydata.Mean();
        int len = xdata.Length;
        double[][] input = new double[len][];
        for(var i = 0; i < len; i++)
        {
            input[i] = new double[] { xdata[i], ydata[i] };
        }

        var pca = new PrincipalComponentAnalysis(method:
            PrincipalComponentMethod.Center);
        pca.Learn(input);
        var ab = pca.Components[0].Eigenvector;

        var b = ab[1] / ab[0];
        var a = yavg - b * xavg;
        List<double[]> data = new List<double[]>();
        double[] predicted = new double[len];
        for (var i = 0; i < len; i++)
        {
            predicted[i] = a + b * xdata[i];
            data.Add(new double[] { xdata[i], ydata[i], predicted[i] });
        }

        return new SlrOutput
        {
            Name1 = name1,
            Name2 = name2,
            Alpha = a,
            Beta = b,
            RSquared = GetRSquared(ydata,predicted),
            Data = data
        };
    }

    private static double GetRSquared(double[] ydata, double[] predicted)
    {
        double avg = ydata.Mean();
        double ss_tot = 0.0;
        double ss_res = 0.0;
        for(var i = 0; i < ydata.Length; i++)
        {
            double p = predicted[i];
            double y = ydata[i];
            ss_tot += (y - avg) * (y - avg);
            ss_res += (y - p) * (y - p);
        }
        return 1.0 - ss_res / ss_tot;
    }
}

// ... other code omitted for brevity ...

}
```

Inside the *GetPca2D* method, we use the *PrincipalComponentAnalysis* class from Accord.NET to perform the PCA computation with the centering method (i.e., subtracting the mean value from the data). We then use the first principal component's eigenvector to calculate intercept and slope for the PCA line. This method returns the *SlrOutput* object, which is the same as that used in the case of simple linear regression.

Here, we also add a private *GetRSquare* method that can be used to calculate the R-squared for our 2D PCA prediction because the PCA in Accord.NET does not implement a method to calculate the R-squared.

Now, I will show you how to perform 2D PCA for some securities and how to convert the results into web services.

Add three new methods to the *LinearAnalysisValuesController* class in the *Controllers* folder with the following code listings:

```
[Route("~/api/Pca2dIndex/{xName}/{yName}")]
[HttpGet]
public SlrOutput Pca2dIndex(string xName, string yName)
{
    var data = context.IndexDatas.OrderBy(d => d.Date);
    double[] xdata = null;
    double[] ydata = null;
    xName = xName.ToLower();
    yName = yName.ToLower();
    if (xName == "ig") xdata = data.Select(x => x.IGSpread).ToArray();
    else if (xName == "hy") xdata = data.Select(x => x.HYSpread).ToArray();
    else if (xName == "spx") xdata = data.Select(x => x.SPX).ToArray();
    else if (xName == "vix") xdata = data.Select(x => x.VIX).ToArray();
    if (yName == "ig") ydata = data.Select(x => x.IGSpread).ToArray();
    else if (yName == "hy") ydata = data.Select(x => x.HYSpread).ToArray();
    else if (yName == "spx") ydata = data.Select(x => x.SPX).ToArray();
    else if (yName == "vix") ydata = data.Select(x => x.VIX).ToArray();
    return LinearAnalysisHelper.GetPca2D(xName.ToUpper(), yName.ToUpper(),
        xdata, ydata);
}


[Route("~/api/Pca2DStock/{xTicker}/{yTicker}/{start}/{end}")]
[HttpGet]
public async Task<SlrOutput> Pca2dStock(string xTicker, string yTicker,
    string start, string end)
{
    xTicker = xTicker.ToUpper();
    yTicker = yTicker.ToUpper();
    var startDate = DateTime.Parse(start);
    var endDate = DateTime.Parse(end);
    var data1 = await Yahoo.GetHistoricalAsync(xTicker, startDate, endDate,
        Period.Daily);
    var data2 = await Yahoo.GetHistoricalAsync(yTicker, startDate, endDate,
        Period.Daily);
            var xdata = data1.Select(x => (double)x.AdjustedClose).ToArray();
            var ydata = data2.Select(x => (double)x.AdjustedClose).ToArray();
            return LinearAnalysisHelper.GetPca2D(xTicker, yTicker, xdata, ydata);
    }
```

```
[Route("~/api/Pca2dStockReturn/{xTicker}/{yTicker}/{start}/{end}")]
[HttpGet]
public async Task<SlrOutput> Pca2dStockReturn(string xTicker, string yTicker,
    string start, string end)
{
    xTicker = xTicker.ToUpper();
    yTicker = yTicker.ToUpper();
    var startDate = DateTime.Parse(start);
    var endDate = DateTime.Parse(end);
    var data1 = await Yahoo.GetHistoricalAsync(xTicker, startDate, endDate,
        Period.Daily);
    var data2 = await Yahoo.GetHistoricalAsync(yTicker, startDate, endDate,
        Period.Daily);
    var xdata1 = data1.Select(x => (double)x.AdjustedClose).ToArray();
    var ydata1 = data2.Select(x => (double)x.AdjustedClose).ToArray();
    int len = xdata1.Length;
    double[] xdata = new double[len - 1];
    double[] ydata = new double[len - 1];
    for (var i = 1; i < len; i++)
    {
        xdata[i - 1] = 100.0 * (xdata1[i] - xdata1[i - 1]) / xdata1[i - 1];
        ydata[i - 1] = 100.0 * (ydata1[i] - ydata1[i - 1]) / ydata1[i - 1];
    }
    return LinearAnalysisHelper.GetPca2D(xTicker, yTicker, xdata, ydata);
}
```

The methods, *Pca2dIndex*, *Pca2dStock* and *Pca2dStockReturn* are very similar to those used in simple linear regression and can be used to perform PCA computations for index data, stock prices, and daily stock price returns.

2D PCA in Angular

The process of sending a request from the Angular application to get the 2D PCA results following the same basic repository patterns as in the simple linear regression presented previously. Add the highlighted code to the *ch6.service.ts* file in the *ClientApp/src/app/models folder*:

```
// ch6-service.ts file:
import { Injectable, Inject } from '@angular/core';
import { HttpClient } from '@angular/common/http';
import { SlrOutput } from './ch6.model'

@Injectable({
  providedIn: 'root'
})
export class Ch6Repository {
  slrIndex: SlrOutput;
  slrStock: SlrOutput;
  slrStockReturn: SlrOutput;
  pca2dIndex: SlrOutput;
  pca2dStock: SlrOutput;
  pca2dStockReturn: SlrOutput;

  private url;
  constructor(private http: HttpClient, @Inject('BASE_URL') baseUrl: string) {
```

```
    this.url = baseUrl;
  }

  // ... other methods omitted for brevity ...

  getPca2dIndex(xname: string, yname: string) {
    let url1 = this.url + 'api/pca2dindex/' + xname + '/' + yname;
    this.http.get<SlrOutput>(url1).subscribe(result => { this.pca2dIndex =
      result });
  }

  getPca2dStock(xticker: string, yticker: string, start: string, end: string) {
    let url1 = this.url + 'api/pca2dstock/' + xticker + '/' + yticker + '/'
      + start + '/' + end;
    this.http.get<SlrOutput>(url1).subscribe(result => { this.pca2dStock = result })
  }

  getPca2dStockReturn(xticker: string, yticker: string, start: string, end: string)
  {
    let url1 = this.url + 'api/pca2dstockreturn/' + xticker + '/' + yticker + '/'
      + start + '/' + end;
    this.http.get<SlrOutput>(url1).subscribe(result => { this.pca2dStockReturn =
      result })
  }
}
```

This service is very similar to the *repository.service.ts* class implemented in Chapter 3. The *getPca2dIndex*, *getPca2dStock*, and *getPca2dStockReturn* methods send HTTP requests to specified URLs, which get the 2D PCA results for index data, stock data, and stock price returns respectively from the ASP.NET Core API service.

2D PCA Results for Index Data

Here, I will use an example to show you how to perform 2D PCA for index data and how to display the regression results.

Run the following command in a command prompt window:

ng g c chapter06/ch6-pca2d-index --module=app.module

This will generate a new component named *ch6-pca2d-index* in the *ClientApp/src/app/chapter06* folder. Open the component class file and replace its content with the following code:

```
// ch6-pca2d-index.component.ts file:
import { Component, OnInit } from '@angular/core';
import { SlrOutput } from '../../models/ch6.model';
import { Ch6Service } from '../../models/ch6.service'

@Component({
  selector: 'app-ch6-pca2d-index',
  templateUrl: './ch6-pca2d-index.component.html',
  styleUrls: ['./ch6-pca2d-index.component.css']
})
export class Ch6Pca2dIndexComponent implements OnInit {
  title: string = '2D PCA';
```

```
xname: string = 'SPX';
yname: string = 'HY';

constructor(private repository: Ch6Service) { }

ngOnInit() {
  this.getPca2dOutput(this.xname, this.yname);
}

get pca2dOutput(): SlrOutput {
  return this.repository.pca2dIndex;
}

getPca2dOutput(xname: string, yname: string) {
  this.repository.getPca2dIndex(xname, yname);
}
}
```

This component simply retrieves the 2D PCA results for the index data specified by the *xname* and *yname* properties with the default values of SPX and HY. We also define a *title* property to be used as input for the *ch6-slr-chart* component.

The following code listing is for this component's template:

```
// ch6-pac2d.component.html file:
<h2>
  ch6-pca2d-index works!
</h2>
<mat-form-field>
  <input matInput placeholder="xname" [(ngModel)]="xname" name="nxname">
</mat-form-field>
<mat-form-field>
  <input matInput placeholder="yname" [(ngModel)]="yname" name="yname">
</mat-form-field>
<button mat-raised-button color="primary" (click)="getPca2dOutput(xname,yname)">Get
PCA2D Index Chart</button>

<div *ngIf="pca2dOutput">
  <div *ngIf="pca2dOutput.data.length>0">
    <mat-card class="card-chart">
      <app-ch6-slr-chart [title]="title" [slrOutput]="pca2dOutput">
      </app-ch6-slr-chart>
    </mat-card>
  </div>
</div>
```

This template allows you to specify a pair of index data for the 2D PCA. We also add an *app-ch6-slr-chart* directive and specify its *title* and *slrOutput* directives using corresponding properties. The *mat-card* container consists of a class named *card-chart* defined in the component's style file:

```
// ch6-pca2d-index.component.css file:
.card-chart {
  margin: 10px;
  width: 800px;
  height: 600px;
}
```

This simply defines the size of the chart.

Finally, we need to add a path for this new component to the *RouterModule* of the root module (i.e., the *app.module.ts* file):

```
{ path: 'chapter06/ch6-pca2d-index, component: Ch6Pca2dIndexComponent },
```

Then add the corresponding URL link to the *home* and *nav-menu* components.

Saving the project and navigating to the */chapter06/ch6-pca2d-index* page produce the default 2D PCA results shown in Fig.6-9.

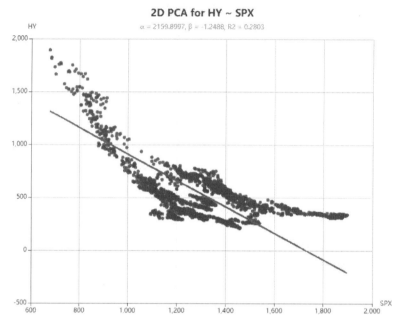

Fig.6-9. 2D PCA results for HY and SPX.

Now, changing the *xname* to VIX, keep HY in the *yname* field and clicking the *Get PCA2D Index Chart* button produce the results shown in Fig.6-10.

Note that the PCA results for SPX and VIX relative to HY have an R-squared = 0.2803 and 0.6743 respectively, indicating that VIX has a higher correlation to HY than SPX does during a 10-year period.

2D PCA Results for Stocks

Similarly, we can create a component to display the 2D PCA results for a pair of stocks. Run the following command in a command prompt window:

```
ng g c chapter06/ch6-pca2d-stock --module=app.module
```

This will generate a new component named *ch6-pca2d-stock* in the *ClientApp/src/app/chapter06* folder. Open the component class file and replace its content with the following code:

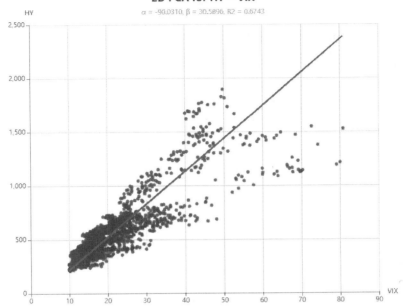

Fig.6-10. 2D PCA results for HY and VIX.

```
// ch6-pca2d-stock.ts file:
import { Component, OnInit } from '@angular/core';
import { SlrOutput } from '../../models/ch6.model';
import { Ch6Service } from '../../models/ch6.service'

@Component({
  selector: 'app-ch6-pca2d-stock',
  templateUrl: './ch6-pca2d-stock.component.html',
  styleUrls: ['./ch6-pca2d-stock.component.css']
})
export class Ch6Pca2dStockComponent implements OnInit {
  title: string = '2D PCA  Prices';
  titleReturn: string = '2D PCA Returns';
  ticker1: string = '^GSPC';
  ticker2: string = 'C';
  start: string = '2013-01-01';
  end: string = '2018-01-01';

  constructor(private repository: Ch6Service) { }

  ngOnInit() {
    this.getPca2dOutput(this.ticker1, this.ticker2, this.start, this.end);
  }

  get pca2dOutput(): SlrOutput {
    return this.repository.pca2dStock;
  }

  get pca2dOutputReturn(): SlrOutput {
```

```
      return this.repository.pca2dStockReturn;
  }

  getPca2dOutput(ticker1: string, ticker2: string, start: string, end: string) {
    this.repository.getPca2dStock(ticker1, ticker2, start, end);
    this.repository.getPca2dStockReturn(ticker1, ticker2, start, end);
  }
}
```

This component simply retrieves the 2D PCA results for the stock price data and price returns specified by the *ticker1, ticker2, start,* and *end* properties with the default stock tickers C (Citi) and ^GSPC. We also define *title* and *titleReturn* properties to be used as input for the *ch6-slr-chart* component.

The following code is for this component's template:

```
// ch6-pca2d-stock.component.html file:
<h2>
  ch6-pca2d-stock works!
</h2>

<mat-form-field>
  <input matInput placeholder="ticker1" [(ngModel)]="ticker1" name="ticker1">
</mat-form-field>
<mat-form-field>
  <input matInput placeholder="ticker2" [(ngModel)]="ticker2" name="ticker2">
</mat-form-field>
<mat-form-field>
  <input matInput placeholder="start" [(ngModel)]="start" name="start">
</mat-form-field>
<mat-form-field>
  <input matInput placeholder="end" [(ngModel)]="end" name="end">
</mat-form-field>
<button mat-raised-button color="primary"
(click)="getPca2dOutput(ticker1,ticker2,start,end)">Get PCA-2D Stock Chart</button>

<div *ngIf="pca2dOutput">
  <div *ngIf="pca2dOutput.data.length>0">
    <div class="cardList">
      <mat-card class="card-border">
        <app-ch6-slr-chart [title]="title" [slrOutput]="pca2dOutput">
        </app-ch6-slr-chart>
      </mat-card>
      <mat-card class="card-border">
        <app-ch6-slr-chart [title]="titleReturn"
          [slrOutput]="pca2dOutputReturn"></app-ch6-slr-chart>
      </mat-card>
    </div>
  </div>
</div>
```

This template allows you to specify a pair of stocks and date range for the 2D PCA. We add two *app-ch6-slr-chart* directives and specify its *title* and *slrOutput* directives using corresponding properties, which are used to display 2D PCA results for stock prices and price returns. The *mat-card* container consists of style classes named *cardList* and *card-border* defined in the component's style file:

```
// ch6-pca2d-stock.component.css file:
```

```
.cardList {
  display: flex;
  flex-direction: row;
  flex-wrap: wrap;
  justify-content: flex-start;
}

.card-border {
  margin: 10px;
  width: 600px;
  height: 500px;
}
```

Finally, we need to add a path for this new component to the *RouterModule* of the root module (i.e., the *app.module.ts* file):

```
{ path: 'chapter06/ch6-pca2d-stock, component: Ch6Pca2dStockComponent },
```

Then add the corresponding URL link to the *home* and *nav-menu* components.

Saving the project and navigating to the */chapter06/ch6-pca2d-stock* page produce the default 2D PCA results shown in Fig.6-11.

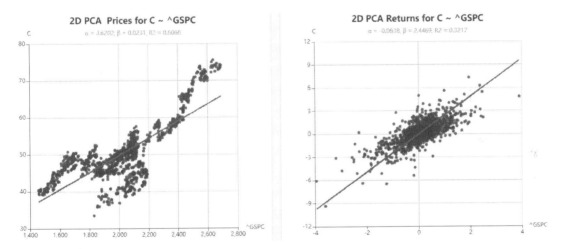

Fig.6-11. 2D PCA results for C and ^GSPC.

Note that the price PCA for C (Citi) and SPX (or ^GSPC) has an R-squared =0.6066, which is higher than their daily return PCA (0.3217).

We can check the ^DJI CPA relative to SPX. Figure 6-12 shows the PCA results for ^DJI and SPX. You can see that both the price (left) and return (right) PCA results have high R-squared (0.9572 and 0.9308), and Dow Jones index is slightly outperforms SPX (*Alpha* = 0.0021 > 0 for the return).

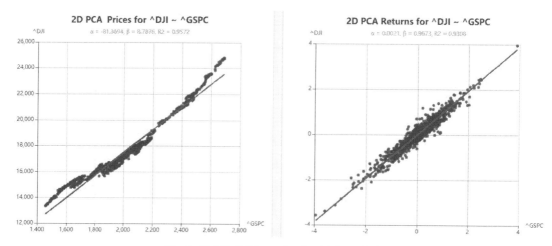

Fig.6-12. 2D PCA results for ^DJI and SPX.

Compare SLR and 2D PCA

In the preceding sections, we discussed the simple linear regression and 2D PCA. By comparing the results from regression and PCA, you may find that they look similar, but you may still wonder what is fundamental difference between the linear regression and the PCA? First, I should point out that the linear regression is not symmetric between $y \sim x$ and $x \sim y$. You can see clearly from Fig. 6-13 that the linear regression (LR) of HY ~ SPX (or $y \sim x$) is not the same as that of SPX ~ HY (or $x \sim y$). The reason for this asymmetry is that the linear regression of $y \sim x$ minimizes error perpendicular to the independent axis (vertical red lines in Fig. 6-13). If you want to regress $x \sim y$, it would minimize error perpendicular to Y-axis (horizontal green lines in Fig. 6-13). In general, these two regressions gives different results.

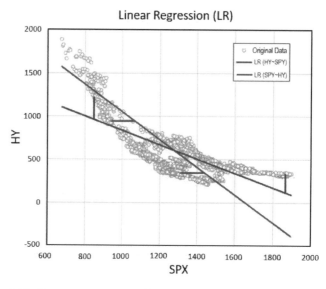

Fig. 6-13. Linear regressions of HY ~ SPX (red) and SPX ~ HY (green).

On the other hand, the PCA effectively minimizes error orthogonal to the principal component axis, as shown in Fig. 6-14 (red lines). Therefore, the PCA results are always symmetric between ($y \sim x$) and ($x \sim y$).

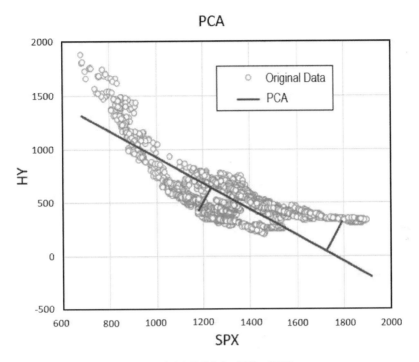

Fig. 6-14. PCA for HY ~ SPX.

Multiple Linear Regressions

In the preceding sections, we discussed the simple linear regression: the dependent variable y depends only on a single independent variable x. In practice, the dependent variable can depend on several independent variables. The purpose of the multivariable (or multiple) linear regression is to find the relationship between the dependent and multiple independent variables. For example, the CDS high yield (HY) spread can depend not only on the equity index (SPX) but also on volatility (VIX), interest rate, and other factors. A real estate agent such as Zillow attempts to collect information for each listing, including the size of the house, the number of bedrooms, and the average income in the respective neighborhood according to census data. Once this information has been compiled for various houses we would like to see whether and how these variables relate to the price for which a house is sold.

Mathematically, a multiple regression model consists of p independent variables:

$$y_i = b_1 x_{i1} + b_2 x_{i2} + \cdots + b_p x_{ip} + \varepsilon_i$$

where x_{ij} is the ith observation on the jth independent variable. We can obtain the least squares parameter estimates from p normal equations. The residual can be written as

$$\varepsilon_i = y_i - b_1 x_{i1} - \cdots - b_p x_{ip}$$

The normal equations become

$$\sum_{i=1}^{n}\sum_{k=1}^{p} X_{ij}X_{ik}\hat{b}_k = \sum_{i=1}^{n} X_{ij}y_i, \quad j = 1,2,\ldots,p$$

In matrix notation, the above equation can be written as

$$(X^T X)\hat{b} = X^T Y$$

Where the *ij* element of *X* is x_{ij}, the *j* element of the column vector *Y* is y_j, and the *j* element of $\hat{b}$ is b_j. Thus, *X* is the *n×p*, *Y* is the *n×1*, and $\hat{b}$ is the *p×1* matrix. The solution is

$$\hat{b} = (X^T X)^{-1} X^T Y$$

We can easily implement the above solution by solving the standard linear equations, as discussed in my previously published book, *Practical Numerical Methods with C#*. In the following sections, I will show you how to use the Accord.NET package to perform the multiple linear regressions for various securities.

Implementation

Here, we will also use Accord.NET, to perform multiple linear regression (MLR). First, add a class named *MlrOutput* to the *LinearAnalysisHelper.cs* file in the *Quant/Models* folder. The *MlrOutput* class defines the output objects from a multiple linear regression. Here is the code for this class:

```
public class MlrOutput
{
    public string[] Tickers { get; set; }
    public double RSquared { get; set; }
    public List<object[]> Data { get; set; }
}
```

Then add a new method named *GetMlr* to the *LinearAnalysisHelper.cs* file:

```
public static MlrOutput GetMlr(DataTable dt, string[] tickers)
{
    string dependentName = tickers[0];
    string[] independentNames = tickers.ToList().GetRange(1,
        tickers.Length - 1).ToArray();
    double[][] input = dt.DefaultView.ToTable(false, independentNames).ToJagged();
    double[] output = (dt.DefaultView.ToTable(false, dependentName))
        .Columns[dependentName].ToArray();
    var mlr = new MultipleLinearRegressionAnalysis(intercept: true)
    {
        Inputs = independentNames,
        Output = dependentName
    };
    mlr.OrdinaryLeastSquares.IsRobust = true;
    mlr.Learn(input, output);

    double[] val = new double[tickers.Length];
    List<object[]> data = new List<object[]>();

    for (int i = 0; i < tickers.Length; i++)
        val[i] = mlr.Coefficients[i].Value;
```

```
foreach (DataRow p in dt.Rows)
{
    double price = val[val.Length - 1];
    for (int i = 0; i < tickers.Length - 1; i++)
        price += val[i] * Convert.ToDouble(p[tickers[i + 1]]);
    data.Add(new object[] {p["Date"], price, p[tickers[0]] });
}

return new MlrOutput
{
    Tickers = tickers,
    RSquared = mlr.RSquared,
    Data = data
};
}
```

This method takes a *DataTable* object, which holds the original market data, and a string array, which holds the securities names, as input parameters. A *DataTable* represents one table in memory relational data and can be created and used independently. Note that we always assume that the first ticker in the *tickers* array is the dependent variable and the rest names in the array are the independent variables.

Next, we convert the data in the *DataTable* into the input and output arrays and call the function named *MultipleLinearRegressionAnalysis* implemented in the Accord.NET libraries to perform the regression. In order to avoid linear dependency errors, we set

mlr.OrdinaryLeastSquares.IsRobust = true;

We then compute the analysis and obtain the estimated regression by calling the **mlr.Learn** method. Finally, we extract the intercept and weights parameters to calculate the predicted values and return the results as an *MlrOutput* object.

The other task is to prepare the input *DataTable* for the *GetMlr* method. Add the following two method, *GetMlrStockData* and *GetStockCloseAdj*, to the *LinearAnalysisHelper.cs* file:

```
public static async Task<DataTable> GetMlrStockData(string[] tickers, string start,
    string end)
{
    var startDate = DateTime.Parse(start);
    var endDate = DateTime.Parse(end);
    DataTable res = new DataTable();
    List<StockCloseAdj> data = new List<StockCloseAdj>();
    foreach(var ticker in tickers)
    {
        var d = await GetStockCloseAdj(ticker, startDate, endDate);
        if(d.Count > 1) data.AddRange(d);
    }

    DateTime date = startDate;
    int count = 0;
    while (date <= endDate)
    {
        var dts = from p in data where p.Date == date orderby p.Ticker select p;
        if (dts.Count() == tickers.Length)
        {
            if (count == 0)
            {
```

```
                res.Columns.Add("Date", typeof(DateTime));
                foreach (var r in dts)
                    res.Columns.Add(r.Ticker, typeof(double));
            }
            res.Rows.Add(date);

            int n = 0;
            foreach (var r in dts)
            {
                res.Rows[res.Rows.Count - 1][n + 1] = r.CloseAdj;
                n++;
            }
            count++;
        }
        date = date.AddDays(1);
    }
    return res;
}

private static async Task<List<StockCloseAdj>> GetStockCloseAdj(string ticker,
    DateTime start, DateTime end)
{
    var data = await Yahoo.GetHistoricalAsync(ticker, start, end, Period.Daily);
    List<StockCloseAdj> res = new List<StockCloseAdj>();
    foreach (var d in data)
    {
        res.Add(new StockCloseAdj
        {
            Ticker = ticker,
            Date = d.DateTime,
            CloseAdj = (double)d.AdjustedClose,
        });
    }
    return res;
}
```

The private *GetStockCloseAdj* method retrieves the stock adjusted close price for single ticker from Yahoo Finance, while the *GetMlrStockData* method prepares the stock data for multiple tickers to be used for multiple linear regression by repeatedly calling the *GetStockCloseAdj* method.

Note that we cannot add the method to prepare the index data for multiple linear regression to the static *LinearAnalysisHelper* class because we cannot retrieve data from database by injecting *QuantDataContext* to the static class's constructor. Here, we will add a private method named *GetMlrIndexData* to the *LinearAnalysisValuesController* class that already had a dependency injection for *QuantDataContext*. Here is the code snippet for this new method:

```
private DataTable GetMlrIndexData()
{
    string[] tickers = new string[] { "HY", "SPX", "VIX", "IG" };
    DataTable res = new DataTable();
    res.Columns.Add("Date", typeof(DateTime));
    foreach (string tk in tickers)
        res.Columns.Add(tk, typeof(double));

    var idx = context.IndexDatas.OrderBy(d => d.Date);
    foreach (var p in idx)
```

```
            res.Rows.Add(p.Date, p.HYSpread, p.SPX, p.VIX, p.IGSpread);
    return res;
}
```

This method retrieves index data from database and formats the data for multiple linear regression. Here, we take HY as dependent variable and the rest (SPX, VIX, and IG) as independent variables.

Now, I will show you how to perform multiple linear regression for some securities and how to convert the results into web services.

Add two new methods to the *LinearAnalysisValuesController* class in the *Controllers* folder with the following code listings:

```
[Route("~/api/MlrIndex")]
[HttpGet]
public MlrOutput MlrIndex()
{
    DataTable dt = GetMlrIndexData();
    string[] tickers = new string[] { "HY", "SPX", "VIX", "IG" };
    return LinearAnalysisHelper.GetMlr(dt, tickers);
}

[Route("~/api/mlrStock/{start}/{end}/{tickers}")]
[HttpGet]
public async Task<MlrOutput> MlrStock(string start, string end, string tickers)
{
    string[] tickers1 = tickers.ToUpper().Split(',');
    DataTable dt = await LinearAnalysisHelper.GetMlrStockData(tickers1, start, end);
    return LinearAnalysisHelper.GetMlr(dt, tickers1);
}
```

These methods, similar to those used in simple linear regression, can be used to perform multiple linear regression for index data and stock data with any number of stocks.

Multiple Linear Regression in Angular

We can use the similar repository service presented in the preceding chapter to send a request from the Angular application to get the MLR results. The first step is to define a model for the regression. Add a TypeScript class called *MlrOutput* to the *ch6.model.ts* file in the *ClientApp/src/app/models* folder. Here is the code listing for this class:

```
export class MlrOutput {
  constructor(
    public tickers: string,
    public rSquared?: number,
    public data?: any[]
  ) { }
}
```

This class corresponds to the C# *MlrOutput.cs* class defined in the preceding section. Next, we need to add the highlighted code snippet to the *ch6.service.ts* file in the *ClientApp/src/app/models folder*:

```
// ch6.repository.ts file:
import { Injectable, Inject } from '@angular/core';
import { HttpClient } from '@angular/common/http';
import { SlrOutput, MlrOutput } from './ch6.model'
```

```
@Injectable({
  providedIn: 'root'
})
export class Ch6Repository {
  slrIndex: SlrOutput;
  slrStock: SlrOutput;
  slrStockReturn: SlrOutput;
  pca2dIndex: SlrOutput;
  pca2dStock: SlrOutput;
  pca2dStockReturn: SlrOutput;
  mlrIndex: MlrOutput;
  mlrStock: MlrOutput;

  private url;
  constructor(private http: HttpClient, @Inject('BASE_URL') baseUrl: string) {
    this.url = baseUrl;
  }

  // ... other methods omitted for brevity ...

  getMlrIndex() {
    let url1 = this.url + 'api/mlrindex';
    this.http.get<MlrOutput>(url1).subscribe(result => { this.mlrIndex = result });
  }

  getMlrStock(start: string, end: string, tickers: string) {
    let url1 = this.url + 'api/mlrstock/' + start + '/' + end + '/' + tickers;
    this.http.get<MlrOutput>(url1).subscribe(result => { this.mlrStock = result })
  }
}
```

The *getMlrIndex* and *getMlrStock* methods send HTTP requests to specified URLs, which retrieve the multiple linear regression results for index data and stock data respectively from the ASP.NET Core API web service.

MLR Results for Index Data

Here, I will use an example to show you how to perform multiple linear regression for index data and how to display the regression results.

First, we create a scatter chart and a line chart to display various MLR results. Run the following command in a command prompt window:

ng g c chapter06/ch6-mlr-chart --module=app.module

This will generate a new component named *ch6-mlr-chart* in the *ClientApp/src/app/chapter06* folder. Open the component class file and replace its content with the following code:

```
// ch6-mlr-chart.component.ts file:
import { Component, OnInit, Input, OnChanges } from '@angular/core';
import * as ecStat from 'echarts-stat/dist/ecStat.min.js';
import { MlrOutput } from '../../models/ch6.model';

@Component({
```

```
  selector: 'app-ch6-mlr-chart',
  templateUrl: './ch6-mlr-chart.component.html',
  styleUrls: ['./ch6-mlr-chart.component.css']
})
export class Ch6MlrChartComponent implements OnInit, OnChanges {
  @Input() title: string;
  @Input() mlrOutput: MlrOutput;
  option1: any;
  option2: any;

  constructor() { }

  ngOnInit() {
  }

  ngOnChanges() {
    this.option1 = this.getOption1();
    this.option2 = this.getOption2();
  }

  getOption1() {
    var dd: any[] = [];
    for (let i in this.mlrOutput.data) {
      dd.push([this.mlrOutput.data[i][1], this.mlrOutput.data[i][2]]);
    }

    let regr = ecStat.regression('linear', dd);
    regr.points.sort(function (a, b) {
      return a[0] - b[0];
    });

    return {
      title: {
        text: this.title + ' for ' + this.mlrOutput.tickers.toString(),
        subtext: 'R2 = ' + this.mlrOutput.rSquared.toFixed(4),
        left: 'center'
      },
      tooltip: {
        trigger: 'axis',
        axisPointer: {
          type: 'cross'
        }
      },
      dataset: {
        source: this.mlrOutput.data
      },
      xAxis: {
        name: this.title + ' Component',
        nameLocation: 'center',
        nameGap: 30,
        scale: true,
        axisLine: { onZero: false }
      },
      yAxis: {
        name: this.mlrOutput.tickers[0],
```

```
          nameLocation: 'center',
          nameGap: 40,
          scale: true,
          axisLine: { onZero: false }
        },
        series: [
          {
            type: 'line',
            data: regr.points,
            showSymbol: false,
            zlevel: 10
          },
          {
            type: 'scatter',
            encode: {
              x: 1,
              y: 2
            },
            symbolSize: 6,
            zlevel: 0
          }
        ]
      }
    }
  }

  getOption2() {
    return {
      title: {
        text: this.title + ' Price',
        left: 'center'
      },
      legend: {
        right: '50px',
        top: '70px',
        orient: 'vertical'
      },
      tooltip: {
        trigger: 'axis',
        axisPointer: {
          type: 'cross'
        }
      },
      dataset: {
        source: this.mlrOutput.data
      },
      xAxis: {
        name: 'Date',
        type: 'category',
        scale: true,
        boundaryGap: false,
        axisLine: { onZero: false },
        axisLabel: {
          formatter: function (value, index) {
            return value.toString().substring(0, 10);
          }
```

```
      },
      nameLocation: 'center',
      nameGap: 30,
    },
    yAxis: {
      name: 'Price',
      scale: true,
      axisLine: { onZero: false },
      nameLocation: 'center',
      nameGap: 35,
    },
    series: [
      {
        name: 'Original ' + this.mlrOutput.tickers[0] + ' Data',
        type: 'line',
        encode: {
          x: 0,
          y: 2
        },
        showSymbol: false,
      }, {
        name: this.title + ' Component',
        type: 'line',
        encode: {
          x: 0,
          y: 1
        },
        showSymbol: false,
      }
    ]
  }
}
}
```

This component takes *title* and *mlrOutput* as input parameters that should be specified in its parent component. We also define two properties, *option1* and *options2*, specified using the *getOption1* and *getOption2* methods respectively. The *option1* property is used to create a scatter chart that displays the dependent variable vs the predicted result from multiple linear regression of independent variables. Inside the *getOption1* method, we employ a statistical and data mining tool for Echarts named *ecStat* to add a regression line. Note that in order to use the *ecStat* tool, we need to install the *echarts-stat* package by adding the following command to the *dependencies* section of the *package.json* file in the *ClientApp* folder:

```
"echarts-stat": "1.1.1",
```

We use the *option2* property to create a line chart that displays the time series of the dependent variable and MLR predicted result.

The template for this component is very simple:

```
// ch6-mlr-chart.component.html file:
<div class="cardList">
  <mat-card class="card-border">
    <div echarts [options]="option1" style="height:100%"></div>
  </mat-card>
  <mat-card *ngIf="title.includes('MLR')" class="card-border">
```

```
     <div echarts [options]="option2" style="height:100%"></div>
   </mat-card>
</div>
```

Here, we add two echarts directives that create two charts specified by *option1* and *option2*. Note that the *ngIf* directive for the second chart:

*ngIf="title.includes('MLR')

This means that the second chart is only visible for the title containing the MLR string. For PCA, this chart will be invisible.

This component also consists of a style file as shown in the following code:

```
// ch6-mlr-chart.component.css file:
.cardList {
  display: flex;
  flex-direction: row;
  flex-wrap: wrap;
  justify-content: flex-start;
}

.card-border {
  margin: 10px;
  width: 550px;
  height: 500px;
}
```

Now, we can use this component to display the MLR results for index and stock data.

Run the following command in a command prompt window:

ng g c chapter06/ch6-mlr-index --module=app.module

This will generate a new component named *ch6-mlr-index* in the *ClientApp/src/app/chapter06* folder. Open the component class file and replace its content with the following code:

```
// ch6-mlr-index.component.ts file:
import { Component, OnInit } from '@angular/core';
import { MlrOutput } from '../../models/ch6.model';
import { Ch6Service } from '../../models/ch6.service'

@Component({
  selector: 'app-ch6-mlr-index',
  templateUrl: './ch6-mlr-index.component.html',
  styleUrls: ['./ch6-mlr-index.component.css']
})
export class Ch6MlrIndexComponent implements OnInit {
  title: string = 'MLR';

  constructor(private repository: Ch6Service) { }

  ngOnInit() {
    this.getMlrOutput();
  }

  get mlrOutput(): MlrOutput {
    return this.repository.mlrIndex;
```

```
  }

  getMlrOutput() {
    this.repository.getMlrIndex();
  }
}
```

This component simply retrieves the MLR results for the index data. We also define a *title* property to be used as input for the *ch6-mlr-chart* component. The following code listing is for this component's template:

```
// ch6-mlr-index.html file:
<h2>
  ch6-mlr-index works!
</h2>

<div *ngIf="mlrOutput">
  <div *ngIf="mlrOutput.data.length>0">
    <app-ch6-mlr-chart [title]="title" [mlrOutput]="mlrOutput"></app-ch6-mlr-chart>
  </div>
</div>
```

This template adds an *app-ch6-mlr-chart* directive and specifies its *title* and *mlrOutput* directives using corresponding properties.

Finally, we need to add a path for this new component to the *RouterModule* of the root module (i.e., the *app.module.ts* file):

```
{ path: 'chapter06/ch6-mlr-index, component: Ch6MlrIndexComponent },
```

Then add the corresponding URL link to the *home* and *nav-menu* components.

Saving the project and navigating to the */chapter06/ch6-mlr-index* page produce the results shown in Fig.6-15.

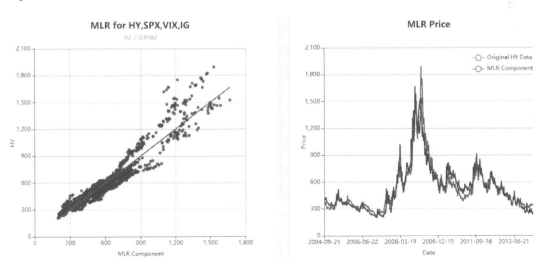

Fig.6-15. Multiple linear regression results for HY ~ SPX, VIX, and IG.

The scatter chart on the left shows the result of HY vs the MLR component with an R-squared = 0.9182. We can compare this result with that from a simple linear regression, where we have R-squared=0.4465 for HY ~ SPX (Fig.6-4), 0.7542 for HY ~ VIX (Fig.6-5), and 0.8727 for HY ~ IG (not shown) respectively. The multiple linear regression indeed gives a better result with a higher correlation.

The line chart on the right in Fig.6-15 shows the time-series of the original HY data and its predicted values from multiple linear regression, which also demonstrates the predicted values are highly correlated with the original data.

MLR Results for Stocks

Similarly, we can create a component to display the multiple linear regression results for a list of stocks. Run the following command in a command prompt window:

```
ng g c chapter06/ch6-mlr-stock --module=app.module
```

This will generate a new component named *ch6-mlr-stock* in the *ClientApp/src/app/chapter06* folder. Open the component class file and replace its content with the following code:

```
// ch6-mlr-stock.component.ts file:
import { Component, OnInit } from '@angular/core';
import { MlrOutput } from '../../models/ch6.model';
import { Ch6Service } from '../../models/ch6.Service'

@Component({
  selector: 'app-ch6-mlr-stock',
  templateUrl: './ch6-mlr-stock.component.html',
  styleUrls: ['./ch6-mlr-stock.component.css']
})
export class Ch6MlrStockComponent implements OnInit {
  tickers: string = 'MS,GS,C';
  start: string = '2004-01-01';
  end: string = '2014-01-01';
  title: string = 'MLR';

  constructor(private repository: Ch6Service) { }

  ngOnInit() {
    this.getMlrOutput(this.tickers, this.start, this.end);
  }

  get mlrOutput(): MlrOutput {
    return this.repository.mlrStock;
  }

  getMlrOutput(tickers: string, start: string, end: string) {
    this.repository.getMlrStock(start, end, tickers);
  }
}
```

This component simply retrieves the MLR results for the stock price data specified by the *tickers, start,* and *end* properties with the default stock tickers MS (Morgan Stanley), GS (Goldman Sachs), and C (Citi). We also define a *title* property to be used as input for the *ch6-mlr-chart* component.

The following code is for this component's template:

```
// ch6-mlr-stock.component.html file:
<h2>
  ch6-mlr-stock works!
</h2>

<mat-form-field>
  <input matInput placeholder="tickers" [(ngModel)]="tickers" name="tickers">
</mat-form-field>
<mat-form-field>
  <input matInput placeholder="start" [(ngModel)]="start" name="start">
</mat-form-field>
<mat-form-field>
  <input matInput placeholder="end" [(ngModel)]="end" name="end">
</mat-form-field>
<button mat-raised-button color="primary"
(click)="getMlrOutput(tickers,start,end)">Get MLR Stock Chart</button>

<div *ngIf="mlrOutput">
  <div *ngIf="mlrOutput.data.length>0">
    <app-ch6-mlr-chart [title]="title" [mlrOutput]="mlrOutput"></app-ch6-mlr-chart>
  </div>
</div>
```

This template allows you to specify a list of stocks and date range for the regression. We add an *app-ch6-mlr-chart* directive and specify its *title* and *mlrOutput* directives using corresponding properties, which is used to display regression results for stock data.

Finally, we need to add a path for this new component to the *RouterModule* of the root module (i.e., the *app.module.ts* file):

```
{ path: 'chapter06/ch6-mlr-stock, component: Ch6MlrStockComponent },
```

Then add the corresponding URL link to the *home* and *nav-menu* components.

Saving the project and navigating to the */chapter06/ch6-mlr-stock* page produce the default MLR results shown in Fig.6-16.

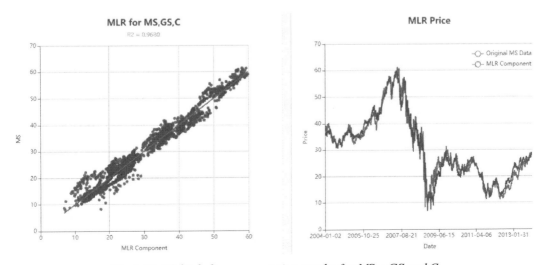

Fig.6-16. Multiple linear regression results for MS ~ GS and C.

You can see from Fig.6-16 that the predicted values have a very high correlation relative to the original MS data with an R-squared = 0.968.

Multiple PCA

Previously, we have discussed the simplest PCA case: a simple 2D PCA. Just like the multiple linear regression, we can also perform a PCA computation with multiple variables (i.e., the number of variables > 2) using the Accord.NET package.

Implementation

Here, we will implement an interface to access the PCA tool in the Accord.NET package. Add a new method named *GetPca* to the *LinearAnalysisHelper* class in the *Quant/models* folder with the following code snippet:

```
public static MlrOutput GetPca(DataTable  dt, string[] tickers)
{
    string[] independentNames = tickers.ToList().GetRange(1,
        tickers.Length - 1).ToArray();
    double[][] input = dt.DefaultView.ToTable(false, independentNames).ToJagged();

    var pca = new PrincipalComponentAnalysis(method:
    PrincipalComponentMethod.Standardize);
    pca.Learn(input);

    var finalData = pca.Transform(input);
    int len = dt.Rows.Count;
    double[] xdata = new double[len];
    double[] ydata = new double[len];
    List<object[]> data = new List<object[]>();

    for (var i = 0; i < len; i++)
    {
        xdata[i] = finalData[i][0];
        ydata[i] = Convert.ToDouble(dt.Rows[i][tickers[0]]);
        data.Add(new object[] { dt.Rows[i]["Date"], finalData[i][0],
            dt.Rows[i][tickers[0]]});
    }

    OrdinaryLeastSquares ols = new OrdinaryLeastSquares();
    SimpleLinearRegression regression = ols.Learn(xdata, ydata);

    return new MlrOutput
    {
        Tickers = tickers,
        RSquared = regression.CoefficientOfDetermination(xdata, ydata),
        Data = data
    };
}
```

Inside this method, we first define the independent variables as *independentNames*. Note that we always use the first ticker in the *tickers* array as the dependent variable. We then convert all data for the independent variables from a *DataTable* into a 2D jagged array. As discussed previously in the simple 2D PCA section, we need to center our input data before performing the PCA calculation. The PCA tool in Accord.NET does this automatically by specifying the *AnalysisMethod* enumeration, which has two options: *Center* and *Standarize*. By default, Accord.NET uses the *Center* method, which subtracts the mean only. However, we can also remove the mean and then divide by the standard deviation by choosing the *Standarize* option. Here we set the *AnalysisMethod* to *Standarize*. Next, we create PCA analysis using the selected method and call the *Learn* method to perform the PCA calculation, which gives the results for eigenvalues and corresponding eigenvectors. In PCA, the eigenvector with the highest eigenvalue is the principal component of the data set. We can choose one or few eigenvectors with higher eigenvalues as the principal components according to the requirement of our applications. For the purpose of demonstration in our example, we will pick the single one eigenvector that has the highest eigenvalue as the principal component.

Next, we need to project the original data on to the selected principal eigenvectors to obtain the predicted data set by PCA. Note that each component in a principal eigenvector will provide weight information about the corresponding security (stock or index in our example); this weight information corresponds to the hedge ratios, which is very important when you develop a trading strategy based on PCA. You can obtain the new PCA data set directly using the *pca.Transform* method, as we did in the preceding code listing.

I should emphasize that here, we just discussed one of the PCA processes – separating dependent and independent variables for making a better comparison with the multiple linear regression. You can also do a PCA analysis for all securities without separation between dependent and independent variables, and the selected principal components will then represent the main features for all securities.

Now, I will show you how to perform multiple PCA for some securities and how to convert the results into web services.

Add two new methods to the *LinearAnalysisValuesController* class in the *Controllers* folder with the following code listings:

```
[Route("~/api/PcaIndex")]
[HttpGet]
public MlrOutput PcaIndex()
{
    DataTable dt = GetMlrIndexData();
    string[] tickers = new string[] { "HY", "SPX", "VIX", "IG" };
    return LinearAnalysisHelper.GetPca(dt, tickers);
}

[Route("~/api/PcaStock/{start}/{end}/{tickers}")]
[HttpGet]
public async Task<MlrOutput> PcaStock(string start, string end, string tickers)
{
    string[] tickers1 = tickers.ToUpper().Split(',');
    DataTable dt = await LinearAnalysisHelper.GetMlrStockData(tickers1, start, end);
    return LinearAnalysisHelper.GetPca(dt, tickers1);
}
```

These methods, similar to those used in multiple linear regression, can be used to perform multiple PCA for index data and stock data with any number of stocks.

PCA in Angular

Now, add the highlighted code snippet to the *ch6.service.ts* file in the *ClientApp/src/app/models folder*:

```
// ch6.service.ts file:
import { Injectable, nject } from '@angular/core';
import { HttpClient } from '@angular/common/http';
import { SlrOutput, MlrOutput } from './ch6.model'

@Injectable({
  providedIn: 'root'
})
export class Ch6Repository {
  slrIndex: SlrOutput;
  slrStock: SlrOutput;
  slrStockReturn: SlrOutput;
  pca2dIndex: SlrOutput;
  pca2dStock: SlrOutput;
  pca2dStockReturn: SlrOutput;
  mlrIndex: MlrOutput;
  mlrStock: MlrOutput;
  pcaIndex: MlrOutput;
  pcaStock: MlrOutput;

  private url;
  constructor(private http: HttpClient, @Inject('BASE_URL') baseUrl: string) {
    this.url = baseUrl;
  }

  // ... other methods omitted for brevity ...

  getPcaIndex() {
    let url1 = this.url + 'api/pcaindex';
    this.http.get<MlrOutput>(url1).subscribe(result => { this.pcaIndex = result });
  }

  getPcaStock(start: string, end: string, tickers: string) {
    let url1 = this.url + 'api/pcastock/' + start + '/' + end + '/' + tickers;
    this.http.get<MlrOutput>(url1).subscribe(result => { this.pcaStock = result })
  }
}
```

The *getPcaIndex* and *getPcaStock* methods send HTTP requests to specified URLs, which retrieve PCA results for index data and stock data respectively from the ASP.NET Core API web service.

PCA Results for Index Data

Run the following command in a command prompt window:

```
ng g c chapter06/ch6-pca-index --module=app.module
```

This will generate a new component named *ch6-pca-index* in the *ClientApp/src/app/chapter06* folder. Open the component class file and replace its content with the following code:

```
// ch6-pca-index.component.ts file:
```

```
import { Component, OnInit } from '@angular/core';
import { MlrOutput } from '../../models/ch6.model';
import { Ch6Service } from '../../models/ch6.service'

@Component({
  selector: 'app-ch6-pca-index',
  templateUrl: './ch6-pca-index.component.html',
  styleUrls: ['./ch6-pca-index.component.css']
})
export class Ch6PcaIndexComponent implements OnInit {
  title: string = 'PCA';

  constructor(private repository: Ch6Service) { }

  ngOnInit() {
    this.getPcaOutput();
  }

  get pcaOutput(): MlrOutput {
    return this.repository.pcaIndex;
  }

  getPcaOutput() {
    this.repository.getPcaIndex();
  }
}
```

This component simply retrieves the PCA results for the index data. It also defines a *title* property to be used as input for the *ch6-mlr-chart* component. The following code listing is for this component's template:

```
// ch6-pca-index.component.html file:
<h2>
  ch6-pca-index works!
</h2>

<div *ngIf="pcaOutput">
  <div *ngIf="pcaOutput.data.length>0">
    <app-ch6-mlr-chart [title]="title" [mlrOutput]="pcaOutput"></app-ch6-mlr-chart>
  </div>
</div>
```

This template adds an *app-ch6-mlr-chart* directive and specifies its *title* and *mlrOutput* directives using corresponding properties.

Finally, we need to add a path for this new component to the *RouterModule* of the root module (i.e., the *app.module.ts* file):

```
{ path: 'chapter06/ch6-pca-index, component: Ch6PcaIndexComponent },
```

Then add the corresponding URL link to the *home* and *nav-menu* components.

Saving the project and navigating to the */chapter06/ch6-mlr-index* page produce the results shown in Fig.6-17.

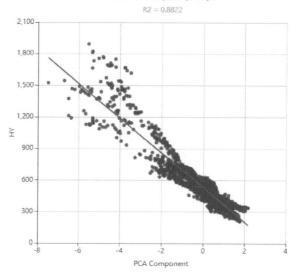

Fig.6-17. Multiple PCA results for HY ~ SPX, VIX, and IG.

This scatter chart simply shows the data points for the original HY data relative to the *PcaComponent* with a line trend line. The PCA result has a high correlation with an R-squared = 0.8822, which can be compared with simple PCA analysis, where we have R-squared = 0.2803 for HY ~ SPX (Fig.6-9), 0.6743 for HY ~ VIX (Fig.6-10), and 0.8551 for HY ~ IG (not shown), respectively. The multiple PCA analysis indeed gives a better result with a higher correlation.

PCA Results for Stocks

Similarly, we can create a component to display the PCA results for a list of stocks. Run the following command in a command prompt window:

ng g c chapter06/ch6-pca-stock --module=app.module

This will generate a new component named *ch6-pca-stock* in the *ClientApp/src/app/chapter06* folder. Open the component class file and replace its content with the following code:

```
// ch6-pac-stock.component.ts file:
import { Component, OnInit } from '@angular/core';
import { MlrOutput } from '../../models/ch6.model';
import { Ch6Service } from '../../models/ch6.service'

@Component({
  selector: 'app-ch6-pca-stock',
  templateUrl: './ch6-pca-stock.component.html',
  styleUrls: ['./ch6-pca-stock.component.css']
})
export class Ch6PcaStockComponent implements OnInit {
  tickers: string = 'MS,GS,C';
  start: string = '2004-01-01';
  end: string = '2014-01-01';
```

```
  title: string = 'PCA';

  constructor(private repository: Ch6Service) { }

  ngOnInit() {
    this.getPcaOutput(this.tickers, this.start, this.end);
  }

  get pcaOutput(): MlrOutput {
    return this.repository.pcaStock;
  }

  getPcaOutput(tickers: string, start: string, end: string) {
    this.repository.getPcaStock(start, end, tickers);
  }
}
```

This component simply retrieves the PCA results for the stock price data specified by the *tickers, start,* and *end* properties with the default stock tickers MS, GS, and C. It also defines a *title* property to be used as input for the *ch6-mlr-chart* component.

The following code is for this component's template:

```
// ch6-pca-stock.component.html file:
<h2>
  ch6-pca-stock works!
</h2>
<mat-form-field>
  <input matInput placeholder="tickers" [(ngModel)]="tickers" name="tickers">
</mat-form-field>
<mat-form-field>
  <input matInput placeholder="start" [(ngModel)]="start" name="start">
</mat-form-field>
<mat-form-field>
  <input matInput placeholder="end" [(ngModel)]="end" name="end">
</mat-form-field>
<button mat-raised-button color="primary"
(click)="getPcaOutput(tickers,start,end)">Get PCA Stock Chart</button>

<div *ngIf="pcaOutput">
  <div *ngIf="pcaOutput.data.length>0">
    <app-ch6-mlr-chart [title]="title" [mlrOutput]="pcaOutput"></app-ch6-mlr-chart>
  </div>
</div>
```

This template allows you to specify a list of stocks and date range for the PCA. We add an *app-ch6-mlr-chart* directive and specify its *title* and *mlrOutput* directives using corresponding properties, which are used to display PCA results for stock data.

Finally, we need to add a path for this new component to the *RouterModule* of the root module (i.e., the *app.module.ts* file):

```
{ path: 'chapter06/ch6-pca-stock, component: Ch6PcaStockComponent },
```

Then add the corresponding URL link to the *home* and *nav-menu* components.

Saving the project and navigating to the */chapter06/ch6-pca-stock* page produce the default PCA results shown in Fig.6-18.

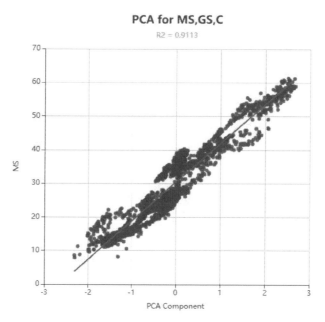

Fig.6-18. Multiple PCA results for MS ~ GS and C.

You can see from Fig.6-18 that the PCA component has a very high correlation relative to the original MS data with an R-squared = 0.9113.

In this chapter, we present two linear analysis techniques, linear regression and PCA, which are most commonly used approaches in quantitative finance. There are many other linear and nonlinear analysis approaches, such as moving average, technical indicators, and machine learning, which will be discussed in following chapters.

Chapter 7
Technical Indicators

Market data for securities, such as price, is the primary resource for technical analysis because it reflects every factor affecting the value of a market. However, market data does not generate just trend lines and basic chart pattern. Quant traders, analysts, and developers have expanded their studies of market data far beyond those basic elements. They have managed and manipulated market data to develop a number of technical indicators (also called technical analysis indicators), which provide more insight into market action than what you see on the surface.

Stock charts, such as the bar and candlestick charts, can provide a lot of information about a market at a glance, but a technical indicator can put a number on those observations and confirm whether a market is strengthening or weakening or becoming overbought or oversold before it becomes evident on a stock chart. Many analytical software packages or even the market data vendors (including Bloomberg and Reuters) now provide a variety of technical indicators as the computation capabilities of computers have evolved.

You should be very careful when applying the technical indicators in your real-life trading. Most traders and analysts do not rely on only one indicator but often use several indicators together to help making a trading decision because of the misleading information one indicator might provide. An indicator that works in one type of market condition may perform poorly in another market condition. There is no perfect indicator for every market in every period in every market condition.

Nevertheless, you, as a quant analyst, developer, or trader, should be familiar with various technical indicators. In this chapter, I will discuss some commonly used technical indicators based mainly on the financial analysis capability provided by a free technical analysis library called TA-Lib. TA-Lib consists of over 200 technical indicators. In most cases, you do not need to implement these commonly used indicators by yourself; instead, you simply need to learn how the math and algorithm work behind each indicator and how to use those indicators in your applications.

Implementation

In this section, I show you how to perform technical analysis in our ASP.NET Core Angular single-page applications. We will implement a helper interface for using TA-Lib as a technical analysis tool, rather than develop our own technical indicators from scratch. TA-Lib is widely used by trading software developers requiring performing technical analysis of financial market data. It includes over 200 indicators such as ADX, MACD, RSI, Stochastic, Bollinger bands, etc. It has an open-source API for C/C++, Java, Perl, Python, and C#.

In this book, we will use a .NET wrapper called *Cryptowatcher.TA-Lib-Core* to deploy C++ TA-Lib-Core library to a .NET core project. This is a NuGet package and can be installed with the following command in a NuGet Package Manager Console window:

```
PM> Install-Package Cryptowatcher.TA-Lib-Core -Version 1.0.0
```

Helper Class

In this section, we will implement some helper methods to help easily employing TA-Lib technical analysis tool in our applications. Add a helper class called *IndicatorHelper* in the *Quant/Models* folder with the following code:

```csharp
using System;
using System.Collections.Generic;
using System.Globalization;
using System.Linq;
using System.Threading.Tasks;
using TicTacTec.TA.Library;
using YahooFinanceApi;

namespace Quant.Models
{
    public static class IndicatorHelper
    {
        public static List<double?> MovingAverage(this List<double> source,
            int period = 30, string maType = "sma")
        {
            var count = source.Count;
            int outBegIdx, outNbElement;
            double[] maValues = new double[count];
            var ma = Core.MovingAverage(0, count - 1, source.ToArray(), period,
                GetMaType(maType), out outBegIdx, out outNbElement, maValues);
            if (ma == Core.RetCode.Success) return FixIndicatorOrdering(
                maValues.ToList(), outBegIdx, outNbElement);
            throw new Exception("Failed to calculate Ma.");
        }

        public static BbandOutput Bbands(this List<double> source, int period = 5,
            double devUp = 2, double devDown = 2, string maType = "sma")
        {
            var count = source.Count;
            int outBegIdx, outNbElement;
            double[] upperValues = new double[count];
            double[] middleValues = new double[count];
            double[] lowerValues = new double[count];
            var bb = Core.Bbands(0, count - 1, source.ToArray(), period, devUp,
                devDown, GetMaType(maType), out outBegIdx, out outNbElement,
                upperValues, middleValues, lowerValues);
            if (bb == Core.RetCode.Success)
            {
                return new BbandOutput()
                {
```

```csharp
                UpperBand = FixIndicatorOrdering(upperValues.ToList(),
                    outBegIdx, outNbElement),
                MiddleBand = FixIndicatorOrdering(middleValues.ToList(),
                    outBegIdx, outNbElement),
                LowerBand = FixIndicatorOrdering(lowerValues.ToList(),
                    outBegIdx, outNbElement)
            };
        }
        throw new Exception("Failed to calculate Bbands.");
    }

    public static List<double?> Sar(this List<Candle> source,
        double acceleration = 0.02, double maximum = 0.2)
    {
        var count = source.Count;
        int outBegIdx, outNbElement;
        double[] maValues = new double[count];
        var ma = Core.Sar(0, count - 1, source.Select(x => x.High).ToArray(),
            source.Select(x => x.Low).ToArray(), acceleration, maximum,
            out outBegIdx, out outNbElement, maValues);
        if (ma == Core.RetCode.Success) return FixIndicatorOrdering(
            maValues.ToList(), outBegIdx, outNbElement);
        throw new Exception("Failed to calculate Sar.");
    }

    public static List<double?> Adx(this List<Candle> source, int period = 14)
    {
        var count = source.Count;
        int outBegIdx, outNbElement;
        double[] indValues = new double[count];

        var highs = source.Select(x => Convert.ToDouble(x.High)).ToArray();
        var lows = source.Select(x => Convert.ToDouble(x.Low)).ToArray();
        var closes = source.Select(x => Convert.ToDouble(x.Close)).ToArray();

        var indicator = Core.Adx(0, source.Count - 1, highs, lows, closes,
            period, out outBegIdx, out outNbElement, indValues);

        if (indicator == Core.RetCode.Success)
        {
            return FixIndicatorOrdering(indValues.ToList(), outBegIdx,
                outNbElement);
        }
        throw new Exception("Failed to calculate Adx.");
    }

    public static List<double?> Apo(this List<double> source,
        int fastPeriod = 12, int slowPeriod = 26, string maType = "sma")
    {
        var count = source.Count;
        int outBegIdx, outNbElement;
        double[] indValues = new double[count];
        var ind = Core.Apo(0, count - 1, source.ToArray(), fastPeriod,
            slowPeriod, GetMaType(maType), out outBegIdx, out outNbElement,
            indValues);
```

```
        if (ind == Core.RetCode.Success) return FixIndicatorOrdering(
            indValues.ToList(), outBegIdx, outNbElement);
        throw new Exception("Failed to calculate Apo.");
}

public static AroonOutput Aroon(this List<Candle> source, int period = 14)
{
    var count = source.Count;
    int outBegIdx, outNbElement;
    double[] downValues = new double[count];
    double[] upValues = new double[count];

    var highs = source.Select(x => Convert.ToDouble(x.High)).ToArray();
    var lows = source.Select(x => Convert.ToDouble(x.Low)).ToArray();

    var ind = Core.Aroon(0, source.Count - 1, highs, lows, period,
        out outBegIdx, out outNbElement, downValues, upValues);

    if (ind == Core.RetCode.Success)
    {
        return new AroonOutput
        {
            AroonDown = FixIndicatorOrdering(downValues.ToList(), outBegIdx,
                outNbElement),
            AroonUp = FixIndicatorOrdering(upValues.ToList(), outBegIdx,
                outNbElement)
        };
    }

    throw new Exception("Failed to calculate Aroon.");
}

public static List<double?> Bop(this List<Candle> source)
{
    var count = source.Count;
    int outBegIdx, outNbElement;
    double[] indValues = new double[count];

    var highs = source.Select(x => Convert.ToDouble(x.High)).ToArray();
    var lows = source.Select(x => Convert.ToDouble(x.Low)).ToArray();
    var opens = source.Select(x => Convert.ToDouble(x.Open)).ToArray();
    var closes = source.Select(x => Convert.ToDouble(x.Close)).ToArray();

    var ind = Core.Bop(0, source.Count - 1, opens, highs, lows, closes,
        out outBegIdx, out outNbElement, indValues);

    if (ind == Core.RetCode.Success)
    {
        return FixIndicatorOrdering(indValues.ToList(), outBegIdx,
            outNbElement);
    }

    throw new Exception("Failed to calculate Bop.");
}
```

```csharp
public static List<double?> Cci(this List<Candle> source, int period = 14)
{
    var count = source.Count;
    int outBegIdx, outNbElement;
    double[] indValues = new double[count];

    var highs = source.Select(x => Convert.ToDouble(x.High)).ToArray();
    var lows = source.Select(x => Convert.ToDouble(x.Low)).ToArray();
    var closes = source.Select(x => Convert.ToDouble(x.Close)).ToArray();

    var ind = Core.Cci(0, source.Count - 1, highs, lows, closes, period,
        out outBegIdx, out outNbElement, indValues);

    if (ind == Core.RetCode.Success)
    {
        return FixIndicatorOrdering(indValues.ToList(), outBegIdx,
            outNbElement);
    }

    throw new Exception("Failed to calculate Cci.");
}

public static MacdOutput Macd(this List<double> source, int fastPeriod = 12,
    int slowPeriod = 26, int signalPeriod = 9)
{
    var count = source.Count;
    int outBegIdx, outNbElement;
    double[] indValues = new double[count];
    double[] ind1Values = new double[count];
    double[] ind2Values = new double[count];

    var ind = Core.Macd(0, source.Count - 1, source.ToArray(), fastPeriod,
        slowPeriod, signalPeriod, out outBegIdx, out outNbElement,
        indValues, ind1Values, ind2Values);

    if (ind == Core.RetCode.Success)
    {
        return new MacdOutput
        {
            Macd = FixIndicatorOrdering(indValues.ToList(), outBegIdx,
                outNbElement),
            Signal = FixIndicatorOrdering(ind1Values.ToList(), outBegIdx,
                outNbElement),
            Hist = FixIndicatorOrdering(ind2Values.ToList(), outBegIdx,
                outNbElement),
        };
    }
    throw new Exception("Failed to calculate Macd.");
}

public static List<double?> Rsi(this List<double> source, int period)
{
    var count = source.Count;
    int outBegIdx, outNbElement;
    double[] indValues = new double[count];
```

```
    var ind = Core.Rsi(0, source.Count - 1, source.ToArray(), period,
        out outBegIdx, out outNbElement, indValues);

    if (ind == Core.RetCode.Success)
    {
        return FixIndicatorOrdering(indValues.ToList(), outBegIdx,
            outNbElement);
    }

    throw new Exception("Failed to calculate Rsi.");
}

public static StochOutput Stoch(this List<Candle> source,
    int fastkPeriod = 5, int slowkPeriod = 3, int slowdPeriod = 3,
    string maType = "sma")
{
    var count = source.Count;
    int outBegIdx, outNbElement;
    double[] indValues = new double[count];
    double[] ind1Values = new double[count];

    var highs = source.Select(x => Convert.ToDouble(x.High)).ToArray();
    var lows = source.Select(x => Convert.ToDouble(x.Low)).ToArray();
    var closes = source.Select(x => Convert.ToDouble(x.Close)).ToArray();

    var indicator = Core.Stoch(0, source.Count - 1, highs, lows, closes,
        fastkPeriod, slowkPeriod, GetMaType(maType), slowdPeriod,
        GetMaType(maType), out outBegIdx, out outNbElement, indValues,
        ind1Values);

    if (indicator == Core.RetCode.Success)
    {
        return new StochOutput
        {
            SlowK = FixIndicatorOrdering(indValues.ToList(), outBegIdx,
                outNbElement),
            SlowD = FixIndicatorOrdering(ind1Values.ToList(), outBegIdx,
                outNbElement)
        };
    }

    throw new Exception("Failed to calculate Stoch.");
}

public static List<double?> WillR(this List<Candle> source, int period = 14)
{
    var count = source.Count;
    int outBegIdx, outNbElement;
    double[] indValues = new double[count];
    var highs = source.Select(x => Convert.ToDouble(x.High)).ToArray();
    var lows = source.Select(x => Convert.ToDouble(x.Low)).ToArray();
    var closes = source.Select(x => Convert.ToDouble(x.Close)).ToArray();
    var indicator = Core.WillR(0, source.Count - 1, highs, lows, closes,
        period, out outBegIdx, out outNbElement, indValues);
```

```csharp
        if (indicator == Core.RetCode.Success)
        {
            return FixIndicatorOrdering(indValues.ToList(), outBegIdx,
            outNbElement);
        }

        throw new Exception("Failed to calculate WilliamsR.");
}

public static List<double?> Ad(this List<Candle> source)
{
        var count = source.Count;
        int outBegIdx, outNbElement;
        double[] indValues = new double[count];
        var highs = source.Select(x => Convert.ToDouble(x.High)).ToArray();
        var lows = source.Select(x => Convert.ToDouble(x.Low)).ToArray();
        var closes = source.Select(x => Convert.ToDouble(x.Close)).ToArray();
        var volumes = source.Select(x => Convert.ToDouble(x.Volume)).ToArray();

        var ind = Core.Ad(0, source.Count - 1, highs, lows, closes, volumes,
            out outBegIdx, out outNbElement, indValues);

        if (ind == Core.RetCode.Success)
        {
            return FixIndicatorOrdering(indValues.ToList(), outBegIdx,
                outNbElement);
        }

        throw new Exception("Failed to calculate Ad.");
}

public static List<double?> Obv(this List<Candle> source, string priceType)
{
        var count = source.Count;
        int outBegIdx, outNbElement;
        double[] indValues = new double[count];
        var closes = source.Select(x => Convert.ToDouble(x.Close)).ToArray();
        priceType = priceType.ToLower();
        if (priceType == "open") closes = source.Select(x =>
            Convert.ToDouble(x.Open)).ToArray();
        else if (priceType == "high") closes = source.Select(x =>
            Convert.ToDouble(x.High)).ToArray();
        else if (priceType == "low") closes = source.Select(x =>
            Convert.ToDouble(x.Low)).ToArray();

        var volumes = source.Select(x => Convert.ToDouble(x.Volume)).ToArray();
        var ind = Core.Obv(0, source.Count - 1, closes, volumes, out outBegIdx,
            out outNbElement, indValues);

        if (ind == Core.RetCode.Success)
        {
            return FixIndicatorOrdering(indValues.ToList(), outBegIdx,
                outNbElement);
        }
```

```
            throw new Exception("Failed to calculate Obv.");
    }

    public static List<double?> Atr(this List<Candle> source, int period = 14)
    {
        var count = source.Count;
        int outBegIdx, outNbElement;
        double[] indValues = new double[count];
        var highs = source.Select(x => Convert.ToDouble(x.High)).ToArray();
        var lows = source.Select(x => Convert.ToDouble(x.Low)).ToArray();
        var closes = source.Select(x => Convert.ToDouble(x.Close)).ToArray();

        var ind = Core.Atr(0, source.Count - 1, highs, lows, closes, period,
            out outBegIdx, out outNbElement, indValues);

        if (ind == Core.RetCode.Success)
        {
            return FixIndicatorOrdering(indValues.ToList(), outBegIdx,
                outNbElement);
        }

        throw new Exception("Failed to calculate Atr.");
    }

    public static List<double?> Natr(this List<Candle> source, int period = 14)
    {
        var count = source.Count;
        int outBegIdx, outNbElement;
        double[] indValues = new double[count];
        var highs = source.Select(x => Convert.ToDouble(x.High)).ToArray();
        var lows = source.Select(x => Convert.ToDouble(x.Low)).ToArray();
        var closes = source.Select(x => Convert.ToDouble(x.Close)).ToArray();

        var ind = Core.Natr(0, source.Count - 1, highs, lows, closes, period,
            out outBegIdx, out outNbElement, indValues);

        if (ind == Core.RetCode.Success)
        {
            return FixIndicatorOrdering(indValues.ToList(), outBegIdx,
                outNbElement);
        }

        throw new Exception("Failed to calculate Natr.");
    }

    public static List<double?> TrueRange(this List<Candle> source)
    {
        var count = source.Count;
        int outBegIdx, outNbElement;
        double[] indValues = new double[count];
        var highs = source.Select(x => Convert.ToDouble(x.High)).ToArray();
        var lows = source.Select(x => Convert.ToDouble(x.Low)).ToArray();
        var closes = source.Select(x => Convert.ToDouble(x.Close)).ToArray();
```

```csharp
        var ind = Core.TrueRange(0, source.Count - 1, highs, lows, closes,
            out outBegIdx, out outNbElement, indValues);

        if (ind == Core.RetCode.Success)
        {
            return FixIndicatorOrdering(indValues.ToList(), outBegIdx,
                outNbElement);
        }

        throw new Exception("Failed to calculate TrueRange.");
}

public static List<Candle> GetCandleData(string ticker, string start,
    string end)
{
    DateTime startDate = DateTime.ParseExact(start, "yyyy-MM-dd",
        CultureInfo.InvariantCulture);
    DateTime endDate = DateTime.ParseExact(end, "yyyy-MM-dd",
        CultureInfo.InvariantCulture);
    var data = Task.Run(() => Yahoo.GetHistoricalAsync(ticker, startDate,
        endDate, Period.Daily)).Result;

    List<Candle> res = new List<Candle>();
    foreach (var r in data)
    {
        var Open = r.Open;
        var High = r.High;
        var Low = r.Low;
        var Close = r.Close;
        var CloseAdj = r.AdjustedClose;
        var Volume = r.Volume;
        if (Open > 0 && High > 0 && Low > 0 && Close > 0 && Volume > 0)
        {
            res.Add(new Candle
            {
                Date = r.DateTime,
                Open = (double)Open,
                High = (double)High,
                Low = (double)Low,
                Close = (double)Close,
                Volume = Volume
            });
        }
    }
    return res;
}

public static List<double> CandleToDoubleList(List<Candle> candles,
    string priceType)
{
    List<double> res = new List<double>();
    switch (priceType.ToLower())
    {
        case "open":
            foreach (var p in candles)
```

```
                    {
                        res.Add(p.Open);
                    }
                    break;
                case "high":
                    foreach (var p in candles)
                    {
                        res.Add(p.High);
                    }
                    break;
                case "low":
                    foreach (var p in candles)
                    {
                        res.Add(p.Low);
                    }
                    break;
                case "close":
                    foreach (var p in candles)
                    {
                        res.Add(p.Close);
                    }
                    break;
                case "volume":
                    foreach (var p in candles)
                    {
                        res.Add(p.Volume);
                    }
                    break;
            }
            return res;
        }

        private static Core.MAType GetMaType(string maType)
        {
            maType = maType.ToLower();
            var type = Core.MAType.Sma;
            if (maType == "sma") type = Core.MAType.Sma;
            else if (maType == "ema") type = Core.MAType.Ema;
            else if (maType == "wma") type = Core.MAType.Wma;
            return type;
        }

        private static List<double?> FixIndicatorOrdering(List<double> items,
            int outBegIdx, int outNbElement)
        {
            var outValues = new List<double?>();
            var validAdx = items.Take(outNbElement);

            for (int i = 0; i < outBegIdx; i++)
                outValues.Add(null);

            foreach (var value in validAdx)
                outValues.Add(value);

            return outValues;
```

```
        }
    }

    public class Candle
    {
        public DateTime Date { get; set; }
        public double High { get; set; }
        public double Low { get; set; }
        public double Open { get; set; }
        public double Close { get; set; }
        public double Volume { get; set; }
    }

    public class BbandOutput
    {
        public List<double?> UpperBand { get; set; }
        public List<double?> MiddleBand { get; set; }
        public List<double?> LowerBand { get; set; }
    }

    public class MacdOutput
    {
        public List<double?> Macd { get; set; }
        public List<double?> Signal { get; set; }
        public List<double?> Hist { get; set; }
    }

    public class AroonOutput
    {
        public List<double?> AroonDown { get; set; }
        public List<double?> AroonUp { get; set; }
    }

    public class StochOutput
    {
        public List<double?> SlowK { get; set; }
        public List<double?> SlowD { get; set; }
    }
}
```

This class has a long code listing. First, we implement various extension method with *this* key word for seventeen commonly used technical indicators. Each method implemented for a specified indicator that takes different set of input arguments and returns different output. Most of these methods simply return a list of double values, such as moving average, ADX, CCI, RSI, etc., while some other methods return different class objects, such as Bollinger bands returns *BbandOutput* and MACD indicator returns *MacdOutput*, etc. These kinds of outputs are defined using corresponding classes at the bottom of the *IndicatorHelper.cs* class. For instance, for MACD indicator, we define its output object in terms of the following class:

```
public class MacdOutput
{
    public List<double?> Macd { get; set; }
    public List<double?> Signal { get; set; }
    public List<double?> Hist { get; set; }
}
```

This means that the output from the MACD indicator consists of three double lists: *Macd*, *Signal*, and *Hist* (or histogram).

For simplifying calculation, we also define a *Candle* class to represent the market data:

```
public class Candle
{
    public DateTime Date { get; set; }
    public double High { get; set; }
    public double Low { get; set; }
    public double Open { get; set; }
    public double Close { get; set; }
    public double Volume { get; set; }
}
```

The indicator methods in the above code use a list of *Candle* object as their data source to perform various technical analysis. We also implement two helper methods, *GetCandleData* and *CandleToDoubleList*. The former method retrieves the historical stock EOD data from Yahoo Finance and converts it into a list of *Candle* object, while the latter extracts the data for a specified price type that will be used in calculating technical indicators. In the current implementation, we will always use the *close* price as the price type. You can change whatever price type you like or make it as a variable to be specified by users.

One important aspect of the output from the TA-Lib Core is the *outBegIdx* and *outNbElement*. For example, the *MovingAverage* method has the following code snippet:

```
public static List<double?> MovingAverage(this List<double> source, int period = 30,
    string maType = "sma")
{
    var count = source.Count;
    int outBegIdx, outNbElement;
    double[] maValues = new double[count];
    var ma = Core.MovingAverage(0, count - 1, source.ToArray(), period,
        GetMaType(maType), out outBegIdx, out outNbElement, maValues);
    if (ma == Core.RetCode.Success) return FixIndicatorOrdering(maValues.ToList(),
        outBegIdx, outNbElement);
    throw new Exception("Failed to calculate Ma.");
}
```

The reason is that even if we want to calculate for the whole range (from 0 to 399 for example) with a period of 30, the moving average is not valid until the 30th day. Consequently, the *outBegIdx* will be 29 (zero based) and the *outNbElement* will be 400−29 = 371. This means that only the first 371 elements of out are valid, and these could be calculated only starting at the 30th element of the input.

In order to align the timestamp of moving average result with the time series calculation, we implement a method called *FixedIndicatorOrdering*, which adds *null* elements for the first 30th day, ensuring the moving average result has the same number of elements as the original price data.

Web Service for Technical Indictors

In this section, I will show you how to convert the technical indicators implemented in the preceding section into a web service.

Add an API controller named *IndicatorValuesController* to the *Controllers* folder and replace its content with the following code:

```csharp
using Microsoft.AspNetCore.Mvc;
using Quant.Models;

namespace Quant.Controllers
{
    [Produces("application/json")]
    public class IndicatorValuesController : Controller
    {
        [Route("~/api/indicatorMa/{ticker}/{start}/{end}/{period}/{maType}")]
        [HttpGet]
        public JsonResult GetMovingAverage(string ticker,string start,string end,
            int period, string maType)
        {
            var candles = IndicatorHelper.GetCandleData(ticker, start, end);
            var dl = IndicatorHelper.CandleToDoubleList(candles, "close");
            var indicator = dl.MovingAverage(period, maType);
            return Json(new { ticker, name = maType, indicator, candles });
        }

        [Route("~/api/indicatorBbands/{ticker}/{start}/{end}/{period}/
            {maType}/{devUp}/{devDown}")]
        [HttpGet]
        public JsonResult GetBbands(string ticker, string start, string end,
            int period, string maType, double devUp, double devDown)
        {
            var candles = IndicatorHelper.GetCandleData(ticker, start, end);
            var dl = IndicatorHelper.CandleToDoubleList(candles, "close");
            var indicator = dl.Bbands(period, devUp, devDown, maType);
            return Json(new { ticker, name = "bbands", indicator, candles });
        }

        [Route("~/api/IndicatorSar/{ticker}/{start}/{end}/{acceleration}/
            {maximum}")]
        [HttpGet]
        public JsonResult GetSar(string ticker, string start, string end,
            double acceleration, double maximum)
        {
            var candles = IndicatorHelper.GetCandleData(ticker, start, end);
            var indicator = candles.Sar(acceleration, maximum);
            return Json(new { ticker, name = "sar", indicator, candles });
        }

        [Route("~/api/indicatorAdx/{ticker}/{start}/{end}/{period}")]
        [HttpGet]
        public JsonResult GetAdx(string ticker, string start, string end,
            int period)
        {
            var candles = IndicatorHelper.GetCandleData(ticker, start, end);
            var indicator = candles.Adx(period);
            return Json(new { ticker, name="adx", indicator, candles });
        }

        [Route("~/api/indicatorApo/{ticker}/{start}/{end}/{fastPeriod}/
            {slowPeriod}/{maType}")]
        [HttpGet]
```

```
public JsonResult GetApo(string ticker, string start, string end,
    int fastPeriod, int slowPeriod, string maType)
{
    var candles = IndicatorHelper.GetCandleData(ticker, start, end);
    var dl = IndicatorHelper.CandleToDoubleList(candles, "close");
    var indicator = dl.Apo(fastPeriod, slowPeriod, maType);
    return Json(new { ticker, name = "apo", indicator, candles });
}


[Route("~/api/indicatorAroon/{ticker}/{start}/{end}/{period}")]
[HttpGet]
public JsonResult GetAroon(string ticker, string start, string end,
    int period)
{
    var candles = IndicatorHelper.GetCandleData(ticker, start, end);
    var indicator = candles.Aroon(period);
    return Json(new { ticker, name="aroon", indicator, candles });
}


[Route("~/api/indicatorBop/{ticker}/{start}/{end}")]
[HttpGet]
public JsonResult GetBop(string ticker, string start, string end)
{
    var candles = IndicatorHelper.GetCandleData(ticker, start, end);
    var indicator = candles.Bop();
    return Json(new { ticker, name="bop", indicator, candles });
}


[Route("~/api/indicatorCci/{ticker}/{start}/{end}/{period}")]
[HttpGet]
public JsonResult GetCci(string ticker, string start, string end,
    int period)
{
    var candles = IndicatorHelper.GetCandleData(ticker, start, end);
    var indicator = candles.Cci(period);
    return Json(new { ticker, name = "cci", indicator, candles });
}


[Route("~/api/indicatorMacd/{ticker}/{start}/{end}/{fastPeriod}/
    {slowPeriod}/{signalPeriod}")]
[HttpGet]
public JsonResult GetMacd(string ticker, string start, string end,
    int fastPeriod, int slowPeriod, int signalPeriod)
{
    var candles = IndicatorHelper.GetCandleData(ticker, start, end);
    var dat = IndicatorHelper.CandleToDoubleList(candles, "close");
    var indicator = dat.Macd(fastPeriod, slowPeriod, signalPeriod);

    return Json(new { ticker, name = "macd", indicator, candles });
}


[Route("~/api/indicatorRsi/{ticker}/{start}/{end}/{period}")]
[HttpGet]
public JsonResult GetRsi(string ticker, string start, string end,
    int period)
```

```
{
    var candles = IndicatorHelper.GetCandleData(ticker, start, end);
    var dl = IndicatorHelper.CandleToDoubleList(candles, "close");
    var indicator = dl.Rsi(period);
    return Json(new { ticker, name="rsi", indicator, candles });
}


[Route("~/api/indicatorStoch/{ticker}/{start}/{end}/{fastkPeriod}/
    {slowkPeriod}/{slowdPeriod}/{maType}")]
[HttpGet]
public JsonResult GetStoch(string ticker, string start, string end,
    int fastkPeriod, int slowkPeriod, int slowdPeriod, string maType)
{
    var candles = IndicatorHelper.GetCandleData(ticker, start, end);
    var indicator = candles.Stoch(fastkPeriod, slowkPeriod, slowdPeriod,
        maType);
    return Json(new { ticker, name="stoch", indicator, candles });
}


[Route("~/api/indicatorWillR/{ticker}/{start}/{end}/{period}")]
[HttpGet]
public JsonResult GetWillR(string ticker, string start, string end,
    int period)
{
    var candles = IndicatorHelper.GetCandleData(ticker, start, end);
    var indicator = candles.WillR(period);
    return Json(new { ticker, name="willR", indicator, candles });
}



[Route("~/api/indicatorAd/{ticker}/{start}/{end}")]
[HttpGet]
public JsonResult GetAd(string ticker, string start, string end,
    int interval)
{
    var candles = IndicatorHelper.GetCandleData(ticker, start, end);
    var indicator = candles.Ad();
    return Json(new { ticker, name="ad", indicator, candles });
}


[Route("~/api/indicatorObv/{ticker}/{start}/{end}")]
[HttpGet]
public JsonResult GetObv(string ticker, string start, string end)
{
    var candles = IndicatorHelper.GetCandleData(ticker, start, end);
    var indicator = candles.Obv("close");
    return Json(new { ticker, name="obv", indicator, candles });
}



[Route("~/api/indicatorAtr/{ticker}/{start}/{end}/{period}")]
[HttpGet]
public JsonResult GetAtr(string ticker, string start, string end,
    int period)
{
```

```
            var candles = IndicatorHelper.GetCandleData(ticker, start, end);
            var indicator = candles.Atr(period);
            return Json(new { ticker, name="atr", indicator, candles });
        }


        [Route("~/api/indicatorNatr/{ticker}/{start}/{end}/{period}")]
        [HttpGet]
        public JsonResult GetNatr(string ticker, string start, string end,
            int period)
        {
            var candles = IndicatorHelper.GetCandleData(ticker, start, end);
            var indicator = candles.Natr(period);
            return Json(new { ticker, name="natr", indicator, candles });
        }


        [Route("~/api/indicatorTrueRange/{ticker}/{start}/{end}")]
        [HttpGet]
        public JsonResult GetTrueRange(string ticker, string start, string end)
        {
            var candles = IndicatorHelper.GetCandleData(ticker, start, end);
            var indicator = candles.TrueRange();
            return Json(new { ticker, name="trueRange", indicator, candles });
        }
    }
}
```

Here, we convert seventeen commonly used technical indicators into a web API service with specified URL routes. The returned result from each indicator is a *JsonResult* object that represents a class used to send JSON-formatted content to the response. For example, the following URL

https://localhost:5001/api/indicatorma/ibm/2018-01-01/2018-02-28/10/sma

will return the moving average results for IBM as shown in Fig.7-1.

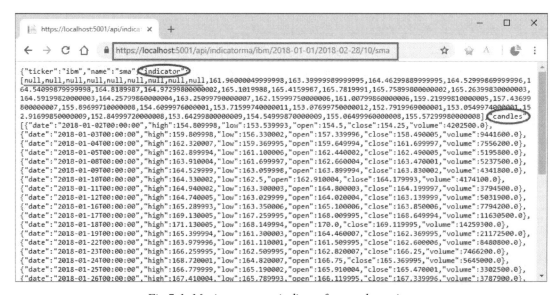

Fig.7-1. Moving average indictor from web service.

Note how the *null* elements are added to the first nine elements of the moving average indicator.

Technical Indicators in Angular

The process of sending a request from the Angular application to get the technical indicator results following the same basic repository patterns presented in the preceding chapters. Here, we need to add a service called *ch7.service.ts* to the *ClientApp/src/app/models* folder by running the following command in a command prompt window:

ng g s models/ch7

Open the *ch7.service.ts* class file and replace its content with the following code:

```
// ch7.service.ts file:
import { Injectable, Inject } from '@angular/core';
import { HttpClient } from '@angular/common/http';

@Injectable({
  providedIn: 'root'
})
export class Ch7Service {
  private url;

  constructor(private http: HttpClient, @Inject('BASE_URL') baseUrl: string) {
    this.url = baseUrl;
  }

  ma: any;
  getMa(ticker: string, start: string, end: string, period: number, maType: string)
  {
    let url1 = this.url + 'api/indicatorma/' + ticker + '/' + start + '/' + end +
      '/' + period + '/' + maType;
    this.http.get<any>(url1).subscribe(result => { this.ma = result });
  }

  bbands: any;
  getBbands(ticker: string, start: string, end: string, period: number, maType:
    string, devUp: number, devDown: number) {
    let url1 = this.url + 'api/indicatorbbands/' + ticker + '/' + start + '/' +
      end + '/' + period + '/' + maType + '/' + devUp + '/' + devDown;
    this.http.get<any>(url1).subscribe(result => { this.bbands = result });
  }

  sar: any;
  getSar(ticker: string, start: string, end: string, acceleration: number,
    maximum: number) {
    let url1 = this.url + 'api/indicatorsar/' + ticker + '/' + start + '/' +
      end + '/' + acceleration + '/' + maximum;
    this.http.get<any>(url1).subscribe(result => { this.sar = result });
  }

  adx: any;
  getAdx(ticker: string, start: string, end: string, period: number) {
    let url1 = this.url + 'api/indicatoradx/' + ticker + '/' + start + '/' +
      end + '/' + period;
```

```
    this.http.get<any>(url1).subscribe(result => { this.adx = result });
  }

  apo: any;
  getApo(ticker: string, start: string, end: string, fastPeriod: number,
    slowPeriod: number, maType: string) {
    let url1 = this.url + 'api/indicatorapo/' + ticker + '/' + start + '/' +
      end + '/' + fastPeriod + '/' + slowPeriod + '/' + maType;
    this.http.get<any>(url1).subscribe(result => { this.apo = result });
  }

  aroon: any;
  getAroon(ticker: string, start: string, end: string, period: number) {
    let url1 = this.url + 'api/indicatoraroon/' + ticker + '/' + start + '/' +
      end + '/' + period;
    this.http.get<any>(url1).subscribe(result => { this.aroon = result });
  }

  bop: any;
  getBop(ticker: string, start: string, end: string) {
    let url1 = this.url + 'api/indicatorbop/' + ticker + '/' + start + '/' + end;
    this.http.get<any>(url1).subscribe(result => { this.bop = result });
  }

  cci: any;
  getCci(ticker: string, start: string, end: string, period: number) {
    let url1 = this.url + 'api/indicatorcci/' + ticker + '/' + start + '/' +
      end + '/' + period;
    this.http.get<any>(url1).subscribe(result => { this.cci = result });
  }

  macd: any;
  getMacd(ticker: string, start: string, end: string, fastPeriod: number,
slowPeriod, signalPeriod) {
    let url1 = this.url + 'api/indicatormacd/' + ticker + '/' + start + '/' +
      end + '/' + fastPeriod + '/' + slowPeriod + '/' + signalPeriod;
    this.http.get<any>(url1).subscribe(result => { this.macd = result });
  }

  rsi: any;
  getRsi(ticker: string, start: string, end: string, period: number) {
    let url1 = this.url + 'api/indicatorrsi/' + ticker + '/' + start + '/' +
      end + '/' + period;
    this.http.get<any>(url1).subscribe(result => { this.rsi = result });
  }

  stoch: any;
  getStoch(ticker: string, start: string, end: string, fastkPeriod: number,
    slowkPeriod: number, slowdPeriod: number, maType: string) {
    let url1 = this.url + 'api/indicatorstoch/' + ticker + '/' + start + '/' +
      end + '/' + fastkPeriod + '/' +
      slowkPeriod + '/' + slowdPeriod + '/' + maType;
    this.http.get<any>(url1).subscribe(result => { this.stoch = result });
  }
```

```
willR: any;
getWillR(ticker: string, start: string, end: string, period: number) {
  let url1 = this.url + 'api/indicatorwillr/' + ticker + '/' + start + '/' +
    end + '/' + period;
  this.http.get<any>(url1).subscribe(result => { this.willR = result });
}

ad: any;
getAd(ticker: string, start: string, end: string) {
  let url1 = this.url + 'api/indicatorad/' + ticker + '/' + start + '/' + end;
  this.http.get<any>(url1).subscribe(result => { this.ad = result });
}

obv: any;
getObv(ticker: string, start: string, end: string) {
  let url1 = this.url + 'api/indicatorobv/' + ticker + '/' + start + '/' + end;
  this.http.get<any>(url1).subscribe(result => { this.obv = result });
}

atr: any;
getAtr(ticker: string, start: string, end: string, period: number) {
  let url1 = this.url + 'api/indicatoratr/' + ticker + '/' + start + '/' +
    end + '/' + period;
  this.http.get<any>(url1).subscribe(result => { this.atr = result });
}

natr: any;
getNatr(ticker: string, start: string, end: string, period: number) {
  let url1 = this.url + 'api/indicatornatr/' + ticker + '/' + start + '/' +
    end + '/' + period;
  this.http.get<any>(url1).subscribe(result => { this.natr = result });
}

trueRange: any;
getTrueRange(ticker: string, start: string, end: string) {
  let url1 = this.url + 'api/indicatortruerange/' + ticker + '/' + start +
    '/' + end;
  this.http.get<any>(url1).subscribe(result => { this.trueRange = result });
}
}
```

This service is very similar to the *repository.service.ts* class implemented in Chapter 3. Various methods implemented in this class send HTTP requests to specified URLs, which retrieve the results for different technical indicators from the ASP.NET Core API service.

Charts for Technical Indicators

In this section, we will implement some Angular helper components to help creating charts for displaying technical indicator results. In a standard indicator chart, we would like to show the stock prices, indictor results, and volume with an aligned date axis, which requires a chart to have three chart areas. However, in a chart for an indicator based on the moving average, we usually want to overlay the indicator results with the stock prices. In this case, the indicator chart has two areas: one is for the stock prices and indicator results, and the other for volume.

Chart with Two Chart Areas

In this section, we will create an interface for the indicators based on the moving average. Technical indicators that use the same scale as stock prices, such as moving average and Bollinger bands, are typically plotted on top of the price bar or candlestick chart and are therefore referred to as *overlap* or *overlay* indicators.

In chapter 5, we already demonstrate how to create a stock chart with two chart areas, that is, the candlestick and volume chart. Here, we need to add the overlap indicators on top of the candlestick chart. Run the following command in a command prompt window from the *ClientApp* folder:

```
ng g c chapter07/ch7-ind2-chart --module=app.module
```

This generates a new component called *ch7-ind2-chart* in the *ClientApp/src/app/chapter07* folder. Open the *ch7-ind2-chart.component.ts* file and replace its content with the following code:

```
// ch7-ind-chart.component.ts file:
import { Component, OnInit, Input, OnChanges } from '@angular/core';
import { StockChartHelper } from '../../models/stockChartHelper';

@Component({
  selector: 'app-ch7-ind2-chart',
  templateUrl: './ch7-ind2-chart.component.html',
  styleUrls: ['./ch7-ind2-chart.component.css']
})
export class Ch7Ind2ChartComponent implements OnInit, OnChanges {
  @Input() indicator: any;

  private helper: StockChartHelper = new StockChartHelper();
  private stock: any;
  private legend: any;
  options: any;

  constructor() { }

  ngOnInit() {
    this.stock = this.helper.processCandleData(this.indicator.candles);
    this.options = this.getOptions();
  }

  ngOnChanges() {
    this.stock = this.helper.processCandleData(this.indicator.candles);
    this.options = this.getOptions();
  }

  getOptions() {
    const downColor = '#ec0000';
    const downBorderColor = '#8A0000';
    const upColor = '#00da3c';
    const upBorderColor = '#008F28';

    let candleSeries = {
      name: 'price',
      type: 'candlestick',
      data: this.stock.values,
      itemStyle: {
```

```
    color: upColor,
    color0: downColor,
    borderColor: upBorderColor,
    borderColor0: downBorderColor
  }
};

let VolumeSeries = {
  name: 'volume',
    type: 'bar',
      xAxisIndex: 1,
        yAxisIndex: 1,
          itemStyle: {
    normal: {
      color: '#7fbe9e'
    },
    emphasis: {
      color: '#140'
    }
  },
  data: this.stock.volume
}

let series = [];
series.push(candleSeries);
let indSeries = this.processIndicatorSeries();
for (let i in indSeries) {
  series.push(indSeries[i]);
}
series.push(VolumeSeries);

return {
  title: {
    text: this.indicator.ticker + ': Stock Price (' + this.indicator.name + ')',
    left: 'center'
  },
  legend: {
    top: 35,
    right: 30,
    data: this.legend
  },
  tooltip: {
    trigger: 'axis',
    axisPointer: {
      type: 'cross'
    }
  },
  axisPointer: {
    link: { xAxisIndex: 'all' }
  },
  grid: [{
    left: 50,
    right: 20,
    top: '10%',
    height: '53%'
```

```
}, {
  left: 50,
  right: 20,
  height: '20%',
  top: '68%'
}],
xAxis: [{
  type: 'category',
  data: this.stock.categoryData,
  scale: true,
  boundaryGap: false,
  axisLine: { onZero: false },
  splitLine: { show: false },
  splitNumber: 20,
  min: 'dataMin',
  max: 'dataMax'
}, {
  type: 'category',
  gridIndex: 1,
  data: this.stock.categoryData,
  scale: true,
  boundaryGap: false,
  splitLine: { show: false },
  axisLabel: { show: false },
  axisTick: { show: false },
  axisLine: { lineStyle: { color: '#777' } },
  splitNumber: 20,
  min: 'dataMin',
  max: 'dataMax'
}
],
yAxis: [{
  scale: true,
  splitArea: {
    show: true
  }
}, {
  scale: true,
  gridIndex: 1,
  splitNumber: 2,
  axisLabel: { show: false },
  axisLine: { show: false },
  axisTick: { show: false },
  splitLine: { show: false }
}
],
dataZoom: [
  {
    show: true,
    type: 'slider',
    y: '93%',
    start: 70,
    end: 100,
    xAxisIndex: [0, 1],
  }
```

```
      ],
      series: series
    };
  }

  private processIndicatorSeries() {
    let indicatorSeries = [];
    switch (this.indicator.name) {
      case 'bbands':
        this.legend = ['price', { name: 'upperBand', icon: 'line' },
          { name: 'middleBand', icon: 'line' }, { name: 'lowerBand', icon: 'line' }];
        indicatorSeries.push({
          name: 'upperBand',
          type: 'line',
          data: this.indicator.indicator.upperBand,
          showSymbol: false
        });
        indicatorSeries.push({
          name: 'middleBand',
          type: 'line',
          data: this.indicator.indicator.middleBand,
          showSymbol: false
        });
        indicatorSeries.push({
          name: 'lowerBand',
          type: 'line',
          data: this.indicator.indicator.lowerBand,
          showSymbol: false
        });
        break;
      default:
        this.legend = ['price', { name: this.indicator.name, icon: 'line' }];
        indicatorSeries.push({
          name: this.indicator.name,
          type: 'line',
          data: this.indicator.indicator,
          showSymbol: false
        });
        break;
    }
    return indicatorSeries;
  }
}
```

This component contains an *Input* argument called *indicator*, which represents the indicator results from the web service. The *Input* argument will be specified in its parent component. First, we process the *candles* data in the *indicator* using the *processCandleData* method implemented in the *stockChartHelper.ts* class in the *ClientApp/src/app/models* folder:

```
// stockChartHelper.ts file:
import { MarketData } from './market-data.model';

export class StockChartHelper {

  processStockData(stockData: MarketData[]) {
    const categoryData = [];
```

```
    const values = [];
    const volume = [];
    for (let i = 0; i < stockData.length; i++) {
      categoryData.push(stockData[i].date.toString().substring(0, 10));
      values.push([stockData[i].open, stockData[i].close, stockData[i].low,
        stockData[i].high]);
      volume.push(stockData[i].volume);
    }
    return {
      categoryData: categoryData,
      values: values,
      volume: volume
    };
  }

  processCandleData(candles: any) {
    const categoryData = [];
    const values = [];
    const volume = [];
    for (let i = 0; i < candles.length; i++) {
      categoryData.push(candles[i].date.toString().substring(0, 10));
      values.push([candles[i].open, candles[i].close, candles[i].low,
        candles[i].high]);
      volume.push(candles[i].volume);
    }
    return {
      categoryData: categoryData,
      values: values,
      volume: volume
    };
  }
}
```

The processed data will be used to create the candlestick and volume charts. We then define a *series* array that consists of *candleSeries*, *indSeries* (for indicator), and *volumeSeries*. The *indSeries* is generated using the *processIndicatorSeries* method. This method includes a switch statement: the default case is for the indicators with a single line, while the other cases are for the indicators with multiple lines. For example, the Bollinger-bands indicator has three lines: *upperBand*, *middleBand*, and *lowerBand*.

We also need to update the component's template:

```
// ch7-ind2-chart.component.html file:
<mat-card class="card-stock">
  <div echarts [options]="options" style="height:100%"></div>
</mat-card>
```

This template has a *card-stock* style class defined in its style file:

```
// ch7-ind2-chart.component.css file:
.card-stock {
  margin: 10px;
  width: 800px;
  height: 600px;
}
```

Chart with Three Chart Areas

For some indicators, such as oscillator indicators, their values have a very different data range from the stock prices, and are hard to be overlaid with the stock prices on the same area. In this case, we usually show the indicators in a separated area, so that the corresponding chart would have three chart areas, which are used to display the stock prices, indicator results, and volume.

Run the following command in a command prompt window from the *ClientApp* folder:

```
ng g c chapter07/ch7-ind3-chart --module=app.module
```

This generates a new component called *ch7-ind3-chart* in the *ClientApp/src/app/chapter07* folder. Open the *ch7-ind3-chart.component.ts* file and replace its content with the following code:

```
// ch7-ind3-chart.component.ts file:
import { Component, OnInit, Input, OnChanges } from '@angular/core';
import { StockChartHelper } from '../../models/stockChartHelper';

@Component({
  selector: 'app-ch7-ind3-chart',
  templateUrl: './ch7-ind3-chart.component.html',
  styleUrls: ['./ch7-ind3-chart.component.css']
})
export class Ch7Ind3ChartComponent implements OnInit, OnChanges {
  @Input() indicator: any;

  private helper: StockChartHelper = new StockChartHelper();
  private stock: any;
  private legend: any;
  options: any;

  constructor() { }
  ngOnInit() {
    this.stock = this.helper.processCandleData(this.indicator.candles);
    this.options = this.getOptions();
  }

  ngOnChanges() {
    this.stock = this.helper.processCandleData(this.indicator.candles);
    this.options = this.getOptions();
  }

  getOptions() {
    const downColor = '#ec0000';
    const downBorderColor = '#8A0000';
    const upColor = '#00da3c';
    const upBorderColor = '#008F28';

    let candleSeries = {
      name: 'price',
      type: 'candlestick',
      data: this.stock.values,
      itemStyle: {
        color: upColor,
        color0: downColor,
        borderColor: upBorderColor,
```

```
      borderColor0: downBorderColor
    }
};

let VolumeSeries = {
  name: 'volume',
  type: 'bar',
  xAxisIndex: 2,
  yAxisIndex: 2,
  itemStyle: {
    normal: {
      color: '#7fbe9e'
    },
    emphasis: {
      color: '#140'
    }
  },
  data: this.stock.volume
}

let series = [];
series.push(candleSeries);
let indSeries = this.processIndicatorSeries();
for (let i in indSeries) {
  series.push(indSeries[i]);
}
series.push(VolumeSeries);

let leftMargin = 50;
if (this.indicator.name == 'ad' || this.indicator.name == 'obv')
  leftMargin = 100;

return {
  title: {
    text: this.indicator.ticker + ': Stock Price (' + this.indicator.name + ')',
    left: 'center'
  },
  legend: {
    top: '49%',
    right: 30,
    data: this.legend
  },
  tooltip: {
    trigger: 'axis',
    axisPointer: {
      type: 'cross'
    }
  },
  axisPointer: {
    link: { xAxisIndex: 'all' }
  },
  grid: [{
    left: leftMargin,
    right: 20,
    top: '6%',
```

```
    height: '37%'
}, {
    left: leftMargin,
  right: 20,
  height: '25%',
  top: '53%'
  }, {
    left: leftMargin,
    right: 20,
    height: '12%',
    top: '80%'
  }],
xAxis: [{
  type: 'category',
  data: this.stock.categoryData,
  scale: true,
  boundaryGap: false,
  axisLine: { onZero: false },
  splitLine: { show: false },
  splitNumber: 20,
  min: 'dataMin',
  max: 'dataMax'
}, {
    type: 'category',
    gridIndex: 1,
    data: this.stock.categoryData,
    scale: true,
    boundaryGap: false,
    axisLine: { onZero: false },
    splitLine: { show: false },
    splitNumber: 20,
    min: 'dataMin',
    max: 'dataMax'
  },
  {
  type: 'category',
  gridIndex: 2,
  data: this.stock.categoryData,
  scale: true,
  boundaryGap: false,
  splitLine: { show: false },
  axisLabel: { show: false },
  axisTick: { show: false },
  axisLine: { lineStyle: { color: '#777' } },
  splitNumber: 20,
  min: 'dataMin',
  max: 'dataMax'
}
],
yAxis: [{
  scale: true,
  splitArea: {
    show: true
  }
},
```

```
        {
          scale: true,
          gridIndex: 1,
          splitArea: {
            show: true
          }
        },{
          scale: true,
          gridIndex: 2,
          splitNumber: 2,
          axisLabel: { show: false },
          axisLine: { show: false },
          axisTick: { show: false },
          splitLine: { show: false }
        }
        ],
        dataZoom: [
          {
            show: true,
            type: 'slider',
            y: '95%',
            start: 70,
            end: 100,
            xAxisIndex: [0, 1, 2],
          }
        ],
        series: series
      };
    }

private processIndicatorSeries() {
    let indicatorSeries = [];
    switch (this.indicator.name) {
      case 'aroon':
        this.legend = [, { name: 'aroonDown', icon: 'line' },
          { name: 'aroonUp', icon: 'line' }];
        indicatorSeries.push({
          name: 'aroonDown',
          type: 'line',
          xAxisIndex: 1,
          yAxisIndex: 1,
          data: this.indicator.indicator.aroonDown,
          showSymbol: false
        });
        indicatorSeries.push({
          name: 'aroonUp',
          type: 'line',
          xAxisIndex: 1,
          yAxisIndex: 1,
          data: this.indicator.indicator.aroonUp,
          showSymbol: false
        });
        break;
      case 'macd':
        this.legend = [, { name: 'macd', icon: 'line' }, { name: 'signal', icon:
```

```
      'line' }, { name: 'histogram', icon: 'rect' }];
    indicatorSeries.push({
      name: 'macd',
      type: 'line',
      xAxisIndex: 1,
      yAxisIndex: 1,
      data: this.indicator.indicator.macd,
      showSymbol: false
    });
    indicatorSeries.push({
      name: 'signal',
      type: 'line',
      xAxisIndex: 1,
      yAxisIndex: 1,
      data: this.indicator.indicator.signal,
      showSymbol: false
    });
    indicatorSeries.push({
      name: 'histogram',
      type: 'bar',
      xAxisIndex: 1,
      yAxisIndex: 1,
      data: this.indicator.indicator.hist,
      itemStyle: {
        normal: {
          color: '#7fbe9e'
        },
        emphasis: {
          color: '#140'
        }
      }
    });
    break;
  case 'stoch':
    this.legend = [, { name: 'slowK', icon: 'line' },
      { name: 'slowD', icon: 'line' }];
    indicatorSeries.push({
      name: 'slowK',
      type: 'line',
      xAxisIndex: 1,
      yAxisIndex: 1,
      data: this.indicator.indicator.slowK,
      showSymbol: false
    });
    indicatorSeries.push({
      name: 'slowD',
      type: 'line',
      xAxisIndex: 1,
      yAxisIndex: 1,
      data: this.indicator.indicator.slowD,
      showSymbol: false
    });
    break;
  default:
    this.legend = [, { name: this.indicator.name, icon: 'line' }];
```

```
        indicatorSeries.push({
          name: this.indicator.name,
          type: 'line',
          data: this.indicator.indicator,
          xAxisIndex: 1,
          yAxisIndex: 1,
          showSymbol: false
        });
        break;
    }
    return indicatorSeries;
  }
}
```

This component class looks similar to that with two chart areas implemented in the preceding section, except that we show the indicator results in a separate chart area. The *processIndicatorSeries* method is much more complicated than that used in the previous section because there are more indicators that have different outputs.

We also need to update the component's template:

```
// ch7-ind3-chart.component.html file:
<mat-card class="card-stock">
  <div echarts [options]="options" style="height:100%"></div>
</mat-card>
```

This template has a *card-stock* style class defined in its style file:

```
// ch7-ind3-chart.component.css file:
.card-stock {
  margin: 10px;
  width: 800px;
  height: 600px;
}
```

In the following sections, we will study various technical indicators and try to understand how they work. We will also demonstrate how to use the methods implemented here to visualize indicator results.

Overlap Indicators

In this section, we will discuss the concept of overlap indicators and explain how they work and how to use them in your quantitative analysis. Technical indicators are mathematical calculations based on a security's past and current price and volume activity. They provide a different perspective to analyze the price action. Some indicators are derived from simple mathematical formulas and their mechanism is relatively easy to understand; while some other indicators have complex formulas and require more study to understand how they work. Regardless of the complexity of the formula, technical indicators can offer a unique perspective on the strength and direction of the underlying price action.

Many quant analysts and traders use technical indicators to identify trading signals' entry and exit points, evaluate historical performance, and predict future prices. Usually, technical indicators do not directly provide any buy and sell signals; you have to interpret the signals to determine trade entry and exit points.

In this section, I will discuss several overlap indicators and explain how the math and algorithm behind indicators work.

Moving Average Based Indicators

Moving averages are often used in analyzing time series data. They are widely applied in finance, especially in technical analysis. They can be also used as a generic smoothing operation, in which case the data need not be a time series.

We can compute a moving average for any time series. In finance, it is most often applied to stock prices, returns, or trading volumes. We use the moving averages to smooth out short-term fluctuations and highlight long-term trends or cycles. The threshold between short-term and long-term depends on the application, and the parameters of the moving average will be set accordingly.

A moving average smooths data by replacing each data point with the average of the neighboring data points defined within the time span. This process is equivalent to low pass filters used in digital signal processing.

A simple moving average (SMA) is the mean value of the previous n data points. For example, a 5-day simple moving average of closing price is the mean of the previous 5 days' closing prices. If those prices are $p_0, p_{-1}, p_{-2}, p_{-3}, p_{-4}$ then the moving average is described by

$$SMA = \frac{p_0 + p_{-1} + p_{-2} + p_{-3} + p_{-4}}{5}$$

In general, for an n-day moving average, we have

$$SMA = \frac{p_0 + p_{-1} + \cdots}{n} = \frac{1}{n}\sum_{i=0}^{n-1} p_{-i}$$

When calculating successive values, a new value comes into the sum and an old value drops out, meaning a full summation each time is unnecessary

$$SMA_{today} = MSA_{yesterday} - \frac{p_{-n+1}}{n} + \frac{p_1}{n}$$

In technical analysis, there are various popular values for n, like 10 days, 40 days, or 100 days. The period selected depends on the kind of movement you are concentrating on, such as short, intermediate, or long term. In any case, moving average levels are interpreted as support in a rising market, or resistance in a falling market.

In all cases, a moving average lags behind the latest data point, simply from the nature of its smoothing. An SMA can lag to an undesirable extent and can be disproportionately influenced by old data points' dropping out of the average. You can address this issue by giving extra weight to more recent data points, as done in the weighted and exponential moving averages.

A weighted average is any average that has multiplying factors to give different weights to different data points. In technical analysis, a weighted moving average (WMA) specifically means weights that decrease arithmetically. In an n-day WMA the latest day has weight n, the second latest $n-1$, etc., down to zero:

$$WMA = \frac{np_0 + (n-1)p_{n-1} + \cdots 2 + p_{-n+1}}{n + (n-1) + \cdots} = \frac{2}{n(n+1)}\sum_{i=0}^{n-1}(n-i)p_{-i}$$

One drawback of both the simple and weighted moving averages is that they include data for only the number of periods the moving average covers. For example, a five-day simple or weighted moving average only uses five days' worth of data. Data prior to those five days are not included in the calculation of the moving average.

In some situations, however, the prior data is an important reflection of prices and should be included in a moving average calculation. You can achieve this by using an exponential moving average (EMA).

An EMA uses weight factors that decrease exponentially. The weight for each older data point decreases exponentially, giving much more importance to recent observations while not discarding older observations entirely.

The degree of weigh decrease is expressed as a constant smoothing factor α, which is a number between 0 and 1. α may be expressed as a percentage, so a smoothing factor of 10% is equivalent to $\alpha = 0.1$. Alternatively, α may be expressed in terms of n time periods, where $\alpha = 2/(n+1)$. For example, $n = 19$ is equivalent to $\alpha = 0.1$.

The observation at a time period t is designated Y_t, and the value of the EMA at any time period t is designated S_t. S_1 is undefined. S_2 may be initialized in a number of different ways, most commonly by setting S_2 to Y_1, though other techniques exist, such as setting S_2 to an average of the first 4 or 5 observations. The prominence of the S_2 initialization's effect on the resultant moving average depends on α; smaller α value makes the choice of S_2 relatively more important than larger α values, since a higher α discounts older observations faster.

The formula for calculating the EMA at time periods $t \geq 2$ is

$$S_t = \alpha Y_{t-1} + (1-\alpha)S_{t-1}$$

This formula can also be expressed in technical analysis terms as follows, showing how the EMA steps towards the latest data point:

$$EMA_{today} = EMA_{yesterday} + \alpha(p_0 - EMA_{yesterday})$$

Where p_0 is the current price. Expanding out $EMA_{yesterday}$ each time results in the following power series, showing how the weighting factor on each data point p_1, p_2, etc., decrease exponentially:

$$EMA = \frac{p_{-1} + (1-\alpha)p_{-2} + (1-\alpha)^2 p_{-3} + \cdots}{1 + (1-\alpha) + (1-\alpha)^2 + \cdots} = \frac{\sum_{j}^{\infty}(1-\alpha)^j p_{-i-1}}{\sum_{i=0}^{\infty}(1-\alpha)^i} = \alpha \sum_{i=0}^{\infty}(1-\alpha)^j p_{-i-1}$$

Theoretically, this is an infinite sum, but because $1-\alpha$ is less than one, the terms become smaller and smaller, and can be ignored once they are small enough.

In the preceding section, we have implemented an indicator chart component called *ch7-ind2-chart*, which allows you to display overlap indicator results. Run the following command in a command prompt window:

```
ng g c chapter07/ch7-ind-ma --module=app.module
```

This generates a new component named *ch7-ind-ma* in the *ClientApp/src/app/chapter07* folder. Open the component class file and replace its content with the following code:

```
// ch7-ind-ma.component.ts file:
import { Component, OnInit } from '@angular/core';
import { Ch7Service } from '../../models/ch7.service';

@Component({
  selector: 'app-ch7-ind-ma',
```

```
  templateUrl: './ch7-ind-ma.component.html',
  styleUrls: ['./ch7-ind-ma.component.css']
})
export class Ch7IndMaComponent implements OnInit {
  ticker = 'IBM';
  start: string = '2018-01-01';
  end: string = '2018-12-31';
  period: number = 10;
  maType: string = 'sma';

  constructor(private reporsitory: Ch7Service) { }

  ngOnInit() {
    this.getIndicator(this.ticker, this.start, this.end, this.period, this.maType);
  }

  get indicator(): any {
    return this.reporsitory.ma;
  }

  getIndicator(ticker: string, start: string, end: string, period: number,
    maType: string) {
    this.reporsitory.getMa(ticker, start, end, period, maType);
  }
}
```

This component should be familiar to you – it simply retrieves the MA indicator results from web service through the repository service. The retrieved *indicator* property will be the input for the *ch7-ind2-chart* component.

Open the *ch7-ind-ma* component's template and replace its content with the following code:

```
//ch7-ind-ma.component.html file:
<h2>
  ch7-ind-ma works!
</h2>

<mat-form-field>
  <input matInput placeholder="ticker" [(ngModel)]="ticker" name="ticker">
</mat-form-field>
<mat-form-field>
  <input matInput placeholder="start" [(ngModel)]="start" name="start">
</mat-form-field>
<mat-form-field>
  <input matInput placeholder="end" [(ngModel)]="end" name="end">
</mat-form-field>
<mat-form-field>
  <input matInput placeholder="period" [(ngModel)]="period" name="period">
</mat-form-field>
<mat-form-field>
  <mat-select [(value)]="maType">
    <mat-option value="sma">sma</mat-option>
    <mat-option value="ema">ema</mat-option>
    <mat-option value="wma">wma</mat-option>
  </mat-select>
</mat-form-field>
```

```
<button mat-raised-button color="primary" (click)="getIndicator(ticker, start, end,
    period, maType)">Get Indicator Chart</button>

<div *ngIf="indicator">
    <app-ch7-ind2-chart [indicator] ="indicator"></app-ch7-ind2-chart>
</div>
```

This template allows you to specify input parameters for retrieving indicator results, which will be the input for the *app-ch7-ind2-chart* directive. Here, you can calculate the MA indicator for any stock traded in the US equity market by specifying a period and choosing a type of moving average from three options: *sma*, *ema*, and *wma*.

Finally, we need to add a path for this new component to the *RouterModule* of the root module (i.e., the *app.module.ts* file):

```
{ path: 'chapter07/ch7-ind-ma, component: Ch7IndMaComponent },
```

Then add the corresponding URL link to the *home* and *nav-menu* components.

Saving the project and navigating to the */chapter07/ch7-ind-ma* page produce the result shown in Fig.7-2.

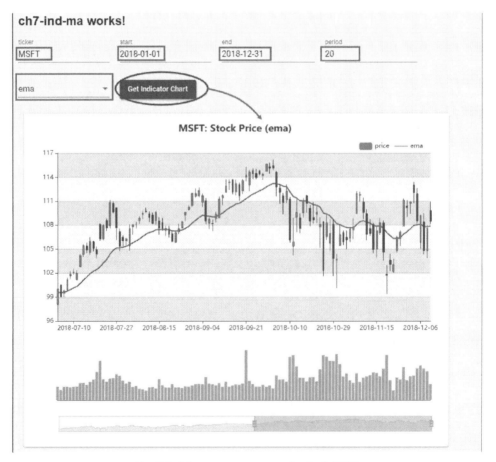

Fig.7-2. Moving average results for MSFT.

Here, you can also zoom in to see the details or get an overview of the entire data range using the *dataZoom* component located at the bottom of the chart.

You can use the moving average indicator to generate the trading signals. Crossovers are one of the moving average based trading strategies. The first type is a price crossover, indicating a potential change in trend when the price above or below a moving average. Another type is to apply two moving averages to a chart, one with a longer period and the other with a shorter period. When the shorter MA crosses above the longer term MA, it shows a buy signal as it indicates the trend is shifting up. When the shorter MA crosses below the longer MA, it is a shell signal as it indicates that the trend is shifting down.

Bollinger Band Indicator

Moving average indicators are a popular trading tool. However, they are prone to providing false signals in choppy markets. The stock's volatility will also affect the parameters. Bollinger band indicator has a built-in mechanism that automatically adjusted to the stock's volatility. Bollinger bands use the standard deviation to set bandwidth. Usually, stocks with a high volatility will require wider bands to encompass most price action. Stocks with a low volatility can use narrower bands. A Bollinger band indicator with two standard deviations will encompass 95% of the price action. Then a stock's price going outside the Bollinger bands should not last and should revert back to the moving average. You can create the trading signals using the Bollinger band indicator. A buy signal will be generated when the stock price falls below the lower Bollinger band, while a sell signal will be created when the price goes outside the upper Bollinger band.

In order to create a chart for display Bollinger band results, run the following command in a command prompt window:

```
ng g c chapter07/ch7-ind-bbands --module=app.module
```

This generates a new component named *ch7-ind-bbands* in the *ClientApp/src/app/chapter07* folder. Open the component class file and replace its content with the following code:

```
// ch7-ind-bbands.component.ts file:
import { Component, OnInit } from '@angular/core';
import { Ch7Service } from '../../models/ch7.service';

@Component({
  selector: 'app-ch7-ind-bbands',
  templateUrl: './ch7-ind-bbands.component.html',
  styleUrls: ['./ch7-ind-bbands.component.css']
})
export class Ch7IndBbandsComponent implements OnInit {
  ticker = 'IBM';
  start: string = '2018-01-01';
  end: string = '2018-12-31';
  period: number = 10;
  maType: string = 'sma';
  devUp: number = 2;
  devDown: number = 2;

  constructor(private reporsitory: Ch7Service) { }

  ngOnInit() {
    this.getIndicator(this.ticker, this.start, this.end, this.period, this.maType,
      this.devUp, this.devDown);
```

```
  }

  get indicator(): any {
    return this.reporsitory.bbands;
  }

  getIndicator(ticker: string, start: string, end: string, period: number, maType,
    devUp: number, devDown: number) {
    this.reporsitory.getBbands(ticker, start, end, period, maType, devUp, devDown);
  }
}
```

This component class simply retrieves the Bollinger band indictor results from the ASP.NET API via a repository service.

We also need to update its template with the following code:

```
// ch7-ind-bbands.component.html file:
<h2>
  ch7-ind-bbands works!
</h2>

<mat-form-field>
  <input matInput placeholder="ticker" [(ngModel)]="ticker" name="ticker">
</mat-form-field>
<mat-form-field>
  <input matInput placeholder="start" [(ngModel)]="start" name="start">
</mat-form-field>
<mat-form-field>
  <input matInput placeholder="end" [(ngModel)]="end" name="end">
</mat-form-field>
<mat-form-field>
  <input matInput placeholder="period" [(ngModel)]="period" name="period">
</mat-form-field>
<mat-form-field>
  <mat-select placeholder="Select an MA type" [(value)]="maType">
    <mat-option value="sma">sma</mat-option>
    <mat-option value="ema">ema</mat-option>
    <mat-option value="wma">wma</mat-option>
  </mat-select>
</mat-form-field>
<mat-form-field>
  <input matInput placeholder="devUp" [(ngModel)]="devUp" name="devUp">
</mat-form-field>
<mat-form-field>
  <input matInput placeholder="devDown" [(ngModel)]="devDown" name="devDown">
</mat-form-field>

<button mat-raised-button color="primary" (click)="getIndicator(ticker, start, end,
  period, maType, devUp, devDown)">Get Indicator Chart</button>

<div *ngIf="indicator">
  <app-ch7-ind2-chart [indicator]="indicator"></app-ch7-ind2-chart>
</div>
```

Here, we can specify various input parameters required for computing the Bollinger band indicator, including a stock ticker, data range, period, and MA type used in moving average calculation, as well as the standard deviation. We then set the resulted *indicator* as the input for the *ch7-ind2-chart* component.

Finally, we need to add a path for this new component to the *RouterModule* of the root module (i.e., the *app.module.ts* file):

```
{ path: 'chapter07/ch7-ind-bbands, component: Ch7IndBbandsComponent },
```

Then add the corresponding URL link to the *home* and *nav-menu* components.

Saving the project and navigating to the */chapter07/ch7-ind-bbands* page produce the result shown in Fig.7-3.

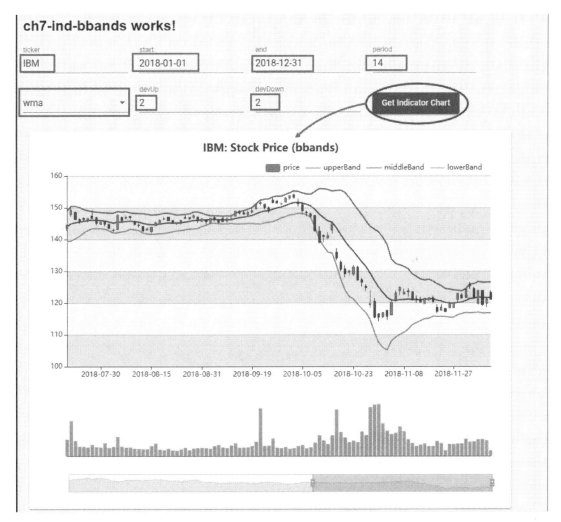

Fig.7-3. Bollinger band indicator for IBM.

SAR Indicator

The parabolic SAR indicator is another overlap technical indicator, which is a price-and-time-based trading system (also called parabolic time/price system). SAR stands for "stop and reverse". This is the actual indicator used as a trading system. SAR trails price as the trend extends over time. The indicator is below prices when prices are rising and above prices when prices are falling. In this regard, the indicator stops and reverses when the price trend reverses and breaks above or below the indicator.

A parabola SAR below the price is generally bullish, while a parabola above the price is generally bearish. A parabola below the price may be used as support, whereas a parabola above the price may represent resistance. These parabolas may be used as price areas for stop losses or profit targets.

The parabolic SAR is calculated almost independently for each trend in the price. When the price is in an uptrend, the SAR emerges below the price and converges upwards towards it. Similarly, on a downtrend, the SAR emerges above the price and converges downwards. At each step within a trend, the SAR is calculated one period in advance. That is, tomorrow's SAR value is built using data available today. The general formula used for this is:

$$SAR_{i+1} = SAR_i + \alpha(EP - SAR_i)$$

Where SAR_i and SAR_{i+1} represent the current period and the next period's SAR values, respectively. EP (the extreme point) is a record kept during each trend that represents the highest value reached by the price during the current uptrend or lowest value during a downtrend. During each period, if a new maximum (or minimum) is observed, the EP is updated with that value.

The α value represents the acceleration factor. Usually, this is set initially to a value of 0.02, but can be chosen by the trader. This factor is increased by 0.02 each time a new EP is recorded, which means that every time a new EP is observed, it will make the acceleration factor go up. The rate will then quicken to a point where the SAR converges towards the price. To prevent it from getting too large, a maximum value for the acceleration factor is normally set to 0.2. The traders can set these numbers depending on their trading style and the instruments being traded. Generally, it is preferable in stocks trading to set the acceleration factor to 0.01, so that it is not too sensitive to local decreases. For commodity or currency trading, the preferred value is 0.02.

The SAR is calculated in this manner for each new period. However, two special cases will modify the SAR value:

- If the next period's SAR value is inside (or beyond) the current period or the previous period's price range, the SAR must be set to the closest price bound. For example, if in an upward trend, the new SAR value is calculated and if it results to be more than today's or yesterday's lowest price, it must be set equal to that lower boundary.

- If the next period's SAR value is inside (or beyond) the next period's price range, a new trend direction is then signaled. The SAR must then switch sides.

Upon a trend switch, the first SAR value for this new trend is set to the last EP recorded on the prior trend, EP is then reset accordingly to this period's maximum, and the acceleration factor is reset to its initial value of 0.01 or 0.02.

Run the following command in a command prompt window:

```
ng g c chapter07/ch7-ind-sar --module=app.module
```

This generates a new component named *ch7-ind-sar* in the *ClientApp/src/app/chapter07* folder. Open the component class file and replace its content with the following code:

```
// ch7-ind-sar.component.ts file:
import { Component, OnInit } from '@angular/core';
import { Ch7Service } from '../../models/ch7.service';

@Component({
  selector: 'app-ch7-ind-sar',
  templateUrl: './ch7-ind-sar.component.html',
  styleUrls: ['./ch7-ind-sar.component.css']
})
export class Ch7IndSarComponent implements OnInit {
  ticker = 'IBM';
  start: string = '2018-01-01';
  end: string = '2018-12-31';
  acceleration: number = 0.01;
  maximum: number = 0.2;

  constructor(private reporsitory: Ch7Service) { }

  ngOnInit() {
    this.getIndicator(this.ticker, this.start, this.end, this.acceleration,
      this.maximum);
  }

  get indicator(): any {
    return this.reporsitory.sar;
  }

  getIndicator(ticker: string, start: string, end: string, acceleration: number,
    maximum: number) {
    this.reporsitory.getSar(ticker, start, end, acceleration, maximum);
  }
}
```

This component simply retrieves the SAR indicator results from web service. We also need to update this component's template with the following code:

```
// ch7-ind-sar.component.html file:
<h2>
  ch7-ind-sar works!
</h2>

<mat-form-field>
  <input matInput placeholder="ticker" [(ngModel)]="ticker" name="ticker">
</mat-form-field>
<mat-form-field>
  <input matInput placeholder="start" [(ngModel)]="start" name="start">
</mat-form-field>
<mat-form-field>
  <input matInput placeholder="end" [(ngModel)]="end" name="end">
</mat-form-field>
<mat-form-field>
  <input matInput placeholder="acceleration" [(ngModel)]="acceleration"
name="acceleration">
</mat-form-field>
<mat-form-field>
  <input matInput placeholder="maximum" [(ngModel)]="maximum" name="maximum">
```

```
</mat-form-field>

<button mat-raised-button color="primary" (click)="getIndicator(ticker, start, end,
acceleration, maximum)">Get Indicator Chart</button>

<div *ngIf="indicator">
  <app-ch7-ind2-chart [indicator]="indicator"></app-ch7-ind2-chart>
</div>
```

This template allows you to specify a stock ticker, date range, acceleration, and maximum EP value as input parameters, which are required in calculating the SAR indicator. The resulted SAR indicator is then as input for the *ch7-ind2-chart* component.

Finally, we need to add a path for this new component to the *RouterModule* of the root module (i.e., the *app.module.ts* file):

```
{ path: 'chapter07/ch7-ind-sar, component: Ch7IndSarComponent },
```

Then add the corresponding URL link to the *home* and *nav-menu* components.

Saving the project and navigating to the */chapter07/ch7-ind-sar* page produce the result shown in Fig.7-4.

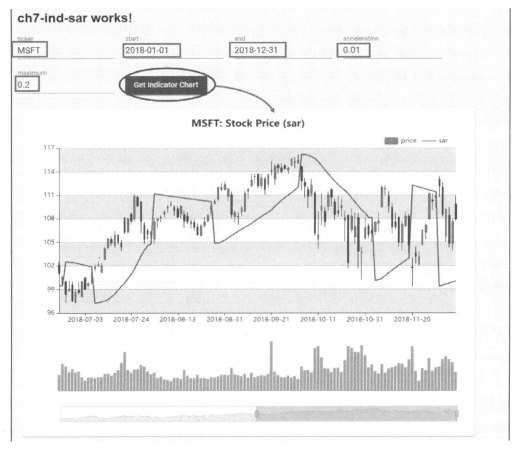

Fig.7-4. SAR Indicator for MSFT.

Note that the SAR indicator tends to produce good results in a treading environment, but it produces many false signals and losing trades when the price starts moving sideways. To help filter out some of the poor trade signals, only trade in the direction of the dominant trend.

Momentum Indicators

Many leading indicators come in the form of momentum oscillators. Generally, momentum measures the rate-of-change of a security's price. As the price of a security rises, price momentum increases. The faster the security rises, the larger the increase in momentum. Once this rise begins to slow, momentum will also slow. As a security begins to trade flat, momentum starts to actually decline from previous high levels. However, declining momentum in the face of sideways trading is not always a bearish signal. It simply means that momentum is returning to a median level.

Since momentum indicators are oscillators, their values have a very different data range from the stock prices, and are hard to be overlaid with the stock prices on the same chart area. In this case, we need to show the indicators in a separated area, so that we need to use the *ch7-ind3-chart* component to display momentum indicators. In this section, we will consider some of the commonly used momentum indicators in an alphabetical order.

ADX Indicator

The average directional index (ADX) indicator is designed to quantify trend strength by measuring the amount of price movement in a single direction. It is part of the directional movement system published by J. Welles Wilder, and is the average resulting from the directional movement indicators.

ADX is a combination of two other indicators developed by Wilder, the positive directional indicator $+DI$ and negative directional indicator $-DI$. ADX combines them and smooths the result with a smoothed moving average.

To calculate $+DI$ and $-DI$, we need price data consisting of high, low, and closing prices. We first need to calculate the directional movement ($+DM$ and $-DM$): Directional movement is defined as the largest part of the current period's price range that lies outside the previous period's price range:

$$+DM = High - \text{Previous } High$$
$$-DM = \text{Previous } Low - Low$$

The smaller of these two values is reset to zero, i.e., if $+DM > -DM$, then $-DM = 0$. On the inside bar (a lower high and higher low), both $+DM$ and $-DM$ are negative values, so both get reset to zero as there was no directional movement for that period.

The true range (TR) can be calculated for each period using the following formula:

$$TR = Max[(high - low), (high - \text{Previous } Close), (\text{Previous } Close - Low)]$$

The $+DM, -DM$, and TR are each accumulated and smoothed using a custom smoothing method. After selecting the number of periods (usually 14), $+DM$ and $-DM$ are given by

$$+DI = 100 \times \text{the smoothed moving average of } (+DM)/TR$$
$$-DI = 100 \times \text{the smoothed moving average of } (-DM)/TR$$

Finally, ADX can be calculated using the following formula:

$$ADX = 100 \times \text{the smoothed moving average of } |[(+DI) - (-DI)]/[(+DI) + (-DI)]|$$

Variations of this calculation typically involve using different types of moving averages, such as SMA, EMA, or WMA.

Note that ADX does not indicate trend direction or momentum, but only trend strength. It is a lagging indicator, that is, a trend must have established before ADX will generate a signal that a trend is under way. ADX will range between 0 and 100. Generally, ADX readings below 20 indicate trend weakness, and readings above 40 indicate trend strength. An extremely strong trend is indicated by readings above 50.

Run the following command in a command prompt window:

```
ng g c chapter07/ch7-ind-adx --module=app.module
```

This generates a new component named *ch7-ind-adx* in the *ClientApp/src/app/chapter07* folder. Open the component class file and replace its content with the following code:

```
// ch7-ind-adx.component.ts file:
import { Component, OnInit } from '@angular/core';
import { Ch7Service } from '../../models/ch7.service';

@Component({
  selector: 'app-ch7-ind-adx',
  templateUrl: './ch7-ind-adx.component.html',
  styleUrls: ['./ch7-ind-adx.component.css']
})
export class Ch7IndAdxComponent implements OnInit {
  ticker = 'IBM';
  start: string = '2018-01-01';
  end: string = '2018-12-31';
  period: number = 14;

  constructor(private reporsitory: Ch7Service) { }

  ngOnInit() {
    this.getIndicator(this.ticker, this.start, this.end, this.period);
  }

  get indicator(): any {
    return this.reporsitory.adx;
  }

  getIndicator(ticker: string, start: string, end: string, period: number) {
    this.reporsitory.getAdx(ticker, start, end, period);
  }
}
```

This component simply retrieves the ADX indicator results from web service. We also need to update this component's template with the following code:

```
// ch7-ind-adx.component.html file:
<h2>
  ch7-ind-adx works!
</h2>

<mat-form-field>
  <input matInput placeholder="ticker" [(ngModel)]="ticker" name="ticker">
</mat-form-field>
```

```
<mat-form-field>
  <input matInput placeholder="start" [(ngModel)]="start" name="start">
</mat-form-field>
<mat-form-field>
  <input matInput placeholder="end" [(ngModel)]="end" name="end">
</mat-form-field>
<mat-form-field>
  <input matInput placeholder="period" [(ngModel)]="period" name="period">
</mat-form-field>
<button mat-raised-button color="primary" (click)="getIndicator(ticker, start, end,
  period)">Get Indicator Chart</button>

<div *ngIf="indicator">
  <app-ch7-ind3-chart [indicator]="indicator"></app-ch7-ind3-chart>
</div>
```

This template allows you to specify a stock ticker, date range, and period as input parameters, which are required in calculating the ADX indicator. The resulted ADX indicator is then as input for the *ch7-ind3-chart* component.

Finally, we need to add a path for this new component to the *RouterModule* of the root module (i.e., the *app.module.ts* file):

```
{ path: 'chapter07/ch7-ind-adx, component: Ch7IndAdxComponent },
```

Then add the corresponding URL link to the *home* and *nav-menu* components. Saving the project and navigating to the */chapter07/ch7-ind-adx* page generate the result shown in Fig.7-5.

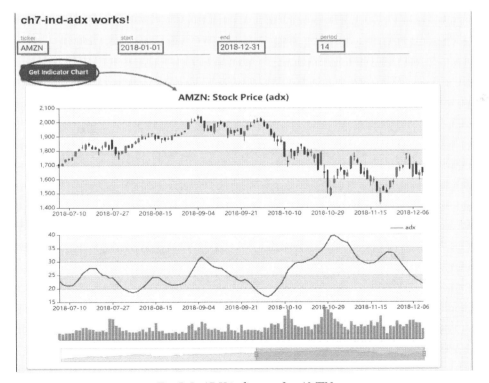

Fig.7-5. ADX indicator for AMZN.

APO Indicator

An absolute price oscillator (APO) is another momentum indicator, which displays the difference between two moving averages with different periods. It can be calculated using the following formula:

$$APO = Fast\ Moving\ Average - Slow\ Moving\ Avreage$$

In the above formula, you can use different types of MAs, such as SMA, EMA, or WMA.

Run the following command in a command prompt window:

```
ng g c chapter07/ch7-ind-apo --module=app.module
```

This generates a new component named *ch7-ind-apo* in the *ClientApp/src/app/chapter07* folder. Open the component class file and replace its content with the following code:

```
// ch7-ind-apo.component.ts file:
import { Component, OnInit } from '@angular/core';
import { Ch7Service } from '../../models/ch7.service';

@Component({
  selector: 'app-ch7-ind-apo',
  templateUrl: './ch7-ind-apo.component.html',
  styleUrls: ['./ch7-ind-apo.component.css']
})
export class Ch7IndApoComponent implements OnInit {
  ticker = 'IBM';
  start: string = '2018-01-01';
  end: string = '2018-12-31';
  fastPeriod: number = 10;
  slowPeriod: number = 20;
  maType: string = 'sma';

  constructor(private reporsitory: Ch7Service) { }

  ngOnInit() {
    this.getIndicator(this.ticker, this.start, this.end, this.fastPeriod,
this.slowPeriod, this.maType);
  }

  get indicator(): any {
    return this.reporsitory.apo;
  }

  getIndicator(ticker: string, start: string, end: string, fastPeriod: number,
    lowPeriod: number, maType: string) {
    this.reporsitory.getApo(ticker, start, end, fastPeriod, slowPeriod, maType);
  }
}
```

This component simply retrieves the APO indicator results from web service. We also need to update this component's template:

```
// ch7-ind-apo.component.html file:
<h2>
  ch7-ind-apo works!
</h2>
```

```
<mat-form-field>
  <input matInput placeholder="ticker" [(ngModel)]="ticker" name="ticker">
</mat-form-field>
<mat-form-field>
  <input matInput placeholder="start" [(ngModel)]="start" name="start">
</mat-form-field>
<mat-form-field>
  <input matInput placeholder="end" [(ngModel)]="end" name="end">
</mat-form-field>
<mat-form-field>
  <input matInput placeholder="fastPeriod" [(ngModel)]="fastPeriod"
name="fastPeriod">
</mat-form-field>
<mat-form-field>
  <input matInput placeholder="slowPeriod" [(ngModel)]="slowPeriod"
name="slowPeriod">
</mat-form-field>
<mat-form-field>
  <mat-select placeholder="Select an MA type" [(value)]="maType">
    <mat-option value="sma">sma</mat-option>
    <mat-option value="ema">ema</mat-option>
    <mat-option value="wma">wma</mat-option>
  </mat-select>
</mat-form-field>
<button mat-raised-button color="primary" (click)="getIndicator(ticker, start, end,
  fastPeriod, slowPeriod, maType)">Get Indicator Chart</button>

<div *ngIf="indicator">
  <app-ch7-ind3-chart [indicator]="indicator"></app-ch7-ind3-chart>
</div>
```

This template allows you to specify a stock ticker, date range, and periods for fast and slow moving averages as input parameters, which are required in calculating the APO indicator. The resulted APO indicator is then as input for the *ch7-ind3-chart* component.

Finally, we need to add a path for this new component to the *RouterModule* of the root module (i.e., the *app.module.ts* file):

```
{ path: 'chapter07/ch7-ind-apo, component: Ch7IndApoComponent },
```

Then add the corresponding URL link to the *home* and *nav-menu* components. Saving the project and navigating to the */chapter07/ch7-ind-apo* page generate the result shown in Fig.7-6.

APO indicator crossing above zero is considered bullish, while crossing below the zero line is bearish. A positive indicator value means an upward movement, while negative readings signal a downward trend.

Divergences will be identified when a new high or low in price is not confirmed by the APO indicator. A bullish divergence forms when price makes a lower low, but the APO forms a higher low. This indicates less downward momentum that could foreshadow a bullish reversal. A bearish divergence forms when price makes a higher high, but the APO forms a lower high. This shows less upward momentum that could foreshadow a bearish reversal.

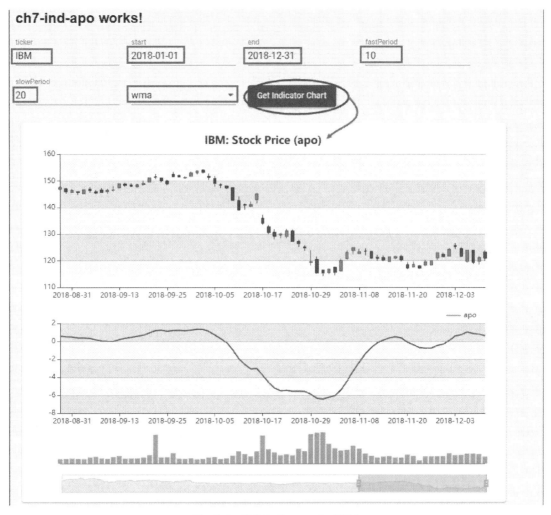

Fig.7-6. APO indicator for IBM.

Aroon Indicator

Aroon indicator is used to identify when trends are likely to change direction. It measures the time that it takes for the price to reach the highest and lowest points over a given timeframe as a percentage of total time. Aroon consists of an "Aroon up" line, which measures the strength of the uptrend, and an "Aroon down" line, which measures the strength of the downtrend.

The two component lines of the Aroon indicator can be calculated as follows:

$$AroonUp = 100 \times \frac{n - \text{number of bars since } n \text{ bar } high}{n}$$

$$aroondown = 100 \times \frac{n - \text{number of bars since } n \text{ bar } low}{n}$$

Where *n* is the number of periods used for the indicator. By default, many traders use the Aroon indicator with $n = 25$.

Run the following command in a command prompt window:

```
ng g c chapter07/ch7-ind-aroon --module=app.module
```

This generates a new component named *ch7-ind-aroon* in the *ClientApp/src/app/chapter07* folder. Open the component class file and replace its content with the following code:

```
// ch7-ind-aroon.component.ts file:
import { Component, OnInit } from '@angular/core';
import { Ch7Service } from '../../models/ch7.service';

@Component({
  selector: 'app-ch7-ind-aroon',
  templateUrl: './ch7-ind-aroon.component.html',
  styleUrls: ['./ch7-ind-aroon.component.css']
})
export class Ch7IndAroonComponent implements OnInit {
  ticker = 'IBM';
  start: string = '2018-01-01';
  end: string = '2018-12-31';
  period: number = 25;

  constructor(private reporsitory: Ch7Service) { }

  ngOnInit() {
    this.getIndicator(this.ticker, this.start, this.end, this.period);
  }

  get indicator(): any {
    return this.reporsitory.aroon;
  }

  getIndicator(ticker: string, start: string, end: string, period: number) {
    this.reporsitory.getAroon(ticker, start, end, period);
  }
}
```

This component simply retrieves the Aroon indicator results from web service. We also need to update this component's template with the following code:

```
// ch7-ind-aroon.component.html file:
<h2>
  ch7-ind-aroon works!
</h2>

<mat-form-field>
  <input matInput placeholder="ticker" [(ngModel)]="ticker" name="ticker">
</mat-form-field>
<mat-form-field>
  <input matInput placeholder="start" [(ngModel)]="start" name="start">
</mat-form-field>
<mat-form-field>
  <input matInput placeholder="end" [(ngModel)]="end" name="end">
</mat-form-field>
```

```
<mat-form-field>
  <input matInput placeholder="period" [(ngModel)]="period" name="period">
</mat-form-field>
<button mat-raised-button color="primary" (click)="getIndicator(ticker, start, end,
  period)">Get Indicator Chart</button>

<div *ngIf="indicator">
  <app-ch7-ind3-chart [indicator]="indicator"></app-ch7-ind3-chart>
</div>
```

This template allows you to specify a stock ticker, date range, and period as input parameters, which are required in calculating the Aroon indicator. The resulted indicator is then as input for the *ch7-ind3-chart* component.

Finally, we need to add a path for this new component to the *RouterModule* of the root module (i.e., the *app.module.ts* file):

```
{ path: 'chapter07/ch7-ind-aroon, component: Ch7IndAroonComponent },
```

Then add the corresponding URL link to the *home* and *nav-menu* components. Saving the project and navigating to the */chapter07/ch7-ind-aroon* page generate the result shown in Fig.7-7.

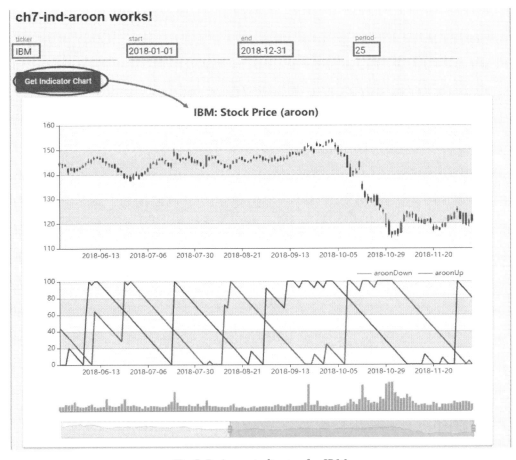

Fig.7-7. Aroon indicator for IBM.

You can see from Fig.7-7 that the Aroon indicator oscillates between a maximum value of 100 and a minimum value of zero. Basically, you can analyze the relationship between Aroon up and Aroon down lines to interpret the price action of a stock in three different ways:

- When the momentum in the market changes from a bullish one to a bearish one, and vice versa, the Aroon up or Aroon down will cross each other and change sides.

- When the market is trending with strong momentum, the Aroon indicator will display extreme readings.

- Lastly, when the market is consolidating, the Aroon up and Aroon down lines will stay parallel to each other.

You can use the crossover of the Aroon up and Aroon down lines to determine the directional movement of price. When the Aroon up crosses above the Aroon down, it generates a signal that the price is about to start a potential bullish move. By contrast, when the Aroon down crosses below the Aroon up line, it indicates a potential bearish move.

However, you should not place a buy or sell order whenever there is a new crossover, because this is an indication that the existing trend has changed. Instead, you should wait for the price of the security to breakout of a range or trend line before opening a new position in the direction that the Aroon suggested.

BOP Indicator

A balance of power (BOP) indicator measures the market strength of buyers against sellers by assessing the ability of each side to drive prices to an extreme level. BOP oscillates around zero line with positive values indicating the dominance of the bulls and negative values pointing to the dominance of the bears. It can be calculated as follows

$$BOP = \frac{\text{Close price} - \text{open price}}{\text{high price} - \text{low price}}$$

The resulted BOP value can be smoothed by a moving average.

Run the following command in a command prompt window:

```
ng g c chapter07/ch7-ind-bop --module=app.module
```

This generates a new component named *ch7-ind-bop* in the *ClientApp/src/app/chapter07* folder. Open the component class file and replace its content with the following code:

```
//ch7-ind-bop.component.ts file:
import { Component, OnInit } from '@angular/core';
import { Ch7Service } from '../../models/ch7.service';

@Component({
  selector: 'app-ch7-ind-bop',
  templateUrl: './ch7-ind-bop.component.html',
  styleUrls: ['./ch7-ind-bop.component.css']
})
export class Ch7IndBopComponent implements OnInit {
  ticker = 'IBM';
  start: string = '2018-01-01';
  end: string = '2018-12-31';

  constructor(private reporsitory: Ch7Service) { }
```

```
ngOnInit() {
  this.getIndicator(this.ticker, this.start, this.end);
}

get indicator(): any {
  return this.reporsitory.bop;
}

getIndicator(ticker: string, start: string, end: string) {
  this.reporsitory.getBop(ticker, start, end);
}
}
```

This component simply retrieves the BOP indicator results from web service. We also need to update this component's template:

```
// ch7-ind-bop.component.html file:
<h2>
  ch7-ind-bop works!
</h2>

<mat-form-field>
  <input matInput placeholder="ticker" [(ngModel)]="ticker" name="ticker">
</mat-form-field>
<mat-form-field>
  <input matInput placeholder="start" [(ngModel)]="start" name="start">
</mat-form-field>
<mat-form-field>
  <input matInput placeholder="end" [(ngModel)]="end" name="end">
</mat-form-field>
<button mat-raised-button color="primary" (click)="getIndicator(ticker, start,
end)">Get Indicator Chart</button>

<div *ngIf="indicator">
  <app-ch7-ind3-chart [indicator]="indicator"></app-ch7-ind3-chart>
</div>
```

This template allows you to specify a stock ticker and date range as input parameters, which are required in calculating the BOP indicator. The resulted indicator is then as input for the *ch7-ind3-chart* component.

Finally, we need to add a path for this new component to the *RouterModule* of the root module (i.e., the *app.module.ts* file):

```
{ path: 'chapter07/ch7-ind-bop, component: Ch7IndBopComponent },
```

Then add the corresponding URL link to the *home* and *nav-menu* components. Saving the project and navigating to the */chapter07/ch7-ind-bop* page generate the result shown in Fig.7-8.

The BOP indicator tells us whether the underlying action in the trading of a stock is characterized by systematic buying (accumulation) or systematic selling (distribution). A key feature of BOP is the ability to contradict price movement. It goes far beyond the divergences that many indicators are capable of. In divergence analysis, the price and the indicator tend to move together. A divergence is detected when the price makes a new high and the indicator fails to confirm.

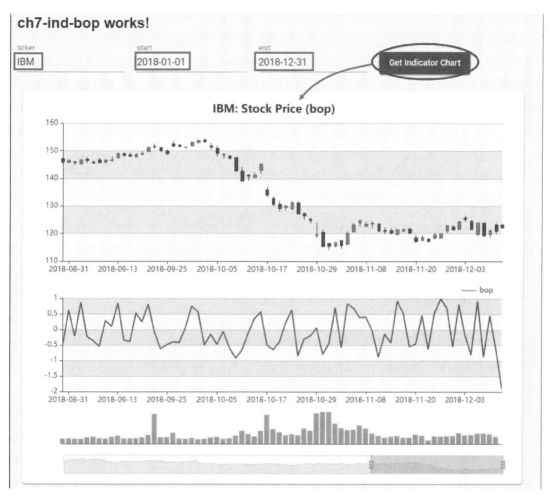

Fig.7-8. BOP indicator for IBM.

BOP is capable of outright contradiction. Thus, while the price is attaining new highs, BOP may very well be attaining new lows. It is possible for BOP to move in the exact opposite direction of price.

Note that although BOP is plotted above and below zero lines, it is not an oscillator. It does not swing up and down with the price. It goes its own way, often independent of price movement. When BOP is above the zero line, it is depicting systematic buying. When it is below the zero line, it is revealing systematic selling.

CCI Indicator

Commodity Channel Index (CCI) indicator is a versatile indicator that can be used to identify a new trend or warn of extreme conditions. In general, CCI measures the current price level relative to an average price level over a given period of time. CCI is relatively high when prices are far above their average and it is relatively low when prices are far below their average. In this manner, CCI can be used to identify overbought and oversold levels. This indicator uses a typical period of 20.

CCI is usually scaled by an inverse factor of 0.015 to provide more readable numbers:

$$CCI = \frac{1}{0.015} \frac{p_t - SMA(p_t)}{MD(p_t)}$$

Where p_t is the typical price:

$$p_t = \frac{High + Low + Close}{3}$$

and *SMA* is the simple moving average; *MD* is the mean absolute deviation.

For scaling purposes, the constant at 0.015 to ensure that approximately 70 to 80 percent of CCI values would fall between −100 and +100. The CCI fluctuates above and below zero. The percentage of CCI values that fall between +100 and −100 will depend on the number of periods used. A shorter CCI will be more volatile with a smaller percentage of values between +100 and −100. Conversely, the more periods used to calculate the CCI, the higher the percentage of values between +100 and −100.

Run the following command in a command prompt window:

ng g c chapter07/ch7-ind-cci --module=app.module

This generates a new component named *ch7-ind-cci* in the *ClientApp/src/app/chapter07* folder. Open the component class file and replace its content with the following code:

```
// ch7-ind-cci.component.ts file:
import { Component, OnInit } from '@angular/core';
import { Ch7Service } from '../../models/ch7.service';

@Component({
  selector: 'app-ch7-ind-cci',
  templateUrl: './ch7-ind-cci.component.html',
  styleUrls: ['./ch7-ind-cci.component.css']
})
export class Ch7IndCciComponent implements OnInit {
  ticker = 'IBM';
  start: string = '2018-01-01';
  end: string = '2018-12-31';
  period: number = 20;

  constructor(private reporsitory: Ch7Service) { }

  ngOnInit() {
    this.getIndicator(this.ticker, this.start, this.end, this.period);
  }

  get indicator(): any {
    return this.reporsitory.cci;
  }

  getIndicator(ticker: string, start: string, end: string, period: number) {
    this.reporsitory.getCci(ticker, start, end, period);
  }
}
```

This component simply retrieves the CCI indicator results from web service. We also need to update this component's template with the following code:

```
// ch7-ind-cci.component.html file:
<h2>
  ch7-ind-cci works!
</h2>

<mat-form-field>
  <input matInput placeholder="ticker" [(ngModel)]="ticker" name="ticker">
</mat-form-field>
<mat-form-field>
  <input matInput placeholder="start" [(ngModel)]="start" name="start">
</mat-form-field>
<mat-form-field>
  <input matInput placeholder="end" [(ngModel)]="end" name="end">
</mat-form-field>
<mat-form-field>
  <input matInput placeholder="period" [(ngModel)]="period" name="period">
</mat-form-field>
<button mat-raised-button color="primary" (click)="getIndicator(ticker, start, end,
period)">Get Indicator Chart</button>

<div *ngIf="indicator">
  <app-ch7-ind3-chart [indicator]="indicator"></app-ch7-ind3-chart>
</div>
```

This template allows you to specify a stock ticker, date range, and period as input parameters, which are required in calculating the CCI indicator. The resulted indicator is then as input for the *ch7-ind3-chart* component.

Finally, we need to add a path for this new component to the *RouterModule* of the root module (i.e., the *app.module.ts* file):

```
{ path: 'chapter07/ch7-ind-cci, component: Ch7IndCciComponent },
```

Then add the corresponding URL link to the *home* and *nav-menu* components. Saving the project and navigating to the */chapter07/ch7-ind-cci* page generate the result shown in Fig.7-9.

The CCI strategy is designed to find cyclical trends in the market and to be used as a bearish or bullish filter. CCI is simply an oscillator that moves the majority of the time between + 100 and -100.

A basic CCI trading strategy is used to track CCI for movement above +100, which generates buy signals, and movements below -100, which generates sell or short trade signals. You may only wish to take the buy signals, exit when the sell signals occur, and then reinvest when the buy signal occurs again.

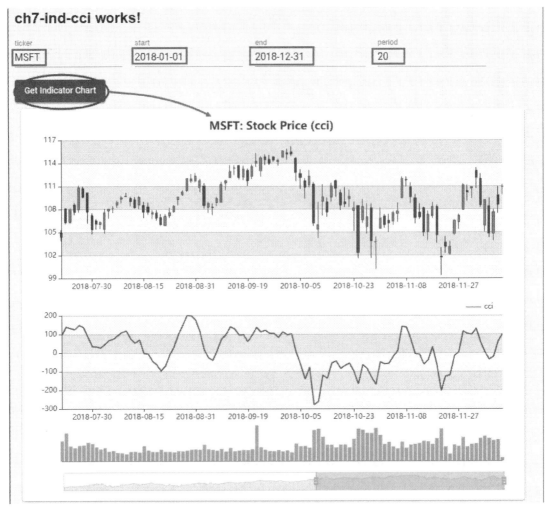

Fig.7-9. CCI indicator for MSFT.

MACD Indicator

The moving average convergence and divergence (MACD) is a popular indicator used in technical analysis. It can identify aspects of a security's overall trend. Most notably these aspects are momentum, as well as trend direction and duration. What makes MACD so informative is that it is actually the combination of two different types of indicators. First, MACD employs two moving averages of different periods to identify trend direction and duration. Then, MACD takes the difference in values between those two moving averages (the MACD line) and an EMA of those moving averages (the Signal line) and plots that difference between the two lines as a histogram, which oscillates above and below a center zero line. The MACD is used as a good indication of a security's momentum.

An approximated MACD can be constructed by subtracting the value of a 26-day exponential moving average (EMA) from a 12 period EMA. The shorter EMA is constantly converging toward, and diverging away from the longer EMA. This causes MACD to oscillate around the zero level. MACD can be calculated as follows:

$$MACD \text{ line} = EMA(12, \text{price}) - EMA(26, \text{price})$$
$$\text{Signal line} = EMA(9, MACD \text{ line})$$
$$MACD \text{ Histogram} = \text{Signal line} - MACD \text{ line}$$

Run the following command in a command prompt window:

```
ng g c chapter07/ch7-ind-macd --module=app.module
```

This generates a new component named *ch7-ind-macd* in the *ClientApp/src/app/chapter07* folder. Open the component class file and replace its content with the following code:

```
// ch7-ind-macd.component.ts file:
import { Component, OnInit } from '@angular/core';
import { Ch7Service } from '../../models/ch7.service';

@Component({
  selector: 'app-ch7-ind-macd',
  templateUrl: './ch7-ind-macd.component.html',
  styleUrls: ['./ch7-ind-macd.component.css']
})
export class Ch7IndMacdComponent implements OnInit {
  ticker = 'IBM';
  start: string = '2018-01-01';
  end: string = '2018-12-31';
  fastPeriod: number = 12;
  slowPeriod: number = 26;
  signalPeriod: number = 9;

  constructor(private reporsitory: Ch7Service) { }

  ngOnInit() {
    this.getIndicator(this.ticker, this.start, this.end, this.fastPeriod,
this.slowPeriod, this.signalPeriod);

  }

  get indicator(): any {
    return this.reporsitory.macd;
  }

  getIndicator(ticker: string, start: string, end: string, fastPeriod: number,
slowPeriod: number, signalPeriod: number) {
    this.reporsitory.getMacd(ticker, start, end, fastPeriod, slowPeriod,
signalPeriod);
  }
}
```

This component simply retrieves the MACD indicator results from web service. We also need to update this component's template:

```
// ch7-ind-macd.component.html file:
<h2>
  ch7-ind-macd works!
</h2>
```

```
<mat-form-field>
  <input matInput placeholder="ticker" [(ngModel)]="ticker" name="ticker">
</mat-form-field>
<mat-form-field>
  <input matInput placeholder="start" [(ngModel)]="start" name="start">
</mat-form-field>
<mat-form-field>
  <input matInput placeholder="end" [(ngModel)]="end" name="end">
</mat-form-field>
<mat-form-field>
  <input matInput placeholder="fastPeriod" [(ngModel)]="fastPeriod"
name="fastPeriod">
</mat-form-field>
<mat-form-field>
  <input matInput placeholder="slowPeriod" [(ngModel)]="slowPeriod"
name="slowPeriod">
</mat-form-field>
<mat-form-field>
  <input matInput placeholder="signalPeriod" [(ngModel)]="signalPeriod"
name="signalPeriod">
</mat-form-field>
<button mat-raised-button color="primary" (click)="getIndicator(ticker, start, end,
fastPeriod, slowPeriod, signalPeriod)">Get Indicator Chart</button>

<div *ngIf="indicator">
  <app-ch7-ind3-chart [indicator]="indicator"></app-ch7-ind3-chart>
</div>
```

This template allows you to specify a stock ticker, date range, and various periods as input parameters, which are required in calculating the MACD indicator. The resulted indicator is then as input for the *ch7-ind3-chart* component.

Finally, we need to add a path for this new component to the *RouterModule* of the root module (i.e., the *app.module.ts* file):

```
{ path: 'chapter07/ch7-ind-macd, component: Ch7IndMacdComponent },
```

Then add the corresponding URL link to the *home* and *nav-menu* components. Saving the project and navigating to the */chapter07/ch7-ind-macd* page generate the result shown in Fig.7-10.

Note from Fig.7-10 that the MACD line is faster than the signal line. Many traders use this line as a proxy for measuring the rate of change of price. The signal line in MACD is slower due to its setting and traders often use it as a trend determination tool.

One of the basic MACD trading strategies is signal line crossovers. This method tends to work well with volatile markets that trend often, such as FX, technology stocks, and volatile ETF's. The signal line is just a 9-day EMA of the MACD line. As a moving average of the indicator, it slowly follows the MACD line. A bullish crossover occurs when the MACD line turns up and crosses above the signal line. While a bearish crossover occurs when the MACD line turns down and crosses below the signal line. Once the crossover occurs, you want to make sure both lines gain as much distance apart from each other as possible. This is a good sign that momentum is continuing in the desired direction. The signal line crossover is the most fundamental way to use the MACD indicator.

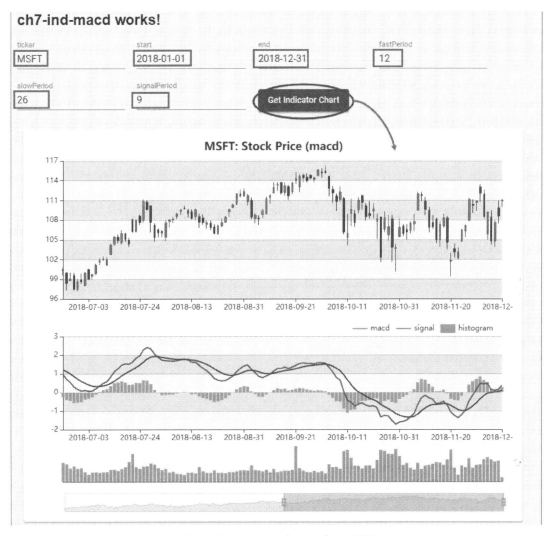

Fig.7-10. MACD indicator for MSFT.

RSI Indicator

The relative strength index (RSI) indicator is one of the classic momentum indicators. RSI measures a market's internal strength by dividing the average of the sum of the up bar closing prices by the average of the sum of the down bar closing prices over a specific period of time. It returns a value within the range of 0 to 100. The RSI is a leading or a coincidental indicator. Popular averaging periods for the RSI are 9, 14 and 25. The indicator becomes more volatile and amplitude widens with fewer periods used.

The indicator is calculated as follows

$$RSI = 100 - \frac{100}{1 + RS}$$

Where *RS* is given by

$$RS = \frac{\text{average of } n \text{ bars' up closes}}{\text{average of } n \text{ bars' down closes}}$$

Where n is the number of bars or period. Note that in calculating the RS values for the total of closes up, we add all price changes where the close is greater than previous close. For closes down, we add all price changes where the close is less than previous close.

Run the following command in a command prompt window:

```
ng g c chapter07/ch7-ind-rsi --module=app.module
```

This generates a new component named *ch7-ind-rsi* in the *ClientApp/src/app/chapter07* folder. Open the component class file and replace its content with the following code:

```
// ch7-ind-rsi.component.ts file:
import { Component, OnInit } from '@angular/core';
import { Ch7Service } from '../../models/ch7.service';

@Component({
  selector: 'app-ch7-ind-rsi',
  templateUrl: './ch7-ind-rsi.component.html',
  styleUrls: ['./ch7-ind-rsi.component.css']
})
export class Ch7IndRsiComponent implements OnInit {
  ticker = 'IBM';
  start: string = '2018-01-01';
  end: string = '2018-12-31';
  period: number = 14;

  constructor(private reporsitory: Ch7Service) { }

  ngOnInit() {
    this.getIndicator(this.ticker, this.start, this.end, this.period);
  }

  get indicator(): any {
    return this.reporsitory.rsi;
  }

  getIndicator(ticker: string, start: string, end: string, period: number) {
    this.reporsitory.getRsi(ticker, start, end, period);
  }
}
```

This component simply retrieves the RSI indicator results from web service. We also need to update this component's template with the following code:

```
// ch7-ind-rsi.component.html file:
<h2>
  ch7-ind-rsi works!
</h2>

<mat-form-field>
  <input matInput placeholder="ticker" [(ngModel)]="ticker" name="ticker">
</mat-form-field>
<mat-form-field>
  <input matInput placeholder="start" [(ngModel)]="start" name="start">
```

```
</mat-form-field>
<mat-form-field>
  <input matInput placeholder="end" [(ngModel)]="end" name="end">
</mat-form-field>
<mat-form-field>
  <input matInput placeholder="period" [(ngModel)]="period" name="period">
</mat-form-field>
<button mat-raised-button color="primary" (click)="getIndicator(ticker, start, end,
period)">Get Indicator Chart</button>

<div *ngIf="indicator">
  <app-ch7-ind3-chart [indicator]="indicator"></app-ch7-ind3-chart>
</div>
```

This template allows you to specify a stock ticker, date range, and period as input parameters, which are required in calculating the RSI indicator. The resulted indicator is then as input for the *ch7-ind3-chart* component.

Finally, we need to add a path for this new component to the *RouterModule* of the root module (i.e., the *app.module.ts* file):

{ path: 'chapter07/ch7-ind-rsi, component: Ch7IndRsiComponent },

Then add the corresponding URL link to the *home* and *nav-menu* components. Saving the project and navigating to the */chapter07/ch7-ind-macd* page generate the result shown in Fig.7-11.

The classic way to interpret RSI is to look for oversold levels below 30 and overbought levels above 70. These normally occur before the underlying price chart forms a top or a bottom. Note that you should change the levels depending on market conditions. Ensure that the level lines cut across the highest peaks and the lowest troughs.

The main problem of the RSI indicator is that the stock may continue to move up despite the indicator hitting the overbought zone, or continue to go down even after the indicator hits the oversold zone. In order to avoid a big loss of using the indicator, Wilder (the inventor of the RSI indicator) developed a new concept called "failure swing" for the RSI. A "bearish failure swing" occurs when the RSI enters the overbought zone (goes above the 70 level) and comes below 70 again. In other words, a short position can be taken only when the RSI cuts the 70 lines from the top. Similarly, a "bullish failure swing" occurs when the RSI enters the oversold zone and comes out. Both the positive and negative failure swings can be clearly seen in the RSI indicator chart.

Stochastic Indicator

The stochastic indicator is a range bound momentum oscillator. It is designed to display the location of the close compared to the high/low range over a user-defined number of periods. Typically, the stochastic oscillator is used for three things: identifying overbought and oversold levels, spotting divergences, and identifying bull and bear set ups or signals.

The stochastic indicator can be calculated as follows:

$$\text{fast }\%K = 100 \times MA\left(\frac{\text{current close} - \text{lowest low}}{\text{highest high} - \text{lowest low}}, \text{fastK period}\right)$$

$$\text{slow }\%K = MA(\text{fast }\%K, \text{slowK period})$$
$$\text{slow }\%D = MA(\text{slow }\%K, \text{slowD period})$$

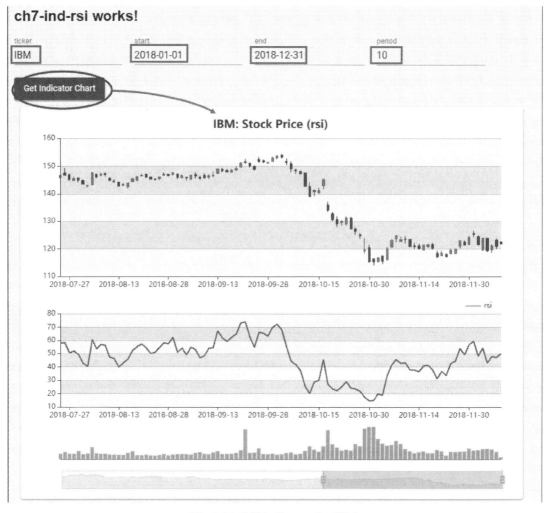

Fig.7-11. RSI indicator for IBM.

Where MA is the moving average, such as SMA, EMA, or WMA. The lowest low (highest high) is the lowest (highest) price within the number of recent bars in the look-back period. The indicator usually shows two lines: slow %*K* and slow %*D*.

Run the following command in a command prompt window:

```
ng g c chapter07/ch7-ind-stoch --module=app.module
```

This generates a new component named *ch7-ind-stoch* in the *ClientApp/src/app/chapter07* folder. Open the component class file and replace its content with the following code:

```
// ch7-ind-stoch.component.ts file:
import { Component, OnInit } from '@angular/core';
import { Ch7Service } from '../../models/ch7.service';

@Component({
  selector: 'app-ch7-ind-stoch',
```

```
  templateUrl: './ch7-ind-stoch.component.html',
  styleUrls: ['./ch7-ind-stoch.component.css']
})
export class Ch7IndStochComponent implements OnInit {
  ticker = 'IBM';
  start: string = '2018-01-01';
  end: string = '2018-12-31';
  fastkPeriod: number = 14;
  slowkPeriod: number = 3;
  slowdPeriod: number = 5;
  maType: string = 'sma';

  constructor(private reporsitory: Ch7Service) { }

  ngOnInit() {
    this.getIndicator(this.ticker, this.start, this.end, this.fastkPeriod,
      this.slowkPeriod, this.slowdPeriod, this.maType);
  }

  get indicator(): any {
    return this.reporsitory.stoch;
  }

  getIndicator(ticker: string, start: string, end: string, fastkPeriod: number,
    slowkPeriod: number, slowdPeriod, maType: string) {
      this.reporsitory.getStoch(ticker, start, end, fastkPeriod, slowkPeriod,
      slowdPeriod, maType);
  }
}
```

This component simply retrieves the stochastic indicator results from web service. We also need to update this component's template:

```html
// ch7-ind-stoch.component.html file:
<h2>
  ch7-ind-stoch works!
</h2>

<mat-form-field>
  <input matInput placeholder="ticker" [(ngModel)]="ticker" name="ticker">
</mat-form-field>
<mat-form-field>
  <input matInput placeholder="start" [(ngModel)]="start" name="start">
</mat-form-field>
<mat-form-field>
  <input matInput placeholder="end" [(ngModel)]="end" name="end">
</mat-form-field>
<mat-form-field>
  <input matInput placeholder="fastkPeriod" [(ngModel)]="fastkPeriod"
name="fastkPeriod">
</mat-form-field>
<mat-form-field>
  <input matInput placeholder="slowkPeriod" [(ngModel)]="slowkPeriod"
name="slowkPeriod">
</mat-form-field>
<mat-form-field>
```

```
    <input matInput placeholder="slowdPeriod" [(ngModel)]="slowdPeriod"
name="slowdPeriod">
</mat-form-field>
<mat-form-field>
    <mat-select placeholder="Select an MA type" [(value)]="maType">
        <mat-option value="sma">sma</mat-option>
        <mat-option value="ema">ema</mat-option>
        <mat-option value="wma">wma</mat-option>
    </mat-select>
</mat-form-field>
<button mat-raised-button color="primary" (click)="getIndicator(ticker, start, end,
    fastkPeriod, slowkPeriod, slowdPeriod, maType)">Get Indicator Chart</button>

<div *ngIf="indicator">
    <app-ch7-ind3-chart [indicator]="indicator"></app-ch7-ind3-chart>
</div>
```

This template allows you to specify a stock ticker, date range, and various periods as input parameters, which are required in calculating the stochastic indicator. The resulted indicator is then as input for the *ch7-ind3-chart* component.

Finally, we need to add a path for this new component to the *RouterModule* of the root module (i.e., the *app.module.ts* file):

```
{ path: 'chapter07/ch7-ind-stoch, component: Ch7IndStochComponent },
```

Then add the corresponding URL link to the *home* and *nav-menu* components. Saving the project and navigating to the */chapter07/ch7-ind-stoch* page generate the result shown in Fig.7-12.

You can see from Fig.7-12 that the stochastics indicator is a range-bound oscillator consisting of two lines that move between 0 and 100. The first line (known as *slowK*) displays the current close in relation to a user-defined period's high/low range. The second line (known as *slowD*) is a moving average of the *slowK* line. Now, as with most indicators, all of the periods used within stochastic can be user defined. The basic understanding is that a stochastic indicator uses closing prices to determine momentum. When prices close in the upper half of the look-back period's high/low range, then the stochastic oscillator (*slowK*) rises, indicating an increase in momentum or buying/selling pressure. When prices close in the lower half of the period's high/low range, *slowK* falls, indicating weakening momentum or buying/selling pressure.

Williams %R Indicator

The Williams %R indicator is a momentum indicator, which is used to measure overbought or oversold levels. This indicator is very similar to the stochastic %K indicator, except that the Williams %R indicator calculates a negative value between 0, −100 and does not smooth the signals. The trading strategy using this indicator is simple: you sell when %R reaches −10% or higher and buy when it reaches −90% or lower. The Williams %R indicator works best in trending markets, either bull or bear trends.

The Williams %R indicator shows the current close price in relation to the high and low of the past *n* days. You need to determine the highest high and lowest low for the past *n* days. This is the trading range for the past *n* days. Once those values are determined, the Williams %R can be calculated using the following formula:

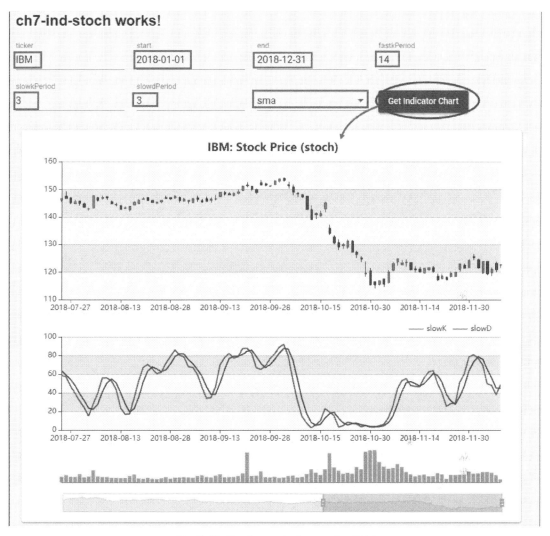

Fig.7-12. Stochastic indicator for IBM.

$$\%R = -100 \times \frac{high_{n-days} - close_{today}}{high_{n-days} - low_{n-days}}$$

You can see that the indicator is on a negative scale. A value of -100 means the close today is the lowest low of the past n days, and zero means today's close is the highest high of the past n days.

Run the following command in a command prompt window:

```
ng g c chapter07/ch7-ind-willr --module=app.module
```

This generates a new component named *ch7-ind-willr* in the *ClientApp/src/app/chapter07* folder. Open the component class file and replace its content with the following code:

```
// ch7-ind-willr.component.ts file:
import { Component, OnInit } from '@angular/core';
```

```
import { Ch7Service } from '../../models/ch7.service';

@Component({
  selector: 'app-ch7-ind-willr',
  templateUrl: './ch7-ind-willr.component.html',
  styleUrls: ['./ch7-ind-willr.component.css']
})
export class Ch7IndWillrComponent implements OnInit {
  ticker = 'IBM';
  start: string = '2018-01-01';
  end: string = '2018-12-31';
  period: number = 14;

  constructor(private reporsitory: Ch7Service) { }

  ngOnInit() {
    this.getIndicator(this.ticker, this.start, this.end, this.period);
  }

  get indicator(): any {
    return this.reporsitory.willR;
  }

  getIndicator(ticker: string, start: string, end: string, period: number) {
    this.reporsitory.getWillR(ticker, start, end, period);
  }
}
```

This component simply retrieves the Williams %R indicator results from web service. We also need to update this component's template:

```
// ch7-ind-willr.component.html file:
<h2>
  ch7-ind-willr works!
</h2>

<mat-form-field>
  <input matInput placeholder="ticker" [(ngModel)]="ticker" name="ticker">
</mat-form-field>
<mat-form-field>
  <input matInput placeholder="start" [(ngModel)]="start" name="start">
</mat-form-field>
<mat-form-field>
  <input matInput placeholder="end" [(ngModel)]="end" name="end">
</mat-form-field>
<mat-form-field>
  <input matInput placeholder="period" [(ngModel)]="period" name="period">
</mat-form-field>
<button mat-raised-button color="primary" (click)="getIndicator(ticker, start, end,
period)">Get Indicator Chart</button>

<div *ngIf="indicator">
  <app-ch7-ind3-chart [indicator]="indicator"></app-ch7-ind3-chart>
</div>
```

This template allows you to specify a stock ticker, date range, and period as input parameters, which are required in calculating the Williams' %R indicator. The resulted indicator is then as input for the *ch7-ind3-chart* component.

Finally, we need to add a path for this new component to the *RouterModule* of the root module (i.e., the *app.module.ts* file):

```
{ path: 'chapter07/ch7-ind-willr, component: Ch7IndWillrComponent },
```

Then add the corresponding URL link to the *home* and *nav-menu* components. Saving the project and navigating to the */chapter07/ch7-ind-willr* page generate the result shown in Fig.7-13.

Fig.7-13. Williams %R indicator for IBM.

The most common use for the Williams %R is for overbought and oversold readings and momentum confirmations and failures. Usually, a security is overbought when the indicator is above -20, and the security is oversold if the indicator is below -80.

During an uptrend, if the Williams %R continually moves above -20 (overbought) that shows strength and confirms the trend. The price is closing in the upper portion of its 14 period range. It follows that if during an uptrend the indicator cannot reach -20, momentum may be failing. If during an uptrend the price falls into oversold territory and then cannot rally back above -20, this shows upside momentum has stalled and potentially reversed.

A downtrend is strong when the indicator consistently reaches -80 or below. If it fails to reach -80, momentum is slowing; if it reaches overbought and then fails to drop back below -80, the downtrend could be reversing.

Volume Indicators

Volume is a measure of how much of a stock has been traded in a given period of time, or how many times the stock has been brought or sold over a particular time span. In this section, we will consider two volume-related indicators: accumulation/distribution (AD) and on balance volume (OBV).

AD Indicator

This is a volume-based indicator designed to measure the cumulative flow of money into and out of a security. It is determined by the changes in price and volume. The volume acts as a weight coefficient at the change of price: the higher the volume is, the greater the contribution of the price change will be in the value of the indicator. This indicator is in fact a variant of the more commonly used OBV indicator. They are both used to confirm price changes by means of measuring the respective volume of sales.

The AD indicator can be calculated as follows:

$$AD = cumulative(MFV)$$

Where *MFV* is the money flow volume, which is given by

$$MFV = \frac{(\text{Close} - \text{Low}) - (\text{High} - \text{Close})}{\text{High} - \text{low}}$$

Run the following command in a command prompt window:

`ng g c chapter07/ch7-ind-ad --module=app.module`

This generates a new component named *ch7-ind-ad* in the *ClientApp/src/app/chapter07* folder. Open the component class file and replace its content with the following code:

```
// ch7-ind-ad.component.ts file:
import { Component, OnInit } from '@angular/core';
import { Ch7Service } from '../../models/ch7.service';

@Component({
  selector: 'app-ch7-ind-ad',
  templateUrl: './ch7-ind-ad.component.html',
  styleUrls: ['./ch7-ind-ad.component.css']
})
export class Ch7IndAdComponent implements OnInit {
  ticker = 'IBM';
  start: string = '2018-01-01';
  end: string = '2018-12-31';

  constructor(private reporsitory: Ch7Service) { }

  ngOnInit() {
    this.getIndicator(this.ticker, this.start, this.end);
  }
```

```
get indicator(): any {
    return this.reporsitory.ad;
}

getIndicator(ticker: string, start: string, end: string) {
    this.reporsitory.getAd(ticker, start, end);
}
}
```

This component simply retrieves the AD indicator results from web service. We also need to update this component's template with the following code:

```
// ch7-ind-ad.component.html file:
<h2>
    ch7-ind-ad works!
</h2>

<mat-form-field>
    <input matInput placeholder="ticker" [(ngModel)]="ticker" name="ticker">
</mat-form-field>
<mat-form-field>
    <input matInput placeholder="start" [(ngModel)]="start" name="start">
</mat-form-field>
<mat-form-field>
    <input matInput placeholder="end" [(ngModel)]="end" name="end">
</mat-form-field>
<button mat-raised-button color="primary" (click)="getIndicator(ticker, start,
end)">Get Indicator Chart</button>

<div *ngIf="indicator">
    <app-ch7-ind3-chart [indicator]="indicator"></app-ch7-ind3-chart>
</div>
```

This template allows you to specify a stock ticker and date range as input parameters, which are required in calculating the AD indicator. The resulted indicator is then as input for the *ch7-ind3-chart* component.

Finally, we need to add a path for this new component to the *RouterModule* of the root module (i.e., the *app.module.ts* file):

```
{ path: 'chapter07/ch7-ind-ad, component: Ch7IndAdComponent },
```

Then add the corresponding URL link to the *home* and *nav-menu* components. Saving the project and navigating to the */chapter07/ch7-ind-ad* page generate the result shown in Fig.7-14.

You can see from Fig.7-14 that when the value of AD indicator increases, it means accumulation (buying) of a particular stock, as the overwhelming share of the trading volume is related to an upward trend of prices. When the value of the indicator drops, it means distribution (selling) of the stock, as most of sales take place during the downward price movement.

Divergences between the AD indicator and the price of the security indicate the upcoming change of prices. As a rule of thumb, in case of such divergences, the price tendency moves in the direction in which the indicator moves. Thus, if the indicator is growing, and the price of the security is dropping, a turnaround of price should be expected.

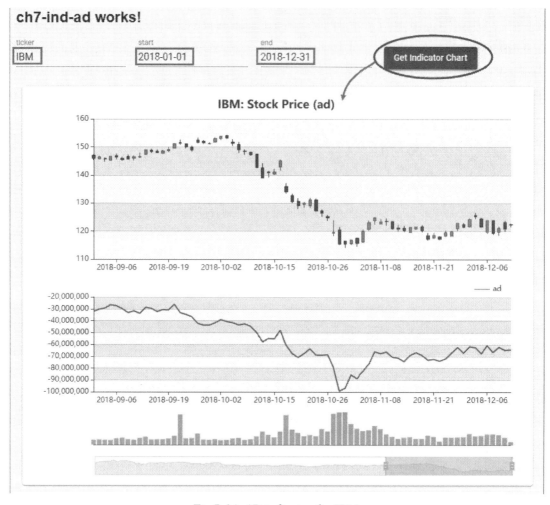

Fig.7-14. AD indicator for IBM.

OBV Indicator

Trading volume itself is a valuable indicator, and the on balance volume (OBV) takes a lot volume information and compiles it into a signal indicator. The OBV indicator measures positive and negative volume flows and tends to relate price and volume in the stock market.

We can calculate the OBV using the following formula:

$$OBV = OBV_{\text{prev}} + \begin{cases} \text{volume} & \text{if close} > \text{close}_{\text{prev}} \\ 0 & \text{if close} = \text{close}_{\text{prev}} \\ -\text{volume} & \text{if close} < \text{close}_{\text{prev}} \end{cases}$$

Since OBV is a cumulative result, the value of OBV depends on the starting point of the calculation. Volume should confirm trends. A rising price should be accompanied by a rising OBV; a failing price should be accompanied by a failing OBV.

Run the following command in a command prompt window:

```
ng g c chapter07/ch7-ind-obv --module=app.module
```

This generates a new component named *ch7-ind-obv* in the *ClientApp/src/app/chapter07* folder. Open the component class file and replace its content with the following code:

```
// ch7-ind-obv.component.ts file:
import { Component, OnInit } from '@angular/core';
import { Ch7Service } from '../../models/ch7.service';

@Component({
  selector: 'app-ch7-ind-obv',
  templateUrl: './ch7-ind-obv.component.html',
  styleUrls: ['./ch7-ind-obv.component.css']
})
export class Ch7IndObvComponent implements OnInit {
  ticker = 'IBM';
  start: string = '2018-01-01';
  end: string = '2018-12-31';

  constructor(private reporsitory: Ch7Service) { }

  ngOnInit() {
    this.getIndicator(this.ticker, this.start, this.end);
  }

  get indicator(): any {
    return this.reporsitory.obv;
  }

  getIndicator(ticker: string, start: string, end: string) {
    this.reporsitory.getObv(ticker, start, end);
  }
}
```

This component simply retrieves the OBV indicator results from web service. We also need to update this component's template with the following code:

```
// ch7-ind-obv.component.html file:
<h2>
  ch7-ind-obv works!
</h2>

<mat-form-field>
  <input matInput placeholder="ticker" [(ngModel)]="ticker" name="ticker">
</mat-form-field>
<mat-form-field>
  <input matInput placeholder="start" [(ngModel)]="start" name="start">
</mat-form-field>
<mat-form-field>
  <input matInput placeholder="end" [(ngModel)]="end" name="end">
</mat-form-field>
<button mat-raised-button color="primary" (click)="getIndicator(ticker, start,
end)">Get Indicator Chart</button>

<div *ngIf="indicator">
```

```
<app-ch7-ind3-chart [indicator]="indicator"></app-ch7-ind3-chart>
</div>
```

This template allows you to specify a stock ticker and date range as input parameters, which are required in calculating the OBV indicator. The resulted indicator is then as input for the *ch7-ind3-chart* component.

Finally, we need to add a path for this new component to the *RouterModule* of the root module (i.e., the *app.module.ts* file):

```
{ path: 'chapter07/ch7-ind-obv, component: Ch7IndObvComponent },
```

Then add the corresponding URL link to the *home* and *nav-menu* components. Saving the project and navigating to the */chapter07/ch7-ind-obv* page generate the result shown in Fig.7-15.

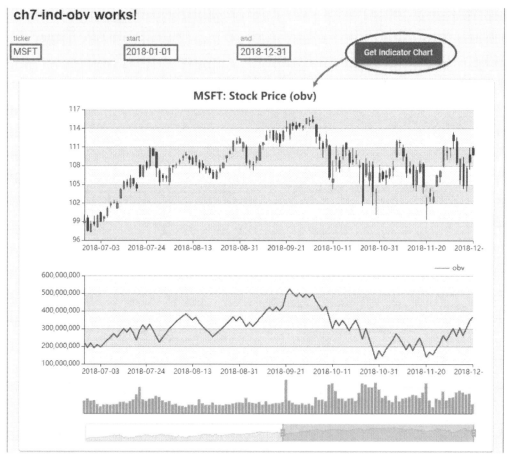

Fig.7-15. OBV indicator for MSFT.

The OBV indicator is a momentum indicator that uses volume flow to predict changes in stock price. When volume increases sharply without a significant change in the stock price, the price will eventually jump upward, and vice versa. The basic assumption is that OBV changes precede price changes. The theory is that smart money can be seen flowing into the stock by a rising OBV. When the public then moves into the stock, both the stock and the OBV will surge ahead.

If the stock price movement precedes OBV movement, a non-confirmation has occurred. Non-confirmations can occur at bull market tops (when the stock rises without or before the OBV) or at bear market bottoms (when the stock falls without or before the OBV). When the OBV changes to a rising or falling trend, a breakout has occurred. Since OBV breakouts normally precede price breakouts, you should buy long on OBV upside breakouts. On the other hand, you should sell short when the OBV makes a downside breakout. You should hold stock position until the trend changes.

Volatility Indicators

Volatility indicators attempt to measure the volatility of a security's price action. Day traders prefer increased volatility as the price is more volatile and more money can be gained (or lost) in a short time. In this section, we consider three volatility indicators, including true range (TR), average true range (ATR), and normalized average true range (NATR).

TR Indicator

The true range (TR) indicator attempts to measure volatility of a stock. It does not provide an indication of price trend, simply the degree of price volatility.

The TR indicator is calculated as follows:

$$TR = Max[(\text{high} - \text{low}), abs(\text{high} - \text{prev close}), abs(\text{prev close} - \text{low})]$$

The absolute values are used to ensure positive numbers.

Run the following command in a command prompt window:

```
ng g c chapter07/ch7-ind-tr --module=app.module
```

This generates a new component named *ch7-ind-tr* in the *ClientApp/src/app/chapter07* folder. Open the component class file and replace its content with the following code:

```
// ch7-ind-tr.component.ts file:
import { Component, OnInit } from '@angular/core';
import { Ch7Service } from '../../models/ch7.service';

@Component({
  selector: 'app-ch7-ind-tr',
  templateUrl: './ch7-ind-tr.component.html',
  styleUrls: ['./ch7-ind-tr.component.css']
})
export class Ch7IndTrComponent implements OnInit {
  ticker = 'IBM';
  start: string = '2018-01-01';
  end: string = '2018-12-31';

  constructor(private reporsitory: Ch7Service) { }

  ngOnInit() {
    this.getIndicator(this.ticker, this.start, this.end);
  }

  get indicator(): any {
    return this.reporsitory.trueRange;
```

```
  }

  getIndicator(ticker: string, start: string, end: string) {
    this.reporsitory.getTrueRange(ticker, start, end);
  }
}
```

This component simply retrieves the TR indicator results from web service. We also need to update this component's template:

```
// ch7-ind-tr.component.html file:
<h2>
  ch7-ind-tr works!
</h2>

<mat-form-field>
  <input matInput placeholder="ticker" [(ngModel)]="ticker" name="ticker">
</mat-form-field>
<mat-form-field>
  <input matInput placeholder="start" [(ngModel)]="start" name="start">
</mat-form-field>
<mat-form-field>
  <input matInput placeholder="end" [(ngModel)]="end" name="end">
</mat-form-field>
<button mat-raised-button color="primary" (click)="getIndicator(ticker, start,
end)">Get Indicator Chart</button>

<div *ngIf="indicator">
  <app-ch7-ind3-chart [indicator]="indicator"></app-ch7-ind3-chart>
</div>
```

This template allows you to specify a stock ticker and date range as input parameters, which are required in calculating the TR indicator. The resulted indicator is then as input for the *ch7-ind3-chart* component.

Finally, we need to add a path for this new component to the *RouterModule* of the root module (i.e., the *app.module.ts* file):

```
{ path: 'chapter07/ch7-ind-tr, component: Ch7IndTrComponent },
```

Then add the corresponding URL link to the *home* and *nav-menu* components. Saving the project and navigating to the */chapter07/ch7-ind-tr* page generate the result shown in Fig.7-16.

ATR Indicator

Average true range (ATR) indicator is an *n*-bar smoothed moving average of the true range indicator discussed in the preceding section.

The *ATR* indicator can be calculated as follows:

$$ATR = MA(TR, n)$$

Where *TR* is defined in the preceding section.

Run the following command in a command prompt window:

```
ng g c chapter07/ch7-ind-atr --module=app.module
```

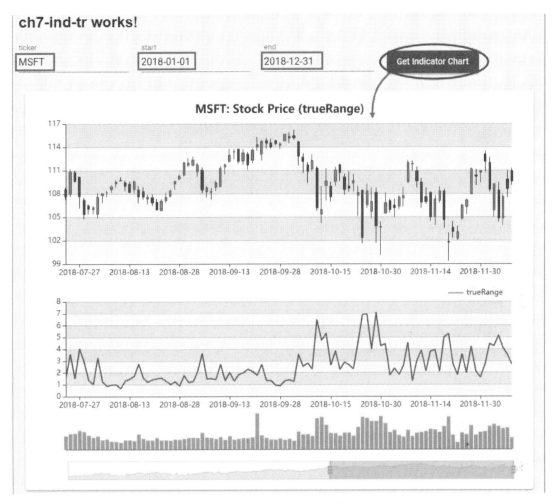

Fig.7-16. True range indicator for MSFT.

This generates a new component named *ch7-ind-atr* in the *ClientApp/src/app/chapter07* folder. Open the component class file and replace its content with the following code:

```
// ch7-ind-atr.component.ts file:
import { Component, OnInit } from '@angular/core';
import { Ch7Service } from '../../models/ch7.service';

@Component({
  selector: 'app-ch7-ind-atr',
  templateUrl: './ch7-ind-atr.component.html',
  styleUrls: ['./ch7-ind-atr.component.css']
})
export class Ch7IndAtrComponent implements OnInit {
  ticker = 'IBM';
  start: string = '2018-01-01';
  end: string = '2018-12-31';
  period: number = 14;
```

```
constructor(private reporsitory: Ch7Service) { }

ngOnInit() {
  this.getIndicator(this.ticker, this.start, this.end, this.period);
}

get indicator(): any {
  return this.reporsitory.atr;
}

getIndicator(ticker: string, start: string, end: string, period: number) {
  this.reporsitory.getAtr(ticker, start, end, period);
}
}
```

This component simply retrieves the ATR indicator results from web service. We also need to update this component's template with the following code:

```
// ch7-ind-atr.component.html file:
<h2>
  ch7-ind-atr works!
</h2>

<mat-form-field>
  <input matInput placeholder="ticker" [(ngModel)]="ticker" name="ticker">
</mat-form-field>
<mat-form-field>
  <input matInput placeholder="start" [(ngModel)]="start" name="start">
</mat-form-field>
<mat-form-field>
  <input matInput placeholder="end" [(ngModel)]="end" name="end">
</mat-form-field>
<mat-form-field>
  <input matInput placeholder="period" [(ngModel)]="period" name="period">
</mat-form-field>
<button mat-raised-button color="primary" (click)="getIndicator(ticker, start, end,
period)">Get Indicator Chart</button>

<div *ngIf="indicator">
  <app-ch7-ind3-chart [indicator]="indicator"></app-ch7-ind3-chart>
</div>
```

This template allows you to specify a stock ticker, date range, and period as input parameters, which are required in calculating the ATR indicator. The resulted indicator is then as input for the *ch7-ind3-chart* component.

Finally, we need to add a path for this new component to the *RouterModule* of the root module (i.e., the *app.module.ts* file):

```
{ path: 'chapter07/ch7-ind-atr, component: Ch7IndAtrComponent },
```

Then add the corresponding URL link to the *home* and *nav-menu* components. Saving the project and navigating to the */chapter07/ch7-ind-atr* page generate the result shown in Fig.7-17.

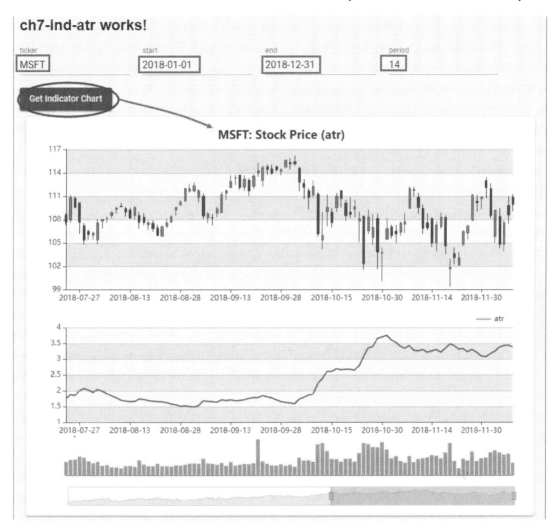

Fig.7-17. ATR indicator for MSFT.

ATR is based on price movement, so the reading is a dollar amount. For example, an ATR reading of 0.25 means that the price moves $0.25, on average, each price bar. Because the ATR value is based on how much each stock moves, the reading for one stock is not compared to other stocks in isolation. For example, an ATR reading of 0.5 may be regarded high if the stock is priced at $10, but on a stock priced at $100, an ATR of 0.5 may be considered low.

NATR Indicator

The ATR indicator is a very useful measure of volatility, but it has downside. Because it is derived from true price range and expressed as absolute dollar value, it cannot be directly comparable across securities and over time. For example, a stock trading at $10 with ATR of 0.5 is actually more volatile than a stock trading at $200 with a much greater ATR of 2.

There is an easy fix for this issue. If you express ATR as percentage of stock price, you get a volatility measure that is directly comparable across stocks with different prices. In our example, the first stock's ATR becomes 0.5/10 = 5% and the second becomes 2/200 = 1%. The first stock, which has 4x smaller ATR, is actually 5x more volatile.

This ATR adjustment is called the normalized ATR (NATR) indicator, which attempts to normalize the ATR values across instruments by using the following formula:

$$NATR = 100 \times \frac{ATR(n)}{Close}$$

Run the following command in a command prompt window:

ng g c chapter07/ch7-ind-natr --module=app.module

This generates a new component named *ch7-ind-natr* in the *ClientApp/src/app/chapter07* folder. Open the component class file and replace its content with the following code:

```
// ch7-ind-natr.component.ts file:
import { Component, OnInit } from '@angular/core';
import { Ch7Service } from '../../models/ch7.service';

@Component({
  selector: 'app-ch7-ind-natr',
  templateUrl: './ch7-ind-natr.component.html',
  styleUrls: ['./ch7-ind-natr.component.css']
})
export class Ch7IndNatrComponent implements OnInit {
  ticker = 'IBM';
  start: string = '2018-01-01';
  end: string = '2018-12-31';
  period: number = 14;

  constructor(private reporsitory: Ch7Service) { }

  ngOnInit() {
    this.getIndicator(this.ticker, this.start, this.end, this.period);
  }

  get indicator(): any {
    return this.reporsitory.natr;
  }

  getIndicator(ticker: string, start: string, end: string, period: number) {
    this.reporsitory.getNatr(ticker, start, end, period);
  }
}
```

This component simply retrieves the NATR indicator results from web service. We also need to update this component's template:

```
// ch7-ind-natr.component.html file:
<h2>
  ch7-ind-natr works!
</h2>

<mat-form-field>
```

```
  <input matInput placeholder="ticker" [(ngModel)]="ticker" name="ticker">
</mat-form-field>
<mat-form-field>
  <input matInput placeholder="start" [(ngModel)]="start" name="start">
</mat-form-field>
<mat-form-field>
  <input matInput placeholder="end" [(ngModel)]="end" name="end">
</mat-form-field>
<mat-form-field>
  <input matInput placeholder="period" [(ngModel)]="period" name="period">
</mat-form-field>
<button mat-raised-button color="primary" (click)="getIndicator(ticker, start, end,
period)">Get Indicator Chart</button>

<div *ngIf="indicator">
  <app-ch7-ind3-chart [indicator]="indicator"></app-ch7-ind3-chart>
</div>
```

This template allows you to specify a stock ticker, date range, and period as input parameters, which are required in calculating the NATR indicator. The resulted indicator is then as input for the *ch7-ind3-chart* component.

Finally, we need to add a path for this new component to the *RouterModule* of the root module (i.e., the *app.module.ts* file):

```
{ path: 'chapter07/ch7-ind-natr, component: Ch7IndNatrComponent },
```

Then add the corresponding URL link to the *home* and *nav-menu* components. Saving the project and navigating to the */chapter07/ch7-ind-natr* page generate the result shown in Fig.7-18.

In this chapter, we simply show you how to apply some commonly used technical indicators to Angular single-page applications. In fact, the TA-Lib library consists of over 200 indicators. Following the procedure presented here, you can easily examine all of these indicators and see how they work. I should point out that the example applications presented in this chapter are a powerful trading tool, which allows you to check different stocks for different periods using the specified indicator.

You can easily customize the indicator charts according to the requirement of your applications. For example, if you want to display signals from several indicators on the same chart, you can modify the C# code in the *IndicatorHelper* class and corresponding TypeScript code in the *ch7.service.ts* file following the procedures we used for creating the indicator charts.

Technical indicators can also be categorized into two types: leading and lagging indicators. Leading indicators are deigned to lead price movements. The majority of leading indicators are momentum oscillators. This means that the values of these indicators are limited within a bounded range. The oscillator will fluctuate into overbought and oversold conditions based on set levels. Some of the more popular leading indicators include CCI, RSI, stochastic, and Williams' %R. A leading indicator is considered to be powerful during periods of sideways or non-trending trading ranges.

Leading indicators usually generate more signals and create more trading opportunities. Early signaling for entry and exit is the main advantage of the leading indicators, which can act to forewarn against a potential strength or weakness. Because they generate more signals, leading indicators are best used in non-trending markets. In a market that is trending up, the best use of the leading indicators is to help identify oversold conditions for buying opportunities. In a market that is trending down, leading indicators can help identify overbought situations for selling opportunities.

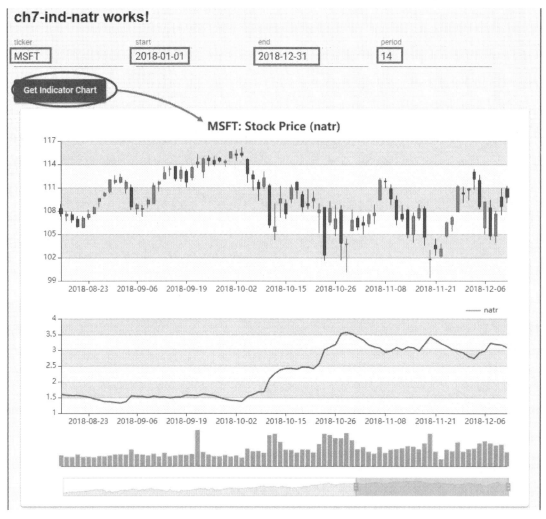

Fig.7-18. NATR indicator for MSFT.

With early signals comes the prospect of higher returns and with higher returns comes the reality of greater risk. More signals and earlier signals mean that the chances of false signals and whipsaws increase. False signals will increase the potential for losses. Whipsaws can generate commissions that can eat away profits and test trading stamina.

Lagging indicators follow price movements and have less predictive qualities. The most well-known lagging indicators include moving average, MACD, envelope, and Bollinger band indicators. The usefulness of these indicators tends to be lower during non-trending periods but highly useful during trending periods. This is because lagging indicators tend to focus more on the trend and generate fewer buy-and-sell signals. This allows you to capture more of the trend instead of being forced out of your positions based on the volatile nature of the leading indicators.

One of the main benefits of lagging indicators is the ability to catch a move and remain in a move. When the market or security in question develops a sustained move, trend-following indicators can be enormously profitable and easy to use. The longer the trend, the fewer the signals and less trading involved.

The benefits of lagging indicators are lost when a security moves in a non-trending range. Another drawback of lagging indicators is that signals tend to be late. By the time a moving average crossover occurs, a significant portion of the move may have already occurred. Late entry and exit points can skew the risk/reward ratio.

Chapter 8
Machine Learning

In recent years, machine-learning (ML) technique has become one of the most promising fields in quantitative finance. ML can be categorized into unsupervised and supervised learning. Unsupervised learning is a type of ML algorithm used to draw inferences from data sets consisting of input data without labeled responses. The most common unsupervised learning method is cluster analysis, which is used for exploratory data analysis to find the hidden patterns or grouping in data.

Supervised learning is a type of ML algorithm that uses a known dataset (called the training dataset) to make predictions. The training dataset includes input data and response values, from which the supervised learning algorithm seeks to build a model that can make predictions of the response values for a new dataset. Supervised learning consists of two types of algorithms: classification and regression. The classification is used for categorical response values, for example, the direction of the next day's stock price movement; while the regression is used for continuous response values, that is, it attempts to predict both the direction and magnitude of a value (i.e., a stock price).

Supervised learning is widely used in quantitative finance for predicting the future stock prices. In this chapter, we will concentrate on the supervised learning, and present several commonly used ML algorithms in finance, including the K-nearest neighbors (KNN), support vector machines (SVM), and neural networks.

For general machine learning problems, you can check our ML playground at https://gincker.com/ai, where over 30 machine-learning algorithms have been implemented.

Prepare Data for Machine learning

Building machine-learning models for predicting stock price movements is neither a straightforward nor an easy task. The first thing we should do is to retrieve and prepare the time-series market data for training ML models. For demonstration purpose, here, I will use three quantities, the close price, typical price, and MA (moving average) as selected features. The typical price provides a simple EOD average price and is calculated by

$$Typical\ Price = \frac{high + low + close}{3} \qquad (8\text{-}1)$$

The typical price carries more information than the close price because it takes into account high, low, and close. In practice, you may add more variables to the selected features, such as the other price types and technical indicators.

In a time series, such as stock price, each value is affected by the values just preceding this value. Sliding (or rolling) window is a temporary approximation over the actual value of the time series data. The size of the window and segment increases until we reached the less error approximation. After selecting the first segment, the next segment is selected from the end of the first segment. The process is repeated until all the time series data are segmented. The process of sliding window is shown in Fig.8-1 with a window size = 3.

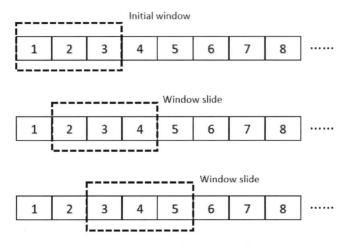

Fig.8-1. Process of sliding window.

Sliding window accumulates the historical time series data to predict next day's movement of stock. Each number (1, 2 ... 8) represents daily observations (typical price, close, and MA in our example) of time series data of day 1, 2 ... 8 respectively. Initial window has covered from 1 to 3, which represents those 3 days historical data being used for predicting next day's stock price movement, then window slides right side by one day to cover another 3 days (from 2 to 4) observations to predict next day's stock price movement. The process will be continued until the entire time series data is covered.

Most ML techniques benefit from scaling the raw time series data. This is because most common activation functions used in the neural network such as tanh or sigmoid are defined on the [-1, 1] or [0, 1] range respectively. Nowadays, rectified line unit (ReLU) activation is often used, which is unbounded on the axis of positive activation values. However, if an ML method does require data scaling, we will use the following equation to normalize the dataset:

$$x_{new} = 2 \times \frac{x - x_{min}}{x_{max} - x_{min}} - 1 \qquad (8\text{-}2)$$

Where x_{min} (x_{max}) is the minimum (maximum) value of the dataset. You can see the normalized values always lie in the range of [-1, 1].

Furthermore, we need split the dataset into training and test data. We will use a *trainDate* parameter to separate the raw time series: the training data is in the range of [*startDate, trainDate*] while the test data is in the range of (*trainDate*, *endDate*]. Note that in order to keep the temporal characteristics of the data, the data is not shuffled but sequentially sliced.

Here, for demonstration purpose, we will scale the entire time series dataset before splitting it into training and test data. However, in real-world technical analysis for stock trading, caution must be undertaken regarding what part of the data is scaled and when. Usually, you should not scale the whole dataset before training and test split are being applied. This is because scaling invokes the computation of the min/max of an observation. When performing time series prediction in real life, you do not have information from future observations at the time of predicting. Therefore, calculation of normalization values has to be conducted on training data and must then be applied to the test data. Otherwise, you use future information at the time of prediction that commonly biases predicting metrics in a positive direction.

Implementation

In this chapter, we will use Accord.NET machine learning and neural network modules to perform ML analysis and predict the stock price movement. Please install the following Accord.NET NuGet packages from the Package Manager Console within the Visual Studio:

```
PM> Install-Package Accord.MachineLearning -Version 3.8.2-alpha
PM> Install-Package Accord.MachineLearning.GPL -Version 3.8.2-alpha
PM> Install-Package Accord.Neuro -Version 3.8.2-alpha
```

Now, we will implement an ML helper class to process the raw stock time-series data. Add a new class called *MachineLearningHelper.cs* to the *Quant/Models* folder with the following code:

```
using System;
using System.Collections.Generic;
using System.Data;
using System.Globalization;
using System.Threading.Tasks;
using System.Linq;
using YahooFinanceApi;
using Accord;
using Accord.Math;
using Accord.MachineLearning;
using Accord.Statistics.Analysis;
using Accord.MachineLearning.VectorMachines.Learning;
using Accord.Statistics.Kernels;
using Accord.MachineLearning.VectorMachines;
using Accord.Math.Optimization.Losses;
using Accord.Neuro;
using Accord.Neuro.Learning;

namespace Quant.Models
{
    public static class MachineLearningHelper
    {
        public static MlInput ProcessMLData(string ticker, string start, string end,
            int period, string maType,
            string mlType, string trainDate, bool isNormalized, int windowSize)
        {
            DataTable dt = GetMlStockData(ticker, start, end, period, maType,
                mlType);
```

```
List<double> minMax = new List<double>();
if(isNormalized) minMax = NormalizeData(dt, mlType);

int n = 3; // num of selected features
string[] inputColNames = new string[n * windowSize];

for (var i = 0; i < windowSize; i++)
{
    inputColNames[n * i] = "Close" + (i + 1).ToString();
    inputColNames[n * i + 1] = "Price" + (i + 1).ToString();
    inputColNames[n * i + 2] = "Ma" + (i + 1).ToString();
}

foreach (var ss in inputColNames)
{
    dt.Columns.Add(ss, typeof(double));
}

int inputSize = dt.Rows.Count - windowSize;
for(int i = 0; i < inputSize; i++)
{
    for(int j = 0; j < windowSize; j++)
    {
        dt.Rows[i + windowSize][inputColNames[n * j]] =
            dt.Rows[i + j]["Close"];
        dt.Rows[i + windowSize][inputColNames[n * j + 1]] =
            dt.Rows[i + j]["Price"];
        dt.Rows[i + windowSize][inputColNames[n * j + 2]] =
            dt.Rows[i + j]["Ma"];
    }
}
dt.Columns["Expected"].SetOrdinal(dt.Columns.Count - 1);

if (mlType.Contains("cla"))
{
    dt.Columns.Add("Predicted", typeof(int));
}
else
{
    dt.Columns.Add("Predicted", typeof(double));
}

DataTable dtTrain = dt.Clone();
DataTable dtTest = dt.Clone();
var tdate = DateTime.ParseExact(trainDate, "yyyy-MM-dd",
    CultureInfo.InvariantCulture);
List<DateTime> dateTrain = new List<DateTime>();
List<DateTime> dateTest = new List<DateTime>();

for (int i = windowSize; i < dt.Rows.Count; i++){
    DateTime date = Convert.ToDateTime(dt.Rows[i]["Date"]);
    if (date <= tdate)
    {
        dateTrain.Add(date);
        dtTrain.ImportRow(dt.Rows[i]);
```

```
            }
            else
            {
                dateTest.Add(date);
                dtTest.ImportRow(dt.Rows[i]);
            }
        }

        int samples = dtTrain.Rows.Count;
        var inputTrain = dtTrain.DefaultView.ToTable(false,
            inputColNames).ToJagged();
        var inputTest = dtTest.DefaultView.ToTable(false,
            inputColNames).ToJagged();
        var outputTrain = dtTrain.DefaultView.ToTable(false,
            "Expected").ToJagged();
        var outputTest = dtTest.DefaultView.ToTable(false,
            "Expected").ToJagged();
        var outputTestClass = outputTest.SelectMany(x => x).ToArray();
        var outputTrainClass = outputTrain.SelectMany(x => x).ToArray();
        if (mlType.Contains("cla"))
        {
            return new MlInput
            {
                DateTrain = dateTrain,
                InputTrain = inputTrain,
                OutputTrainClass = outputTrainClass.Select(x =>
                    (int)x).ToArray(),
                DateTest = dateTest,
                InputTest = inputTest,
                OutputTestClass = outputTestClass.Select(x => (int)x).ToArray(),
                StockTable = dt
            };
        }
        else
        {
            return new MlInput
            {
                DateTrain = dateTrain,
                InputTrain = inputTrain,
                OutputTrain = outputTrain,
                DateTest = dateTest,
                InputTest = inputTest,
                OutputTest = outputTest,
                StockTable = dt,
                MinMax = minMax
            };
        }
    }

    public static DataTable GetMlStockData(string ticker, string start,
        string end, int period, string maType, string mlType)
    {
        DataTable dt = new DataTable();
        var stock = GetYahooStockEodData(ticker, start, end);
        var dl = stock.Select(x => x.Close).ToList();
```

```
        var ma = dl.MovingAverage(period, maType);

        dt.Columns.Add("Date", typeof(DateTime));
        dt.Columns.Add("Close", typeof(double));
        dt.Columns.Add("Price", typeof(double));
        dt.Columns.Add("Ma", typeof(double));
        if (mlType.Contains("cla"))
        {
            dt.Columns.Add("Expected", typeof(int));

            for (int i = period - 1; i < ma.Count; i++)
            {
              var price = (stock[i].High + stock[i].Low + stock[i].Close) / 3.0;
                double p0 = stock[i - 1].Close;
                double p1 = stock[i].Close;
                int c1 = 0;
                if (p1 > p0) c1 = 1;
                else if (p1 < p0) c1 = 2;
                dt.Rows.Add(stock[i].Date, stock[i].Close, price, ma[i], c1);
            }
        }
        else
        {
            dt.Columns.Add("Expected", typeof(double));
            for (int i = period - 1; i < ma.Count - 1; i++)
            {
              var price = (stock[i].High + stock[i].Low + stock[i].Close) / 3.0;
                dt.Rows.Add(stock[i].Date, stock[i].Close, price, ma[i],
                    stock[i].Close);
            }
        }
        return dt;
}

private static List<double> NormalizeData(DataTable dt, string mlType)
{
    double minPrice = dt.Compute("Min([Price])", string.Empty).To<double>();
    double maxPrice = dt.Compute("Max([Price])", string.Empty).To<double>();
    double minClose = dt.Compute("Min([Close])", string.Empty).To<double>();
    double maxClose = dt.Compute("Max([Close])", string.Empty).To<double>();
    double minMa = dt.Compute("Min([Ma])", string.Empty).To<double>();
    double maxMa = dt.Compute("Max([Ma])", string.Empty).To<double>();

    foreach(DataRow row in dt.Rows)
    {
        row["Close"] = 2.0 * (row["Close"].To<double>() - minClose) /
            (maxClose - minClose) - 1.0;
        row["Price"] = 2.0 * (row["Price"].To<double>() - minPrice) /
            (maxPrice - minPrice) - 1.0;
        row["Ma"] = 2.0 * (row["Ma"].To<double>() - minMa) / (maxMa - minMa)
            - 1.0;
        if (!mlType.Contains("cla")) row["Expected"] = row["Close"];
    }

    var minMax = new List<double>();
```

```
            minMax.Add(minClose);
            minMax.Add(maxClose);
            return minMax;
        }

        private static List<StockData> GetYahooStockEodData(string ticker,
            string start, string end)
        {
            var startDate = DateTime.Parse(start);
            var endDate = DateTime.Parse(end);
            var hist = Task.Run(() => Yahoo.GetHistoricalAsync(ticker, startDate,
                endDate, Period.Daily)).Result;
            List<StockData> prices = new List<StockData>();
            foreach (var r in hist)
            {
                prices.Add(new StockData
                {
                    Ticker = ticker,
                    Date = r.DateTime,
                    Open = (double)r.Open,
                    High = (double)r.High,
                    Low = (double)r.Low,
                    Close = (double)r.Close,
                    CloseAdj = (double)r.AdjustedClose,
                    Volume = r.Volume
                });
            }
            return prices;
        }
    }

    public class MlInput
    {
        public List<DateTime> DateTrain { get; set; }
        public double[][] InputTrain { get; set; }
        public double[][] OutputTrain { get; set; }
        public int[] OutputTrainClass { get; set; }
        public List<DateTime> DateTest { get; set; }
        public double[][] InputTest { get; set; }
        public double[][] OutputTest { get; set; }
        public int[] OutputTestClass { get; set; }
        public DataTable StockTable { get; set; }
        public List<double> MinMax { get; set; }
    }

    public class MlOutput
    {
        public DataTable TrainTable { get; set; }
        public DataTable TestTable { get; set; }
        public DataTable StockTable { get; set; }
        public GeneralConfusionMatrix CmTrain { get; set; }
        public GeneralConfusionMatrix CmTest { get; set; }
        public List<double> Errors { get; set; }
    }
}
```

Here, the *MlInput* and *MlOutput* classes define various input and output properties from machine learning respectively. First, we retrieve raw stock data from Yahoo Finance using a private method called *GetYahooStockEodData*, and then use the *GetMlStockData* method to extract the data for machine learning with three features, i.e., the close price, typical price, and moving average, stored in a DataTable with the column names, *Close*, *Price*, and *MA*, respectively. Inside the *GetMlStockData* method, we use the *mlType* parameter to specify whether machine learning is for classification or regression. For classification, we set the next day's stock market direction as the target (stored in DataTable as the *Expected* column). We define the next day's market direction as the difference between next day's close price and today's close price and assign three values (0, 1, 2) to represent the market direction: 0 – no market movement, 1 – market up, and 2 – market down. For regression, we set the next day's close price as the target.

In the *ProcessMLData* method, we apply a sliding window to process the time-series data specified by the *windowSize* parameter. We also split the time series into training and test data, and then transform the data stored in DataTable into jagged arrays, which are formats required by the machine learning package. This method also contains an *isNormalized* parameter that specifies whether the normalized data is used or not. If the parameter is set to true, the data is normalized using a method called *NormalizeData* based on the formula given in Eq.(8.2).

Web Service

Now, we can convert the above methods into web service. Add a new API controller named *MachineLearningValuesController* to the *Quant/Controllers* folder with the following code:

```
using Microsoft.AspNetCore.Mvc;
using Quant.Models;

namespace Quant.Controllers
{
    [Produces("application/json")]
    public class MachineLearningValuesController : Controller
    {
        [Route("~/api/mlStockData/{ticker}/{start}/{end}/{period}/{mlType}")]
        [HttpGet]
        public JsonResult GetMlStockData(string ticker, string start, string end,
            int period, string mlType)
        {
            var res = MachineLearningHelper.GetMlStockData(ticker, start, end,
                period, "sma", mlType);
            return Json(new { Name = "ML Stock Data", Result = res });
        }

        [Route("~/api/mlProcessedData/{ticker}/{start}/{end}/{period}/{mlType}/
            {trainDate}/{isNormalized}/{windowSize}")]
        [HttpGet]
        public JsonResult GetMlProcessedData(string ticker, string start,
            string end, int period, string mlType, string trainDate,
            bool isNormalized, int windowSize)
        {
            var res = MachineLearningHelper.ProcessMLData(ticker, start, end,
                period, "sma", mlType, trainDate, isNormalized, windowSize);
            return Json(new { Name = "ML Processed Data", Result = res });
        }
    }
```

```
      }
}
```

Here, we use web service to retrieve processed ML data with specified URLs by calling the methods defined in the *MachineLearningHelper* class. To use this service in Angular applications, we need to implement a corresponding service class in Angular. Add a TypeScript class named *ch8.service.ts* in the *ClientApp/src/app/models* folder by running the following command in a command prompt window:

`ng g s models/ch8`

Open the ch8.service.ts file and replace its content with the following code:

```
// ch8.service.ts file:
import { Inject } from '@angular/core';
import { HttpClient } from '@angular/common/http';

export class Ch8Repository {
  private url;

  constructor(private http: HttpClient, @Inject('BASE_URL') baseUrl: string) {
    this.url = baseUrl;
  }

  mlStockData: any;
  getMlStockData(ticker: string, start: string, end: string, period: number,
    mlType: string) {
    let url1 = this.url + 'api/mlstockdata/' + ticker + '/' + start + '/' + end +
      '/' + period + '/' + mlType;
    this.http.get<any>(url1).subscribe(result => { this.mlStockData = result });
  }

  mlProcessedData: any;
  getMlProcessedData(ticker: string, start: string, end: string, period: number,
    mlType: string, trainDate: string, isNormalized: boolean, windowSize: number) {
    let url1 = this.url + 'api/mlprocesseddata/' + ticker + '/' + start + '/' + end
      + '/' + period + '/' + mlType + '/' + trainDate + '/' + isNormalized + '/' +
      windowSize;
    this.http.get<any>(url1).subscribe(result => { this.mlProcessedData = result });
  }
}
```

This service is very similar to the repository service classes used in preceding chapters. The methods implemented in this class send HTTP requests to specified URLs, which retrieve the results for processed ML data from the ASP.NET Core API service.

Examine Processed ML Data

We can now examine the processed ML data using an Angular component. To display a large dataset, here we will use a new data grid named *ag-Grid*. You can install the package by adding the following statement to the *dependencies* section of the *package.json* file in the *ClientApp* folder:

```
"ag-grid-community": "19.1.4",
"ag-grid-angular": "19.1.2"
```

You also need to add the *ag-Grid* Angular module named *AgGridModule* to the *app.module.ts* file following the same procedure as that we used previously.

The next step is to add the *ag-Grid* style by adding following statements to the *style.css* file in the *ClientApp/src* folder:

```
@import 'ag-grid-community/dist/styles/ag-grid.css';
@import 'ag-grid-community/dist/styles/ag-theme-balham.css';
```

Now, run the following command in a command prompt window:

```
ng g c chapter08/ch8-ml-data --module=app.module
```

This generates a new component named *ch8-ml-data* in the *ClientApp/src/app/chapter08* folder. Open the component class file and replace its content with the following code:

```
// ch8-ml-data.ts file:
import { Component, OnInit } from '@angular/core';
import { Ch8Service } from '../../models/ch8.service';

@Component({
  selector: 'app-ch8-ml-data',
  templateUrl: './ch8-ml-data.component.html',
  styleUrls: ['./ch8-ml-data.component.css']
})
export class Ch8MlDataComponent implements OnInit {
  ticker = 'FB';
  start: string = '2018-01-01';
  end: string = '2018-12-31';
  trainDate: string = '2018-07-31';
  period: number = 14;
  mlType: string = 'classification';
  isNormalized: boolean = false;
  windowSize: number = 3;

  columnDefs = [
    { headerName: "Date", field: "date", width: 100 },
    { headerName: "Close", field: "close", width: 80 },
    { headerName: "Price", field: "price", width: 80 },
    { headerName: "MA", field: "ma", width: 80 },
    { headerName: "Expect", field: "expected", width: 80 },
  ]
  columnDefs2: any;

  constructor(private repository: Ch8Service) { }

  ngOnInit() {
    this.columnDefs2 = this.getColDef2();
    this.getMlData(this.ticker, this.start, this.end, this.period, this.mlType,
      this.trainDate, this.isNormalized, this.windowSize);
  }

  get mlStockData(): any {
    return this.repository.mlStockData;
  }

  get mlProcessedData(): any {
    return this.repository.mlProcessedData;
  }
```

```
getMlData(ticker: string, start: string, end: string, period: number,
  mlType: string, trainDate: string, isNormalized: boolean, windowSize: number) {
  this.repository.getMlStockData(ticker, start, end, period, mlType);
  this.repository.getMlProcessedData(ticker, start, end, period, mlType,
    trainDate, isNormalized, windowSize);
}

getColDef2() {
  let col2 = [
    { headerName: "Date", field: "date", width: 100, pinned: true  },
    { headerName: "Close", field: "close", width: 80 },
    { headerName: "Price", field: "price", width: 80 },
    { headerName: "MA", field: "ma", width: 80 },
    { headerName: "Expect", field: "expected", width: 80 }
  ];

  for (let i = 0; i < this.windowSize; i++) {
    col2.push({ headerName: "Close" + (i + 1).toString(), field: "close" +
      (i + 1).toString(), width: 80 });
    col2.push({ headerName: "Price" + (i + 1).toString(), field: "price" +
      (i + 1).toString(), width: 80 });
    col2.push({ headerName: "MA" + (i + 1).toString(), field: "ma" +
      (i + 1).toString(), width: 80 });
  }
  return col2;
}
}
```

This component first retrieves processed ML data from the Web service with specified input parameters. It then defines two properties, *columnDefs* and *columnDefs2*, which are used to display the original ML data and processed ML data respectively using *ag-Grid* tables. These two properties contain column definitions with each column entry specifying the header label and the data field to be displayed in the body of the table.

We also need to update the component's template with the following code:

```
// ch8-ml-data.component.html file:
<h2>
  ch8-ml-data works!
</h2>

<mat-form-field>
  <input matInput placeholder="ticker" [(ngModel)]="ticker" name="ticker">
</mat-form-field>
<mat-form-field>
  <input matInput placeholder="start" [(ngModel)]="start" name="start">
</mat-form-field>
<mat-form-field>
  <input matInput placeholder="trainDate" [(ngModel)]="trainDate" name="trainDate">
</mat-form-field>
<mat-form-field>
  <input matInput placeholder="end" [(ngModel)]="end" name="end">
</mat-form-field>
<mat-form-field>
  <input matInput placeholder="period" [(ngModel)]="period" name="period">
</mat-form-field>
```

```
<mat-form-field>
  <mat-select [(value)]="mlType">
    <mat-option value="classification">classification</mat-option>
    <mat-option value="regression">regression</mat-option>
  </mat-select>
</mat-form-field>
<mat-form-field>
  <input matInput placeholder="isNormalized" [(ngModel)]="isNormalized"
name="isNormalized">
</mat-form-field>
<mat-form-field>
  <input matInput placeholder="windowSize" [(ngModel)]="windowSize"
name="windowSize">
</mat-form-field>

<button mat-raised-button color="primary" (click)="getMlData(ticker, start, end,
  period, mlType,trainDate, isNormalized, windowSize)">Get ML Data</button>

<br />
<p>Original Stock Data:</p>
<ag-grid-angular *ngIf="mlStockData" style="height:400px;width:600px;"
  class="ag-theme-balham" [rowData]="mlStockData.result" [columnDefs]="columnDefs">
</ag-grid-angular>

<p><span *ngIf="isNormalized">Normalized,</span> Processed Stock Data:</p>
<ag-grid-angular *ngIf="mlProcessedData" style="height:400px;width:1200px;
  margin-bottom:100px" class="ag-theme-balham"
  [rowData]="mlProcessedData.result.stockTable" [columnDefs]="columnDefs2">
</ag-grid-angular>
```

This template first defines input parameters and then adds two *ag-Gird* component directives, each with two property bindings, *rowData* and *columnDefs*. Note that we directly bind the C# DataTable objects, *mlStockData.result* and *mlProcessedData.result.stockTable* to the *rowData* property, which is much simpler than the *mat-table* directive as we used previously.

Finally, we need to add a path for this new component to the *RouterModule* of the root module (i.e., the *app.module.ts* file):

```
{ path: 'chapter08/ch8-ml-data, component: Ch8MlDataComponent },
```

Then add the corresponding URL link to the *home* and *nav-menu* components.

Saving the project and navigating to the */chapter08/ch8-ml-data* page produce the result shown in Fig.8-2, where the original ML data is displayed with the default parameters. The *Expect* column shows today's market direction, which is determined by comparing the today's close with previous day's close.

The *ch8-ml-data* component also displays the results of processed ML data, as shown in Fig.8-3. Here, we process ML data using the default parameters with *windowSize* = 3. You can see that before 2018-01-24, there is no input data because we need 3-day historical data to make a prediction for next day. Note how we put the 3-day historical data into the same row as the prediction day's data.

Now, set the *isNormalized* field to *true* and click the *Get ML Data* button to obtain the normalized market data shown in Fig.8-4.

Stock Data:

Date	Close	Price	MA	Expect
2018-01-22...	185.369...	183.723...	183.632...	1
2018-01-23...	189.350...	188.150...	184.198...	1
2018-01-24...	186.550...	187.910...	184.332...	2
2018-01-25...	187.479...	187.566...	184.557...	1
2018-01-26...	190	188.936...	184.782...	1
2018-01-29...	185.979...	186.816...	184.618...	2
2018-01-30...	187.119...	185.713...	184.564...	1
2018-01-31...	186.889...	187.313...	184.497...	2
2018-02-01...	193.089...	192.100...	184.877...	1
2018-02-02...	190.279...	191.490...	185.656...	2
2018-02-05...	181.259...	184.159...	185.861...	2
2018-02-06...	185.309...	182.940...	186.412...	1
2018-02-07...	180.179...	181.736...	186.439...	2

Fig.8-2. Original ML data for FB.

Processed Stock Data:

				target		inputs							
Date	Close	Price	MA	Expect	Close1	Price1	MA1	Close2	Price2	MA2	Close3	Price3	MA3
2018-01-22...	185.369...	183.723...	183.632...	1									
2018-01-23...	189.350...	188.150...	184.198...	1									
2018-01-24...	186.550...	187.910...	184.332...	2									
2018-01-25...	187.479...	187.566...	184.557...	1	185.369...	183.723...	183.632...	189.350...	188.150...	184.198...	186.550...	187.910...	184.332...
2018-01-26...	190	188.936...	184.782...	1	189.350...	188.150...	184.198...	186.550...	187.910...	184.332...	187.479...	187.566...	184.557...
2018-01-29...	185.979...	186.816...	184.618...	2	186.550...	187.910...	184.332...	187.479...	187.566...	184.557...	190	188.936...	184.782...
2018-01-30...	187.119...	185.713...	184.564...	1	187.479...	187.566...	184.557...	190	188.936...	184.782...	185.979...	186.816...	184.618...
2018-01-31...	186.889...	187.313...	184.497...	2	190	188.936...	184.782...	185.979...	186.816...	184.618...	187.119...	185.713...	184.564...
2018-02-01...	193.089...	192.100...	184.877...	1	185.979...	186.816...	184.618...	187.119...	185.713...	184.564...	186.889...	187.313...	184.497...
2018-02-02...	190.279...	191.490...	185.656...	2	187.119...	185.713...	184.564...	186.889...	187.313...	184.497...	193.089...	192.100...	184.877...
2018-02-05...	181.259...	184.159...	185.861...	2	186.889...	187.313...	184.497...	193.089...	192.100...	184.877...	190.279...	191.490...	185.656...
2018-02-06...	185.309...	182.940...	186.412...	1	193.089...	192.100...	184.877...	190.279...	191.490...	185.656...	181.259...	184.159...	185.861...
2018-02-07...	180.179...	181.736...	186.439...	2	190.279...	191.490...	185.656...	181.259...	184.159...	185.861...	185.309...	182.940...	186.412...

Fig.8-3. Processed ML data for FB.

Normalized, Processed Stock Data:

Date	Close	Price	MA	Expect	Close1	Price1	MA1	Close2	Price2	MA2	Close3	Price3	MA3
2018-01-22...	0.29306...	0.24742...	0.31140...	1									
2018-01-23...	0.38063...	0.34814...	0.32722...	1									
2018-01-24...	0.31903...	0.34268...	0.33097...	2									
2018-01-25...	0.33949...	0.33487...	0.33726...	1	0.29306...	0.24742...	0.31140...	0.38063...	0.34814...	0.32722...	0.31903...	0.34268...	0.33097...
2018-01-26...	0.39493...	0.36604...	0.34354...	1	0.38063...	0.34814...	0.32722...	0.31903...	0.34268...	0.33097...	0.33949...	0.33487...	0.33726...
2018-01-29...	0.30649...	0.31780...	0.33895...	2	0.31903...	0.34268...	0.33097...	0.33949...	0.33487...	0.33726...	0.39493...	0.36604...	0.34354...
2018-01-30...	0.33157...	0.29270...	0.33746...	1	0.33949...	0.33487...	0.33726...	0.39493...	0.36604...	0.34354...	0.30649...	0.31780...	0.33895...
2018-01-31...	0.32651...	0.32911...	0.33556...	2	0.39493...	0.36604...	0.34354...	0.30649...	0.31780...	0.33895...	0.33157...	0.29270...	0.33746...
2018-02-01...	0.46292...	0.43803...	0.34618...	1	0.30649...	0.31780...	0.33895...	0.33157...	0.29270...	0.33746...	0.32651...	0.32911...	0.33556...
2018-02-02...	0.40110...	0.42415...	0.36794...	2	0.33157...	0.29270...	0.33746...	0.32651...	0.32911...	0.33556...	0.46292...	0.43803...	0.34618...
2018-02-05...	0.20264...	0.25735...	0.37367...	2	0.32651...	0.32911...	0.33556...	0.46292...	0.43803...	0.34618...	0.40110...	0.42415...	0.36794...
2018-02-06...	0.29174...	0.22959...	0.38905...	1	0.46292...	0.43803...	0.34618...	0.40110...	0.42415...	0.36794...	0.20264...	0.25735...	0.37367...
2018-02-07...	0.17887...	0.20221...	0.38981...	2	0.40110...	0.42415...	0.36794...	0.20264...	0.25735...	0.37367...	0.29174...	0.22959...	0.38905...

Fig.8-4. Normalized ML data for FB.

KNN Classification

The K-nearest neighbors (KNN) classifier is one of the simplest machine learning algorithms. It is a non-parametric algorithm, which can be used for either classification or regression. Non-parametric means that it makes no assumption about the underlying data or its distribution. It has applications in a variety of fields, ranging from the healthcare industry and IT industry with pattern recognition to the finance industry.

The KNN algorithm is simply based on the idea that objects that are near each other will also have similar characteristics. Thus, if we know the characteristic features of one of the objects, we can also predict it for its nearest neighbor. This indicates that any new instance can be classified by the majority vote of its k-neighbors, where k is a positive integer, usually a small number.

The KNN algorithm looks for k nearest records in the training dataset and uses the majority of the classes of the identified neighbors for classifying a new record. It is commonly based on the Euclidean distance between a test sample and the specified training samples. Let $\mathbf{x}_i$ be an input sample with p features $(x_{i1}, x_{i2}, \ldots, x_{ip})$, n be the total number of input samples $(i = 1,2, \cdots, n)$, and p the total number of features $(j = 1,2, \cdots, p)$. The Euclidean distance between sample $\mathbf{x}_i$ and $\mathbf{x}_l$ $(l = 1,2, \cdots, n)$ is given by the following formula

$$d(\mathbf{x}_i, \mathbf{x}_l) = \sqrt{(x_{i1} - x_{l1})^2 + (x_{i2} - x_{l2})^2 + \cdots + \left(x_{ip} - x_{lp}\right)^2}$$

If you use the KNN algorithm for classification, for each data point, the algorithm finds k closet observations, and then classifies the data point to the majority. For example, if $k = 4$ and four nearest observations to a specific data point belong to the classes A, B, C, and B respectively, the KNN will classify this data point into class B. If k is an even number, there might be ties. To avoid this, you can add weights to the observations, so that observations with a shorter distance are more influential in determining which class the data point belongs to.

Implementation

Here, we will use the Accord.NET machine-learning module to perform the classification computation using the KNN algorithm.

Add a new method called *GetKnn* to the *MachineLearningHelper* class in the *Quant/Models* folder with the following code:

```
public static MlOutput GetKnn(string ticker, string start, string end, int period,
    string maType, string trainDate, bool isNormalized, int windowSize, int knum)
{
    var ml = ProcessMLData(ticker, start, end, period, maType, "classification",
        trainDate, isNormalized, windowSize);
    var knn = new KNearestNeighbors(k: knum * windowSize);
    knn.Learn(ml.InputTrain, ml.OutputTrainClass);

    DataTable trainTable = new DataTable();
    trainTable.Columns.Add("Date", typeof(string));
    trainTable.Columns.Add("Expected", typeof(int));
    trainTable.Columns.Add("Predicted", typeof(int));
    DataTable testTable = trainTable.Clone();

    for(int i = 0; i < ml.OutputTrainClass.Length; i++)
    {
        trainTable.Rows.Add(ml.DateTrain[i].ToString("yyyy-MM-dd"),
            ml.OutputTrainClass[i], knn.Decide(ml.InputTrain[i]));
    }
    for(int i = 0; i < ml.OutputTestClass.Length; i++)
    {
        testTable.Rows.Add(ml.DateTest[i].ToString("yyyy-MM-dd"),
            ml.OutputTestClass[i], knn.Decide(ml.InputTest[i]));
    }

    var cmTrain = GeneralConfusionMatrix.Estimate(knn, ml.InputTrain,
        ml.OutputTrainClass);
    var cmTest = GeneralConfusionMatrix.Estimate(knn, ml.InputTest,
        ml.OutputTestClass);

    return new MlOutput
    {
        TrainTable = trainTable,
        TestTable = testTable,
        StockTable = ml.StockTable,
        CmTrain = cmTrain,
        CmTest = cmTest
    };
}
```

This method first retrieves the processed ML data and then creates the KNN algorithm with $k = knum *$ *windowSize*, where *knum* is specified by user. This means that, for a given instance, its nearest k neighbors will be used to cast a decision. Next, we learn the KNN algorithm using the training inputs and training target. After the algorithm has been created, we classify the results using the training and test data, and compute corresponding confusion matrices.

We can now convert the KNN results into a web service. Add a new method named *GetKnnResult* to the *MachineLearningValuesController* class in the *Quant/Controllers* folder with the following code:

```
[Route("~/api/mlknn/{ticker}/{start}/{end}/{period}/{trainDate}/{isNormalized}
    /{windowSize}/{knum}")]
[HttpGet]
public JsonResult GetKnnResult(string ticker, string start, string end, int period,
    string mlType, string trainDate, bool isNormalized, int windowSize, int knum)
{
    var res = MachineLearningHelper.GetKnn(ticker, start, end, period, "sma",
        trainDate, isNormalized, windowSize, knum);

    return Json(new { Name = "knn classification", Results = res });
}
```

KNN in Angular Application

To use KNN web service in Angular applications, we need to add a method named *getKnnClass* to the *ch8.service.ts* file in the *ClientApp/src/app/models* folder with the following code:

```
mlKnnClass: any;
getMlKnnClass(ticker: string, start: string, end: string, period: number,
  mlType: string, trainDate: string, isNormalized: boolean, windowSize: number,
  knum: number) {
  let url1 = this.url + 'api/mlknn/' + ticker + '/' + start + '/' + end + '/' +
    period + '/' + mlType + '/' + trainDate + '/' + isNormalized + '/' +
    windowSize + '/' + knum;
  this.http.get<any>(url1).subscribe(result => { this.mlKnnClass = result });
}
```

Here, we will create a common component called *ch8-class-res* used for displaying the classification results. Run the following command in a command prompt window:

ng g c chapter08/ch8-class-res --module=app.module

Open the *ch8-class-res* component class and replace its content with the following code:

```
// ch8-class-res.component.ts file:
import { Component, OnInit, Input} from '@angular/core';

@Component({
  selector: 'app-ch8-class-res',
  templateUrl: './ch8-class-res.component.html',
  styleUrls: ['./ch8-class-res.component.css']
})
export class Ch8ClassResComponent implements OnInit {
  @Input() mlResult

  colDefs = [
    { headerName: "Date", field: "date", width: 100 },
    { headerName: "Expect", field: "expected", width: 100 },
    { headerName: "Predict", field: "predicted", width: 100 },
  ];

  constructor() { }
```

```
  ngOnInit() {
  }
}
```

This component takes the *mlResult* property as input parameter. The *colDefs* property is used to display the *mlResult* with an *ag-Grid* component.

We also need to update the template of the *ch8-class-res* component with the following code:

```
// ch8-class-res.component.html file:
<div *ngIf="mlResult">
  <br />Classification Result Summary:
  <ul>
    <li>
      Train Data: Accuracy = {{mlResult.results.cmTrain.accuracy.toFixed(4)}},
      Error = {{mlResult.results.cmTrain.error.toFixed(4)}},
      kappa = {{mlResult.results.cmTrain.kappa.toFixed(4)}}
    </li>
    <li>
      Test Data: Accuracy = {{mlResult.results.cmTest.accuracy.toFixed(4)}},
      Error = {{mlResult.results.cmTest.error.toFixed(4)}},
      kappa = {{mlResult.results.cmTest.kappa.toFixed(4)}}
    </li>
  </ul>
  <div class="cardList">
    <mat-card class="card-border">
      <p>Classification result for training data:</p>
      <ag-grid-angular style="height:90%" class="ag-theme-balham"
        [rowData]="mlResult.results.trainTable" [columnDefs]="colDefs">
      </ag-grid-angular>
    </mat-card>
    <mat-card class="card-border">
      <p>Classification result for test data:</p>
      <ag-grid-angular style="height:90%" class="ag-theme-balham"
        [rowData]="mlResult.results.testTable" [columnDefs]="colDefs">
      </ag-grid-angular>
    </mat-card>
    <mat-card class="card-border">
      <p>Confusion matrix for train data:</p>
      <table>
        <tr><td></td><td>C0</td><td>C1</td><td>C2</td><td>Total</td></tr>
        <tr>
          <td>R0</td>
          <td>{{mlResult.results.cmTrain.matrix[0][0]}}</td>
          <td>{{mlResult.results.cmTrain.matrix[1][0]}}</td>
          <td>{{mlResult.results.cmTrain.matrix[2][0]}}</td>
          <td>{{mlResult.results.cmTrain.columnTotals[0]}}</td>
        </tr>
        <tr>
          <td>R1</td>
          <td>{{mlResult.results.cmTrain.matrix[0][1]}}</td>
          <td>{{mlResult.results.cmTrain.matrix[1][1]}}</td>
          <td>{{mlResult.results.cmTrain.matrix[2][1]}}</td>
          <td>{{mlResult.results.cmTrain.columnTotals[1]}}</td>
        </tr>
        <tr>
```

```html
      <td>R2</td>
      <td>{{mlResult.results.cmTrain.matrix[0][2]}}</td>
      <td>{{mlResult.results.cmTrain.matrix[1][2]}}</td>
      <td>{{mlResult.results.cmTrain.matrix[2][2]}}</td>
      <td>{{mlResult.results.cmTrain.columnTotals[2]}}</td>
    </tr>
    <tr>
      <td>Total</td>
      <td>{{mlResult.results.cmTrain.rowTotals[0]}}</td>
      <td>{{mlResult.results.cmTrain.rowTotals[1]}}</td>
      <td>{{mlResult.results.cmTrain.rowTotals[2]}}</td>
      <td>{{mlResult.results.cmTrain.samples}}</td>
    </tr>
    </table>
  </mat-card>
  <mat-card class="card-border">
    <p>Confusion matrix for test data:</p>
    <table>
      <tr><td></td><td>C0</td><td>C1</td><td>C2</td><td>Total</td></tr>
      <tr>
        <td>R0</td>
        <td>{{mlResult.results.cmTest.matrix[0][0]}}</td>
        <td>{{mlResult.results.cmTest.matrix[1][0]}}</td>
        <td>{{mlResult.results.cmTest.matrix[2][0]}}</td>
        <td>{{mlResult.results.cmTest.columnTotals[0]}}</td>
      </tr>
      <tr>
        <td>R1</td>
        <td>{{mlResult.results.cmTest.matrix[0][1]}}</td>
        <td>{{mlResult.results.cmTest.matrix[1][1]}}</td>
        <td>{{mlResult.results.cmTest.matrix[2][1]}}</td>
        <td>{{mlResult.results.cmTest.columnTotals[1]}}</td>
      </tr>
      <tr>
        <td>R2</td>
        <td>{{mlResult.results.cmTest.matrix[0][2]}}</td>
        <td>{{mlResult.results.cmTest.matrix[1][2]}}</td>
        <td>{{mlResult.results.cmTest.matrix[2][2]}}</td>
        <td>{{mlResult.results.cmTest.columnTotals[2]}}</td>
      </tr>
      <tr>
        <td>Total</td>
        <td>{{mlResult.results.cmTest.rowTotals[0]}}</td>
        <td>{{mlResult.results.cmTest.rowTotals[1]}}</td>
        <td>{{mlResult.results.cmTest.rowTotals[2]}}</td>
        <td>{{mlResult.results.cmTest.samples}}</td>
      </tr>
    </table>
  </mat-card>
  </div>
</div>

<div style="height:600px" *ngIf="!mlResult">
  <mat-spinner></mat-spinner>
</div>
```

This template displays various ML results, including a result summary, classification results, and confusion matrices for both the training and test datasets.

This template also uses the following styling classes defined in the component's styling file:

```
// ch8-class-res.component.css file:
.cardList {
  display: flex;
  flex-direction: row;
  flex-wrap: wrap;
  justify-content: flex-start;
}

.card-border {
  margin: 10px;
  width: 400px;
  height: 400px;
}

table {
  border-collapse: collapse;
}

table, th, td {
  border: 1px solid lightgrey;
}

th, td {
  padding: 7px;
  text-align: center;
}

.mat-spinner {
  margin-left: 50%;
  margin-right: 50%;
}
```

In the following, I will use an example to demonstrate how to use the web service to perform KNN classification for stock moving direction.

Run the following command in a command prompt window:

```
ng g c chapter08/ch8-knn-class --module=app.module
```

This generates a new component named *ch8-knn-class* in the *ClientApp/src/app/chapter08* folder. Open the component class and replace its content with the following code:

```
// ch8-knn-class.component.ts file:
import { Component, OnInit } from '@angular/core';
import { Ch8Service } from '../../models/ch8.service';

@Component({
  selector: 'app-ch8-knn-class',
  templateUrl: './ch8-knn-class.component.html',
  styleUrls: ['./ch8-knn-class.component.css']
})
export class Ch8KnnClassComponent implements OnInit {
```

```
ticker = 'AMAT';
start: string = '2000-01-01';
end: string = '2015-12-31';
trainDate: string = '2014-12-31';
period: number = 14;
isNormalized: boolean = false;
windowSize: number = 3;
knum: number = 4;

constructor(private repository: Ch8Service) { }

ngOnInit() {
  this.getMlResult(this.ticker, this.start, this.end, this.period, this.trainDate,
    this.isNormalized, this.windowSize, this.knum);
}

get mlResult(): any {
  return this.repository.mlKnnClass;
}

getMlResult(ticker: string, start: string, end: string, period: number,
  trainDate: string, isNormalized: boolean, windowSize: number, knum: number) {
  this.repository.getMlKnnClass(ticker, start, end, period, trainDate,
  isNormalized, windowSize, knum);
  }
}
```

This component retrieves the KNN output from web service using the repository service created previously.

We also need to update the component's template file using the following code:

```
// ch8-knn-class.component.html file:
<h2>
  ch8-knn-class works!
</h2>

<mat-form-field>
  <input matInput placeholder="ticker" [(ngModel)]="ticker" name="ticker">
</mat-form-field>
<mat-form-field>
  <input matInput placeholder="start" [(ngModel)]="start" name="start">
</mat-form-field>
<mat-form-field>
  <input matInput placeholder="end" [(ngModel)]="end" name="end">
</mat-form-field>
<mat-form-field>
  <input matInput placeholder="trainDate" [(ngModel)]="trainDate" name="trainDate">
</mat-form-field>
<mat-form-field>
  <input matInput placeholder="period" [(ngModel)]="period" name="period">
</mat-form-field>
<mat-form-field>
  <input matInput placeholder="isNormalized" [(ngModel)]="isNormalized"
name="isNormalized">
</mat-form-field>
```

```
<mat-form-field>
  <input matInput placeholder="windowSize" [(ngModel)]="windowSize"
name="windowSize">
</mat-form-field>
<mat-form-field>
  <input matInput placeholder="knum" [(ngModel)]="knum" name="knum">
</mat-form-field>
<button mat-raised-button color="primary" (click)="getMlResult(ticker, start, end,
period,trainDate, isNormalized, windowSize, knum)">Get ML Result</button>
```

<app-ch8-class-res [mlResult]="mlResult"></app-ch8-class-res>

This template first defines the input fields required by the KNN computation and then displays various KNN output results using the common component called *ch8-class-res* that we created previously.

Finally, we need to add a path for this new component to the *RouterModule* of the root module (i.e., the *app.module.ts* file):

{ path: 'chapter08/ch8-knn-class, component: Ch8KnnClassComponent },

Then add the corresponding URL link to the *home* and *nav-menu* components.

Saving the project and navigating to the */chapter08/ch8-knn-class* page produce the default results shown in Fig.8-5.

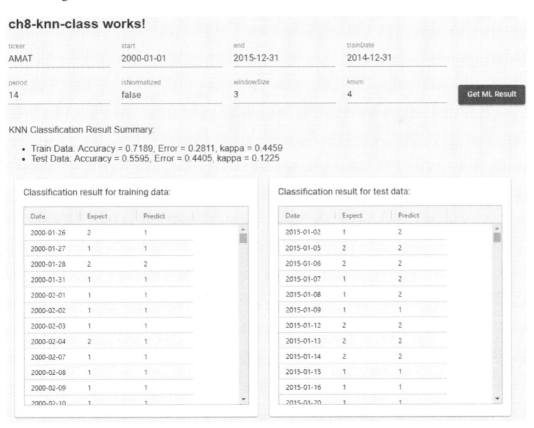

Fig.8-5. KNN classification results for AMAT.

You can see that the accuracy is 71.89% for the training data set and 55.95% for the test data set, which is a very good result for the prediction. However, this result depends strongly on the stock names, the training and prediction periods. Here, we will not concentrate on the prediction results, but on how to implement the machine learning approach in the ASP.NET Core Angular applications.

Confusion Matrix

In the field of machine learning, the confusion matrix, also known as the contingency table or the error matrix, is a specific table layout that allows you to examine the performance of a machine-learning algorithm. Each column of the matrix represents the instances in a predicted class while each row represents the instances in an actual class (or vice-versa). The simplest description of the machine-learning algorithm is the overall prediction accuracy, which is computed by dividing the total correctness (i.e., the sum of the major diagonal) by the total number of data records in the confusion matrix. In addition, accuracies of individual classes can be computed in a similar manner. However, this case is a little more complex in that we have a choice of dividing the number of correctness in that class by either the total number of records in the corresponding row or the corresponding column.

The *ch8-knn-class* component also displays two confusion matrices for training and test datasets respectively. Let us consider these two matrices with *the default parameters*, as shown in Figure 8-6.

		Predicted			
		C0	C1	C2	Total
Expected	R0	0	26	30	56
	R1	0	1288	538	1826
	R2	0	530	1345	1875
	Total	0	1844	1913	3757

		Predicted			
		C0	C1	C2	Total
Expected	R0	0	1	0	1
	R1	0	69	56	125
	R2	0	55	71	126
	Total	0	125	127	252

Fig.8-6. Confusion matrices for training data (left) and test data (right).

In the confusion matrix for the training data set, the total in each row represents the number of records for the expected (or actual) class. In this example, there are total of 56, 1826, and 1875 records for the expected class 0 (no market movement), 1 (market up), and 2 (market down), respectively. While the total in each column represents the number of records for the predicted class. You can see from Figure 8-6 that there are total of 0, 1844, and 1913 records for the predicted class 0, 1, and 2, respectively.

In this confusion matrix, of the 56 actual class 0, the KNN algorithm predicts that 0 are class 0, 26 are class 1, and 30 are class 2, which is really bad prediction for the training data set. However, of the 1826 actual class 1, it predicts that 0 is class 0, 1288 are class 1, and 538 are class 2; and of the 1875 actual class 2, it predicts that 0 is class 0, 530 are class 1, and 1345 are class 2, which is a reasonably good prediction.

In the confusion matrix for the test data set, of the 1 actual class 0, the KNN algorithm predicts that 1 for class 1. Of the 125 actual class 1, it predicts that 0 is class 0, 69 are class 1, and 56 are class 2. Of the 126 actual class 2, it predicts that 0 is class 0, 55 are class 1, and 71 are class 2.

You can see from these confusion matrices that the KNN algorithm has trouble to identify the class 0 (i.e., no market movement), but can make reasonably good prediction for the class 1 (market up) and class 2 (market down). All correct predictions are located in the diagonal of the shaded table, so it is easy to visually inspect the table for errors, as they will be represented by values outside the diagonal of the shaded table.

In Fig.8-5, we obtain the accuracy and error from the KNN outputs. In fact, we can extract the accuracy directly from the confusion matrices. We know from Fig.8-5 that the accuracies from the KNN algorithm are 0.7189 and 0.5595 for the training and test data sets respectively. We can extract the accuracy from the confusion matrix by dividing the total correctness (i.e., the sum of the major diagonal) by the total number of data records in the confusion matrix:

$$Accuracy_{training} = \frac{0 + 1315 + 1386}{3757} = 0.7189$$

$$Accuracy_{test} = \frac{0 + 70 + 71}{252} = 0.5595$$

Which are consistent with those obtained from the KNN outputs directly. You can see that the confusion matrix is a good description for the performance of the classification model on a set of test data for which the true classification values are known.

Support Vector Machine

In machine learning, the support vector machine (SVM) is a supervised learning model with associated algorithms that analyze data and recognize patterns, which can be used for both classification and regression analysis. SVM was originally used as a discriminative classifier defined by separating hyperplane. The SVM algorithm is based on finding the hyperplane that gives the largest minimum distance to the data points in the training data set. This distance is called margin in the SVM theory. Therefore, the optimal separating hyperplane maximizes the margin of the training data. In addition to performing linear classification, SVM can efficiently perform a non-linear classification using the kernel trick, implicitly mapping their inputs into high-dimensional feature space.

The large-margin separation and the kernel function are two key features of SVM. The large-margin separation means that only the relative position or similarity of the data points to each other is important. Such a similarity can be computed using a so-called kernel function. The simplest kernel function is the dot-product between two feature vectors (known as the linear kernel), which leads to a linear decision boundary between the two classes. Nonlinear kernels, such as the polynomial and Gaussian kernels, provide additional flexibility for large-margin separation between different classes.

SVM can be applied not only to the classification problems but also to the case of regression by introducing an alternative loss function. Still it contains all the main features that characterize maximum margin algorithm: a nonlinear function is learned by linear learning machine mapping into high dimensional kernel induced feature space. The loss function in SVM should be modified to include a distance measure. This type of function is often called epsilon intensive loss function. Using the epsilon intensive loss function ensures existence of the global minimum.

There are two steps for the SVM training. The first step is to transform input data to a high-dimensional feature space by specifying a kernel function. The next step is to solve a quadratic optimization problem to fit an optimal hyperplane to classify the transformed features into different classes. The number of transformed features is determined by the number of support vectors.

The SVM algorithm implemented in Accord.NET allows you to solve both the classification and regression problems. The algorithm also has several built-in kernel functions, including Gaussian, linear, polynomial, and sigmoid. In the following sections, I will show you how to use the SVM models in Accord.NET to predict the next day's stock prices.

SVM for Classification

In this section, I will use an example to illustrate how to use the SVM model in Accord.NET to predict the next day's stock price direction. This example looks very similar to the KNN method presented previously.

Add a new method called *GetSvmClassification* to the *MachineLearningHelper* class in the *Quant/Models* folder with the following code:

```
public static MlOutput GetSvmClassification(string ticker, string start, string end,
    int period, string maType, string trainDate, bool isNormalized, int windowSize)
{
    var ml = ProcessMLData(ticker, start, end, period, maType, "classification",
        trainDate, isNormalized, windowSize);

    var teacher = new MulticlassSupportVectorLearning<Linear>()
    {
        Learner = (p) => new LinearDualCoordinateDescent()
        {
            Loss = Loss.L2
        }
    };
    teacher.ParallelOptions.MaxDegreeOfParallelism = 1;
    var svm = teacher.Learn(ml.InputTrain, ml.OutputTrainClass);

    DataTable trainTable = new DataTable();
    trainTable.Columns.Add("Date", typeof(string));
    trainTable.Columns.Add("Expected", typeof(int));
    trainTable.Columns.Add("Predicted", typeof(int));
    DataTable testTable = trainTable.Clone();

    var trainResult = svm.Decide(ml.InputTrain);
    var testResult = svm.Decide(ml.InputTest);

    for (int i = 0; i < ml.OutputTrainClass.Length; i++)
    {
        trainTable.Rows.Add(ml.DateTrain[i].ToString("yyyy-MM-dd"),
            ml.OutputTrainClass[i], trainResult[i]);
    }
    for (int i = 0; i < ml.OutputTestClass.Length; i++)
    {
        testTable.Rows.Add(ml.DateTest[i].ToString("yyyy-MM-dd"),
        ml.OutputTestClass[i], testResult[i]);
    }

    var cmTrain = new GeneralConfusionMatrix(classes: 3,
        expected: ml.OutputTrainClass, predicted: trainResult);
    var cmTest = new GeneralConfusionMatrix(classes:3, expected: ml.OutputTestClass,
        predicted: testResult);
```

```
    return new MlOutput
    {
        TrainTable = trainTable,
        TestTable = testTable,
        CmTrain = cmTrain,
        CmTest = cmTest
    };
}
```

This method first retrieves processed ML data and then creates a one-vs-one multi-class SVM learning algorithm with a linear kernel function. Next, we train the SVM algorithm using the training inputs and training target. After creating the algorithm, we classify the results using the training and test data, and compute corresponding confusion matrices.

We can now convert the SVM results into a web service. Add a new method named *GetKnnResult* to the *MachineLearningValuesController* class in the *Quant/Controllers* folder with the following code:

```
[Route("~/api/mlSvm/{ticker}/{start}/{end}/{period}/{trainDate}/{isNormalized}
    /{windowSize}")]
[HttpGet]
public JsonResult GetSvmClassification(string ticker, string start, string end,
    int period, string trainDate, bool isNormalized, int windowSize)
{
    var res = MachineLearningHelper.GetSvmClassification(ticker, start, end, period,
        "sma", trainDate, isNormalized, windowSize);
    return Json(new { Name = "svm classification", Results = res });
}
```

To use SVM web service in Angular applications, we need to add a TypeScript method named *getMlSvmClass* to the *ch8.service.ts* file in the *ClientApp/src/app/models* folder with the following code:

```
mlSvmClass: any;
getMlSvmClass(ticker: string, start: string, end: string, period: number,
    trainDate: string, isNormalized: boolean, windowSize: number) {
    let url1 = this.url + 'api/mlsvm/' + ticker + '/' + start + '/' + end + '/'
        + period + '/' + trainDate + '/' + isNormalized + '/' + windowSize;
    this.http.get<any>(url1).subscribe(result => { this.mlSvmClass = result });
}
```

In the following, I will use an example to demonstrate how to use above service to perform SVM classification for stock moving direction.

Run the following command in a command prompt window:

ng g c chapter08/ch8-svm-class --module=app.module

This generates a new component named *ch8-svm-class* in the *ClientApp/src/app/chapter08* folder. Open the component class and replace its content with the following code:

```
// ch8-svm-class.component.ts file:
import { Component, OnInit } from '@angular/core';
import { Ch8Service } from '../../models/ch8.service';

@Component({
    selector: 'app-ch8-svm-class',
    templateUrl: './ch8-svm-class.component.html',
    styleUrls: ['./ch8-svm-class.component.css']
})
```

```
export class Ch8SvmClassComponent implements OnInit {
  ticker = 'AMAT';
  start: string = '2000-01-01';
  end: string = '2015-12-31';
  trainDate: string = '2014-12-31';
  period: number = 14;
  isNormalized: boolean = false;
  windowSize: number = 3;

  constructor(private repository: Ch8Service) { }

  ngOnInit() {
    this.getMlResult(this.ticker, this.start, this.end, this.period, this.trainDate,
      this.isNormalized, this.windowSize);
  }

  get mlResult(): any {
    return this.repository.mlSvmClass;
  }

  getMlResult(ticker: string, start: string, end: string, period: number,
    trainDate: string, isNormalized: boolean, windowSize: number) {
    this.repository.getMlSvmClass(ticker, start, end, period, trainDate,
      isNormalized, windowSize);
  }
}
```

This component retrieves the SVM output from web service using the repository created previously. It also defines a *colDefs* property that will be used to display the classification results using the *ag-Grid* component.

We also need to update the component's template with the following code:

```
// ch8-svm-class.component.html file:
<h2>
  ch8-svm-class works!
</h2>

<mat-form-field>
  <input matInput placeholder="ticker" [(ngModel)]="ticker" name="ticker">
</mat-form-field>
<mat-form-field>
  <input matInput placeholder="start" [(ngModel)]="start" name="start">
</mat-form-field>
<mat-form-field>
  <input matInput placeholder="end" [(ngModel)]="end" name="end">
</mat-form-field>
<mat-form-field>
  <input matInput placeholder="trainDate" [(ngModel)]="trainDate" name="trainDate">
</mat-form-field>
<mat-form-field>
  <input matInput placeholder="period" [(ngModel)]="period" name="period">
</mat-form-field>
<mat-form-field>
  <input matInput placeholder="isNormalized" [(ngModel)]="isNormalized"
name="isNormalized">
```

```
</mat-form-field>
<mat-form-field>
  <input matInput placeholder="windowSize" [(ngModel)]="windowSize"
name="windowSize">
</mat-form-field>
<button mat-raised-button color="primary" (click)="getMlResult(ticker, start, end,
period,trainDate, isNormalized, windowSize)">Get ML Result</button>
```

<app-ch8-class-res [mlResult]="mlResult"></app-ch8-class-res>

This template first defines the input fields required by the SVM computation and then displays various SVM output results using the common component called *ch8-class-res* that we created previously.

Finally, we need to add a path for this new component to the *RouterModule* of the root module (i.e., the *app.module.ts* file):

```
{ path: 'chapter08/ch8-svm-class, component: Ch8SvmClassComponent },
```

Then add the corresponding URL link to the *home* and *nav-menu* components.

Saving the project and navigating to the */chapter08/ch8-svm-class* page produce the default results shown in Fig.8-7.

ch8-svm-class works!

ticker	start	end	trainDate
AMAT	2000-01-01	2015-12-31	2014-12-31

period	isNormalized	windowSize	
14	false	3	Get ML Result

Classification Result Summary:

- Train Data: Accuracy = 0.5036, Error = 0.4964, kappa = 0.0149
- Test Data: Accuracy = 0.5317, Error = 0.4683, kappa = 0.0648

Classification result for training data:

Date	Expect	Predict
2000-01-26	2	2
2000-01-27	1	2
2000-01-28	2	2
2000-01-31	1	2
2000-02-01	1	2
2000-02-02	1	2
2000-02-03	1	2
2000-02-04	2	2
2000-02-07	1	2
2000-02-08	1	2
2000-02-09	1	2
2000-02-10	1	2

Classification result for test data:

Date	Expect	Predict
2015-01-02	1	2
2015-01-05	2	2
2015-01-06	2	2
2015-01-07	1	1
2015-01-08	1	1
2015-01-09	1	2
2015-01-12	2	2
2015-01-13	2	2
2015-01-14	2	1
2015-01-15	1	1
2015-01-16	1	2
2015-01-20	1	2

Confusion matrix for train data:

	C0	C1	C2	Total
R0	0	16	40	56
R1	0	432	1394	1826
R2	0	415	1460	1875
Total	0	863	2894	3757

Confusion matrix for test data:

	C0	C1	C2	Total
R0	0	1	0	1
R1	0	25	100	125
R2	0	17	109	126
Total	0	43	209	252

Fig.8-7. SVM classification results for AMAT.

SVM for Regression

As mentioned previously, we can also apply SVM to regression problems. Add a new method called *GetSvmRegression* to the *MachineLearningHelper.cs* class in the *Quant/Models* folder with the following code:

```
public static object GetSvmRegression(string ticker, string start, string end,
    int period, string maType, string trainDate, bool isNormalized, int windowSize)
{
    var ml = ProcessMLData(ticker, start, end, period, maType, "regression",
        trainDate, isNormalized, windowSize);

    var learn = new SequentialMinimalOptimizationRegression<Linear>()
    {
        Kernel = new Linear(),
        Complexity = 1
    };
    SupportVectorMachine<Linear> svm = learn.Learn(ml.InputTrain,
        ml.OutputTrain.SelectMany(x=>x).ToArray());

    DataTable trainTable = new DataTable();
    trainTable.Columns.Add("Date", typeof(string));
    trainTable.Columns.Add("Expected", typeof(double));
    trainTable.Columns.Add("Predicted", typeof(double));
    DataTable testTable = trainTable.Clone();
    var trainResult = svm.Score(ml.InputTrain);
    var testResult = svm.Score(ml.InputTest);

    for (int i = 0; i < ml.OutputTrain.Length; i++)
    {
        var target = NormalizedBack(ml.OutputTrain[i][0], ml.MinMax, isNormalized);
        var pred = NormalizedBack(trainResult[i], ml.MinMax, isNormalized);
        trainTable.Rows.Add(ml.DateTrain[i].ToString("yyyy-MM-dd"), target, pred);
    }
    for (int i = 0; i < ml.OutputTest.Length; i++)
    {
        var target = NormalizedBack(ml.OutputTest[i][0], ml.MinMax, isNormalized);
        var pred = NormalizedBack(testResult[i], ml.MinMax, isNormalized);
        testTable.Rows.Add(ml.DateTest[i].ToString("yyyy-MM-dd"),target, pred);
    }
```

```
        return new MlOutput
        {
            TrainTable = trainTable,
            TestTable = testTable,
            Errors = GetRegressionErrors(trainTable,testTable)
        };
}
```

This method first retrieves the processed ML data and then creates a sequential minimal optimization learner with the simplest *Linear* kernel, where we set *Complexity* = 1. Increasing the *Complexity* value forces the creation of a more accurate model that takes longer time to finish. You can also try the other kernel functions, such as *Polynomial* or *Gaussian*. Next, we run the SVM learning algorithm using the training dataset and compute the predicted scores for both the training and test datasets. Note that we use the *NormalizedBack* method to convert the SVM regression results back to original scale if the normalized data is used:

```
public static double NormalizedBack(double x, List<double> minMax,
    bool isNormalized)
{
    if (isNormalized) return minMax[0] + 0.5 * (minMax[1] - minMax[0]) * (1 + x);
    else return x;
}
```

Finally, we calculate various error functions using the *GetRegressionErrors* method with the following code:

```
public static List<double> GetRegressionErrors(DataTable trainTable,
    DataTable testTable)
{
    List<double> errors = new List<double>();
    var expect = trainTable.DefaultView.ToTable(false,
        "Expected").ToJagged().SelectMany(x => x).ToArray();
    var predict = trainTable.DefaultView.ToTable(false,
        "Predicted").ToJagged().SelectMany(x => x).ToArray();
    errors.Add(new SquareLoss(expect).Loss(predict) / (1.0 * expect.Length));
    expect = testTable.DefaultView.ToTable(false,
        "Expected").ToJagged().SelectMany(x => x).ToArray();
    predict = testTable.DefaultView.ToTable(false,
        "Predicted").ToJagged().SelectMany(x => x).ToArray();
    errors.Add(new SquareLoss(expect).Loss(predict) / (1.0 * expect.Length));
    errors.Add(GetRmse(trainTable));
    errors.Add(GetRmse(testTable));
    return errors;
}
```

Where the root-mean-square error (RMSE) is calculated using a private method called *GetRmse* with the following code:

```
private static double GetRmse(DataTable dt)
{
    double avg = dt.Compute("Avg(Expected)", "").To<double>();
    double mse = 0;
    foreach (DataRow row in dt.Rows)
    {
        double expected = row["Expected"].To<double>();
        double predicted = row["Predicted"].To<double>();
```

```
        mse += (expected - predicted) * (expected - predicted);
    }
    return Math.Sqrt(mse / dt.Rows.Count) / avg;
}
```

We can now convert the *GetSvmRegression* method into a web service. Add a new method named *GetSvmRegr* to the *MeachineLearningValueController* class in the *Quant/Controllers* folder with the following code:

```
[Route("~/api/mlSvmRegr/{ticker}/{start}/{end}/{period}/{trainDate}/{isNormalized}
    /{windowSize}")]
[HttpGet]
public JsonResult GetSvmRegr(string ticker, string start, string end, int period,
    string trainDate, bool isNormalized, int windowSize)
{
    var res = MachineLearningHelper.GetSvmRegression(ticker, start, end, period,
        "sma", trainDate, isNormalized, windowSize);
    return Json(new { Name = "svm regression", Results = res });
}
```

To use the SVM regression web service in Angular applications, we need to add a method named *getSvmRegr* to the *ch8.service.ts* file in the *ClientApp/src/app/models* folder with the following code:

```
getMlSvmRegr(ticker: string, start: string, end: string, period: number,
    trainDate: string, isNormalized: boolean, windowSize: number): Observable<any> {
    let url1 = this.url + 'api/mlsvmregr/' + ticker + '/' + start + '/' + end +
        '/' + period + '/' + trainDate + '/' + isNormalized + '/' + windowSize;
    return this.http.get<any>(url1);
}
```

Note that this method is different from those we used previously, where we assigned the result from web service to a property. Here, the *getMlSvmRegr* method returns a promise, which allows you to execute your code sequentially. Since SVM regression may take a longer time (few minutes for example), we need to wait for the regression to finish before updating UI using the regression results.

Now, I will use an example to illustrate how to use this web service in an Angular application. First, we want to create a common component called *ch8-regr-chart* that will be used to display the regression results graphically. Run the following statement in a command prompt window:

ng g c chapter08/ch8-regr-chart --module=app.module

Open the component class file and replace its content with the following code:

```
// ch8-regr-chart.component.ts file:
import { Component, OnInit, Input, OnChanges } from '@angular/core';

@Component({
    selector: 'app-ch8-regr-chart',
    templateUrl: './ch8-regr-chart.component.html',
    styleUrls: ['./ch8-regr-chart.component.css']
})
export class Ch8RegrChartComponent implements OnInit, OnChanges {
    @Input() title: string;
    @Input() mlData: any;
    options: any;

    constructor() { }
```

```
ngOnInit() {
  this.options = this.getOptions(this.mlData, this.title);
}

ngOnChanges() {
  this.options = this.getOptions(this.mlData, this.title);
}

getOptions(mlData: any, title: string) {
  let data1 = [];
  let data2 = [];
  mlData.forEach(function (d) {
    data1.push([d.date, d.expected]);
    data2.push([d.date, d.predicted]);
  });

  return {
    legend: {
      top: '8%',
      right: 20
    },
    grid: {
      left: '15%',
      right: '5%',
      bottom: 50
    },
    title: {
      text: title,
      left: 'center'
    },
    tooltip: {
      trigger: 'axis',
      axisPointer: {
        type: 'cross'
      },
      backgroundColor: 'rgba(120, 120, 120, 0.9)',
      borderWidth: 1,
      borderColor: '#aaa',
      padding: 10,
      textStyle: {
        color: 'white'
      }
    },
    xAxis: {
      type: 'category',
      name: 'Date',
      nameLocation: 'center',
      nameGap: 30,
      boundaryGap: false,
    },
    yAxis: {
      type: 'value',
      name: 'Stock Price',
      nameLocation: 'center',
```

```
          nameGap: 40,
          scale: true,
        },
        series: [{
          name: 'Expected',
          type: 'scatter',
          data: data1,
          symbol: 'circle',
          symbolSize: 6,
          zlevel: 0
        },
        {
          name: 'Predicted',
          type: 'line',
          data: data2,
          showSymbol: false,
          zlevel: 10
        }
        ]
    };
  }
}
```

This component takes the *title* and *mlData* as input, which contains the expected and predicted data from ML regression. The *options* property, specified using the *getOptions* method, will be used to create a chart (using ECharts) that displays the expected and predicted stock prices.

The template for this component is very simple:

```
// ch8-regr-chart.html file:
<div echarts [options]="options" style="height:100%"></div>
```

Now, run the following command in a command prompt window:

ng g c chapter08/ch8-svm-regr --module=app.module

This generates a new component called *ch8-svm-regr*. Open this component class file and replace its content with the following code:

```
// ch8-svm-regr.component.ts file:
import { Component, OnInit } from '@angular/core';
import { Ch8Service } from '../../models/ch8.service';

@Component({
  selector: 'app-ch8-svm-regr',
  templateUrl: './ch8-svm-regr.component.html',
  styleUrls: ['./ch8-svm-regr.component.css']
})
export class Ch8SvmRegrComponent implements OnInit {
  ticker = 'IBM';
  start: string = '2016-01-01';
  end: string = '2018-12-31';
  trainDate: string = '2017-12-31';
  period: number = 14;
  isNormalized: boolean = false;
  windowSize: number = 2;
```

```
  titleTrain: string;
  titleTest: string;
  mlResult: any;

  colDefs = [
    { headerName: "Date", field: "date", width: 100 },
    { headerName: "Expect", field: "expected", width: 100 },
    { headerName: "Predict", field: "predicted", width: 100 },
  ];

  constructor(private repository: Ch8Service) { }

  ngOnInit() {
    this.getMlResult(this.ticker, this.start, this.end, this.period, this.trainDate,
      this.isNormalized, this.windowSize);
  }

  getMlResult(ticker: string, start: string, end: string, period: number,
    trainDate: string, isNormalized: boolean, windowSize: number) {
    this.mlResult = null;
    this.titleTrain = ticker + ": Regression for Training Data";
    this.titleTest = ticker + ":  Regression for Test Data";
    this.repository.getMlSvmRegr(ticker, start, end, period, trainDate,
      isNormalized, windowSize).subscribe(result => {
      this.mlResult = result;
    });
  }
}
```

This component retrieves the SVM regression output from web service using the repository created previously. Inside the *getMlResult* method, we use the promise to reset the *mlResult* property from null to the regression result. If we use the old repository method without promise, it is impossible to reset mlResult because it is a *get*-only property.

This component also defines a *colDefs* property that will be used to display the results using the *ag-Grid* component.

We also need to update the component's template file using the following code:

```
// ch8-svm-regr.component.html file:
<h2>
  ch8-svm-regr works!
</h2>
<mat-form-field>
  <input matInput placeholder="ticker" [(ngModel)]="ticker" name="ticker">
</mat-form-field>
<mat-form-field>
  <input matInput placeholder="start" [(ngModel)]="start" name="start">
</mat-form-field>
<mat-form-field>
  <input matInput placeholder="end" [(ngModel)]="end" name="end">
</mat-form-field>
<mat-form-field>
  <input matInput placeholder="trainDate" [(ngModel)]="trainDate" name="trainDate">
</mat-form-field>
<mat-form-field>
```

```
  <input matInput placeholder="period" [(ngModel)]="period" name="period">
</mat-form-field>
<mat-form-field>
  <input matInput placeholder="isNormalized" [(ngModel)]="isNormalized"
name="isNormalized">
</mat-form-field>
<mat-form-field>
  <input matInput placeholder="windowSize" [(ngModel)]="windowSize"
name="windowSize">
</mat-form-field>
<button mat-raised-button color="primary" (click)="getMlResult(ticker, start, end,
  period,trainDate, isNormalized, windowSize)">Get ML Result</button>

<div *ngIf="mlResult">
  <br />{{ticker}}: Train Data: Error = {{mlResult.results.errors[0].toFixed(6)}},
  RMSE = {{mlResult.results.errors[2].toFixed(6)}} |
  Test Data: Error = {{mlResult.results.errors[1].toFixed(6)}},
  RMSE = {{mlResult.results.errors[3].toFixed(6)}}

  <div class="cardList">
    <mat-card class="card-border">
      <p>Regression result for training data:</p>
      <ag-grid-angular style="height:90%" class="ag-theme-balham"
        [rowData]="mlResult.results.trainTable" [columnDefs]="colDefs">
      </ag-grid-angular>
    </mat-card>
    <mat-card class="card-border">
      <app-ch8-regr-chart [title]="titleTrain" [mlData]=
        "mlResult .results.trainTable"></app-ch8-regr-chart>
    </mat-card>
    <mat-card class="card-border">
      <p>Regression result for test data:</p>
      <ag-grid-angular style="height:90%" class="ag-theme-balham"
        [rowData]="mlResult.results.testTable" [columnDefs]="colDefs">
      </ag-grid-angular>
    </mat-card>
    <mat-card class="card-border">
      <app-ch8-regr-chart [title]="titleTest" [mlData]
        ="mlResult.results.testTable"></app-ch8-regr-chart>
    </mat-card>
  </div>
</div>

<div style="height:600px" *ngIf="!mlResult">
  <mat-spinner></mat-spinner>
</div>
```

This template first defines the input fields required by the SVM regression and then displays various regression results, including regression errors, regression results for both the training and test datasets. Note that the highlighted code snippet shows how we use the *app-ch8-regr-chart* directive to display the regression results.

This template also uses the following styling classes defined in the component's styling file:

```
// ch8-svm-regr.component.css file:
.cardList {
```

```
  display: flex;
  flex-direction: row;
  flex-wrap: wrap;
  justify-content: flex-start;
}

.card-border {
  margin: 10px;
  width: 400px;
  height: 400px;
}

.mat-spinner {
  position: relative;
  margin-left: 50%;
  margin-right: 50%;
}
```

Finally, we need to add a path for this new component to the *RouterModule* of the root module (i.e., the *app.module.ts* file):

```
{ path: 'chapter08/ch8-svm-regr, component: Ch8SvmRegrComponent },
```

Then add the corresponding URL link to the *home* and *nav-menu* components.

Saving the project and navigating to the */chapter08/ch8-svm-regr* page produce the default results shown in Fig.8-8.

You can see that the SVM regression gives a reasonably good prediction for the next day's stock price. You can perform SVM regression for any stock ticker traded in the US equity market by specifying different sets of input parameters.

Artificial Neural Networks

In machine learning, artificial neural networks (ANNs), also called deep learning techniques, are a family of models inspired by biological neural networks. ANNs are generally presented as systems of interconnected neurons that exchange massages between each other. The connections have numeric weights that can be tuned based on experience, making neural nets adaptive to inputs and capable of learning.

In numeric computation and related symbol manipulation, the modern computers usually outperform humans. However, humans can intuitively solve complex perceptual problems much more quickly than the world's fastest computer does. For instance, human can easily recognize a man in a crowd from a mere glimpse of his face. Why is there such a remarkable difference in their performance? This is because the fact that the biological neural system is completely different from the von Neumann architecture of computers.

Inspired by biological neural networks, ANNs are massively parallel computing systems consisting of an extremely large number of simple processors with many interconnections. ANN models attempt to use some organizational principles believed to be used in the human brain. However, the human brain as a whole is far too complex to model. Rather, ANNs study individual cells that make up the human brain.

ch8-svm-regr works!

ticker	start	end	trainDate
IBM	2016-01-01	2018-12-31	2017-12-31

period	isNormalized	windowSize	
14	false	2	Get ML Result

IBM: Train Data: Error = 0.005534, RMSE = 0.010614 | Test Data: Error = 0.021011, RMSE = 0.015639

Regression result for training data:

Date	Expect	Predict
2016-01-26	122.589996	122.871687...
2016-01-27	120.959999	123.343488...
2016-01-28	122.220001	121.626473...
2016-01-29	124.790001	122.974977...
2016-02-01	124.830002	125.420924...
2016-02-02	122.940002	125.227435...
2016-02-03	124.720001	123.333902...
2016-02-04	127.650002	125.244487...
2016-02-05	128.570007	128.008706...
2016-02-08	126.980003	128.758447...
2016-02-09	124.07	127.092107...
2016-02-10	120.190002	124.541816

Regression result for test data:

Date	Expect	Predict
2018-01-02	154.25	153.521662...
2018-01-03	158.490005	154.388556...
2018-01-04	161.699997	158.600813...
2018-01-05	162.490005	161.623991...
2018-01-08	163.470001	162.238735...
2018-01-09	163.830002	163.259169...
2018-01-10	164.179993	163.617581...
2018-01-11	164.199997	163.965720...
2018-01-12	163.139999	164.030165...
2018-01-16	163.850006	163.100901...
2018-01-17	168.649994	163.940672...
2018-01-18	169.119995	168.785511

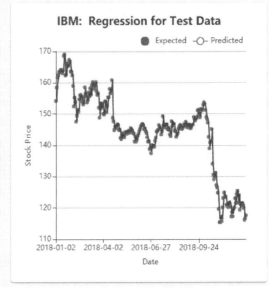

Fig.8-8. SVM regression results for IBM.

Introduction to Neural Networks

ANN is basically a mathematical model of what goes in our brain. Let us consider a supervised learning problem where we have access to labeled training examples (x_i, y_i). ANNs provide a way of defining a complex, nonlinear form of hypotheses $h_{W,b}(x)$, with the weight W and bias b parameters that we can fit to our data.

The simplest possible ANN consists of a single neuron, as shown in Fig.8-9.

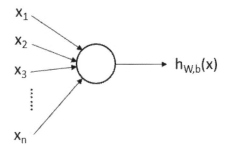

Fig.8-9. The simplest ANN with a single neuron.

This neuron is a computational unit that takes $(x_1, x_2, \ldots, x_n)$ as inputs. The output $h_{W,b}(x)$ can be written in the form:

$$h_{W,b}(x) = f\left(\sum_{i=1}^{n} W_i x_i + b\right)$$

Where f is called the activation function, which limits the output of a neuron. The activation function plays an important role in the schema of a neuron. It can be chosen as a unit step, piecewise linear, sigmoid, or Gaussian function. The sigmoid function is by far the most frequently used in ANNs. It is a strictly increasing function, which exhibits smoothness and has the desired asymptotic properties. The standard sigmoid function is the logistic function, defined by

$$f(z) = \frac{1}{1 + e^{-z}}$$

Thus, the single neuron corresponds exactly to the input-output mapping defined by logistic regression.

Another popular activation function in deep learning is the rectified linear unit (ReLU), which is given by a piecewise formula:

$$f(z) = \max(0, z) = \begin{cases} z & \text{if } z > 0 \\ 0 & \text{otherwise} \end{cases}$$

Which is unbounded on the axis of positive activation values. In this case, you do not need to scale the inputs and outputs to a certain range to perform ANN analysis. It has been demonstrated that ReLU enables better and faster training for deep-learning neural networks, compared to the other widely used activation functions, including sigmoid and tanh functions. Currently, ReLU finds applications in computer version, speech recognition, stock market predictions, etc. using deep neural networks.

We can construct a neural network by hooking many of the simple neurons so that the output of a neuron can be the input of another, as shown in Fig.8-10.

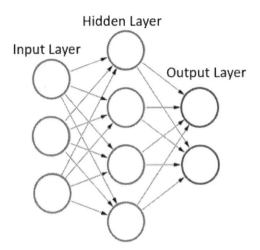

Fig. 8-10. A multilayer neural network.

In Fig.8-10, each circle represents a neuron and an arrow represents a connection from the output of one neuron to the input of another. We call the leftmost layer of the network the input layer, the rightmost layer the output layer, and the middle layer of nodes the hidden layer.

In this section, we will use the so-called multilayer feed forward network that is the best choice for predicting the stock price movement. In a feed forward ANN, neurons are only connected forward. Each layer of the neural network contains connections to the next layer, but there are no connections back, as shown in Fig.8-10. Multilayer feed forward ANNs use a variety of learning techniques, the most popular being back-propagation, where the weights and biases are updated in the direction of the negative gradient of predefined error-function and the error is then fed back through the network. Using this information, the algorithm adjusts the weights of each connection in order to reduce the value of the error function by some small amount. After repeating this process for a sufficiently large number of training cycles, the network will usually converge to some state where the error of the calculations is small. In this case, one would say that the network has learned a certain target function.

One of the problem with the back-propagation training algorithm is the speed of convergence and the possibility of ending up in a local minimum of the error function. In order to overcome this difficulty, the resilient back-propagation (Rprop), Levenberg-Marquardt (LM), evolutionary, and other learning algorithms have been introduced. Rprop algorithm is a modification of the back-propagation. It uses only the sign of the partial derivative to determine the direction of the weight update multiplied by the step size. The LM algorithm, also known as the damped least-squares method, is used to solve nonlinear least squares problems. It blends the steepest gradient decent method and the Gauss-Newton algorithm. The basic idea of the LM algorithm is that it performs a combined training process: around the area with complex curvature, the LM algorithm switches to the steepest decent algorithm, until the local curvature is proper to make a quadratic approximation; then it approximately becomes the Gauss-Newton algorithm, which can speed up the convergence significantly. The LM algorithm is usually used for training small- and medium-sized ANN problems. The evolutionary learning is based on genetic algorithms. For a given neural network, it creates a population of chromosomes, which represent neural network's weights. Then, during the learning process, the genetic population evolves and weights are set to the source neural network.

 In this section, we will use all of these four algorithms to train the ANNs and predict the next day's stock price.

Helper Classes

Neural networks can be applied to both classification and regression problems and involve many input and output parameters. In order to simplify the process, we will define some helper classes and methods before performing any analysis using neural networks.

Add following three classes to the *MachineLearningHelper.cs* file in the *Quant/Models* folder:

```
public class AnnInput
{
    public string Ticker { get; set; }
    public string Start { get; set; }
    public string End { get; set; }
    public int Period { get; set; }
    public string TrainDate { get; set; }
    public bool IsNormalized { get; set; }
    public int WindowSize { get; set; }
    public string LearningType { get; set; }
    public int Seed { get; set; }
    public double LearningRate { get; set; }
    public double Momentum { get; set; }
    public int PopulationSize { get; set; }
    public int Iterations { get; set; }
    public double Loss { get; set; }
}

public class AnnData
{
    public MlInput MlInput { get; set; }
    public ISupervisedLearning Teacher { get; set; }
    public ActivationNetwork Network { get; set; }
}

public class AnnOutput
{
    public MlOutput MlOutput { get; set; }
    public List<object[]> LossFunction { get; set; }
    public string Status { get; set; }
}
```

These classes will be used when setting up the input parameters, processing the neural network data, and returning outputs.

We also need to implement a TypeScript model that corresponds to the C# *AnnInput* class. Add a TypeScript class named *ml.model.ts* in the *ClientApp/src/app/models* folder with the following code:

```
export class AnnInputModel {
  constructor(
    public ticker: string,
    public start: string,
    public end: string,
    public period: number,
```

```
    public trainDate: string,
    public isNormalized: boolean,
    public windowSize: number,
    public learningType: string,
    public seed: number,
    public learningRate: number,
    public momentum: number,
    public populationSize: number,
    public iterations: number,
    public loss: number
  ) { }
}
```

Next, add a helper method named *GetAnnData* to the *MachineLearningHelper* class in the *Quant/Models* folder with the following code:

```
public static AnnData GetAnnData(AnnInput model, string mlType)
{
    Accord.Math.Random.Generator.Seed = model.Seed;
    var ml = ProcessMLData(model.Ticker, model.Start, model.End, model.Period,
        "sma", mlType, model.TrainDate, model.IsNormalized, model.WindowSize);

    IActivationFunction af = null;
    if (model.IsNormalized) af = new BipolarSigmoidFunction(2.0);
    else af = new RectifiedLinearFunction();
    var net = new ActivationNetwork(af, 3 * model.WindowSize, 6 * model.WindowSize,
        mlType.Contains("cla") ? 3 : 1);

    NguyenWidrow initializer = new NguyenWidrow(net);
    initializer.Randomize();
    ISupervisedLearning teacher = null;
    model.LearningType = model.LearningType.ToLower();
    if (model.LearningType.Contains("leven")) // Levenberg-Marquardt
    {
        teacher = new LevenbergMarquardtLearning(net)
        {
            LearningRate = model.LearningRate
        };
    }
    else if (model.LearningType.Contains("back")) // BackPropagation
    {
        teacher = new BackPropagationLearning(net)
        {
            LearningRate = model.LearningRate,
            Momentum = model.Momentum
        };
    }
    else if (model.LearningType.Contains("res")) // Resilient Backpropagation
    {
        teacher = new ResilientBackpropagationLearning(net)
        {
            LearningRate = model.LearningRate,
        };
    }
    else if (model.LearningType.Contains("evo")) // Evolutionary
    {
```

```
        teacher = new EvolutionaryLearning(net, model.PopulationSize);
    }

    return new AnnData
    {
        MlInput = ml,
        Teacher = teacher,
        Network = net
    };
}
```

This method prepares data for both classification and regression using ANNs. It takes an *AnnInput* object as the input argument, which contains a variety of input parameters required by the market data processing and neural network training. The method first retrieves the processed ML data by calling the *ProcessMLData* method and then introduces two different activation functions, *bipolar sigmoid* (or tanh) and *rectified linear* (or ReLU) functions, which will be used for normalized data and unscaled data respectively. Next, it creates a multi-layer neural network and randomizes the network heuristically using the Nguyen window. We then create four learning algorithms for the network using the *Levenberg-Marquardt*, *Back Propagation*, *Resilient Back Propagation*, and *Evolutionary* learning algorithms.

Neural Networks for Classification

In this section, we will consider how to use the neural network classification to predict the next day's stock price direction. Training a neural network is complicated and time consuming. It is better to monitor the progress in real-time. To this end, we will use the SignalR streaming capability to monitor the loss function during the process of training the neural network.

In order to use SignalR to monitor the progress of neural network training in real time, we need to create a SignalR Hub class. Add a new Hub class called *Ch8Hub.cs* in the *Quant/Hubs* folder with the following code:

```
using Accord;
using Accord.Math;
using Accord.Math.Optimization.Losses;
using Accord.Statistics.Analysis;
using Microsoft.AspNetCore.SignalR;
using Quant.Models;
using System;
using System.Collections.Generic;
using System.Data;
using System.Linq;
using System.Threading;
using System.Threading.Channels;
using System.Threading.Tasks;

namespace Quant.Hubs
{
    public class Ch8Hub : Hub
    {
        public ChannelReader<AnnOutput> SendAnnClassResult(AnnInput model,
            CancellationToken token)
        {
            var channel = Channel.CreateUnbounded<AnnOutput>();
            _ = GetAnnClassResult(channel.Writer, model, token);
```

```csharp
        return channel.Reader;
    }


    private async Task GetAnnClassResult(ChannelWriter<AnnOutput> writer,
        AnnInput model, CancellationToken token)
    {
        var ann = MachineLearningHelper.GetAnnData(model, "classification");
        var ml = ann.MlInput;
        var outputTrain = Jagged.OneHot(ml.OutputTrainClass);
        var samples = outputTrain.Length;
        var res = new AnnOutput();

        res.Status = "starting";
        res.LossFunction = new List<object[]>();
        double loss = 10000.0;
        int iteration = 0;
        while (iteration <= model.Iterations)
        {
            token.ThrowIfCancellationRequested();
            if (loss < model.Loss) break;
            loss = ann.Teacher.RunEpoch(ml.InputTrain, outputTrain) / samples;
            if (iteration % 5 == 0)
            {
                res.LossFunction.Add(new object[] { iteration, loss });
                await writer.WriteAsync(res);
                await Task.Delay(100, token);
            }
            iteration++;
        }
        res.Status = "finished";

        DataTable trainTable = new DataTable();
        trainTable.Columns.Add("Date", typeof(string));
        trainTable.Columns.Add("Expected", typeof(int));
        trainTable.Columns.Add("Predicted", typeof(int));
        DataTable testTable = trainTable.Clone();

        int answer;
        double[] comp;
        double response;
        int[] trainResult = new int[samples];
        int[] testResult = new int[ml.OutputTestClass.Length];

        for (int i = 0; i < samples; i++)
        {
            comp = ann.Network.Compute(ml.InputTrain[i]);
            response = comp.Max(out answer);
            trainResult[i] = answer;
            trainTable.Rows.Add(ml.DateTrain[i].ToString("yyyy-MM-dd"),
                ml.OutputTrainClass[i], answer);
        }
        for (int i = 0; i < ml.OutputTestClass.Length; i++)
        {
            comp = ann.Network.Compute(ml.InputTest[i]);
```

```
                response = comp.Max(out answer);
                testResult[i] = answer;
                testTable.Rows.Add(ml.DateTest[i].ToString("yyyy-MM-dd"),
                    ml.OutputTestClass[i], answer);
            }
            var cmTrain = new GeneralConfusionMatrix(classes: 3,
                expected: ml.OutputTrainClass, predicted: trainResult);
            var cmTest = new GeneralConfusionMatrix(classes: 3,
                expected: ml.OutputTestClass, predicted: testResult);

            res.MlOutput = new MlOutput
            {
                TrainTable = trainTable,
                TestTable = testTable,
                CmTrain = cmTrain,
                CmTest = cmTest,
            };
            var istrue = true;
            while (istrue)
            {
                await Task.Delay(100);
                if (res.Status == "finished")
                {
                    await writer.WriteAsync(res);
                    istrue = false;
                }
            }
            writer.TryComplete();
        }
    }
}
```

Here, the *Ch8Hub* inherits from the SignalR *Hub* class. The *SendAnnClassResult* method can be called by any connected client. A hub method automatically supports a streaming hub method when it returns a **ChannelReader<T>** or a **Task<ChannelReader<T>>**. Inside the *GetAnnClassResult* method, we first retrieve the processed neural network data from the *GetAnnData* method implemented in the *MachineLearningHelper* class previously and then stream each iteration's loss function value of training the neural network within a *while* loop in every 100 milliseconds.

The learning process of the neural network is controlled by either the iterations or the loss. After training the network, we can classify new instances by calling the *ann.Network.Compute* method and extracting the results using the *Max* method. We perform this calculation and extract the confusion matrices for both the training and prediction datasets. Finally, we stream ANN results via the SignalR Hub.

Next, we need to convert our SignalR Hub into a service in Angular. Add the following highlighted code to the *signalr.service.ts* file in the *ClientApp/src/app/models* folder:

```
// signalr.service.ts file:
import { HubConnection, HubConnectionBuilder, IStreamResult } from
  '@aspnet/signalr';
import { AnnInputModel } from '../models/ml.model';

@Injectable({
  providedIn: 'root'
})
```

```
export class Ch5HubService {
  private connection: HubConnection;

  constructor() {
    this.connection = new HubConnectionBuilder().withUrl('/ch5Hub').build();
    this.connection.start();
  }

  startStream(ticker: string, start: string, end: string, interval: number):
IStreamResult<any> {
    if (this.connection.state == 0) this.connection.start();
    return this.connection.stream("SendStock", ticker, start, end, interval);
  }
}

@Injectable({
  providedIn: 'root'
})
export class Ch8AnnClassHubService {
  private connection: HubConnection;

  constructor() {
    this.connection = new HubConnectionBuilder().withUrl('/ch8Hub').build();
    this.connection.start();
  }

  startStream(model: AnnInputModel): IStreamResult<any> {
    if (this.connection.state == 0) this.connection.start();
    return this.connection.stream("SendAnnClassResult", model);
  }
}
```

The *Ch8AnnClassHubService* class is similar to the *Ch5HubService* class that was used in creating real-time stock charts in Chapter 5. Inside the constructor, we define and start the connection, which is responsible for creating connection with the SignalR hub, while the *startStream* method calls the *SendAnnClassResult* method defined in server to subscribe the stream data.

Now, we can use an example to test the SignalR service. Run the following command in a command prompt window from the *ClientApp* directory:

ng g c chapter08/ch8-ann-class --module=app.module

This creates a new component named *ch8-ann-class* in the *ClientApp/src/app/chapter08* folder. Open the component class file and replace its content with the following code:

```
// ch8-ann-class.component.ts file:
import { Component, OnInit } from '@angular/core';
import { Ch8AnnClassHubService } from '../../models/signalr.service';
import { AnnInputModel } from '../../models/ml.model';

@Component({
  selector: 'app-ch8-ann-class',
  templateUrl: './ch8-ann-class.component.html',
  styleUrls: ['./ch8-ann-class.component.css']
})
export class Ch8AnnClassComponent implements OnInit {
```

```
ticker = 'AMAT';
start: string = '2000-01-01';
end: string = '2015-12-31';
trainDate: string = '2014-12-31';
period: number = 14;
isNormalized: boolean = true;
windowSize: number = 3;
learningType: string = 'levenbergMarquardt';
seed: number = 3;
learningRate: number = 0.1;
momentum: number = 0.1;
populationSize: number = 100;
iterations: number = 100;
loss: number = 0.001;

private model: AnnInputModel;
private subscription: any;
private data: any;
options: any;
updateOptions: any;

mlResult: any;

constructor(private service: Ch8AnnClassHubService) { }

ngOnInit() {
}

getMlResult(ticker: string, start: string, end: string, period: number,
  trainDate: string, isNormalized: boolean, windowSize: number,
  learningType: string, seed: number, learningRate: number, momentum: number,
  populationSize: number, iterations: number, loss: number) {

  this.data = [];
  this.options = this.getOptions(this.data);
  this.model = new AnnInputModel(ticker, start, end, period, trainDate,
    isNormalized, windowSize, learningType, seed, learningRate, momentum,
    populationSize, iterations, loss);

  this.subscription = this.service.startStream(this.model).subscribe({
      next: (item) => {
        if (item.status == 'starting') {
          this.data = item.lossFunction;
          this.updateOptions = {
            series: [{ data: this.data }]
          }
        } else if (item.status == 'finished') {
          this.mlResult = { results: item.mlOutput };
        }
      },
      complete: () => {
      },
      error: (err) => {
        console.log(err);
      }
```

```
      });
  }

  stopService() {
    this.subscription.dispose();
  }

  getOptions(data: any) {
    return {
      title: {
        text: 'Loss Function',
        left: 'center'
      },
      grid: {
        right: 50
      },
      xAxis: {
        type: 'value',
        name: 'epoch',
      },
      yAxis: {
        type: 'value',
        name: 'loss',
        scale: true,
      },
      series: [
        {
          name: 'loss',
          type: 'line',
          data: data,
          showSymbol: false,
        }
      ]
    }
  }
}
```

In order to use the SignalR service, this component's constructor injects the *Ch8AnnClassHubService* defined in the *signalr.service.ts* file. Inside the *getMlResult* method, we first define the options specified by the *getOptions* method. Next, we call the SignalR service's *startStream* method that returns an *IStreamResult*, which contains a subscribe method; and pass an *IStreamSubscriber* to *subscribe* and set the *next*, *error*, and *complete* callbacks to get notifications from the stream invocation.

In the *next* section, we can access the stream loss function via *item.lossFunction*. In the real-time loss function chart, we only need to update the data for the *series*. After completing the training process for the neural network, we retrieve the final results via *item.mlOutput* and assign it to the *mlResult* property.

To stop the SignalR service, we implement a *stopService* method where we end the stream by calling the *dispose* method on the *ISubscription* that is returned from the *subscribe* method. Calling this *dispose* method will cause the *CancellationToken* parameter of the *Hub* method to be cancelled.

Now, we need to update the component's template with the following code:

```
// ch8-ann-class.component.html file:
<h2>
  ch8-ann-class works!
```

```
</h2>

<mat-form-field>
  <input matInput placeholder="ticker" [(ngModel)]="ticker" name="ticker">
</mat-form-field>
<mat-form-field>
  <input matInput placeholder="start" [(ngModel)]="start" name="start">
</mat-form-field>
<mat-form-field>
  <input matInput placeholder="end" [(ngModel)]="end" name="end">
</mat-form-field>
<mat-form-field>
  <input matInput placeholder="trainDate" [(ngModel)]="trainDate" name="trainDate">
</mat-form-field>
<mat-form-field>
  <input matInput placeholder="period" [(ngModel)]="period" name="period">
</mat-form-field>
<mat-form-field>
  <input matInput placeholder="isNormalized" [(ngModel)]="isNormalized"
name="isNormalized">
</mat-form-field>
<mat-form-field>
  <input matInput placeholder="windowSize" [(ngModel)]="windowSize"
name="windowSize">
</mat-form-field>
<mat-form-field>
  <mat-select [(value)]="learningType">
    <mat-option value="levenbergMarquardt">Levenberg-Marquardt</mat-option>
    <mat-option value="backPropagation">Backpropagation</mat-option>
    <mat-option value="resilientBackpropagation">Resilient Backpropagation</mat-
option>
    <mat-option value="evolutionary">Evolutionary</mat-option>
  </mat-select>
</mat-form-field>
<mat-form-field *ngIf="!learningType.includes('evo')" >
  <input matInput placeholder="learningRate" [(ngModel)]="learningRate"
name="learningRate">
</mat-form-field>
<mat-form-field *ngIf="learningType.includes('back')" >
  <input matInput placeholder="momentum" [(ngModel)]="momentum" name="momentum">
</mat-form-field>
<mat-form-field *ngIf="learningType.includes('evo')" >
  <input matInput placeholder="populationSize" [(ngModel)]="populationSize"
name="populationSize">
</mat-form-field>
<mat-form-field>
  <input matInput placeholder="iterations" [(ngModel)]="iterations"
name="iterations">
</mat-form-field>
<mat-form-field>
  <input matInput placeholder="loss" [(ngModel)]="loss" name="loss">
</mat-form-field>
<mat-form-field>
  <input matInput placeholder="seed" [(ngModel)]="seed" name="seed">
</mat-form-field>
```

```
<button mat-raised-button color="primary" (click)="getMlResult(ticker, start, end,
  period, trainDate, isNormalized, windowSize, learningType, seed, learningRate,
  momentum, populationSize, iterations, loss)">Get ML Result</button>
<button mat-raised-button color="primary" style="margin-left:10px"
  (click)="stopService()">Stop Computation</button>
```

<div echarts [options]="options" [merge]="updateOptions" style="height:350px;
width:450px;margin-top:30px"></div>
<app-ch8-class-res *ngIf="mlResult" [mlResult]="mlResult"></app-ch8-class-res>

This template first defines various input parameters required for retrieving market data and training neural networks, and then creates a line chart to monitor the progress in real time. Finally, it displays the ANN results using an *app-ch8-class-res* directive implemented previously.

Finally, we need to add a path for this new component to the *RouterModule* of the root module (i.e., the *app.module.ts* file):

{ path: 'chapter08/ch8-ann-class, component: Ch8AnnClassComponent },

Then add the corresponding URL link to the *home* and *nav-menu* components.

Saving the project, navigating to the */chapter08/ch8-ann-class* page, and clicking the *Get ML Result* button produce the default results shown in Fig.8-11 and Fig.8-12.

Fig.8-11. Monitor neural network training in real time.

Classification Result Summary:

- Train Data: Accuracy = 0.5888, Error = 0.4112, kappa = 0.1897
- Test Data: Accuracy = 0.5357, Error = 0.4643, kappa = 0.0742

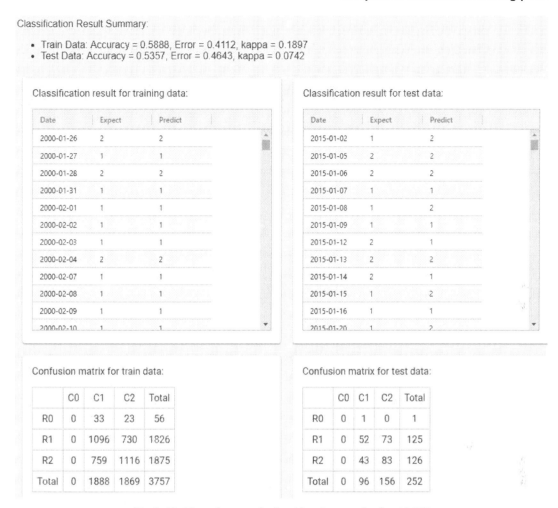

Fig.8-12. Neural network classification results for AMAT.

Neural Network for Regression

ANNs are commonly used for classification because of the relationship to logistic regressions: they typically use a logistic activation function and output values from 0 to 1 (sigmoid) or from -1 to $+1$ (bipolar sigmoid) like logistic regression. However, the worth of ANNs to model complex, nonlinear hypothesis is desirable for many real world problems, including regression.

Note that the outputs from ANNs have a limited range $[-1, +1]$ for bipolar sigmoid activation function while they have no limitation in the positive axis for the ReLU activation function. Here, we will use both functions to solve regression problems with neural network. Therefore, if the bipolar sigmoid function is used, you must use the normalized data to training the neural network, while for the ReLU function, you can use the original data directly.

Be careful when you use the ANNs with the bipolar sigmoid activation function to predict the stock price values. You can make prediction using the trained ANNs when the future stock price you want to predict is within the range of your training data set. However, if the future price is beyond the range of your training data set, (say, it will reach the historical high or low), your prediction will get cutoff, i.e., you cannot get reasonable prediction in this case. That is different from the other machine learning algorithms, such as SVM. SVM has a kernel function (linear, polynomial, etc.), and it can always extrapolate the results using the kernel function even the future price is beyond the range of the training data set. The reason for ANNs cannot make correct prediction in this case is that they use the activation function with a limited range. In order to solve this problem, you can always use the ReLU function instead.

Add the following two methods to the *Ch8Hub* class in the *Quant/Hubs* folder with the following code:

```
public ChannelReader<AnnOutput> SendAnnRegrResult(AnnInput model,
    CancellationToken token)
{
    var channel = Channel.CreateUnbounded<AnnOutput>();
    _ = GetAnnRegrResult(channel.Writer, model, token);
    return channel.Reader;
}


private async Task GetAnnRegrResult(ChannelWriter<AnnOutput> writer, AnnInput model,
    CancellationToken token)
{
    var ann = MachineLearningHelper.GetAnnData(model, "regression");
    var ml = ann.MlInput;
    var samples = ml.OutputTrain.Length;
    var res = new AnnOutput();
    res.Status = "starting";
    res.LossFunction = new List<object[]>();
    double loss = 10000.0;
    int iteration = 0;
    while (iteration <= model.Iterations)
    {
        token.ThrowIfCancellationRequested();
        if (loss < model.Loss) break;
        loss = ann.Teacher.RunEpoch(ml.InputTrain, ml.OutputTrain) / samples;
        if (iteration % 5 == 0)
        {
            res.LossFunction.Add(new object[] { iteration, loss });
            await writer.WriteAsync(res);
            await Task.Delay(100, token);
        }
        iteration++;
    }
    res.Status = "finished";
    DataTable trainTable = new DataTable();
    trainTable.Columns.Add("Date", typeof(string));
    trainTable.Columns.Add("Expected", typeof(double));
    trainTable.Columns.Add("Predicted", typeof(double));
    DataTable testTable = trainTable.Clone();

    for (int i = 0; i < samples; i++)
    {
        var pred1 = ann.Network.Compute(ml.InputTrain[i])[0];
        var target = MachineLearningHelper.NormalizedBack(ml.OutputTrain[i][0],
            ml.MinMax, model.IsNormalized);
```

```
        var pred = MachineLearningHelper.NormalizedBack(pred1, ml.MinMax,
            model.IsNormalized);
        trainTable.Rows.Add(ml.DateTrain[i].ToString("yyyy-MM-dd"), target, pred);
    }
    for (int i = 0; i < ml.OutputTest.Length; i++)
    {
        var pred1 = ann.Network.Compute(ml.InputTest[i])[0];
        var target = MachineLearningHelper.NormalizedBack(ml.OutputTest[i][0],
            ml.MinMax, model.IsNormalized);
        var pred = MachineLearningHelper.NormalizedBack(pred1, ml.MinMax,
            model.IsNormalized);
        testTable.Rows.Add(ml.DateTest[i].ToString("yyyy-MM-dd"), target, pred);
    }
    res.MlOutput = new MlOutput
    {
        TrainTable = trainTable,
        TestTable = testTable,
        Errors = MachineLearningHelper.GetRegressionErrors(trainTable, testTable)
    };
    var istrue = true;
    while (istrue)
    {
        await Task.Delay(100);
        if (res.Status == "finished")
        {
            await writer.WriteAsync(res);
            istrue = false;
        }
    }
    writer.TryComplete();
}
```

These methods are very similar to those we used for ANN classification presented in the preceding section. The *SendAnnRegrResult* method can be called by any connected client. Inside the *GetAnnRegrResult* method, we first retrieve the processed neural network data from the *GetAnnData* method implemented in the *MachineLearningHelper* class previously and then stream each iteration's loss function value of training the neural network within a *while* loop in every 100 milliseconds.

The learning process of the neural network is controlled by either the iterations or the loss. After training the network, we calculate the regression values for new instances by calling the *ann.Network.Compute* method and convert the results back if the normalized data was used. We perform this calculation and extract the error functions for both the training and prediction datasets. Finally, we stream ANN results via the SignalR Hub.

Next, we need to convert our SignalR Hub into a service in Angular. Add the following highlighted code to the *signalr.service.ts* file in the *ClientApp/src/app/models* folder:

```
// signalr.service.ts file:
import { HubConnection, HubConnectionBuilder, IStreamResult } from
  '@aspnet/signalr';
import { AnnInputModel } from '../models/ml.model';

// ... other classes omitted for brevity ...

@Injectable({
```

```
  providedIn: 'root'
})
export class Ch8AnnRegrHubService {
  private connection: HubConnection;

  constructor() {
    this.connection = new HubConnectionBuilder().withUrl('/ch8Hub').build();
    this.connection.start();
  }

  startStream(model: AnnInputModel): IStreamResult<any> {
    if (this.connection.state == 0) this.connection.start();
    return this.connection.stream("SendAnnRegrResult", model);
  }
}
```

The *Ch8AnnRegrHubService* class is similar to the *Ch8AnnClassHubService* class that was used in ANN classification in the preceding section. Inside the constructor, we define and start the connection, which is responsible for creating connection with the SignalR hub, while the *startStream* method calls the *SendAnnRegrResult* method defined in server to subscribe the stream data.

Now, we can use an example to test the SignalR service. Run the following command in a command prompt window from the *ClientApp* directory:

ng g c chapter08/ch8-ann-regr --module=app.module

This creates a new component named *ch8-ann-regr* in the *ClientApp/src/app/chapter08* folder. Open the component class file and replace its content with the following code:

```
// ch8-ann-regr.component.ts file:
import { Component, OnInit } from '@angular/core';
import { Ch8AnnRegrHubService } from '../../models/signalr.service';
import { AnnInputModel } from '../../models/ml.model';

@Component({
  selector: 'app-ch8-ann-regr',
  templateUrl: './ch8-ann-regr.component.html',
  styleUrls: ['./ch8-ann-regr.component.css']
})
export class Ch8AnnRegrComponent implements OnInit {
  ticker = 'IBM';
  start: string = '2010-01-01';
  end: string = '2015-12-31';
  trainDate: string = '2014-12-31';
  period: number = 14;
  isNormalized: boolean = true;
  windowSize: number = 3;
  learningType: string = 'levenbergMarquardt';
  seed: number = 3;
  learningRate: number = 0.1;
  momentum: number = 0.1;
  populationSize: number = 100;
  iterations: number = 50;
  loss: number = 0.00001;

  private model: AnnInputModel;
```

```typescript
private subscription: any;
private data: any;
options: any;
updateOptions: any;

mlResult: any;
colDefs = [
  { headerName: "Date", field: "date", width: 100 },
  { headerName: "Expect", field: "expected", width: 100 },
  { headerName: "Predict", field: "predicted", width: 100 },
];

constructor(private service: Ch8AnnRegrHubService) { }

ngOnInit() {
}

getMlResult(ticker: string, start: string, end: string, period: number,
  trainDate: string, isNormalized: boolean, windowSize: number,
  learningType: string, seed: number, learningRate: number, momentum: number,
  populationSize: number, iterations: number, loss: number) {

  this.data = [];
  this.options = this.getOptions(this.data);
  this.model = new AnnInputModel(ticker, start, end, period, trainDate,
    isNormalized, windowSize, learningType, seed, learningRate,
    momentum, populationSize, iterations, loss);

  this.subscription = this.service.startStream(this.model).subscribe({
      next: (item) => {
        this.mlResult = null;
        if (item.status == 'starting') {
          this.data = item.lossFunction;
          this.updateOptions = {
            series: [{ data: this.data }]
          }
        } else if (item.status == 'finished') {
          this.mlResult = { results: item.mlOutput };
        }
      },
      complete: () => {
      },
      error: (err) => {
        console.log(err);
      }
    });
}

stopService() {
  this.subscription.dispose();
}

getOptions(data: any) {
  return {
    title: {
```

```
      text: 'Loss Function',
      left: 'center'
    },
    grid: {
      right: 50
    },
    xAxis: {
      type: 'value',
      name: 'epoch',
    },
    yAxis: {
      type: 'value',
      name: 'loss',
      scale: true,
    },
    series: [
      {
        name: 'loss',
        type: 'line',
        data: data,
        showSymbol: false,
      }
    ]
  }
}
}
```

This component is very similar to that used for ANN classification in the preceding section. Inside the *getMlResult* method, we first define the options specified by the *getOptions* method. Next, we call the SignalR service's *startStream* method that returns an *IStreamResult*, which contains a subscribe method; and pass an *IStreamSubscriber* to *subscribe* and set the *next*, *error*, and *complete* callbacks to get notifications from the stream invocation.

In the *next* section, we can access the stream loss function via *item.lossFunction*. In the real-time loss function chart, we only need to update the data for the *series*. After completing the training process for the neural network, we retrieve the final results via *item.mlOutput* and assign it to the *mlResult* property.

To stop the SignalR service, we implement a *stopService* method where we end the stream by calling the *dispose* method on the *ISubscription* that is returned from the *subscribe* method. Calling this *dispose* method will cause the *CancellationToken* parameter of the *Hub* method to be cancelled.

Now, we need to update the component's template with the following code:

```
// ch8-ann-regr.component.html file:
<h2>
  ch8-ann-regr works!
</h2>
<mat-form-field>
  <input matInput placeholder="ticker" [(ngModel)]="ticker" name="ticker">
</mat-form-field>
<mat-form-field>
  <input matInput placeholder="start" [(ngModel)]="start" name="start">
</mat-form-field>
<mat-form-field>
  <input matInput placeholder="end" [(ngModel)]="end" name="end">
</mat-form-field>
```

```html
<mat-form-field>
  <input matInput placeholder="trainDate" [(ngModel)]="trainDate" name="trainDate">
</mat-form-field>
<mat-form-field>
  <input matInput placeholder="period" [(ngModel)]="period" name="period">
</mat-form-field>
<mat-form-field>
  <input matInput placeholder="isNormalized" [(ngModel)]="isNormalized"
name="isNormalized">
</mat-form-field>
<mat-form-field>
  <input matInput placeholder="windowSize" [(ngModel)]="windowSize"
name="windowSize">
</mat-form-field>
<mat-form-field>
  <mat-select [(value)]="learningType">
    <mat-option value="levenbergMarquardt">Levenberg-Marquardt</mat-option>
    <mat-option value="backPropagation">Backpropagation</mat-option>
    <mat-option value="resilientBackpropagation">Resilient Backpropagation
    </mat-option>
    <mat-option value="evolutionary">Evolutionary</mat-option>
  </mat-select>
</mat-form-field>
<mat-form-field *ngIf="!learningType.includes('evo')">
  <input matInput placeholder="learningRate" [(ngModel)]="learningRate"
name="learningRate">
</mat-form-field>
<mat-form-field *ngIf="learningType.includes('back')">
  <input matInput placeholder="momentum" [(ngModel)]="momentum" name="momentum">
</mat-form-field>
<mat-form-field *ngIf="learningType.includes('evo')">
  <input matInput placeholder="populationSize" [(ngModel)]="populationSize"
    name="populationSize">
</mat-form-field>
<mat-form-field>
  <input matInput placeholder="iterations" [(ngModel)]="iterations"
    name="iterations">
</mat-form-field>
<mat-form-field>
  <input matInput placeholder="loss" [(ngModel)]="loss" name="loss">
</mat-form-field>
<mat-form-field>
  <input matInput placeholder="seed" [(ngModel)]="seed" name="seed">
</mat-form-field>

<button mat-raised-button color="primary" (click)="getMlResult(ticker, start, end,
  period, trainDate, isNormalized, windowSize, learningType, seed, learningRate,
  momentum, populationSize, iterations, loss)">Get ML Result</button>
<button mat-raised-button color="primary" style="margin-left:10px"
  (click)="stopService()">Stop Computation</button>

<div echarts [options]="options" [merge]="updateOptions"
style="height:350px;width:450px;margin-top:30px"></div>

<div *ngIf="mlResult">
```

```
<br />{{ticker}}: Train Data: Error = {{mlResult.results.errors[0].toFixed(6)}},
    RMSE = {{mlResult.results.errors[2].toFixed(6)}} |
    Test Data: Error = {{mlResult.results.errors[1].toFixed(6)}},
    RMSE = {{mlResult.results.errors[3].toFixed(6)}}

<div class="cardList">
  <mat-card class="card-border">
    <p>Regression result for training data:</p>
    <ag-grid-angular style="height:90%" class="ag-theme-balham"
      [rowData]="mlResult.results.trainTable" [columnDefs]="colDefs">
    </ag-grid-angular>
  </mat-card>
  <mat-card class="card-border">
    <app-ch8-regr-chart [title]="titleTrain"
      [mlData]="mlResult.results.trainTable"></app-ch8-regr-chart>
  </mat-card>
  <mat-card class="card-border">
    <p>Regression result for test data:</p>
    <ag-grid-angular style="height:90%" class="ag-theme-balham"
      [rowData]="mlResult.results.testTable" [columnDefs]="colDefs">
    </ag-grid-angular>
  </mat-card>
  <mat-card class="card-border">
    <app-ch8-regr-chart [title]="titleTest"
      [mlData]="mlResult.results.testTable"></app-ch8-regr-chart>
  </mat-card>
</div>
</div>
```

This template first defines various input parameters required for retrieving market data and training neural networks, and then creates a line chart to monitor the progress in real time. Next, it displays various regression results, including regression errors and regression results for both the training and test datasets. Note that the highlighted code snippet shows how we use the *app-ch8-regr-chart* directive to display the regression results.

This template also uses the following styling classes defined in the component's styling file:

```
// ch8-ann-regr.component.css file:
.cardList {
  display: flex;
  flex-direction: row;
  flex-wrap: wrap;
  justify-content: flex-start;
}

.card-border {
  margin: 10px;
  width: 400px;
  height: 400px;
}
```

Now, we need to add a path for this new component to the *RouterModule* of the root module (i.e., the *app.module.ts* file):

```
{ path: 'chapter08/ch8-ann-regr, component: Ch8AnnRegrComponent },
```

Then add the corresponding URL link to the *home* and *nav-menu* components.

Saving the project, navigating to the */chapter08/ch8-ann-regr* page, and clicking the *Get ML Result* button produce the default results shown in Fig.8-13 and Fig.8-14.

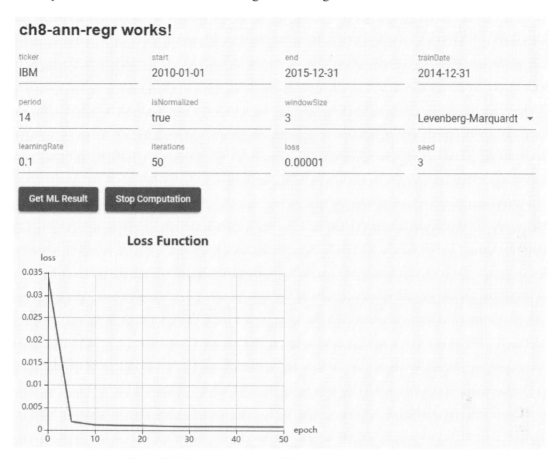

Fig.8-13. Monitor progress of ANN regression in real time.

Fig.13 shows the loss function as a function of iteration (epoch), which is used to monitor the progress of the ANN regression in real time. This is very useful when you perform an ANN regression that takes a long time.

Note from Fig.8-14 that for IBM with normalized data (*isNormalized* is set to *true* in Fig.8-13), our trained network with the 5-year training period (from 1/1/2010 to 12/31/2014) gives reasonable predictions for next one year (from 1/1/2015 to 12/31/2015). This is because the range of our prediction data is covered by our training data. However, if the prediction data are beyond the range of the training data, the network will not give good predictions. For example, using the same training and prediction periods as used for IBM, you will obtain very bad predictions for JPM, as shown in Figure 8-15.

Fig.8-14. ANN regression results for IBM with normalized data.

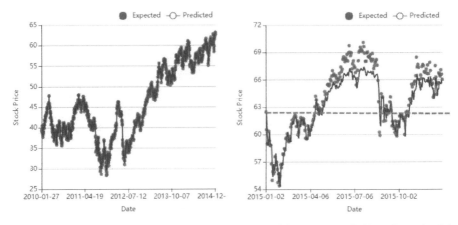

Fig.8-15. ANN regression for JPM using bipolar sigmoid for training (left) and test (right) data.

You can see that when the prediction data are beyond the range of the training data, that is, above 62 in this example (above the dashed line), the neural network fails to make prediction. As discussed previously, in order to make reasonable predictions for the prediction data beyond the range of the training data set, you need to use the ReLU activation function with unscaled data.

Now, running the same regression for JPM by setting the *isNormalized* property to false generates the results shown in Fig.8-16.

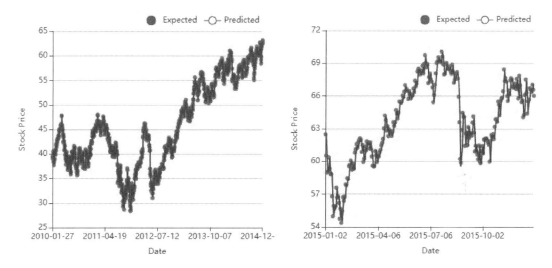

Fig.8-16. ANN regression for JPM with ReLU for training (left) and test (right) data.

You can see from Fig.8-16 that the ANN regression with a ReLU activation function can always extrapolate the results even the future stock price in the test dataset is beyond the range of the training dataset.

The examples presented in this chapter are used for demonstration purpose only. In order to apply ANNs to real-world stock market, you may need to include much more features than the stock prices and moving average, such as other indicators, volume, PE ratio, volatility, risk premium, interest rate, S&P 500 index, and other sector related data. In our examples, we only use a single hidden layer to construct the neural network, whereas for more complicated real-world problems, you may need multiple hidden layers. However, by following the procedure presented in our examples, you should be able to apply the neural network and other machine learning techniques to your financial applications without any difficulty.

Chapter 9
Options Pricing

Options are derivative contracts that give the holder the right, but not the obligation, to buy or sell the underlying instrument at a specified price on or before a specified future date. Although the buyer of the option is not obligated to exercise the option, the option seller has an obligation to buy or sell the underlying instrument if the option is exercised. Option trading can provide a variety of benefits including the security of limited risk and the advantage of leverage. Before you start trading options, it is important to understand the factors that determine the value of an option. In this chapter, I will show you how to pricing options.

Introduction to Options

An option, just like a stock or bond, is a security. It is also a binding contract with strictly defined terms and properties. The underlying assets of an option can be stocks, stock indices, currencies, debt instruments, commodities, etc. Options are security derivatives because they derive their value from an underlying asset.

There are two basic types of options: calls and puts. A call option gives the holder the right to buy an underlying asset at a certain price within a specific period of time. The call options are similar to having a long position on a stock. Buyers of the call options hope that the stock will increase before the option expires. A put option gives the holder the right to sell an asset at a certain price within a specific period of time. The put options are very similar to having a short position on a stock. Buyers of the put options hope that the price of the stock will fall before the option expires. There are four types of participants in option markets: buyers of calls, sellers of calls, buyers of puts, and sellers of puts.

The price in the option contract is called the exercise price or strike price; the total cost of an option is called the premium; the date in the contract is called the expiration date, exercise date, or maturity. Options can be categorized into two types: American options and European options according to their exercise characteristics. American options can be exercised at any time between the date of purchase and expiration date. Most exchange-traded options are American options. European options can only be exercised on the expiration date. Both American and European options are standard derivatives or "plain vanilla" options. Other types of options are called exotic or non-standard derivatives, which include Asian, Lookback, and Barrier options among others. Please note that the distinction between American and European options has nothing to do with geographic location.

Option Payoffs

As mentioned previously, a European call (put) option gives the holder the right but not the obligation to buy (sell) the underlying asset with an initial price S, at a given maturity date T, and for a fixed price (strike) K. Let the price of a European call (put) option be denoted by c (p). The payoff of a European call at maturity time T is:

$$c = \max(S_T - K, 0)$$

Where S_T is the price of the underlying asset at maturity. If $S_T < K$, the call will be worthless and the holder will not exercise the right. The payoff of a European put is

$$p = \max(K - S_T, 0)$$

If $S_T > K$, the put will be worthless and the holder will not exercise the right. The call-put parity is the relationship between a European call and put, given by

$$c + Ke^{-rt} = p + S$$

Where r is the risk free interest rate and S the underlying asset price.

American call (put) option gives the holder the right but not the obligation to buy (sell) the underlying asset at any time t $(0 < t < T)$ between the date of purchase and expiration date T, for a strike price K. Let the price of the American call (put) option be denoted by C (P). The payoff of an American call (put) at maturity T is the same as that of corresponding European option. The price boundary and put-call parity for the American option is given by

$$S - K \leq C - P \leq S - Ke^{-rt}$$

Option Value

In option pricing, the value of an option is a function of both the underlying asset and time, $c_t = f(S_t, t)$. The calculation of the option price (premium) is the option buyers' prime concern. The premium is the fair value of an option contract determined in the competitive market, which the option buyers pay to the option writer (seller).

The intrinsic value of a call option is $\max(S_t - K, 0)$ and that of the put option is $\max(K - S_t, 0)$ for $0 < t < T$. This value represents the profit and loss (P&L) you can make by immediately exercising the option. The time value of a call is the difference between the price of the call and its intrinsic value. The time value of an option decreases as the time approaches expiration. The European options do not have time value because they can only be exercised at maturity, at which the time value of the option becomes zero.

The sum of an option intrinsic and time values is the total value of an option. The intrinsic value is the possible profit resulting from selling the option at the current time and does not take a negative value. If the current value of the underlying asset is lower than the strike price the intrinsic value of the call vanishes. For instance, if the premium of a stock call option is $5.5 and the price of the stock is $100 with a strike price of $97, the intrinsic value is $3 and the time value is $2.5. When an option is in-the-money (ITM), the intrinsic value is non-zero. When the strike price is the same as the spot price, the option is at-the-money (ATM) and the intrinsic is zero. Otherwise, the option is out-of-the-money (OTM) when the underlying asset is priced cheaper than the call option's strike price.

Although options have a reputation for being more risky investments that only expert traders or financial institution can understand, they can be useful to the individual investor. Options can provide several key advantages as listed below:

- *Cost Efficiency*: Options have great leveraging power. As such, you can obtain an option position that will mimic a stock position almost identically, but at a huge cost savings. For instance, in order to buy 100 shares of a $100 stock, you must pay out $10,000. However, if you were to buy one $20 call (with each contract representing 100 shares), the total outlay would be only $2,000. You would then have an additional $8,000 to use at your discretion. Of course, it is not quite as simple as that. You have to pick the right call option to purchase in order to mimic the stock position properly. However, this strategy, known as stock replacement, is not only viable but also practical and cost efficient.

- *Less Risk*: People usually believe that buying options is riskier than owning equities, but there are also times when options can be used to reduce risk. It really depends on how you use them. Options can be less risky because they require less financial commitment than equities, and they can also be less risky due to their relative imperviousness to the potentially catastrophic effects of gap openings. Options are the most dependable form of hedge, and this also makes them safer than stocks. When you purchase stocks, a stop-loss-order is frequently placed to protect the position. The stop order is designed to stop losses below a predetermined price. The problem with these orders lies in the nature of the order itself. It is still possible for a considerable loss if the stock has a sudden drop because your order will become a market order when the price drops below the predetermined price level. Had you purchased a put option for protection, you would not have had to suffer the catastrophic loss. Unlike stop-loss orders, options do not shut down when the market closes. They give you insurance 24 hours a day, seven days a week. This is something that stop orders cannot do. This is why options are considered a dependable form of hedging.

- *Possible Higher Returns*: It is easy to figure out that if you spend much less money and make almost the same profit, you will have a higher percentage return. When they pay off, that is what options typically offer to you.

QuantLib

In my previous published book "*Practical C# and WPF for Financial Markets*", I implemented several models from scratch to pricing various options including vanilla European and American options as well as exotic barrier options. You can follow the sample procedure provided in that book to implement some simple Black-Scholes models by yourself. This way, you will get a better understanding on how the algorithm of pricing options works. Even if you are working in a quant group within a financial institution where you do not need to create the pricing engine from scratch, implementing some programming functions for pricing simple vanilla options is always a good practice. This will give you confidence when you use the pricing engines provided by commercial package, internal libraries, or free-source tools.

Options, especially the exotic derivatives, are complex security instruments and usually do not have analytic solutions. You have to use different approximations or various numerical approaches to price them. It is almost impossible to create pricing engines by your own for pricing various complex instruments. In this chapter, I will show you how to use a free open-source tool, QuantLib, to price options.

QuantLib has been used as a base reference for modeling various financial instruments. It is a free open-source library for trading strategy development and risk management in real-life. It is written in C++

with a clean object model, and is then exported to different languages (including C#), which are automatically generated using SWIG (simplified wrapper and interface generator). I should point out that QuantLib SWIG C# version does not have 100 percent support for all of the features in original QuantLib. Some .NET developers started a new QlNet project and have being trying to port QuantLib to .NET by writing the code in C# directly. Again, QlNet cannot access the full features in QuantLib, and is quite limited in some areas. In this regards, QuantLib SWIG C# has much more features than QlNet.

In this book, I will use the latest QuantLib version as a pricing engine. At the time of writing, the latest version of QuantLib SWIG C# is 1.14. You can download it from the following URL:

`https://bintray.com/quantlib/releases/QuantLib-SWIG`

and build your own binary following the instruction provided with the download. Here, for your convenience, I have created the binary files that are included in the *Quant* project, as shown in Fig.9-1.

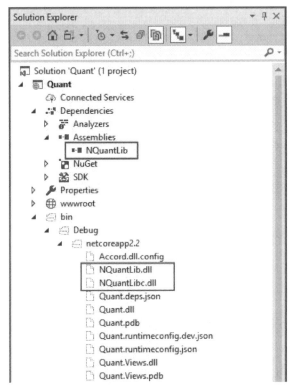

Fig.9-1. Include the QuantLib SWIG binary files.

Here, we add two files, *NQuantLib.dll* and *NQuantLibc.dll*, to the *Quant/bin/Debug/netcoreapp2.2* folder and then include the SWIG C# wrapper file, *NQuantLib.dll*, in *Dependencies*. The *NQuantLibc.dll* file is the native QuantLib C++ component, which is required to access QuantLib features.

After installing the QuantLib SWIG C# package, we can now use it to pricing various options.

Dates, Calendars, and Day Counters

In order to process financial data, the software packages, such as QuantLib, require an efficient way of dealing with dates, time periods, and calendars. QuantLib provides several helper classes in order to support this feature.

Date in QuantLib represents a day, which can lie between 1/1/1901 and 12/31/2199. Internally dates are stored in the same way as they are stored in Microsoft Excel, by an integer number that counts the days from 1/1/1900. By not allowing any dates before 1901, QuantLib avoids the leap year bug of Excel, in which the year 1900 is counted as a leap year. You can initialize dates using Excel data number, or by explicitly stating the day, month, and year:

```
Date date1 = new Date(25, Month.November, 2015);
Date date2 = new Date(42333);
```

The above variables, *date1* and *date2*, represent the same date: 11/25/2015. You can query more information from *Date*:

```
date1.weekdayNumber();   //output: 4
date1.weekday();         //output: Wednesday
date1.dayOfMonth();      //output: 25
date1.dayOfYear();       //output: 329
date1.serialNumber();    //output: 42333
```

It is also possible to add and subtract time periods to or from dates by adding or subtracting an integer. This integer represents the number of days by which the date should be shifted:

```
Date newDate = date1 + 5; //output: 11/30/2015
newDate = date1 - 5;      //output: 11/20/2015
```

In order to handle date intervals, QuantLib defines the *Period* class. This class stores an arbitrary time period corresponding to a full number of days. You can create *Period* object using an integer number and a time unit, or using a frequency. In QuantLib, available time units are *Days, Weeks, Months,* and *Years*; while available frequencies are *Daily, Weekly, Biweekly, EveryFourthWeek, Monthly, Bimonthly, Quarterly, EveryFourthMonth, Semiannual, Annual, Once,* and *NoFrequency*. All of these identifiers can be used to construct the corresponding periods. There are a few accessor methods that let you access the values stored in the period, including *length()*, *units()*, and *frequency()*:

```
Period p1 = new Period(5, TimeUnit.Weeks);     //p1.length()= 5, p1.units()=Weeks
Period p2 = new Period(Frequency.Bimonthly);   //p2.length()= 2, p2.units()=Months
newDate = date1.Add(p1);                       //output: 12/30/2015
```

One of the crucial objects in finance is a calendar for different countries, which shows the holidays, business days, and weekends for the respective country. In QuantLib, a calendar for US can be set up easily by

```
Calendar cal = new UnitedStates();
```

Various other calendars are available, for instance, UK, Germany, Switzerland, Ukraine, Turkey, China, Japan, Canada, Australia, etc. In addition, special exchange calendars can be initialized for several countries. You can also query information about a calendar or a particular date in context of a calendar using various methods:

```
Calendar cal = new Germany(Germany.Market.FrankfurtStockExchange);
Date d = new Date(6, Month.December, 2015);
cal.name();              //output: Frankfurt stock exchange
cal.isBusinessDay(d);    //output: False
```

```
cal.isHoliday(d);                    //output: True
cal.isEndOfMonth(d);                 //output: False
```

You can also adjust calendars by adding or removing user defined holidays using the *addHoliday* and *removeHoliday* methods.

In order to perform financial calculations involving date intervals, day counting conventions have to be properly taken care of. QuantLib handles these using several helper classes based on the *DayCounter* interface. There are a number of predefined day counters in QuantLib, which should be sufficient for most calculations. These predefined day counters include:

- *SimpleDayCounter*: This day counter does not correspond to any conversion in the real world. It is used for theoretical calculations only.

- *Thirty360*: implements the 30/360 day counting convention and its variations. In the pure 30/360 convention a starting date on or after the 30th of a month becomes the 30th of that month. An ending date on the 31st becomes the 1st of the following month if the starting date is before the 30th of a month, otherwise the ending date will become the 30th of its month. This variant is called the USA or *BondBasis* variant. The European variant of the 30/360, the 30E/360 convention will always shift the ending date to the 30th of its month if it falls on the 31st.

- *Actual360*: implements the Actual/360 day count convention.

- *Actual365Fixed*: implements the Actual/365 (fixed) day count convention.

- *ActualActual*: implements the Actual/Actual day count convention and its variants. The ISDA convention, which is the same as Actual/Actual (Historical), Actual/Actual, and Actual/365.

- *Business252*: implements the Business252 day count convention used in Brazil. By default, this convention uses the Brazil calendar but any other calendar can be passed in the constructor.

Term Structures in QuantLib

In a well-known Black-Scholes model for European vanilla options, we usually use a constant interest rate, dividend yield, and volatility as input parameters. However, in real world, these parameters are not constant. For example, the interest rate is different for one month than that for 5 years. The term structure of interest rates is simply the series of interest rates ordered by term-to-maturity at a given time. In Chapter 4, I have shown you how to download the ISDA interest rate from Markit. Fig. 9-2 shows the yield curve of the ISDA interest rates for USD on 12/7/2015. You can see from the figure that the interest rates depend strongly on the times to maturity. In order to pricing options in real-world market, we should use different interest rates for different times to expiration. This is why we need to introduce the concept of term structures.

QuantLib defines an abstract class called *TermStructure*, which is the base class for any kind of term structure. The *TermStructure* class is inherited by a number of classes such as *YieldTermStructure*, *InflationTermStructure*, or *DefaultProbabilityTermStructure*. The *YieldTermStructure* defines the base for all yield curves, *InflationTermStructure* acts as a base for all inflation term structures, and the *DefaultProbabilityTermStructure* is the base for term structures of the default risk. Term structures are an important tool for analyzing the real-world market, and many different term structures are defined in the library.

Term structures need to track of a reference date. This reference date either can be fixed to a specific date, which can be provided by a fixed number of business days after the evaluation date, or it can be linked to the reference date of an underlying structure.

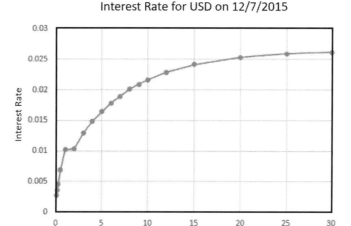

Fig. 9-2. *ISDA interest rate yield curve for USD.*

European Options

The price, or cost, of an option is called premium, which is non-refundable whether or not the option is exercised. You pay this premium to the seller in exchange for the right granted by the option. Premiums are priced per share. For example, the premium on a GOOG call option with a strike price of $800 might be quoted as $3.4. Since equity option contracts are based on 100 stock shares, this particular contract would cost the buyer $3.4×100, or $340 dollars. While supply and demand ultimately determine the option premium, other factors, such as the strike price, interest rate, and time to maturity, do play a role. We can apply these factors to mathematical models to help determine what an option should be worth.

Black-Scholes Model

The Black-Scholes model is a partial differential equation that governs the price evolution of a European call or put option. For a European option on an underlying stock paying no dividends, the equation is:

$$dS = \mu S dt + \sigma S dz$$

Where μ is the expected instantaneous rate of return on the underlying asset, σ is the instantaneous volatility of the rate of return, and dz is a Wiener process. You can find the derivation of the above formula from various textbooks, such as Hull's *Options, Futures,* and *Other Derivatives*. I will omit the derivation here.

Once the Black-Scholes equation with boundary and terminal conditions is derived for a derivative, you can solve it numerically using standard methods of numerical analysis, such as the finite-difference method. In certain cases, it is possible to solve for an exact formula, such as in the case of a European option, which was done by Black and Scholes. Letting c and p denote the price of European call and put options, respectively, the formula states that

$$c = SN(d_1) - Ke^{-rT}N(d_2)$$
$$p = Ke^{rT}N(-d_2) - SN(-d_1)$$

$$d_1 = \frac{\ln\left(\frac{S}{K}\right) + \left(r + \frac{\sigma^2}{2}\right)T}{\sigma\sqrt{T}}$$

$$d_2 = \frac{\ln\left(\frac{S}{K}\right) + \left(r - \frac{\sigma^2}{2}\right)T}{\sigma\sqrt{T}} = d_1 - \sigma\sqrt{T}$$

where S is the stock price, K the strike price, r the risk-free interest rate, T the time to expiration in years, σ the volatility of the relative price change of the underlying stock price, and $N(x)$ the cumulative normal distribution function. The cumulative normal distribution function is given by the integral:

$$N(x) = \frac{1}{\sqrt{2\pi}} \int_{-\infty}^{x} e^{-z^2/2} dz$$

This integral has no analytic solution, so you have to solve it numerically.

Generalized Black-Scholes Model

The Black-Scholes model can be generalized by incorporating a cost-of-carry rate b. This model can be used to pricing European options on stocks, stocks paying a continuous dividend yield, options on futures contracts, and currency options. Here are solutions to this generalized model:

$$c = Se^{(b-r)T}N(d_1) - Ke^{-rT}N(d_2)$$

$$p = Ke^{-rT}N(-d_2) - Se^{(b-r)T}N(-d_1)$$

$$d_1 = \frac{\ln\left(\frac{S}{K}\right) + \left(b + \frac{\sigma^2}{2}\right)T}{\sigma\sqrt{T}}$$

$$d_2 = d_1 - \sigma\sqrt{T}$$

The generalized model will reduce to different models depending how you choose the parameter b:

- $b = r$: gives the standard Black-Scholes (1973) stock option model.
- $b = r - q$: gives the Merton (1973) stock option model with continuous dividend yield q.
- $b = 0$: gives the Black (1976) futures option model.
- $b = 0$ and $r = 0$: gives the Asay (1982) margined futures option model.
- $b = r - r_f$: gives the Garman and Kohlhagen (1983) currency option model, where r_f is the risk-free rate of the foreign currency.

Black-Scholes Greeks

In quantitative finance, the Greeks are the quantities representing the partial derivatives of the generalized Black-Scholes formula introduced in preceding sections. The Greeks are a measure of the sensitivity of the option price to a small change in a parameter of the formula. The name is used because these sensitivities are commonly denoted by Greek letters. Sometimes, they have been also called the risk sensitivities, risk measures, or hedge parameters.

Delta

Delta measures the rate of change of the option price with respect to the underlying asset's price.

$$\Delta_{call} = \frac{\partial c}{\partial S} = e^{(b-r)T} N(d_1) > 0$$

$$\Delta_{put} = \frac{\partial p}{\partial S} = e^{(b-r)T} [N(d_1) - 1] < 0$$

For example, consider a stock option with 6 months to expiration. The stock price is 100, the strike price = 110, the risk-free interest rate is 0.1 per year, the continuous dividend yield is 0.06, and the volatility is 0.3. Then we obtain $c = 5.2515$, and $\Delta_{call} = 0.3898$, $p = 12.8422$, and $\Delta_{put} = -0.5806$.

Delta measures the expected price change of the option given a $1 change in the underlying asset, and can be used in evaluating buying and selling opportunities. Call options have positive deltas with a range of $(0, 1)$ and puts have negative deltas with a range of $(-1, 0)$. For example, a call option has a spot price at $45.2 and has a delta of 0.4. If the underlying stock goes up to 46.2, the option should increase by $0.4. Delta also gives a measure of the probability that an option will expire in the money. In the above example, the call option has a 40% probability of expiring in the money.

Delta can be used to evaluate alternatives when buying options. At-the-money options have deltas of roughly 0.5, meaning that the options have a 50% chance of going up or down. Deep in-the-money options have very high deltas (~ 1), indicating that they will essentially trade dollar for dollar with the stock. Some traders use these as stock substitutes, though there are clearly different risks involved. On the other hand, deep out-of-the-money options have very low deltas (~ 0) and therefore change very little with a $1 move in the underlying stock. Taking into account for commissions and bid/ask spread, low delta options may not make a profit even despite large moves in the underlying. Thus, comparing the delta to the options price across different strikes is one way of measuring the potential returns on a trade.

Gamma

Gamma is the delta's sensitivity to small changes in the underlying asset's price. Gamma is identical for both the call and put options:

$$\Gamma_{call,put} = \frac{\partial^2 c}{\partial S^2} = \frac{\partial^2 p}{\partial S^2} = \frac{n(d_1)e^{(b-r)T}}{S\sigma\sqrt{T}} > 0$$

Where $n(x)$ is the standard normal density:

$$n(x) = \frac{1}{2\pi} e^{-x^2/2}$$

Gamma measures the change in delta for a $1 change in the price of the underlying asset price. This is really the rate of change of the option price, and is most closely watched by those who sell options, as the gamma gives an indication of potential risk exposure if the stock price moves against the position.

For example, consider a stock option with 6 months to expiration. The stock price is 100, the strike price = 110, the risk-free interest rate is 0.1 per year, the continuous dividend yield is 0.06, and the volatility is 0.3. Then we obtain $c = 5.2515$, and $\Gamma_{call} = 0.01769$, $p = 12.8422$, and $\Gamma_{put} = 0.01769$.

Theta

Theta is the option's sensitivity to a small change in time to expiration, i.e., the time decay. At time approaches expiration, we can express theta as minus the partial derivative with respect to time:

$$\Theta_{call} = -\frac{\partial c}{\partial T} = -\frac{Se^{(b-r)T}n(d_1)\sigma}{2\sqrt{T}} - (b-r)Se^{(b-r)T}N(d_1) - rKe^{-rT}N(d_2)$$

$$\Theta_{put} = -\frac{\partial p}{\partial T} = -\frac{Se^{(b-r)T}n(d_1)\sigma}{2\sqrt{T}} + (b-r)Se^{(b-r)T}N(-d_1) + rKe^{-rT}N(-d_2)$$

For example, consider a stock option with 6 months to expiration. The stock price is 100, the strike price = 110, the risk-free interest rate is 0.1 per year, the continuous dividend yield is 0.06, and the volatility is 0.3. Then we obtain $c = 5.2515$, and $\Theta_{call} = -8.9963$, $p = 12.8422$, and $\Theta_{put} = -4.3554$. Thus, theta for a one-day time decay is, *call*: $-8.9963/365 = -0.02465$, *put*: $-4.3554/365 = -0.01193$.

Rho

Rho is the option's sensitivity to small changes in the risk-free interest rate:

$$\rho_{call} = \frac{\partial c}{\partial r} = TKe^{-rT}N(d_2) > 0$$

$$\rho_{put} = \frac{\partial p}{\partial r} = -TKe^{-rT}N(-d_2) < 0$$

In the case of an option on a futures contract, we have carry $(b) = 0$. The rho will be given by the following formulas:

$$\rho_{call} = -Tc < 0, \quad \rho_{put} = -Tp < 0$$

When interest rates rise, call prices will rise and put prices will fall. Just the reverse occurs when interest rates fall. Rho is a risk measure that simply tells us by how much call and put prices changes as a result of the rise or fall in interest rates. The rho values for ITM options will be largest due to arbitrary activity with such options. You are willing to pay more for call options and less for put options when interest rates rise because of the interest earnings potential on short sales made to hedge long calls and opportunity costs of not earning that interest.

Vega

Vega is the option's sensitivity to a small change in the volatility of the underlying asset. Vega is the same for both the call and put options:

$$Vega_{call,put} = \frac{\partial^2 c}{\partial \sigma^2} = \frac{\partial^2 p}{\partial \sigma^2} = Se^{(b-r)T}n(d_1)\sqrt{T} > 0$$

When any position is taken on options, not only is there risk from changes in the underlying asset but there is risk from changes in implied volatility. Vega is the measure of that risk.

Implied Volatility

For a given option price, we can also calculate the implied volatility based on the Black-Scholes model using various numerical methods, such as the Newton-Raphson and Bisection methods. The Newton-Raphson method requires knowledge of the partial derivative of the option pricing formula with respect to volatility (Vega) when searching for the implied volatility. For some options, such as American and exotic options, Vega is not known analytically. The bisection method can be used to estimate implied volatility when Vera is unknown.

Pricing European Options Using QuantLib

In this section, we will use QuantLib as a pricing engine to evaluate European options.

Helper Class and Web Service

In order to use QuantLib to pricing European options, we will create an interface to easily access QuantLib's option pricing engine. Add a new helper class named *OptionHelper* in the *Quant/Models* folder with the following code:

```
using QuantLib;
using System;

namespace Quant.Models
{
    public static class OptionHelper
    {
        public static object[] EuropeanOption(string optionType, string evalDate,
            double yearsToMaturity, double strike, double spot, double q, double r,
            double vol, string priceEngineType, int timeSteps)
        {
            DateTime evalDate1 = DateTime.Parse(evalDate);
            Date startDate = new Date((int)evalDate1.ToOADate());
            Date maturity = startDate + Convert.ToInt32(
                yearsToMaturity * 360 + 0.5);
            priceEngineType = char.ToUpper(priceEngineType[0]) +
                priceEngineType.Substring(1);
            Enum.TryParse(priceEngineType, out EuropeanEngineType engineType);
            return EuropeanOptionResult(optionType, startDate, maturity, strike,
                spot, q, r, vol, engineType, timeSteps);
        }

        private static object[] EuropeanOptionResult(string optionType,
            Date evalDate, Date maturity, double strike, double spot, double q,
            double r, double vol, EuropeanEngineType priceEngineType, int timeSteps)
        {
            optionType = optionType.ToUpper();
            Option.Type otype = Option.Type.Call;
            if (optionType == "P" || optionType == "PUT") otype = Option.Type.Put;

            Settings.instance().setEvaluationDate(evalDate);
            Date settlementDate = evalDate;
            Calendar calendar = new TARGET();
```

```
DayCounter dc = new Actual360();
QuoteHandle spot1 = new QuoteHandle(new SimpleQuote(spot));
YieldTermStructureHandle qTS = new YieldTermStructureHandle(
    new FlatForward(settlementDate, q, dc));
YieldTermStructureHandle rTS = new YieldTermStructureHandle(
    new FlatForward(settlementDate, r, dc));
BlackVolTermStructureHandle volTS = new BlackVolTermStructureHandle(
    new BlackConstantVol(settlementDate, calendar, vol, dc));
Payoff payoff = new PlainVanillaPayoff(otype, strike);
Exercise exercise = new EuropeanExercise(maturity);
BlackScholesMertonProcess bsmProcess =
    new BlackScholesMertonProcess(spot1, qTS, rTS, volTS);

PricingEngine engine;
switch (priceEngineType)
{
    case EuropeanEngineType.Analytic:
        engine = new AnalyticEuropeanEngine(bsmProcess);
        break;
    case EuropeanEngineType.BinomiallJarrowRudd:
        engine = new BinomialVanillaEngine(bsmProcess, "jarrowrudd",
            (uint)timeSteps);
        break;
    case EuropeanEngineType.BinomialCoxRossRubinstein:
        engine = new BinomialVanillaEngine(bsmProcess,
            "coxrossrubinstein", (uint)timeSteps);
        break;
    case EuropeanEngineType.BinomialAdditiveEquiprobabilities:
        engine = new BinomialVanillaEngine(bsmProcess, "eqp",
            (uint)timeSteps);
        break;
    case EuropeanEngineType.BinomialTrigeorgis:
        engine = new BinomialVanillaEngine(bsmProcess, "trigeorgis",
            (uint)timeSteps);
        break;
    case EuropeanEngineType.BinomialTian:
        engine = new BinomialVanillaEngine(bsmProcess, "tain",
            (uint)timeSteps);
        break;
    case EuropeanEngineType.BinomialLeisenReimer:
        engine = new BinomialVanillaEngine(bsmProcess, "leisenreimer",
            (uint)timeSteps);
        break;
    case EuropeanEngineType.BinomialJoshi:
        engine = new BinomialVanillaEngine(bsmProcess, "joshi4",
            (uint)timeSteps);
        break;
    case EuropeanEngineType.FiniteDifference:
        engine = new FDEuropeanEngine(bsmProcess, (uint)timeSteps,
            (uint)timeSteps - 1);
        break;
    case EuropeanEngineType.Integral:
        engine = new IntegralEngine(bsmProcess);
        break;
    case EuropeanEngineType.PseudoMonteCarlo:
```

```
            string traits = "pseudorandom";
            int mcTimeSteps = 1;
            int timeStepsPerYear = int.MaxValue;
            bool brownianBridge = false;
            bool antitheticVariate = false;
            int requiredSamples = int.MaxValue;
            double requiredTolerance = 0.05;
            int maxSamples = int.MaxValue;
            int seed = 42;
            engine = new MCEuropeanEngine(bsmProcess, traits, mcTimeSteps,
                timeStepsPerYear, brownianBridge, antitheticVariate,
                requiredSamples, requiredTolerance, maxSamples, seed);
            break;
        case EuropeanEngineType.QuasiMonteCarlo:
            traits = "lowdiscrepancy";
            mcTimeSteps = 1;
            timeStepsPerYear = int.MaxValue;
            brownianBridge = false;
            antitheticVariate = false;
            requiredSamples = 32768;   // 2^15
            requiredTolerance = double.MaxValue;
            maxSamples = int.MaxValue;
            seed = 0;
            engine = new MCEuropeanEngine(bsmProcess, traits, mcTimeSteps,
                timeStepsPerYear, brownianBridge, antitheticVariate,
                requiredSamples, requiredTolerance, maxSamples, seed);
            break;

    default:
        throw new ArgumentException("unknown engine type");
}

VanillaOption option = new VanillaOption(payoff, exercise);
option.setPricingEngine(engine);

object value = null;
object delta = null;
object gamma = null;
object theta = null;
object rho = null;
object vega = null;

try
{
    value = option.NPV();
    delta = option.delta();
    gamma = option.gamma();
    theta = option.theta();
    rho = option.rho();
    vega = option.vega();
}
catch { }

return new object[] { value, delta, gamma, theta, rho, vega };
}
```

```
    public static object EuropeanOptionImpliedVol(string optionType,
        string evalDate, double yearsToMaturity, double strike, double spot,
        double q, double r, double targetPrice)
    {
        Date startDate = new Date((int)DateTime.Parse(evalDate).ToOADate());
        Date maturity = startDate + Convert.ToInt32(
            yearsToMaturity * 360 + 0.5);
        return EuropeanOptionImpliedVol(optionType, startDate, maturity,
            strike, spot, q, r, targetPrice);
    }

    public static object EuropeanOptionImpliedVol(string optionType, Date
        evalDate, Date maturity, double strike, double spot, double q, double r,
        double targetPrice)
    {
        optionType = optionType.ToUpper();
        Option.Type otype = Option.Type.Call;
        if (optionType == "P" || optionType == "PUT")
            otype = Option.Type.Put;

        Settings.instance().setEvaluationDate(evalDate);
        Date settlementDate = evalDate;
        Calendar calendar = new TARGET();
        DayCounter dc = new Actual360();
        QuoteHandle spot1 = new QuoteHandle(new SimpleQuote(spot));
        YieldTermStructureHandle qTS = new YieldTermStructureHandle(
            new FlatForward(settlementDate, q, dc));
        YieldTermStructureHandle rTS = new YieldTermStructureHandle(
            new FlatForward(settlementDate, r, dc));
        BlackVolTermStructureHandle volTS = new BlackVolTermStructureHandle(
            new BlackConstantVol(settlementDate, calendar, 0.3, dc));
        Payoff payoff = new PlainVanillaPayoff(otype, strike);
        Exercise exercise = new EuropeanExercise(maturity);
        BlackScholesMertonProcess bsmProcess =
            new BlackScholesMertonProcess(spot1, qTS, rTS, volTS);
        VanillaOption option = new VanillaOption(payoff, exercise);

        object v = null;
        try
        {
            v = option.impliedVolatility(targetPrice, bsmProcess,
                1.0e-6, 10000, 0, 4.0);
        }
        catch { }

        return v;
    }
}

public enum EuropeanEngineType
{
    Analytic,
    BinomiallJarrowRudd,
    BinomialCoxRossRubinstein,
```

```
        BinomialAdditiveEquiprobabilities,
        BinomialTrigeorgis,
        BinomialTian,
        BinomialLeisenReimer,
        BinomialJoshi,
        FiniteDifference,
        Integral,
        PseudoMonteCarlo,
        QuasiMonteCarlo
    };
}
```

The *EuropeanEngineType* enum specifies various approaches in QuantLib to calculate European options. The *EuropeanOptionResult* method uses several QuantLib specific objects, including dates, calendars, day counters, and term structures. Here, we set the settlement date to the evaluation date, and use the *Actual360* day count convention. We also use the flat term structures for the interest rate, dividend yield, and volatility, and then create the flat term structures using the corresponding term structure handles. We construct both the interest rate and dividend yield term structures using a *FlatForward* as the *YieldTermStructure* object; while for the volatility, we create its term structure using the *BlackConstantVol* as the *BlackVolTermStructure* object. Here, you should understand how we relate the constant interest rate, dividend yield, and volatility to corresponding term structures in QuantLib. For real-world options pricing, you should replace the flat term structures with the curves from market.

After constructing the term structures, we create a *BlackScholesMertonProcess* named *bsmProcess*, which is to be used in the selected pricing engine. Next, we need to select the *priceEngineType* from 12 types of pricing engines for European options, including analytic, a variety of binomial vanilla models, finite difference, integral, and Monte Carlo engines. We then create a new *VanillaOption* object named *option* and call the *setPricingEngine* method with the specified pricing engine as input to calculate the option price. Finally, the *EuropeanOptionResult* method returns the calculated results including the option price (from *NPV* method, NPV standards for the net present value) and Greeks. Note that only the *Analytic* engine returns all five Greeks, some other engines do not return all of them, while the Monte Carlo engine returns only the price without Greeks.

Please note that the *EuropeanOptionResult* method takes the maturity date (or expiration date) as input. Sometimes, it is more convenient to use a double variable called *yearsToMaturity* to replace the maturity date, as we did in the *EuropeanOption* method.

Note that the *evalDate* parameter in both the *EuropeanOptionResult* and *EuropeanOption* methods does not affect the calculation results for the flat term structures. However, it will play an important role in the calculation for curved term structures because the yield curve will be different for different *evalDate*.

QuantLib also allows you to calculate implied volatility for a specified (or targeted) option price. The overloaded method, *EuropenOptionImpliedVol*, can be used to calculate the implied volatility. This method does not specify the pricing engine because the option price is the input parameter. You can see that after creating the *VanillaOption* object, we immediately call the *impliedVolatility* method to calculate the implied volatility. Internally, the *impliedVolatility* method is based on the Newton-Raphson algorithm, where the accuracy, maximum number of evaluations, and the volatility range are specified.

Next, we will convert the above methods implemented in the *OptionHelper* class into web services. Add a new API controller called *OptionValuesController* in the *Quant/Controllers* folder with the following code:

```
using Microsoft.AspNetCore.Mvc;
using Quant.Models;
```

```csharp
using System;
using System.Collections.Generic;

namespace Quant.Controllers
{
    [Produces("application/json")]
    public class OptionValuesController : Controller
    {
        [Route("~/api/EuropeanOption/{optionType}/{yearsToMaturity}/{strike}/{spot}
            /{q}/{r}/{vol}/{engineType}/{timeSteps}")]
        [HttpGet]
        public JsonResult GetEuropeanOption(string optionType,
            double yearsTomaturity, double strike, double spot, double q, double r,
            double vol, string engineType, int timeSteps)
        {
            var startDate = DateTime.Today.ToString("yyyy-MM-dd");
            var res = OptionHelper.EuropeanOption(optionType, startDate,
                yearsTomaturity, strike, spot, q, r, vol, engineType, timeSteps);
            return Json(new { Name = "European Options", Result = res });
        }

        [Route("~/api/EuropeanOptions/{optionType}/{strike}/{spot}/{q}/{r}
            /{vol}/{engineType}/{timeSteps}")]
        [HttpGet]
        public JsonResult GetEuropeanOptions(string optionType, double strike,
            double spot, double q, double r,
            double vol, string engineType, int timeSteps)
        {
            var startDate = DateTime.Today.ToString("yyyy-MM-dd");
            var mat = new double[] { 0.1, 0.2, 0.3, 0.4, 0.5, 0.6, 0.7, 0.8,
                0.9, 1.0 };
            List<object> objs = new List<object>();
            for (int i = 0; i < mat.Length; i++)
            {
                var opt = OptionHelper.EuropeanOption(optionType, startDate, mat[i],
                    strike, spot, q, r, vol, engineType, timeSteps);
                objs.Add(new { Maturity = mat[i], Price = opt[0], Delta = opt[1],
                    Gamma = opt[2], Theta = opt[3], Rho = opt[4], Vega = opt[5] });
            }
            return Json(new { Name = "European Options", Result = objs });
        }

        [Route("~/api/EuropeanImpliedVol/{optionType}/{yearsToMaturity}
            /{strike}/{spot}/{q}/{r}/{targetPrice}")]
        [HttpGet]
        public JsonResult GetEuropeanImpliedVol(string optionType,
            double yearsTomaturity, double strike, double spot, double q,
            double r, double targetPrice)
        {
            var startDate = DateTime.Today.ToString("yyyy-MM-dd");
            var res = OptionHelper.EuropeanOptionImpliedVol(optionType, startDate,
                yearsTomaturity, strike, spot, q, r, targetPrice);
            return Json(new { Name = "European Option: Implied Volatility",
                Result = res });
        }
```

```
[Route("~/api/EuropeanImpliedVols/{optionType}/{strike}/{spot}/{q}/{r}")]
[HttpGet]
public JsonResult GetEuropeanImpliedVols(string optionType, double strike,
    double spot, double q, double r)
{
    var startDate = DateTime.Today.ToString("yyyy-MM-dd");
    var mat = new double[] { 0.1, 0.2, 0.3, 0.4, 0.5, 0.6, 0.7, 0.8,
        0.9, 1.0 };
    var price = new double[] { 0.15, 0.2, 0.25, 0.3, 0.35, 0.4, 0.45,
        0.5, 0.55, 0.6 };
    List<object> objs = new List<object>();

    for (int i = 0; i < mat.Length; i++)
    {
        var vol = OptionHelper.EuropeanOptionImpliedVol(optionType,
            startDate, mat[i], strike, spot, q, r, price[i]);
        objs.Add(new { Maturity = mat[i], Price = price[i],
            Volatility = vol });
    }
    return Json(new { Name = "European Option: Implied Volatility",
        Result = objs });
}
}
}
```

The *GetEuropeanOption* method simply returns the option price and Greeks by calling the *EuropeanOption* method implemented in the *OptionHelper* class. Note that we set the *evalDate* to today and encapsulate it internally because it has no effect on the results with flat term structures. The other method, *GetEuropeanOptions*, calculates option prices for a specified maturity array, which will be convenient for displaying the results of different maturities.

The *GetEuropeanImpliedVol* method returns volatility results for a single maturity and targeted price by calling the *EuropeanOptionImpliedVol* method implemented in the *OptionHelper* class. While the *GetEuropeanImpliedVols* method returns results for a specified maturity array and a targeted-price array, which will be used to display the results in an Angular applications.

Option Repository in Angular

The process of sending a request from the Angular application to get the option results following the same basic repository patterns presented in the preceding chapters. Here, we need to add a repository service called *ch9.service.ts* to the *ClientApp/src/app/models* folder by running the following command in a command prompt window:

ng g s models/ch9

Open the *ch9.service.ts* class file and replace its content with the following code:

```
// ch9.service.ts file:
import { Inject } from '@angular/core';
import { HttpClient } from '@angular/common/http';

@Injectable({
  providedIn: 'root'
})
```

```
export class Ch9Repository {
  private url;

  constructor(private http: HttpClient, @Inject('BASE_URL') baseUrl: string) {
    this.url = baseUrl;
  }

  getEuropeanOption(optionType: string, yearsToMaturity: number, strike: number,
    spot: number, q: number, r: number, vol: number, engineType: string,
    timeSteps: number) {
    let url1 = this.url + 'api/europeanoption/' + optionType + '/' + yearsToMaturity
      + '/' + strike + '/' + spot + '/' + q + '/' + r + '/' + vol + '/' + engineType
      + '/' + timeSteps;
    return this.http.get<any>(url1);
  }

  getEuropeanOptions(optionType: string, strike: number, spot: number, q: number,
    r: number, vol: number, engineType: string, timeSteps: number) {
    let url1 = this.url + 'api/europeanoptions/' + optionType + '/' + strike + '/'
      + spot + '/' + q + '/' + r + '/' + vol + '/' + engineType + '/' + timeSteps;
    return this.http.get<any>(url1);
  }

  getEuropeanImpliedVol(optionType: string, yearsToMaturity: number, strike: number,
    spot: number, q: number, r: number, targetPrice: number) {
    let url1 = this.url + 'api/europeanimpliedvol/' + optionType + '/' +
      yearsToMaturity + '/' + strike + '/' + spot + '/' + q + '/' + r + '/' +
      targetPrice;
    return this.http.get<any>(url1);
  }

  getEuropeanImpliedVols(optionType: string, strike: number, spot: number,
    q: number, r: number) {
    let url1 = this.url + 'api/europeanimpliedvols/' + optionType + '/' + strike +
      '/' + spot + '/' + q + '/' + r;
    return this.http.get<any>(url1);
  }
}
```

Note that these methods return promises, which allow you to execute your code sequentially and create responsive UI.

Option Pricing in Angular

Now, I will use an example to illustrate how to pricing European options in an Angular application. Run the following statement in a command prompt window:

```
ng g c chapter09/ch9-option-eu --module=app.module
```

This generates a new component called *ch9-option-eu* in the *ClientApp/src/app/Chapter09* folder. Open the component class and replace its content with the following code:

```
// ch9-option-eu.component.ts file:
import { Component, OnInit } from '@angular/core';
import { Ch9Service } from '../../models/ch9.service';
```

```
@Component({
  selector: 'app-ch9-option-eu',
  templateUrl: './ch9-option-eu.component.html',
  styleUrls: ['./ch9-option-eu.component.css']
})
export class Ch9OptionEuComponent implements OnInit {
  optionType: string = 'call';
  strike: number = 100;
  spot: number = 100;
  q: number = 0.06;
  r: number = 0.1;
  vol: number = 0.3;
  engineType: string = 'analytic';
  timeSteps: number = 100;
  optionResult: any;

  colDefs = [
    { headerName: "Maturity", field: "maturity", width: 100 },
    { headerName: "Price", field: "price", width: 100 },
    { headerName: "Delta", field: "delta", width: 100 },
    { headerName: "Gamma", field: "gamma", width: 100 },
    { headerName: "Theta", field: "theta", width: 100 },
    { headerName: "Rho", field: "rho", width: 100 },
    { headerName: "Vega", field: "vega", width: 100 },
  ];

  constructor(private repository: Ch9Service) { }

  ngOnInit() {
    this.getOptionResult(this.optionType, this.strike, this.spot, this.q, this.r,
      this.vol, this.engineType, this.timeSteps);
  }

  getOptionResult(optionType: string, strike: number, spot: number, q: number,
    r: number, vol: number, engineType: string, timeSteps: number) {
    this.optionResult = null;
    this.repository.getEuropeanOptions(optionType, strike, spot, q, r, vol,
      engineType, timeSteps).subscribe(result => {
      this.optionResult = result.result;
    });
  }
}
```

This component retrieves the option output results from web service using the repository created previously. Inside the *getOptionResult* method, we use the promise to reset the *optionResult* property from null to the option output. If we use the old repository method without promise, it is impossible to reset *optionResult* because it is a *get*-only property.

This component also defines a *colDefs* property that will be used to display the results using the *ag-Grid* component.

We also need to update the component's template file using the following code:

```
// ch9-option-eu.component.html file:
<h2>
```

```
  ch9-option-eu works!
</h2>
<mat-form-field>
  <input matInput placeholder="optionType" [(ngModel)]="optionType"
name="optionType">
</mat-form-field>
<mat-form-field>
  <input matInput placeholder="strike" [(ngModel)]="strike" name="strike">
</mat-form-field>
<mat-form-field>
  <input matInput placeholder="spot" [(ngModel)]="spot" name="spot">
</mat-form-field>
<mat-form-field>
  <input matInput placeholder="q" [(ngModel)]="q" name="q">
</mat-form-field>
<mat-form-field>
  <input matInput placeholder="r" [(ngModel)]="r" name="r">
</mat-form-field>
<mat-form-field>
  <input matInput placeholder="vol" [(ngModel)]="vol" name="vol">
</mat-form-field>
<mat-form-field>
  <input matInput placeholder="timeSteps" [(ngModel)]="timeSteps" name="timeSteps">
</mat-form-field>
<mat-form-field>
  <mat-select [(value)]="engineType">
    <mat-option value="analytic">Analytic</mat-option>
    <mat-option value="binomialJarrowRudd">Binomial Jarrow-Rudd</mat-option>
    <mat-option value="binomialCoxRossRubinstein">Binomial Cox-Ross-Rubinstein
    </mat-option>
    <mat-option value="binomialAdditiveEquiprobabilities">Binomial
      Additive-Equiprobabilities</mat-option>
    <mat-option value="binomialTrigeorgis">Binomial Trigeorgis</mat-option>
    <mat-option value="binomialTian">Binomial Tian</mat-option>
    <mat-option value="binomialLeisenReimer">Binomial Leisen-Reimer</mat-option>
    <mat-option value="binomialJoshi">Binomial Joshi</mat-option>
    <mat-option value="finiteDifference">Finite Difference</mat-option>
    <mat-option value="integral">Integral</mat-option>
    <mat-option value="pseudoMonteCarlo">Pseudo Monte Carlo</mat-option>
    <mat-option value="quasiMonteCarlo">Quasi Monte Carlo</mat-option>
  </mat-select>
</mat-form-field>
<button mat-raised-button color="primary" click)="getOptionResult(optionType,strike,
  spot,q,r,vol,engineType,timeSteps)">Get Option Result</button>

<ag-grid-angular *ngIf="optionResult" style="height:330px;width:720px;
  margin-top:30px" class="ag-theme-balham" [rowData]="optionResult"
  [columnDefs]="colDefs">
</ag-grid-angular>
```

This template first defines the input fields required by the option pricing and then displays option price and Greeks using *ag-Grid*.

Finally, we need to add a path for this new component to the *RouterModule* of the root module (i.e., the *app.module.ts* file):

```
{ path: 'chapter09/ch9-option-eu, component: Ch9OptionEuComponent },
```

Then add the corresponding URL link to the *home* and *nav-menu* components.

Saving the project and navigating to the */chapter09/ch9-option-eu* page produce the default results shown in Fig.9-3.

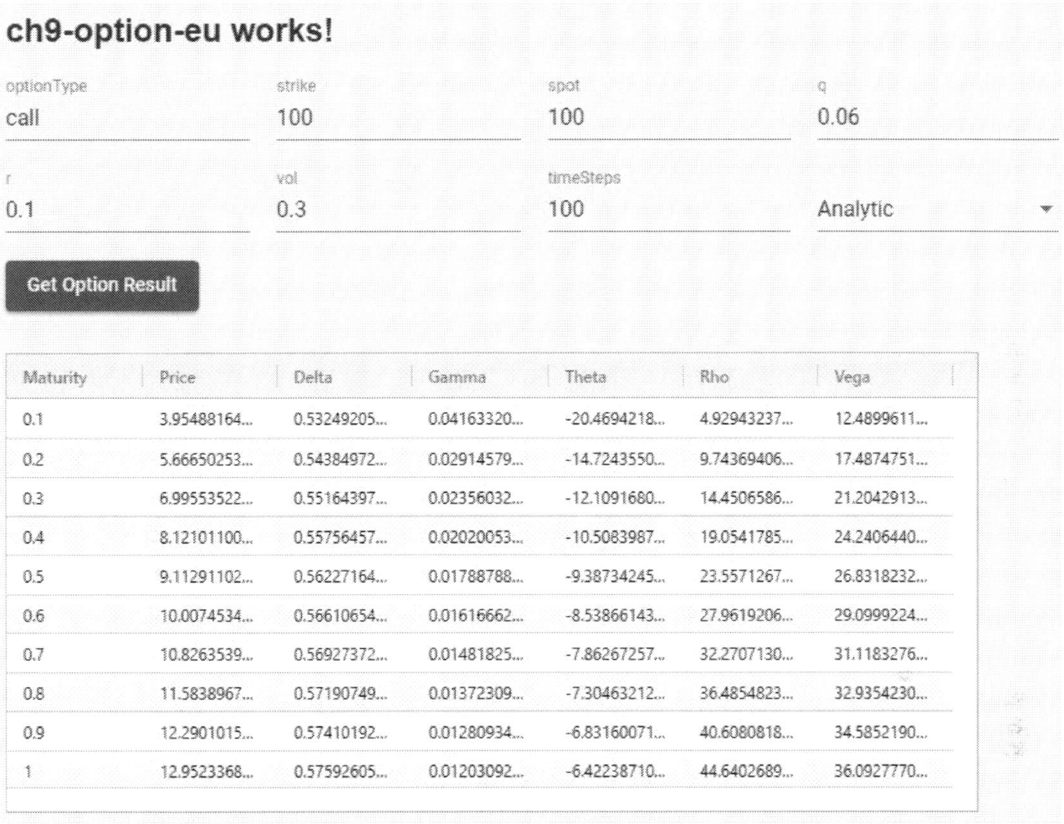

ch9-option-eu works!

optionType	strike	spot	q
call	100	100	0.06

r	vol	timeSteps	
0.1	0.3	100	Analytic ▼

Get Option Result

Maturity	Price	Delta	Gamma	Theta	Rho	Vega
0.1	3.95488164...	0.53249205...	0.04163320...	-20.4694218...	4.92943237...	12.4899611...
0.2	5.66650253...	0.54384972...	0.02914579...	-14.7243550...	9.74369406...	17.4874751...
0.3	6.99553522...	0.55164397...	0.02356032...	-12.1091680...	14.4506586...	21.2042913...
0.4	8.12101100...	0.55756457...	0.02020053...	-10.5083987...	19.0541785...	24.2406440...
0.5	9.11291102...	0.56227164...	0.01788788...	-9.38734245...	23.5571267...	26.8318232...
0.6	10.0074534...	0.56610654...	0.01616662...	-8.53866143...	27.9619206...	29.0999224...
0.7	10.8263539...	0.56927372...	0.01481825...	-7.86267257...	32.2707130...	31.1183276...
0.8	11.5838967...	0.57190749...	0.01372309...	-7.30463212...	36.4854823...	32.9354230...
0.9	12.2901015...	0.57410192...	0.01280934...	-6.83160071...	40.6080818...	34.5852190...
1	12.9523368...	0.57592605...	0.01203092...	-6.42238710...	44.6402689...	36.0927770...

Fig.9-3. Pricing European call options using QuantLib.

Note that the default pricing engine is *Analytic*, which is what we derived various analytic formulas for option price and Greeks previously. You can also choose different pricing engine from the dropdown combo box to price options. Fig.9-4 shows the calculated results from different pricing engines, including using the binomial Joshi and Monte Carlo engines. Note that the binomial Joshi pricing engine does not calculate the Greeks *Rho* and *Vega*, while the Monte Carlo engine does not return any Greeks but price. You can improve the calculated results of using these pricing engines by varying the time step parameter.

Results from Binomial Joshi:

Maturity	Price	Delta	Gamma	Theta	Rho	Vega	
0.1	3.91575094...	0.53223460...	0.04226729...	-20.7576463...			
0.2	5.61040452...	0.54349638...	0.02959345...	-14.9299991...			
0.3	6.92622491...	0.55122251...	0.02392528...	-12.2786445...			
0.4	8.04047613...	0.55708980...	0.02051611...	-10.6565649...			
0.5	9.02244965...	0.56175324...	0.01816970...	-9.52113716...			
0.6	9.90800728...	0.56555154...	0.01642348...	-8.66197409...			
0.7	10.7186514...	0.56868754...	0.01505567...	-7.97793656...			
0.8	11.4685265...	0.57129451...	0.01394480...	-7.41348667...			
0.9	12.1675538...	0.57346575...	0.01301800...	-6.93521048...			
1	12.8230303...	0.57526977...	0.01222852...	-6.52161360...			

Results from Monte Carlo:

Maturity	Price	Delta	Gamma	Theta	Rho	Vega	
0.1	3.93905949...						
0.2	5.64232633...						
0.3	6.96416867...						
0.4	8.08302679...						
0.5	9.06865964...						
0.6	9.95717772...						
0.7	10.7702280...						
0.8	11.5220497...						
0.9	12.2226471...						
1	12.8793519...						

Fig.9-4. Pricing European options using binomial Joshi (top) and Monte Carlo (bottom) engines.

Implied Volatility in Angular

Following the same procedure as that presented in the preceding section, we can easily calculate the implied volatility for European options using QuantLib. Run the following statement in a command prompt window:

```
ng g c chapter09/ch9-vol-eu --module=app.module
```

This generates a new component called *ch9-vol-eu* in the *ClientApp/src/app/Chapter09* folder. Open the component class and replace its content with the following code:

```
// ch9.vol.eu.component.ts file:
import { Component, OnInit } from '@angular/core';
import { Ch9Service } from '../../models/ch9.service';

@Component({
  selector: 'app-ch9-vol-eu',
  templateUrl: './ch9-vol-eu.component.html',
  styleUrls: ['./ch9-vol-eu.component.css']
})
export class Ch9VolEuComponent implements OnInit {
  optionType: string = 'call';
  strike: number = 10.5;
  spot: number = 10;
  q: number = 0.04;
  r: number = 0.1;

  volResult: any = [];
  colDefs = [
    { headerName: "Maturity", field: "maturity", width: 100 },
    { headerName: "Option Price", field: "price", width: 100 },
    { headerName: "Implied Vol", field: "volatility", width: 150 },
  ];

  constructor(private repository: Ch9Service) { }

  ngOnInit() {
    this.getVolResult(this.optionType, this.strike, this.spot, this.q, this.r);
  }

  getVolResult(optionType: string, strike: number, spot: number, q: number,
    r: number) {
    this.volResult = null;
    this.repository.getEuropeanImpliedVols(optionType, strike, spot, q, r)
      .subscribe(result => { this.volResult = result.result; });
  }
}
```

This component retrieves the implied volatility results from web service using the repository service created previously. Inside the *getVolResult* method, we use the promise to reset the *volResult* property from null to the implied volatility output.

This component also defines a *colDefs* property that will be used to display the results using the *ag-Grid* component.

We also need to update the component's template file using the following code:

```
// ch9-vol.eu.component.html file:
<h2>
  ch9-vol-eu works!
</h2>
<mat-form-field>
  <input matInput placeholder="optionType" [(ngModel)]="optionType"
name="optionType">
</mat-form-field>
<mat-form-field>
  <input matInput placeholder="strike" [(ngModel)]="strike" name="strike">
```

```
</mat-form-field>
<mat-form-field>
  <input matInput placeholder="spot" [(ngModel)]="spot" name="spot">
</mat-form-field>
<mat-form-field>
  <input matInput placeholder="q" [(ngModel)]="q" name="q">
</mat-form-field>
<mat-form-field>
  <input matInput placeholder="r" [(ngModel)]="r" name="r">
</mat-form-field>

<button mat-raised-button color="primary"
  (click)="getVolResult(optionType,strike,spot,q,r)">Get Option Result</button>

<ag-grid-angular *ngIf="volResult" style="height:330px;width:400px;margin-top:30px"
  class="ag-theme-balham" [rowData]="volResult" [columnDefs]="colDefs">
</ag-grid-angular>
```

This template first defines the input fields required by calculating the implied volatility and then displays the results using *ag-Grid*.

Finally, we need to add a path for this new component to the *RouterModule* of the root module (i.e., the *app.module.ts* file):

```
{ path: 'chapter09/ch9-vol-eu, component: Ch9VolEuComponent },
```

Then add the corresponding URL link to the *home* and *nav-menu* components.

Saving the project and navigating to the */chapter09/ch9-vol-eu* page produce the default results shown in Fig.9-5.

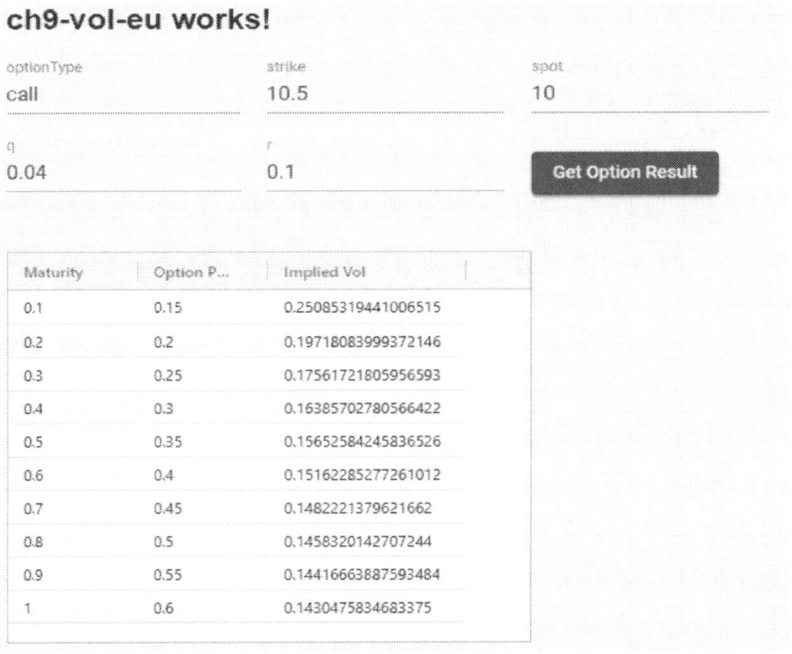

ch9-vol-eu works!

optionType	strike	spot
call	10.5	10

q	r	
0.04	0.1	**Get Option Result**

Maturity	Option P...	Implied Vol	
0.1	0.15	0.25085319441006515	
0.2	0.2	0.197180839993372146	
0.3	0.25	0.17561721805956593	
0.4	0.3	0.16385702780566422	
0.5	0.35	0.15652584245836526	
0.6	0.4	0.15162285277261012	
0.7	0.45	0.1482221379621662	
0.8	0.5	0.1458320142707244	
0.9	0.55	0.14416663887593484	
1	0.6	0.1430475834683375	

Fig.9-5. Volatility results for European call options from QuantLib.

American Options

Unlike European options, American options can be exercised at any time up to its maturity. This flexibility complicates the valuation of American options relative to their European counterparts. In general, American options do not have analytical solutions. However, some excellent closed-form approximations have been proposed. The approximations have become especially popular because they execute quickly compared to numerical methods. Here, I will present one of the approximations, the Barone-Adesi and Whaley (BAW) method, and then show you how to use QuantLib to pricing American options.

BAW Approximation

The BAW method, based on the quadratic approximation, can be used to price American options on an underlying asset with carry rate b. When $b \geq r$, the American call price is equal to the European call price and can then be found by using the generalized Black-Scholes formula. The model is fast and accurate for most practical input values. The BAW approximation for American call options can be written in the form:

$$c(S,K,T) = \begin{cases} c_{GBS}(S,K,T) + A_2(S/S^*)^{q_2} & \text{for } S < S^* \\ S - K & \text{for } S \geq S^* \end{cases}$$

Where $c_{GBS}(S,K,T)$ is the generalized Black-Scholes call formula, and

$$A_2 = \frac{S^*}{q_2}\{1 - e^{(b-r)T}N[d_1(S^*)]\}$$

$$d_1(S) = \frac{\ln\left(\frac{S}{K}\right) + \left(b + \frac{\sigma^2}{2}\right)T}{\sigma\sqrt{T}}$$

$$q_2 = \frac{-(N-1) + \sqrt{(N-1)^2 + 4M/L}}{2}$$

$$M = \frac{2r}{\sigma^2}, \quad N = \frac{2b}{\sigma^2}, \quad L = 1 - e^{-rT}$$

For American put, we have:

$$p(S,K,T) = \begin{cases} p_{GBS}(S,K,T) + A_1(S/S^{**})^{q_1} & \text{for } S > S^{**} \\ K - S & \text{for } S \leq S^{**} \end{cases}$$

Where $p_{GBS}(S,K,T)$ is the generalized Black-Scholes call formula, and

$$A_1 = -\frac{S^{**}}{q_1}\{1 - e^{(b-r)T}N[-d_1(S^{**})]\}$$

$$q_1 = \frac{-(N-1) - \sqrt{(N-1)^2 + 4M/L}}{2}$$

Where S^* (S^{**}) is the critical commodity price for the call (put) option that satisfies

$$S^* - K = c(S^*,K,T) + \{1 - e^{(b-r)T}N[d_1(S^*)]\}\frac{S^*}{q_2}$$

$$K - S^{**} = p(S^{**}, K, T) - \left\{1 - e^{(b-r)T} N[-d_1(S^{**})]\right\} \frac{S^{**}}{q_1}$$

The above equations for S^* and S^{**} can be solved by using the Newton-Raphson algorithm. Calculating the price for American options will be straightforward as long as S^* and S^{**} are known.

In this book, I will not show you how to implement the program using the above formulas (if you are interested in the implementation, please refer to my previously published book "*Practical C# and WPF for Financial Markets*"); instead, I will demonstrate how to use QuantLib to pricing American options in the following sections.

Helper Methods and Web Service

In order to use QuantLib to pricing American options, we will create some helper methods to easily access QuantLib's option pricing engine. First, add an enum called *AmericanEngineType* to the *OptionHelper* class in the *Quant/Models* folder:

```
public enum AmericanEngineType
{
    BaroneAdesiWhaley,
    BjerksundStensland,
    FiniteDifference,
    BinomialJarrowRudd,
    BinomialCoxRossRubinstein,
    BinomialAdditiveEquiprobabilities,
    BinomialTrigeorgis,
    BinomialTian,
    BinomialLeisenReimer,
    BinomialJoshi,
};
```

This enum specifies various price engines for pricing American options available in QuantLib.

Next, add the following methods to the *OptionHelper* class in the *Quant/Models* folder with the following code:

```
public static object[] AmericanOption(string optionType, string evalDate,
    double yearsToMaturity, double strike, double spot, double q, double r,
    double vol, string priceEngineType, int timeSteps)
{
    DateTime evalDate1 = DateTime.Parse(evalDate);
    Date startDate = new Date((int)evalDate1.ToOADate());
    Date maturity = startDate + Convert.ToInt32(yearsToMaturity * 360 + 0.5);
    priceEngineType = char.ToUpper(priceEngineType[0])+priceEngineType.Substring(1);
    Enum.TryParse(priceEngineType, out AmericanEngineType engineType);
    return AmericanOptionResult(optionType, startDate, maturity, strike, spot, q, r,
        vol, engineType, timeSteps);
}

public static object[] AmericanOptionResult(string optionType, Date evalDate,
    Date maturity, double strike, double spot, double q, double r, double vol,
    AmericanEngineType priceEngineType, int timeSteps)
{
    optionType = optionType.ToUpper();
    Option.Type otype = Option.Type.Call;
```

```
if (optionType == "P" || optionType == "PUT")
    otype = Option.Type.Put;
Settings.instance().setEvaluationDate(evalDate);
Date settlementDate = evalDate;
Calendar calendar = new TARGET();
DayCounter dc = new Actual360();
QuoteHandle spot1 = new QuoteHandle(new SimpleQuote(spot));
YieldTermStructureHandle qTS = new YieldTermStructureHandle(new
    FlatForward(settlementDate, q, dc));
YieldTermStructureHandle rTS = new YieldTermStructureHandle(new
    FlatForward(settlementDate, r, dc));
BlackVolTermStructureHandle volTS = new BlackVolTermStructureHandle(new
    BlackConstantVol(settlementDate, calendar, vol, dc));
Payoff payoff = new PlainVanillaPayoff(otype, strike);
Exercise exercise = new AmericanExercise(settlementDate, maturity);
BlackScholesMertonProcess bsmProcess = new BlackScholesMertonProcess(spot1,
    qTS, rTS, volTS);

PricingEngine engine;
switch (priceEngineType)
{
    case AmericanEngineType.BaroneAdesiWhaley:
        engine = new BaroneAdesiWhaleyEngine(bsmProcess);
        break;
    case AmericanEngineType.BjerksundStensland:
        engine = new BjerksundStenslandEngine(bsmProcess);
        break;
    case AmericanEngineType.FiniteDifference:
        engine = new FDAmericanEngine(bsmProcess, (uint)timeSteps,
            (uint)timeSteps - 1);
        break;
    case AmericanEngineType.BinomialJarrowRudd:
        engine = new BinomialVanillaEngine(bsmProcess, "jarrowrudd",
            (uint)timeSteps);
        break;
    case AmericanEngineType.BinomialCoxRossRubinstein:
        engine = new BinomialVanillaEngine(bsmProcess, "coxrossrubinstein",
            (uint)timeSteps);
        break;
    case AmericanEngineType.BinomialAdditiveEquiprobabilities:
        engine = new BinomialVanillaEngine(bsmProcess, "eqp", (uint)timeSteps);
        break;
    case AmericanEngineType.BinomialTrigeorgis:
        engine = new BinomialVanillaEngine(bsmProcess, "trigeorgis",
            (uint)timeSteps);
        break;
    case AmericanEngineType.BinomialTian:
        engine = new BinomialVanillaEngine(bsmProcess, "tian", (uint)timeSteps);
        break;
    case AmericanEngineType.BinomialLeisenReimer:
        engine = new BinomialVanillaEngine(bsmProcess, "leisenreimer",
            (uint)timeSteps);
        break;
    case AmericanEngineType.BinomialJoshi:
        engine = new BinomialVanillaEngine(bsmProcess, "joshi4",
```

```
                    (uint)timeSteps);
            break;
        default:
            throw new ArgumentException("unknown engine type");
    }

    VanillaOption option = new VanillaOption(payoff, exercise);
    option.setPricingEngine(engine);
    object value = null;
    object delta = null;
    object gamma = null;
    object theta = null;
    object rho = null;
    object vega = null;

    try
    {
        value = option.NPV();
        delta = option.delta();
        gamma = option.gamma();
        theta = option.theta();
        rho = option.rho();
        vega = option.vega();
    }
    catch { }
    return new object[] { value, delta, gamma, theta, rho, vega };
}

public static object AmericanOptionImpliedVol(string optionType, string evalDate,
    double yearsToMaturity, double strike, double spot, double q, double r,
    double targetPrice)
{
    Date startDate = new Date((int)DateTime.Parse(evalDate).ToOADate());
    Date maturity = startDate + Convert.ToInt32(yearsToMaturity * 360 + 0.5);
    return AmericanOptionImpliedVol(optionType, startDate, maturity, strike, spot,
        q, r, targetPrice);
}

public static object AmericanOptionImpliedVol(string optionType, Date evalDate,
    Date maturity, double strike, double spot, double q, double r,
    double targetPrice)
{
    optionType = optionType.ToUpper();
    Option.Type otype = Option.Type.Call;
    if (optionType == "P" || optionType == "PUT")
        otype = Option.Type.Put;

    Settings.instance().setEvaluationDate(evalDate);
    Date settlementDate = evalDate;
    Calendar calendar = new TARGET();
    DayCounter dc = new Actual360();
    QuoteHandle spot1 = new QuoteHandle(new SimpleQuote(spot));
    YieldTermStructureHandle qTS = new YieldTermStructureHandle(new
        FlatForward(settlementDate, q, dc));
    YieldTermStructureHandle rTS = new YieldTermStructureHandle(new
```

```
            FlatForward(settlementDate, r, dc));
        BlackVolTermStructureHandle volTS = new BlackVolTermStructureHandle(new
        BlackConstantVol(settlementDate, calendar, 0.3, dc));
        Payoff payoff = new PlainVanillaPayoff(otype, strike);
        Exercise exercise = new AmericanExercise(settlementDate, maturity);
        BlackScholesMertonProcess bsmProcess = new BlackScholesMertonProcess(spot1, qTS,
            rTS, volTS);
        VanillaOption option = new VanillaOption(payoff, exercise);

        object v = null;
        try
        {
            v = option.impliedVolatility(targetPrice, bsmProcess, 1.0e-6, 10000,
                0, 4.0);
        }
        catch { }
        return v;
    }
```

Here, we implement several helper methods, which allow you to calculate the option price and implied volatility for American options using a variety of pricing engines (over 10 types). These helper methods are very similar to those we implemented previously for the European options.

Next, we will convert the above methods into web services. Add the following methods to the *OptionValuesController* class in the *Quant/Controllers* folder with the following code:

```
[Route("~/api/americanOption/{optionType}/{yearsToMaturity}/{strike}/{spot}/{q}
    /{r}/{vol}/{engineType}/{timeSteps}")]
[HttpGet]
public JsonResult GetAmericanOption(string optionType, double yearsTomaturity,
    double strike, double spot, double q, double r, double vol, string engineType,
    int timeSteps)
{
    var startDate = DateTime.Today.ToString("yyyy-MM-dd");
    var res = OptionHelper.AmericanOption(optionType, startDate, yearsTomaturity,
        strike, spot, q, r, vol, engineType, timeSteps);
    return Json(new { Name = "American Option", Result = res });
}

[Route("~/api/americanImpliedVol/{optionType}/{yearsToMaturity}/{strike}/{spot}
    /{q}/{r}/{targetPrice}")]
[HttpGet]
public JsonResult GetAmericanImpliedVol(string optionType, double yearsTomaturity,
    double strike, double spot, double q, double r, double targetPrice)
{
    var startDate = DateTime.Today.ToString("yyyy-MM-dd");
    var res = OptionHelper.AmericanOptionImpliedVol(optionType, startDate,
        yearsTomaturity, strike, spot, q, r, targetPrice);
    return Json(new { Name = "American Option: Implied Volatility", Result = res });
}

[Route("~/api/americanOptionTest")]
[HttpGet]
public JsonResult GetAmericanOptionTest()
{
    var optionTable = new DataTable();
```

```csharp
optionTable.Columns.Add("OptionType", typeof(string));
optionTable.Columns.Add("Strike", typeof(float));
optionTable.Columns.Add("Spot", typeof(float));
optionTable.Columns.Add("DivYield", typeof(float));
optionTable.Columns.Add("Rate", typeof(float));
optionTable.Columns.Add("Maturity", typeof(float));
optionTable.Columns.Add("Vol", typeof(float));
optionTable.Columns.Add("BAWValue", typeof(float));
optionTable.Columns.Add("BaroneAdesi", typeof(float));
optionTable.Columns.Add("FiniteDifference", typeof(double));
optionTable.Columns.Add("BinomialJarrowRudd", typeof(double));
optionTable.Columns.Add("BinomialCRR", typeof(double));

optionTable.Rows.Add("Call", 100.00, 90.00, 0.10, 0.10, 0.10, 0.15, 0.0206);
optionTable.Rows.Add("Call", 100.00, 100.00, 0.10, 0.10, 0.10, 0.15, 1.8771);
optionTable.Rows.Add("Call", 100.00, 110.00, 0.10, 0.10, 0.10, 0.15, 10.0089);
optionTable.Rows.Add("Call", 100.00, 90.00, 0.10, 0.10, 0.10, 0.25, 0.3159);
optionTable.Rows.Add("Call", 100.00, 100.00, 0.10, 0.10, 0.10, 0.25, 3.1280);
optionTable.Rows.Add("Call", 100.00, 110.00, 0.10, 0.10, 0.10, 0.25, 10.3919);
optionTable.Rows.Add("Call", 100.00, 90.00, 0.10, 0.10, 0.10, 0.35, 0.9495);
optionTable.Rows.Add("Call", 100.00, 100.00, 0.10, 0.10, 0.10, 0.35, 4.3777);
optionTable.Rows.Add("Call", 100.00, 110.00, 0.10, 0.10, 0.10, 0.35, 11.1679);
optionTable.Rows.Add("Call", 100.00, 90.00, 0.10, 0.10, 0.50, 0.15, 0.8208);
optionTable.Rows.Add("Call", 100.00, 100.00, 0.10, 0.10, 0.50, 0.15, 4.0842);
optionTable.Rows.Add("Call", 100.00, 110.00, 0.10, 0.10, 0.50, 0.15, 10.8087);
optionTable.Rows.Add("Call", 100.00, 90.00, 0.10, 0.10, 0.50, 0.25, 2.7437);
optionTable.Rows.Add("Call", 100.00, 100.00, 0.10, 0.10, 0.50, 0.25, 6.8015);
optionTable.Rows.Add("Call", 100.00, 110.00, 0.10, 0.10, 0.50, 0.25, 13.0170);
optionTable.Rows.Add("Call", 100.00, 90.00, 0.10, 0.10, 0.50, 0.35, 5.0063);
optionTable.Rows.Add("Call", 100.00, 100.00, 0.10, 0.10, 0.50, 0.35, 9.5106);
optionTable.Rows.Add("Call", 100.00, 110.00, 0.10, 0.10, 0.50, 0.35, 15.5689);
optionTable.Rows.Add("Put", 100.00, 90.00, 0.10, 0.10, 0.10, 0.15, 10.0000);
optionTable.Rows.Add("Put", 100.00, 100.00, 0.10, 0.10, 0.10, 0.15, 1.8770);
optionTable.Rows.Add("Put", 100.00, 110.00, 0.10, 0.10, 0.10, 0.15, 0.0410);
optionTable.Rows.Add("Put", 100.00, 90.00, 0.10, 0.10, 0.10, 0.25, 10.2533);
optionTable.Rows.Add("Put", 100.00, 100.00, 0.10, 0.10, 0.10, 0.25, 3.1277);
optionTable.Rows.Add("Put", 100.00, 110.00, 0.10, 0.10, 0.10, 0.25, 0.4562);
optionTable.Rows.Add("Put", 100.00, 90.00, 0.10, 0.10, 0.10, 0.35, 10.8787);
optionTable.Rows.Add("Put", 100.00, 100.00, 0.10, 0.10, 0.10, 0.35, 4.3777);
optionTable.Rows.Add("Put", 100.00, 110.00, 0.10, 0.10, 0.10, 0.35, 1.2402);
optionTable.Rows.Add("Put", 100.00, 90.00, 0.10, 0.10, 0.50, 0.15, 10.5595);
optionTable.Rows.Add("Put", 100.00, 100.00, 0.10, 0.10, 0.50, 0.15, 4.0842);
optionTable.Rows.Add("Put", 100.00, 110.00, 0.10, 0.10, 0.50, 0.15, 1.0822);
optionTable.Rows.Add("Put", 100.00, 90.00, 0.10, 0.10, 0.50, 0.25, 12.4419);
optionTable.Rows.Add("Put", 100.00, 100.00, 0.10, 0.10, 0.50, 0.25, 6.8014);
optionTable.Rows.Add("Put", 100.00, 110.00, 0.10, 0.10, 0.50, 0.25, 3.3226);
optionTable.Rows.Add("Put", 100.00, 90.00, 0.10, 0.10, 0.50, 0.35, 14.6945);
optionTable.Rows.Add("Put", 100.00, 100.00, 0.10, 0.10, 0.50, 0.35, 9.5104);
optionTable.Rows.Add("Put", 100.00, 110.00, 0.10, 0.10, 0.50, 0.35, 5.8823);

var startDate = DateTime.Today.ToString("yyyy-MM-dd");

foreach (DataRow row in optionTable.Rows)
{
    string optionType = row["OptionType"].ToString();
```

```
        double spot = Convert.ToDouble(row["Spot"]);
        double strike = Convert.ToDouble(row["Strike"]);
        double rate = Convert.ToDouble(row["Rate"]);
        double div = Convert.ToDouble(row["DivYield"]);
        double maturity = Convert.ToDouble(row["Maturity"]);
        double vol = Convert.ToDouble(row["Vol"]);
        row["BaroneAdesi"] = OptionHelper.AmericanOption(optionType, startDate,
            maturity, strike, spot, div, rate, vol, "BaroneAdesiWhaley", 0)[0];
        row["FiniteDifference"] = OptionHelper.AmericanOption(optionType, startDate,
            maturity, strike, spot, div, rate, vol, "FiniteDifference", 100)[0];
        row["BinomialJarrowRudd"] = OptionHelper.AmericanOption(optionType,
            startDate, maturity, strike, spot, div, rate, vol, "BinomialJarrowRudd",
            100)[0];
        row["BinomialCRR"] = OptionHelper.AmericanOption(optionType, startDate,
            maturity, strike, spot, div, rate, vol, "BinomialCoxRossRubinstein",
            100)[0];
    }
    return Json(new { Name = "American Option", result = optionTable });
}
```

You can use the *GetAmericanOption* and *GetAmericanImpliedVol* methods to calculate the price, Greeks, and implied volatility for American options.

The *GetAmericanOptionTest* method calculates prices for American call and put options with fixed strike = 100, dividend yield = 0.1, interest rate = 0.1, and varying the parameters of the spot, times to maturity, and volatility. The last column in the input table shows the results from the BAW approximation in the literature. Here, we calculate option prices using several different pricing engines, and compare the calculated results with those in the literature.

Option Pricing in Angular

The process of sending a request from the Angular application to get results for American options following the same basic repository patterns presented in the preceding chapters. Add the following methods to the *ch9.service.ts* file in the *ClientApp/src/app/models* folder with the following code:

```
// ch9-service.ts file:
getAmericanOption(optionType: string, yearsToMaturity: number, strike: number,
  spot: number, q: number, r: number, vol: number, engineType: string,
  timeSteps: number) {
  let url1 = this.url + 'api/americanoption/' + optionType + '/' + yearsToMaturity
    + '/' + strike + '/' + spot + '/' + q + '/' + r + '/' + vol + '/' +
    engineType + '/' + timeSteps;
  return this.http.get<any>(url1);
}

getAmericanImpliedVol(optionType: string, yearsToMaturity: number, strike: number,
  spot: number, q: number, r: number, targetPrice: number) {
  let url1 = this.url + 'api/americanimpliedvol/' + optionType + '/' +
    yearsToMaturity + '/' + strike + '/' + spot + '/' + q + '/' + r + '/' +
    targetPrice;
  return this.http.get<any>(url1);
}

getAmericanOptionTest() {
```

```
    return this.http.get<any>(this.url + 'api/americanoptiontest');
  }
```

Note that these methods also return promises, which allow you to execute your code sequentially and create responsive UI.

Now, I will use an example to illustrate how to pricing American options in an Angular application. Run the following statement in a command prompt window:

ng g c chapter09/ch9-option-am --module=app.module

This generates a new component called *ch9-option-am* in the *ClientApp/src/app/Chapter09* folder. Open the component class and replace its content with the following code:

```
// ch9-option-am.component.ts file:
import { Component, OnInit } from '@angular/core';
import { Ch9Service } from '../../models/ch9.service';
import { ModelHelper } from '../../models/model.helper';

@Component({
  selector: 'app-ch9-option-am',
  templateUrl: './ch9-option-am.component.html',
  styleUrls: ['./ch9-option-am.component.css']
})
export class Ch9OptionAmComponent implements OnInit {
  optionResult: any;
  colDefs: any;
  private helper: ModelHelper;

  constructor(private repository: Ch9Service) { }

  ngOnInit() {
    this.getOptionResult();
  }

  getOptionResult() {
    this.optionResult = null;
    this.repository.getAmericanOptionTest().subscribe(result => {
      this.optionResult = result.result;
      this.helper = new ModelHelper();
      this.colDefs = this.helper.setColDefs(result.result, 100);
    });
  }
}
```

Here, to extract the columns names automatically for displaying option results using *ag-Grid*, we implement a TypeScript helper class called *model.helper.ts* in the *ClientApp/src/app/models* folder with the following code:

```
// model.helper.ts file:
export class ModelHelper {
  setColDefs(data: any, colWidth: number) {
    var keys = Object.keys(data[0]);
    let cols = [];
    for (let k of keys) {
      cols.push({ headerName: this.FirstLetterCapitalize(k), field: k,
        width: colWidth });
```

```
    }
    return cols;
  }
  private FirstLetterCapitalize(s: string): string {
    return s.charAt(0).toUpperCase() + s.slice(1);
  }
}
```

We also need to update the *ch9-option-am* component's template:

```
<h2>
  ch9-option-am works!
</h2>

<ag-grid-angular *ngIf="optionResult" style="height:700px;width:1220px;"
  class="ag-theme-balham" [rowData]="optionResult" [columnDefs]="colDefs">
</ag-grid-angular>
```

Finally, we need to add a path for this new component to the *RouterModule* of the root module (i.e., the *app.module.ts* file):

```
{ path: 'chapter09/ch9-option-am, component: Ch9OptionAmComponent },
```

Then add the corresponding URL link to the *home* and *nav-menu* components.

Saving the project and navigating to the */chapter09/ch9-option-am* page produce the default results shown in Fig.9-6.

ch9-option-am works!

OptionTy...	Strike	Spot	DivYield	Rate	Maturity	Vol	BawValue	BaroneA...	FiniteDiff...	Binomial...	Binomial...
Call	100	90	0.1	0.1	0.1	0.15	0.0206	0.0227944851	0.02264326...	0.02155761...	0.02156899...
Call	100	100	0.1	0.1	0.1	0.15	1.8771	1.9024117	1.90177170...	1.89690836...	1.89743775...
Call	100	110	0.1	0.1	0.1	0.15	10.0089	10.0077362	10.0118193...	10.0115466...	10.0116415...
Call	100	90	0.1	0.1	0.1	0.25	0.3159	0.332877547	0.33217149...	0.32549117...	0.32251494...
Call	100	100	0.1	0.1	0.1	0.25	3.128	3.17013955	3.16910384...	3.15938035...	3.16185531...
Call	100	110	0.1	0.1	0.1	0.25	10.3919	10.410181	10.4160088...	10.4099726...	10.4117015...
Call	100	90	0.1	0.1	0.1	0.35	0.9495	0.9856709	0.98449675...	0.97535732...	0.97058326...
Call	100	100	0.1	0.1	0.1	0.35	4.3777	4.43706274	4.43561831...	4.41864737...	4.42546146...
Call	100	110	0.1	0.1	0.1	0.35	11.1679	11.2095232	11.2135302...	11.2058281...	11.2019128...
Call	100	90	0.1	0.1	0.5	0.15	0.8208	0.820821762	0.81120674...	0.81127731...	0.80560391...
Call	100	100	0.1	0.1	0.5	0.15	4.0842	4.084117	4.06768896...	4.07424866...	4.06001120...
Call	100	110	0.1	0.1	0.5	0.15	10.8087	10.808527	10.8082961...	10.8128350...	10.8159742...
Call	100	90	0.1	0.1	0.5	0.25	2.7437	2.74360037	2.72178071...	2.73231930...	2.71087595...
Call	100	100	0.1	0.1	0.5	0.25	6.8015	6.80134153	6.77398797...	6.79139242...	6.76112372...
Call	100	110	0.1	0.1	0.5	0.25	13.017	13.01673	12.9988859...	13.0093509...	13.0112425...
Call	100	90	0.1	0.1	0.5	0.35	5.0063	5.00615835	4.97274601...	4.98202391...	4.97065416...
Call	100	100	0.1	0.1	0.5	0.35	9.5106	9.510307	9.47199545...	9.49417704...	9.45390258...
Call	100	110	0.1	0.1	0.5	0.35	15.5689	15.5684271	15.5355254...	15.5551405...	15.5307578...
Put	100	90	0.1	0.1	0.1	0.15	10	10	10.0003345...	10.0007276...	10.0007341...
Put	100	100	0.1	0.1	0.1	0.15	1.877	1.9024092	1.90177167...	1.89687620...	1.89743794...
Put	100	110	0.1	0.1	0.1	0.15	0.041	0.0447037481	0.04448491...	0.04261966...	0.04280279...
Put	100	90	0.1	0.1	0.1	0.25	10.2533	10.2680483	10.2744309...	10.2696256...	10.2669546...
Put	100	100	0.1	0.1	0.1	0.25	3.1277	3.1701417	3.16910365...	3.15929894...	3.16185680...
Put	100	110	0.1	0.1	0.1	0.25	0.4562	0.478178233	0.47729458...	0.46928679...	0.47120902...

Fig.9-6. Calculated results for American options using different QuantLib pricing engines.

You can also pricing American options by calling the *getAmericanOption* and *getAmericanImpliedVol* methods implemented in the *ch9.service.ts* file, which expose input parameters that can be specified by users.

Barrier Options

We usually call the straight call or put options, such as European or American options, non-exotic or vanilla options. Whereas we consider the barrier options a type of exotic option because it is more complex than basic vanilla options. Their payoff depends on whether or not the underlying asset has reached or exceeded a predetermined price. A barrier option can be a knockout, meaning it can expire worthless if the underlying exceeds a certain price, limiting profits for the holder but limiting losses for the writer. It can also be a knock-in, meaning it has no value until the underlying reaches a certain price. Barrier options are also considered a type of path-dependent option because their value fluctuates as the underlying's price changes during the option's contract term. In other words, a barrier option's payoff is based on the underlying asset's price path.

Barrier options are always cheaper than a similar option without barrier. For example, if you believe that GOOG will go up this year, but are willing to bet that it will not go above $850, then you can buy the barrier and pay less premium than the vanilla option.

Standard Barrier Option Formulas

Here, we will discuss how to pricing the standard barrier options using the formulas provided in the literature (for example: D. R. Rich, *Advances in Futures and Options Research*, 7, 267, 1994, and E. G. Haug's book *The complete Guide to Option Pricing Formulas*). The formulas for pricing the standard barrier options use the following common set of factors:

$$A = \phi S e^{(b-r)T} N(\phi x_1) - \phi K e^{-rT} N(\phi x_1 - \phi \sigma \sqrt{T})$$

$$B = \phi S e^{(b-r)T} N(\phi x_2) - \phi K e^{-rT} N(\phi x_2 - \phi \sigma \sqrt{T})$$

$$C = \phi S e^{(b-r)T} \left(\frac{H}{S}\right)^{2(\mu+1)} N(\eta y_1) - \phi K e^{-rT} \left(\frac{H}{S}\right)^{2\mu} N(\eta y_1 - \eta \sigma \sqrt{T})$$

$$D = \phi S e^{(b-r)T} \left(\frac{H}{S}\right)^{2(\mu+1)} N(\eta y_2) - \phi K e^{-rT} \left(\frac{H}{S}\right)^{2\mu} N(\eta y_2 - \eta \sigma \sqrt{T})$$

$$E = K e^{-rT} \left[N(\eta x_2 - \eta \sigma \sqrt{T}) - \left(\frac{H}{S}\right)^{2\mu} N(\eta y_2 - \eta \sigma \sqrt{T}) \right]$$

$$F = K \left[\left(\frac{H}{S}\right)^{\mu+\lambda} N(\eta z) + \left(\frac{H}{S}\right)^{\mu-\lambda} N(\eta z - 2\eta \lambda \sigma \sqrt{T}) \right]$$

$$x_1 = \frac{\ln\left(\frac{S}{K}\right)}{\sigma \sqrt{T}} + (1+\mu)\sigma\sqrt{T}, \quad x_2 = \frac{\ln\left(\frac{S}{H}\right)}{\sigma \sqrt{T}} + (1+\mu)\sigma\sqrt{T}$$

$$y_1 = \frac{\ln\left(\frac{H^2}{SK}\right)}{\sigma \sqrt{T}} + (1+\mu)\sigma\sqrt{T}, \quad y_2 = \frac{\ln\left(\frac{H}{S}\right)}{\sigma \sqrt{T}} + (1+\mu)\sigma\sqrt{T}$$

$$z = \frac{\ln\left(\frac{H}{S}\right)}{\sigma\sqrt{T}} + \lambda\sigma\sqrt{T}, \quad \mu = \frac{b - \sigma^2/2}{\sigma^2}, \quad \lambda = \sqrt{\mu^2 + \frac{2r}{\sigma^2}}$$

In Barriers:

In options are paid for today but first come into existence if the asset price S hits the barrier H before expiration. It is possible to include a pre-specified cash rebate L, which is paid out at option expiration if the option has not been knocked in during its lifetime.

Down-and-in call for $S > H$:

Payoff: $\max(S-K, 0)$ if $S \leq H$ before T else L at expiration.

$$c_{di(K>H)} = C + E \qquad\qquad\qquad \eta = 1, \phi = 1$$
$$c_{di(K<H)} = A - B + D + E \qquad\qquad \eta = 1, \phi = 1$$

Up-and-in call for $S < H$:

Payoff: $\max(S-K, 0)$ if $S \geq H$ before T else L at expiration.

$$c_{ui(K>H)} = A + E \qquad\qquad\qquad \eta = -1, \phi = 1$$
$$c_{ui(K<H)} = B - C + D + E \qquad\qquad \eta = -1, \phi = 1$$

Down-and-in put for $S > H$:

Payoff: $\max(K-S, 0)$ if $S \leq H$ before T else L at expiration.

$$p_{di(K>H)} = B - C + D + E \qquad\qquad \eta = 1, \phi = -1$$
$$p_{di(K<H)} = A + E \qquad\qquad\qquad \eta = 1, \phi = -1$$

Up-and-in put for $S < H$:

Payoff: $\max(K-S, 0)$ if $S \geq H$ before T else L at expiration.

$$p_{ui(K>H)} = A - B + D + E \qquad\qquad \eta = -1, \phi = -1$$
$$p_{ui(K<H)} = C + E \qquad\qquad\qquad \eta = -1, \phi = -1$$

Out Barriers:

Out options are similar to standard options except that the option becomes worthless if the asset price S hits the barrier before expiration. It is possible to include a pre-specified cash rebate L, which is paid out if the option is knocked out before expiration.

Down-and-out call for $S > H$:

Payoff: $\max(S-K, 0)$ if $S > H$ before T else L at hit.

$$c_{do(K>H)} = A - C + F \qquad\qquad\qquad \eta = 1, \phi = 1$$
$$c_{do(K<H)} = B - D + F \qquad\qquad\qquad \eta = 1, \phi = 1$$

Up-and-out call for $S < H$:

Payoff: $\max(S-K, 0)$ if $S < H$ before T else L at hit.

$$c_{uo(K>H)} = F \qquad\qquad\qquad\qquad \eta = -1, \phi = 1$$
$$c_{uo(K<H)} = A - B + C - D + F \qquad\qquad \eta = -1, \phi = 1$$

Down-and-out put for $S > H$:

Payoff: $\max(K-S, 0)$ if $S > H$ before T else L at hit.

$$p_{do(K>H)} = A - B + C - D + F \qquad\qquad \eta = 1, \phi = -1$$
$$p_{do(K<H)} = F \qquad\qquad \eta = 1, \phi = -1$$

Up-and-out put for $S < H$:

Payoff: $\max(K-S, 0)$ if $S < H$ before T else L at hit.

$$p_{uo(K>H)} = B - D + F \qquad\qquad \eta = -1, \phi = -1$$
$$p_{uo(K<H)} = A - C + F \qquad\qquad \eta = -1, \phi = -1$$

In this book, I will not show you how to implement the program using the above formulas; instead, I will demonstrate how to use QuantLib to pricing barrier options in the following sections.

Helper Methods and Web Service

In order to use QuantLib to pricing barrier options, we will create some helper methods to easily access QuantLib's option pricing engine. First, add an enum called *BarrierEngineType* to the *OptionHelper* class in the *Quant/Models* folder:

```
public enum BarrierEngineType
{
    Analytic = 0,
    MonteCarlo = 1,
};
```

This enum only contains two types of pricing engines for barrier options available in QuantLib.

Next, add the following methods to the *OptionHelper* class in the *Quant/Models* folder with the following code:

```
public static object BarrierOption(string optionType, string evalDate,
    double yearsToMaturity, double strike, double spot, double barrierLevel,
    double rebate, double q, double r, double vol, string barrierType,
    string priceEngineType)
{
    DateTime evalDate1 = DateTime.Parse(evalDate);
    Date startDate = new Date((int)evalDate1.ToOADate());
    Date maturity = startDate + 2 + Convert.ToInt32(yearsToMaturity * 365 + 0.5);
    barrierType = char.ToUpper(barrierType[0]) + barrierType.Substring(1);
    Enum.TryParse(barrierType, out Barrier.Type barrierType1);
    priceEngineType = char.ToUpper(priceEngineType[0]) +
        priceEngineType.Substring(1);
    Enum.TryParse(priceEngineType, out BarrierEngineType engineType);

    return BarrierOptionResult(optionType, startDate, maturity, strike, spot,
        barrierLevel, rebate, q, r, vol, barrierType1, engineType);
}

private static object BarrierOptionResult(string optionType, Date evalDate,
    Date maturity, double strike, double spot, double barrierLevel, double rebate,
    double q, double r, double vol, Barrier.Type barrierType,
    BarrierEngineType priceEngineType)
```

```
{
    optionType = optionType.ToUpper();
    Option.Type otype = Option.Type.Call;
    if (optionType == "P" || optionType == "PUT")
        otype = Option.Type.Put;
    Calendar calendar = new TARGET();
    Date settleDate = evalDate;
    Settings.instance().setEvaluationDate(evalDate);
    DayCounter dc = new Actual365Fixed();
    Exercise exercise = new EuropeanExercise(maturity);
    QuoteHandle underlyingH = new QuoteHandle(new SimpleQuote(spot));
    YieldTermStructureHandle flatTermStructure = new YieldTermStructureHandle(
        new FlatForward(settleDate, r, dc));
    var flatDividendTS = new YieldTermStructureHandle(
        new FlatForward(settleDate, q, dc));
    var flatVolTS = new BlackVolTermStructureHandle(new BlackConstantVol(settleDate,
        calendar, vol, dc));
    var payoff = new PlainVanillaPayoff(otype, strike);
    var bsmProcess = new BlackScholesMertonProcess(underlyingH, flatDividendTS,
        flatTermStructure, flatVolTS);
    BarrierOption option = new BarrierOption(barrierType, barrierLevel, rebate,
        payoff, exercise);
    PricingEngine engine;

    switch (priceEngineType)
    {
        case BarrierEngineType.Analytic:
            engine = new AnalyticBarrierEngine(bsmProcess);
            break;
        case BarrierEngineType.MonteCarlo:
            string traits = "pseudorandom";
            uint mcTimeSteps = 1;
            uint timeStepsPerYear = int.MaxValue;
            bool brownianBridge = false;
            bool antitheticVariate = false;
            int requiredSamples = int.MaxValue;
            double requiredTolerance = 0.05;
            int maxSamples = int.MaxValue;
            int seed = 42;
            engine = new MCBarrierEngine(bsmProcess, traits, mcTimeSteps,
                timeStepsPerYear, brownianBridge, antitheticVariate,
                requiredSamples, requiredTolerance, maxSamples, false, seed);
            break;
        default:
            throw new ArgumentException("unknown engine type");
    }
    option.setPricingEngine(engine);
    object v = null;
    try
    {
        v = option.NPV();
    }
    catch { }
    return v;
}
```

Here, we create two helper methods, which allow you to calculate the option price for barrier options using different pricing engines. These two helper methods are very similar to those we implemented previously for the European options.

Next, we will convert the above methods into web services. Add the following methods to the *OptionValuesController* class in the *Quant/Controllers* folder with the following code:

```
[Route("~/api/barrierOption/{optionType}/{yearsToMaturity}/{strike}
    /{spot}/{barrierLevel}/{rebate}/{q}/{r}/{vol}/{barrierType}/{engineType}")]
[HttpGet]
public JsonResult GetBarrierOption(string optionType, double yearsTomaturity,
    double strike, double spot, double barrierLevel, double rebate, double q,
    double r, double vol, string barrierType, string engineType)
{
    var startDate = DateTime.Today.ToString("yyyy-MM-dd");
    var res = OptionHelper.BarrierOption(optionType, startDate, yearsTomaturity,
        strike, spot, barrierLevel, rebate, q, r, vol, barrierType, engineType);
    return Json(new { Name = "Barrier Option", Result = res });
}


[Route("~/api/barrierOptions/{optionType}/{strike}/{spot}/{barrierLevel}/{rebate}
    /{q}/{r}/{vol}/{engineType}")]
[HttpGet]
public JsonResult GetBarrierOptions(string optionType, double strike, double spot,
    double barrierLevel, double rebate, double q, double r, double vol,
    string engineType)
{
    var startDate = DateTime.Today.ToString("yyyy-MM-dd");
    var mat = new double[] { 0.1, 0.2, 0.3, 0.4, 0.5, 0.6, 0.7, 0.8, 0.9, 1.0 };
    List<object> objs = new List<object>();
    for (int i = 0; i < mat.Length; i++)
    {
        var downIn = OptionHelper.BarrierOption(optionType, startDate, mat[i],
            strike, spot, barrierLevel, rebate, q, r,vol, "downIn", engineType);
        var downOut = OptionHelper.BarrierOption(optionType, startDate, mat[i],
            strike, spot, barrierLevel, rebate, q, r, vol, "downOut", engineType);
        var upIn = OptionHelper.BarrierOption(optionType, startDate, mat[i],
            strike, spot, barrierLevel, rebate, q, r, vol, "upIn", engineType);
        var upOut = OptionHelper.BarrierOption(optionType, startDate, mat[i],
            strike, spot, barrierLevel, rebate, q, r, vol, "upOut", engineType);

        objs.Add(new { Maturity = mat[i], downIn, downOut, upIn, upOut });
    }
    return Json(new { Name = "Barrier Options", Result = objs });
}
```

You can use the *GetBarrierOption* method to calculate the option price for barrier options.

The *GetBarrierOptions* method calculates the prices for barrier call and put options with an array of times to maturity and different types of barriers (*downIn, downOutp, upIn,* and *upOut*).

Option Pricing in Angular

The process of sending a request from the Angular application to get results for barrier options following the same basic repository patterns presented in the preceding chapters. Add the following methods to the *ch9.service.ts* file in the *ClientApp/src/app/models* folder with the following code:

```
getBarrierOption(optionType: string, yearsToMaturity: number, strike: number,
  spot: number, barrierLevel: number, rebate: number, q: number, r: number,
  vol: number, barrierType: string, engineType: string) {
    let url1 = this.url + 'api/barrieroption/' + optionType + '/' + yearsToMaturity
      + '/' + strike + '/' + spot + '/' + barrierLevel + '/' + rebate + '/' + q
      + '/' + r + '/' + vol + '/' + barrierType + '/' + engineType;
    return this.http.get<any>(url1);
}

getBarrierOptions(optionType: string, strike: number, spot: number,
  barrierLevel: number, rebate: number, q: number, r: number, vol: number,
  engineType: string) {
    let url1 = this.url + 'api/barrieroptions/' + optionType  + '/' + strike + '/'
      + spot + '/' + barrierLevel + '/' + rebate + '/' + q + '/' + r + '/' + vol
      + '/' + engineType;
    return this.http.get<any>(url1);
}
```

Note that these methods also return promises, which allow you to execute your code sequentially and create responsive UI.

Now, I will use an example to illustrate how to pricing barrier options in an Angular application. Run the following statement in a command prompt window:

```
ng g c chapter09/ch9-option-barrier --module=app.module
```

This generates a new component called *ch9-option-barrier* in the *ClientApp/src/app/Chapter09* folder. Open the component class and replace its content with the following code:

```
// ch9-option-barrier.component.ts file:
import { Component, OnInit } from '@angular/core';
import { Ch9Service } from '../../models/ch9.service';
import { ModelHelper } from '../../models/model.helper';

@Component({
  selector: 'app-ch9-option-barrier',
  templateUrl: './ch9-option-barrier.component.html',
  styleUrls: ['./ch9-option-barrier.component.css']
})
export class Ch9OptionBarrierComponent implements OnInit {
  optionResult: any;
  colDefs: any;

  inputColDefs: any = [
    { headerName: "Parameter", field: "param", width: 100 },
    { headerName: "Value", field: "value", width: 100, editable: true },
    { headerName: "Description", field: "desc", width: 300 },
  ];

  inputRows: any = [
```

```
    { param: 'Option Type', value: 'C', desc: 'P for a put option, otherwise
      a call option' },
    { param: 'Spot', value: 100, desc: 'Current price of the underlying asset' },
    { param: 'Strike', value: 100, desc: 'Strike price' },
    { param: 'Rate', value: 0.1, desc: 'Interest rate' },
    { param: 'Div Yield', value: 0.06, desc: 'Continuous dividend yield' },
    { param: 'Vol', value: 0.3, desc: 'Volatility' },
    { param: 'Barrier', value: 90, desc: 'Barrier level' },
    { param: 'Rebate', value: 0, desc: 'Paid off if barrier is not knocked in
      during if life' },
    { param: 'Engine Type', value: 'analytic', desc: 'Pricing engine type' },
  ];

  private helper: ModelHelper;

  constructor(private repository: Ch9Service) { }

  ngOnInit() {
    this.getOptionResult(this.inputRows);
  }

  getOptionResult(rows: any) {
    this.optionResult = null;

    this.repository.getBarrierOptions(rows[0].value, rows[2].value, rows[1].value,
      rows[6].value, rows[7].value, rows[4].value, rows[3].value, rows[5].value,
      rows[8].value).subscribe(result => {
        this.optionResult = result.result;
        this.helper = new ModelHelper();
        this.colDefs = this.helper.setColDefs(result.result, 100);
      });
  }
}
```

Here, we use an *ag-Grid* component to display the input parameters, which is much cleaner than using multiple input fields. Note that we enable editing in the *Value* column of the input *ag-Grid* by setting the *editable* property to *true* inside the *inputColDefs* property.

Next, we need to update the *ch9-option-barrier* component's template:

```
// ch9-option-barrier.component.ts file:
<h2>
  ch9-option-barrier works!
</h2>

<button mat-raised-button color="primary" (click)="getOptionResult(inputRows)">
  Get Option Result</button>
<div class="cardList">
  <mat-card class="card-border">
    <p>Input Parameters</p>
    <ag-grid-angular *ngIf="optionResult" style="height:90%;"
      class="ag-theme-balham" [rowData]="inputRows" [columnDefs]="inputColDefs">
    </ag-grid-angular>
  </mat-card>
  <mat-card class="card-border">
    <p>Barrier option price</p>
```

```
<ag-grid-angular *ngIf="optionResult" style="height:90%;"
  class="ag-theme-balham" [rowData]="optionResult" [columnDefs]="colDefs">
</ag-grid-angular>
  </mat-card>
</div>
```

This template adds two *ag-grid-angular* directives that are used to display the input parameters and output option prices respectively.

Finally, we need to add a path for this new component to the *RouterModule* of the root module (i.e., the *app.module.ts* file):

```
{ path: 'chapter09/ch9-option-barrier, component: Ch9OptionBarrierComponent },
```

Then add the corresponding URL link to the *home* and *nav-menu* components.

Saving the project and navigating to the */chapter09/ch9-option-barrier* page produce the default results shown in Fig.9-7.

Fig.9-7. Calculated prices for a barrier option using the analytic pricing engine.

You can see from Fig.9-7 that there are no values for the *UpIn* and *UpOut* fields because the barrier level is lower than the *spot* value. If you enter a barrier that is higher than the *spot* value (say 110), both the *UpIn* and *UpOut* fields will then have values, but no values for the fields *DownIn* and *DownOut*, as shown in Fig.9-8.

You can also use the *MonteCarlo* engine to calculate the option prices for a barrier option, as shown in Fig.9-9.

ch9-option-barrier works!

Fig.9-8. Barrier option prices when barrier level > spot.

ch9-option-barrier works!

Fig.9-9. Calculate prices for a barrier option using the Monte Carlo engine.

Bermudan Options

Bermudan options are a type of exotic options that can only be exercised on predetermined dates, e.g. at 1st of each month. They fall somewhere between American and European options because the holder has the right but not the obligation to exercise the option at a specific time (as with a European option), but there are multiple opportunities to exercise before expiration (as with an American option). As the Bermuda option lies between American and European options, its premium should also fall between those of American and European options, i.e., European premium < Bermudan premium < American premium.

Helper Methods and Web Service

In order to use QuantLib to pricing Bermudan options, we will implement some helper methods to easily access QuantLib's option pricing engine. First, add an enum called *BarrierEngineType* to the *OptionHelper* class in the *Quant/Models* folder:

```
public enum BermudanEngineType
{
    FiniteDifference,
    BinomialJarrowRudd,
    BinomialCoxRossRubinstein,
    BinomialAdditiveEquiprobabilities,
    BinomialTrigeorgis,
    BinomialTian,
    BinomialLeisenReimer,
    BinomialJoshi,
};
```

This enum specify various pricing engine types for pricing Bermudan options available in QuantLib.

Next, add the following methods to the *OptionHelper* class with the following code:

```
public static object[] BermudanOption(string optionType, string evalDate,
    int exerciseFrequency, int exerciseTimes, double strike, double spot, double q,
    double r, double vol, string priceEngineType, int timeSteps)
{
    priceEngineType = char.ToUpper(priceEngineType[0]) +
        priceEngineType.Substring(1);
    Enum.TryParse(priceEngineType, out BermudanEngineType engineType);
    Date evalDate1 = new Date((int)DateTime.Parse(evalDate).ToOADate());
    Settings.instance().setEvaluationDate(evalDate1);
    Date settlementDate = evalDate1 + 2;

    DateVector exerciseDates = new DateVector(exerciseTimes);
    for (int i = 1; i <= exerciseTimes; i++)
    {
        Period forwordPeriod = new Period(exerciseFrequency * i, TimeUnit.Months);
        Date forwordDate = settlementDate.Add(forwordPeriod);
        exerciseDates.Add(forwordDate);
    }
    return BermudanOptionResult(optionType, evalDate1, settlementDate,
        exerciseDates, strike, spot, q, r, vol, engineType, timeSteps);
}

private static object[] BermudanOptionResult(string optionType, Date evalDate,
    Date settlementDate, DateVector exerciseDates, double strike, double spot,
    double q, double r, double vol, BermudanEngineType priceEngineType,
    int timeSteps)
{
    optionType = optionType.ToUpper();
    Option.Type otype = Option.Type.Call;
    if (optionType == "P" || optionType == "PUT")
        otype = Option.Type.Put;

    Calendar calendar = new TARGET();
    Exercise exercise = new BermudanExercise(exerciseDates);
```

```
DayCounter dc = new Actual360();
QuoteHandle spot1 = new QuoteHandle(new SimpleQuote(spot));
YieldTermStructureHandle qTS = new YieldTermStructureHandle(new
    FlatForward(settlementDate, q, dc));
YieldTermStructureHandle rTS = new YieldTermStructureHandle(new
    FlatForward(settlementDate, r, dc));
BlackVolTermStructureHandle volTS = new BlackVolTermStructureHandle(new
    BlackConstantVol(settlementDate, calendar, vol, dc));
PlainVanillaPayoff payoff = new PlainVanillaPayoff(otype, strike);
BlackScholesMertonProcess bsmProcess = new BlackScholesMertonProcess(spot1,
    qTS, rTS, volTS);

PricingEngine engine;
switch (priceEngineType)
{
    case BermudanEngineType.BinomialJarrowRudd:
        engine = new BinomialVanillaEngine(bsmProcess, "jarrowrudd",
            (uint)timeSteps);
        break;
    case BermudanEngineType.BinomialCoxRossRubinstein:
        engine = new BinomialVanillaEngine(bsmProcess, "coxrossrubinstein",
            (uint)timeSteps);
        break;
    case BermudanEngineType.BinomialAdditiveEquiprobabilities:
        engine = new BinomialVanillaEngine(bsmProcess, "eqp", (uint)timeSteps);
        break;
    case BermudanEngineType.BinomialTrigeorgis:
        engine = new BinomialVanillaEngine(bsmProcess, "trigeorgis",
            (uint)timeSteps);
        break;
    case BermudanEngineType.BinomialTian:
        engine = new BinomialVanillaEngine(bsmProcess, "tain", (uint)timeSteps);
        break;
    case BermudanEngineType.BinomialLeisenReimer:
        engine = new BinomialVanillaEngine(bsmProcess, "leisenreimer",
            (uint)timeSteps);
        break;
    case BermudanEngineType.BinomialJoshi:
        engine = new BinomialVanillaEngine(bsmProcess, "joshi4",
            (uint)timeSteps);
        break;
    case BermudanEngineType.FiniteDifference:
        engine = new FDBermudanEngine(bsmProcess, (uint)timeSteps,
            (uint)timeSteps - 1);
        break;
    default:
        throw new ArgumentException("unknown engine type");
}

VanillaOption option = new VanillaOption(payoff, exercise);
option.setPricingEngine(engine);
object value = null;
object delta = null;
object gamma = null;
object theta = null;
```

```
    object rho = null;
    object vega = null;
    try
    {
        value = option.NPV();
        delta = option.delta();
        gamma = option.gamma();
        theta = option.theta();
        rho = option.rho();
        vega = option.vega();
    }
    catch { }
    return new object[] { value, delta, gamma, theta, rho, vega };
}
```

Here, we create two helper methods, which allow you to calculate the option price for Bermudan options using a variety of pricing engines. Note that for Bermudan options, the input parameters do not contain the maturity or expiration date; instead, you need to specify the exercise frequency (in unit of month) and the total exercise times. These two parameters allow you to set the predetermined exercise dates for Bermudan options. For instance, if you set *exerciseFrequency* = 3 and *exerciseTimes* = 4, you then specify the exercise date quarterly, i.e., you can exercise the Bermudan option every three months starting from the settlement date, and you have total four exercise opportunities before expiration.

Now, we will convert the above methods into web services. Add the following methods to the *OptionValuesController* class in the *Quant/Controllers* folder with the following code:

```
[Route("~/api/bermudanOption/{optionType}/{exerciseFrequency}/{exerciseTimes}/
    {strike}/{spot}/{q}/{r}/{vol}/{engineType}/{timeSteps}")]
[HttpGet]
public JsonResult GetBermudanOption(string optionType, int exerciseFrequency,
    int exerciseTimes, double strike, double spot, double q, double r, double vol,
    string engineType, int timeSteps)
{
    var startDate = DateTime.Today.ToString("yyyy-MM-dd");
    var res = OptionHelper.BermudanOption(optionType, startDate, exerciseFrequency,
        exerciseTimes, strike, spot, q, r, vol, engineType, timeSteps);
    return Json(new { Name = "Bermudan Option", Result = res });
}


[Route("~/api/bermudanOptions/{optionType}/{exerciseFrequency}/{exerciseTimes}/
    {spot}/{q}/{r}/{vol}/{engineType}/{timeSteps}")]
[HttpGet]
public JsonResult GetBermudanOptions(string optionType, int exerciseFrequency,
    int exerciseTimes, double spot, double q, double r, double vol,
    string engineType, int timeSteps)
{
    var startDate = DateTime.Today.ToString("yyyy-MM-dd");
    List<object> objs = new List<object>();
    for (int i = 1; i < 11; i++)
    {
        double strike = 20.0 * i;
        var opt = OptionHelper.BermudanOption(optionType, startDate,
            exerciseFrequency, exerciseTimes, strike, spot, q, r, vol, engineType,
            timeSteps);
        objs.Add(new { Strike = strike, Price = opt[0], Delta = opt[1],
```

```
            Gamma = opt[2], Theta = opt[3], Rho = opt[4], Vega = opt[5] });
    }
    return Json(new { Name = "Bermudan Options", Result = objs });
}
```

You can use the *GetBermudanOption* method to calculate the price and Greeks for Bermudan options. The *GetBermudanOptions* method calculates the prices and Greeks for Bermudan options with an array of strike values.

Option Pricing in Angular

The process of sending a request from the Angular application to get results for Bermudan options following the same basic repository patterns presented in the preceding chapters. Add the following methods to the *ch9.service.ts* file in the *ClientApp/src/app/models* folder with the following code:

```
getBermudanOption(optionType: string, exerciseFrequency: number,
  exerciseTimes: number, strike: number, spot: number, q: number, r: number,
  vol: number, engineType: string, timeSteps) {
    let url1 = this.url + 'api/bermudanoption/' + optionType + '/' + exerciseFrequency
      + '/' + exerciseTimes + '/' + strike + '/'
      + spot + '/' + q + '/' + r + '/' + vol + '/' + engineType + '/' + timeSteps;
    return this.http.get<any>(url1);
}

getBermudanOptions(optionType: string, exerciseFrequency: number,
  exerciseTimes: number, spot: number, q: number, r: number, vol: number,
  engineType: string, timeSteps) {
    let url1 = this.url + 'api/bermudanoptions/' + optionType + '/' +
      exerciseFrequency + '/' + exerciseTimes + '/' + spot + '/' + q + '/' + r + '/' +
      vol + '/' + engineType + '/' + timeSteps;
    return this.http.get<any>(url1);
}
```

Note that these methods also return promises, which allow you to execute your code sequentially and create responsive UI.

Now, I will use an example to illustrate how to pricing Bermudan options in an Angular application. Run the following statement in a command prompt window:

ng g c chapter09/ch9-option-bermudan --module=app.module

This generates a new component called *ch9-option-bermudan* in the *ClientApp/src/app/Chapter09* folder. Open the component class and replace its content with the following code:

```
//ch9-option-bermudan.component.ts file:
import { Component, OnInit } from '@angular/core';
import { Ch9Service } from '../../models/ch9.service';
import { ModelHelper } from '../../models/model.helper';

@Component({
  selector: 'app-ch9-option-bermudan',
  templateUrl: './ch9-option-bermudan.component.html',
  styleUrls: ['./ch9-option-bermudan.component.css']
})
export class Ch9OptionBermudanComponent implements OnInit {
  optionResult: any;
```

```
  engineType: string = 'binomialJoshi';
  colDefs: any;

  inputColDefs: any = [
    { headerName: "Parameter", field: "param", width: 100 },
    { headerName: "Value", field: "value", width: 100, editable: true },
    { headerName: "Description", field: "desc", width: 300 },
  ];

  inputRows: any = [
    { param: 'Option Type', value: 'C', desc: 'P for a put option, otherwise
       a call option' },
    { param: 'Spot', value: 100, desc: 'Current price of the underlying asset' },
    { param: 'Rate', value: 0.1, desc: 'Interest rate' },
    { param: 'Div Yield', value: 0.06, desc: 'Continuous dividend yield' },
    { param: 'Vol', value: 0.3, desc: 'Volatility' },
    { param: 'Exercise Frequency', value: 3, desc: 'Exercise frequency
       (in Month)' },
    { param: 'Exercise Times', value: 4, desc: 'Total exercise times' },
    { param: 'Time Steps', value: 200, desc: 'Time steps used in binomial
       engines' },
  ];

  private helper: ModelHelper;

  constructor(private repository: Ch9Service) { }

  ngOnInit() {
    this.getOptionResult(this.inputRows, this.engineType);
  }

  getOptionResult(rows: any, engineType: string) {
    this.optionResult = null;
    this.repository.getBermudanOptions(rows[0].value, rows[5].value, rows[6].value,
      rows[1].value, rows[3].value, rows[2].value, rows[4].value, engineType,
      rows[7].value).subscribe(result => {
      this.optionResult = result.result;
      this.helper = new ModelHelper();
      this.colDefs = this.helper.setColDefs(result.result, 100);
    });
  }
}
```

Here, we use an *ag-Grid* component to display the input parameters, which is much cleaner than using multiple input fields. Note that we enable editing in the *Value* column of the input *ag-Grid* by setting the *editable* property to true inside the *inputColDefs* property.

Next, we need to update the *ch9-option-bermudan* component's template:

```
// ch9-option-bermudan.component.html file:
<h2>
  ch9-option-bermudan works!
</h2>

<mat-form-field>
  <mat-select  placeholder="Select a pricing engine" [(value)]="engineType">
```

```
    <mat-option value="finiteDifference">Finite Difference</mat-option>
    <mat-option value="binomialJarrowRudd">Binomial Jarrow-Rudd</mat-option>
    <mat-option value="binomialCoxRossRubinstein">Binomial Cox-Ross-Rubinstein
    </mat-option>
    <mat-option value="binomialAdditiveEquiprobabilities">Binomial
      Additive-Equiprobabilities</mat-option>
    <mat-option value="binomialTrigeorgis">Binomial Trigeorgis</mat-option>
    <mat-option value="binomialTian">Binomial Tian</mat-option>
    <mat-option value="binomialLeisenReimer">Binomial Leisen-Reimer</mat-option>
    <mat-option value="binomialJoshi">Binomial Joshi</mat-option>
  </mat-select>
</mat-form-field>

<button mat-raised-button color="primary" (click)="getOptionResult(inputRows)">Get
Option Result</button>
<div class="cardList">
  <mat-card class="card-border">
    <p>Input Parameters</p>
    <ag-grid-angular *ngIf="optionResult" style="height:90%;"
      class="ag-theme-balham" [rowData]="inputRows" [columnDefs]="inputColDefs">
    </ag-grid-angular>
  </mat-card>
  <mat-card class="card-border">
    <p>Bermudan option price</p>
    <ag-grid-angular *ngIf="optionResult" style="height:90%;"
      class="ag-theme-balham" [rowData]="optionResult" [columnDefs]="colDefs">
    </ag-grid-angular>
  </mat-card>
</div>
```

This template first specifies the price engines and then adds two *ag-grid-angular* directives that are used to display the input parameters and output option prices respectively.

Finally, we need to add a path for this new component to the *RouterModule* of the root module (i.e., the *app.module.ts* file):

```
{ path: 'chapter09/ch9-option-bermudan, component: Ch9OptionBermudanComponent },
```

Then add the corresponding URL link to the *home* and *nav-menu* components.

Saving the project and navigating to the */chapter09/ch9-option-bermudan* page produce the default results shown in Fig.9-10.

You can also use the other pricing engines to calculate the prices and Greeks for the Bermudan options, as shown in Fig.9-11, where the finite difference engine is used for pricing a Bermudan put options.

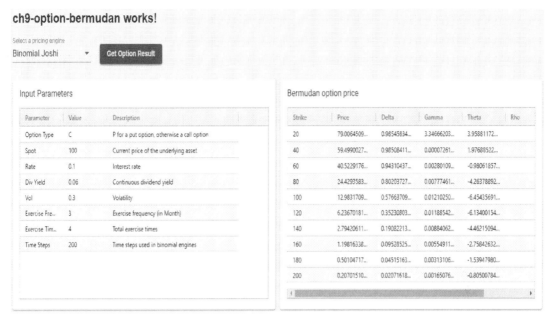

Fig.9-10. Calculated results for a Bermudan call option using the Binomial Joshi engine.

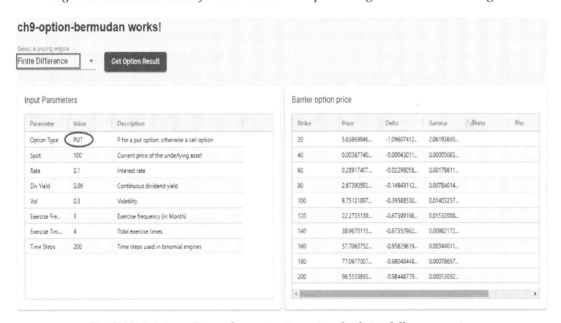

Fig.9-11. Pricing a Bermudan put option using the finite difference engine.

American Options in Real-World

Up to now, in our discussion on options pricing, we always use the continuous dividend yield and the flat term structures for interest rates and volatility. However, in real-world market, the dividends are not paid in a continuous way but in a predetermined format, such as quarterly; both the interest rate and volatility are not constants and you cannot use the flat term structures for them.

In this section, I will show you how to price American options in real-world market with discrete dividend payments using the interest rate curve and volatility surface. I will present the detailed procedure on how to bootstrap the required dividend, interest rate, and volatility curves from real market data. This will give you an idea for what is required to price options in real-world markets. By following the steps and templates described here, you should be able to price various options in real-world markets.

Term Structure for Interest Rates

Here, we are only interested in the short-term options (expiration < one year), so the USD LIBOR interest rate should be enough to build the term structure for the interest rates. Fig.9-12 shows a sample Libor data from https://www.theice.com/marketdata/reports/170 website.

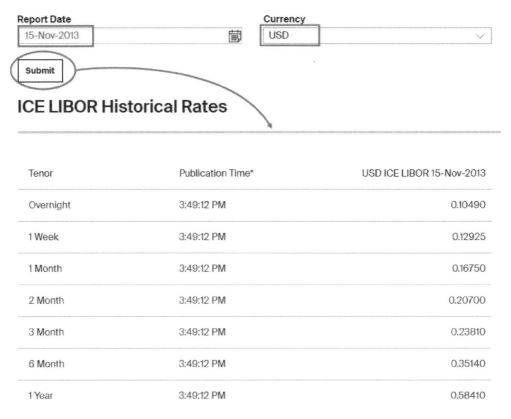

Tenor	Publication Time*	USD ICE LIBOR 15-Nov-2013
Overnight	3:49:12 PM	0.10490
1 Week	3:49:12 PM	0.12925
1 Month	3:49:12 PM	0.16750
2 Month	3:49:12 PM	0.20700
3 Month	3:49:12 PM	0.23810
6 Month	3:49:12 PM	0.35140
1 Year	3:49:12 PM	0.58410

Fig. 9-12. USD LIBOR interest rates.

From this ICE website, you can get the LIBOR rates by specifying the report date and currency, and then clicking the submit button. You can see that for each day, the USD LIBOR rate usually contains seven quantities for overnight, 1 week, 1 month, 2 months, 3 months, 6 months, and 1 year respectively. We can build a term structure using the USD LIBOR data format. Add a private method called *GetYieldCurve* to the *OptionHelper* class in the *Quant/Models* folder with the following code:

```
private static YieldTermStructure GetYieldCurve(Date settlementDate,
    uint fixingDays, double[] rates, Calendar calendar, DayCounter dc)
{
    Period[] periods = new Period[]
    {
        new Period(1, TimeUnit.Days),
        new Period(1, TimeUnit.Weeks),
        new Period(1, TimeUnit.Months),
        new Period(2, TimeUnit.Months),
        new Period(3, TimeUnit.Months),
        new Period(6, TimeUnit.Months),
        new Period(12, TimeUnit.Months)
    };

    RateHelperVector liborRates = new RateHelperVector();
    for (int i = 0; i < rates.Length; i++)
        liborRates.Add(new DepositRateHelper(rates[i], periods[i], (uint)fixingDays,
            calendar, BusinessDayConvention.ModifiedFollowing, true, dc));
    return new PiecewiseCubicZero(settlementDate, liborRates, dc);
}
```

This method takes a double array called *rates* as input parameter, which holds the USD LIBOR rate data on the settlement date. Note that the *rates* array data should be stored in the same order as the *periods* array. We then create the *DepositRateHelper* objects for the USD LIBOR rate and add them to the *RateHelperVector* object named *liborRates*. Finally, we bootstrap on the USD LIBOR rate using a cubic spline interpolation algorithm, in which each segment is determined sequentially starting from the earliest period to the latest period.

If you want to price a long-term option (> one year), the LIBOR rate data are not enough, and you may need to add some swap rate data to the yield curve using the *SwapRateHelper* object. Following the template specified in the *GetYieldCurve* method, you can easily build various yield term structures according to the requirement of your applications.

Dividend Yield Curve

In this section, we will create a dividend yield curve for a given dividend yield and a dividend paid frequency (i.e., quarterly, semiannually, etc.). Add a private method named *GetDividendCurve* to the *OptionHelper* class. Here is the code for this method:

```
private static ZeroCurve GetDividendCurve(Date evalDate, Date maturity,
    Date exDivDate, double spot, double dividend, int dividendFrequency,
    Calendar calendar)
{
    Double annualDividend = dividend * 12.0 / dividendFrequency;
    Settings.instance().setEvaluationDate(evalDate);
    int settlementDays = 2;
    int dividendDiscountDays = settlementDays + lendar.businessDaysBetween(evalDate,
        maturity);
    double dividendYield = (annualDividend / spot) * dividendDiscountDays / 252;
    DateVector exDivDates = new DateVector();
    DoubleVector dividendYields = new DoubleVector();

    //Last ex div date and yield
    exDivDates.Add(calendar.advance(exDivDate, new Period(-dividendFrequency,
```

```
        TimeUnit.Months), BusinessDayConvention.ModifiedPreceding, true));
    dividendYields.Add(dividendYield);

    //Currently announced ex div date and yield
    exDivDates.Add(exDivDate);
    dividendYields.Add(dividendYield);

    //Next ex div date (projected) and yield
    Date projectedNextExDivDate = calendar.advance(exDivDate,
        new Period(dividendFrequency, TimeUnit.Months),
        BusinessDayConvention.ModifiedPreceding, true);
    exDivDates.Add(projectedNextExDivDate);
    dividendYields.Add(dividendYield);

    return new ZeroCurve(exDivDates, dividendYields, new ActualActual(), calendar);
}
```

This method takes the *dividend* and *dividendFrequency* (in months) as inputs and returns a *ZeroCurve* object as the dividend curve. For our short-term options, we simply create three dividend data points: last dividend, current dividend, and next dividend; and use these data to build the *ZeroCurve* object.

Volatility Smile

Conventionally, the relationship between the implied volatility and strike is called the volatility smile. Both the shape and level of the smile provide useful information about the current market price of risk for a particular underlying asset. Usually the low delta options are trading at a higher implied volatility than the ATM options. The OTM puts are often priced with a higher implied volatility than the OTM calls, which is called the *skew* phenomenon.

Since the implied volatility changes with the strike and times to maturity, we need to construct the volatility surface for the option pricing engines. Add a new static method named *GetVolCurve* to the *OptionHelper* class. Here is the code for this method:

```
private static BlackVolTermStructure GetVolCurve(Date evalDate, Date maturity,
    double[] strikes, double[] vols, Calendar calendar, DayCounter dc)
{
    DoubleVector strikes1 = new DoubleVector();
    for (int i = 0; i < strikes.Length; i++)
        strikes1.Add(strikes[i]);

    DateVector expirations = new DateVector();
    expirations.Add(maturity);

    Matrix volMatrix = new Matrix((uint)strikes1.Count, 1);
    for (int i = 0; i < vols.Length; i++)
    {
        volMatrix.set((uint)i, 0, vols[i]);
    }

    return new BlackVarianceSurface(evalDate, calendar, expirations, strikes1,
        volMatrix, dc);
}
```

This method takes the volatility smile (*strikes* and *vols*) as input parameters. The volatility smile data should be provided by the market, or market data vendors. By creating various vectors and matrix objects, this method finally return a *BlackVarianceSurface* instance to create the *BlackVolTermStructure* object. The *BlackVarianceSurface* class simulates the Black volatility surface as a variance surface and calculates time and strike dependent Black volatility using the matrix of Black volatilities observed in the market. Note that the calculation is performed interpolating on the variance surface using a bilinear algorithm.

Helper Methods and Web Service

In the preceding sections, we have implemented the code to bootstrap all of our market data curves. Now, we are ready to price American options in a real-world market. Add the following two methods to the *OptionHelper* class with the following code:

```
public static DataTable AmericanOptionRealWorld(string optionType, string evalDate,
    string maturity, double spot, double[] strikes, double[] vols, double[] rates,
    double dividend, int dividendFrequency, string exDivDate,
    string priceEngineType, int timeSteps)
{
    Date evalDate1 = new Date((int)DateTime.Parse(evalDate).ToOADate());
    Date maturity1 = new Date((int)DateTime.Parse(maturity).ToOADate());
    Date exDivDate1 = new Date((int)DateTime.Parse(exDivDate).ToOADate());
    priceEngineType = char.ToUpper(priceEngineType[0])+priceEngineType.Substring(1);
    Enum.TryParse(priceEngineType, out AmericanEngineType engineType);
    return AmericanOptionRealWorldResult(optionType, evalDate1, maturity1, spot,
        strikes, vols, rates, dividend, dividendFrequency,exDivDate1, engineType,
        timeSteps);
}


public static DataTable AmericanOptionRealWorld(string optionType, Date evalDate,
    Date maturity, double spot, double[] strikes, double[] vols, double[] rates,
    double dividend, int dividendFrequency, Date exDivDate,  AmericanEngineType
    priceEngineType, int timeSteps)
{
    optionType = optionType.ToUpper();
    Option.Type otype = Option.Type.Call;
    if (optionType == "P" || optionType == "PUT")
        otype = Option.Type.Put;

    Calendar calendar = new UnitedStates(UnitedStates.Market.NYSE);
    Settings.instance().setEvaluationDate(evalDate);
    Date settlementDate = evalDate + 2;
    settlementDate = calendar.adjust(settlementDate);
    DayCounter dc = new ActualActual();

    // build yield term structure from Libor rates
    YieldTermStructureHandle yieldTS = new YieldTermStructureHandle(
        GetYieldCurve(settlementDate, 2, rates, calendar, dc));

    //build dividend term structure
    YieldTermStructureHandle dividendTS = new YieldTermStructureHandle(
        GetDividendCurve(evalDate, maturity, exDivDate, spot, dividend,
        dividendFrequency, calendar));
```

```
//build vol term structure:
BlackVolTermStructureHandle volTS = new BlackVolTermStructureHandle(
    GetVolCurve(evalDate, maturity, strikes, vols, calendar, dc));

QuoteHandle spot1 = new QuoteHandle(new SimpleQuote(spot));
Exercise exercise = new AmericanExercise(settlementDate, maturity);
BlackScholesMertonProcess bsmProcess =
    new BlackScholesMertonProcess(spot1, dividendTS, yieldTS, volTS);

PricingEngine engine;
switch (priceEngineType)
{
    case AmericanEngineType.Barone_Adesi_Whaley:
        engine = new BaroneAdesiWhaleyEngine(bsmProcess);
        break;
    case AmericanEngineType.Bjerksund_Stensland:
        engine = new BjerksundStenslandEngine(bsmProcess);
        break;
    case AmericanEngineType.FiniteDifference:
        engine = new FDAmericanEngine(bsmProcess, (uint)timeSteps,
            (uint)timeSteps - 1);
        break;
    case AmericanEngineType.Binomial_Jarrow_Rudd:
        engine = new BinomialVanillaEngine(bsmProcess, "jarrowrudd",
            (uint)timeSteps);
        break;
    case AmericanEngineType.Binomial_Cox_Ross_Rubinstein:
        engine = new BinomialVanillaEngine(bsmProcess,
            "coxrossrubinstein", (uint)timeSteps);
        break;
    case AmericanEngineType.Binomial_Additive_Equiprobabilities:
        engine = new BinomialVanillaEngine(bsmProcess, "eqp",
            (uint)timeSteps);
        break;
    case AmericanEngineType.Binomial_Trigeorgis:
        engine = new BinomialVanillaEngine(bsmProcess, "trigeorgis",
            (uint)timeSteps);
        break;
    case AmericanEngineType.Binomial_Tian:
        engine = new BinomialVanillaEngine(bsmProcess, "tian",
            (uint)timeSteps);
        break;
    case AmericanEngineType.Binomial_Leisen_Reimer:
        engine = new BinomialVanillaEngine(bsmProcess, "leisenreimer",
            (uint)timeSteps);
        break;
    case AmericanEngineType.Binomial_Joshi:
        engine = new BinomialVanillaEngine(bsmProcess, "joshi4",
            (uint)timeSteps);
        break;
    default:
        throw new ArgumentException("unknown engine type");
}
```

```
DataTable res = new DataTable();
res.Columns.Add("Strike", typeof(double));
res.Columns.Add("Price", typeof(double));
res.Columns.Add("Delta", typeof(double));
res.Columns.Add("Gamma", typeof(double));
res.Columns.Add("Theta", typeof(double));
res.Columns.Add("Rho", typeof(double));
res.Columns.Add("Vega", typeof(double));

for (int i = 0; i < strikes.Length; i++)
{
    Payoff payoff = new PlainVanillaPayoff(otype, strikes[i]);
    VanillaOption option = new VanillaOption(payoff, exercise);
    option.setPricingEngine(engine);
    object value = null;
    object delta = null;
    object gamma = null;
    object theta = null;
    object rho = null;
    object vega = null;
    object impliedVol = null;
    try
    {
        value = option.NPV();
        delta = option.delta();
        gamma = option.gamma();
        theta = option.theta();
        rho = option.rho();
        vega = option.vega();
    }
    catch { }
    res.Rows.Add(strikes[i], value, delta, gamma, theta, rho, vega);
}
return res;
}
```

The above pricing code looks very similar to that used in the *AmericanOption* and *AmericanOptionResult* methods, except that here, we use curved term structures for the interest rate, dividend yield, and volatility.

Now, I will use an example to show you how to pricing real world American options using the helper methods implemented in the preceding code. Specifically, we will calculate the value of a series of Intel (INTC) call options expiring on 2/21/2014, where a dividend of $0.22 is expected to be paid on 2/5/2014. Since this example has been discussed in the internet by Mick Hittesdorf at the following URL:

https://mhittesdorf.wordpress.com/2013/11/17/introducing-quantlib-american-option-pricing-with-dividends/

We can compare our results with his. As Mick did, we use the volatility smile data from Interactive Brokers, as shown in Fig. 9-13.

Here, we will use a web service to implement this example.

Add a new method called *GetAmericanOptionRealWorld* to the *OptionValuesControllers* class in the *Quant/Controllers* folder with the following code:

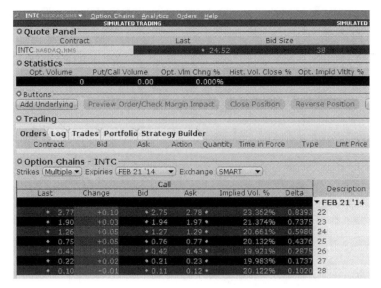

Fig. 9-13. INTC option data from Interactive Brokers.

```
[Route("~/api/americanOptionRealWorld/{engineType}")]
[HttpGet]
public JsonResult GetAmericanOptionRealWorld(string engineType)
{
    string evalDate = "2013-11-15";
    string maturity = "2014-02-21";
    string exDivDate = "2014-02-05";
    double spot = 24.52;
    double[] strikes = new double[] { 22.0, 23.0, 24.0, 25.0, 26.0, 27.0, 28.0 };
    double dividend = 0.22;
    int dividendFrequency = 3; // Dividend paid quanterly
    double[] rates = new double[] { 0.001049, 0.0012925, 0.001675, 0.00207,
        0.002381, 0.003514, 0.005841 };
    double[] vols = new double[] { 0.23362, 0.21374, 0.20661, 0.20132, 0.19921,
        0.19983, 0.20122 };
    var res = OptionHelper.AmericanOptionRealWorld("CALL", evalDate, maturity, spot,
        strikes, vols, rates, dividend, dividendFrequency, exDivDate,
        engineType, 200);

    return Json(new { Name = "Real World American Option", Result = res });
}
```

Within this method, the data for the *spot*, *strikes*, and *vols* are the market data directly from Interactive Brokers, and the data for *rates* are from www.theice.com as shown in Fig. 9-12.

Option Pricing in Angular

The process of sending a request from the Angular application to get results for real-world American options following the same basic repository patterns presented in the preceding chapters. Add the following methods to the *ch9.service.ts* file in the *ClientApp/src/app/models* folder with the following code:

```
getAmericanOptionRealWorld(engineType: string) {
    return this.http.get<any>(this.url + 'api/americanoptionrealworld/' + engineType);
}
```

Note that this method also returns a promise, which allows you to execute your code sequentially and create responsive UI.

Now, I will use an example to illustrate how to pricing real world American options in an Angular application. Run the following statement in a command prompt window:

ng g c chapter09/ch9-option-realworld --module=app.module

This generates a new component called *ch9-option-realworld* in the *ClientApp/src/app/Chapter09* folder. Open the component class and replace its content with the following code:

```
//ch9-option-realworld.component.ts file:
import { Component, OnInit } from '@angular/core';
import { Ch9Repository } from '../../models/ch9.repository';
import { ModelHelper } from '../../models/model.helper';

@Component({
    selector: 'app-ch9-option-realworld',
    templateUrl: './ch9-option-realworld.component.html',
    styleUrls: ['./ch9-option-realworld.component.css']
})
export class Ch9OptionRealworldComponent implements OnInit {
    optionResult: any;
    engineType: string = 'binomialJarrowRudd';
    colDefs: any;
    private helper: ModelHelper;

    constructor(private repository: Ch9Repository) { }

    ngOnInit() {
        this.getOptionResult(this.engineType);
    }
    getOptionResult(engineType: string) {
        this.optionResult = null;
        this.repository.getAmericanOptionRealWorld(engineType).subscribe(result => {
            this.optionResult = result.result;
            this.helper = new ModelHelper();
            this.colDefs = this.helper.setColDefs(result.result, 100);
        });
    }
}
```

This method defines an *engineType* property that allows you to select a pricing engine, and then uses an *ag-Grid* component to display the output results.

Next, we need to update the *ch9-option-realworld* component's template:

```
// ch9-option-realworld.component.html file:
<h2>
    ch9-option-realworld works!
</h2>
<mat-form-field>
    <mat-select placeholder="Select a pricing engine" [(value)]="engineType">
```

```
      <mat-option value="baroneAdesiWhaley">Barone-Adesi-Whaley</mat-option>
      <mat-option value="bjerksundStensland">Bjerksund-Stensland</mat-option>
      <mat-option value="finiteDifference">Finite Difference</mat-option>
      <mat-option value="binomialJarrowRudd">Binomial Jarrow-Rudd</mat-option>
      <mat-option value="binomialCoxRossRubinstein">Binomial Cox-Ross-Rubinstein
      </mat-option>
      <mat-option value="binomialAdditiveEquiprobabilities">Binomial
        Additive-Equiprobabilities</mat-option>
      <mat-option value="binomialTrigeorgis">Binomial Trigeorgis</mat-option>
      <mat-option value="binomialTian">Binomial Tian</mat-option>
      <mat-option value="binomialLeisenReimer">Binomial Leisen-Reimer</mat-option>
      <mat-option value="binomialJoshi">Binomial Joshi</mat-option>
    </mat-select>
  </mat-form-field>

<button mat-raised-button color="primary" (click)="getOptionResult(engineType)">
  Get Option Result</button>

<ag-grid-angular *ngIf="optionResult" style="height:250px;width:720px;
  margin-top:30px" class="ag-theme-balham" [rowData]="optionResult"
  [columnDefs]="colDefs">
</ag-grid-angular>
```

This template first specifies the price engines and then adds an *ag-grid-angular* directive that is used to display the output option prices and Greeks.

Finally, we need to add a path for this new component to the *RouterModule* of the root module (i.e., the *app.module.ts* file):

```
{ path: 'chapter09/ch9-option-realworld, component: Ch9OptionRealworldComponent },
```

Then add the corresponding URL link to the *home* and *nav-menu* components.

Saving the project and navigating to the */chapter09/ch9-option-realworld* page produce the default results shown in Fig.9-14.

ch9-option-realworld works!

Select a pricing engine

Binomial Jarrow-Rudd ▼   **Get Option Result**

Strike	Price	Delta	Gamma	Theta	Rho	Vega
22	2.67591344...	0.86327538...	0.08954785...	-0.93634160...		
23	1.89777251...	0.74417527...	0.12826927...	-1.44579402...		
24	1.26240478...	0.59596158...	0.15331807...	-1.79031659...		
25	0.78633969...	0.43973440...	0.15539513...	-1.84930329...		
26	0.45744125...	0.29835324...	0.13631591...	-1.64069074...		
27	0.24668780...	0.18551220...	0.10522221...	-1.27588699...		
28	0.12581811...	0.10696940...	0.07231707...	-0.88121208...		

Fig.9-14. Pricing INTC call options using a binomial Jarrow-Rudd price engine.

Our calculated prices for INTC options are reasonably good, which are within or just outside the bid-ask spread for each strike in the Interactive Brokers screenshot (see Fig. 9-13). You can also change the pricing engines to re-pricing the INTC options. Fig.9-15 shows the results calculated using a finite-difference pricing engine.

ch9-option-realworld works!

Select a pricing engine

Finite Difference ▼   **Get Option Result**

Strike	Price	Delta	Gamma	Theta	Rho	Vega
22	2.76756261...	0.82813169...	0.08777055...			
23	1.94514777...	0.73169670...	0.12282077...			
24	1.28703477...	0.59289779...	0.14864149...			
25	0.78522221...	0.43868524...	0.15451464...			
26	0.44727783...	0.29540803...	0.13657128...			
27	0.24291805...	0.18393746...	0.10481781...			
28	0.12582770...	0.10703154...	0.07213427...			

Fig.9-15. pricing INTC call options using a finite-difference pricing engine.

Chapter 10
Pricing Fixed-Income Instruments

Fixed income securities are usually regarded as complex financial instruments. This may be because they have a more complex structure, or include some form of derivative component. Although the fixed income market is more than twice as large as the equity market, it is generally followed less closely by the media and is less well understood by the general public.

The major difference between fixed income and equities is in the area of price transparency. Stock prices are publicly known and the price changes are relayed instantly to all market participants. Thus, in the stock market, you can get a fair market price at the time of your buy or sell stocks. On the other hand, in the fixed income market, such as the bond market, trades are usually executed dealer-to-dealer or dealer-to-investor. This means that there is no central record of all of the transaction prices in the bond market. Therefore, instruments pricing in the fixed income market is more important than that in the equity market.

In this chapter, I will show you how to price some of fixed income instruments, including bond, credit swaps, and interest rates. The purpose of this chapter is more on technical approaches, implementation, and pricing engine applications, rather than an introduction or complete explanation about the fixed income instruments. You can always find good introductions on the topics from textbooks.

Simple Bonds Pricing

A bond, or a debt security, is a financial instrument, under which the issuer owes the holders a debt and is obliged to pay them interest (the coupon) and to repay the principal at a maturity date. Interest is usually payable at fixed intervals (annual, semiannual, monthly). Bonds and stocks are both securities, but the major difference between the two is that stockholders have an equity stake in the company (i.e. they are investors), whereas bondholders have a creditor stake in the company (i.e. they are lenders). Being a creditor, bondholders have priority over stockholders. This means they will be repaid in advance of stockholders in the event of bankruptcy. This is the reason why a bond is less risky than an equity. Another difference is that bonds usually have a defined term, or maturity, after which the bond is redeemed, whereas stocks are typically outstanding indefinitely. A standard bond is a fixed coupon bond without any embedded option, delivering its coupons on periodic dates and principal on the maturity date.

In this section, we will discuss simplified or hypothetical bonds, which has flat rate or simple rate curve term structures. Bond pricing can be viewed as a three-step process: obtain the cash flows the bondholder is entitled to; obtain the discount rates for the maturities corresponding to the cash flow dates; obtain the bond price as the discounted value of the cash flow.

The cash flow of a bond depends on two parameters: maturity and coupon rate. For example, a government bond pays one-half of its coupon rate times its principal value every 6 months up to and including the maturity date. Thus, a bond with a 6% coupon and $1,000 face value maturing on 12/1/2017, will make future coupon payments of 3% of principal value, that is $30 on every June 1 and December 1 between the purchase date and the maturity date.

Then, we need to apply some kind of discounted value type of formula to obtain the current value of the bond. Given that the cash flows are known with certainty ex ante, only the time-value needs to be accounted for, using the present value rule, which can be written in the form:

$$PV(CF_t) = B(0, t)CF_t$$

Where $PV(CF_t)$ is the present value of the cash flow CF_t received at date t and $B(0, t)$ is the price at date 0 (today) of $1 to be received on date t. $B(t, 0)$ is called discount factor. You might be more familiar with an expression of the kind

$$PV(CF_t) = \frac{CF_t}{[1 + R(0, t)]^t}$$

Where $R(0, t)$ is the annual spot rate (or discount rate or interest rate) at date 0 for an investment up to date t. Thus, we can write the price for a bond as

$$PV(\text{bond}) = \sum_{t=1}^{T} \frac{CF_t}{[1 + R(0, t)]^t} = \sum_{t=1}^{T} B(0, t)CF_t \qquad (10\text{-}1)$$

You may ask how much exactly is worth the $1 received in a year from now? The answer to this question is simply $1/[1 + R(0,1)]$. Indeed, note that if you start with $1/[1 + R(0,1)]$ and invest it at the rate of $R(0,1)$, you will end up with $1 at the end of the period. Therefore, there is no difference between getting $1/[1 + R(0,1)]$ today or $1 in a year from now, so you should be willing to exchange one for the other. In other words, the fair price of a contract that promises to pay $1 in 1 year from now is $1/[1 + R(0,1)]$. It is the present value of $1. Of course, you may extend the principle to obtain the present value of a series of cash flows, which is just the bond pricing formula as shown in above equation.

Discounting Factors

There is a very convenient formula that allows you to compute the present value of a series of cash flows when all cash flows and all discount rates across various maturities are identical and equal to CF and y. Then the formula become

$$P_0 = \sum_{t=1}^{T} \frac{CF}{(1 + y)^t} = CF \times \frac{1}{y} \times \left[1 - \frac{1}{(1 + y)^T}\right] \qquad (10\text{-}2)$$

More generally, we have

$$P_0 = C \times \frac{1}{y} \times \left[1 - \frac{1}{(1+y)^T} \right] + \frac{N}{(1+y)^T} \qquad (10\text{-}3)$$

Where P_0 is the present value of the bond, T is the maturity of the bond, N is the nominal value of the bond, $C = c \times N$ is the coupon payment, and c is the coupon rate and y is the discount rate.

As an illustration, we consider the problem of valuing a series of cash flows promised by a bond with a 5% annual coupon rate, a 10-year maturity and a \$1,000 face value. We also assume all discount rates equal to 6%. Before we compute the present value of this bond, denoted by P_0, we first identify the cash flows. We have $CF_1 = CF_2 = \ldots = CF_9 = 50$ and $CF_{10} = 1{,}050$. Therefore, the value of this bond is

$$P_0 = \sum_{t=1}^{9} \frac{50}{(1+0.06)^t} + \frac{1050}{(1+0.06)^{10}} = \$926.3991 \qquad (10\text{-}4)$$

It is useful to note the following result. When the discount rate is equal to the coupon rate, then the bond value is equal to the face value.

The quoted price (or market price) of a bond in the market is usually its clean price, that is, its gross price minus the accrued interest. When you purchase a bond, you are actually entitled to receive all the future cash flows of this bond, until you no longer own it. If you buy the bond between two coupon payment dates, you logically must pay it at a price reflecting the fraction of the next coupon that the seller of the bond is entitled to receive for having held it until the sale. This price is called the gross price or dirty price, which is the sum of the clean price and the portion of the coupon that is due to the seller of the bond. This portion is called the accrued interest. Note that the accrued interest is computed from the settlement data on. In convention, the clean price, dirty price, and accrued interest are calculated for the face value of 100. Therefore, the present value of a bond should be equal to the face value times dirty price divided by 100.

Pricing Bonds with Flat Rates

The above example for a bond is very simple. Now we will try to reproduce the above results using the QuantLib bond-pricing engine, which should give you an idea what are the steps you need to take when pricing a simple bond using the pricing engine in QuantLib.

Add a new QuantLib fixed income helper class named *FixedIncomeHelper* to the *Quant/Models* folder with the following code:

```
using QuantLib;
using System;
using System.Data;

namespace Quant.Models
{
    public static class FixedIncomeHelper
    {
        public static object[] BondPrice(string evalDate, string issueDate,
            int timeToMaturity, int settlementDays, double faceValue, double rate,
            string coupon, string frequency)
        {
            Date evalDate1 = DateTime.Parse(evalDate).To<Date>();
```

```
Settings.instance().setEvaluationDate(evalDate1);
Date issueDate1 = DateTime.Parse(issueDate).To<Date>();
var maturity = DateTime.Parse(issueDate).AddYears(timeToMaturity);
Date maturity1 = maturity.To<Date>();
var couponStr = coupon.Split(',');
double[] coupons = new double[couponStr.Length];
for (int i = 0; i < couponStr.Length; i++)
    coupons[i] = couponStr[i].To<double>();

frequency = char.ToUpper(frequency[0]) + frequency.Substring(1);
Enum.TryParse(frequency, out Frequency frequency1);

Calendar calendar = new UnitedStates(
    UnitedStates.Market.GovernmentBond);
Date settlementDate = evalDate1.Add(settlementDays);
settlementDate = calendar.adjust(settlementDate);
DoubleVector coupon1 = new DoubleVector();
for (int i = 0; i < coupons.Length; i++)
    coupon1.Add(coupons[i]);

DayCounter dc = new ActualActual(ActualActual.Convention.Bond);
Schedule schedule = new Schedule(issueDate1, maturity1,
    new Period(frequency1), calendar, BusinessDayConvention.Unadjusted,
    BusinessDayConvention.Unadjusted, DateGeneration.Rule.Backward,
    false);
var fixedRateBond = new FixedRateBond(settlementDays, faceValue,
    schedule, coupon1, dc);
var flatCurve = new FlatForward(settlementDate, rate, dc,
    Compounding.Compounded, Frequency.Annual);
YieldTermStructureHandle discountingTermStructure =
    new YieldTermStructureHandle(flatCurve);
var bondEngine = new DiscountingBondEngine(discountingTermStructure);
fixedRateBond.setPricingEngine(bondEngine);

object npv = null;
object cprice = null;
object dprice = null;
object accrued = null;
object ytm = null;

try
{
    npv = fixedRateBond.NPV();
    cprice = fixedRateBond.cleanPrice();
    dprice = fixedRateBond.dirtyPrice();
    accrued = fixedRateBond.accruedAmount();
    ytm = fixedRateBond.yield(fixedRateBond.dayCounter(),
        Compounding.Compounded, frequency1);
}
catch { }
return new object[] { npv, cprice, dprice, accrued, ytm };
}

private static T To<T>(this object text)
{
```

```
        if (text == null) return default(T);
        if (text.Equals(DBNull.Value)) return default(T);
        if (text is string) if (string.IsNullOrWhiteSpace(text as string))
            return default(T);

        var type = typeof(T);
        if (type.ToString().Contains("QuantLib.Date"))
        {
            var dt = (DateTime)text;
            Date date = new Date((int)dt.ToOADate());
            return (T)Convert.ChangeType(date, type);
        }
        else if(type.ToString().Contains("DateTime"))
        {
            var date = text as Date;
            if (date!=null)
            {
                DateTime dt = Convert.ToDateTime(date.month() + " " +
                    date.dayOfMonth().ToString() + ", " +
                    date.year().ToString());
                return (T)Convert.ChangeType(dt, typeof(T));
            }
            else
            {
                DateTime dt = Convert.ToDateTime(text);
                return (T)Convert.ChangeType(dt, typeof(T));
            }
        }
        var underlyingType = Nullable.GetUnderlyingType(type) ?? type;
        return (T)Convert.ChangeType(text, underlyingType);
    }
  }
}
```

Here, we implement a private extension *To* method that is used to convert the *QuantLib.Date* object into *System.DateTime* object or vice versa. The *BondPrice* method takes the face value, discount rate, and coupon rate as inputs and returns the NPV (net present value), clean price, dirty price, accrued amount, and yield to maturity (YTM). Within this method, we first create a *Schedule* object, which generates coupon payment dates by taking into account a supplied calendar to determine business dates and holidays. We then set a *FixedRateBond* instance that takes face value of the bond, schedule, and coupon rate as its input parameters. Next, we create a flat term structure for the discount rate because the discount rate is a constant for a simple bond. Finally, the *DiscountingBondEngine* takes the *discountTermStruture* (or yield curve) as an argument, from which the pricing engine extracts the interest rates required to discount the bond's coupons.

Note that we also define the settlement date using the input parameter, *settlementDays*. The settlement date is the date on which payment is due in exchange for the bond. It is generally equal to the trade date (*evalDate*) plus a number of working days (*settlementDays*). For example, in Japan, *settlementDays* = 3 for Treasury bonds and T-bills. On the other hand, in the United States, *settlementDays* = 1 for Treasury bonds and T-bills. In UK, settlementDays = 1 and 2 for Treasury bonds and T-bills respectively. In the Euro zone, *settlementDays* = 3 for Treasury bonds, as it can be 1, 2, or 3 for T-bills, depending on the country under consideration. We also adjust the settlement date to be a business day using the *adjust* method of the calendar.

Now, we can convert the *BondPrice* method into a web service. Add a new API controller named *FixedIncomeValuesController* to the *Quant/Controllers* folder with the following code:

```
using Microsoft.AspNetCore.Mvc;
using Quant.Models;

namespace Quant.Controllers
{
    [Produces("application/json")]
    public class FixedIncomeValuesController : Controller
    {
        [Route("~/api/bondPrice/{evalDate}/{issueDate}/{timeToMaturity}
            /{settlementDays}/{faceValue}/{rate}/{coupon}/{frequency}")]
        [HttpGet]
        public JsonResult GetBondPrice(string evalDate, string issueDate,
            int timeToMaturity, int settlementDays, double faceValue,
            double rate, string coupon, string frequency)
        {
            var res = FixedIncomeHelper.BondPrice(evalDate, issueDate,
                timeToMaturity, settlementDays, faceValue, rate, coupon, frequency);
            return Json(new
            {
                Name = "Bond Price",
                Result = new
                {
                    presentValue = res[0],
                    cleanPrice = res[1],
                    dirtyPrice = res[2],
                    accuedValue = res[3],
                    ytm = res[4]
                }
            });
        }
    }
}
```

Running this project by pressing F5 and entering the following URL:

**https://localhost:5001/api/bondprice/2015-12-16/2015-12-16/ 10/1/1000/0.06/0.05
/annual**

Which produces the results shown in Fig.10-1.

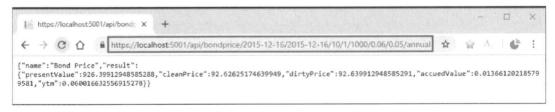

Fig.10-1. Results for a simple bond.

You can see that the present value for this simple bond from QuantLib is the same as our previous analytic result [see Eq. (10-4)]. Note that the dirty price is consistent with the present value of the bond. Also the dirty price is the sum of the clean price and accrued amount. Now, you may ask how does the pricing engine calculate the accrued amount? We know that the evaluation (trade) date is on 12/16/2015, and the settlement days = 1, indicating the settlement date is on 12/17/2015. This means you cannot collect the coupon rate until the settlement date, so you need to pay back one-day coupon to the seller, which is just the one day accrued amount. For the $100 face value and 5% annual coupon rate, the one-year coupon payment will be $5. Since we use the *ActualActual* day counter convention in the *BondPrice* method. There are 366 days from 12/16/2015 to 12/16/2016. In this case, the accrued interest is equal to $5 \times \left(\frac{1}{366}\right) = \$0.0136612$, which is the exact the same result shown in Fig.10-1.

Fig.10-2 shows the results when you change the discount rate to 0.05, which is the same as the coupon rate. In this case, the present value is equal to the face value, as expected.

Fig.10-2. Results for a simple bond with the discount rate equal to coupon rate.

Compounding Frequency Conventions

In calculating the present value of a bond, you should pay special attention to the question of how the interest rate is defined. To apply present value formulas, you need information about both the time basis (usually interest rates are expressed on an annual basis) and the compounding frequency.

In general, if you invest x amount at the interest rate R_n expressed on an annual basis and compounded n times per year, you would get $x(1 + \frac{R_n}{n})^{nT}$ after T years. Then, the effective equivalent annual (i.e., compounded once a year) rate $R_1 = R$ is defined as the solution to

$$x \left(1 + \frac{R_n}{n}\right)^{nT} = x(1 + R)^T$$

or

$$R = \left(1 + \frac{R_n}{n}\right)^n - 1 \tag{10-5}$$

For example, bond yields are often expressed on a yearly basis with semiannual compounding in the United States and UK, as they are expressed on a yearly basis with annual compounding in France and Germany. One can always convert a bond yield into an effective annual yield (EAY), that is, an interest rate expressed on a yearly basis with annual compounding.

In Eq. (10-5), if we let the compounding frequency increase without bound, we will perform a continuous compounding. In this case, the amount of money obtained per x invested after T years is

$$\lim_{n \to \infty} x \left(1 + \frac{R_n}{n}\right)^{nT} = xe^{R_c T}$$

Where R_c expressed on an annual basis is a continuously compounded rate. This allows you to obtain a very easy derivation of the future or present value of any cash flow, using

$$FV_t(CF_0) = CF_0 e^{R_c t}, \qquad PV(CF_t) = CF_t e^{-R_c t}$$

Where $FV_t(CF_0)$ is the future value at date t of a cash flow CF_0 invested at date 0 at an R_c continuously compounded rate, and $PV(CF_t)$ is the present value at date 0 of a cash flow CF_t received at date t.

You can also easily obtain the effective equivalent annual rate R:

$$R = e^{R_c} - 1$$

When R is small, we have $R \approx R_c$ as a first-order approximation. For example, the equivalent annual rate of a 5% continuously compounded interest rate is $R = e^{0.05} - 1 = 5.1271\%$. Note that $R - R^c > 0$, which makes sense; it means that we should invest at a higher rate when compounding is less frequent to generate the same amount of cash at the end of a given period.

Pricing Bonds with a Rate Curve

In the preceding section, we discussed the frequency compounding. Here I will show you how to price a bond with an interest curve instead of a constant rate. In this case, we need to build a curved term structure for the interest rate instead of a flat one. Specifically, we want to consider a simple hypothetical bond with a face value of $100, which pays 5% coupon semiannually issued on 1/15/2015 and maturity on 1/15/2017. To make things simpler, we assume that we know the interest rates of the treasury as of 1/15/2015. The annualized rates are 0.4% for 6 months, 0.6% for 1 year, 0.65% for 1.5 years, and 0.7% for 2 years. We can calculate the present value for this bond easily using the formula in Eq. (10-1):

$$PV = \frac{2.5}{(1 + 0.004)^{0.5}} + \frac{2.5}{1 + 0.006} + \frac{2.5}{(1 + 0.0065)^{1.5}} + \frac{102.5}{(1 + 0.007)^2} = 108.53 \qquad (10\text{-}6)$$

Now, we try to reproduce the above result using the pricing engine in QuantLib. Add a new method, *BondPriceCurveRate*, to the *FixedIncomeHelper* class. Here is the code for this method:

```
public static DataTable BondPriceCurveRate()
{
    Date evalDate = new Date(15, Month.January, 2015);
    Settings.instance().setEvaluationDate(evalDate);
    Date issueDate = new Date(15, Month.January, 2015);
    Date maturity = new Date(15, Month.January, 2017);
    Calendar calendar = new UnitedStates(UnitedStates.Market.GovernmentBond);
    int settlementDays = 1;
    Date settlementDate = evalDate.Add(settlementDays);
    settlementDate = calendar.adjust(settlementDate);

    Date[] rateDates = new Date[]
    {
        new Date(15, Month.January, 2015),
        new Date(15, Month.July, 2015),
        new Date(15, Month.January, 2016),
        new Date(15, Month.July, 2016),
        new Date(15, Month.January, 2017)
    };
    double[] rates = new double[] { 0, 0.004, 0.006, 0.0065, 0.007 };
```

```
DateVector rateDates1 = new DateVector();
DoubleVector rates1 = new DoubleVector();
for(int i =0;i<rates.Length;i++)
{
    rateDates1.Add(rateDates[i]);
    rates1.Add(rates[i]);
}
DoubleVector coupon = new DoubleVector();
coupon.Add(0.05);
DayCounter dc = new ActualActual(ActualActual.Convention.Bond);

Schedule schedule = new Schedule(issueDate, maturity, new Period(
    Frequency.Semiannual), calendar, BusinessDayConvention.Unadjusted,
    BusinessDayConvention.Unadjusted, DateGeneration.Rule.Backward, false);
var fixedRateBond = new FixedRateBond(settlementDays, 100, schedule,coupon, dc);
var rateCurve = new ZeroCurve(rateDates1, rates1, dc, calendar, new Linear(),
    Compounding.Compounded, Frequency.Annual);
YieldTermStructureHandle discountingTermStructure =
    new YieldTermStructureHandle(rateCurve);
var bondEngine = new DiscountingBondEngine(discountingTermStructure);
fixedRateBond.setPricingEngine(bondEngine);

DataTable dt = new DataTable();
dt.Columns.Add("Name", typeof(string));
dt.Columns.Add("Value", typeof(string));
dt.Rows.Add("Pricing Bond", "Using QuantLib");
dt.Rows.Add("Issue Date", "1/15/2015");
dt.Rows.Add("Evaluation Date", "1/15/2015");
dt.Rows.Add("Times to Maturity in Years", 2);
dt.Rows.Add("Face Value", 100);
dt.Rows.Add("Discount Rate", "0.004, 0.006, 0.0065, 0.007");
dt.Rows.Add("Coupon", "5%");

try
{
    fixedRateBond.setPricingEngine(bondEngine);
    dt.Rows.Add("Present Value", fixedRateBond.NPV());
    dt.Rows.Add("Present Value", fixedRateBond.cleanPrice());
    dt.Rows.Add("Dirty Price", fixedRateBond.dirtyPrice());
    dt.Rows.Add("Accrued Value",fixedRateBond.accruedAmount());
    dt.Rows.Add("YTM", fixedRateBond.yield(fixedRateBond.dayCounter(),
        Compounding.Compounded, Frequency.Semiannual));
}
catch { }
return dt;
}
```

The key step in this method is to create a curved term structure for the interest rates using the *ZeroCurve* class. This class takes the rate dates and rate data points as its arguments. The zero curve is a special type of yield curve that maps interest rates on zero-coupon bonds to different maturities across time. Zero-coupon bonds have a single payment at maturity, so these curves enable you to price arbitrary cash flows, fixed income instruments, and derivatives. Another type of interest rate curve, the forward curve, is constructed using the forward rates derived from this curve.

Zero curves should be separately constructed for government securities and for inter-bank markets. Zero-coupon bonds are available for a limited number of maturities, so you typically construct zero curves with a combination of boostrapping and interpolation techniques in order to build a continuous curve. Inside the *BondPriceCurveRate* method, we use the linear approach to interpolate our zero curve. Once you construct these curves, you can then use them to derive other curves such as the forward curve and price financial instruments.

We can now convert the *BondPriceCurveRate* method into a web service. Add a new method called *getBondPriceCurveRate* to the *FixedIncomeValuesController* class with the following code:

```
[Route("~/api/bondPriceCurveRate")]
[HttpGet]
public JsonResult GetBondPriceCurveRate()
{
    var res = FixedIncomeHelper.BondPriceCurveRate();
    return Json(new { Name = "Bond Price with Curve Rate", Result = res });
}
```

Running this project by pressing F5 and entering the following URL:

https://localhost:5001/api/bondpricecurverate

Which produces the results shown in Fig.10-3.

Fig.10-3. Computed results for a hypothetical bond using QuantLib.

You can see that the calculated result for the present value of the bond is consistent with the analytic calculation in Eq. (10-6).

Yield to Maturity

The coupon rate is the yield paid by a fixed-income security, referred to as an annual percentage of the face value. It is commonly paid twice a year in the United States or once a year in France and Germany. Please do not confuse it with the actual current yield. The current yield y_c is obtained using the following formula:

$$y_c = \frac{cN}{P}$$

Where c is the coupon rate, N is the nominal value, and P is the current price.

The yield to maturity (YTM) is the single rate that sets the present value of the cash flows equal to the bond price. More precisely, the bond price P can be obtained by discounting future cash flows back to their present value as indicated in the following formula:

$$P = \sum_{t=1}^{T} \frac{CF_t}{(1 + y)^t} \tag{10-7}$$

Where y is the yield expressed on a yearly basis and T is the number of periods.

Previously, we calculated the present value for a bond directly using the different interest rates for different periods. Now, we can calculate it again using Eq. (10-7) with a single YTM rate. In Fig.10-3, we have obtained $ytm = 0.00695281$ from the pricing engine in QuantLib, and we can then calculate the present value with Eq. (10-7)

$$P = \frac{2.5}{(1 + ytm)^{0.5}} + \frac{2.5}{1 + ytm} + \frac{2.5}{(1 + ytm)^{1.5}} + \frac{102.5}{(1 + ytm)^2} = 108.53$$

Which is consistent with the direct calculation in Eq. (10-6).

In fact, the YTM is the internal rate of return of the series of cash flows. Hence, each cash flow is discounted using the same rate. Generally, there exists a one-to-one correspondence between the price and the YTM of a bond. Therefore, giving the YTM for a bond is equivalent to giving the price for the bond. The YTM is a complex average of pure discount rates that makes the present value of the bond's payment equal to its price. Unless the term structure of interest rates is flat, there is no reason one would consider the YTM on a 10-year bond as the relevant discount rate for a 10-year horizon. You may consider the YTM as just a convenient way of re-expressing the bond price.

Pricing Bonds in Angular

In the preceding sections, we convert the bond pricing methods into a web service. In order to access this web service from Angular applications, we can create a repository service called *ch10.service.ts* by running the following command in a command prompt window:

```
ng g s models/ch10
```

Open the *ch10.service.ts* class file and replace its content with the following code:

```
// ch10.service.ts file:
import { Injectable, Inject } from '@angular/core';
import { HttpClient } from '@angular/common/http';

@Injectable({
  providedIn: 'root'
})
export class Ch10Service {
  private url;
  constructor(private http: HttpClient, @Inject('BASE_URL') baseUrl: string) {
    this.url = baseUrl;
  }

  getBondPrice(evalDate: string, issueDate: string, timeToMaturity: number,
```

```
        settlementDays: number, faceValue: number,
        rate: number, coupon: string, frequency: string) {
        let url1 = this.url + 'api/bondprice/' + evalDate + '/' + issueDate + '/'
            + timeToMaturity + '/' + settlementDays + '/' + faceValue +
            '/' + rate + '/' + coupon + '/' + frequency;
        return this.http.get<any>(url1);
    }

    getBondPriceCurveRate() {
        return this.http.get<any>(this.url + 'api/bondpricecurverate');
    }
}
```

Note that these methods return promises, which allow you to execute your code sequentially and create responsive UI.

Now, I will use an example to illustrate how to pricing a simple bond in an Angular application. Run the following statement in a command prompt window:

ng g c chapter10/ch10-simple-bond --module=app.module

This generates a new component called *ch10-simple-bond* in the *ClientApp/src/app/Chapter10* folder. Open the component class and replace its content with the following code:

```
// ch10-simple-bond.component.ts file:
import { Component, OnInit } from '@angular/core';
import { Ch10Service } from '../../models/ch10.service';
import { ModelHelper } from '../../models/model.helper';

@Component({
    selector: 'app-ch10-simple-bond',
    templateUrl: './ch10-simple-bond.component.html',
    styleUrls: ['./ch10-simple-bond.component.css']
})
export class Ch10SimpleBondComponent implements OnInit {
    evalDate: string = '2015-12-16';
    issueDate: string = '2015-12-16';
    timeToMaturity: number = 10;
    settlementDays: number = 1;
    faceValue: number = 1000;
    rate: number = 0.06;
    coupon: string = '0.05';
    frequency: string = 'annual'
    bondResult: any;
    curveRateResult: any;
    bondCols: any;
    curveRateCols: any;
    private helper: ModelHelper;

    constructor(private service: Ch10Service) { }

    ngOnInit() {
        this.getBondPrice(this.evalDate, this.issueDate, this.timeToMaturity,
            this.settlementDays, this.faceValue, this.rate, this.coupon, this.frequency);
        this.getBondPriceCurveRate();
    }
```

```
getBondPrice(evalDate: string, issueDate: string, timeToMaturity: number,
  settlementDays: number, faceValue: number, rate: number, coupon: string,
  frequency: string) {
  this.bondResult = null;
  this.service.getBondPrice(evalDate, issueDate, timeToMaturity, settlementDays,
    faceValue, rate, coupon, frequency).subscribe(result => {
    this.bondResult = [result.result];
    this.helper = new ModelHelper();
    this.bondCols = this.helper.setColDefs([result.result], 120);
  });
}

getBondPriceCurveRate() {
  this.curveRateResult = null;
  this.service.getBondPriceCurveRate().subscribe(result => {
    this.curveRateResult = result.result;
    this.helper = new ModelHelper();
    this.curveRateCols = this.helper.setColDefs(result.result, 250);
  });
}
}
```

Here, we retrieve bond prices for flat and curved rates from web service and display the results using *ag-Grid* components.

Next, we need to update the component's template with the following code:

```html
// ch10-simple-bond.component.html file:
<h2>
  ch10-simple-bond works!
</h2>
<h3>A bond with a flat rate:</h3>
<mat-form-field>
  <input matInput placeholder="evalDate" [(ngModel)]="evalDate" name="evalDate">
</mat-form-field>
<mat-form-field>
  <input matInput placeholder="issueDate" [(ngModel)]="issueDate" name="issueDate">
</mat-form-field>
<mat-form-field>
  <input matInput placeholder="timeToMaturity (in years)"
    [(ngModel)]="timeToMaturity" name="timeToMaturity">
</mat-form-field>
<mat-form-field>
  <input matInput placeholder="settlementDays" [(ngModel)]="settlementDays"
    name="settlementDays">
</mat-form-field>
<mat-form-field>
  <input matInput placeholder="faceValue" [(ngModel)]="faceValue" name="faceValue">
</mat-form-field>
<mat-form-field>
  <input matInput placeholder="discountRate" [(ngModel)]="rate" name="rate">
</mat-form-field>
<mat-form-field>
  <input matInput placeholder="coupon" [(ngModel)]="coupon" name="coupon">
</mat-form-field>
<mat-form-field>
```

```
  <input matInput placeholder="frequency" [(ngModel)]="frequency" name="frequency">
</mat-form-field>
<button mat-raised-button color="primary"
(click)="getBondPrice(evalDate,issueDate,timeToMaturity,
        settlementDays,faceValue,rate,coupon,frequency)">Get Bond Result</button>
<ag-grid-angular *ngIf="bondResult" style="height:70px;width:700px;margin-top:20px"
  class="ag-theme-balham" [rowData]="bondResult" [columnDefs]="bondCols">
</ag-grid-angular>
<br />
<h3>A bond with curved rates:</h3>
<ag-grid-angular *ngIf="curveRateResult" style="height:400px;width:700px;"
  class="ag-theme-balham" [rowData]="curveRateResult" [columnDefs]="curveRateCols">
</ag-grid-angular>
```

This template adds two *ag-grid-angular* directives that are used to display the bond prices for a bond with flat and curved rates respectively.

Finally, we need to add a path for this new component to the *RouterModule* of the root module (i.e., the *app.module.ts* file):

```
{ path: 'chapter10/ch10-simple-bond, component: Ch10SimpleBondComponent },
```

Then add the corresponding URL link to the *home* and *nav-menu* components.

Saving the project and navigating to the */chapter10/ch10-smple-bond* page produce the default results shown in Fig.10-4.

Zero-Coupon Yield Curve

When you attempt to price whatever financial securities, you always need to construct various term structures for the interest rates. In Chapter 9, we have already introduced term structures when we discussed options pricing. The term structure of interest rates is simply the series of interest rates ordered by term-to-maturity at a given time. The nature of interest rate determines the nature of the term structure.

There are several different types of yield curves, including the yield to maturity curve, swap rate curve, zero-coupon curve, forward rate curve, etc. The yield to maturity and swap rate curves are market data, whereas zero-coupon and forward rate curves can be constructed using market data.

The zero-coupon yield curve is especially important in practice because it allows you to calculate the discount factor and price any fixed-income security delivering known cash flows in the future such as a fixed coupon bond. It also allows you to derive other implicit curves such as the forward rate curve and par yield curve.

In Eq. (10-1), we have defined the discount factor $B(0, t)$ as

$$B(0, t) = \frac{1}{[1 + R(0, t)]^t} \tag{10-8}$$

Where $B(0, t)$ is the market price at date 0 of a bond paying off \$1 at date t. $B(0, t)$ is also called the spot zero-coupon rate or discount rate. In practice, when we know the spot zero-coupon yield curve $R(0, t)$, we can obtain spot prices for all fixed income securities with known future cash flows.

If $R(0, t)$ is the rate at which you can invest today in a t period bond, we can define an implied forward rate (also called forward zero-coupon rate) between years x and y as

$$F(0, x, y - x) = \left\{ \frac{[1 + R(0,y)]^y}{[1 + R(0,x)]^x} \right\}^{\frac{1}{y-x}} - 1 \qquad (10\text{-}9)$$

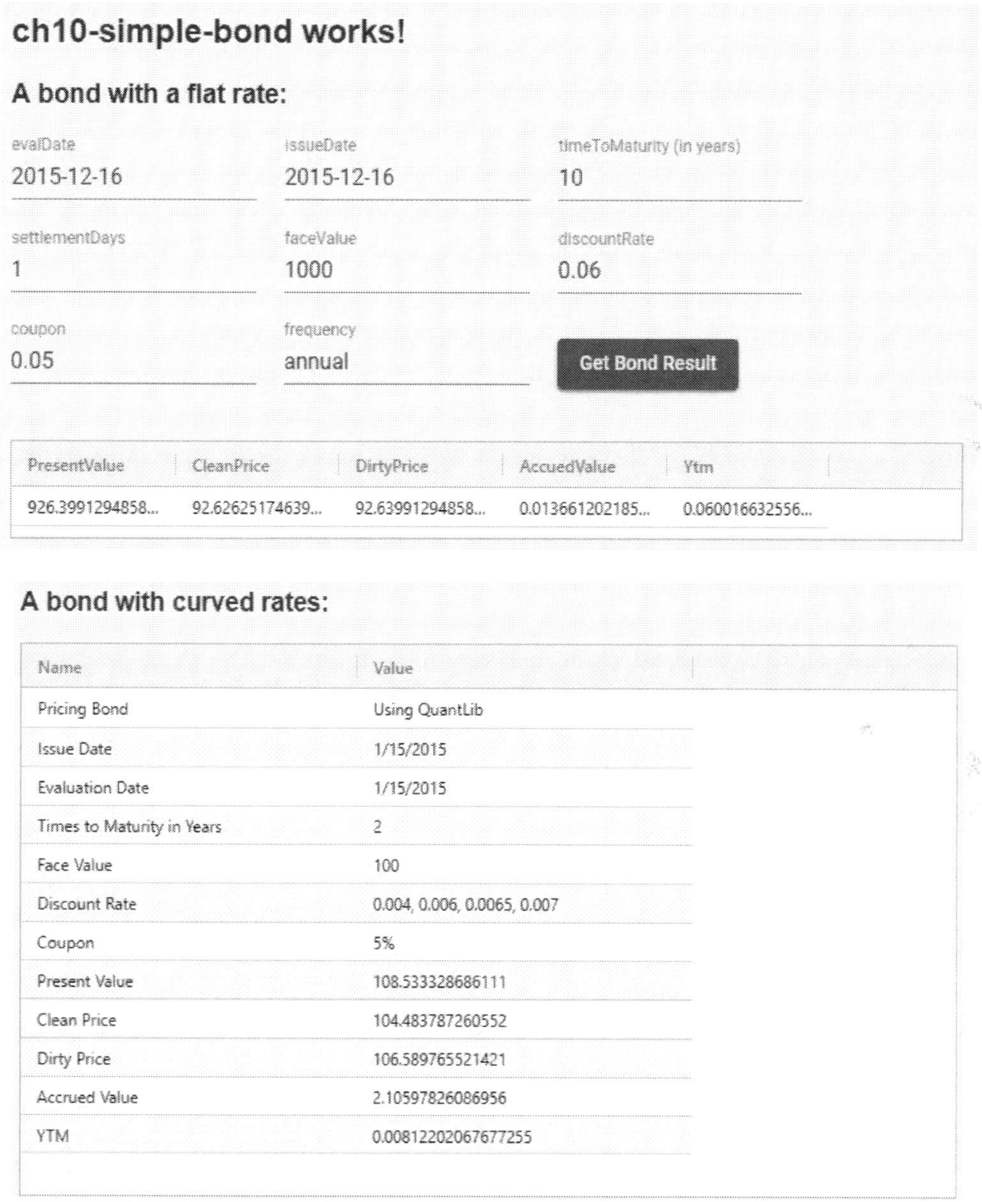

ch10-simple-bond works!

A bond with a flat rate:

evalDate	issueDate	timeToMaturity (in years)
2015-12-16	2015-12-16	10

settlementDays	faceValue	discountRate
1	1000	0.06

coupon	frequency	
0.05	annual	Get Bond Result

PresentValue	CleanPrice	DirtyPrice	AccuedValue	Ytm
926.3991294858...	92.62625174639...	92.63991294858...	0.013661202185...	0.060016632556...

A bond with curved rates:

Name	Value
Pricing Bond	Using QuantLib
Issue Date	1/15/2015
Evaluation Date	1/15/2015
Times to Maturity in Years	2
Face Value	100
Discount Rate	0.004, 0.006, 0.0065, 0.007
Coupon	5%
Present Value	108.533328686111
Clean Price	104.483787260552
Dirty Price	106.589765521421
Accrued Value	2.10597826086956
YTM	0.00812202067677255

Fig.10-4. Pricing a simple bond with flat rates (top) and curved rates (bottom).

Where $F(0, x, y - x)$ is the forward rate as seen from date $t = 0$, starting at date $t = x$, and with residual maturity $y - x$. In practice, it is very common to draw the forward curve $F(0, x, \theta)$ with rates starting at date x.

In this section, we will try to build the zero-coupon yield curve for three types of market data. First curve is the non-default Treasury zero-coupon curve, which is derived from Treasury bond market prices. The second curve is the interbank zero-coupon yield curve, which is derived from money-market rates, futures contracts rates, and swap rates. The third yield curve is the credit zero-coupon curve for a given rating and economic sector, which is derived from corporate bond market prices. Note that by subtracting the Treasury or the interbank zero-coupon curve from the credit curve, we can obtain the credit spread zero-coupon yield curve.

Treasury Zero-Coupon Yield Curve

We can derive the Treasury zero-coupon curve directly from the current fixed coupon bearing bond prices. This method allows us to recover exactly the prices of the selected bonds. If n distinct zero-coupon rates are required, we need to first collect the prices of n coupon (or even better the zero coupon if existing) bonds. The default-free coupon bonds (like US Treasury bonds) are usually preferred, because they provide information about the risk-free structure of interest rates.

Suppose, we pick up n coupon bonds. We need to figure out the cash flows (coupons and principal) for each bond, and then relate the zero-coupon bond prices to the bond market prices via the cash flows:

$$P_t^j = \sum_{i=1}^{n} CF_{t_i}^j B(t, t_i)$$ (10-10)

where P_t^j is the jth bond price at date t, $CF_{t_i}^j$ is the cash flows of the jth bond at date t_i, and $B(t, t_i)$ is the zero-coupon bond price at date t of \$1 to be received on date t_i. Thus, in order to determine the value of the zero-coupon bond price, we need to solve the linear equation (10-10). The zero-coupon bond prices derived here are not real market values, but, rather, implied zero-coupon bond values consistent with the set of market prices of fixed coupon bonds. From these zero-coupon bond prices, we can easily extract at date t the annual compounded zero-coupon rate $R(t, t_i - t)$ with maturity $t_i - t$ using

$$R(t, t_i - t) = e^{-\frac{1}{t_i - t} \ln[B(t, t_i)]} - 1$$ (10-11)

and its continuously compounded equivalent $R_c(t, t_i - t)$ by using

$$R_c(t, t_i - t) = -\frac{1}{t_i - t} \ln[B(t, t_i)]$$ (10-12)

Now, let us look at an example. On 1/15/2015, we want to derive the zero-coupon curve until 4-year maturity. For this purpose, we obtain from the market four bonds with the following features:

Bond	Annual Coupon	Maturity (Years)	Price
1	5%	1	101
2	5.50%	2	101.5
3	5%	3	99
4	6%	4	100

Here I will show you how to use QuantLib to calculate the zero-coupon rate (R), continuously compounded equivalent rate (R_c), and discount rate (B).

Add a new public method named *ZeroCouponDirect* to the *FixedIncomeHelper* class. Here is the code for this method:

```
public static DataTable ZeroCouponDirect()
{
    DataTable res = new DataTable();
    Date evalDate = new Date(15, Month.January, 2015);
    double[] coupons = new double[] { 0.05, 0.055, 0.05, 0.06 };
    double[] bondPrices = new double[] { 101.0, 101.5, 99.0, 100.0 };
    Date[] maturities = new Date[]
    {
        new Date(15, Month.January, 2016),
        new Date(15, Month.January, 2017),
        new Date(15, Month.January, 2018),
        new Date(15, Month.January, 2019)
    };
    Settings.instance().setEvaluationDate(evalDate);
    Calendar calendar = new UnitedStates();
    DayCounter dc = new ActualActual(ActualActual.Convention.Bond);
    RateHelperVector rateHelpers = new RateHelperVector();
    for (int i = 0; i < maturities.Length;i++ )
    {
        QuoteHandle quote = new QuoteHandle(new SimpleQuote(bondPrices[i]));
        DoubleVector coupon = new DoubleVector();
        coupon.Add(coupons[i]);
        Schedule schedule = new Schedule(evalDate, maturities[i],
            new Period(Frequency.Annual), calendar,
            BusinessDayConvention.Unadjusted,
            BusinessDayConvention.Unadjusted, DateGeneration.Rule.Backward,
            true);
        FixedRateBondHelper helper = new FixedRateBondHelper(quote, 0, 100,
            schedule, coupon, dc, BusinessDayConvention.Unadjusted, 100.0,
            evalDate);
        rateHelpers.Add(helper);
    }
    var discountTS = new PiecewiseLinearZero(evalDate, rateHelpers, dc);
    res = new DataTable();
    res.Columns.Add("Maturity", typeof(string));
    res.Columns.Add("Zero Coupon Rate: R", typeof(string));
    res.Columns.Add("Equivalent Rate: Rc", typeof(string));
    res.Columns.Add("Discount Rate: B", typeof(string));
    foreach(var d in discountTS.dates())
    {
        var years = dc.yearFraction(evalDate, d);
        var zeroRate = discountTS.zeroRate(years, Compounding.Compounded,
            Frequency.Annual);
        var discount = discountTS.discount(d);
        var eqRate = zeroRate.equivalentRate(dc, Compounding.Compounded,
            Frequency.Daily, evalDate, d).rate();
        res.Rows.Add(d.ToDatetime<string>(), zeroRate.rate(), eqRate, discount);
    }
    return res;
}
```

This method is very simple. It first defines various input parameters according to the QuantLib SWIG format, including the maturities, coupons, and prices for the selected four bonds. Then, it creates the *FixedRateBondHelper* objects to hold bond properties for each bond and add them to a *RateHelperVector*. Next, it defines the discount term structure using the *PiecewiseLinearZero* class, in which the term structure is bootstrapped and interpolated linearly on a number of interest rate instruments. QuantLib implemented various bootstrapping and interpolation functions, and you can choose different methods to build the term structures, such as *PiecewiseLogCubicDiscount*, or *PiecewiseCubicZero*.

Finally, the method extracts the results from this discounting term structure and saves the results to a *DataTable*. Note that it extracts the continuously compounded equivalent rate by setting the compounding frequency to daily, the smallest possible date unit.

Now, we can convert the method into a web service. Add a new method named *GetZeroCouponDirect* to the *FixedIncomeValuesController* class in the *Quant/Controllers* folder with the following code:

```
[Route("~/api/zeroCouponDirect")]
[HttpGet]
public JsonResult GetZeroCouponDirect()
{
    var res = FixedIncomeHelper.ZeroCouponDirect();
    return Json(new { Name = "Zero-Coupon Direct", Result = res });
}
```

Next, add a TypeScript method named *getZeroCouponDirect* to the *ch10.service.ts* file in the *ClientApp/ src/app/models* folder with the following code:

```
getZeroCouponDirect() {
  return this.http.get<any>(this.url + 'api/zerocoupondirect');
}
```

Here, I will use an example to illustrate how to construct a treasury zero-coupon yield curve in an Angular application. Run the following statement in a command prompt window:

ng g c chapter10/ch10-zc-direct --module=app.module

This generates a new component called *ch10-zc-direct* in the *ClientApp/src/app/Chapter10* folder. Open the component class and replace its content with the following code:

```
// ch10-zc-direct.component.ts file:
import { Component, OnInit } from '@angular/core';
import { Ch10Service } from '../../models/ch10.service';
import { ModelHelper } from '../../models/model.helper';

@Component({
  selector: 'app-ch10-zc-direct',
  templateUrl: './ch10-zc-direct.component.html',
  styleUrls: ['./ch10-zc-direct.component.css']
})
export class Ch10ZcDirectComponent implements OnInit {
  zcResult: any;
  zcCols: any;
  private helper: ModelHelper;

  constructor(private service: Ch10Service) { }

  ngOnInit() {
```

```
    this.getZcResult();
  }

  getZcResult() {
    this.zcResult = null;
    this.service.getZeroCouponDirect().subscribe(result => {
      this.zcResult = result.result;
      this.helper = new ModelHelper();
      this.zcCols = this.helper.setColDefs(result.result, 170);
    });
  }
}
```

We also need to update the component's template with the following code:

```
// ch10-zc-direct.component.html file:
<h2>
  ch10-zc-direct works!
</h2>

<ag-grid-angular *ngIf="zcResult" style="height:160px;width:700px;"
  class="ag-theme-balham" [rowData]="zcResult" [columnDefs]="zcCols">
</ag-grid-angular>
```

This template adds an *ag-grid-angular* directive that is used to display zero-coupon results.

Finally, we need to add a path for this new component to the *RouterModule* of the root module (i.e., the *app.module.ts* file):

```
{ path: 'chapter10/ch10-zc-direct, component: Ch10ZcDirectComponent },
```

Then add the corresponding URL link to the *home* and *nav-menu* components.

Saving the project and navigating to the */chapter10/ch10-zc-direct* page produce the results shown in Fig.10-5.

ch10-zc-direct works!

Maturity	Zero Coupon Rate: R	Equivalent Rate: Rc	Discount Rate: B
1/15/2016	0.0396039603962934	0.038841899872919	0.961904761904527
1/15/2017	0.04711700132389423	0.04460942102933981	0.91193861430792
1/15/2018	0.05417013270767	0.0527576549968156	0.853626505894645
1/15/2019	0.061033793960152	0.05924851839983337	0.789011138748655

Fig.10-5. Calculated results for the zero-coupon yield curve.

You can see that the continuously equivalent rate (compounded daily) is always smaller than the corresponding zero-coupon rate (compounded annually). This makes sense; it means that we should invest at a higher rate when compounding is less frequent to generate the same amount of cash at the end of a given period.

This direct method is fairly simple. Unfortunately, finding many distinct linearly independent bonds with the same coupon dates is almost impossible in practice. This is why we need to use a more powerful approach called the bootstrapping technique.

Bootstrapping is the term for building a zero-coupon yield curve from existing market data such as bond prices. Bootstrapping can be regarded as a repetitive double-step procedure.

- Extract directly zero-coupon rates with maturity inferior or equal to one year from corresponding zero-coupon bond prices. We then use interpolation to create a continuous zero-coupon yield curve for maturities inferior or equal to one year.

- Consider the bond with nearest maturity between one and two years. The bond has two cash flows and its price is logically the discounted value of these two cash flows. We know the first discount factor needed to obtain the discounted value of the first cash flow. The unknown variable is the second discount factor. By solving a nonlinear equation, we get this discount factor and corresponding zero-coupon rate. We begin again with the same process considering the next bond with nearest maturity between one and two years. We then use interpolation to create a continuous zero-coupon yield curve for maturities between one and two years, using the zero-coupon rates obtained from market prices.

- Consider the bond with nearest maturity between two and three years and repeat the same process. The unknown factors are always reduced to one and solving one equation enables to determine it as well as the corresponding zero-coupon rate. Repeat the process as necessary…

Here, I will create a helper method called *ZeroCouponBootstrap* in the *FixedIncomeHelper* class and show how we can construct a Zero-coupon yield curve using the deposit rates and bond prices. The following is the code for this method:

```
public static DataTable ZeroCouponBootstrap(double[] depositRates,
    Period[] depositMaturities, double[] bondPrices, double[] bondCoupons,
    Period[] bondMaturities, string curveType)
{
    DataTable res = new DataTable();
    Date evalDate = new Date(15, Month.January, 2015);
    Settings.instance().setEvaluationDate(evalDate);
    Calendar calendar = new UnitedStates();
    DayCounter dc = new ActualActual(ActualActual.Convention.Bond);

    RateHelperVector rateHelpers = new RateHelperVector();
    for (int i = 0; i < depositMaturities.Length; i++)
    {
        rateHelpers.Add(new DepositRateHelper(depositRates[i],
        depositMaturities[i], 0, calendar,
        BusinessDayConvention.Unadjusted, true, dc));
    }

    for (int i = 0; i < bondMaturities.Length; i++)
    {
        QuoteHandle quote = new QuoteHandle(new SimpleQuote(bondPrices[i]));
        DoubleVector coupon = new DoubleVector();
        coupon.Add(bondCoupons[i]);
        Date maturity = evalDate.Add(bondMaturities[i]);
        Schedule schedule = new Schedule(evalDate, maturity,
            new Period(Frequency.Annual), calendar,BusinessDayConvention.Unadjusted,
            BusinessDayConvention.Unadjusted, DateGeneration.Rule.Backward, true);
```

```
        FixedRateBondHelper helper = new FixedRateBondHelper(quote, 0, 100.0,
            schedule, coupon, dc, BusinessDayConvention.Unadjusted, 100.0,
            evalDate);
        rateHelpers.Add(helper);
    }

    var ts = new PiecewiseLinearZero(evalDate, rateHelpers, dc);
    res = new DataTable();
    res.Columns.Add("Maturity", typeof(string));
    res.Columns.Add("TimesToMaturity", typeof(string));
    res.Columns.Add("Zero Coupon Rate: R", typeof(string));
    res.Columns.Add("Equivalent Rate: Rc", typeof(string));
    res.Columns.Add("Discount Rate: B", typeof(string));

    if (curveType == "dataPoints")
    {
        foreach (var d in ts.dates())
        {
            if (d > evalDate)
            {
                var years = dc.yearFraction(evalDate, d);
                var zeroRate = ts.zeroRate(years, Compounding.Compounded,
                    Frequency.Annual);
                var discount = ts.discount(d);
                var eqRate = zeroRate.equivalentRate(dc, Compounding.Compounded,
                    Frequency.Daily, evalDate, d).rate();
                res.Rows.Add(d.To<DateTime>().ShortDateString(), years,
                    zeroRate.rate(), eqRate, discount);
            }
        }
        return res;
    }
    else
    {
        Date d = evalDate.Add(depositMaturities[0]);
        Date lastDate = evalDate.Add(new Period(3, TimeUnit.Years));
        while (d < lastDate)
        {
            var years = dc.yearFraction(evalDate, d);
            var zeroRate = ts.zeroRate(years, Compounding.Compounded,
                Frequency.Annual);
            var discount = ts.discount(d);
            var eqRate = zeroRate.equivalentRate(dc, Compounding.Compounded,
                Frequency.Daily, evalDate, d).rate();
            res.Rows.Add(d.To<DateTime>().ToShortDateString(), years,
                zeroRate.rate(), eqRate, discount);
            d = d.Add(new Period(1, TimeUnit.Months));
        }
        return res;
    }
}
```

This method takes the deposit rates and fixed coupon bonds as input arguments. First, we define the deposit rates using the *DepositRateHelper* and add them to the *RateHelperVector* object named *rateHelpers*. Next, we create a *FixedRateBondHelper* object for each bond and add the bond helper to the *rateHelpers*. The zero-coupon yield curve is then constructed by putting this *rateHelpers* into a bootstrapping and linear interpolation object named *PiecewiseLinearZero*. Finally, we obtain the yield rates from the *ts* (term structure) object using the *zeroRate* method.

Note that you can specify the *curveType* parameter, which controls the output results. If you set it to "*DataPoints*", the results are only extracted from the curve at the maturities provided from input. Otherwise, you will get the output monthly. In fact, QuantLib generates a continuous yield curve, so you can extract the results at any maturities.

Here, I will show you an example on how to use the *ZeroCouponBootstrap* method to build a zero-coupon yield curve. Suppose we know from market prices the following deposit rates (zero-coupon) with maturities less or equal to 1 year:

Maturity	Deposit Rates (%)
1 Day	4.4
1 Month	4.5
2 Months	4.6
3 Months	4.7
6 Months	4.9
9 Months	5.1
12 Months	5.3

The following are bonds priced by the market until 3-year maturity:

Maturity	Coupon (%)	Price
12 Months	5	99.55
21 Months	6	100.55
2 Years	5.5	99.5
3 Years	5	97.6

Now, add a new method called *GetZeroCouponBootstrap* to the *FixedIncomeValuesController* class with the following code:

```
[Route("~/api/zeroCouponBootstrap/{curveType}")]
[HttpGet]
public JsonResult GetZeroCouponBootstrap(string curveType)
{
    double[] depositRates = new double[] { 0.044, 0.045, 0.046, 0.047, 0.049,
        0.051, 0.053 };
    Period[] depositMaturities = new Period[]
    {
        new Period(1, TimeUnit.Days),
        new Period(1, TimeUnit.Months),
        new Period(2, TimeUnit.Months),
        new Period(3, TimeUnit.Months),
        new Period(6, TimeUnit.Months),
        new Period(9, TimeUnit.Months),
        new Period(12, TimeUnit.Months),
    };

    double[] bondCoupons = new double[] { 0.05, 0.06, 0.055, 0.05 };
    double[] bondPrices = new double[] { 99.55, 100.55, 99.5, 97.6 };
    Period[] bondMaturities = new Period[]
```

```
    {
        new Period(14, TimeUnit.Months),
        new Period(21, TimeUnit.Months),
        new Period(2, TimeUnit.Years),
        new Period(3, TimeUnit.Years),
    };

    var res = FixedIncomeHelper.ZeroCouponBootstrap(depositRates, depositMaturities,
        bondPrices, bondCoupons, bondMaturities, curveType);
    return Json(new { Name = "Zero-Coupon Bootstrap", Result = res });
}
```

Next, add a TypeScript method named *getZeroCouponBootstrap* to the *ch10.service.ts* file in the *ClientApp/ src/app/models* folder with the following code:

```
getZeroCouponBootstrap(curveType: string) {
    return this.http.get<any>(this.url + 'api/zerocouponbootstrap/' + curveType);
}
```

Here, I will use an example to illustrate how to construct a treasury zero-coupon yield curve in an Angular application. First, we will create a line chart component that is used to plot the zero-coupon yield results.

Run the following statement in a command prompt window:

ng g c chapter10/ch10-line-chart --module=app.module

This generates a new component called *ch10-line-chart* in the *ClientApp/src/app/Chapter10* folder. Open the component class and replace its content with the following code:

```
// ch10-line-chart.component.ts file:
import { Component, OnInit, Input, OnChanges } from '@angular/core';

@Component({
    selector: 'app-ch10-line-chart',
    templateUrl: './ch10-line-chart.component.html',
    styleUrls: ['./ch10-line-chart.component.css']
})
export class Ch10LineChartComponent implements OnInit, OnChanges {
    @Input() data: any;
    zcOptions: any;
    discOptions: any;

    constructor() { }

    ngOnInit() {
        this.zcOptions = this.getZcOptions(this.data)
        this.discOptions = this.getDiscOptions(this.data);
    }

    ngOnChanges() {
        this.zcOptions = this.getZcOptions(this.data)
        this.discOptions = this.getDiscOptions(this.data);
    }

    getZcOptions(data: any) {
        let data1 = [];
```

```
    let data2 = [];
    data.forEach(function (d) {
      data1.push([d['timesToMaturity'], d['zero Coupon Rate: R']]);
      data2.push([d['timesToMaturity'], d['equivalent Rate: Rc']]);
    });
    return {
      legend: {
        top: '11%',
        left: '17%',
        orient: 'vertical',
        data: [{ name: 'R', icon: 'line' }, { name: 'Rc', icon: 'line' }]
      },
      grid: {
        top: 35,
        left: 70,
        right: 10
      },
      title: {
        text: 'Zero-Coupon Yield',
        left: 'center'
      },
      xAxis: {
        type: 'value',
        name: 'Times to Maturity',
        nameLocation: 'center',
        nameGap: '30',
        axisLine: { onZero: false }
      },
      yAxis: {
        type: 'value',
        scale: true,
        name: 'Zero-Coupon Rate',
        nameLocation: 'center',
        nameGap: '50'
      },
      series: [{
        name: 'R',
        type: 'line',
        data: data1,
        showSymbol: false
      },
      {
        name: 'Rc',
        type: 'line',
        data: data2,
        showSymbol: false
      }]
    };
  }

  getDiscOptions(data: any) {
    let data1 = [];
    data.forEach(function (d) {
      data1.push([d['timesToMaturity'], d['discount Rate: B']]);
    });
```

```
    return {
      title: {
        text: 'Discount Yield',
        left: 'center'
      },
      grid: {
        top: 35,
        left: 70,
        right: 10
      },
      xAxis: {
        type: 'value',
        name: 'Times to Maturity',
        nameLocation: 'center',
        nameGap: '30',
        axisLine: { onZero: false }
      },
      yAxis: {
        type: 'value',
        scale: true,
        name: 'Discount Rate',
        nameLocation: 'center',
        nameGap: '50'
      },
      series: [{
        name: 'Discount Rate',
        type: 'line',
        data: data1,
        showSymbol: false
      }]
    };
  }
}
```

This component takes data as input and then creates two line charts: one is used to display the zero-coupon yield and the other is used to display the discount rate.

Next, we need also update this component's template with the following code:

```
// ch10-line-chart.component.html file:
<div class="cardList">
  <mat-card class="card-border">
    <div echarts [options]="zcOptions" style="height:100%"></div>
  </mat-card>
  <mat-card class="card-border">
    <div echarts [options]="discOptions" style="height:100%"></div>
  </mat-card>
</div>
```

This template is styled by the following file:

```
// ch10-line-chart.component.css file:
.cardList {
  display: flex;
  flex-direction: row;
  flex-wrap: wrap;
  justify-content: flex-start;
```

```
}

.card-border {
  width: 450px;
  height: 400px;
}
```

Now, run the following statement in a command prompt window:

ng g c chapter10/ch10-zc-bootstrap --module=app.module

This generates a new component called *ch10-zc-bootstrap* in the *ClientApp/src/app/Chapter10* folder. Open the component class and replace its content with the following code:

```
// ch10-zc-bootstrap.component.ts file:
import { Component, OnInit } from '@angular/core';
import { Ch10Service } from '../../models/ch10.service';
import { ModelHelper } from '../../models/model.helper';

@Component({
  selector: 'app-ch10-zc-bootstrap',
  templateUrl: './ch10-zc-bootstrap.component.html',
  styleUrls: ['./ch10-zc-bootstrap.component.css']
})
export class Ch10ZcBootstrapComponent implements OnInit {
  zcResult: any;
  zcCols: any;
  curveType: string = 'dataPoints'
  private helper: ModelHelper;

  constructor(private service: Ch10Service) { }

  ngOnInit() {
    this.getZcResult(this.curveType);
  }

  getZcResult(curveType: string) {
    this.zcResult = null;
    this.service.getZeroCouponBootstrap(curveType).subscribe(result => {
      this.zcResult = result.result;
      this.helper = new ModelHelper();
      this.zcCols = this.helper.setColDefs(result.result, 170);
    });
  }
}
```

We also need to update the component's template with the following code:

```
// ch10-zc-bootstrap.component.html file:
<h2>
  ch10-zc-bootstrap works!
</h2>

<mat-form-field>
  <mat-select placeholder="Select a curve type" [(value)]="curveType">
    <mat-option value="dataPoints">Data Points</mat-option>
    <mat-option value="notDataPoints">Not Data Points</mat-option>
```

```
  </mat-select>
</mat-form-field>
<button mat-raised-button color="primary" (click)="getZcResult(curveType)">Get Zero-
Coupon Curve</button>
<ag-grid-angular *ngIf="zcResult" style="height:400px;width:900px;"
  class="ag-theme-balham" [rowData]="zcResult" [columnDefs]="zcCols">
</ag-grid-angular>
<app-ch10-line-chart *ngIf="zcResult" [data]="zcResult"></app-ch10-line-chart>
```

This template adds an *ag-grid-angular* directive and a *ch10-line-chart* directive, which are used to display zero-coupon results.

Finally, we need to add a path for this new component to the *RouterModule* of the root module (i.e., the *app.module.ts* file):

```
{ path: 'chapter10/ch10-zc-bootstrap, component: Ch10ZcBootstrapComponent },
```

Then add the corresponding URL link to the *home* and *nav-menu* components.

Saving the project and navigating to the */chapter10/ch10-zc-bootstrap* page produce the default results shown in Fig.10-6.

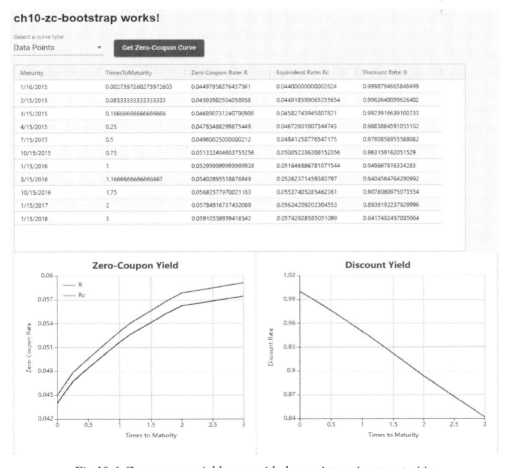

Fig.10-6. Zero-coupon yield curve with data points at input maturities.

If selecting the *Not Data Points* option from the dropdown menu and clicking the *Get Zero-Coupon Curve* button, you will get results with data points distributed monthly.

You can see from Fig.10-6 that zero-coupon curve (compounded annually) is always located above its continuously equivalent rate (compounded daily) as expected, and the discount rate curve looks like a straight line and decreases with the increase of maturity.

Interbank Zero-Coupon Yield Curve

Generally, the input basket for deriving the interbank zero-coupon curve contains three types of instruments: money-market rates, futures contracts, and swap rates. Money-market rates have maturities ranging from 1 day to 1 year, such as Euribor and Libor rates. These rates, expressed on an Actual/360 (or 365) basis, are first converted into equivalent zero-coupon rates with Actual/365 (or 30/360) basis. For example, on 1/1/2015, we assume that the 1-month Libor rate was equal to 1.5%. Using the Actual/365 basis, the equivalent zero-coupon rate is given by

$$R\left(0, \frac{1}{12}\right) = \left(1 + \frac{31}{360} \times 1.5\%\right)^{\frac{365}{31}} - 1$$

We only need to consider futures contracts depending on money-market rates, for example, 3-month Libor or 3-month Euribor contracts, and find zero-coupon rates from raw data. The price of a 3-month Libor contract is given by 100 minus the underlying 3-month forward rate. For instance, on 3/15/2015, the 3-month Libor rate was 1.5%, and the 3-month Libor contract with maturity date June 2015 had a price equal to 97.5. Hence, on 3/15/2015, the 3-month forward rate, starting on 6/15/2015, is 2.5%. The 6-month spot (or zero-coupon) rate can be obtained as follows:

$$R\left(0, \frac{6}{12}\right) = \left[\left(1 + \frac{92}{360} \times 1.5\%\right)\left(1 + \frac{92}{360} \times 2.5\%\right)\right]^{\frac{365}{184}} - 1$$

Similarly, from the prices of futures contracts with maturity date September 2015, December 2015 and March 2016, respectively, we can obtain the zero-coupon rates $R(0, 9/12)$, $R(0, 1)$, and $R(0, 15/12)$.

For the swap rates, we consider 3-or-6 month Libor (or Euribor) swap yields with maturities ranging from 1 year to 30 years and find recursively equivalent zero-coupon rates. Swap yields are par yields; so the zero-coupon rate with maturity 2 years $R(0, 2)$ is obtained as the solution to the following equation

$$\frac{Swap(2)}{1 + R(0,1)} + \frac{1 + Swap(2)}{[(1 + R(0,2)]^2} = 1$$

Where *Swap*(2) is the 2-year swap yield and $R(0, 1)$ is equal to *Swap*(1). The other zero-coupon rates can be obtained recursively in a similar fashion.

Thus, the input basket for deriving the interbank zero-rate curve contains many different instruments with maturities ranging from 1 day to 30 years. If you need a continuous zero-coupon term structure, you can achieve this using either linear, cubic, log linear, or log cubic interpolations in QuantLib.

Add two new helper methods, *InterbankTermStructure* and *InterbankZeroCoupon*, to the *FixedIncomeHelper* class. Here is code for these two methods:

```
public static YieldTermStructure InterbankTermStructure (
    DateTime settlementDate1, double[] depositRates, Period[] depositMaturities,
```

```
        double[] futPrices, double[] swapRates, Period[] swapMaturities)
{
    Calendar calendar = new JointCalendar(
        new UnitedKingdom(UnitedKingdom.Market.Exchange),
        new UnitedStates(UnitedStates.Market.Settlement));
    Date settlementDate = settlementDate1.To<Date>();
    int fixingDays = 2;
    Date evalDate = calendar.advance(settlementDate, -fixingDays, TimeUnit.Days);
    Settings.instance().setEvaluationDate(evalDate);
    RateHelperVector rateHelpers = new RateHelperVector();

    // Money market - Deposit:
    DayCounter depositDayCounter = new Actual360();
    for (int i = 0; i < depositRates.Length; i++)
        rateHelpers.Add(new DepositRateHelper(depositRates[i], depositMaturities[i],
            (uint)fixingDays, calendar, BusinessDayConvention.ModifiedFollowing, true,
            depositDayCounter));

    // Futures contracts:
    DayCounter futDayCounter = new Actual360();
    Date imm = IMM.nextDate(settlementDate);
    uint futMonths = 3;
    for (int i = 0; i < futPrices.Length; i++)
    {
        rateHelpers.Add(new FuturesRateHelper(futPrices[i], imm, futMonths,
            calendar, BusinessDayConvention.ModifiedFollowing, true,
            futDayCounter));
        imm = IMM.nextDate(imm + 1);
    }

    // Swap rates:
    Frequency swFixedLegFrequency = Frequency.Annual;
    BusinessDayConvention swFixedLegConvention = BusinessDayConvention.Unadjusted;
    DayCounter swFixedLegDayCounter = new Actual360();
    IborIndex swFloatingLegIndex = new USDLibor(new Period(3, TimeUnit.Months));
    for (int i = 0; i < swapRates.Length; i++)
        rateHelpers.Add(new SwapRateHelper(swapRates[i], swapMaturities[i],
            calendar, swFixedLegFrequency, swFixedLegConvention,
            swFixedLegDayCounter, swFloatingLegIndex));

    // Term structure:
    DayCounter tsDayCounter = new Actual360();
    var yieldTS = new PiecewiseCubicZero(settlementDate, rateHelpers, tsDayCounter);
    return yieldTS;
}

public static DataTable InterbankZeroCoupon(DateTime settlementDate1,
    double[] depositRates, Period[] depositMaturities, double[] futPrices,
    double[] swapRates, Period[] swapMaturities)
{
    Date settlementDate = settlementDate1.To<Date>();
    DataTable res = new DataTable();
    var ts = (PiecewiseCubicZero)InterbankTermStructure(settlementDate1,
        depositRates, depositMaturities, futPrices, swapRates, swapMaturities);
    res = new DataTable();
```

```
res.Columns.Add("Maturity", typeof(string));
res.Columns.Add("TimesToMaturity", typeof(double));
res.Columns.Add("Zero Coupon Rate: R", typeof(double));
res.Columns.Add("Equivalent Rate: Rc", typeof(double));
res.Columns.Add("Discount Rate: B", typeof(double));

DayCounter dc = new Actual360();
foreach (var d in ts.dates())
{
    if (d > settlementDate && d < settlementDate.
        Add(swapMaturities[swapMaturities.Length-1]))
    {
        var years = dc.yearFraction(settlementDate, d);
        var zeroRate = ts.zeroRate(years, Compounding.Compounded,
            Frequency.Annual);
        var discount = ts.discount(d);
        var eqRate = zeroRate.equivalentRate(dc, Compounding.Compounded,
            Frequency.Daily, settlementDate, d).rate();
        res.Rows.Add(d.To<DateTime>().ToShortString(), years, zeroRate.rate(),
            eqRate, discount);
    }
}
return res;
}
```

The *InterbankTermStructure* method takes the money market (deposit), futures contracts, and swap rate market data as input arguments and returns a *YieldTermStructure* object. Note how we create the *FuturesRateHelper* instance with the IMM (international money market) dates. The IMM dates are four quarterly dates of each year, which most futures and option contracts use as their scheduled maturity date. The dates are the third Wednesday of March, June, September, and December.

The credit default swaps (CDS) also use the IMM dates. From 2002, the CDS market began to standardize CDS contracts so that they would all mature on one of the four IMM dates of March 20, June 20, September 20, and December 20. These IMM dates are used both as maturity dates for the contracts and as the dates for quarterly coupon payments.

The *InterbankZeroCoupon* method simply extract the zero-coupon and discount yield curves from the term structure returned by the *InterbankTermStructure* method.

We can test these methods using a web service. Add a new method called *GetZeroCouponInterbank* to the *FixedIncomeValuesController* class in the *Quant/Controllers* folder with the following code:

```
[Route("~/api/zeroCouponInterbank")]
[HttpGet]
public JsonResult GetZeroCouponInterband()
{
    DateTime settlementDate = new DateTime(2015, 2, 18);
    double[] depositRates = new double[] { 0.001375, 0.001717, 0.002112, 0.002581 };
    Period[] depositeMaturities = new Period[]
    {
        new Period(1,TimeUnit.Weeks),
        new Period(1,TimeUnit.Months),
        new Period(2,TimeUnit.Months),
        new Period(3,TimeUnit.Months)
    };
```

```
double[] futRates = new double[] { 99.725, 99.585, 99.385, 99.16, 98.93,
    98.715 };
double[] swapRates = new double[] { 0.0089268, 0.0123343, 0.0147985, 0.0165843,
    0.0179191 };
Period[] swapMaturities = new Period[]
{
    new Period(2,TimeUnit.Years),
    new Period(3,TimeUnit.Years),
    new Period(4,TimeUnit.Years),
    new Period(5,TimeUnit.Years),
    new Period(6,TimeUnit.Years)
};

var res = FixedIncomeHelper.InterbankZeroCoupon(settlementDate, depositRates,
    depositeMaturities, futRates, swapRates, swapMaturities);
return Json(new { Name = "Zero-Coupon Interbank", Result = res });
}
```

Here, we just select few of market data points for demonstration purpose. In practice, you should use all of the relevant market data to build the zero-coupon curve.

Next, add a TypeScript method named *getZeroCouponInterbank* to the *ch10.service.ts* file in the *ClientApp/ src/app/models* folder with the following code:

```
getZeroCouponInterbank() {
  return this.http.get<any>(this.url + 'api/zerocouponinterbank');
}
```

Here, I will use an example to illustrate how to construct an interbank zero-coupon yield curve in an Angular application. Run the following statement in a command prompt window:

ng g c chapter10/ch10-zc-interbank --module=app.module

This generates a new component called *ch10-zc-interbank* in the *ClientApp/src/app/Chapter10* folder. Open the component class and replace its content with the following code:

```
// ch10-zc-interbank.component.ts file:
import { Component, OnInit } from '@angular/core';
import { Ch10Service } from '../../models/ch10.service';
import { ModelHelper } from '../../models/model.helper';

@Component({
  selector: 'app-ch10-zc-interbank',
  templateUrl: './ch10-zc-interbank.component.html',
  styleUrls: ['./ch10-zc-interbank.component.css']
})
export class Ch10ZcInterbankComponent implements OnInit {
  zcResult: any;
  zcCols: any;
  private helper: ModelHelper;

  constructor(private service: Ch10Service) { }

  ngOnInit() {
    this.getZcResult();
  }
```

```
getZcResult() {
  this.zcResult = null;
  this.service.getZeroCouponInterbank().subscribe(result => {
    this.zcResult = result.result;
    this.helper = new ModelHelper();
    this.zcCols = this.helper.setColDefs(result.result, 170);
  });
}
}
```

We also need to update the component's template with the following code:

```
// ch10-zc-interbank.component.html file:
<h2>
  ch10-zc-interbank works!
</h2>
<ag-grid-angular *ngIf="zcResult" style="height:400px;width:900px;"
  class="ag-theme-balham" [rowData]="zcResult" [columnDefs]="zcCols">
</ag-grid-angular>
<app-ch10-line-chart *ngIf="zcResult" [data]="zcResult"></app-ch10-line-chart>
```

This template adds an *ag-grid-angular* directive and a *ch10-line-chart* directive, which are used to display zero-coupon results.

Finally, we need to add a path for this new component to the *RouterModule* of the root module (i.e., the *app.module.ts* file):

```
{ path: 'chapter10/ch10-zc-Interbank, component: Ch10ZcInterbankComponent },
```

Then add the corresponding URL link to the *home* and *nav-menu* components.

Saving the project and navigating to the */chapter10/ch10-zc-interbank* page produce the default results shown in Fig.10-7.

Credit Spread Term Structures

We can derive a term structure of credit spreads for a given rating class and a given sector from market data by the following steps – First, we derive the benchmark zero-coupon yield curve, which can be taken as either the Treasury zero-coupon yield curve or the Interbank zero-coupon yield curve, using the approaches described in the preceding sections. Next, we constitute a homogeneous basket of bonds for the risky class studied, using the same method as we did for deriving the Treasury zero-coupon curve. Finally, we obtain the zero-coupon credit spread curve by subtracting the benchmark zero-coupon yield curve from the risky zero-coupon yield curve.

The nominal spread (*n*-spread) and the zero-volatility spread (*z*-spread) are often used to measure the spread that the investor will receive from a non-Treasury bond over the Treasury yield curve. The nominal spread, or the nominal yield spread, is the simple yield spread for non-Treasury bonds. It measures the difference between the yield of a bond and the yield to maturity of a similar maturity Treasury bond. For example, consider two 10-year bonds: a Treasury bond with an YTM of 3.5%, and a non-Treasury bond with an YTM of 6%. The *n*-spread = non-Treasury YTM – Treasury YTM = 6% – 3.5% = 2.5%. The difference between the YTM for the two bonds is 2.5% (250 bps or basis points). This is the *n*-spread.

ch10-zc-interbank works!

Maturity	TimesToMaturity	Zero Coupon Rate: R	Equivalent Rate: Rc	Discount Rate: B
2/25/2015	0.019444444444444445	0.0013759273398739058	0.001374984209054908	0.9999732646036894
3/18/2015	0.077777777777777778	0.0017183600538137611	0.0017168894002483892	0.9998664733872928
4/20/2015	0.16944444444444445	0.0021138532271565147	0.002111628291107115	0.9996422613560693
5/18/2015	0.24722222222222223	0.0025835084282817	0.0025801860267848.92	0.999362326331613
6/18/2015	0.3333333333333333	0.002511347583568524	0.002508208037768078	0.9991642829328984
9/17/2015	0.5861111111111111	0.0032284209089279425	0.003223234979091716	0.9981126178563563
12/16/2015	0.8361111111111111	0.004108918641638537	0.004100523121409738	0.9965773968200701
3/16/2016	1.0888888888888888	0.005109540363417597	0.0050965665397972.87	0.9944658144075246
6/16/2016	1.3444444444444446	0.006177882341604102	0.006158929421254955	0.9917539184150767
9/15/2016	1.5972222222222223	0.007242456702645228	0.007216427396373737	0.9885400470321849
2/21/2017	2.0388888888888888	0.008908173235258277	0.008868837281149622	0.9820801506945267
2/20/2018	3.05	0.012370934025799939	0.01229525169917367	0.9631945274455526
2/19/2019	4.0611111111111111	0.0148979301279204	0.014788345561110864	0.9417118924254216

Fig.10-7. Interbank zero-coupon and discount yield curves.

A non-Treasury bond usually provides a higher yield compared to a Treasury bond because of the additional risk involved. The n-spread is a way to price the bonds. Even though the n-spread is easy to calculate, it is not a very strong measure because it does not consider the spot rates for different maturities and it also ignores the effect of embedded options. Due to this reason, the other spread measures such as the z-spread are more popular.

The problem with the n-spread is that it measures the spread at just one point on the yield curve. The z-spread solves this problem by considering the spot yield curve instead of the standard yield curve. Calculating the z-spread requires the present value of the cash flows. We start with an assumption for the z-spread: taking the Treasury yield rates for each maturity, adding the z-spread to it, and using this new rate as a discount rate for each maturity to price the bond. The correct z-spread is the one that makes the present value of cash flows equal to the price of the bond:

$$P = \sum_{t=1}^{T} \frac{CF_t}{[1 + R(0,t) + z]^t}$$

Where z is called the z-spread. The z-spread represents the additional risk the investor is taking in the form of credit risk, liquidity risk, and option risk.

In most case, such as the fixed coupon bonds, the z-spread will only slightly diverge from the n-spread. The difference mainly comes from the shape of the term structure and the bond characteristics. For instance, the difference will be high for amortizing bonds for which the principal is repaid over time, bonds with high coupon, and when the yield curve is steep.

QuantLib provides a z-spread feature, which allows you to shift the yield curve and to reprice the bonds with specified z-spread. First, I will use an example to show you how to shift a zero-coupon curve by modified the *ZeroCouponBootstrap* method in the *FixedIncomeHelper* class discussed previously (see Fig.10-6). Here is the code snippet for the z-spread related parts of the modified method named *ZeroCouponBootstrapZSpread*:

```
public static DataTable ZeroCouponBootstrapZSpread(double[] depositRates,
    Period[] depositMaturities, double[] bondPrices, double[] bondCoupons,
    Period[] bondMaturities, string curveType, double zSpread)
{
    DataTable res = new DataTable();
    Date evalDate = new Date(15, Month.January, 2015);

    ... ...

    var ts = new PiecewiseLinearZero(evalDate, rateHelpers, dc);
    YieldTermStructureHandle tsHandle = new YieldTermStructureHandle(ts);
    QuoteHandle zsHandle = new QuoteHandle( new SimpleQuote(zSpread/10000.0));
    ZeroSpreadedTermStructure zs = new ZeroSpreadedTermStructure(tsHandle,
        zsHandle);

    ... ...

    return res;
}
```

The most part of the code in this method is identical to that used in the original *ZeroCouponBootstrap* method. Here, we add the *zSpread* parameter as input. The key step is to use the z-spread and the original term structure *ts* as inputs to create a *ZeroSpreadTermStructure* named *zs*, which will shift the original term structure by an amount of *zSpread*. Note that we divide the input *zSpread* by 10,000, which means that the input z-spread should be in units of bps (basis points).

We can now convert the above method into a web service. Add a new method called *GetZeroCouponBootstrapZSpread* to the *FixedIncomeValuesController* class with the following code:

```
[Route("~/api/zeroCouponBootstrapZspread/{zSpread}/{curveType}")]
[HttpGet]
public JsonResult GetZeroCouponBootstrapZSpread(double zSpread, string curveType)
{
    double[] depositRates = new double[] { 0.0525, 0.055 };
    Period[] depositMaturities = new Period[]
    {
        new Period(6, TimeUnit.Months),
        new Period(12, TimeUnit.Months),
```

```
    };
    double[] bondCoupons = new double[] { 0.0575, 0.06, 0.0625, 0.065, 0.0675,
        0.068, 0.07, 0.071, 0.0715, 0.072, 0.073, 0.0735, 0.074, 0.075, 0.076,
        0.076, 0.077, 0.078 };
    Period[] bondMaturities = new Period[bondCoupons.Length];
    for (int i = 0; i < bondCoupons.Length; i++)
    {
        bondMaturities[i] = new Period((i + 3) * 6, TimeUnit.Months);
    }
    double[] bondPrices = new double[bondCoupons.Length];
    for (int i = 0; i < bondPrices.Length; i++)
        bondPrices[i] = 100.0;

    var res = FixedIncomeHelper.ZeroCouponBootstrapZSpread(depositRates,
        depositMaturities, bondPrices, bondCoupons, bondMaturities, curveType,
        zSpread);
    return Json(new { Name = "Zero-Coupon Bootstrap", Result = res });
}
```

This method is similar to the *GetZeroCouponBootstrap* method, except that we call the *ZeroCouponBootstrapZSpread* here instead of the *ZeroCouponBootstrap* method.

Next, add a TypeScript method named *getZeroCouponBootstrapZspread* to the *ch10.service.ts* file in the *ClientApp/ src/app/models* folder with the following code:

```
getZeroCouponBootstrapZspread(zSpread: number, curveType: string) {
  return this.http.get<any>(this.url + 'api/zerocouponbootstrapzspread/' +
    zSpread + '/' + curveType);
}
```

Here, I will use an example to illustrate how to construct a credit spread zero-coupon yield curve in an Angular application. First, we need to add a chart component that is used to display the zero-coupon results:

Run the following statement in a command prompt window:

ng g c chapter10/ch10-line-chart2 --module=app.module

This generates a new component called *ch10-line-chart2* in the *ClientApp/src/app/Chapter10* folder. Open the component class and replace its content with the following code:

```
// ch10-line-chart2.component.ts file:
import { Component, OnInit, Input, OnChanges } from '@angular/core';
@Component({
  selector: 'app-ch10-line-chart2',
  templateUrl: './ch10-line-chart2.component.html',
  styleUrls: ['./ch10-line-chart2.component.css']
})
export class Ch10LineChart2Component implements OnInit, OnChanges {
  @Input() data: any;
  zcOptions: any;
  discOptions: any;
  constructor() { }

  ngOnInit() {
    this.zcOptions = this.getOptions(this.data, 'zc');
    this.discOptions = this.getOptions(this.data, 'disc');
```

```
  }

  ngOnChanges() {
    this.zcOptions = this.getOptions(this.data, 'zc');
    this.discOptions = this.getOptions(this.data, 'disc');
  }

  getOptions(data: any, chartType: string) {
    let title = 'Zero-Coupon Yield';
    let ylabel = 'Zero-Coupon Rate';
    let seriesNames = ['R', 'R with ZSpread'];
    let top = '11%';
    let data1 = [];
    let data2 = [];

    if (chartType == 'zc') {
      data.forEach(function (d) {
        data1.push([d['timesToMaturity'], d["zero Coupon Rate: R"]]);
        data2.push([d['timesToMaturity'], d["zero Coupon Rate: R with ZSpread"]]);
      })
    } else if (chartType == 'disc') {
      title = 'Discount Yield';
      ylabel = 'Disount Rate';
      seriesNames = ['B', 'B with ZSpread'];
      top = "70%";
      data.forEach(function (d) {
        data1.push([d['timesToMaturity'], d["discount Rate: B"]]);
        data2.push([d['timesToMaturity'], d["discount Rate: B with ZSpread"]]);
      })
    }

    return {
      legend: {
        top: top,
        left: '17%',
        orient: 'vertical',
        data: [{ name: seriesNames[0], icon: 'line' }, { name: seriesNames[1],
          icon: 'line' }]
      },
      grid: {
        top: 35,
        left: 70,
        right: 10
      },
      title: {
        text: title,
        left: 'center'
      },
      xAxis: {
        type: 'value',
        name: 'Times to Maturity',
        nameLocation: 'center',
        nameGap: '30',
        axisLine: { onZero: false }
      },
```

```
      yAxis: {
        type: 'value',
        scale: true,
        name: ylabel,
        nameLocation: 'center',
        nameGap: '50'
      },
      series: [{
        name: seriesNames[0],
        type: 'line',
        data: data1,
        showSymbol: false
      },
      {
        name: seriesNames[1],
        type: 'line',
        data: data2,
        showSymbol: false
      }]
    };
  }
}
```

This component takes *data* as input and then creates two line charts used to display the zero-coupon yield and discount yield respectively.

We also need to update the component's template with the following code:

```
// ch10-line-chart2.component.html file:
<div class="cardList">
  <mat-card class="card-border">
    <div echarts [options]="zcOptions" style="height:100%"></div>
  </mat-card>
  <mat-card class="card-border">
    <div echarts [options]="discOptions" style="height:100%"></div>
  </mat-card>
</div>
```

This template is styled with the following *css* file:

```
// ch10-line-chart2.component.css file:
.cardList {
  display: flex;
  flex-direction: row;
  flex-wrap: wrap;
  justify-content: flex-start;
}

.card-border {
  width: 450px;
  height: 400px;
}
```

Now, run the following statement in a command prompt window:

```
ng g c chapter10/ch10-zc-zspread --module=app.module
```

This generates a new component called *ch10-zc-zspread* in the *ClientApp/src/app/Chapter10* folder. Open the component class and replace its content with the following code:

```
// ch10-zc-zspread.component.ts file:
import { Component, OnInit } from '@angular/core';
import { Ch10Service } from '../../models/ch10.service';

@Component({
  selector: 'app-ch10-zc-zspread',
  templateUrl: './ch10-zc-zspread.component.html',
  styleUrls: ['./ch10-zc-zspread.component.css']
})
export class Ch10ZcZspreadComponent implements OnInit {
  zcResult: any;
  zSpread: number = 50;
  curveType: string = 'notDataPoints';

  constructor(private service: Ch10Service) { }

  ngOnInit() {
    this.getZcResult(this.zSpread, this.curveType);
  }

  getZcResult(zSpread: number, curveType: string) {
    this.zcResult = null;
    this.service.getZeroCouponBootstrapZspread(zSpread, curveType).subscribe(
    result => { this.zcResult = result.result; });
  }
}
```

We also need to update the component's template with the following code:

```
// ch10-zc-zspread.component.html file:
<h2>
  ch10-zc-zspread works!
</h2>

<mat-form-field>
  <input matInput placeholder="zSpread" [(ngModel)]="zSpread" name="zSpread">
</mat-form-field>
<mat-form-field>
  <mat-select placeholder="Select a curve type" [(value)]="curveType">
    <mat-option value="dataPoints">Data Points</mat-option>
    <mat-option value="notDataPoints">Not Data Points</mat-option>
  </mat-select>
</mat-form-field>
<button mat-raised-button color="primary" (click)="getZcResult(zSpread,
curveType)">Get Zero-Coupon Curve</button>

<app-ch10-line-chart2 *ngIf="zcResult" [data]="zcResult"></app-ch10-line-chart2>
```

This template adds a *ch10-line-chart2* directive that is used to display the zero-coupon and discount yield curves.

Finally, we need to add a path for this new component to the *RouterModule* of the root module (i.e., the *app.module.ts* file):

```
{ path: 'chapter10/ch10-zc-zspread, component: Ch10ZcZspreadComponent },
```

Then add the corresponding URL link to the *home* and *nav-menu* components.

Saving the project and navigating to the */chapter10/ch10-zc-zspread* page produce the default results shown in Fig.10-8.

Fig.10-8. Zero-coupon and discount yield curves with and without z-spread.

You can see from Fig.10-8 that the zero-coupon yield with the *z*-spread is always higher than the original curve, while the discount yield with the *z*-spread is always lower than the original discount curve, as expected.

QuantLib also enables you to reprice the bond with the *z*-spread. Here, I will use an example to illustrate how to do it. Here, we modify the *BondPriceCurveRate* method used previously (see Figure 10-3). Add a new method named *BondPriceCurveRateZSpread* to the *FixedIncomeHelper* class. The most part of the code in this method is identical to that used in original *BondPriceCurveRate* method. Here I list only the code snippet related to the *z*-spread:

```
public static DataTable BondPriceCurveRateZSpread()
{
    ... ...

    var rateCurve = new ZeroCurve(rateDates1, rates1, dc, calendar,
        new Linear(), Compounding.Compounded, Frequency.Semiannual);

    ... ...

    DataTable dt = new DataTable();
    dt.Columns.Add("ZSpread", typeof(double));
    dt.Columns.Add("Price", typeof(double));
    fixedRateBond.setPricingEngine(bondEngine);
```

```
double[] zSpreads = new double[21];
for (int i = 0; i < zSpreads.Length; i++)
    zSpreads[i] = 250.0 * i;

Leg leg = fixedRateBond.cashflows();
for (int i = 0; i < zSpreads.Length; i++)
{
    object zNPV = CashFlows.npv(leg, rateCurve, zSpreads[i] / 10000.0, dc,
        Compounding.Compounded, Frequency.Semiannual, true, settlementDate,
        evalDate);
    dt.Rows.Add(zSpreads[i], zNPV);
}

    return dt;
}
```

Here, we first define a double array for the z-spreads. We then extract the leg of cash flows from the original *fixedRateBond*. QuantLib provides a number of functions that calculate the *NPV* of a series of cash flows. These functions are defined as static methods inside the *CashFlows* class. Here, we use the *CashFlows.npv* method to recalculate the bond price for different z-spreads. This method takes the cash flow leg and original term structure (*rateCurve*) as inputs.

We can test this method by converting it into a web service. Add a new method called *GetBondPriceCurveRateZSpread* to the *FixedIncomeValuesController* class with the following code:

```
[Route("~/api/bondPriceCurveRateZspread")]
[HttpGet]
public JsonResult GetBondPriceCurveRateZSpread()
{
    var res = FixedIncomeHelper.BondPriceCurveRateZSpread();
    return Json(new { Name = "Bond Price with Curve Rate and Z-Spread",
        Result = res });
}
```

Now, running our project and enter the following URL

https://localhost:5001/api/bondpricecurveratezspread

Which generates the following results shown in Fig.10-9.

Fig.10-9. Bond price with z-spreads.

You can see that the bond price drops with the increase of the z-spread – the bond becomes very cheap when its z-spread approaches 5000 bps (near default).

Bonds with Embedded Options

In the preceding sections, we discussed simple fixed-coupon bonds pricing and yield term structures. However, most corporate bonds are not straight bonds; they usually contain all kinds of embedded options. For example, a callable bond is a bond with embedded option that would give the issuer the right (but not the obligation) to redeem the bond before its scheduled maturity. In a convertible bond, however, an embedded option may give the holder the right to exchange the bond for shares in the underlying common stock. The presence of embedded options affects the value of the security, and you should be aware of any embedded options and the potential outcome or impact. In this section, I will show you how to price the callable and convertible bonds using QuantLib.

Callable Bonds

Buying a callable bond comes down to buying an option-free bond and selling a call option to the issuer of the bond. For example, the US Treasury bond with coupon 5.5% and maturity date 2/15/2018 can be called on coupon dates only, at a price of $100, from 2/15/2016 on. Such a bond is said to be discretely callable.

A callable bond allows its issuer to buy back his debt at par value prior to maturity in case interest rates fall below the coupon rate of issue. Therefore, the issuer will have the opportunity to issue a new bond at a lower option rate. A callable bond could be less valuable than a non-callable bond. This is because you could lose out on interest payments to which you would otherwise be entitled if the bond were held to maturity.

Unlike an option-free fixed coupon bond, a callable bond is a contingent claim, that is, you do not know its future cash flows with certainty, because they are dependent on the future values of interest rates. Therefore, pricing the callable bonds requires not only the knowledge on discount factors at the present date but also some kind of understanding of how these discount factors or the term structure of discount rates are going to evolve over time. Some dynamic model of the term structure of interest rates is therefore needed to describe the explicit nature of the variables of interest in the valuation formula.

The Hull-White model is one of the most popular models of future interest rates. One version of the extended Vasicek's model is

$$dr(t) = [\theta(t) - a\,r(t)]dt + \sigma dz \qquad (10\text{-}13)$$

where r is the short-term interest rate at time t, dz is the Wiener process driving the term structure movements, σ is a constant representing the instantaneous standard deviation of the short rate, a is a constant, θ is a function of time chosen to ensure that the model fits the initial term structure.

QuantLib implemented a class named *HullWhite*, which simulates the future interest rates using the Hull-White model described in Eq. (10-13). After creating the term structure for the future interest rates using this model, we can then use the bond-pricing engine, *TreeCallableFixedRateBondEngine*, to price the callable fixed coupon bonds. This pricing engine for the callable bonds is based on the trinomial tree model.

Add a new helper method named *CallableBondPrice* to the *FixedIncomeHelper* class with the following code:

```
public static DataTable CallableBondPrice(string evalDate, string issueDate, string
    callDate, string maturity, double coupon, double sigma, double a, double rate)
{
    Date evalDate1 = DateTime.Parse(evalDate).To<Date>();
    Settings.instance().setEvaluationDate(evalDate1);
    Date issueDate1 = DateTime.Parse(issueDate).To<Date>();
    Date callDate1 = DateTime.Parse(callDate).To<Date>();
    Date maturity1 = DateTime.Parse(maturity).To<Date>();

    uint maxIterations = 1000;
    double accuracy = 1e-8;
    uint gridIntervals = 40;
    DayCounter dc = new ActualActual(ActualActual.Convention.Bond);

    var flatCurve = new FlatForward(evalDate1, rate, dc, Compounding.Compounded,
        Frequency.Semiannual);
    YieldTermStructureHandle discountingTermStructure =
        new YieldTermStructureHandle(flatCurve);
    CallabilitySchedule callSchedule = new CallabilitySchedule();
    double callPrice = 100.0;
    int numberOfCallDates = 24;
    Calendar nullCalendar = new NullCalendar();
    for (int i = 0; i < numberOfCallDates; i++)
    {
        CallabilityPrice myPrice = new CallabilityPrice(callPrice,
            CallabilityPrice.Type.Clean);
        callSchedule.Add(new Callability(myPrice, Callability.Call, callDate1));
        callDate1 = nullCalendar.advance(callDate1, 3, TimeUnit.Months);
    }

    int settlementDays = 3;
    Calendar bondCalendar = new UnitedStates(UnitedStates.Market.GovernmentBond);
    Frequency frequency = Frequency.Quarterly;
    double redemption = 100.0;
    double faceAmount = 100.0;

    DayCounter bondDayCounter = new ActualActual(ActualActual.Convention.Bond);
    BusinessDayConvention accrualConvention = BusinessDayConvention.Unadjusted;
    BusinessDayConvention paymentConvention = BusinessDayConvention.Unadjusted;
    Schedule sch = new Schedule(issueDate1, maturity1, new Period(frequency),
        bondCalendar, accrualConvention, accrualConvention,
        DateGeneration.Rule.Backward, false);
    ShortRateModel hw = new HullWhite(discountingTermStructure, a, sigma);
    DoubleVector couponsVector = new DoubleVector();
    couponsVector.Add(coupon);
    var engine = new TreeCallableFixedRateBondEngine(hw, gridIntervals,
        discountingTermStructure);
    CallableFixedRateBond callableBond = new CallableFixedRateBond(settlementDays,
        faceAmount, sch, couponsVector, bondDayCounter, paymentConvention,
        redemption, issueDate1, callSchedule);

    DataTable dt = new DataTable();
```

```
    dt.Columns.Add("Name", typeof(string));
    dt.Columns.Add("Value", typeof(string));
    try
    {
        callableBond.setPricingEngine(engine);
        dt.Rows.Add("Present Value", callableBond.NPV());
        dt.Rows.Add("Clean Price", callableBond.cleanPrice());
        dt.Rows.Add("Dirty Price", callableBond.dirtyPrice());
        dt.Rows.Add("Accrued Value", callableBond.accruedAmount());
        dt.Rows.Add("YTM", callableBond.yield(bondDayCounter,
            Compounding.Compounded, frequency, accuracy, maxIterations));
    }
    catch { }
    return dt;
}
```

Here, we first set up the schedule (quarterly) for the callable bond; then use the flat interest rate to create the future interest rate term structure by calling the *HullWhite* instance. We next create the pricing engine using *TreeCallableFixedRateBondEngine* class; and finally create a *CallableFixedRateBond* object and set up its pricing engine.

We can convert this method into a web service. Add a new method named *GetCallableBondPrice* to the *FixedIncomeValuesController* class with the following code:

```
[Route("~/api/callableBondPrice/{evalDate}/{issueDate}/{callDate}/{maturity}/
    {coupon}/{sigma}/{a}/{rate}")]
[HttpGet]
public JsonResult GetCallableBondPrice(string evalDate, string issueDate, string
    callDate, string maturity, double coupon, double sigma, double a, double rate)
{
    var res = FixedIncomeHelper.CallableBondPrice(evalDate, issueDate, callDate,
        maturity, coupon, sigma, a, rate);
    return Json(new { Name = "Callable Bond Price", Result = res });
}
```

Now, add a TypeScript method named *getCallableBondPrice* to the *ch10.service.ts* file in the *ClientApp /src/app/models* folder with the following code:

```
getCallableBondPrice(evalDate: string, issueDate: string, callDate: string,
  maturity: string, coupon: number, sigma: number, a: number, rate: number) {
    let url1 = this.url + 'api/callableBondprice/' + evalDate + '/' + issueDate +
      '/' + callDate + '/' + maturity + '/' + coupon + '/' + sigma + '/' + a + '/' +
      rate;
  return this.http.get<any>(url1);
}
```

Run the following statement in a command prompt window:

ng g c chapter10/ch10-callable-bond --module=app.module

This generates a new component called *ch10-callable-bond* in the *ClientApp/src/app/Chapter10* folder. Open the component class and replace its content with the following code:

```
// ch10-callable-bond.component.ts file:
import { Component, OnInit } from '@angular/core';
import { Ch10Service } from '../../models/ch10.service';
import { ModelHelper } from '../../models/model.helper';
```

```
@Component({
  selector: 'app-ch10-callable-bond',
  templateUrl: './ch10-callable-bond.component.html',
  styleUrls: ['./ch10-callable-bond.component.css']
})
export class Ch10CallableBondComponent implements OnInit {
  bondResult: any;
  colDefs: any;

  inputCols: any = [
    { headerName: "Parameter", field: "param", width: 100 },
    { headerName: "Value", field: "value", width: 100, editable: true },
  ];
  inputRows: any = [
    { param: 'Eval Date', value: '2007-10-16' },
    { param: 'Issue Date', value: '2004-09-16' },
    { param: 'Call Date', value: '2006-09-15' },
    { param: 'Maturity', value: '2012-09-15' },
    { param: 'Coupon', value: 0.0465 },
    { param: 'Sigma', value: 0.06 },
    { param: 'Reversion a', value: 0.03 },
    { param: 'Rate', value: 0.055 }
  ];

  private helper: ModelHelper;

  constructor(private service: Ch10Service) { }

  ngOnInit() {
    this.getBondResult(this.inputRows);
  }

  getBondResult(rows: any) {
    this.bondResult = null;
    this.service.getCallableBondPrice(rows[0].value, rows[1].value, rows[2].value,
      rows[3].value, rows[4].value, rows[5].value, rows[6].value, rows[7].value)
      .subscribe(result => {
        this.bondResult = result.result;
        this.helper = new ModelHelper();
        this.colDefs = this.helper.setColDefs(result.result, 120);
      });
  }
}
```

Here, we use an *ag-Grid* component to display the input parameters, which is much cleaner than using multiple input fields. Note that we enable editing in the *Value* column of the input *ag-Grid* by setting the *editable* property to true inside the *inputCols* property.

Next, we need to update the component's template with the following code:

```
// ch10-callable-bond.component.html file:
<h2>
  ch10-callable-bond works!
</h2>
```

```
<button mat-raised-button color="primary" (click)="getBondResult(inputRows)">Get
Option Result</button>
<div class="cardList">
  <mat-card class="card-border">
    <p>Input Parameters</p>
    <ag-grid-angular *ngIf="bondResult" style="height:90%;" class="ag-theme-balham"
[rowData]="inputRows" [columnDefs]="inputCols">
    </ag-grid-angular>
  </mat-card>
  <mat-card class="card-border">
    <p>Results</p>
    <ag-grid-angular *ngIf="bondResult" style="height:90%;" class="ag-theme-balham"
[rowData]="bondResult" [columnDefs]="colDefs">
    </ag-grid-angular>
  </mat-card>
</div>
```

This template is styled by the following *css* file:

```
.cardList {
  display: flex;
  flex-direction: row;
  flex-wrap: wrap;
  justify-content: flex-start;
}

.card-border {
  margin: 10px;
  margin-left: 0;
  margin-bottom: 0;
  width: 300px;
  height: 300px;
}
```

Finally, we need to add a path for this new component to the *RouterModule* of the root module (i.e., the *app.module.ts* file):

```
{ path: 'chapter10/ch10-callable-bond, component: Ch10CallableBondComponent },
```

Then add the corresponding URL link to the *home* and *nav-menu* components.

Saving the project and navigating to the */chapter10/ch10-callable-bond* page produce the default results shown in Fig.10-10.

You can change the sigma parameter and compare the results directly with those from Bloomberg screen, as shown in the following list:

sigma (%)	0	1	3	6	12
QuantLib Clean Price	96.47	95.64	93.31	87.08	77.34
Bloomberg Clean Price	96.5	95.68	92.34	87.16	77.31
QuantLib YTM (%)	5.48	5.67	6.49	7.85	10.64
Bloomberg YTM (%)	5.47	5.66	6.49	7.83	10.65

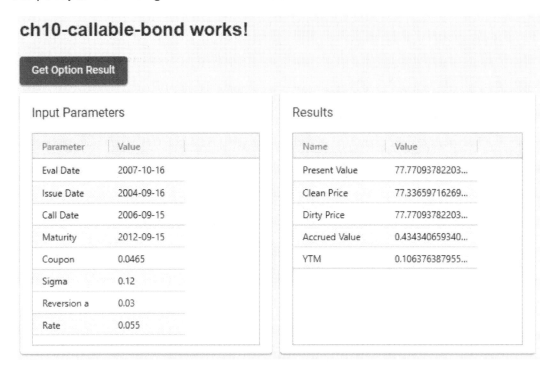

Fig.10-10. Calculated results for a callable bond.

You can see the QuantLib results are very close to the Bloomberg results, which should give you some confidence when you use QuantLib in your applications.

Convertible Bonds

A convertible bond or convertible note is a type of bond that the bondholder can convert it into a specified number of shares of common stock in the issuing company or cash of equal value. It is a hybrid security with debt- and equity-like features. Convertible bonds are most often issued by company with a relatively low credit rating and high growth potential. From the investor's perspective, a convertible bond has a value-added component built into it; it is essentially a bond with a stock option hidden inside. Thus, it tends to offer a lower rate of return in exchange for the value of the option to trade the bond into stock.

Due to their relative complexity, you should be familiar with terminology associated with the convertible bonds.

- The convertible price is the price of the convertible bond.

- The bond floor is the price of the bond if there is no conversion option.

- The conversion ratio is the number of shares a bond is exchanged for.

- The conversion price is the shares price at which the face amount of the bond may be exchanged for shares; it is the strike price of the embedded equity option, and it is given by: Conversion Price = Par Value of Convertible Bond/Conversion Ratio.

- The conversion value (also called parity) is equal to: Conversion Value = Current Share Price × Conversion Ratio.

- The conversion premium is equal to: (Convertible Price – Conversion Value)/Conversion Value.

- The income pickup is the amount by which the YTM of the convertible bond exceeds the dividend yield of the share.

A convertible bond is similar to a normal coupon bond plus a call option on the underlying stock, with an important difference: the effective strike price of the call option will vary with the price of the bond, which itself varies with interest rates. Because of this characteristic, it is difficult to price the conversion option using a Black-Scholes formula or other similar models that assume constant interest rates.

QuantLib implemented several binomial based models that enable you to price the convertible bonds. Add an enum called *ConvertibleBondEngineType* to the *FixedIncomeHelper* class with the following code:

```
public enum ConvertableBondEngineType
{
    BinomialJarrowRudd,
    BinomialCoxRossRubinstein,
    BinomialAdditiveEquiprobabilities,
    BinomialTrigeorgis,
    BinomialTian,
    BinomialLeisenReimer,
    BinomialJoshi,
};
```

This enum is used to specify the pricing engine type. Here I will implement a helper method named *ConvertibleBondPrice* in the *FixedIncomeHelper* class with the following code:

```
public static DataTable ConvertibleBondPrice(string priceEngineType)
{
    priceEngineType = char.ToUpper(priceEngineType[0]) +
        priceEngineType.Substring(1);
    Enum.TryParse(priceEngineType, out ConvertableBondEngineType engineType);
    double spot = 36.0;
    double spreadRate = 0.005;
    double dividendYield = 0.02;
    double riskFreeRate = 0.06;
    double vol = 0.2;
    int settlementDays = 3;
    int length = 5;
    double redemprion = 100.0;
    double conversionRatio = redemprion / spot;
    Calendar calendar = new TARGET();
    Date today = calendar.adjust(Date.todaysDate());
    Settings.instance().setEvaluationDate(today);
    Date settlementDate = calendar.advance(today, new Period(settlementDays,
        TimeUnit.Days));
    Date exerciseDate = calendar.advance(settlementDate,
        new Period(length, TimeUnit.Years));
    Date issueDate = calendar.advance(exerciseDate,
        new Period(-length, TimeUnit.Years));
    BusinessDayConvention convention = BusinessDayConvention.ModifiedFollowing;
    Frequency frequency = Frequency.Annual;
    Schedule schedule = new Schedule(issueDate, exerciseDate, new Period(frequency),
        calendar, convention, convention, DateGeneration.Rule.Backward, false);
    DividendSchedule dividends = new DividendSchedule();
```

```
CallabilitySchedule callability = new CallabilitySchedule();
DoubleVector coupons = new DoubleVector();
coupons.Add(0.05);
DayCounter bondDayCounter = new Thirty360();
uint[] callLength = new uint[] { 2, 4 };
uint[] putLength = new uint[] { 3 };
double[] callPrices = new double[] { 101.5, 100.85 };
double[] putPrices = new double[] { 105.0 };
for(int i = 0;i<callLength.Length;i++)
{
    callability.Add(new SoftCallability(
        new CallabilityPrice(callPrices[i],CallabilityPrice.Type.Clean),
        schedule.date(callLength[i]),1.2));
}
for (int i = 0; i < putLength.Length; i++)
{
    callability.Add(new Callability(new CallabilityPrice(putPrices[i],
        CallabilityPrice.Type.Clean), Callability.Put,
        schedule.date(putLength[i])));
}

// Assume dividends are paid every 6 months.
for (Date d = today.Add(new Period(6, TimeUnit.Months));
    d < exerciseDate; d = d.Add(new Period(6, TimeUnit.Months)))
{
    dividends.Add(new FixedDividend(1.0, d));
}
DayCounter dayCounter = new Actual365Fixed();
double maturity = dayCounter.yearFraction(settlementDate, exerciseDate);
Exercise exercise = new EuropeanExercise(exerciseDate);
Exercise amExercise = new AmericanExercise(settlementDate, exerciseDate);

QuoteHandle underlyingH = new QuoteHandle(new SimpleQuote(spot));
YieldTermStructureHandle flatTS = new YieldTermStructureHandle(
    new FlatForward(settlementDate, riskFreeRate, dayCounter));
YieldTermStructureHandle flatDividendTS =
    new YieldTermStructureHandle(new FlatForward(settlementDate, dividendYield,
    dayCounter));
BlackVolTermStructureHandle flatVolTS = new BlackVolTermStructureHandle( new
    BlackConstantVol(settlementDate, calendar, vol, dayCounter));
BlackScholesMertonProcess bsmProcess = new BlackScholesMertonProcess(
    underlyingH, flatDividendTS, flatTS, flatVolTS);

uint timeSteps = 801;
QuoteHandle creditSpread = new QuoteHandle(new SimpleQuote(spreadRate));
PricingEngine engine = new BinomialConvertibleEngine(bsmProcess, "jarrowrudd",
    timeSteps);
ConvertibleFixedCouponBond europeanBond =
    new ConvertibleFixedCouponBond(exercise, conversionRatio, dividends,
    callability, creditSpread, issueDate, settlementDays, coupons,
    bondDayCounter, schedule, redemprion);
europeanBond.setPricingEngine(engine);
ConvertibleFixedCouponBond americanBond =
    new ConvertibleFixedCouponBond(amExercise, conversionRatio,
        dividends, callability, creditSpread, issueDate, settlementDays,
```

```
        coupons, bondDayCounter, schedule, redemprion);
    americanBond.setPricingEngine(engine);

    // select pricing engine
    if (engineType == ConvertableBondEngineType.BinomialJarrowRudd)
        engine = new BinomialConvertibleEngine(bsmProcess, "jarrowrudd", timeSteps);
    else if (engineType == ConvertableBondEngineType.BinomialCoxRossRubinstein)
        engine = new BinomialConvertibleEngine(bsmProcess, "coxrossrubinstein",
            timeSteps);
    else if (engineType == ConvertableBondEngineType.
        BinomialAdditiveEquiprobabilities)
        engine = new BinomialConvertibleEngine(bsmProcess, "eqp", timeSteps);
    else if (engineType == ConvertableBondEngineType.BinomialTrigeorgis)
        engine = new BinomialConvertibleEngine(bsmProcess, "trigeorgis", timeSteps);
    else if (engineType == ConvertableBondEngineType.BinomialTian)
        engine = new BinomialConvertibleEngine(bsmProcess, "tian", timeSteps);
    else if (engineType == ConvertableBondEngineType.BinomialLeisenReimer)
        engine = new BinomialConvertibleEngine(bsmProcess, "leisenreimer",
            timeSteps);
    else if (engineType == ConvertableBondEngineType.BinomialJoshi)
        engine = new BinomialConvertibleEngine(bsmProcess, "joshi4", timeSteps);
    europeanBond.setPricingEngine(engine);
    americanBond.setPricingEngine(engine);

    DataTable dt = new DataTable();
    dt.Columns.Add("Name", typeof(string));
    dt.Columns.Add("Value", typeof(string));
    dt.Rows.Add("Pricing Engine", engineType);
    dt.Rows.Add("Times To Maturity", Math.Round(maturity,0));
    dt.Rows.Add("Spot", spot);
    dt.Rows.Add("Risk Free Interest Rate", riskFreeRate);
    dt.Rows.Add("Dividend Yield", dividendYield);
    dt.Rows.Add("Volatility", vol);
    dt.Rows.Add("European Bond Price", europeanBond.NPV());
    dt.Rows.Add("American Bond Price", americanBond.NPV());
    return dt;
}
```

Inside the *ConvertibleBondPrice* method, we define various parameters, create the *call* and *put* schedules, and build flat term structures for interest rates, dividend yield, and volatility. We then setup seven binomial based pricing engines, from which you can choose to price the convertible bonds.

We can convert this method into a web service by adding the following method to the *FixedIncomeValuesController* class:

```
[Route("~/api/convertibleBondPrice/{engineType}")]
[HttpGet]
public JsonResult GetConvertibleBondPrice(string engineType)
{
    var res = FixedIncomeHelper.ConvertibleBondPrice(engineType);
    return Json(new { Name = "Convertible Bond Price", Result = res });
}
```

Now, add a TypeScript method named *getConvertibleBondPrice* to the *ch10.service.ts* file in the *ClientApp /src/app/models* folder with the following code:

```
getConvertibleBondPrice(engineType: string) {
    return this.http.get<any>(this.url + 'api/convertiblebondprice/' + engineType);
}
```

We can test this web service in an Angular application. Run the following statement in a command prompt window:

ng g c chapter10/ch10-conv-bond --module=app.module

This generates a new component called *ch10-conv-bond* in the *ClientApp/src/app/Chapter10* folder. Open the component class and replace its content with the following code:

```
// ch10-conv-bond.component.ts file:
import { Component, OnInit } from '@angular/core';
import { Ch10Service } from '../../models/ch10.service';
import { ModelHelper } from '../../models/model.helper';

@Component({
    selector: 'app-ch10-conv-bond',
    templateUrl: './ch10-conv-bond.component.html',
    styleUrls: ['./ch10-conv-bond.component.css']
})
export class Ch10ConvBondComponent implements OnInit {
    bondCols: any;
    bondResult: any;
    engineType: string = 'binomialJarrowRudd';
    private helper: ModelHelper;

    constructor(private service: Ch10Service) { }

    ngOnInit() {
        this.getBondPrice(this.engineType);
    }

    getBondPrice(engineType: string) {
        this.bondResult = null;
        this.service.getConvertibleBondPrice(engineType).subscribe(result => {
            this.bondResult = result.result;
            this.helper = new ModelHelper();
            this.bondCols = this.helper.setColDefs(result.result, 150);
        });
    }
}
```

We also need to update this component's template with the following code:

```
// ch10-conv-bond.component.html file:
<h2>
    ch10-conv-bond works!
</h2>

<mat-form-field>
    <mat-select placeholder="Select a pricing engine" [(value)]="engineType">
        <mat-option value="binomialJarrowRudd">Binomial Jarrow-Rudd</mat-option>
        <mat-option value="binomialCoxRossRubinstein">Binomial Cox-Ross-Rubinstein</mat-option>
        <mat-option value="binomialAdditiveEquiprobabilities">Binomial
```

```
  Additive-Equiprobabilities</mat-option>
  <mat-option value="binomialTrigeorgis">Binomial Trigeorgis</mat-option>
  <mat-option value="binomialTian">Binomial Tian</mat-option>
  <mat-option value="binomialLeisenReimer">Binomial Leisen-Reimer</mat-option>
  <mat-option value="binomialJoshi">Binomial Joshi</mat-option>
  </mat-select>
</mat-form-field>
<button mat-raised-button color="primary" (click)="getBondPrice(engineType)">Get
Bond Result</button>

<ag-grid-angular *ngIf="bondResult" style="height:270px;width:350px;"
  class="ag-theme-balham" [rowData]="bondResult" [columnDefs]="bondCols">
</ag-grid-angular>
```

Finally, we need to add a path for this new component to the *RouterModule* of the root module (i.e., the *app.module.ts* file):

```
{ path: 'chapter10/ch10-conv-bond, component: Ch10ConvBondComponent },
```

Then add the corresponding URL link to the *home* and *nav-menu* components.

Saving the project and navigating to the */chapter10/ch10-conv-bond* page produce the default results shown in Fig.10-11.

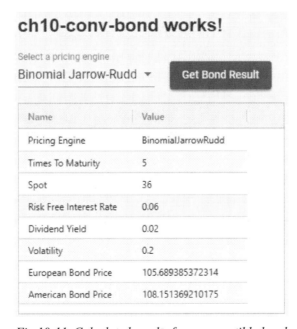

Fig.10-11. Calculated results for a convertible bond.

CDS Pricing

In the previous sections, we discussed how to build the term structures for interest rate, dividend yield, and volatility, and how to price the fixed coupon bonds, callable bonds, and convertible bonds.

Following the similar procedure, you can price the other types of fixed income instruments. In this section, I will discuss CDS (credit default swap) pricing.

CDS is an agreement between two parties to exchange the credit risk of an issuer (reference entity). The buyer of CDS is said to buy protection, and needs to pay a periodic fee (coupon) and profits if the reference entity has a default event, or if the credit worsens while the swap is outstanding. A credit event includes bankruptcy, failing to pay outstanding debt obligations, or in some CDS contracts, a restructuring of a bond or loan. Buying protection has a similar credit risk position to selling a bond short, or "going short risk".

The seller of CDS is said to sell protection. The seller collects the coupon and profits if the credit of the reference entity remains stable or improves while the swap is outstanding. Selling protection has a similar credit risk position to owning a bond or loan, or "going long risk".

The most commonly traded and therefore the most liquid tenors, or maturity lengths, for CDS contracts are five, seven, and ten years, though liquidity across the maturity curve continues to develop. Standard trading sizes vary depending on the reference entity. For example, in US, $10-20 million notional is typical for investment grade (IG) credits and $2-5 million notional is typical for high yield (HY) credits.

Hazard Rate and Default Probability

The CDS valuation is similar to other fixed-income instruments, i.e., the future cash flows are discounted to the present value. What is different in CDS is that the cash flows are further discount by the credit risk. If there is a credit event, the CDS contract is settled and the cash flows then stop. The valuation of CDS can be thought of as a scenario analysis where the credit survives or default. The protection seller (long risk) hopes the credit survives, and discounts the expected annual payments by the probability of this scenario (called the fee leg). The protection buyer (short risk) hopes the credit default, and discounts the expected contingent payment (notional − recovery rate) by the probability of this scenario (called the contingent leg).

CDS usually has a credit curve because the spread demanded for buying or selling protection varies with the length of that protection. Fig. 10-12 shows each spread against the time the protection covers (1Y, 2Y...10Y) for IG index on 12/22/2015 to give us a credit curve.

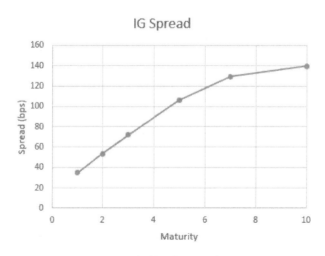

Fig. 10-12. IG spread.

Each point along this credit curve represents a spread that ensures the present value of the expected spread payments (Fee Leg) equals the present value of the payment on default (contingent Leg).

Given that the spread will be paid as long as the credit has not defaulted and the contingent leg payment occurs only if there is a default in a period, we can write for a par CDS contract (with a notional of 1):

$$S_n \sum_{i=1}^{n} \Delta_i \cdot P_{si} \cdot DF_i + accrual\ on\ default = (1 - R) \cdot \sum_{i=1}^{n} \left[P_{s(i-1)} - P_{si}\right] \cdot DF_i \qquad (10\text{-}14)$$

Where the left hand side is the present value for fee leg and the right hand side represents the present value for the contingent leg. S_n is the spread for protection to period n; Δ_i is the length of time period i in years; P_{si} is the probability of survival to time i; DF_i is the risk-free discount factor to time i; R is the recovery rate on default; and the accrual on default is given by

$$Accrual\ on\ default = S_n \sum_{i=1}^{n} \frac{\Delta_i}{2} \cdot \left[P_{s(i-1)} - P_{si}\right] \cdot DF_i$$

We can model survival probabilities by making them a function of a hazard rate. The hazard rate (denoted as λ) as the conditional probability of default in a period. For the first period $i = 1$, the probability of survival (P_s) is the probability of not having defaulted in the period, or $(1 - \lambda)$. So, we can write:

$$P_{s1} = (1 - \lambda_1) \quad for\ i = 1$$

For the next period, $i = 2$, the probability of survival is the probability of surviving period 1 and the probability of surviving period 2, i.e.:

$$P_{s2} = (1 - \lambda_1) \cdot (1 - \lambda_2) \quad for\ i = 2$$

The probability of default (P_d) in a given period is then just the probability of surviving to the start of the period minus the probability of surviving to the end of it, i.e.:

$$P_{d2} = P_{s1} - P_{s2} = (1 - \lambda_1) \cdot \lambda_2$$

This shows how we can build up the probabilities of survival used for CDS pricing in Eq. (10-14). In theory, that means we could calculate a CDS spread from probabilities of survival. In practice, the spread is readily observable in the market and instead we can back out the probability of survival to any time period implied by the market spread, which means we can back out the hazard rates for each period using market spreads.

In terms of pricing a CDS contract, we could in theory solve Eq. (10-14) using a single hazard rate. However, we can also bootstrap a hazard rate implied for each period from the market-observed credit curve. To do this we use the period 1 spread to imply the hazard rate for period 1. For period 2 we use the period 1 hazard rate to calculate the survival probability for period 1 and use the spread observed for period 2 to calculate the hazard rate for period 2. In that way, we are using the market data of default risk in period 1 when we price our period 2 CDS contract (i.e. when we back out the survival probability for period 2). Continuing this process, we can bootstrap the hazard rates implied for each period.

Now, let me show you how to calculate the CDS hazard rate and survival probability from the CDS market spread data using QuantLib. Add a new helper method called *CdsHazardRate* to the *FixedIncomeHelper* class with the following code:

```
public static DataTable CdsHazardRate(DateTime evalDate, double recoveryRate,
```

```
      string spreadsStr, string tenors)
{
      Calendar calendar = new TARGET();
      var evalDate1 = evalDate.To<Date>();
      evalDate1 = calendar.adjust(evalDate1);
      Settings.instance().setEvaluationDate(evalDate1);
      var spreads = spreadStr.To<double[]>();
      var periods = tenors.To<PeriodVector>();

      // dummy curve
      QuoteHandle flatRateH = new QuoteHandle(new SimpleQuote(0.01));
      YieldTermStructureHandle tsCurve = new YieldTermStructureHandle(new
          FlatForward(evalDate1, flatRateH, new Actual365Fixed()));
      DateVector maturities = new DateVector();
      for (int i = 0; i < periods.Count; i++)
          maturities.Add(calendar.adjust(evalDate1.Add(periods[i]),
              BusinessDayConvention.Following));

      DefaultProbabilityHelperVector instruments =
          new DefaultProbabilityHelperVector();
      for (int i = 0; i < periods.Count; i++)
      {
          QuoteHandle qh = new QuoteHandle(new SimpleQuote(spreads[i] / 10000.0));
          instruments.Add(new SpreadCdsHelper(qh, periods[i], 0, calendar,
              Frequency.Quarterly, BusinessDayConvention.Following,
              DateGeneration.Rule.TwentiethIMM, new Actual365Fixed(), recoveryRate,
              tsCurve));
      }

      // bootstrap hazard rates
      var hazardRateStructure = new PiecewiseFlatHazardRate(evalDate1, instruments,
          new Actual365Fixed());

      DataTable res = new DataTable();
      res.Columns.Add("Maturity", typeof(string));
      res.Columns.Add("TimesToMaturity", typeof(double));
      res.Columns.Add("Hazard Rate (%)", typeof(double));
      res.Columns.Add("Survival Probability (%)", typeof(double));
      res.Columns.Add("Default Probability (%)", typeof(double));
      DayCounter dc = new Actual365Fixed();
      Date dd = evalDate1;
      Date lastDate = maturities[maturities.Count - 1];
      while (dd < lastDate)
      {
          var years = dc.yearFraction(evalDate1, dd);
          var hazard = Math.Round(100.0 * hazardRateStructure.hazardRate(dd), 5);
          var survive = Math.Round(100.0 * azardRateStructure.survivalProbability(dd),
              5);
          var def = Math.Round(100.0 * hazardRateStructure.defaultProbability(dd), 5);
          res.Rows.Add(dd.To<DateTime>().ToShortDateString(), Math.Round(years, 4),
              hazard, survive, def);
          dd = dd.Add(new Period(1, TimeUnit.Days));
      }
      return res;
}
```

```
private static T To<T>(this string text)
{
    var ss = text.Split('_');
    var type = typeof(T);
    var ts = type.ToString().ToLower();
    if (ts == "system.double[]")
    {
        double[] res = new double[ss.Length];
        for (int i = 0; i < ss.Length; i++)
            res[i] = ss[i].To<double>();
        return (T)Convert.ChangeType(res, type);
    } else if (ts.Contains("periodvector"))
    {
        PeriodVector periods = new PeriodVector();
        foreach (string s in ss)
        {
            int num = s.Remove(s.Length - 1, 1).To<int>();
            string sub = s.Substring(s.Length - 1, 1).ToUpper();
            if (sub == "M")
                periods.Add(new Period(num, TimeUnit.Months));
            else if (sub == "Y")
                periods.Add(new Period(num, TimeUnit.Years));
        }
        return (T)Convert.ChangeType(periods, type);
    }
    var underlyingType = Nullable.GetUnderlyingType(type) ?? type;
    return (T)Convert.ChangeType(text, underlyingType);
}
```

The *CdsHazardRate* method uses a dummy flat term structure for interest rates and takes an array of spread data and recovery rate from market as inputs. We then create a *SpreadCdsHelper* object for the spread at each tenor. Finally, we bootstrap the hazard rates using the *PiecewiseFlatHazardRate* class and interpolate the hazard rate and survival probability with daily continuous curves. The private extension *To* method converts a string into a *PeriodVector* object or into a double array object, which allows you to input tenors and spreads using a simple string with a delimiter of _ (an underscore character). The reason to use the underscore rather than a comma is that the comma character is reserved for URL.

We can convert the *CdsHazardRate* method into a web service by adding a new method named *GetCdsHazardRate* method to the *FixedIncomeValuesController* class with the following code:

```
[Route("~/api/cdsHazardRate")]
[HttpGet]
public JsonResult GetCdsHazardRate()
{
    var evalDate = new DateTime(2015, 3, 20);
    var spreads = "34.93_53.60_72.02_106.39_129.39_139.46";
    var tenors = "1Y_2Y_3Y_5Y_7Y_10Y";
    var recoveryRate = 0.4;
    var res = FixedIncomeHelper.CdsHazardRate(evalDate, recoveryRate, spreads,
        tenors);
    return Json(new { Name = "Convertible Bond Price", Result = res });
}
```

Here, we first define various input parameters and set their default values. Please note that the elements in spreads must align with the elements in tenors, i.e., the first element in spreads corresponds to the first element in tenors, the second in spreads to the second in tenors, and so on.

Now, add a TypeScript method named *getCdsHazardRate* to the *ch10.service.ts* file in the *ClientApp /src/app/models* folder with the following code:

```
getCdsHazardRate() {
  return this.http.get<any>(this.url + 'api/cdshazardrate');
}
```

Here, I will use an example to illustrate how to display the CDS hazard rate results in an Angular application. First, we will create a line chart component that is used to plot the hazard rate and survival probability. Run the following statement in a command prompt window:

```
ng g c chapter10/ch10-line-chart3 --module=app.module
```

This generates a new component called *ch10-line-chart3* in the *ClientApp/src/app/Chapter10* folder. Open the component class and replace its content with the following code:

```
// ch10-line-chart3.component.ts file:
import { Component, OnInit, Input, OnChanges  } from '@angular/core';

@Component({
  selector: 'app-ch10-line-chart3',
  templateUrl: './ch10-line-chart3.component.html',
  styleUrls: ['./ch10-line-chart3.component.css']
})
export class Ch10LineChart3Component implements OnInit, OnChanges {
  @Input() data: any;
  hazardOptions: any;
  survivalOptions: any;
  constructor() { }

  ngOnInit() {
    this.hazardOptions = this.getOptions(this.data, 'hazard');
    this.survivalOptions = this.getOptions(this.data, 'survival');
  }

  ngOnChanges() {
    this.hazardOptions = this.getOptions(this.data, 'hazard');
    this.survivalOptions = this.getOptions(this.data, 'survival');
  }

  getOptions(data: any, chartType: string) {
    let title = 'Hazard Rate';
    let ylabel = 'Hazard Rate (%)';
    let data1 = [];
    if (chartType == 'hazard') {
      data.forEach(function (d) {
        data1.push([d['timesToMaturity'], d['hazard Rate (%)']]);
      });
    } else if (chartType == 'survival') {
      title = 'Survival Probability';
      ylabel = 'Survival Probability (%)';
      data.forEach(function (d) {
```

```
      data1.push([d['timesToMaturity'], d['survival Probability (%)']]);
    });
  }

  return {
    title: {
      text: title,
      left: 'center'
    },
    grid: {
      top: 35,
      left: 55,
      right: 10
    },
    xAxis: {
      type: 'value',
      name: 'Maturity (Years)',
      nameLocation: 'center',
      nameGap: '30',
      axisLine: { onZero: false }
    },
    yAxis: {
      type: 'value',
      scale: true,
      name: ylabel,
      nameLocation: 'center',
      nameGap: '35'
    },
    series: [{
      name: 'Discount Rate',
      type: 'line',
      data: data1,
      showSymbol: false
    }]
  };
  }
}
```

This component takes the *data* property as input and then creates two line charts to display the CDS hazard rate and survival probability.

We also need to update the component's template and styling files:

```
// ch10-line-chart3.component.html file:
<div class="cardList">
  <mat-card class="card-border">
    <div echarts [options]="hazardOptions" style="height:100%"></div>
  </mat-card>
  <mat-card class="card-border">
    <div echarts [options]="survivalOptions" style="height:100%"></div>
  </mat-card>
</div>

// ch10-line-chart3.component.css file:
.cardList {
  display: flex;
```

```
  flex-direction: row;
  flex-wrap: wrap;
  justify-content: flex-start;
}

.card-border {
  width: 420px;
  height: 360px;
}
```

Now, run the following statement in a command prompt window:

ng g c chapter10/ch10-cds-hazard --module=app.module

This generates a new component called *ch10-cds-hazard* in the *ClientApp/src/app/Chapter10* folder. Open the component class and replace its content with the following code:

```
// ch10-cds-hazard.component.ts file:
import { Component, OnInit } from '@angular/core';
import { Ch10Service } from '../../models/ch10.service';
import { ModelHelper } from '../../models/model.helper';

@Component({
  selector: 'app-ch10-cds-hazard',
  templateUrl: './ch10-cds-hazard.component.html',
  styleUrls: ['./ch10-cds-hazard.component.css']
})
export class Ch10CdsHazardComponent implements OnInit {
  data: any;
  colDefs: any;
  private helper: ModelHelper;

  constructor(private service: Ch10Service) { }

  ngOnInit() {
    this.getCds();
  }

  getCds() {
    this.data = null;
    this.service.getCdsHazardRate().subscribe(result => {
      this.data = result.result;
      this.helper = new ModelHelper();
      this.colDefs = this.helper.setColDefs(result.result, 170);
    });
  }
}
```

We also need to update the component's template file with the following code:

```
// ch10-cds-hazard.component.ts file:
<h2>
  ch10-cds-hazard works!
</h2>

<ag-grid-angular *ngIf="data" style="height:300px;width:900px;"
  class="ag-theme-balham" [rowData]="data" [columnDefs]="colDefs">
```

```
</ag-grid-angular>
<br />
<app-ch10-line-chart3 *ngIf="data" [data]="data"></app-ch10-line-chart3>
```

This template includes an *ag-Grid* directive and a *ch10-line-chart3* directive that are used to display CDS hazard results.

Finally, we need to add a path for this new component to the *RouterModule* of the root module (i.e., the *app.module.ts* file):

```
{ path: 'chapter10/ch10-cds-hazard, component: Ch10CdsHazardComponent },
```

Then add the corresponding URL link to the *home* and *nav-menu* components.

Saving the project and navigating to the */chapter10/ch10-cds-hazard* page produce the default results shown in Fig.10-13.

ch10-cds-hazard works!

Maturity	TimesToMaturity	Hazard Rate (%)	Survival Probability (%)	Default Probability (%)
3/20/2015	0	0.58143	100	0
3/21/2015	0.0027	0.58143	99.99841	0.00159
3/22/2015	0.0055	0.58143	99.99681	0.00319
3/23/2015	0.0082	0.58143	99.99522	0.00478
3/24/2015	0.011	0.58143	99.99363	0.00637
3/25/2015	0.0137	0.58143	99.99204	0.00796
3/26/2015	0.0164	0.58143	99.99044	0.00956
3/27/2015	0.0192	0.58143	99.98885	0.01115
3/28/2015	0.0219	0.58143	99.98726	0.01274

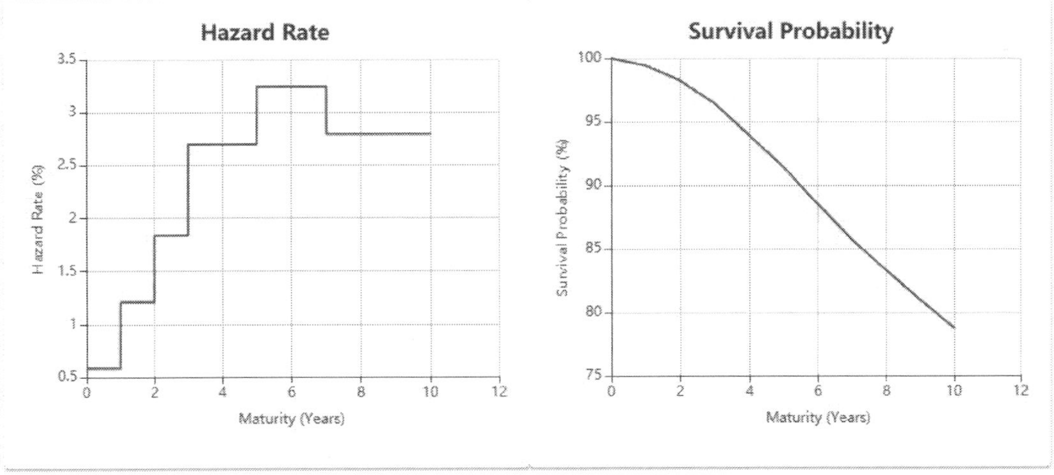

Fig.10-13. Calculated results for CDS hazard rate and survival probability.

You can see that the survival probability always decreases as time goes on, while the hazard rate is bootstrapped as a piecewise flat curve. QuantLib models hazard rates as a step function, indicating it holds them constant between changes in spreads. This means that we have constant hazard rates between every period.

Risky Annuities and Risky Durations

The risky annuity is the present value of a 1 bp risky annuity stream:

$$RiskyAnnuity = A_s \approx 1 \cdot \sum_{i=1}^{n} \Delta_i P_{si} DF_i + 1 \cdot \sum_{i=1}^{n} \frac{\Delta_i}{2} \left[P_{s(i-1)} - P_{si} \right] \cdot DF_i$$

Where A_s is the risky annuity for an annuity lasting n periods, given spread level S.

The risky duration (DV01) relates to a trade and is the change in mark-to-market (MTM) of a CDS trade for a 1bp parallel shift in spreads. The MTM for a long risk CDS trade with notional = 1 is:

$$MTM_{S\ current} = (S_{Initial} - S_{Current}) \cdot A_{s\ current}$$

$$MTM_{1bp\ shift} = (S_{Initial} - S_{Current+1bp}) \cdot A_{s\ current+1bp}$$

$$DV01 = MTM_{1bp\ shift} - MTM_{S\ current}$$

Using $S_{Current+1bp} \cdot A_{S\ current+1bp} = S_{Current} \cdot A_{S\ current+1bp} + 1bp \cdot A_{S\ current+1bp}$, we can show that:

$$DV01 = -A_{S\ current+1bp} + (S_{Initial} - S_{Current}) \cdot (A_{S\ current+1bp} - A_{S\ current})$$

For a par trade $S_{Initial} = S_{Current}$, and since the risky annuities do not change by a large amount for a 1bp change in spread, we get:

$$DV01 = -A_{S\ current+1bp} \approx -A_{S\ current}$$

This means that the risky duration is equal to the risky annuity. This approximation can become inaccurate if we are looking at a trade that is far off-market, where $S_{Initial} - S_{Current}$ becomes significant, causing the risky duration to move away from the risky annuity.

CDS Pricing Engine

As shown in Eq. (10-14), pricing CDS involves calculating the present value of the two legs of the transaction, i.e., the premium leg or fee leg (the regular fee payments) and the contingent leg (the payment at the time of defaults). If the trade made at the fair spread, the fees associated with these two legs should be equal. However, starting on 4/8/2009, the new ISDA CDS standardization initiatives, i.e. the 100/500 standard fixed coupon CDS contracts, take effect. The 100/500 standard is a change in the practice of trading single name CDS from a traded coupon and T+1 accrual period to a bond like fixed coupon (fixed to 100 or 500 bps) with standardized bond like accrual periods, paid upfront, on the settlement of the trade. Here are the key features of the new standard:

- Fixed coupons of 100 bps and 500 bps.

- Buyer pays the full first coupon period (e.g. accrual) for the previous quarterly coupon period T+1 fall into.

- Maturity dates always match a quarterly roll date.

We can simply regard the new ISDA standard CDS model as a quoting convention, and it provides a way to map a spread quote into an upfront cash amount, which is the actual "price" or present value of the CDS.

QuantLib's CDS pricing engine enables you to price both the conventional and the new 100/500 fixed coupon CDS contracts. Instead of using the flat rate term structure for the discount curve shown in the previous example for the default probability and hazard rate, here we will use a full ISDA rate curve for building the discount term structure. To achieve this, we add the following helper method called *IsdaZeroCurve* to the *FixedIncomeHelper* class:

```csharp
private static YieldTermStructure IsdaZeroCurve(DateTime evalDate, string ccy)
{
    DateTime rateDate = GetPreviousWorkday(evalDate);
    Calendar calendar = new TARGET();
    var isdaRates = IsdaHelper.GetIsdaRates(ccy, rateDate.ToString("yyyyMMdd"));
    Date date = rateDate.To<Date>();
    RateHelperVector rateHelpers = new RateHelperVector();
    PeriodVector depositMaturities = new PeriodVector();
    DoubleVector depositRates = new DoubleVector();
    PeriodVector swapMaturities = new PeriodVector();
    DoubleVector swapRates = new DoubleVector();
    DayCounter depositDayCounter = new Actual360();
    DayCounter swapDayCounter = new Thirty360(Thirty360.Convention.USA);
    int fixedDays = 0;

    foreach (var item in isdaRates)
    {
        fixedDays = GetNumberCalendarDays(item.SnapTime.Date,
            Convert.ToDateTime(item.SpotDate).Date);
        int num = 0;
        if (string.IsNullOrEmpty(item.FixedDayCountConvention))
        {
            if (item.Tenor.Contains("M"))
            {
                num = item.Tenor.Split('M')[0].To<int>();
                depositMaturities.Add(new Period(num, TimeUnit.Months));
                depositRates.Add(item.Rate.To<double>());
            }
            else if (item.Tenor.Contains("Y"))
            {
                num = item.Tenor.Split('Y')[0].To<int>();
                depositMaturities.Add(new Period(num, TimeUnit.Years));
                depositRates.Add(item.Rate.To<double>());
            }
        }
        else
        {
            num = item.Tenor.Split('Y')[0].To<int>();
            swapMaturities.Add(new Period(num, TimeUnit.Years));
            swapRates.Add(item.Rate.To<double>());
        }
    }

    for (int i = 0; i < depositRates.Count; i++)
        rateHelpers.Add(new DepositRateHelper(depositRates[i], depositMaturities[i],
```

```
                    0, calendar, BusinessDayConvention.Unadjusted, false,
                    depositDayCounter));
    Frequency swFixedLegFrequency = Frequency.Semiannual;
    BusinessDayConvention swFixedLegConvention = BusinessDayConvention.Unadjusted;
    IborIndex swFloatingLegIndex = new USDLibor(new Period(3, TimeUnit.Months));
    for (int i = 0; i < swapRates.Count; i++)
    {
        QuoteHandle qh = new QuoteHandle(new SimpleQuote(swapRates[i]));
        rateHelpers.Add(new SwapRateHelper(qh, swapMaturities[i], calendar,
            swFixedLegFrequency, swFixedLegConvention, swapDayCounter,
            swFloatingLegIndex));
    }
    return new PiecewiseLogCubicDiscount(date, rateHelpers, new Actual365Fixed());
}
```

Here, we first set *rateDate* to previous workday of the original *evalDate*, which is because the ISDA rates on *evalDate* are not available yet, we have to use the rates at the previous workday, i.e., *rateDate*. We then load the ISDA rate curve directly from Markit's website using the *GetIsdaRates* method in *IsdaHelper* class, implemented in Chapter 4. Here, we can specify *ccy* (i.e. "USD", "EUR", "JPY", etc.) and rate date. Next, we separate the money market (deposit) rates and swap rates. Finally, we use the *PiecewiseLogCubicDiscount* object to build the yield term structure for the discount curve.

Now, we will add another helper method named *CdsPV* to the *FixedIncomeHelper* class. This method enables you to calculate the present value and fair (or par) spread for a CDS contract. Here is the code for this method:

```
public static DataTable CdsPV(string protectionSide1, string ccy, string evalDate1,
    string effectiveDate1, string maturity1, double recoveryRate, string spreadStr,
    string tenors, double notional, string couponFrequency1, double coupon,
    double flatRate = -1.0)
{
    Date evalDate = DateTime.Parse(evalDate1).To<Date>();
    Date effectiveDate = DateTime.Parse(effectiveDate1).To<Date>();
    Date maturity = DateTime.Parse(maturity1).To<Date>();
    var periods = tenors.To<PeriodVector>();
    var spreads = spreadStr.To<double[]>();
    couponFrequency1 = char.ToUpper(couponFrequency1[0]) +
        couponFrequency1.Substring(1);
    Enum.TryParse(couponFrequency1, out Frequency couponFrequency);
    protectionSide1 = char.ToUpper(protectionSide1[0]) +
        protectionSide1.Substring(1);
    Enum.TryParse(protectionSide1, out Protection.Side protectionSide);
    Calendar calendar = new TARGET();
    evalDate = calendar.adjust(evalDate);
    Settings.instance().setEvaluationDate(evalDate);
    YieldTermStructureHandle tsCurve;
    if (flatRate <= 0)
        tsCurve = new
            YieldTermStructureHandle(IsdaZeroCurve(evalDate.To<DateTime>(), ccy));
    else
        tsCurve = new YieldTermStructureHandle(new FlatForward(evalDate,
            new QuoteHandle(new SimpleQuote(flatRate)), new Actual365Fixed()));

    DefaultProbabilityHelperVector instruments =
        new DefaultProbabilityHelperVector();
```

```csharp
    for (int i = 0; i < periods.Count; i++)
    {
        QuoteHandle qh = new QuoteHandle(new SimpleQuote(spreads[i] / 10000.0));
        instruments.Add(new SpreadCdsHelper(qh, periods[i], 1, calendar,
            couponFrequency, BusinessDayConvention.Following,
            DateGeneration.Rule.TwentiethIMM, new Actual365Fixed(),
            recoveryRate, tsCurve));
    }

    // bootstrap hazard rates
    var hazardRateStructure = new PiecewiseFlatHazardRate(evalDate, instruments,
        new Actual365Fixed());
    DefaultProbabilityTermStructureHandle probability = new
        DefaultProbabilityTermStructureHandle(hazardRateStructure);

    DataTable res = new DataTable();
    res.Columns.Add("Name", typeof(string));
    res.Columns.Add("Value", typeof(string));
    res.Rows.Add("Maturity", maturity.To<DateTime>().ToShortDateString());
    res.Rows.Add("Coupon", coupon);

    try
    {
        Schedule cdsSchedule = new Schedule(effectiveDate, maturity,
            new Period(couponFrequency), calendar, BusinessDayConvention.Following,
            BusinessDayConvention.Following, DateGeneration.Rule.TwentiethIMM,
            false);
        CreditDefaultSwap cds = new CreditDefaultSwap(protectionSide, notional,
            coupon / 10000.0, cdsSchedule, BusinessDayConvention.ModifiedFollowing,
            new ActualActual(), false);
        PricingEngine engine = new MidPointCdsEngine(probability, recoveryRate,
            tsCurve);
        cds.setPricingEngine(engine);
        var surv = 100.0 * hazardRateStructure.survivalProbability(maturity);
        var hazard = 100.0 * hazardRateStructure.hazardRate(maturity);
        var def = 100.0 * hazardRateStructure.defaultProbability(maturity);
        var npv = cds.NPV();
        var fairSpread = 10000.0 * cds.fairSpread();
        res.Rows.Add("SurvivalProb", surv);
        res.Rows.Add("HazardRate", hazard);
        res.Rows.Add("DefaultProb", def);
        res.Rows.Add("FairSpread", fairSpread);
        res.Rows.Add("PresentValue", npv);
    }
    catch { }
    return res;
}
```

This method takes various input parameters including protection side, evaluation data, effective date, maturity, recovery rate, spreads, notional, and coupon. The optional parameter *flatRate* allows you to specify a flat rate for the discount term structure if the *flatRate* parameter is a positive number; while for *flatRate* <= 0, the ISDA rate curve will be used for the discount term structure. The effective date is the date from which the CDS trade provided the buyer of protection with coverage. For the new 100/500 standard trades, this will typically be the most recently passed IMM date. The input spread array (or single spread point) must be paired and aligned with the tenor array. This spread curve at different tenors will be used to calculate the hazard rate and default probability. Note that the spread data are different from the coupon. For conventional CDS contracts, coupon = fair (or par) spread, while for the 100/500 standard CDS contracts, coupon = 100 or 500, depending on the CDS name types. If the CDS name belongs to the IG (investment grade) type, then coupon = 100, otherwise, if the name belongs to the HY (high yield) type, then coupon = 500.

Inside the *CdsPV* method, we use the spread array data to bootstrap the hazard rate and construct the default probability term structure, which will be used by the CDS pricing engine. Next, we create the CDS schedule and the *CreditDefaultSwap* instance. Finally, we set the CDS pricing engine using the *MidPointCdsEngine* class. The two important results from the pricing engine are the fair (or par) spread and the present value of the CDS contract. The former is independent of the coupon while the latter does depend on the coupon.

We can now convert this method into a web service by adding a new method called *GetCdsPV* to the *FixedIncomeValuesController* class with the following code:

```
[Route("~/api/cdsPv/{protectionSide}/{ccy}/{evalDate}/{effectiveDate}/{maturity}/
    {recoveryRate}/{spreads}/{tenors}/{notional}/{couponFrequency}/{coupon}/
    {flatRate}")]
[HttpGet]
public JsonResult GetCdsPV(string protectionSide, string ccy, string evalDate,
    string effectiveDate, string maturity, double recoveryRate, string spreads,
    string tenors, double notional, string couponFrequency, double coupon,
    double flatRate)
{
    var res = FixedIncomeHelper.CdsPV(protectionSide, ccy, evalDate, effectiveDate,
        maturity, recoveryRate, spreads, tenors, notional, couponFrequency, coupon,
        flatRate);
    return Json(new { Name = "CDS PV", Result = res });
}
```

Add a TypeScript method called *GetCdsPv* to the *ch10.service.ts* file with the following code:

```
getCdsPv(protectionSide: string, ccy: string, evalDate: string, effectiveDate:
    string, maturity: string, recoveryRate: number, spreads: string, tenors: string,
    notional: number, couponFrequency: string, coupon: number, flatRate: number) {
    let url1 = this.url + 'api/cdspv/' + protectionSide + '/' + ccy + '/' + evalDate +
        '/' + effectiveDate + '/' + maturity + '/' + recoveryRate + '/' + spreads +
        '/' + tenors + '/' + notional + '/' + couponFrequency + '/' + coupon +
        '/' + flatRate;
    return this.http.get<any>(url1);
}
```

Now, I will use an example to show you how to access CDS pricing engine using this web service. Run the following statement in a command prompt window:

ng g c chapter10/ch10-cds-pv --module=app.module

This generates a new component called *ch10-cds-pv* in the *ClientApp/src/app/Chapter10* folder. Open the component class and replace its content with the following code:

```
// ch10-cds-pv.component.ts file:
import { Component, OnInit } from '@angular/core';
import { Ch10Service } from '../../models/ch10.service';
import { ModelHelper } from '../../models/model.helper';

@Component({
```

```
    selector: 'app-ch10-cds-pv',
    templateUrl: './ch10-cds-pv.component.html',
    styleUrls: ['./ch10-cds-pv.component.css']
})
export class Ch10CdsPvComponent implements OnInit {
  cdsResult: any;
  colDefs: any;
  private helper: ModelHelper;

  inputCols: any = [
    { headerName: "Parameter", field: "param", width: 150 },
    { headerName: "Value", field: "value", width: 150, editable: true },
  ];
  inputRows: any = [
    { param: 'Protection Size', value: 'buyer' },
    { param: 'CCY', value: 'USD' },
    { param: 'Eval Date', value: '2009-06-15' },
    { param: 'Effective Date', value: '2009-03-20' },
    { param: 'Maturity', value: '2014-06-20' },
    { param: 'Recovery Rate', value: 0.4 },
    { param: 'Spreads', value: '210' },
    { param: 'Tenors', value: '5Y' },
    { param: 'Notional', value: 10000 },
    { param: 'Coupon Frequency', value: 'quarterly' },
    { param: 'Coupon (in bps)', value: 100 },
    { param: 'Flat Rate', value: -1.0  },
  ];
  constructor(private service: Ch10Service) { }

  ngOnInit() {
    this.getCds(this.inputRows);
  }

  getCds(rows: any) {
    this.cdsResult = null;
    this.service.getCdsPv(rows[0].value, rows[1].value, rows[2].value,
      rows[3].value, rows[4].value, rows[5].value, rows[6].value,
      rows[7].value, rows[8].value, rows[9].value, rows[10].value,
      rows[11].value).subscribe(result => {
        this.cdsResult = result.result;
        this.helper = new ModelHelper();
        this.colDefs = this.helper.setColDefs(result.result, 170);
      });
  }
}
```

Here, we use an *ag-Grid* component to display the input parameters, which is much cleaner than using multiple input fields. Note that we enable editing in the *Value* column of the input *ag-Grid* by setting the *editable* property to true inside the *inputCols* property.

Next, we need to update the component's template and styling files with the following code:

```
// ch10-cds-pv.component.html file:
<h2>
  ch10-cds-pv works!
</h2>
```

```
<button mat-raised-button color="primary" (click)="getCds(inputRows)">Get CDS
PV</button>
<div class="cardList">
  <mat-card class="card-border">
    <p>Input Parameters</p>
    <ag-grid-angular *ngIf="cdsResult" style="height:90%;"
      class="ag-theme-balham" [rowData]="inputRows" [columnDefs]="inputCols">
    </ag-grid-angular>
  </mat-card>
  <mat-card class="card-border">
    <p>Results</p>
    <ag-grid-angular *ngIf="cdsResult" style="height:90%;" class="ag-theme-balham"
      [rowData]="cdsResult" [columnDefs]="colDefs">
    </ag-grid-angular>
  </mat-card>
</div>

// ch10-cds-pv.component.css file:
.cardList {
  display: flex;
  flex-direction: row;
  flex-wrap: wrap;
  justify-content: flex-start;
}
.card-border {
  margin: 10px;
  margin-left: 0;
  margin-bottom: 0;
  width: 350px;
  height: 450px;
}
```

Finally, we need to add a path for this new component to the *RouterModule* of the root module (i.e., the *app.module.ts* file):

```
{ path: 'chapter10/ch10-cds-pv, component: Ch10CdsPvComponent },
```

Then add the corresponding URL link to the *home* and *nav-menu* components.

Saving the project and navigating to the */chapter10/ch10-cds-hazard* page produce the default results shown in Fig.10-14.

You can see from Fig.10-14 that the buyer needs to pay the present value of $453.39 (the upfront cash value) for the CDS contract with a notional of $10000 and a fixed coupon of 100 bps. This contract is under the new ISDA100/500 standard.

However, the conventional CDS contract with coupon = the fair spread should have no upfront fee, i.e. the present value should be zero. You can double check the results by enter the fair spread value of 199.943457 in the coupon field and recalculate the CDS present value, as shown in Fig.10-15.

You can see the present value is basically zero, i.e. the buyer does not need to pay any upfront for a conventional CDS contract. Please note that all of the CDS contracts for North American Corporates must use the new 100/500 standard agreement after 4/8/2009.

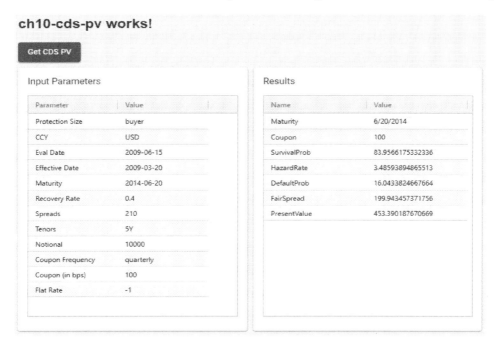

Fig.10-14. Calculated present value and fair spreads for a CDS contract.

Fig.10-15. Calculated present value for a CDS contract with coupon = the fair spread.

For CDS buyers or sellers, the present value of a CDS contract is all what they are care about. However, as a quant analyst or quant developer, you want to know more about the CDS contracts, such as how to calculate the accrual amount and risky annuity (or DV01). You also want to know the dirty price and clean price for a notional of $100, just like a bond with a face value of $100. This can be achieved easily using the following helper method named *CdsPrice* in the FixedIncomeHelper class:

```
public static DataTable CdsPrice(string protectionSide, string ccy, string evalDate,
    string effectiveDate, string maturity, double recoveryRate, string spreads,
    string tenors, string couponFrequency, double coupon, double flatRate = -1)
{
    double notional = 100.0;
    int numDays = GetNumberCalendarDays(effectiveDate.To<DateTime>(),
        evalDate.To<DateTime>()) + 1;
    double accrual = coupon * numDays / 360.0 / 100.0;
    DataTable dtCds = CdsPV(protectionSide, ccy, evalDate, effectiveDate, maturity,
        recoveryRate, spreads, tenors, notional, couponFrequency, coupon, flatRate);
    double upfront = 0;
    foreach (DataRow r in dtCds.Rows)
    {
        if (r["Name"].ToString() == "PresentValue")
            upfront = r["Value"].To<double>();
    }
    double cleanPrice = 100;
    double dirtyPrice = 100;
    if (protectionSide.ToLower().Contains("buyer"))
    {
        accrual = -accrual;
        dirtyPrice = 100 - upfront;
        cleanPrice = dirtyPrice + accrual;
    }
    else if (protectionSide.ToLower().Contains("seller"))
    {
        dirtyPrice = 100 + upfront;
        cleanPrice = dirtyPrice - accrual;
    }
    double coupon1 = 0;
    double parSpread = 0;
    foreach (DataRow r in dtCds.Rows)
    {
        if (r["Name"].ToString() == "FairSpread")
        {
            parSpread = r["Value"].To<double>();
            coupon1 = parSpread + 1.0;
        }
    }
    DataTable dt = CdsPV(protectionSide, ccy, evalDate, effectiveDate, maturity,
        recoveryRate, spreads, tenors, notional, couponFrequency, coupon1,
        flatRate);
    double dv01 = 0;
    foreach (DataRow r in dt.Rows)
    {
        if (r["Name"].ToString() == "PresentValue")
            dv01 = r["Value"].To<double>();
    }
    DataTable res = new DataTable();
```

```
res.Columns.Add("Name", typeof(string));
res.Columns.Add("Value", typeof(string));
res.Rows.Add("Accrual", accrual);
res.Rows.Add("Upfront", upfront);
res.Rows.Add("CleanPrice", cleanPrice);
res.Rows.Add("DirtyPrice", dirtyPrice);
res.Rows.Add("RiskyAnnuity", dv01);
return res;
}
```

Here, we first calculate accrual between the effective date and the evaluation date plus one business day (T+1 rule). For buyer, the dirty price for CDS with a notional of $100 should be $100 − $ upfront, while the clean price should be equal to the dirty price with the accrual removal. Similar derivation applies to the seller side. Next, we want to calculate the risky annuity (or DV01) by setting the coupon equal to *parSpread* + 1bp, and the corresponding present price will be the risky annuity (see the definition of the risky annuity in the preceding section). Thus, this helper method enables you to extract several important quantities, which are widely used in CDS trading.

We can now convert this method into a web service by adding a new method called *GetCdsPrice* to the *FixedIncomeValuesController* class with the following code:

```
[Route("~/api/cdsPrice/{protectionSide}/{ccy}/{evalDate}/{effectiveDate}/{maturity}
    /{recoveryRate}/{spreads}/{tenors}/{couponFrequency}/{coupon}/{flatRate}")]
[HttpGet]
public JsonResult GetCdsPrice(string protectionSide, string ccy, string evalDate,
    string effectiveDate, string maturity, double recoveryRate, string spreads,
    string tenors, string couponFrequency, double coupon, double flatRate)
{
    var res = FixedIncomeHelper.CdsPrice(protectionSide, ccy, evalDate,
        effectiveDate, maturity, recoveryRate, spreads, tenors, couponFrequency,
        coupon, flatRate);
    return Json(new { Name = "CDS Price", Result = res });
}
```

Add a TypeScript method called *GetCdsPrice* to the *ch10.service.ts* file with the following code:

```
getCdsPrice(protectionSide: string, ccy: string, evalDate: string, effectiveDate:
    string, maturity: string, recoveryRate: number, spreads: string, tenors: string,
    couponFrequency: string, coupon: number, flatRate: number) {
    let url1 = this.url + 'api/cdsprice/' + protectionSide + '/' + ccy +
        '/' + evalDate + '/' + effectiveDate + '/' + maturity + '/' + recoveryRate +
        '/' + spreads + '/' + tenors + '/' + couponFrequency + '/' + coupon +
        '/' + flatRate;
    return this.http.get<any>(url1);
}
```

Now, I will use an example to show you how to access CDS pricing engine using this web service. Run the following statement in a command prompt window:

ng g c chapter10/ch10-cds-price --module=app.module

This generates a new component called *ch10-cds-price* in the *ClientApp/src/app/Chapter10* folder. Open the component class and replace its content with the following code:

```
// ch10-cds-price.component.ts file:
import { Component, OnInit } from '@angular/core';
import { Ch10Service } from '../../models/ch10.service';
```

```
import { ModelHelper } from '../../models/model.helper';

@Component({
  selector: 'app-ch10-cds-price',
  templateUrl: './ch10-cds-price.component.html',
  styleUrls: ['./ch10-cds-price.component.css']
})
export class Ch10CdsPriceComponent implements OnInit {
  cdsResult: any;
  colDefs: any;
  private helper: ModelHelper;
  inputCols: any = [
    { headerName: "Parameter", field: "param", width: 150 },
    { headerName: "Value", field: "value", width: 250, editable: true },
  ];
  inputRows: any = [
    { param: 'Protection Size', value: 'buyer' },
    { param: 'CCY', value: 'USD' },
    { param: 'Eval Date', value: '2009-06-15' },
    { param: 'Effective Date', value: '2009-03-20' },
    { param: 'Maturity', value: '2014-06-20' },
    { param: 'Recovery Rate', value: 0.4 },
    { param: 'Spreads', value: '210' },
    { param: 'Tenors', value: '5Y' },
    { param: 'Coupon Frequency', value: 'quarterly' },
    { param: 'Coupon (in bps)', value: 100 },
    { param: 'Flat Rate', value: -1.0 },
  ];
  constructor(private service: Ch10Service) { }

  ngOnInit() {
    this.getCds(this.inputRows);
  }

  getCds(rows: any) {
    this.cdsResult = null;
    this.service.getCdsPrice(rows[0].value, rows[1].value, rows[2].value,
      rows[3].value, rows[4].value, rows[5].value, rows[6].value,
      rows[7].value, rows[8].value, rows[9].value, rows[10].value)
      .subscribe(result => {
        this.cdsResult = result.result;
        this.helper = new ModelHelper();
        this.colDefs = this.helper.setColDefs(result.result, 170);
      });
  }
}
```

This component is similar to that used in the previous example.

We also need to update the component's template and styling files with the following code:

```
// ch10-cds-price.component.html file:
<h2>
  ch10-cds-price works!
</h2>
```

```
<button mat-raised-button color="primary" (click)="getCds(inputRows)">Get CDS
Price</button>
<div class="cardList">
  <mat-card class="card-border">
    <p>Input Parameters</p>
    <ag-grid-angular *ngIf="cdsResult" style="height:90%;" class="ag-theme-balham"
      [rowData]="inputRows" [columnDefs]="inputCols">
    </ag-grid-angular>
  </mat-card>
  <mat-card class="card-border">
    <p>Results</p>
    <ag-grid-angular *ngIf="cdsResult" style="height:90%;" class="ag-theme-balham"
    [rowData]="cdsResult" [columnDefs]="colDefs">
    </ag-grid-angular>
  </mat-card>
</div>

// ch10-cds-price.component.css file:
.cardList {
  display: flex;
  flex-direction: row;
  flex-wrap: wrap;
  justify-content: flex-start;
}
.card-border {
  margin:5px;
  width: 420px;
  height: 400px;
}
```

Finally, we need to add a path for this new component to the *RouterModule* of the root module (i.e., the *app.module.ts* file):

{ path: 'chapter10/ch10-cds-price, component: Ch10CdsPriceComponent },

Then add the corresponding URL link to the *home* and *nav-menu* components.

Saving the project and navigating to the */chapter10/ch10-cds-price* page produce the default results shown in Fig.10-16.

You can see that for this CDS contract, the clean price is 95.22, which is less than 100. This is because its fair spread (199.94) is well above the coupon (100) level. If the fair spread is less than the coupon, we should expect the clean price would be above 100. For example, if we change the spread from 210 to 90, we will obtain the results shown in Fig.10-17, confirming our expectation: clean price > 100.

In the preceding discussion, we always use a single spread data point as input. In practice, the market quoted CDS data are often a spread curve. Our helper methods implemented above allow you to take the spread curve with corresponding tenor array as input parameters. In this case, the program will bootstrap the hazard rates using the spread curve to calculate the default probability. The CDS pricing engine will then use this default probability to calculate the present value and the other quantities for a CDS contract.

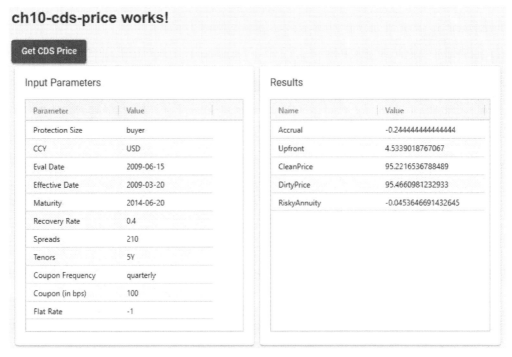

Fig.10-16. Calculated results for a CDS contract with a notional of $100.

Figure 10-17. Calculation for a CDS contract with a 5Y spread of 90 bps.

For example, specifying the input parameters as shown in the left table of Fig.10-18, where the spread curve and a tenor array are used with the underscore as delimiter, and clicking the *Get CDS Price* button, you will get the results shown in the right table of Fig.10-18.

ch10-cds-price works!

Get CDS Price

Input Parameters

Parameter	Value
Protection Size	buyer
CCY	USD
Eval Date	2015-05-18
Effective Date	2015-03-20
Maturity	2018-06-20
Recovery Rate	0.4
Spreads	34.93_53.60_72.02_106.39_129.39_139.46
Tenors	1Y_2Y_3Y_5Y_7Y_10Y
Coupon Frequency	quarterly
Coupon (in bps)	100
Flat Rate	-1

Results

Name	Value
Accrual	-0.166666666666667
Upfront	-0.996260082155231
CleanPrice	100.829593415489
DirtyPrice	100.996260082155
RiskyAnnuity	-0.0315959393171035

Fig.10-18. Calculation for a CDS with a spread curve.

Here, we simply set the maturity about 3 years from the evaluation date, i.e. we want to enter a 3Y CDS contract. The spread data should be the market data on the previous workday of the evaluation date.

In this chapter, we have discussed the basic procedure for pricing CDS contracts using the QuantLib CDS pricing engine. In order to apply this pricing engine in your real-word CDS trading, there is still a lot of calibration work need to be done. In practice, the CDS pricing requires very high accuracy (up to 7 to 9 decimals) because CDS contracts usually involve a very large notional, meaning that a small discrepancy in CDS price may leads to a big difference in P&L (profit and loss). In this regard, it is better to use the ISDA standard CDS model directly. However, regardless of whatever pricing engine you are going to use, I believe that the concept and procedure for CDS pricing presented here will be useful in your applications.

In this chapter, we discussed how to price some of fixed-income instruments. The basic steps are clear: specifying cash flows; build various term structures for discount curves, yield curves, credit risk, and volatility; and select proper pricing engines. Using this procedure, you should be able to price other types of fixed-income instruments, such as swaps and swaptions, without much trouble.

Chapter 11
Trading Strategies and Backtesting

Quantitative trading is usually considered as the rocket science in finance because it is an extremely sophisticated area of quantitative finance. It can take a significant amount of time to gain the necessary knowledge to develop your own trading strategies. It also requires strong background in math, physical modeling, statistics, and extensive programming expertise. A successful quantitative trading system consists of several major components, including trading strategy development, backtesting, automatic algorithm execution, and risk management.

The key step for quantitative trading is to develop and identify the trading strategies. Some strategies do require advanced background knowledge on math and finance, while most trading ideas can easily be found through various public resources, such as blogs, books, magazines, and online communities. After identifying your trading strategies, you need to backtest them to see how they would have performed in the past. Even if you find a strategy with all the historical performance data available, you still need to backtest it yourself, which ensures that you understand the strategy completely and can reproduce its results.

In this chapter, I will show you how to develop several trading strategies using the simple quantitative analysis techniques, including the moving average and linear regression, as well as the commonly used technical indicators. I will also present a long-short based backtesting framework, which allows you to examine the historical performance of your trading strategies.

Trading Strategy Identification

All quantitative trading processes begin with an initial period of research. Reference books, financial courses, blogs, and online trader forums can save your valuable time, but quantitative trading can also be a "do it yourself" career. Contrary to common belief, building strategies can be easy and quick. In fact, you can find good strategies through various public sources. You may question why traders are keen to publicize their trading strategies if the strategies are profitable. The reason lies in the fact that the fundamentals of the published strategies are quite well known to professional traders, so they can discuss the principles of the strategies publicly. However, they will not often discuss the exact parameters and optimization methods that they have carried out. These optimizations are the key to turning a relatively mediocre strategy into a highly profitable one. In fact, one of the best ways to build your own unique strategies is to find similar strategies from public sources and then perform your own optimization procedure.

Many of the trading strategies can broadly divided into the mean-reversion and trend-following categories. A mean-reverting strategy attempts to exploit the fact that a stock price eventually returns to its long-term average price after a temporary deviation. The strategy takes advantage of such price movement, that is, buying low and selling high. On the other hand, trend-following strategies are devised on the promise that strong moves in the market in either direction will be most likely followed by higher highs and lower lows. Trend-following strategies attempt to capitalize on big market movements by buying stocks that are showing an upward trend and selling stocks that are on a downward trend.

To illustrate the difference between these two strategies, take for example the chart below:

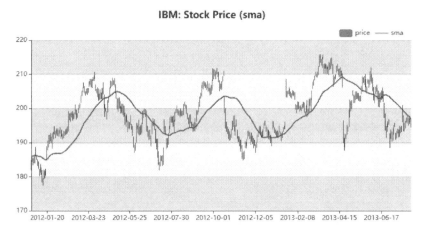

Fig.11-1. IBM stock price from 1/3/2012 to 8/1/2013.

You can see from Fig.11-1 that IBM is very mean-reversion during the period of 1/3/2012 to 8/1/2013. It was moving in a range of 180 to 215. Additionally, its 40-day moving average serves as a guide on its mean or average. In this case, you can enter a short position when the price of the stock moves above MA; and take on a long position when the price moves below MA. A mean reversion strategy like this will prove to be very profitable if the stock has been oscillating in this price range.

Fig.11-2 shows GS stock price and 300-day MA in a period of 3 years from 7/31/2012 to 7/31/2015.

Fig.11-2. GS stock price from 7/31/2012 to 7/31/2015.

GS is a good candidate for trend-following strategies for the period of 7/31/2012 to 7/31/2015. A good trend-following strategy would exploit this opportunity when the stock made higher highs. For example, you can go long once the price goes above the 300-day MA and exit the position once the price is below the MA.

In this book, we do not distinguish between the momentum and the trend-following strategies. Strictly speaking, even though both momentum and trend following have many similarities, they are in fact are two different noncompeting techniques aimed at identifying chances to buy on the upswing and sell on the downswing, serving to support or reject each other.

Momentum investing relies on predictive (forward-looking) fundamental analysis, such as sales and earnings. Momentum is the acceleration in stock prices that can be due to earnings, sentiment, news, greed, or fear. Momentum traders will take a long or short position in the stock in the hope that its momentum will continue in either an upward or downward direction in the time frame they are trading.

Some traders have a different definition for momentum strategies. They believe that momentum is the observation that stock prices have performed well relative to other stock prices (peers) on average continue to outperform, and that prices that have performed relatively poorly tend to continue to underperform. Here, the word *relative* is crucial as momentum is calculated by ranking a stock's price movement against other stocks.

On the other hand, trend-following strategies take a backward-looking approach and focus on the price. Trend-following traders ignore predictions, whatever they are based on. They believe that any change in fundamentals, such as sales and earnings, will eventually reflect on the price. Comparing to the momentum strategies with relative stock prices, trend-following concentrates on the absolute price change (i.e., stock price changes against market). Momentum always takes long position relative past outperformance and short relative past underperformance, while trend following involves increasing your investment exposure during market upswings and decreasing exposure during downswings.

In this book, we will ignore the subtle difference between the momentum and trend-following strategies and will use trend following to represent the strategies of buying high and selling low.

Another important aspect of quantitative trading is the frequency of the trading strategies. Low frequency trading (LFT) generally refers to any strategy that holds positions longer than a trading day. Correspondingly, high frequency trading (HFT) generally refers to a strategy that holds positions intraday. Ultra-high frequency trading (UHFT) refers to strategies that hold positions on the order of seconds and milliseconds. In this chapter, we will only discuss the low frequency trading.

Crossover Trading Signals

In Chapters 6-8, we discussed various quantitative analysis approaches used in finance, including moving average, linear analysis, PCA, a variety of technical indicators, and advanced machine learning techniques. These analysis techniques are very powerful when you use them to study the market trends, price pattern, and correlation between different stocks. However, the ultimate goal of the quantitative analysis is to generate trading signals. Here, we will consider two types of trading signals: crossover (trend following) and z-score (mean-reversion). In this section, we first discuss the crossover trading signals.

Trading Strategy Objects

Before discussing trading signals, we define some class objects that will be used in creating trading signals and implementing a backtesting system. Add a new class called *StrategyObjects* to the *Quant/Models* folder with the following code:

```
using System;
using System.Collections.Generic;

namespace Quant.Models
{
    public class StrategyObjects
    {
        public class StrategySignal
        {
            public string Ticker { get; set; }
            public DateTime Date { get; set; }
            public double Open { get; set; }
            public double High { get; set; }
            public double Low { get; set; }
            public double Close { get; set; }
            public double Volume { get; set; }
            public List<double?> Indicators { get; set; }
            public TradeAdvice TradeAdvise { get; set; }
        }

        public enum TradeAdvice
        {
            Buy,
            Sell,
            Hold
        }

        public class PnLSummary
        {
            public double PnL { get; set; }
            public int NumberTrades { get; set; }
            public double Sharpe { get; set; }
            public double MaxDrawdown { get; set; }
            public double PnL1 { get; set; }
            public double Sharpe1 { get; set; }
            public double MaxDrawdown1 { get; set; }
        }

        public class BacktestResult
        {
            public string Date { get; set; }
            public StrategySignal Signal { get; set; }
            public DateTime? DateIn { get; set; }
            public double PriceIn { get; set; }
            public int NumTrades { get; set; }
            public double PnLPerTrade { get; set; }
            public double PnLAllTrades { get; set; }
            public double PnL { get; set; }
            public double PnLCum { get; set; }
```

```
            public double PnL1 { get; set; }
            public double PnLCum1 { get; set; }
    }

    public class PnLDrawdown
    {
        public DateTime Date { get; set; }
        public double PnL { get; set; }
        public double PnLCum { get; set; }
        public double Drawdown { get; set; }
        public double MaxDrawdown { get; set; }
        public double Drawup { get; set; }
        public double MaxDrawup { get; set; }
        public double PnL1 { get; set; }
        public double PnLCum1 { get; set; }
        public double Drawdown1 { get; set; }
        public double MaxDrawdown1 { get; set; }
        public double Drawup1 { get; set; }
        public double MaxDrawup1 { get; set; }
    }
  }
}
```

This class consists of an enum and several class objects that will be used in creating trading signals and building trading strategies in the following sections. Note that the *StrategySignal* class contains an *Indicators* property, which stores indicators that will be used to generate trading signals.

Two-MA Crossover

Crossover trading signals are simple and popular in quantitative finance. The simplest crossover signal is the crossover of two moving averages. You enter the market when the fast MA crosses the slow MA. This 2-MA crossover strategy uses two moving averages on the chart, as shown in Fig.11-3.

Fig.11-3. Long-short signals in MA crossover strategy.

The trading rules for this 2-MA crossover signals are:

- *Long Entry, Short Exit* – When the fast MA crosses above the slow MA, enter *long* at current bar if the *short* position is empty; or exit the short position at the current bar and enter long at the next bar if the short position has been filled.

- *Short Entry, Long Exit* – When the fast MA crosses below the slow MA, enter *short* at the current bar if the *long* position is empty; or exit the *long* position at the current bar and enter *short* at the next bar if the *long* position has been filled.

Here, we always check whether a *long* or *short* position has been filled or not when a trading signal is triggered. If the position was filled previously, we first flat this position at the current bar to make the fund available before we enter a new position at the next bar. Otherwise, if the position is empty, meaning that the cash fund is available, we can then enter a new position at the current bar.

Now, we will implement this 2-MA crossover trading strategy. Add a new class called *StrategySignalHelper* to the *Quant/Models* folder with the following code:

```
using System;
using System.Collections.Generic;
using static Quant.Models.StrategyObjects;

namespace Quant.Models
{
    public static class StrategySignalHelper
    {
        public static List<StrategySignal> Signal2MaCrossover(string ticker,
            string start, string end, int fastPeriod = 10, int slowPeriod = 30,
            string maType = "sma", string tradeType = "long", double tolerance = 0.0)
        {
            var result = new List<StrategySignal>();
            var candles = IndicatorHelper.GetCandleData(ticker, start, end);
            var dat = IndicatorHelper.CandleToDoubleList(candles, "close");
            var maFast = dat.MovingAverage(fastPeriod, maType);
            var maSlow = dat.MovingAverage(slowPeriod, maType);
            int i, count = candles.Count;

            TradeAdvice[] advices = new TradeAdvice[count];

            tradeType = tradeType.ToLower();
            switch (tradeType)
            {
                case "long":
                    for (i = 0; i < count; i++)
                    {
                        advices[i] = TradeAdvice.Hold;
                        if (i > slowPeriod + 1)
                        {
                            if (maFast[i - 1] > maSlow[i - 1] * (1 + tolerance))
                                advices[i] = TradeAdvice.Buy;
                        }
                    }
                    break;
                case "short":
                    for (i = 0; i < count; i++)
                    {
```

```
                    advices[i] = TradeAdvice.Hold;
                    if (i > slowPeriod + 1)
                    {
                        if (maFast[i - 1] * (1 + tolerance) < maSlow[i - 1])
                            advices[i] = TradeAdvice.Sell;
                    }
                }
                break;
            case "longshort":
                for (i = 0; i < count; i++)
                {
                    advices[i] = TradeAdvice.Hold;
                    if (i > slowPeriod + 1)
                    {
                        if (maFast[i - 1] > maSlow[i - 1] * (1 + tolerance))
                            advices[i] = TradeAdvice.Buy;
                        else if (maFast[i - 1] * (1 + tolerance) <
                            maSlow[i - 1]) advices[i] = TradeAdvice.Sell;
                    }
                }
                break;
        }

        for (i = 1; i < count; i++)
        {
            if ((advices[i - 1] == TradeAdvice.Buy &&
                advices[i] == TradeAdvice.Sell) ||
                (advices[i - 1] == TradeAdvice.Sell &&
                advices[i] == TradeAdvice.Buy))
                advices[i] = TradeAdvice.Hold;
        }

        for (i = 0; i < count; i++)
        {
            result.Add(new StrategySignal
            {
                Ticker = ticker,
                Date = candles[i].Date,
                Open = candles[i].Open,
                High = candles[i].High,
                Low = candles[i].Low,
                Close = candles[i].Close,
                Volume = candles[i].Volume,
                Indicators = new List<double?> { maFast[i], maSlow[i] },
                TradeAdvise = advices[i],
                Position = advices[i] == TradeAdvice.Buy ? 1 :
                    advices[i] == TradeAdvice.Sell ? -1 : 0
            });
        }
        return result;
    }
}
}
```

Note that we always use the previous day's moving averages to generate today's entry or exit points because today's moving averages are not available yet before today's market close. We also introduce a *tolerance* parameter when we apply the 2-MA crossover strategy, that is, we delay our entry into the market after the fast MA crosses the slow MA. So, when the fast MA crosses the slow MA we do not open our position immediately, but delay for several bars when the fast MA crosses slow MA by a certain amount that is controlled by *tolerance*. By doing this we eliminate some rapid whipsaws at the expense of entering the trade later than the original MA cross.

We can convert this 2-MA crossover strategy into a web service by adding an API controller named *StrategyValuesController* to the *Quant/Controllers* folder with the following code:

```
using Microsoft.AspNetCore.Mvc;
using Quant.Models;

namespace Quant.Controllers
{
    [Produces("application/json")]
    public class StrategyValuesController : Controller
    {
        [Route("~/api/strategySignal2MaCrossover/{ticker}/{start}/{end}/
            {fastPeriod}/{slowPeriod}/{maType}/{tradeType}/{tolerance}")]
        [HttpGet]
        public JsonResult GetStrategy2MaCrossover(string ticker, string start,
            string end, int fastPeriod, int slowPeriod, string maType,
            string tradeType, double tolerance)
        {
            var signal = StrategySignalHelper.Signal2MaCrossover(ticker, start, end,
                fastPeriod, slowPeriod, maType, tradeType, tolerance);

            return Json(new { name = ticker + ": 2-MA Crossover", indicatorNames =
                new string[]{"fastMa", "slowMa" }, Signal = signal });
        }
    }
}
```

Two-MA Crossover in Angular

Here, we will create an angular service to access the 2-MA trading signals from the C# API web service. Run the following command in a command prompt window from the *ClientApp* folder:

ng g s models/ch11

This generates an Angular service named *ch11.service.ts* in the *ClientApp/src/app/models* folder. Open the service class file and replace its content with the following code:

```
// ch11.service.ts file:
import { Injectable, Inject } from '@angular/core';
import { HttpClient } from '@angular/common/http';

@Injectable({
  providedIn: 'root'
})
export class Ch11Service {
  private url;
  constructor(private http: HttpClient, @Inject('BASE_URL') baseUrl: string) {
```

```
    this.url = baseUrl;
  }

  getStrategy2MaCrossover(ticker: string, start: string, end: string, fastPeriod:
    number, slowPeriod: number, maType: string, tradeType: string, tolerance:
    number) {
      let url1 = this.url + 'api/strategysignal2macrossover/' + ticker + '/' + start
        + '/' + end + '/' + fastPeriod + '/' + slowPeriod + '/' + maType + '/' +
        tradeType + '/' + tolerance;
      return this.http.get<any>(url1);
  }
}
```

In order to share the code for creating various charts that will be used to display different trading signals,
here, we implement a helper class named *strategy.helper.ts* class in the *ClientApp/src/app/models* folder
with the following code:

```
// strategy.helper.ts file:
export class StrategyHelper {
  chartPrice2(data: any, isMaSeries, indicatorIndex: number, marks: any) {
    let stock = this.processCandleData(data.signal);
    let series = [];
    let showLegend = false;
    let candleSeries = this.processCandlestickSeries(stock);
    series.push(candleSeries);
    if (isMaSeries) {
      let maSeries = this.process2MaSeries(data);
      for (let i in maSeries) {
        series.push(maSeries[i]);
      }
      showLegend = true;
    }
    let signalSeries = this.processSignalSeries(data, indicatorIndex, marks);
    series.push(signalSeries);
    let positionSeries = this.processTradePositionSeries(data, 2);
    series.push(positionSeries);

    let yname = data.indicatorNames[indicatorIndex];
    if (marks.length == 2)
      yname = data.indicatorNames[1] + '-' + data.indicatorNames[0];

    return {
      title: {
        text: data.name,
        left: 'center'
      },
      legend: {
        show: showLegend,
        top: 20,
        right: 45,
        data: ['price', { name: 'fastMa', icon: 'line' },
          { name: 'slowMa', icon: 'line' }]
      },
      tooltip: {
        trigger: 'axis',
        axisPointer: {
```

```
        type: 'cross'
      }
    },
    axisPointer: {
      link: { xAxisIndex: 'all' }
    },
    grid: [{
      left: 50,
      right: 40,
      top: '6%',
      height: '27%'
    }, {
      left: 50,
      right: 40,
      height: '23%',
      top: '42%'
    }, {
      left: 50,
      right: 40,
      height: '13%',
      top: '75%'
    }
    ],
    xAxis: [{
      type: 'category',
      data: stock.categoryData,
      scale: true,
      boundaryGap: false,
      axisLine: { onZero: false },
      splitLine: { show: false },
      splitNumber: 20,
      min: 'dataMin',
      max: 'dataMax'
    }, {
      type: 'category',
      gridIndex: 1,
      data: stock.categoryData,
      scale: true,
      boundaryGap: false,
      axisLine: { onZero: false },
      splitLine: { show: false },
      splitNumber: 20,
      min: 'dataMin',
      max: 'dataMax'
    }, {
      type: 'category',
      gridIndex: 2,
      data: stock.categoryData,
      scale: true,
      boundaryGap: false,
      axisLine: { onZero: false },
      splitLine: { show: false },
      splitNumber: 20,
      min: 'dataMin',
      max: 'dataMax'
```

```
    }
    ],
    yAxis: [{
      scale: true,
      name: 'Price',
      splitArea: {
        show: true
      }
    },
    {
      scale: true,
      name: yname,
      gridIndex: 1,
      splitArea: {
        show: true
      }
    },
    {
      scale: true,
      name: 'Trading Position',
      gridIndex: 2,
      splitArea: {
        show: true
      }
    }
    ],
    dataZoom: {
      show: true,
      type: 'slider',
      y: '93%',
      start: 70,
      end: 100,
      xAxisIndex: [0, 1, 2],
    },
    series: series
  }
}

chartPrice(data: any, isMaSeries) {
  let stock = this.processCandleData(data.signal);
  let series = [];
  let showLegend = false;
  let candleSeries = this.processCandlestickSeries(stock);
  series.push(candleSeries);
  if (isMaSeries) {
    let maSeries = this.process2MaSeries(data);
    for (let i in maSeries) {
      series.push(maSeries[i]);
    }
    showLegend = true;
  }
  let positionSeries = this.processTradePositionSeries(data, 1);
  series.push(positionSeries);

  return {
```

```
title: {
  text: data.name,
  left: 'center'
},
legend: {
  show: showLegend,
  top: 55,
  right: 45,
  data: ['price', { name: 'fastMa', icon: 'line' },
    { name: 'slowMa', icon: 'line' }]
},
tooltip: {
  trigger: 'axis',
  axisPointer: {
    type: 'cross'
  }
},
axisPointer: {
  link: { xAxisIndex: 'all' }
},
grid: [{
  left: 50,
  right: 40,
  top: '7%',
  height: '46%'
}, {
  left: 50,
  right: 40,
  height: '25%',
  top: '63%'
}],
xAxis: [{
  type: 'category',
  data: stock.categoryData,
  scale: true,
  boundaryGap: false,
  axisLine: { onZero: false },
  splitLine: { show: false },
  splitNumber: 20,
  min: 'dataMin',
  max: 'dataMax'
}, {
  type: 'category',
  gridIndex: 1,
  data: stock.categoryData,
  scale: true,
  boundaryGap: false,
  axisLine: { onZero: false },
  splitLine: { show: false },
  splitNumber: 20,
  min: 'dataMin',
  max: 'dataMax'
}],
yAxis: [{
  scale: true,
```

```
          name: 'Price',
          splitArea: {
            show: true
          }
        },
        {
          scale: true,
          name: 'Trading Position',
          gridIndex: 1,
          splitArea: {
            show: true
          }
        }],
        dataZoom: {
          show: true,
          type: 'slider',
          y: '93%',
          start: 70,
          end: 100,
          xAxisIndex: [0, 1],
        },
        series: series
      }
  }

  private processCandlestickSeries(stock: any) {
    const downColor = '#ec0000';
    const downBorderColor = '#8A0000';
    const upColor = '#00da3c';
    const upBorderColor = '#008F28'

    return {
      name: 'price',
      type: 'candlestick',
      data: stock.values,
      itemStyle: {
        color: upColor,
        color0: downColor,
        borderColor: upBorderColor,
        borderColor0: downBorderColor
      }
    };
  }

  private processSignalSeries(data: any, IndicatorIndex: number, marks: any) {
    let dat = [];
    data.signal.forEach(function (d) {
      dat.push(d.indicators[IndicatorIndex]);
    });
    let markLine = {};
    if (marks) {
      if (marks.length == 1) {
        markLine = {
          label: 'NATR',
          data: [{
```

```
            name: 'level', yAxis: marks[0],
            lineStyle: { normal: { color: "red" } }
          }]
        }
      } else if (marks.length == 2) {
        markLine = {
          label: 'Z-Score',
          data: [{
            name: 'zEntry', yAxis: marks[0],
            lineStyle: { normal: { color: "red" } }
          }, {
              name: '-zEntry', yAxis: -marks[0],
              lineStyle: { normal: { color: "red" } }
            },
            {
              name: 'zExit', yAxis: marks[1],
              lineStyle: { normal: { color: "green" } }
            }, {
              name: '-zExit', yAxis: -marks[1],
              lineStyle: { normal: { color: "green" } }
            }
          ]
        }
      }
    }
    return {
      name: data.indicatorNames[IndicatorIndex],
      type: 'line',
      data: dat,
      xAxisIndex: 1,
      yAxisIndex: 1,
      showSymbol: false,
      lineStyle: { color: 'steelblue' },
      markLine: markLine
    }
  }

  private processTradePositionSeries(data: any, axisIndex) {
    let dat = [];
    data.signal.forEach(function (d) {
      dat.push(d.position);
    });
    return {
      name: 'trade position',
      type: 'line',
      step: 'start',
      data: dat,
      xAxisIndex: axisIndex,
      yAxisIndex: axisIndex,
      showSymbol: false,
      lineStyle: { color: 'steelblue' }
    }
  }

  private process2MaSeries(data: any) {
```

```
let fastData = [];
let slowData = [];
let indicatorSeries = [];

data.signal.forEach(function (d) {
  fastData.push(d.indicators[0]);
  slowData.push(d.indicators[1]);
});

indicatorSeries.push(
  {
    name: 'fastMa',
    type: 'line',
    data: fastData,
    showSymbol: false
  });
indicatorSeries.push(
  {
    name: 'slowMa',
    type: 'line',
    data: slowData,
    showSymbol: false
  });

return indicatorSeries;
}

private processCandleData(candles: any) {
  const categoryData = [];
  const values = [];
  const volume = [];
  for (let i = 0; i < candles.length; i++) {
    categoryData.push(candles[i].date.toString().substring(0, 10));
    values.push([candles[i].open, candles[i].close, candles[i].low,
      candles[i].high]);
    volume.push(candles[i].volume);
  }
  return {
    categoryData: categoryData,
    values: values,
    volume: volume
  };
}
}
```

You should be familiar with the above code for creating various charts based on ECharts library. Next, run the following command in a command prompt window:

ng g c chapter11/ch11-crossover-ma --module=app.module

This generates a new component named *ch11-crossover-ma* in the *ClientApp/src/app/chapter11* folder. Open the component class file and replace its content with the following code:

```
// ch11-crossover-ma.component.ts file:
import { Component, OnInit } from '@angular/core';
import { Ch11Service } from '../../models/ch11.service';
```

```
import { StrategyHelper } from '../../models/strategy.helper';

@Component({
  selector: 'app-ch11-crossover-ma',
  templateUrl: './ch11-crossover-ma.component.html',
  styleUrls: ['./ch11-crossover-ma.component.css']
})
export class Ch11CrossoverMaComponent implements OnInit {
  ticker: string = 'SPY';
  start: string = '2016-06-01';
  end: string = '2018-07-01';
  fastPeriod: number = 20;
  slowPeriod: number = 50;
  maType: string = 'sma';
  tradeType: string = 'longshort';
  tolerance: number = 0;
  data: any;
  options: any;
  private helper: StrategyHelper;

  constructor(private service: Ch11Service) { }

  ngOnInit() {
    this.getData(this.ticker, this.start, this.end, this.fastPeriod,
this.slowPeriod, this.maType, this.tradeType, this.tolerance);
  }

  getData(ticker: string, start: string, end: string, fastPeriod: number,
    slowPeriod: number, maType: string,
    tradeType: string, tolerance: number) {
    this.data = null;
    this.helper = new StrategyHelper();
    this.service.getStrategy2MaCrossover(ticker, start, end, fastPeriod, slowPeriod,
      maType, tradeType, tolerance).subscribe(
      result => {
        this.data = result;
        this.options = this.helper.chartPrice(this.data, true);
      });
  }
}
```

Next, update the component's template with the following code:

```
// ch11-crossover-ma.component.html file:
<h2>
  ch11-crossover-ma works!
</h2>
<mat-form-field>
  <input matInput placeholder="ticker" [(ngModel)]="ticker" name="ticker">
</mat-form-field>
<mat-form-field>
  <input matInput placeholder="start" [(ngModel)]="start" name="start">
</mat-form-field>
<mat-form-field>
  <input matInput placeholder="end" [(ngModel)]="end" name="end">
</mat-form-field>
```

```
<mat-form-field>
  <input matInput placeholder="fastPeriod" [(ngModel)]="fastPeriod"
name="fastPeriod">
</mat-form-field>
<mat-form-field>
  <input matInput placeholder="slowPeriod" [(ngModel)]="slowPeriod"
name="slowPeriod">
</mat-form-field>
<mat-form-field>
  <mat-select placeholder="Select an MA type" [(value)]="maType">
    <mat-option value="sma">sma</mat-option>
    <mat-option value="ema">ema</mat-option>
    <mat-option value="wma">wma</mat-option>
  </mat-select>
</mat-form-field>
<mat-form-field>
  <mat-select placeholder="Select a trade type" [(value)]="tradeType">
    <mat-option value="long">Long</mat-option>
    <mat-option value="longshort">Long-Short</mat-option>
    <mat-option value="short">Short</mat-option>
  </mat-select>
</mat-form-field>
<mat-form-field>
  <input matInput placeholder="tolerance" [(ngModel)]="tolerance" name="tolerance">
</mat-form-field>
<button mat-raised-button color="primary" (click)="getData(ticker, start, end,
  fastPeriod, slowPeriod, maType, tradeType, tolerance)">Get Trading Signal</button>
<br /><br />
<div *ngIf="data" echarts [options]="options" style="height:600px;width:1000px">
</div>
```

This template first defines various input parameters and then creates the chart using the ECharts directive to display the trading signals.

Finally, we need to add a path for this new component to the *RouterModule* of the root module (i.e., the *app.module.ts* file):

```
{ path: 'chapter11/ch11-crossover-ma, component: Ch11CrossoverMaComponent },
```

Then add the corresponding URL link to the *home* and *nav-menu* components.

Saving the project and navigating to the */chapter11/ch11-crossover-ma* page produce the default results shown in Fig.11-4.

You can see that the long (corresponding 1) and short (corresponding to -1) entry and exit points in the trading position plot (the bottom chart of Fig.11-4) correspond exactly to the crossovers of the two moving averages (the top chart of Fig.11-4).

Note that in the long-short trading type, we always holding a trading position, either a long or short position after starting trading. If selecting a long-only trade type, and clicking the *Get Trading Signal* button, we will obtain two states: long (corresponding to 1) and no-trading (corresponding to 0) in the trading position plot, as shown in Fig.11-5.

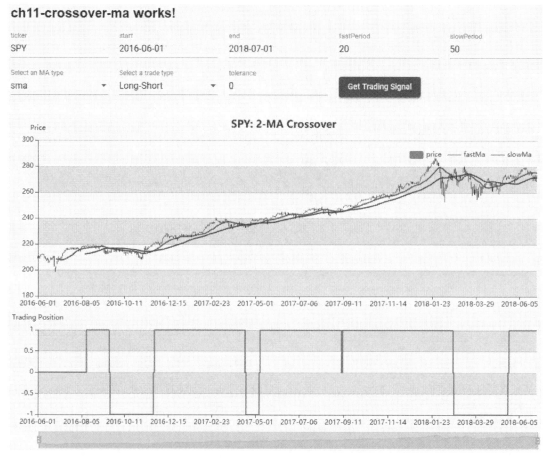

Fig.11-4. 2-MA crossover trading signals and trading positions for long-short trading type.

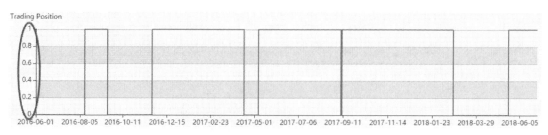

Fig.11-5. Trading positions for long-only trading type.

Two-MA Crossover with NATR Filter

The 2-MA crossover strategy discussed in the preceding section can work well in trending market, but the results are not good in choppy market. Traders usually use this simple MA crossover strategy to indicate the strength and direction of the market trend, and combine it with the other indicators that are used to identify whether the market is in the trending market or not. For example, the NATR (normalized average true range) indicator (see Chapter 7) can be used to measure the stock price volatility. Usually, the NATR has a lower value when the market is in trending while it tends to have a higher value for the choppy market.

Fig.11-6 shows stock prices with two moving averages and NATR indicator for SPY from 1/3/2017 to 4/12/2018.

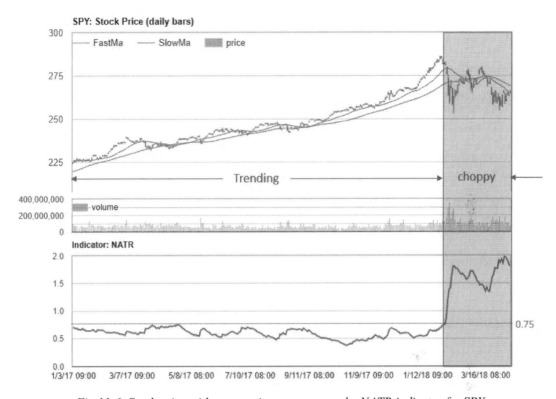

Fig.11-6. Stock price with two moving averages and a NATR indicator for SPY.

You can see that before February 1, 2018, SPY is in a strong uptrend, while the price fluctuates dramatically after that date. These trending and choppy regions are clearly identified by the NATR values. When NATR < 0.75, the market is in trending region, while the market becomes choppy when NATR > 0.75. This suggests that we can combine MA crossover with the NATR indicator to create a new trading strategy. The trading rules become:

- *Long Entry, Short Exit* - When fast MA crosses above the slow MA and NATR < 0.75, enter long at current bar if the short position is empty; or exit the short position at the current bar and enter long at the next bar if the short position has been filled.

- *Short Entry, Long Exit* - When fast MA crosses below the slow MA and NATR < 0.75, enter short at the current bar if the long position is empty; or exit the long position at the current bar and enter short at the next bar if the long position has been filled.

- *Flat* - When NATR ≥ 0.75, close all positions if filled and stay out of the market.

Now, we will implement this 2-MA crossover + NART trading strategy. Add a new helper method called *Signal2MaCrossoverNatr* to the *StrategySignalHelper* class in the *Quant/Models* folder with the following code:

```
public static List<StrategySignal> Signal2MaCrossoverNatr(string ticker,
    string start, string end, int natrPeriod = 14, int fastPeriod = 10,
    int slowPeriod = 30, string maType = "sma", double natrLevel = 0.75,
    string tradeType = "long", double tolerance = 0.0)
{
    var result = new List<StrategySignal>();
    var candles = IndicatorHelper.GetCandleData(ticker, start, end);
    var dat = IndicatorHelper.CandleToDoubleList(candles, "close");
    var maFast = dat.MovingAverage(fastPeriod, maType);
    var maSlow = dat.MovingAverage(slowPeriod, maType);
    var tr = candles.Natr(natrPeriod);

    int i, count = candles.Count;
    TradeAdvice[] advices = new TradeAdvice[count];
    var period = Math.Max(slowPeriod, natrPeriod);

    tradeType = tradeType.ToLower();
    switch (tradeType)
    {
        case "long":
            for (i = 0; i < count; i++)
            {
                advices[i] = TradeAdvice.Hold;
                if (i > period + 1 && i > slowPeriod + 1)
                {
                    if (maFast[i - 1] > maSlow[i - 1] * (1 + tolerance) &&
                        tr[i - 1] < natrLevel) advices[i] = TradeAdvice.Buy;
                }
            }
            break;
        case "short":
            for (i = 0; i < count; i++)
            {
                advices[i] = TradeAdvice.Hold;
                if (i > period + 1 && i > slowPeriod + 1)
                {
                    if (maFast[i - 1] * (1 + tolerance) < maSlow[i - 1] &&
                        tr[i - 1] < natrLevel) advices[i] = TradeAdvice.Sell;
                }
            }
            break;
        case "longshort":
            for (i = 0; i < count; i++)
            {
                advices[i] = TradeAdvice.Hold;
                if (i > period + 1 && i > slowPeriod + 1)
                {
                    if (maFast[i - 1] > maSlow[i - 1] * (1 + tolerance) &&
                        tr[i - 1] < natrLevel) advices[i] = TradeAdvice.Buy;
                    else if (maFast[i - 1] * (1 + tolerance) < maSlow[i - 1] &&
                        tr[i - 1] < natrLevel) advices[i] = TradeAdvice.Sell;
```

```
                }
            }
            break;
    }

    for (i = 1; i < count; i++)
    {
        if ((advices[i - 1] == TradeAdvice.Buy && advices[i] == TradeAdvice.Sell) ||
            (advices[i - 1] == TradeAdvice.Sell && advices[i] == TradeAdvice.Buy))
            advices[i] = TradeAdvice.Hold;
    }
    for (i = 0; i < count; i++)
    {
        result.Add(new StrategySignal
        {
            Ticker = ticker,
            Date = candles[i].Date,
            Open = candles[i].Open,
            High = candles[i].High,
            Low = candles[i].Low,
            Close = candles[i].Close,
            Volume = candles[i].Volume,
            Indicators = new List<double?> { maFast[i], maSlow[i], tr[i] },
            TradeAdvise = advices[i],
            Position = advices[i] == TradeAdvice.Buy ? 1 :
                advices[i] == TradeAdvice.Sell ? -1 : 0
        });
    }
    return result;
}
```

This strategy is similar to the original 2-MA crossover strategy, except that here we use the NATR value as a filter, which controls whether we should open a position or not when an entry occurs in the MA crossover.

Following the procedure presented here, you can create more trading signals based on crossover. For example, you can easily build a trading rule for crossover signals using three moving averages, or combining with other technical indicators.

Now, we can convert our trading signal into a web service. Add a new method called *GetStrategy2MACrossoverNatr* to the *StrategyValuesController* class in the *Quant/Controllers* folder with the following core:

```
[Route("~/api/strategySignal2MaCrossoverNatr/{ticker}/{start}/{end}/{fastPeriod}/
    {slowPeriod}/{maType}/{natrPeriod}/{natrLevel}/{tradeType}/{tolerance}")]
[HttpGet]
public JsonResult GetStrategy2MaCrossoverNatr(string ticker, string start,
    string end, int fastPeriod, int slowPeriod, string maType, int natrPeriod,
    double natrLevel, string tradeType, double tolerance)
{
    var signal = StrategySignalHelper.Signal2MaCrossoverNatr(ticker, start, end,
        fastPeriod, slowPeriod, maType, natrPeriod, natrLevel, tradeType,
        tolerance);
    return Json(new { name = "Signal: 2 MA Crossover + NATR", indicatorNames
        = new string[] { "fastMa", "slowMa", "natr" }, Signal = signal });
}
```

Two-MA Crossover with NATR in Angular

Add a TypeScript method called *getStrategy2MaCrossoverNatr* to the *ch11.service.ts* file with the following code:

```
getStrategy2MaCrossoverNatr(ticker: string, start: string, end: string, fastPeriod:
  number, slowPeriod: number, maType: string, natrPeriod: number, natrLevel: number,
  tradeType: string, tolerance: number) {
  let url1 = this.url + 'api/strategysignal2macrossovernatr/' + ticker + '/' + start
    + '/' + end + '/' + fastPeriod + '/' + slowPeriod + '/' + maType + '/' +
    natrPeriod + '/' + natrLevel + '/' + tradeType + '/' + tolerance;
  return this.http.get<any>(url1);
}
```

This method allows you to access the trading signals generated by the 2-MA crossover strategy with an NATR filter in Angular applications.

Now, run the following command in a command prompt window:

ng g c chapter11/ch11-crossover-ma-natr --module=app.module

This generates a new component named *ch11-crossover-ma-natr* in the *ClientApp/src/app/chapter11* folder. Open the component class file and replace its content with the following code:

```
// ch11-crossover-ma-natr.component file:
import { Component, OnInit } from '@angular/core';
import { Ch11Service } from '../../models/ch11.service';
import { StrategyHelper } from '../../models/strategy.helper';

@Component({
  selector: 'app-ch11-crossover-ma-natr',
  templateUrl: './ch11-crossover-ma-natr.component.html',
  styleUrls: ['./ch11-crossover-ma-natr.component.css']
})
export class Ch11CrossoverMaNatrComponent implements OnInit {
  ticker: string = 'SPY';
  start: string = '2016-06-01';
  end: string = '2018-07-01';
  fastPeriod: number = 20;
  slowPeriod: number = 50;
  maType: string = 'sma';
  natrPeriod: number = 14;
  natrLevel: number = 0.75;
  tradeType: string = 'longshort';
  tolerance: number = 0;
  data: any;
  options: any;
  private helper: StrategyHelper;

  constructor(private service: Ch11Service) { }

  ngOnInit() {
    this.getData(this.ticker, this.start, this.end, this.fastPeriod,
      this.slowPeriod, this.maType, this.natrPeriod, this.natrLevel,
      this.tradeType, this.tolerance);
  }
```

```
getData(ticker: string, start: string, end: string, fastPeriod: number,
  slowPeriod: number, maType: string, natrPeriod: number, natrLevel: number,
  tradeType: string, tolerance: number) {
  this.data = null;
  this.helper = new StrategyHelper();
  this.service.getStrategy2MaCrossoverNatr(ticker, start, end, fastPeriod,
    slowPeriod, maType, natrPeriod, natrLevel, tradeType, tolerance)
    .subscribe(result => {
      this.data = result;
      this.options = this.helper.chartPrice2(this.data, true, 2, [natrLevel]);
    });
  }
}
```

Next, update the component's template with the following code:

```
// ch11-crossover-ma-natr.component file:
<h2>
  ch11-crossover-ma-natr works!
</h2>

<mat-form-field>
  <input matInput placeholder="ticker" [(ngModel)]="ticker" name="ticker">
</mat-form-field>
<mat-form-field>
  <input matInput placeholder="start" [(ngModel)]="start" name="start">
</mat-form-field>
<mat-form-field>
  <input matInput placeholder="end" [(ngModel)]="end" name="end">
</mat-form-field>
<mat-form-field>
  <input matInput placeholder="fastPeriod" [(ngModel)]="fastPeriod"
name="fastPeriod">
</mat-form-field>
<mat-form-field>
  <input matInput placeholder="slowPeriod" [(ngModel)]="slowPeriod"
name="slowPeriod">
</mat-form-field>
<mat-form-field>
  <mat-select placeholder="Select an MA type" [(value)]="maType">
    <mat-option value="sma">sma</mat-option>
    <mat-option value="ema">ema</mat-option>
    <mat-option value="wma">wma</mat-option>
  </mat-select>
</mat-form-field>
<mat-form-field>
  <input matInput placeholder="natrPeriod" [(ngModel)]="natrPeriod"
name="natrPeriod">
</mat-form-field>
<mat-form-field>
  <input matInput placeholder="natrLevel" [(ngModel)]="natrLevel" name="natrLevel">
</mat-form-field>
<mat-form-field>
  <mat-select placeholder="Select a trade type" [(value)]="tradeType">
    <mat-option value="long">Long</mat-option>
    <mat-option value="longshort">Long-Short</mat-option>
```

```
      <mat-option value="short">Short</mat-option>
    </mat-select>
</mat-form-field>
<mat-form-field>
    <input matInput placeholder="tolerance" [(ngModel)]="tolerance" name="tolerance">
</mat-form-field>
<button mat-raised-button color="primary" (click)="getData(ticker, start, end,
    fastPeriod, slowPeriod, maType, natrPeriod, natrLevel, tradeType, tolerance)">
    Get Trading Signal</button>
<br /><br />
<div *ngIf="data" echarts [options]="options"
style="height:700px;width:1000px"></div>
```

This template first defines various input parameters and then creates the chart using the ECharts directive to display the trading signals.

Finally, we need to add a path for this new component to the *RouterModule* of the root module (i.e., the *app.module.ts* file):

{ path: 'chapter11/ch11-crossover-ma-natr, component: Ch11CrossoverMaNatrComponent }

Then add the corresponding URL link to the *home* and *nav-menu* components.

Saving the project and navigating to the */chapter11/ch11-crossover-ma-natr* page produce the default results shown in Fig.11-7.

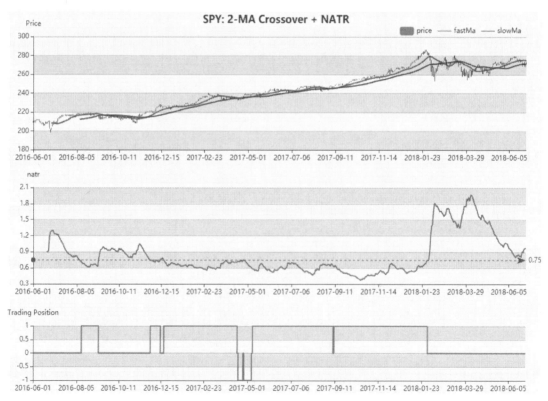

Fig.11-7. 2-MA crossover +NATR trading signals and trading positions for a long-short type.

Note that here we set the NATR level to 0.75, meaning that we will close all positions when NATR > 0.75. In practice, you should adjust the NATR values for different stocks or different periods even for the same stock.

Z-Score Trading Signals

The crossover-based trading strategies are basically trend-following strategies. To apply crossover strategies, a strong trend must be in place. You usually use these strategies to trade in the price direction – you buy when prices are rising and sell when prices are falling. The basic assumption behind a trend-following strategy is that markets underreact.

However, the market is not always in trending conditions. Whether we realize it or not, nature is filled with examples of mean reversion. A mean reverting strategy is one where you trade in the opposite direction of the price. If prices rise, you sell, and vice versa. The oscillator-based indicators such as RSI are usually used to identify when reversals are likely to occur. For example, a high value for the RSI is a sell signal, and vice versa. The assumption behind the mean reverting strategy is the markets overreact. For example, the price falls due to a market panic. If the fall is overdone, we expect the price to recover and move in the opposite direction. To trade this scenario, you should use a mean reverting based strategy.

As we all know, different oscillator-like indicators have very different value ranges. In order to develop a unified backtesting framework for mean reverting-based trading strategies, we rescale the value ranges for different indicators so that their values fall in the similar value range. We call these rescaled indicators as z-score.

MA-Based Z-Score

First, we show how to convert a Bollinger band indicator into a z-score model. Bollinger band indicator is based on the moving average, where we enter a position only when the price deviates by more than *zEntry* standard deviations from the mean value. *zEntry* is a free parameter to be optimized in a training data set. The mean and standard deviation can be computed within a moving window, whose length again can be optimized. We can exit positions when the price returns to *zExit* standard deviations from the mean. We often set *zExit* = 0, which means we will exit when the price returns back to its current mean. If we set the moving window size to a shorter period, and set *zEntry* and *zExit* to smaller values, we will get a shorter holding period and more trades.

We can define the MA-based z-score using the following formula:

$$MAZScore = \frac{price - mean}{standard\ deviation}$$

We can construct a mean-reversion trading rules based on z-score:

- *Long Entry* – when z-score <= *zEntry*, enter long.

- *Long Exit* – When z-score > -*zExit*, exit the long position at the current bar if the long position is filled.

- *Short Entry* – when z-score >= *zEntry*, enter short.

- *Short Exit* – When z-score < -*zExit*, exit the short position at the current bar if the short position is filled.

Now, we will implement this MA-based z-score trading strategy. Add the following helper methods to the *StrategySignalHelper* class in the *Quant/Models* folder with the following code:

```
public static List<StrategySignal> SignalMaZscore(string ticker, string start,
    string end, int period = 14, string maType = "sma", double zEntry = -2.0,
    double zExit = 0)
{
    var result = new List<StrategySignal>();
    var candles = IndicatorHelper.GetCandleData(ticker, start, end);
    var dat = IndicatorHelper.CandleToDoubleList(candles, "close");
    var bb = dat.Bbands(period, 1.0, 1.0, maType);
    int i, count = candles.Count;
    double zscore, std;
    List<double?> zscores = new List<double?>();
    for (i = 0; i < count; i++)
    {
        if (bb.MiddleBand[i] == null)
        {
            zscores.Add(null);
        }
        else
        {
            std = (double)bb.UpperBand[i] - (double)bb.MiddleBand[i];
            zscore = (candles[i].Close - (double)bb.MiddleBand[i]) / std;
            zscores.Add(zscore);
        }
    }
    var advices = ComputeSignalZscore(zscores, period, zEntry, zExit);
    for (i = 0; i < count; i++)
    {
        result.Add(new StrategySignal
        {
            Ticker = ticker,
            Date = candles[i].Date,
            Open = candles[i].Open,
            High = candles[i].High,
            Low = candles[i].Low,
            Close = candles[i].Close,
            Volume = candles[i].Volume,
            Indicators = new List<double?> { zscores[i], bb.MiddleBand[i] },
            TradeAdvise = advices[i],
            Position = advices[i] == TradeAdvice.Buy ? 1 :
                advices[i] == TradeAdvice.Sell ? -1 : 0
        });
    }
    return result;
}

private static TradeAdvice[] ComputeSignalZscore(List<double?> zscores, int start,
    double zEntry = -2.0, double zExit = 0)
{
    int i, count = zscores.Count;
    TradeAdvice[] advices = new TradeAdvice[count];
    for (i = 0; i < count; i++)
    {
```

```
        advices[i] = TradeAdvice.Hold;
        if (i > start + 2)
        {
            // long:
            if (zscores[i - 2] <= -zEntry && zscores[i - 1] > -zEntry)
                advices[i] = TradeAdvice.Buy;
            if (advices[i - 1] == TradeAdvice.Buy)
            {
                if (zscores[i - 1] < -zExit) advices[i] = TradeAdvice.Buy;
            }

            // short:
            if (zscores[i - 2] > zEntry && zscores[i - 1] < zEntry)
                advices[i] = TradeAdvice.Sell;
            if (advices[i - 1] == TradeAdvice.Sell)
            {
                if (zscores[i - 1] > zExit) advices[i] = TradeAdvice.Sell;
            }
        }
    }
    return advices;
}
```

Inside the *SignalMaZscore* method, we use the Bollinger-band indicator to calculate the moving average and the standard deviation, which are required to calculate z-score. The private *ComputeSignalZscore* method implements the trading rules using the z-score signals.

We can convert this MA-based z-score trading signals into a web service by adding the following method to the *StrategyValuesController* class in the *Quant/Controllers* folder:

```
[Route("~/api/strategySignalMaZscore/{ticker}/{start}/{end}/{period}/{maType}/
    {zEntry}/{zExit}")]
[HttpGet]
public JsonResult GetStrategyMaZscore(string ticker, string start, string end,
    int period, string maType, double zEntry, double zExit)
{
    var signal = StrategySignalHelper.SignalMaZscore(ticker, start, end, period,
        maType, zEntry, zExit);
    return Json(new { name = ticker +  ": MA Zscore", indicatorNames =
        new string[] { "zScore", "ma" }, Signal = signal });
}
```

MA-Based Z-Score in Angular

Add a new TypeScript method called *getStrategyMaZscore* to the *ch11.service.ts* file in the *ClientApp/src/app/models* folder with the following code:

```
getStrategy2MaCrossoverNatr(ticker: string, start: string, end: string, fastPeriod:
    number, slowPeriod: number, maType: string, natrPeriod: number, natrLevel: number,
    tradeType: string, tolerance: number) {
    let url1 = this.url + 'api/strategysignal2macrossovernatr/' + ticker + '/' + start
        + '/' + end + '/' + fastPeriod + '/' + slowPeriod + '/' + maType + '/' +
        natrPeriod + '/' + natrLevel + '/' + tradeType + '/' + tolerance;
    return this.http.get<any>(url1);
}
```

Next, run the following command in a command prompt window:

```
ng g c chapter11/ch11-zscore-ma --module=app.module
```

This generates a new component called *ch11-zscore-ma* in the *ClientApp/src/app/chapter11* folder. Open this component class file and replace its content with the following code:

```
// ch11-zscore-ma.component.ts file:
import { Component, OnInit } from '@angular/core';
import { Ch11Service } from '../../models/ch11.service';
import { StrategyHelper } from '../../models/strategy.helper';

@Component({
  selector: 'app-ch11-zscore-ma',
  templateUrl: './ch11-zscore-ma.component.html',
  styleUrls: ['./ch11-zscore-ma.component.css']
})
export class Ch11ZscoreMaComponent implements OnInit {
  ticker: string = 'IBM';
  start: string = '2011-06-01';
  end: string = '2013-08-01';
  period: number = 40;
  maType: string = 'sma';
  zEntry: number = 2;
  zExit: number = 0;
  data: any;
  options: any;
  private helper: StrategyHelper;

  constructor(private service: Ch11Service) { }

  ngOnInit() {
    this.getData(this.ticker, this.start, this.end, this.period, this.maType,
      this.zEntry, this.zExit);
  }

  getData(ticker: string, start: string, end: string, period: number, maType:
    string, zEntry: number, zExit: number) {
    this.data = null;
    this.helper = new StrategyHelper();
    this.service.getStrategyMaZscore(ticker, start, end, period, maType, zEntry,
      zExit).subscribe(result => {
        this.data = result;
        this.options = this.helper.chartPrice2(this.data, false, 0,
          [zEntry, zExit]);
      });
  }
}
```

Next, update the component's template with the following code:

```
// ch11-zscore-ma.component.html file:
<h2>
  ch11-zscore-ma works!
</h2>
<mat-form-field>
  <input matInput placeholder="ticker" [(ngModel)]="ticker" name="ticker">
```

```
</mat-form-field>
<mat-form-field>
  <input matInput placeholder="start" [(ngModel)]="start" name="start">
</mat-form-field>
<mat-form-field>
  <input matInput placeholder="end" [(ngModel)]="end" name="end">
</mat-form-field>
<mat-form-field>
  <input matInput placeholder="period" [(ngModel)]="period" name="period">
</mat-form-field>
<mat-form-field>
  <mat-select placeholder="Select an MA type" [(value)]="maType">
    <mat-option value="sma">sma</mat-option>
    <mat-option value="ema">ema</mat-option>
    <mat-option value="wma">wma</mat-option>
  </mat-select>
</mat-form-field>
<mat-form-field>
  <input matInput placeholder="zEntry" [(ngModel)]="zEntry" name="zEntry">
</mat-form-field>
<mat-form-field>
  <input matInput placeholder="zExit" [(ngModel)]="zExit" name="zExit">
</mat-form-field>
<button mat-raised-button color="primary" (click)="getData(ticker, start, end,
  period, maType, zEntry, zExit)"> Get Trading Signal
</button>
<br /><br />
<div *ngIf="data" echarts [options]="options" style="height:700px;width:1000px">
</div>
```

This template first defines various input parameters and then creates the chart using the ECharts directive to display the trading signals.

Finally, we need to add a path for this new component to the *RouterModule* of the root module (i.e., the *app.module.ts* file):

```
{ path: 'chapter11/ch11-zscore-ma, component: Ch11ZscoreMaComponent }
```

Then add the corresponding URL link to the *home* and *nav-menu* components.

Saving the project and navigating to the */chapter11/ch11-zscore-ma* page produce the default results shown in Fig.11-8.

You can adjust the period and entry/exit z-score level to improve performance. Note that the MA-based z-score is applied to the closing prices, which is an irregular curve that can be smoothed by applying moving average on it. In this book, we will not discuss how to optimize the trading strategies. If you are interested in trading strategy optimization, you can refer to my previously published book "*Practical C# and WPF for Financial Markets*".

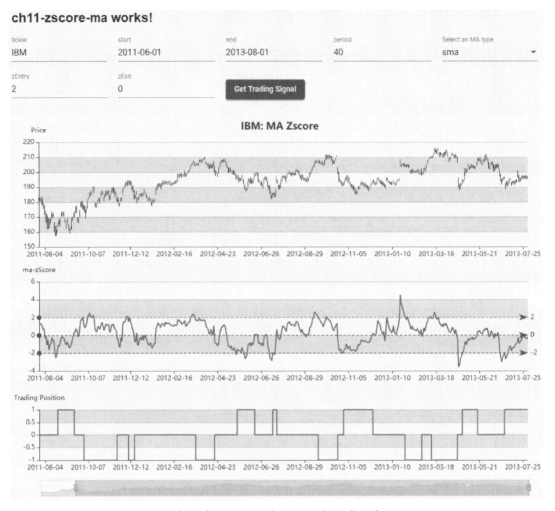

Fig.11-8. Ma-based z-score trading signals and trading positions.

RSI-Based Z-Score

RSI (relative strength Index) indicator is a momentum oscillator that measures the speed and change of price movement. RSI oscillates between 0 and 100. Traditionally, RSI is considered overbought when above 70 and oversold when below 30. You can calculate RSI using the following formula

$$RSI = 100 - \frac{100}{1 + RS}, \quad RS = \frac{Average\ Gain}{Average\ Loss}$$

Note that RSI has been broken down into its basic components: RS, average gain, and average loss. The losses are expressed as positive values, not negative values.

In order to extract the trading signal from the RSI indicator, we need to renormalize it into a proper value range using the following formula:

$$Signal = \frac{RSI - 50}{12.5}$$

You can see that the most part of the signal will be concentrated in the range of $[-2, 2]$. The trading rules for this RSI-based z-score is the same as that used in the MA-based z-score presented in the preceding section.

Add a new helper method called *SignalRsiZscore* to the *StrategySignalHelper* class in the *Quant/Models* folder with the following code:

```
public static List<StrategySignal> SignalRsiZscore(string ticker, string start,
    string end, int period = 14, double zEntry = -2.0, double zExit = 0)
{
    var result = new List<StrategySignal>();
    var candles = IndicatorHelper.GetCandleData(ticker, start, end);
    var dat = IndicatorHelper.CandleToDoubleList(candles, "close");
    var rsi = dat.Rsi(period);
    int i, count = candles.Count;
    List<double?> zscores = new List<double?>();
    for (i = 0; i < count; i++)
    {
        if (rsi[i] == null) zscores.Add(null);
        else zscores.Add((rsi[i] - 50.0) / 12.5);
    }
    var advices = ComputeSignalZscore(zscores, period, zEntry, zExit);
    for (i = 0; i < count; i++)
    {
        result.Add(new StrategySignal
        {
            Ticker = ticker,
            Date = candles[i].Date,
            Open = candles[i].Open,
            High = candles[i].High,
            Low = candles[i].Low,
            Close = candles[i].Close,
            Volume = candles[i].Volume,
            Indicators = new List<double?> { zscores[i], rsi[i] },
            TradeAdvise = advices[i],
            Position = advices[i] == TradeAdvice.Buy ? 1 :
                advices[i] == TradeAdvice.Sell ? -1 : 0
        });
    }
    return result;
}
```

Inside this method, we call the RSI indicator function from the TA-Lib library and then use the result to calculate the RSI-based z-score.

Next, we convert this method into a web service by adding a new method called *GetStrategyRsiZscore* to the *StrategyValuesController* class with the following code:

```
[Route("~/api/strategySignalRsiZscore/{ticker}/{start}/{end}/{period}/
    {zEntry}/{zExit}")]
[HttpGet]
public JsonResult GetStrategyRsiZscore(string ticker, string start, string end,
    int period, double zEntry, double zExit)
```

```
{
    var signal = StrategySignalHelper.SignalRsiZscore(ticker, start, end, period,
        zEntry, zExit);
    return Json(new { name = ticker + ": RSI Zscore", indicatorNames =
        new string[] { "zScore", "rsi" }, Signal = signal });
}
```

RSI-Based Z-Score in Angular

Add a new TypeScript method called *getStrategyRsiZscore* to the *ch11.service.ts* file in the *ClientApp/src/app/models* folder with the following code:

```
getStrategyRsiZscore(ticker: string, start: string, end: string, period: number,
  zEntry: number, zExit: number) {
  let url1 = this.url + 'api/strategysignalrsizscore/' + ticker + '/' + start + '/'
    + end + '/' + period + '/' + zEntry + '/' + zExit;
  return this.http.get<any>(url1);
}
```

Now, run the following command in a command prompt window:

ng g c chapter11/ch11-zscore-rsi --module=app.module

This generates a new component called *ch11-zscore-rsi* in the *ClientApp/src/app/chapter11* folder. Open the component class file and replace its content with the following code:

```
// ch11-zscore-rsi.component.ts file:
import { Component, OnInit } from '@angular/core';
import { Ch11Service } from '../../models/ch11.service';
import { StrategyHelper } from '../../models/strategy.helper';

@Component({
    selector: 'app-ch11-zscore-rsi',
    templateUrl: './ch11-zscore-rsi.component.html',
    styleUrls: ['./ch11-zscore-rsi.component.css']
})
export class Ch11ZscoreRsiComponent implements OnInit {
    ticker: string = 'IBM';
    start: string = '2011-06-01';
    end: string = '2013-08-01';
    period: number = 14;
    zEntry: number = 1.5;
    zExit: number = 0;
    data: any;
    options: any;
    private helper: StrategyHelper;

    constructor(private service: Ch11Service) { }

    ngOnInit() {
        this.getData(this.ticker, this.start, this.end, this.period, this.zEntry,
            this.zExit);
    }

    getData(ticker: string, start: string, end: string, period: number,
    zEntry: number, zExit: number) {
```

```
this.data = null;
this.helper = new StrategyHelper();
this.service.getStrategyRsiZscore(ticker, start, end, period, zEntry, zExit)
  .subscribe(result => {
    this.data = result;
    this.options = this.helper.chartPrice2(this.data, false, 0, [zEntry, zExit]);
  });
  }
}
```

Next, update the component's template with the following code:

```
// ch11-zscore-rsi.component.html file:
<h2>
  ch11-zscore-rsi works!
</h2>
<mat-form-field>
  <input matInput placeholder="ticker" [(ngModel)]="ticker" name="ticker">
</mat-form-field>
<mat-form-field>
  <input matInput placeholder="start" [(ngModel)]="start" name="start">
</mat-form-field>
<mat-form-field>
  <input matInput placeholder="end" [(ngModel)]="end" name="end">
</mat-form-field>
<mat-form-field>
  <input matInput placeholder="period" [(ngModel)]="period" name="period">
</mat-form-field>
<mat-form-field>
  <input matInput placeholder="zEntry" [(ngModel)]="zEntry" name="zEntry">
</mat-form-field>
<mat-form-field>
  <input matInput placeholder="zExit" [(ngModel)]="zExit" name="zExit">
</mat-form-field>
<button mat-raised-button color="primary" (click)="getData(ticker, start, end,
  period, zEntry, zExit)"> Get Trading Signal</button>
<br /><br />
<div *ngIf="data" echarts [options]="options" style="height:700px;width:1000px">
</div>
```

This template first defines various input parameters and then creates the chart using the ECharts directive to display the trading signals.

Finally, we need to add a path for this new component to the *RouterModule* of the root module (i.e., the *app.module.ts* file):

```
{ path: 'chapter11/ch11-zscore-rsi, component: Ch11ZscoreRsiComponent }
```

Then add the corresponding URL link to the *home* and *nav-menu* components.

Saving the project and navigating to the */chapter11/ch11-zscore-rsi* page produce the default results shown in Fig.11-9.

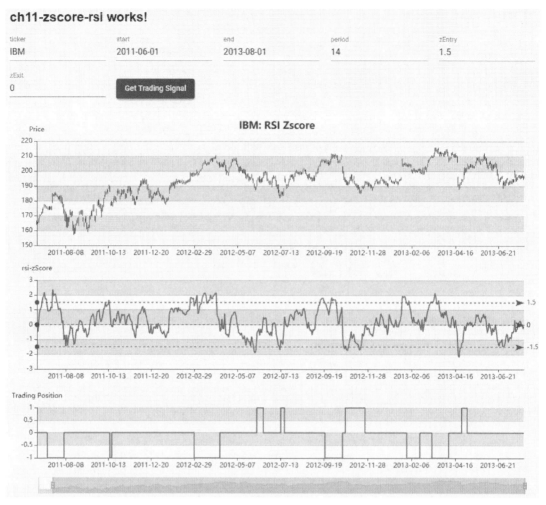

Fig.11-9. RSI-based z-score trading signals and trading positions for IBM.

PPO-Based Z-Score

The percentage price oscillator (PPO) is a momentum oscillator that measures the difference between two moving averages as a percentage of the slower moving average. PPO is very similar to the MACD indicator, except that MACD measures the absolute difference between two moving averages, whereas PPO expresses this difference as a relative value. This allows you to use PPO indicator to compare stocks with different prices more easily. This is useful if the stocks vary significantly in price.

Add a new helper method called *SignalPpoZscore* to the *StrategySignalHelper* class in the *Quant/Models* folder with the following code:

```
public static List<StrategySignal> SignalPpoZscore(string ticker, string start,
    string end, int fastPeriod = 12, int slowPeriod = 26, string maType = "sma",
    double zEntry = -2.0, double zExit = 0)
{
    var result = new List<StrategySignal>();
```

```
var candles = IndicatorHelper.GetCandleData(ticker, start, end);
var dat = IndicatorHelper.CandleToDoubleList(candles, "close");
var ppo = dat.Ppo(fastPeriod, slowPeriod, maType);
int i, count = candles.Count;
List<double?> zscores = new List<double?>();
for (i = 0; i < count; i++)
{
    if (ppo[i] == null) zscores.Add(null);
    else zscores.Add(ppo[i]);
}
var advices = ComputeSignalZscore(zscores, slowPeriod, zEntry, zExit);
for (i = 0; i < count; i++)
{
    result.Add(new StrategySignal
    {
        Ticker = ticker,
        Date = candles[i].Date,
        Open = candles[i].Open,
        High = candles[i].High,
        Low = candles[i].Low,
        Close = candles[i].Close,
        Volume = candles[i].Volume,
        Indicators = new List<double?> { zscores[i], ppo[i] },
        TradeAdvise = advices[i],
        Position = advices[i] == TradeAdvice.Buy ? 1 :
            advices[i] == TradeAdvice.Sell ? -1 : 0
    });
}
return result;
}
```

Inside this method, we call the PPO indicator function from the TA-Lib library and then use the result to calculate the PPO-based z-score.

Next, we convert this method into a web service by adding a new method called *GetStrategyPPOZscore* to the *StrategyValuesController* class with the following code:

```
[Route("~/api/strategySignalPpoZscore/{ticker}/{start}/{end}/{fastPeriod}/
    {slowPeriod}/{maType}/{zEntry}/{zExit}")]
[HttpGet]
public JsonResult GetStrategyppoZscore(string ticker, string start, string end,
    int fastPeriod, int slowPeriod, string maType, double zEntry, double zExit)
{
    var signal = StrategySignalHelper.SignalPpoZscore(ticker, start, end,
        fastPeriod, slowPeriod, maType, zEntry, zExit);
    return Json(new { name = ticker + ": PPO Zscore", indicatorNames =
        new string[] { "zScore", "ppo" }, Signal = signal });
}
```

PPO-Based Z-Score in Angular

Add a new TypeScript method called *getStrategyPpoZscore* to the *ch11.service.ts* file in the *ClientApp/src/app/models* folder with the following code:

```
getStrategyPpoZscore(ticker: string, start: string, end: string, fastPeriod: number,
```

```
 slowPeriod: number, maType: string,
  zEntry: number, zExit: number) {
  let url1 = this.url + 'api/strategysignalppozscore/' + ticker + '/' + start + '/'
    + end + '/' + fastPeriod + '/' + slowPeriod + '/' + maType + '/' + zEntry + '/'
    + zExit;
  return this.http.get<any>(url1);
}
```

Now, run the following command in a command prompt window:

ng g c chapter11/ch11-zscore-ppo --module=app.module

This generates a new component called *ch11-zscore-ppo* in the *ClientApp/src/app/chapter11* folder. Open the component class file and replace its content with the following code:

```
// ch11-zscore-ppo.component.ts file:
import { Component, OnInit } from '@angular/core';
import { Ch11Service } from '../../models/ch11.service';
import { StrategyHelper } from '../../models/strategy.helper';

@Component({
  selector: 'app-ch11-zscore-ppo',
  templateUrl: './ch11-zscore-ppo.component.html',
  styleUrls: ['./ch11-zscore-ppo.component.css']
})
export class Ch11ZscorePpoComponent implements OnInit {
  ticker: string = 'IBM';
  start: string = '2011-06-01';
  end: string = '2013-08-01';
  fastPeriod: number = 12;
  slowPeriod: number = 26;
  maType: string = 'sma';
  zEntry: number = 2.0;
  zExit: number = 0;
  data: any;
  options: any;
  private helper: StrategyHelper;

  constructor(private service: Ch11Service) { }

  ngOnInit() {
    this.getData(this.ticker, this.start, this.end, this.fastPeriod,
      this.slowPeriod, this.maType, this.zEntry, this.zExit);
  }

  getData(ticker: string, start: string, end: string, fastPeriod: number,
    slowPeriod: number, maType: string, zEntry: number, zExit: number) {
    this.data = null;
    this.helper = new StrategyHelper();
    this.service.getStrategyPpoZscore(ticker, start, end, fastPeriod, slowPeriod,
      maType, zEntry, zExit).subscribe(result => {
        this.data = result;
        this.options = this.helper.chartPrice2(this.data, false, 0,
          [zEntry, zExit]);
      });
  }
}
```

Next, update the component's template with the following code:

```
// ch11-zscore-ppo.component.html file:
<h2>
  ch11-zscore-ppo works!
</h2>
<mat-form-field>
  <input matInput placeholder="ticker" [(ngModel)]="ticker" name="ticker">
</mat-form-field>
<mat-form-field>
  <input matInput placeholder="start" [(ngModel)]="start" name="start">
</mat-form-field>
<mat-form-field>
  <input matInput placeholder="end" [(ngModel)]="end" name="end">
</mat-form-field>
<mat-form-field>
  <input matInput placeholder="fastPeriod" [(ngModel)]="fastPeriod"
name="fastPeriod">
</mat-form-field>
<mat-form-field>
  <input matInput placeholder="slowPeriod" [(ngModel)]="slowPeriod"
name="slowPeriod">
</mat-form-field>
<mat-form-field>
  <mat-select placeholder="Select an MA type" [(value)]="maType">
    <mat-option value="sma">sma</mat-option>
    <mat-option value="ema">ema</mat-option>
    <mat-option value="wma">wma</mat-option>
  </mat-select>
</mat-form-field>
<mat-form-field>
  <input matInput placeholder="zEntry" [(ngModel)]="zEntry" name="zEntry">
</mat-form-field>
<mat-form-field>
  <input matInput placeholder="zExit" [(ngModel)]="zExit" name="zExit">
</mat-form-field>
<button mat-raised-button color="primary" (click)="getData(ticker, start, end,
  fastperiod, slowPeriod, maType, zEntry, zExit)">Get Trading Signal</button>
<br /><br />
<div *ngIf="data" echarts [options]="options" style="height:700px;width:1000px">
</div>
```

This template first defines various input parameters and then creates the chart using the ECharts directive to display the trading signals.

Finally, we need to add a path for this new component to the *RouterModule* of the root module (i.e., the *app.module.ts* file):

```
{ path: 'chapter11/ch11-zscore-ppo, component: Ch11ZscorePpoComponent }
```

Then add the corresponding URL link to the *home* and *nav-menu* components.

Saving the project and navigating to the */chapter11/ch11-zscore-ppo* page produce the default results shown in Fig.11-10.

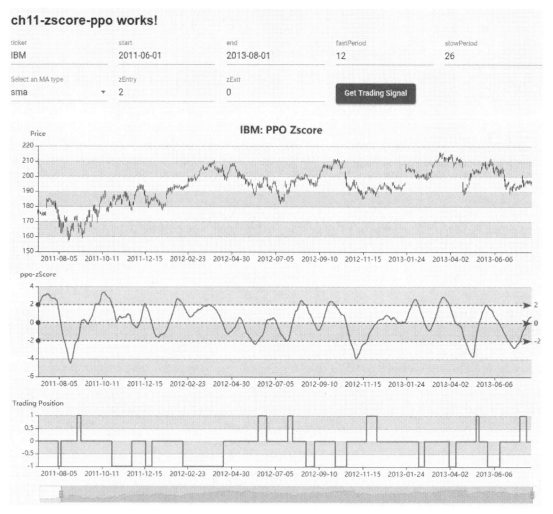

Fig.11-10. PPO-based z-score trading signals and trading positions.

Backtesting System

In this section, we will build a backtesting system that allows you to backtest the historical performance using the trading signals. Typically, you can use this system to calculate the daily and cumulated P&L (profit and loss) and other risk measures for a given trading strategy. For simplicity's sake, we will neglect the transaction costs, which includes brokers' commission and the bid/ask spreads. In addition, we assume that the orders can be filled fully at a specified price (i.e., the close price). We all know that in practice, this is impossible. You have to use proper algorithms to execute your orders, such as the popular TWAP (time-weighted average price) or VWAP (volume-weighted average price) algorithms.

P&L Computation

Here, we will implement a simple long/short method to compute the P&L (profit and loss). Add a new class named Strategy*BacktestHelper* to the *Quant*/*Models* folder. Here is the code for this class:

```
using System;
using System.Collections.Generic;
using System.Linq;
using static Quant.Models.StrategyObjects;

namespace Quant.Models
{
    public static class StrategyBacktestHelper
    {
        public static List<BacktestResult> ComputePnL(List<StrategySignal> signals,
            double notional, double stopLoss = 0.1, double protectProfit = 0.3)
        {
            List<BacktestResult> results = new List<BacktestResult>();
            int numTrades = 0;
            double pnlCum = 0.0;
            double pnlAllTrades = 0.0;
            double priceIn = 0.0;
            DateTime? dateIn = null; ;
            double shares = 0;
            double shares1 = 0;
            double pnlCum1 = 0;
            int i, count = signals.Count;
            for (i = 1; i < count; i++)
            {
                var signal = signals[i];
                var signal0 = signals[i - 1];
                double pnlDaily = 0.0;
                double pnlDaily1 = 0.0;
                double pnlPerTrade = 0.0;
                var pRatio = (signal.Close - signal0.Close) / signal0.Close;
                var pRatio1 = -pRatio;

                // buy and hold pnl:
                if (signal.Indicators[0] != null)
                {
                    shares1 = notional / signal.Close;
                    pnlDaily1 = shares1 * (signal.Close - signal0.Close);
                    pnlCum1 += pnlDaily1;
                }

                // enter buy position:
                if (signal.TradeAdvise == TradeAdvice.Buy &&
                    signal.TradeAdvise != signal0.TradeAdvise)
                {
                    numTrades++;
                    dateIn = signal.Date;
                    priceIn = signal.Close;
                    shares = (pnlCum + notional) / priceIn;
                }
```

```
// if in buy position, calculate daily PnL:
if (signal.TradeAdvise == TradeAdvice.Buy &&
    signal0.TradeAdvise == TradeAdvice.Buy && i != count - 1)
{
    pnlDaily = shares * (signal.Close - signal0.Close);
    pnlCum += pnlDaily;
}

// exit buy position:
if ((signal0.TradeAdvise == TradeAdvice.Buy &&
     signal.TradeAdvise != signal0.TradeAdvise)
    || pRatio < -stopLoss || pRatio > protectProfit ||
    i == count - 1)
{
    pnlDaily = shares * (signal.Close - signal0.Close);
    pnlCum += pnlDaily;
    pnlPerTrade = shares * (signal.Close - priceIn);
    pnlAllTrades += pnlPerTrade;
    numTrades++;
    priceIn = 0;
    shares = 0;
    dateIn = null;
}

// enter sell position:
if (signal.TradeAdvise == TradeAdvice.Sell &&
    signal.TradeAdvise != signal0.TradeAdvise)
{
    numTrades++;
    dateIn = signal.Date;
    priceIn = signal.Close;
    shares = (pnlCum + notional) / priceIn;
}

// if in sell position, calculate daily PnL:
if (signal.TradeAdvise == TradeAdvice.Sell &&
    signal0.TradeAdvise == TradeAdvice.Sell && i != count - 1)
{
    pnlDaily = -shares * (signal.Close - signal0.Close);
    pnlCum += pnlDaily;
}

// exit sell position:
if ((signal0.TradeAdvise == TradeAdvice.Sell &&
     signal.TradeAdvise != signal0.TradeAdvise) ||
     pRatio1 < -stopLoss || pRatio1 > protectProfit ||
     i == count - 1)
{
    pnlDaily = -shares * (signal.Close - signal0.Close);
    pnlCum += pnlDaily;
    pnlPerTrade = -shares * (signal.Close - priceIn);
    pnlAllTrades += pnlPerTrade;
    numTrades++;
    priceIn = 0;
    shares = 0;
```

```
                    dateIn = null;
                }
                results.Add(new BacktestResult
                {
                    Date = signal.Date.ToShortDateString(),
                    Signal = signal,
                    DateIn = dateIn,
                    PriceIn = priceIn,
                    NumTrades = numTrades,
                    PnLPerTrade = pnlPerTrade,
                    PnLAllTrades = pnlAllTrades,
                    PnL = pnlDaily,
                    PnLCum = pnlCum,
                    PnL1 = pnlDaily1,
                    PnLCum1 = pnlCum1
                });
            }
            return results;
        }
    }
}
```

This method returns a list of *BacktestResult* object, which holds the P&L related properties, including daily and cumulated P&L, number of trades, and the P&L per trade. The *BacktestResult* object also defines the *PnLDaily1* and *PnLCum1* properties, which represent the P&L for simply buying-and-holding the stock position. We will use the buying-and-holding P&L to compare with the P&L from the specified trading strategy.

The *ComputePnL* method takes the signal list, *notional*, *stopLoss*, and *protectProfit* as input arguments. The signal list contains the date stamp, stock price, and trading signal information. The *notional* is the initial invest capital. Note that we reinvest the returns from trades we have made based on the trading strategy.

Another rule you need to follow is that you can enter a new trade only after exiting the current position, which ensure that, for any given date, only one trade at most is allowed. Otherwise, the initial invest capital will be not enough to support multiple trades.

Based on this basic method, you can easily add more features to it, such as transaction costs.

Risk Measures

In order to backtest the historical performance of a strategy, in addition to the P&L (or returns) we need to calculate some important risk measures. The commonly used risk metrics for quantitative strategies are the Sharpe ratio and the maximum drawdown. The Sharpe ratio is defined as the average of the excess daily returns divided by the standard deviation of those excess daily returns. Here, the excess returns refer to the return of the strategy above the risk-free rate. For simplicity's sake, here we will neglect the risk-free rate in computing the Sharpe ratio.

Add the following helper methods to the *StrategyBacktestHelper* class:

```
public static PnLSummary ComputeRsik(List<BacktestResult> dt, double notional)
{
    List<PnLDrawdown> pnlDaily = new List<PnLDrawdown>();
    foreach (var r in dt)
```

```
    {
        pnlDaily.Add(new PnLDrawdown
        {
            Date = r.Signal.Date,
            PnL = r.PnL,
            PnL1 = r.PnL1,
            PnLCum = r.PnLCum,
            PnLCum1 = r.PnLCum1
        });
    }
    var sharpes = GetSharpe(pnlDaily);
    ComputeDrawdown(pnlDaily, notional);
    var count = dt.Count;
    var count1 = pnlDaily.Count;
    var last = dt[count - 1];
    var last1 = pnlDaily[count1 - 1];
    return new PnLSummary
    {
        NumberTrades = last.NumTrades,
        PnL = last.PnLCum,
        Sharpe = sharpes[0],
        MaxDrawdown = last1.MaxDrawdown,
        PnL1 = last.PnLCum1,
        Sharpe1 = sharpes[1],
        MaxDrawdown1 = last1.MaxDrawdown1
    };
}

private static double[] GetSharpe(List<PnLDrawdown> pnl)
{
    double avg = pnl.Average(x => x.PnL);
    var pnlList = pnl.Select(x => x.PnL);
    double std = pnlList.StdDev();
    double avg1 = pnl.Average(x => x.PnL1);
    var pnlList1 = pnl.Select(x => x.PnL1);
    double std1 = pnlList1.StdDev();
    var sp = Math.Round(Math.Sqrt(252.0) * avg / std, 4);
    var sp1 = Math.Round(Math.Sqrt(252.0) * avg1 / std1, 4);
    return new double[] { sp, sp1 };
}

private static void ComputeDrawdown(List<PnLDrawdown> dt, double notional)
{
    double max = 0;
    double min = 2.0 * notional;
    double max1 = 0;
    double min1 = 2.0 * notional;
    foreach (var r in dt)
    {
        double pnl = r.PnLCum + notional;
        double pnl1 = r.PnLCum1 + notional;
        max = Math.Max(max, pnl);
        min = Math.Min(min, pnl);
        max1 = Math.Max(max1, pnl1);
        min1 = Math.Min(min1, pnl1);
```

```
            r.Drawdown = 100.0 * (max - pnl) / max;
            r.Drawdown1 = 100.0 * (max1 - pnl1) / max1;
            r.Drawup = 100.0 * (pnl - min) / pnl;
            r.Drawup1 = 100.8 * (pnl1 - min1) / pnl1;
        }
        max = 0;
        max1 = 0;
        double maxu = 0;
        double maxu1 = 0;
        foreach (var r in dt)
        {
            max = Math.Max(max, r.Drawdown);
            max1 = Math.Max(max1, r.Drawdown1);
            r.MaxDrawdown = max;
            r.MaxDrawdown1 = max1;
            maxu = Math.Max(maxu, r.Drawup);
            maxu1 = Math.Max(maxu1, r.Drawup1);
            r.MaxDrawup = maxu;
            r.MaxDrawup1 = maxu1;
        }
    }

    private static double StdDev(this IEnumerable<double> values)
    {
        double mean = 0.0;
        double sum = 0.0;
        double stdDev = 0.0;
        int n = 0;
        foreach (double val in values)
        {
            n++;
            double delta = val - mean;
            mean += delta / n;
            sum += delta * (val - mean);
        }
        if (1 < n)
            stdDev = Math.Sqrt(sum / (n - 1));
        return stdDev;
    }
```

Here, the *GetSharpe* method computes the annualized Sharpe ratios using the daily P&L data from both the strategy (*sp*) and the buying-and-holding position (*sp1*).

The maximum drawdown characterizes the largest peak-to-trough drop in the cumulated return curve over a particular period. It is often quoted as a percentage. The historical backtesting results will show the past maximum drawdown, which is a good guide for the future drawdown performance of the strategy.

The risk measures that depend on the maximum drawdown can directly be observable at the end of the given period because they are functions of the price data, and thus could be traded. For example, the price of a futures contract on maximum drawdown can serve as an important risk measure indicator that could be quoted by the market. When the market is in a bubble, the prices of drawdown contracts would be significantly higher. On the other hand, when the market is stable, or when it exhibits mean reversion behavior, the prices of drawdown contracts would become cheaper.

The *ComputeDrawdown* method first calculates the rolling maximum and rolling minimum. The drawdown (drawup) is defined as the drop (jump) of the price from its rolling maximum (minimum). The maximum drawdown (drawup) is defined as the maximal drop (jump) of the price from its rolling maximum (minimum) over a given period of time.

The *ComputeRisk* method returns a *PnLSummary* object that contains risk measures such as Sharpe rate and maximum drawdown, which are calculated by calling the *GetSharpe* and *ComputeDrawdown* methods.

Backtesting in Web Service

Now, we can convert our backtesting system implemented in the preceding section into a web service for different trading signals.

Add the following methods to the *StrategyValuesController* class in the *Quant/Controllers* folder:

```
[Route("~/api/pnlCrossover/{ticker}/{start}/{end}/{fastPeriod}/{slowPeriod}/
    {maType}/{natrPeriod}/{natrLevel}/{tradeType}/{tolerance}/{notional}/{stopLoss}/
    {protectProfit}/{signalType}")]
[HttpGet]
public JsonResult GetPnlCrossover(string ticker, string start, string end,
    int fastPeriod, int slowPeriod, string maType, int natrPeriod, double natrLevel,
    string tradeType, double tolerance, double notional, double stopLoss,
    double protectProfit, string signalType)
{
    List<StrategyObjects.StrategySignal> signal =
        new List<StrategyObjects.StrategySignal>();
    if (signalType.ToLower().Contains("natr"))
    {
        signal = StrategySignalHelper.Signal2MaCrossoverNatr(ticker, start, end,
            fastPeriod, slowPeriod, maType, natrPeriod, natrLevel, tradeType,
            tolerance);
    }
    else
    {
        signal = StrategySignalHelper.Signal2MaCrossover(ticker, start, end,
            fastPeriod, slowPeriod, maType, tradeType, tolerance);
    }
    var pnl = StrategyBacktestHelper.ComputePnL(signal, notional, stopLoss,
        protectProfit);
    var risk = StrategyBacktestHelper.ComputeRsik(pnl, notional);
    return Json(new { name = ticker + ": " + signalType.ToUpper() +
        " Crossover", pnl, risk });
}


[Route("~/api/pnlZscore/{ticker}/{start}/{end}/{period}/{fastPeriod}/{slowPeriod}/
    {maType}/{zEntry}/{zExit}/{notional}/{stopLoss}/{protectProfit}/{signalType}")]
[HttpGet]
public JsonResult GetPnlZscore(string ticker, string start, string end, int period,
    int fastPeriod, int slowPeriod, string maType, double zEntry, double zExit,
    double notional, double stopLoss, double protectProfit, string signalType)
{
    List<StrategyObjects.StrategySignal> signal =
```

```
        new List<StrategyObjects.StrategySignal>();
    signalType = signalType.ToLower();
    if (signalType.Contains("ma"))
    {
        signal = StrategySignalHelper.SignalMaZscore(ticker, start, end, period,
            maType, zEntry, zExit);
    }
    else if (signalType.Contains("rsi"))
    {
        signal = StrategySignalHelper.SignalRsiZscore(ticker, start, end, period,
            zEntry, zExit);
    }
    else
    {
        signal = StrategySignalHelper.SignalPpoZscore(ticker, start, end,
            fastPeriod, slowPeriod, maType, zEntry, zExit);
    }
    var pnl = StrategyBacktestHelper.ComputePnL(signal, notional, stopLoss,
        protectProfit);
    var risk = StrategyBacktestHelper.ComputeRsik(pnl, notional);
    return Json(new { name = ticker + ": " + signalType.ToUpper() +
        " Z-Score", pnl, risk });
}
```

Next, add the following TypeScript methods to the *ch11.service.ts* file in order to access the backtesting results in Angular applications:

```
getPnl2MaCrossoverNatr(ticker: string, start: string, end: string, fastPeriod:
    number, slowPeriod: number, maType: string, natrPeriod: number, natrLevel: number,
    tradeType: string, tolerance: number, notional: number, stopLoss: number,
    protectProfit: number, signalType: string) {
    let url1 = this.url + 'api/pnl2macrossovernatr/' + ticker + '/' + start + '/' +
        end + '/' + fastPeriod + '/' + slowPeriod + '/' + maType + '/' + natrPeriod +
        '/' + natrLevel + '/' + tradeType + '/' + tolerance + '/' + notional + '/' +
        stopLoss + '/' + protectProfit + '/' + signalType;
    return this.http.get<any>(url1);
}
```

```
getPnlPpoZscore(ticker: string, start: string, end: string, period: number,
    fastPeriod: number, slowPeriod: number, maType: string, zEntry: number, zExit:
    number, notional: number, stopLoss: number, protectProfit: number,
    signalType: string) {
    let url1 = this.url + 'api/pnlppozscore/' + ticker + '/' + start + '/' +
        end + '/' + period + '/' + fastPeriod + '/' + slowPeriod + '/' + maType + '/' +
        zEntry + '/' + zExit + '/' + notional + '/' + stopLoss + '/' +
        protectProfit + '/' + signalType;
    return this.http.get<any>(url1);
}
```

Backtesting System Applications

In the preceding sections, we have demonstrated how to generate trading signals and how to build a backtesting system that can be used to compute the P&L and risk measures. Now, we will apply this backtesting system to examine the historical performance of the trading strategies for various US stocks and ETFs.

In order to share the code for creating various charts that will be used to display P&L results for different trading strategies, here, we will add a TypeScript helper method called *chartPnl* to the *strategy.helper.ts* class file with the following code:

```
chartPnl(data: any) {
  const categoryData = [];
  const pnlData = [];
  const pnlData1 = [];
  const positionData = [];
  data.pnl.forEach(function (d) {
    categoryData.push(d.signal.date.toString().substring(0, 10));
    pnlData.push(d.pnLCum);
    pnlData1.push(d.pnLCum1);
    positionData.push(d.signal.position);
  });

  return {
    title: {
      text: data.name,
      left: 'center'
    },
    legend: {
      top: 20,
      right: 45,
      data: [{ name: 'PnL for Strategy', icon: 'line' },
             { name: 'PnL for Buy-Hold', icon: 'line' },]
    },
    tooltip: {
      trigger: 'axis',
      axisPointer: {
        type: 'cross'
      }
    },
    axisPointer: {
      link: { xAxisIndex: 'all' }
    },
    grid: [{
      left: 50,
      right: 40,
      top: '7%',
      height: '46%'
    }, {
      left: 50,
      right: 40,
      height: '25%',
      top: '63%'
    }],
    xAxis: [{
      type: 'category',
      data: categoryData,
      scale: true,
      boundaryGap: false,
```

```
      axisLine: { onZero: false },
      splitLine: { show: false },
      splitNumber: 20,
      min: 'dataMin',
      max: 'dataMax'
    }, {
      type: 'category',
      gridIndex: 1,
      data: categoryData,
      scale: true,
      boundaryGap: false,
      axisLine: { onZero: false },
      splitLine: { show: false },
      splitNumber: 20,
      min: 'dataMin',
      max: 'dataMax'
    }],
    yAxis: [{
      scale: true,
      name: 'PnL',
      splitArea: {
        show: true
      }
    },
    {
      scale: true,
      name: 'Trading Position',
      gridIndex: 1,
      splitArea: {
        show: true
      }
    }
    ],
    dataZoom: {
      show: true,
      type: 'slider',
      y: '93%',
      start: 70,
      end: 100,
      xAxisIndex: [0, 1],
    },
    series: [
      {
        name: 'PnL for Strategy',
        type: 'line',
        data: pnlData,
        showSymbol: false
      },
      {
        name: 'PnL for Buy-Hold',
        type: 'line',
        data: pnlData1,
        showSymbol: false
      },
      {
```

```
        name: 'Trading Position',
        type: 'line',
        step: 'start',
        data: positionData,
        xAxisIndex: 1,
        yAxisIndex: 1,
        showSymbol: false,
        lineStyle: { color: 'steelblue' }
      }
    ]
  }
}
```

This helper method can be used to display the P&L results and trading positions.

Backtesting for MA Crossover Strategies

In this section, I will use an example to show you how to use the backtesting system for MA-crossover (trend-following) signals.

Run the following command in a command prompt window:

ng g c chapter11/ch11-pnl-crossover --module=app.module

This generates a new component called *ch11-pnl-crossover* in the *ClientApp/src/app/chapter11* folder. Open the component class file and replace its content with the following code:

```
// ch11-pnl-crossover.component.ts file:
import { Component, OnInit } from '@angular/core';
import { Ch11Service } from '../../models/ch11.service';
import { StrategyHelper } from '../../models/strategy.helper';

@Component({
  selector: 'app-ch11-pnl-crossover',
  templateUrl: './ch11-pnl-crossover.component.html',
  styleUrls: ['./ch11-pnl-crossover.component.css']
})
export class Ch11PnlCrossoverComponent implements OnInit {
  ticker: string = 'SPY';
  start: string = '2017-01-01';
  end: string = '2018-12-31';
  fastPeriod: number = 30;
  slowPeriod: number = 70;
  maType: string = 'sma';
  natrPeriod: number = 14;
  natrLevel: number = 0.75;
  tradeType: string = 'long';
  tolerance: number = 0;
  notional: number = 10000;
  stopLoss: number = 0.1;
  protectProfit: number = 0.3;
  signalType: string = 'ma';
  data: any;
  options: any;
  private helper: StrategyHelper;
```

```
colDefs: any = [
  { headerName: "Strategy", field: "strategy", width: 150 },
  { headerName: "P&L", field: "pnl", width: 100 },
  { headerName: "# of Trades", field: "numTrades", width: 100 },
  { headerName: "Sharpe Ratio", field: "sharpe", width: 110 },
  { headerName: "Max Drawdown", field: "drawdown", width: 130 },
];
rowDefs: any;

constructor(private service: Ch11Service) { }

ngOnInit() {
  this.getData(this.ticker, this.start, this.end, this.fastPeriod,
    this.slowPeriod, this.maType, this.natrPeriod, this.natrLevel,
    this.tradeType, this.tolerance, this.notional, this.stopLoss,
    this.protectProfit, this.signalType);
}

getData(ticker: string, start: string, end: string, fastPeriod: number,
  slowPeriod: number, maType: string, natrPeriod: number, natrLevel: number,
  tradeType: string, tolerance: number, notional: number, stopLoss: number,
  protectProfit: number, signalType: string) {
  this.data = null;
  this.helper = new StrategyHelper();
  this.rowDefs = [];
  let strategy = "MA Crossover";
  if (signalType == 'natr') strategy = 'MA Corssover + NATR';
  this.service.getPnlCrossover(ticker, start, end, fastPeriod, slowPeriod, maType,
    natrPeriod, natrLevel, tradeType, tolerance, notional, stopLoss,
    protectProfit, signalType).subscribe(result => {
      this.data = result;
      let risk = result.risk;
      this.options = this.helper.chartPnl(this.data);
      this.rowDefs.push({
        strategy: strategy, pnl: risk.pnL.toFixed(0),
          numTrades: risk.numberTrades,
        sharpe: risk.sharpe, drawdown: risk.maxDrawdown.toFixed(2)
      });
      this.rowDefs.push({
        strategy: 'Buy-Hold', pnl: risk.pnL1.toFixed(0), numTrades: 1,
        sharpe: risk.sharpe1, drawdown: risk.maxDrawdown1.toFixed(2)
      });
    });
}
}
```

Next, update the component's template with the following code:

```
// ch11-pnl-crossover.component.html file:
<h2>
  ch11-pnl-crossover works!
</h2>

<mat-form-field>
  <input matInput placeholder="ticker" [(ngModel)]="ticker" name="ticker">
</mat-form-field>
```

```html
<mat-form-field>
  <input matInput placeholder="start" [(ngModel)]="start" name="start">
</mat-form-field>
<mat-form-field>
  <input matInput placeholder="end" [(ngModel)]="end" name="end">
</mat-form-field>
<mat-form-field>
  <input matInput placeholder="fastPeriod" [(ngModel)]="fastPeriod"
name="fastPeriod">
</mat-form-field>
<mat-form-field>
  <input matInput placeholder="slowPeriod" [(ngModel)]="slowPeriod"
name="slowPeriod">
</mat-form-field>
<mat-form-field>
  <mat-select placeholder="Select an MA type" [(value)]="maType">
    <mat-option value="sma">sma</mat-option>
    <mat-option value="ema">ema</mat-option>
    <mat-option value="wma">wma</mat-option>
  </mat-select>
</mat-form-field>
<mat-form-field *ngIf="signalType=='natr'">
  <input matInput placeholder="natrPeriod" [(ngModel)]="natrPeriod"
name="natrPeriod">
</mat-form-field>
<mat-form-field *ngIf="signalType=='natr'">
  <input matInput placeholder="natrLevel" [(ngModel)]="natrLevel" name="natrLevel">
</mat-form-field>
<mat-form-field>
  <mat-select placeholder="Select a trade type" [(value)]="tradeType">
    <mat-option value="long">Long</mat-option>
    <mat-option value="longshort">Long-Short</mat-option>
    <mat-option value="short">Short</mat-option>
  </mat-select>
</mat-form-field>
<mat-form-field>
  <input matInput placeholder="tolerance" [(ngModel)]="tolerance" name="tolerance">
</mat-form-field>
<mat-form-field>
  <input matInput placeholder="notional" [(ngModel)]="notional" name="notional">
</mat-form-field>
<mat-form-field>
  <input matInput placeholder="stopLoss" [(ngModel)]="stopLoss" name="stopLoss">
</mat-form-field>
<mat-form-field>
  <input matInput placeholder="protectProfit" [(ngModel)]="protectProfit"
name="protectProfit">
</mat-form-field>
<mat-form-field>
  <mat-select placeholder="Select a signal type" [(value)]="signalType">
    <mat-option value="ma">MA Crossover</mat-option>
    <mat-option value="natr">MA Crossover + NATR</mat-option>
  </mat-select>
</mat-form-field>
<button mat-raised-button color="primary" (click)="getData(ticker, start, end,
```

```
      fastPeriod, slowPeriod, maType, natrPeriod, natrLevel, tradeType, tolerance,
         notional, stopLoss, protectProfit, signalType)">Get PnL</button>
<br /><br />
<div *ngIf="data" echarts [options]="options" style="height:600px;width:1000px">
</div>

<p>Risk Measures</p>
<ag-grid-angular *ngIf="rowDefs.length>0" style="height:90px;width:600px;
   margin-bottom:100px" class="ag-theme-balham" [rowData]="rowDefs"
   [columnDefs]="colDefs">
</ag-grid-angular>
```

This template first defines various input parameters and then displays the P&L results and risk measures using an ECharts element and *ag-Grid* table component respectively.

Finally, we need to add a path for this new component to the *RouterModule* of the root module (i.e., the *app.module.ts* file):

{ path: 'chapter11/ch11-pnl-crossover, component: Ch11PnlCrossoverComponent }

Then add the corresponding URL link to the *home* and *nav-menu* components.

Saving the project and navigating to the */chapter11/ch11-pnl-crossover* page produce the default P&L results shown in Fig.11-11 and risk measures shown in Fig.11-12.

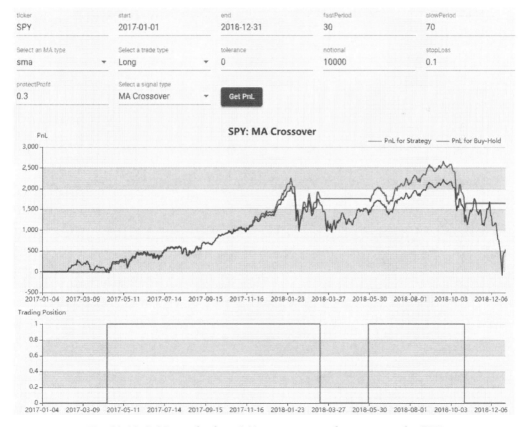

Fig.11-11. P&L results from MA-crossover trading strategy for SPY.

Risk Measures

Strategy	P&L	# of Trades	Sharpe Ratio	Max Drawdown
MA Crossover	1650	6	0.7962	10.10
Buy-Hold	543	1	0.2097	18.92

Fig.11-12. Risk measures from MA-crossover trading strategy for SPY.

You can see that the P&L result from the MA-crossover trading strategy outperforms the P&L result from buying-and-holding the position with the same initial notional of $10,000. The Sharpe ratio ~ 0.8 and maximum drawdown ~ 10.1 for this strategy. While for the buying-and-holding position, the Shape ratio is about 0.2 and maximum drawdown is about 18.9, which is much worse than that from the MA-crossover trading strategy.

Now, if selecting the *MA Crossover + NATR* strategy from the signal-type dropdown menu, using the default parameters in the input fields, and clicking the *Get PnL* button, you will get the P&L results shown in Fig.11-13 and risk measures shown in Fig.11-14.

Fig.11-13. P&L results from MA-crossover + NATR trading strategy for SPY.

Risk Measures

Strategy	P&L	# of Trades	Sharpe Ratio	Max Drawdown
MA Corssover + NATR	2044	14	1.8919	2.93
Buy-Hold	543	1	0.2097	18.92

Fig.11-14. Risk measures from MA-crossover + NATR trading strategy for SPY.

You can see from the above results that the MA-crossover + NATR strategy outperform both the buying-and-holding and MA crossover strategies. At the same time, the MA-crossover + NATR strategy can avoid the large maximum drawdown after February of 2018 and effectively stops trading in the choppy market when NATR value > 0.75. The MA-Crossover + NATR strategy also has highest Shape ratio (~ 1.89) and the lowest maximum drawdown (2.93%).

Backtesting for Z-Score Strategies

In this section, I will use an example to show you how to use the backtesting system for z-score (mean-reversion) based trading strategies.

Run the following command in a command prompt window:

```
ng g c chapter11/ch11-pnl-zscore --module=app.module
```

This generates a new component called *ch11-pnl-zscore* in the *ClientApp/src/app/chapter11* folder. Open the component class file and replace its content with the following code:

```
// ch11-pnl-zscore.component.ts file:
import { Component, OnInit } from '@angular/core';
import { Ch11Service } from '../../models/ch11.service';
import { StrategyHelper } from '../../models/strategy.helper';

@Component({
  selector: 'app-ch11-pnl-zscore',
  templateUrl: './ch11-pnl-zscore.component.html',
  styleUrls: ['./ch11-pnl-zscore.component.css']
})
export class Ch11PnlZscoreComponent implements OnInit {
  ticker: string = 'IBM';
  start: string = '2010-01-01';
  end: string = '2015-12-31';
  period: number = 40;
  fastPeriod: number = 7;
  slowPeriod: number = 25;
  maType: string = 'sma';
  zEntry: number = 1.0;
  zExit: number = 0.0;
  notional: number = 10000;
  stopLoss: number = 0.1;
  protectProfit: number = 0.3;
  signalType: string = 'ma';
  data: any;
```

```
options: any;
private helper: StrategyHelper;

colDefs: any = [
  { headerName: "Strategy", field: "strategy", width: 150 },
  { headerName: "P&L", field: "pnl", width: 100 },
  { headerName: "# of Trades", field: "numTrades", width: 100 },
  { headerName: "Sharpe Ratio", field: "sharpe", width: 110 },
  { headerName: "Max Drawdown", field: "drawdown", width: 130 },
];
rowDefs: any;

constructor(private service: Ch11Service) { }

ngOnInit() {
  this.getData(this.ticker, this.start, this.end, this.period, this.fastPeriod,
    this.slowPeriod, this.maType, this.zEntry, this.zExit, this.notional,
    this.stopLoss, this.protectProfit, this.signalType);
}

getData(ticker: string, start: string, end: string, period: number, fastPeriod:
  number, slowPeriod: number, maType: string, zEntry: number, zExit: number,
  notional: number, stopLoss: number, protectProfit: number, signalType: string) {
  this.data = null;
  this.helper = new StrategyHelper();
  this.rowDefs = [];
  let strategy = "MA Zscore";
  if (signalType == 'rsiZscore') strategy = 'RSI Z-Score';
  else if (signalType == 'ppoZscore') strategy = 'PPO Z-Score';
  this.service.getPnlZscore(ticker, start, end, period, fastPeriod, slowPeriod,
    maType, zEntry, zExit, notional, stopLoss, protectProfit, signalType)
    .subscribe(result => {
      this.data = result;
      let risk = result.risk;
      this.options = this.helper.chartPnl(this.data);
      this.rowDefs.push({
        strategy: strategy, pnl: risk.pnL.toFixed(0), numTrades:
        risk.numberTrades, sharpe: risk.sharpe, drawdown:
        risk.maxDrawdown.toFixed(2)
      });
      this.rowDefs.push({
        strategy: 'Buy-Hold', pnl: risk.pnL1.toFixed(0), numTrades: 1,
        sharpe: risk.sharpe1, drawdown: risk.maxDrawdown1.toFixed(2)
      });
    });
}
}
```

Next, update the component's template with the following code:

```
// ch11-pnl-zscore.component.html file:
<h2>
  ch11-pnl-zscore works!
</h2>

<mat-form-field>
```

```html
  <input matInput placeholder="ticker" [(ngModel)]="ticker" name="ticker">
</mat-form-field>
<mat-form-field>
  <input matInput placeholder="start" [(ngModel)]="start" name="start">
</mat-form-field>
<mat-form-field>
  <input matInput placeholder="end" [(ngModel)]="end" name="end">
</mat-form-field>
<mat-form-field *ngIf="signalType != 'ppo'">
  <input matInput placeholder="period" [(ngModel)]="period" name="period">
</mat-form-field>
<mat-form-field *ngIf="signalType == 'ppo'">
  <input matInput placeholder="fastPeriod" [(ngModel)]="fastPeriod"
name="fastPeriod">
</mat-form-field>
<mat-form-field *ngIf="signalType == 'ppo'">
  <input matInput placeholder="slowPeriod" [(ngModel)]="slowPeriod"
name="slowPeriod">
</mat-form-field>
<mat-form-field *ngIf="signalType != 'rsi'">
  <mat-select placeholder="Select an MA type" [(value)]="maType">
    <mat-option value="sma">sma</mat-option>
    <mat-option value="ema">ema</mat-option>
    <mat-option value="wma">wma</mat-option>
  </mat-select>
</mat-form-field>
<mat-form-field>
  <input matInput placeholder="zEntry" [(ngModel)]="zEntry" name="zEntry">
</mat-form-field>
<mat-form-field>
  <input matInput placeholder="zExit" [(ngModel)]="zExit" name="zExit">
</mat-form-field>
<mat-form-field>
  <input matInput placeholder="notional" [(ngModel)]="notional" name="notional">
</mat-form-field>
<mat-form-field>
  <input matInput placeholder="stopLoss" [(ngModel)]="stopLoss" name="stopLoss">
</mat-form-field>
<mat-form-field>
  <input matInput placeholder="protectProfit" [(ngModel)]="protectProfit"
name="protectProfit">
</mat-form-field>
<mat-form-field>
  <mat-select placeholder="Select a signal type" [(value)]="signalType">
    <mat-option value="ma">MA Z-Score</mat-option>
    <mat-option value="rsi">RSI Z-Score</mat-option>
    <mat-option value="ppo">PPO Z-Score</mat-option>
  </mat-select>
</mat-form-field>
<button mat-raised-button color="primary" (click)="getData(ticker, start, end,
  period, fastPeriod, slowPeriod, maType, zEntry, zExit, notional, stopLoss,
  protectProfit, signalType)">Get PnL</button>
<br /><br />
<div *ngIf="data" echarts [options]="options"
style="height:600px;width:1000px"></div>
```

```
<p>Risk Measures</p>
<ag-grid-angular *ngIf="rowDefs.length>0" style="height:90px;width:600px;
  margin-bottom:100px"  class="ag-theme-balham" [rowData]="rowDefs"
  [columnDefs]="colDefs">
</ag-grid-angular>
```

This template first defines various input parameters and then displays the P&L results and risk measures using an ECharts element and *ag-Grid* table component respectively.

Finally, we need to add a path for this new component to the *RouterModule* of the root module (i.e., the *app.module.ts* file):

```
{ path: 'chapter11/ch11-pnl-zscore, component: Ch11PnlZscoreComponent }
```

Then add the corresponding URL link to the *home* and *nav-menu* components.

Saving the project and navigating to the */chapter11/ch11-pnl-zscore* page produce the default P&L results shown in Fig.11-15 and risk measures shown in Fig.11-16.

Fig.11-15. P&L results from MA Z-score trading strategy for IBM.

Risk Measures

Strategy	P&L	# of Trades	Sharpe Ratio	Max Drawdown
MA Zscore	7095	122	0.5461	20.59
Buy-Hold	-393	1	-0.0345	37.23

Fig.11-16. Risk measures from MA Z-score trading strategy for IBM.

You can see that the P&L from the MA Z-score signal outperforms the P&L from simply buying-and-holding the position with the same initial notional of $10,000. The maximum drawdown is 20.59% for this strategy, while it is 37.23% for the buying-and-holding position.

We obtain a positive return ($7,095) for this strategy with a Sharpe ratio of 0.5461. However, we get a negative return (-$393) for the buying-and-holding position with a negative Sharpe ratio of -0.0345. The results from our MA z-score based trading strategy outperform those from a simply buying-and-holding position.

Next, we can examine the RSI z-score strategy by selecting the *RSI Z-Score* option from the *signal-type* dropdown menu, and setting *period* to 14 *zEntry* to 1.5, which produces the results shown in Fig.11-17 and Fig.11-18.

Fig.11-17. P&L results from RSI Z-score trading strategy for IBM.

Risk Measures

Strategy	P&L	# of Trades	Sharpe Ratio	Max Drawdown
MA Zscore	3565	52	0.5841	11.87
Buy-Hold	-163	1	-0.0143	36.65

Fig.11-18. Risk measures from RSI Z-score trading strategy for IBM.

Finally, let us examine the PPO z-score trading strategy. Selecting the *PPO Z-Score* option from the *signal-type* dropdown menu and set *zEntry* to 2 produce the results shown in Fig.11-19 and Fig.11-20.

Fig.11-19. P&L results from PPO Z-score trading strategy for IBM.

Risk Measures

Strategy	P&L	# of Trades	Sharpe Ratio	Max Drawdown
MA Zscore	8981	86	1.1751	9.30
Buy-Hold	3	1	0.0003	36.25

Fig.11-20. Risk measures from PPO Z-score trading strategy for IBM.

You can see that among three z-score based trading strategies, the PPO z-score strategy gives the highest P&L ($8,981) and Sharpe ratio (1.1751) as well as the lowest max drawdown of 9.3%.

In this section, we simply presented the mean-reversion trading strategy based on z-score, and did not address whether the mean reversion strategy is applicable to a specified stock price series. In fact, most stock price series are not mean reverting, but are geometric random walks. The returns, not the prices, are the ones that actually randomly distributed around a mean of zero. Unfortunately, we cannot trade on the mean reversion of returns. In certain periods of time, those few prices series that are found to be mean reverting are called stationary. There are several techniques available to test whether a time series is in stationary state or not, including augmented Dickey-Fuller (ADF) test, Hurst exponent, variance ratio test, etc.

Therefore, before applying the mean-reverting trading strategies based on z-score to live trading, you should perform stationary tests to make sure the stock price series is a stationary time series. After various stationary tests, you will find there are not too many stock price series that are stationary. Fortunately, we can manufacture many more mean-reverting price series because we can combine two or more individual stock price series that are not mean reverting into a portfolio whose net market value (i.e., price) is mean reverting. Trading those combined price series is often called pair trading, which will not be discussed further in this book. If you are interested in pair trading, please refer to my previously published book "*Practical C# and WPF for Financial Markets*".

There are several important areas in quantitative finance, which are not covered in this book, including real-time automatic order execution as well as the portfolio optimization and management. If you are interested in these topics, please refer to my previously published book: *Practical Quantitative Finance with R*.

Index

Made in the USA
Las Vegas, NV
21 February 2021